The Metaphors of
Consciousness

The Metaphors of
Consciousness

Edited by
Ronald S. Valle
*Center for the Development of
Consciousness and Personal Growth
Wexford, Pennsylvania*

and
Rolf von Eckartsberg
*Duquesne University
Pittsburgh, Pennsylvania*

Plenum Press · New York and London

Library of Congress Cataloging in Publication Data

Main entry under title:

The Metaphors of consciousness.

Includes bibliographical references and indexes.
 1. Consciousness. 2. Knowledge, Theory of. I. Valle, Ronald S. II. Von Eckartsberg, Rolf, 1932-
BF311.M449   150.1   80-24803
ISBN 0-306-40520-2

© 1981 Plenum Press, New York
A Division of Plenum Publishing Corporation
227 West 17th Street, New York, N.Y. 10011

Printed in the United States of America

To Alexa and those who Believe   *R. V.*

To e. v. e. metaphora   *R. v. E.*

Contributors

Puran Khan Bair • Serapis Corporation, 84 State Street, Boston, Massachusetts 02109

Fritjof Capra • Lawrence Berkeley Laboratory, University of California, Berkeley, California 94720

John M. Carpenter • 1017 Milton Avenue, Pittsburgh, Pennsylvania 15218

Padmasiri de Silva • Department of Philosophy and Psychology, University of Sri Lanka, Peradeniya, Sri Lanka

Silvio E. Fittipaldi • Religious Studies Department, Villanova University, Villanova, Pennsylvania 19085

James G. Holland • Department of Psychology, University of Pittsburgh, Pittsburgh, Pennsylvania 15260

Ernest Keen • Department of Psychology, Bucknell University, Lewisburg, Pennsylvania 17837

Elizabeth L. Kruger • Carpenter Road, South Wales, New York 14139

Timothy Leary • c/o Peace Press, 3828 Willat Avenue, Culver City, California 90230

David Ben Leavitt • 8044 Germantown Avenue, Philadelphia, Pennsylvania 19118

Paul A. Lee ● The Platonic Academy, Box 409, Santa Cruz, California 95061

David M. Levin ● Department of Philosophy, Northwestern University, Evanston, Illinois 60201

John C. Lilly ● Human Software Inc., 33307 Decker School Road, Malibu, California 90265

Stanton Marlan ● Pittsburgh Center for Psychotherapy and Psychoanalysis, 4527 Winthrop Avenue, Pittsburgh, Pennsylvania 15213

Donald M. Moss ● Ottawa County Community Mental Health, CMH-1111 Fulton, Grand Haven, Michigan 49417

Karl H. Pribram ● Department of Psychology, Stanford University, Stanford, California 94305

Swami Rama ● The Himalayan International Institute of Yoga Science and Philosophy, R.D. 1, Box 88, Honesdale, Pennsylvania 18431

Robert D. Romanyshyn ● Department of Psychology, University of Dallas, Irving, Texas 75061

Neil E. Schore ● Department of Chemistry, University of California at Davis, Davis, California 95616

Charles T. Tart ● Department of Psychology, University of California at Davis, Davis, California 95616

Ronald S. Valle ● Center for the Development of Consciousness and Personal Growth, 501 Wallace Road, Wexford, Pennsylvania 15090

Valerie A. Valle ● Center for the Development of Consciousness and Personal Growth, 501 Wallace Road, Wexford, Pennsylvania 15090

Elsa von Eckartsberg ● Department of German, University of Pittsburgh, Pittsburgh, Pennsylvania 15213

Rolf von Eckartsberg ● Department of Psychology, Duquesne University, Pittsburgh, Pennsylvania 15219

Renée Weber ● Department of Philosophy, Rutgers University, New Brunswick, New Jersey 08903

Foreword

As we move into the 1980s, there is an increasing awareness that our civilization is going through a profound cultural transformation. At the heart of this transformation lies what is often called a "paradigm shift"—a dramatic change in the thoughts, perceptions, and values which form a particular vision of reality. The paradigm that is now shifting comprises a large number of ideas and values that have dominated our society for several hundred years; values that have been associated with various streams of Western culture, among them the Scientific Revolution of the seventeenth century, The Enlightenment, and the Industrial Revolution. They include the belief in the scientific method as the only valid approach to knowledge, the split between mind and matter, the view of nature as a mechanical system, the view of life in society as a competitive struggle for survival, and the belief in unlimited material progress to be achieved through economic and technological growth. All these ideas and values are now found to be severely limited and in need of radical revision.

Physics has played a major role in shaping the old paradigm. Ever since the seventeenth century, it has been the shining example of an "exact" science, and has served as the model for all the other sciences. For two and a half centuries, physicists developed a mechanistic view of the world, based on the philosophy of Descartes and the mechanics of Newton. The universe was seen as a machine assembled from separate objects which, in turn, were composed of elementary material building blocks. Other sciences accepted this view as the correct description of reality and modeled their own theories accordingly.

In the twentieth century, however, physics went through several conceptual revolutions that clearly revealed the limitations of the mechanistic world-view and that led to an organic, ecological view of the world, showing great similarities to the views of mystics of all ages and traditions. The universe is no longer seen as a machine made up of a multitude of separate objects but appears as a harmonious, indivisible whole; a network of dynamic relationships which does not involve any basic building blocks, nor any material substance, but generates dynamic patterns continually changing into one another—a continuous dance of energy.

The dramatic changes in the philosophy of physics will necessarily affect scientists in other disciplines, who will have to reexamine the foundations of their conceptual framework in the light of these new developments. In this process of reevaluation, the study of the nature of consciousness and of the relation between mind and matter will play a crucial role. The division of nature into two separate and independent realms—that of mind and that of matter—has had the most profound effect on Western thought. It formed the very basis of the Cartesian paradigm and has dominated most of the sciences to the present day. Transcending the Cartesian division will thus be an essential aspect of the current conceptual and cultural transformation.

In modern physics, the question of consciousness has risen in quantum theory with the problem of observation and measurement. The recognition that human consciousness determines, to a large extent, the properties of the observed atomic phenomena has forced physicists to accept the fact that the sharp Cartesian division between mind and matter, between the observer and the observed, can no longer be maintained. In atomic physics, we can never speak about nature without, at the same time, speaking about ourselves. The pragmatic formulation of quantum theory, used by scientists in their day-to-day research, does not refer to the mind of the observer explicitly. However, several physicists have come to see consciousness as an essential aspect of the universe and have argued that we may be blocked from further progress in our understanding of natural phenomena if we insist on excluding it. Thus, the question of the nature of consciousness has come into the forefront of scientific research, even in the natural sciences.

The nature of consciousness, a problem so central to the current paradigm shift, is the focus of the present book. It is explored, in the following pages, from many different points of view—scientific, philosophical, religious, artistic, and others. This broad range of approaches reflects another important aspect of the emerging new paradigm: the recognition that all rational approaches to reality are limited, and that scientific knowledge is not the only valid kind of knowledge. Broad acceptance of this fact will be a necessary step toward a more balanced culture. In such a culture, science will be only one of many ways pursued by men and women to deepen their understanding of the cosmos. It will be complemented by the intuitive ways of poets, mystics, philosophers, and many other, equally valid, approaches.

The recognition that all concepts and theories we use to describe nature are limited has been one of the main lessons that physicists have had to learn in this century. It has given rise to the idea that the science of the future may not produce any more broad unified theories but may well consist of a network of interlocking and mutually consistent models, none of them being any more fundamental than the others. Such an approach seems to be suited ideally to describe the multileveled, interrelated fabric of reality. Ultimately, the various models will go beyond disciplinary distinctions, using whatever language will be appropriate to describe different aspects and levels of reality.

I would like to suggest that the contributions to this book should be read in such a spirit. They represent a wide spectrum of models, based on the exploration of inner and outer realms through scientific analysis, intuitive insight, religious experience, and artistic sensitivity—very often through a combination of several of these approaches. The resulting descriptions should be regarded as the first patches on a large canvas. Many of them will have to be modified, some of them erased, and all of them developed further. But I feel that they do represent an important step toward a future mosaic of interlocking models that will be able to deal with the many aspects and levels of one of the oldest problems in the history of human thought—the nature of consciousness.

In reading *The Metaphors of Consciousness*, it was very gratifying for me to see that the fundamental relationship between the views of modern science and of mystical traditions—an idea which seemed to be very farfetched when I began to explore it a decade ago—is acknowledged, explicitly or implicitly, throughout the book. I think that this, too, is a significant aspect of the new paradigm. In the past, mystical, paranormal, and other transpersonal experiences were not taken seriously in our culture, because they contradicted the basic concepts of classical Western science. People who had experiences of that kind were often diagnosed as schizophrenic by psychiatrists who lacked the conceptual framework for dealing with the transpersonal realm. This situation is now changing rapidly. As Buddhism is establishing itself as the religion of a significant number of Americans, and meditation is no longer viewed with ridicule or suspicion, mysticism is being found worthy of serious consideration even within the scientific community. This has made an increasing number of scientists aware that mystical thought provides a consistent and relevant philosophical background to the theories of contemporary science.

This development may be extremely significant for the further evolution of our culture. Contributions, like the ones collected in this volume, which acknowledge and explore the kinship between science and mysticism, will be not only intellectually stimulating but also therapeutic and culturally unifying.

FRITJOF CAPRA

Contents

Introduction

It seems that a book with the title *The Metaphors of Consciousness* should naturally begin with an introductory discussion of both "consciousness" and "metaphor." Both of these terms have acquired so many different, and ofttimes conflicting, meanings and interpretations that a clarifying discussion of each is not only appropriate but, in fact, necessary.

Consciousness is examined by a diverse group of disciplines—psychology, philosophy, and the religious and spiritual traditions—but it is not unequivocally defined. Concepts like consciousness, mind, awareness, soul, and spirit are too often used interchangeably, inadvertently masking important distinctions that must be made in order to do justice to the complexity of the phenomena involved. Many psychologists, for example, equate consciousness and mind. The rational mind is considered as merely an emergent property of neurological functioning (i.e., the brain), and these physiological processes serve as the causal explanation for all experiential phenomena. In this view, the mind is somehow contained in the brain (see Chapter 8); consciousness *is* mind *is* brain.

The psychologist Charles Tart (see Chapter 10), on the other hand, espouses emergent interactionism; that is, brain and mind as dualistic aspects combine to form a system. Consciousness is an emergent property of this system (not just of brain alone) and manifests itself as "states." Rather than simply equating consciousness with brain, Tart describes a spectrum of different states of consciousness, of which rational, conceptual thought is only one.

Still other psychologists (the existential-phenomenologists, see Chapter 4) and many philosophers regard consciousness as intentional; that is, consciousness is always a consciousness *of* (it always has an object which is not consciousness itself). In this sense, consciousness is the process in which meaning is revealed—consciousness *is* intentionality *is* meaning. Human experience and meaning constitute the primary reality, whatever form the nonexperiential, neurological substrata may take.

In the religious and spiritual realms, consciousness is identified with a transpersonal, nondualistic reality. Pure consciousness is the absolute, noumenal (Kantian) ground which underlies all apparent phenomenal distinctions. Brain, mind, matter, and meaning become simply conceptualizations, mere reflections or manifestations of an underlying, all encompassing unity or *transcendent* consciousness (see Chapter 15). From this perspective, which distinguishes everyday experience from mystical union (this union being the true origin and ultimate goal), consciousness is consciousness *without* an object—pure, undifferentiated bliss. Intentionality may indeed characterize mind, but it is not a hallmark of consciousness! The traditional dualisms are also seen in a new light. Subject–object, mind–matter, idealism–realism, and knower–known are all considered to be illusory dichotomies, their fundamental unity being more basic than their apparent difference.

It is interesting to note that these many different interpretations of consciousness seem to be coming full circle. From within the most "physicalistic" disciplines, such as quantum physics and neuropsychology, come holistic theoretical formulations (see Chapters 5 and 6) which treat consciousness in a way that is remarkably similar to the mystical approaches just discussed. A promising movement toward integration, an integration which will unite the noumenal and phenomenal realms, has appeared on the horizon. The chapters which comprise this volume are offered as representative examples of this very same integrative activity.

Let us now examine the nature of metaphor, emphasizing in particular its essential role in understanding human consciousness. Why, in fact, do we need to talk about metaphors at all?

In order to discuss any issue or describe any experience, one must use language. Inherent in the very structure of language itself is the figure of speech, of which metaphor is the primary one, metaphor being a way of seeing something in terms of something else and, thereby, extending our range of meanings. It takes us from the familiar to the unfamiliar and, speaking metaphorically, serves as a bridge. "Language develops by metaphorical extension, in borrowing words from the realm of the corporeal, visible, tangible and applying them by analogy to the realm of the incorporeal, invisible, intangible."[1] Language articulates and expresses human experience, and metaphors lie at the heart of language. Metaphors, therefore, form the very ground of human consciousness; per-

---

[1]Burke, K. *A Grammar of Motives.* Berkeley: University of California Press, 1969, p.506.

ceived reality *is* metaphorical. Every act of perception carries us *beyond* ourselves into the world. Metaphor literally means "to carry" (*pherein*) "beyond" (*meta*).

Metaphors serve in the creation of theories. As the title of this book indicates, each theory can be understood as a particular metaphorical construction of consciousness. Theories are also metastructures that go beyond the immediacy of experience, becoming, in this way, analogies of human consciousness. In psychology, for example, we find many co-existing theories which articulate human awareness, each one characterized by a different set of ruling metaphors. Hence, psychology is essentially a polyparadigmatic discipline—no single theory can be completely reduced to the terms of any other. Each theory is valid in that it reveals an essential aspect or facet of the structure of human reality, and "truth" is revealed in the discussion of these theoretical differences. This book, therefore, is intended to be an invitation to the ongoing, creative dialogue of theoretical differences and the mutual visitation of metaphors.

Although each theory is originally formulated by one author or founder, its continuing existence depends on *social* institutions or organizations, what we call "schools of thought." In the acceptance of and commitment to any particular theory, there is also an implicit choice of a community of belief. Thus, there is a transrational foundation of theorizing—the faith one has in the truth-revealing power of the theory's unique selection of metaphors and constructs—a decision which cannot be justified in purely logical terms but, rather, reflects an existential choice and social commitment.

The contents of this book and the selection of contributors also represent such a choice. We have included not only the range of subject matter *we* consider most relevant to the understanding of consciousness, but also those individuals with whom we have become most familiar and professionally involved. The editors are well aware that many other "models" could have been included with equal justification: for example, the forever-progressing fugues of Bach, the metaperspectives offered in an Escher print, or Gregory Bateson's vision of the ecology of mind. In addition, there are many other relevant psychological approaches that are not specifically addressed. We are all limited by time, space, and the sociality of choice.

Within the domain of these foundational restrictions of any choice, the contents describe the structure which has slowly but painlessly evolved for this book. The foreword is written by Fritjof Capra, a high-energy particle physicist whose interest and work in describing the remarkable similarities between the findings of the new physics and Eastern philosophy are well known. The twenty-five chapters that comprise the main body of the book are divided into seven major parts. Each part begins with an editorial commentary that describes the reasons for the selection and division. The reader will note that several chapters discuss issues that probably would have justified their inclusion in another part as well. The editors assume full responsibility for decisions regarding chapter placement, their choices reflecting an attempt to make the various approaches to the book as clear and balanced as possible.

The editors hope that this volume will contribute to the fruitful discussion of the most central question of human concern: What is the nature of human consciousness?

> You ask, how can we know the Infinite?
> I answer, not by reason.
> —Plotinus

RONALD S. VALLE
ROLF VON ECKARTSBERG

Pittsburgh, Pennsylvania
December, 1979

I

Metaphors and Maps

The first two chapters present introductory issues that must be addressed in order to understand why "metaphor" is a useful concept in understanding human consciousness. Both of these chapters present foundational considerations which serve as a ground for all of the other chapters which follow.

The first chapter, by Robert Romanyshyn, presents the notion that not only is human experience metaphorical in nature, but also that metaphor is an essential constituent of the structure of human experience. That is, part of the meaning of any experience is elusive, and it is the use of *metaphor* that formulates this elusive meaning and makes it available to us as an understandable figure of speech.

The second chapter, by Rolf von Eckartsberg, examines a broad range of psychological theories as cognitive maps. After presenting each theory in its original diagrammatic form, a heuristic framework is offered in order to integrate these various theories. This framework illustrates the multidimensional nature of human existence, emphasizing its corporeal, imaginative, and spiritual aspects.

Science and Reality
METAPHORS OF EXPERIENCE AND EXPERIENCE AS METAPHORICAL

Robert D. Romanyshyn

An Historical Example

On May 24, 1832, the Swiss naturalist L. A. Necker (1832, p. 336) wrote a letter to Sir David Brewster in which he described the "sudden and involuntary change in the apparent position of a crystal" during its observation. Illustrating his point (see Figure 1), Necker stated that repeated observations of the same figure resulted in a change in its configuration. At one moment the face ACDB was foremost with the face XDC behind it, and at another moment XDC came forward while ACDB receded. Admittedly puzzled, and confessing that for a long time he had been "at a loss to understand the reason of the apparently accidental and involuntary change," Necker added that the only thing which he could observe was that "at the time the change took place, a particular sensation was felt in the eye." This observation was, however, an important one, because it proved to him that an optical and not merely mental operation was involved. It was "an involuntary change in the adjustment of the eye for obtaining distinct vision (pp. 336, 337)," which explained the phenomenon. It was the moving eye searching for a clear vision which accounted for the observation, and, in a test of this explanation, Necker discovered that he could bring about the change by focusing his vision in a certain fashion. If he wanted to see the face ACDB as foremost, he had to

Robert D. Romanyshyn ● Department of Psychology, University of Dallas, Irving, Texas 75061.

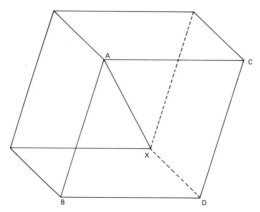

Figure 1 (from Necker, 1832, p. 336).

direct his gaze toward angle A. Conversely, if he wished to see the face XDC as foremost, he had to focus his vision on angle X.

The Necker cube, like a host of other reversible figures and perceptual illusions, has had a long history in psychology. It is a history which continues today. As recently as April, 1976, the cover of *Scientific American* illustrated an article by Gaetano Kanizsa, entitled "Subjective Contours," which dealt with similar phenomena. This endurance is impressive, but certainly it cannot be attributed to the complexities of the empirical problems which these phenomena raise. Empirically they are understood, even if the technical details of their investigation can always be advanced. A physics of nature and a physiology of the body are the contexts within which their empirical solutions are found. If at times such solutions seem inadequate, one needs only to add an *attentive* mind to account for the phenomena. They are nestled between the objective world of empirical facts and the subjective experience of the perceiver, and situated in this fashion, the empirical challenge of such figures is minimal. But if not an empirical challenge, then why do they endure? Is it perhaps because these figures quietly challenge the very foundations upon which our empirical approach to experience and reality rest? Do these phenomena force us beyond the dualism of empirical things and rational mind? Do they implicitly bring into question the most fundamental questions of what is an experienced thing, what is the experiencing body, and what is the relation between the thing experienced and the experience of a thing, if it is not a relation of matter, in the sense of material things in themselves, and mind, in the sense of an immaterial reality for itself? The philosopher of science Norwood Hanson (1972), from whom I have borrowed this opening example, seems to suggest as much. He states, for example, with regard to the Necker cube, that it is important "to note that this observational phenomenon began life not as a psychologist's trick, but at the very frontiers of observational science" (pp. 178–179). For Hanson, then, there is no doubt that this phenomenon raises a fundamental issue. It concerns the question of observing and the philosophical status of the observed.

Already with Necker it is clear that it is not just mind which directs this change in the cube's configuration. He declares that he cannot adequately account for what he sees in terms of a mental operation. One or the other face appears with an *involuntary* change in the adjustment of the eye. The face which is seen, and one's experience of it, do not lead a mental existence. But, on the other hand, it is also clear that it is more than a mechanical, retinal eye which sees. Necker can *voluntarily* experience one or the other face of the cube. He can look with an attentive eye. The face which is seen, and one's experience of it, also do not lead an empirical existence. Indeed, it is impossible to choose either of these alternatives in order to explain the phenomenon, and Necker's account more closely resembles a movement between them. The figure not only sets one's eye in motion, but also one's understanding. The experience of seeing can lead the "see-er" to the appearance of a particular face, and yet the experience of seeing can also be led to a face which appears. The experience seems to be actively mindful and passively recorded. The phenomenon seems to be a created, rational idea and a discovered, empirical fact. The phenomenon and the experience of it seem to be mental and material.

But what is not understandable through *either* alternative is even less comprehensible as an addition of the two. If Necker's account suggests this movement between a realism of the eye—the anatomical eye which records the figure and whose involuntary movement is only a muscular response to stimuli—and a rationalism of the mind, then it is a movement which eventually begins to break down these alternatives rather than to join them. I am not suggesting that Necker himself speaks in this way, but I am suggesting that the "logic of the phenomenon" leads us in this direction. Moving between an empiricism of the world and a rationalism of the mind, this simple figure pushes the observer beyond the boundaries of these terms toward another reality. Or stated in a better way, this moving little figure which appears on the frontiers of observational science reawakens the observer to that sense of reality as it initially appears before the terms of matter and mind are applied. It reawakens the observer to experienced reality, or to what Merleau-Ponty (1962) calls "the phenomenal field," that "layer of living experience through which other people and things are first given to us" (p. 57).

The Necker cube is neither a mental nor a material reality. It is neither a fact in the world nor an idea of the mind. On the contrary, it is an illustration of that first opening of reality, and *as such*, an illustration of the metaphorical character of the world. The phenomenal field about which Merleau-Ponty so eloquently writes, the experienced world about which phenomenology speaks, is a metaphorical reality, and, in this light, the Necker cube and phenomena like it endure because, through their ambiguity and this movement of breakdown, they return us to the originary metaphorical character of the world. Through this example, then, we are set on the path toward recovering this world. Along the way, we also shall have reason to recognize how this original presentation of reality is lost or forgotten, and thus how matter and mind pass from metaphors of experience to philosophical definitions about it.

Experience and Metaphorical Reality

The claim of this chapter is that the original presentation of reality is metaphorical. Ambiguous or reversible perceptual figures like the Necker cube vividly illustrate this point. Let us, therefore, interrogate this figure as it is experienced, in order to see what it can teach us about the metaphorical character of reality.

Reflection

The first thing which we learn if we stay with the figure as it is experienced is that the configuration which is seen *reflects* an attitude or position of the see-er. The see-er and seen form an indissoluble system, one gestalt, so that *what* is seen is always inextricably bound up with *how* one sees, that is, with the concrete anthropological conditions of the perceiver. Necker notices a movement of the eye with the change in appearance, and what is this movement, voluntary or involuntary, if it is not a shift in a way of seeing? When I visit an art museum to look at a Cézanne landscape, my eye searches the canvas, asking it to show itself and being told by the painting how to look. In this case, moreover, the shift in attitude or posture is quite clear, since I actually conduct myself toward the painting in visible ways. Now I stand before it, and then I draw away before I move slightly to the side and tilt my head to see it in another fashion. With each attitude the painting appears in a new way. I change my perspective, and the painting changes; or the painting solicits another look and invites me to change my way of seeing.

But the leap from Necker cubes and art objects to the world outside, to nature, seems too great. Is the original presentation of natural reality also metaphorical? Consider the following imaginative variation of history.

Johannes Kepler and Tycho Brahe are standing on an early morning hillside awaiting the dawn. When that moment finally comes, they both turn toward the east, and, looking in the same direction, they see . . .? The sentence cannot be finished, because, although both men are looking at the same event, they see a different reality. Hanson (1972), from whom this example is taken, quotes the philosopher of science Philip Frank who says that "sense observation shows only that in the morning the distance between horizon and sun is increasing" (p. 182, n. 6). This increasing distance is the same event which Kepler and Brahe see, and yet, in another sense, neither of them sees this event at all. Kepler and Brahe live in different worlds. They stand and see in different ways. Kepler, who already lives in a Copernican universe, sees, therefore, a moving earth. Brahe, who lives in a Ptolemaic world, sees a rising sun. For each of them, this increasing distance is a different world. What each one sees reflects the see-er. How each one looks, one with the eyes of modern science, the other with the eyes of an older world-view, is inextricably related to what one sees.

Does the earth move? Or does the sun rise and set? The questions do not *initially* allow an *empirical* reply, because originally they involve a metaphorical vision. The answers first depend, therefore, on the metaphorical perspective within which one is. The answers presume and reflect that perspective. Given the perspective, however, empirical evidence can then be attained in support of or in opposition to the metaphor. Empirical facts are generated within a metaphorical vision. A metaphor opens up a world which reflects a way of seeing. It binds together a way of seeing and what is there to be seen.

I look at my friend and I say, "Tom is a wolf." This metaphor is neither factually true about Tom in himself nor merely my idea of him. On the contrary, like every metaphor, it says as much about the speaker as it does about the spoken. It says, implicitly if not explicitly, how to see in order to see that Tom is a wolf. To see what I say about Tom, I must look in a certain way. I must notice this and neglect that. But when I see in this way, I do see that indeed he is a wolf. The metaphor has a bite to it. It rings true. I can show another what to see by indicating how to look. Tom's wolfishness, like the increasing distance between horizon and sun, is originally a metaphorical reality. What is seen does reflect a way of seeing.

Paradox

In the story of Johannes Kepler and Tycho Brahe, I mentioned that they see the *same* reality *differently*. The increasing distance is for one a moving earth and for the other a rising sun. The world in its original presentation as a metaphorical reality is paradoxical. Like the reversible figure, it changes its face and yet remains the same.

Consider this example: Two friends decide to take a walk on a bright summer day. One, Mr. A, is a botanist, and the other, Mr. B, is a geologist. They approach a shaded forest, and, as they enter this field,

they fall into silence. Continuing their walk, they emerge finally upon a
clearing, and, as they sit down, they engage in the following conversation:

> Mr. A: Did you notice the many species of flowers, trees, and plants in the
> forest?
> Mr. B: Flowers? Trees? Plants? Were there flowers in the forest? Funny! I did
> not see them. But did you notice the strata markings on the many
> broken rocks which we passed? They were really interesting.
> Mr. A: Rocks? There were no rocks in that forest. There were flowers and
> plants and trees. You must have seen them.
> Mr. B: What? No rocks! That is ridiculous. You could not have missed them.

The conversation continues. The sun sets (or the earth moves). It
grows cold. The two friends decide to walk back home. They enter the
forest again. On the way back, Mr. A stumbles over the rocks, while Mr. B
steps on the flowers.

It is admittedly a simple example, and yet it makes the point. The
same forest is also a different forest, or, in the differences, it is nevertheless the same. For both A and B there is no doubt that they have walked
together through the same woods, and yet for each of them there is also
no doubt about the forest which was seen. There are not two forests.
There is only one. But this one forest is a multiple reality, a paradoxical
reality, which *is* what it is not, and *is not* what it is. "The forest," the
Spanish philosopher José Ortega y Gasset (1963) says, "flees from one's
eyes" (p. 59). It is an *elusive* reality. Reality in its original metaphorical
presentation is elusive. It shows itself to be this, and then, through that
appearance, alludes to something other than what appears.

It is not difficult to show that this paradox of identity-difference beats
at the heart of metaphor. Indeed, a metaphor succeeds only because it
also fails. It tells us what something is only because it also says, at least
implicitly, that this something is not what it is. For example, the great
seventeenth-century, English physician William Harvey (1943) says that
the heart is a pump, and he writes an astonishing book with empirical
support for his point of view, which historically has transformed our
vision of ourselves, of our bodies, and of our medical achievements. But
certainly, though it is empirically true that the heart is a pump, can we fail
to recognize that it is true empirically only because this truth is a
metaphor? If the heart were *not* a pump, could this work have been
written? Is it a pumping heart which knows itself as a pumping heart?
Harvey confesses in the dedication to his text that the publication of his
views took some courage, while a little later in the text he describes the
experience of courage from the point of view of the pumping heart. Is the
courageous heart which writes the text the same mechanical heart whose
courage is a matter of an increase in pulsific power? A negative answer

seems undeniable. The heart which has the courage to write the text *is not* the heart which is described. Nevertheless, while they are not identical, they are not absolutely different either. As I have argued elsewhere, a courageous heart which failed to pump blood could no more have written that work than a heart which was only a pump.[1] The heart is a paradoxical reality of identity–difference.

The heart is a pump! This is a metaphorical truth which affirms that the heart is not a pump. It is a truth about the heart precisely because it is also not true. But this "not true" is not a negation, a mere denial of what is previously affirmed. It is, on the contrary, an allusion to a difference. Reality in its original metaphorical presentation *is what it is not* and/or *is not what it is.* Either of those phrases is meant to describe that elusive character of reality according to which in showing itself to be what it is, it alludes to being something more, something else, a difference.

Illusion, Allusion, and the Elusive

Although the Necker cube is not, strictly speaking, classified as an illusion, it does belong with all those ambiguous figures which are classified as perceptual *tricks.* Kanizsa (1976) presents many of these figures, and what is common between them and the reversible figure is the instability of their appearance. They move, they change, they are disruptive in their presentation. In this sense, we may accept the reversible figure as an *illusion,* and, insofar as we do, we tacitly acknowledge that the changing appearances which are seen are not real. That is, these changes do not belong to the order of things but to the perceptual apparatus of the subject. The eye moves, but not the figure. The figure remains a fixed and stable given. Its movement is illusory, an apparent movement. Regarding the changing appearances as an illusion, we preserve our belief in the immutability of things. What appears is divorced from how and when it is seen. The small, early morning sun with its diffuse, pink light is the same sun which sets at night with a swollen, fiery face.

Attention to the figure as it is experienced belies, however, this judgment of illusion. Indeed, what is *judged* as illusion is more readily *seen* as elusive. The figure which appears eludes us. What it offers at one moment is retracted at another moment as it presents a second face, and, in relation to this elusive character of the thing, one's perceiving becomes

---

[1]This argument is developed in my recently completed book, *The Metaphorical Texture of Psychological Life,* which deals with psychological life as a metaphorical reality. It appears in a chapter devoted to the recovery of the psychological body, the body as metaphor. Much of this chapter draws on the arguments presented in that book.

an allusion. The perceiving eye invites a way in which the thing may appear. It does not define. Between the seeing eye and the thing which is seen, there is a mutual impregnation rather than a passive recording.

But what is true of the cube figure in this fashion is even more true of the things of the world as they are experienced. The scientific eye which sees a spectrum in a rainbow opens a world which is never seen by the eye of science, the recording eye of anatomy. That scientific eye whose vision is an allusion is not the scientific eye which is seen. The former brings forth from the rainbow the elusive appearance of the spectrum which is and is not there in the rainbow, while the latter, if one ever could see with this eye, merely records an isolated datum, a bare thing which is in fact not a thing at all but an abstraction. "How unimportant a thing would be," Ortega y Gasset (1963) asks, "if it were only what it is in isolation?" (pp. 176–177). The rainbow would be only the rainbow, and the spectrum only the spectrum. Worlds would be lost. Reality would be diminished. Metaphorical vision would disappear.

Things, however, resist this literal gaze of the eye which would lock each thing in itself. They persist in showing themselves only through other things, and in this regard the elusiveness of things is betrayed in the most fundamental fashion. This elusive character of reality involves not only the changing face of things—the sun at night and in the morning—or the paradox of identity/difference—the forest of flowers and rocks; it also involves the way in which one thing is what it is, only through something else. The tree, for example, shimmers in the water which flows beneath it, and through that reflection the tree *is* the water, just as the water in visiting the tree on a hot summer day is the tree. Indeed, as I have argued elsewhere (Romanyshyn, 1978), reflections and shadows are peculiarly well suited to demonstrate this elusiveness of things and to indicate how each thing does establish a network of allusions to other things. The reflection visibly shows that the tree *is* the water, and in this regard can one ask for a more visible demonstration of the originally *metaphorical* character of things? To say that the tree *is* the water affirms only what we see, this metaphorical play of things, the founding source of human imagination. Through reflections and shadows, things *deepen* each other. The originary metaphorical character of things is the depth of reality. It is nothing less than the way in which *material* reality *matters*.

A metaphor matters! It counts, and it is the way in which the material world initially comes into being. To illustrate this point, consider Figure 2, a painting by Raoul Dufy entitled "Old Houses at Honfleur." Notice the reflections of the houses in the water, and then consider for a moment the painting presented in exactly the same way but without those reflections. What would become of the houses? Without those reflections, would not

Figure 2 (from Elderfield, 1976, p. 93).

those houses simply float away? Would they not become inhuman houses, without any anchor in the world? Would they not seem unreal? I think the point is unarguable. It is the reflections which convince us of the reality of the houses (and the water). The reflections, this play of allusions, the visible evidence of the elusiveness of things, makes matter matter. Reflections, this presence of one thing through something else, is not an illusion, but a visible display of the originary metaphorical character of things.

Transition

A visit to a museum, an imaginary conversation between Johannes Kepler and Tycho Brahe, a walk taken by two friends in a wood, the rainbow, and the reflections of things have illustrated how reality in its original appearance is metaphorical. Each of these examples, however, has had to work against a resistance, the tendency to take for granted this metaphorical display of the world. We do tend to disregard as immaterial the reflections and shadows of things, and in the course of everyday life we do tend to forget how we the see-ers are implicated in what is seen.

The effort of recovery must be balanced, therefore, with some attention to this forgetfulness of things as they appear. The forgetfulness of the originary metaphorical character of things is as much a part of our experience of reality as is the original presentation.

Experience and the Forgetfulness of Metaphor

Newton's Rainbow

In 1666, Isaac Newton crossed the threshold of his room, and pulling the shade to darken the room, he proceeded to cut a small hole in that shade to admit a ray of the daylight sun. Placing a prism between the entering light and the far wall of the room, Newton turned his back on the light and saw displayed on that wall the sunlight dispersed as a spectrum (Schwartz & Bishop, 1958, pp. 393–400). A remarkable achievement at the early beginnings of modern science, this simple and elegant experiment methodically portrays that natural tendency to forget how the concrete conditions of experience are essentially related to what is experienced.

What is the spectrum? It is the component parts of the white light of the sun, an empirical fact of the natural world. The experiment uncovers the spectrum which is hidden in the light of day. It discovers the true reality of the light. But is the experiment really a discovery? Does the spectrum hide in the daylight sun? Is it there *before* Newton looks?

These questions initially seem inappropriate, because the apparent converse of them commits us to an untenable position. The spectrum is there *before* Newton looks, because we rightly do not believe that it is there *because* he looks. Science and our perceptual life focus on the world. Of this we rightly have no doubt. Moreover, in addition to this consideration, the evidence of daily experience seems to confirm that the experiment is a discovery. We take a walk after a light spring rain and see the rainbow. Newton himself makes this second point. The rainbow is the spectrum in the world, the refraction of the daylight sun, the visible evidence that the spectrum lies *in* nature.

It requires, however, only a brief reflection to realize that this second point is not quite acceptable. Although the spectrum may explain the rainbow, the rainbow *is not* the spectrum. Or, to be more precise here, the rainbow *is* the spectrum, provided that this "is" is understood as a metaphor. In other words, the statement is correctly understood when one comprehends that it indicates *a way of seeing,* and not simply something to be seen. "The rainbow is the spectrum" is a prescription about *how* to look. But how is one to look in order to see that the rainbow is the spectrum?

The experiment prescribes the conditions, and in this regard the spectrum too is also revealed as originally a metaphorical reality. It too is a way of seeing, and not simply something to be seen. More precisely, one sees the light of day as a spectrum when one turns away from this light, narrows one's vision, and looks with a special eye. Newton turns his back on the light, cuts a small hole in his window shade, and looks through a prism. These arrangements which he makes, these procedures and instruments which he uses, these anthropological conditions of experience, are the concrete, embodied postures of this metaphorical vision. They are the specific ways in which we are told how to see, if we are to see that the sunlight is a spectrum.

But if we speak in this fashion, then are we not committed again to that first untenable position previously mentioned? Are we not admitting that the spectrum is there *because* he looks? Are we not implying that these conditions *create* the spectrum?

Newton himself makes a passing reference to this concern. He wonders if "the various thicknesses of the glass" (p. 394), for example, produce this effect of the spectrum, and he experiments in a way which allows him to dismiss this condition. The thickness of the prism does not matter, which comes to mean that the prism itself does not matter, in the sense of creating the spectrum. The point is, of course, quite correct. But though these conditions do not create the spectrum, they cannot be dismissed. Without them there is no spectrum. Without this way of seeing, the rainbow is not and can never be the spectrum. These conditions figure that reality which is experienced. These conditions which embody a metaphor, a figure of speech, as we say, present the spectrum as a figure of the light.

It would seem, therefore, that we must acknowledge that the spectrum is there neither *because* nor *before* Newton looks, but *when* and in relation to *how* he looks. This acknowledgement, moreover, alters nothing of the validity of the achievement. On the contrary, it "only" illustrates the temporality of human experience, a temporality which is marked by the passage to the literal from the metaphorical. A reality which originally appears metaphorically is forgotten and as such becomes a literal, empirical fact. A spectrum which is also a way of seeing becomes only something to be seen. A reality which is neither *in* us nor *in* the world but between the world and us in a *relation of experience* becomes a fact *in* the world of which we *have an experience*.

This literalizing of experience as illustrated in the domain of science is also characteristic, however, of the experience of everyday life. Experience is an awareness of the world precisely as it is a forgetfulness of itself, or there is, so to speak, a natural unconsciousness at the heart of experience.[2] In our daily concerns, we pass into the things in themselves and pass over how things reveal themselves only in relation to our attitudes, intentions, and dispositions. The city in which one lives, for example, quickly assumes a habitual character, and it is often only with the arrival of a visitor that it appears in another way, which awakens one to his or her original way of seeing. At that moment, through the eyes of the stranger, the reality which my city is loses its taken-for-granted character. Through his eyes, the city opens up in another way. The visit of the stranger invites a clash of metaphors.

I do not wish to dwell, however, on the forgetfulness of everyday experience. Rather, I offer an example of it only to indicate that scientific experience is not peculiar in this regard. Indeed, scientific experience is, *in this regard,* a methodic extension of everyday experience, a point which phenomenologists like Husserl (1970), Merleau-Ponty (1962), Straus (1963), and van den Berg (1970) make with convincing clarity. Describing everyday experience as a "perceptual faith," for example, Merleau-Ponty (1968) shows how "science presupposes the perceptual faith and does not elucidate it" (p. 14). Another issue, however, is raised by the use of the Newton example to illustrate this perceptual faith, this transition from an original metaphorical presentation of reality to a forgetfulness of metaphor. If the *origins* of modern science illustrate this theme, is it a theme which also characterizes scientific experience today? Is contemporary science aware of the metaphorical character of its work, and, if so, does it lead to a revisioning of our understanding of reality?

In large measure, I believe that it can be stated that contemporary science remains *unaware* of its metaphorical character, and I will illustrate this point with a brief presentation of the work of the Nobel laureate Sir John Eccles. Before I turn to this consideration, I would like to add two points. The first one is that quantum theory, especially as it takes its inspiration from the work of Niels Bohr (1966), implies a radical recovery of the metaphorical character of reality. Insofar as Bohr argues that "a particle and an instrument adjusted to make a specific measurement on it constitute in some respects a single system" (d'Espagnat, 1979, p. 177), he acknowledges that *what is seen* (the state of a particle, for example) is always in relation to a *way of seeing* (the experimental arrangements).[3] The

---

[2]This point is elaborated in my article entitled "Unconsciousness: Reflection and the Primacy of Perception" (Romanyshyn, 1977). The painting by Dufy also appears in that article, where it is used to illustrate the theme of unconsciousness as an absence of reflections. *The unconscious,* in the sense of repression, is an "un-image-able" existence, a style of life caught in literalism. Neurosis is a form of literalism.

[3]See R. Valle, Chapter 21, for another discussion of this insight.—Eds.

second point is that this volume itself offers interesting alternatives to the direction of contemporary science presented below.

Eccles's Self-Conscious Mind

Eccles affirms a strong dualist–interactionist position with regard to the question of mind and brain, or, more broadly, matter and mind. His hypothesis is that the self-conscious mind is an *independent* entity, which is actively engaged in a reading-out process with respect to the neural events occurring in the dominant cerebral hemisphere, the so-called liaison-brain. He emphasizes an *interaction* between mind and brain, without committing himself to an *identity* between them. He affirms a dualism to avoid any simple-minded reductionism. Thus, the self-conscious mind plays an active and dominant role with regard to the liaison-brain, even to the point of being able to effect changes in the neuronal events (Popper & Eccles, 1977). When one tries to recapture a memory, for example, "it is proposed that the self-conscious mind is actively engaged in searching and in probing through specially selected zones of the neural machinery, and so is able to deflect and mould the dynamic patterned activities in accord with its desire or interest" (pp. 363–364). On the other hand, however, even while the mind is active in its own right with regard to brain events, and hence is not simply the consequence of them, there is no doubt that self-conscious life is brain dependent. "I think that my personal life is given to me by my brain," Eccles (1973) writes, "and is undoubtedly dependent upon my brain, coming to an end, for all I know, when my brain ceases to be" (p. 223). Dependent upon and yet independent of the brain, Eccles's self-conscious mind affirms the position adopted by Sperry, according to which mind is restored to its "old prestigious position over matter, in the sense that the mental phenomena are seen to transcend the phenomena of physiology and biochemistry" (Popper & Eccles, 1977, p. 374).

I do not contest the empirical validity of Eccles's impressive work. My discussion is not focused upon *what he sees*. Rather, my concern is how this work *forgets* that the terms matter and mind, the liaison-brain and the self-conscious mind, are initially *ways of seeing*, in relation to which the empirical data are established. In other words, liaison-brain and self-conscious mind become realities in themselves. The human organism, man, the human person, becomes this interacting-dualism, when in fact this dualism is a metaphor of human action, a means of envisioning it, a *vehicle* through which the *tenor* of human embodied life may be seen (Richards, 1936). When one compares the experimental context out of which these terms appear with the terms themselves which are applied to this context, their status as metaphors, as ways of seeing the events in question, rather than as empirical facts which are demanded by the events themselves, becomes clear.

As an example, consider what Eccles has to say about dreaming. Like every other embodied human action, dreaming is a dual function. During the dream, the self-conscious mind is engaged in reading out neural events, as it is with every other activity. There is the activity which occurs in the liaison-brain and the activity of the self-conscious mind which continuously scans these events. Obviously, this process of neural activity being read out by a mind is not the experience of the dreamer. Without the observing scientist who is watching the dreamer's brain activity as an EEG recording to tell the dreamer of the occurrence of these events, the dreamer would never know of them or of their relation to dreaming, even when he is awake. His ignorance here is not an ignorance of fact, but an ignorance in principle. It springs from the *difference* between his experience of dreaming and its explanation. For the dreamer, his experience of dreaming and/or his experience of his own dreaming brain is given *through* the world of the dream, the figures and events which comprise the landscape of the dream. It is given *through* this world (as a world), and not *in* those neural events. In like manner, moreover, the observing scientist who is watching the dreamer's brain activity and who sees in that activity the presence of self-conscious mind acting on brain events is not aware of his own perceptual activity in this way. The hypothesis self-conscious mind/liaison-brain is not the experience of the observing scientist. On the contrary, his experience of his own brain activity is given *through* the things which he experiences, the dreaming subject which he sees, the clock on the wall which he hears, and the coffee which he smells brewing in the laboratory. Notwithstanding the serious issue of how the chief function of the self-conscious mind—this process of reading out brain events—is not itself a conscious process, the more important issue here is this *difference*. There is a difference between what the observing scientist sees and says of the dreamer's brain and the experience of his own brain, just as there is a difference between what is seen and said of the dreamer's brain and his experience of his brain.

The observing scientist sees in the events of the dreamer's brain the activity of the self-conscious mind/liaison-brain, and, quite naturally, his intention is to apply this vision to his own brain. Eccles does not exclude himself from the hypothesis which he advances about others. But this vision, as we have seen, does not apply to the observing scientist's own experience of the dreamer's brain. Hence, *between* his brain and the dreamer's brain, there is an intended identity and an experienced difference. Human functioning is a self-conscious mind reading out the liaison-brain, and it is not this interacting-dualism. Self-conscious mind and liaison-brain are paradoxes of identity/difference. The interactive dualism of matter and mind is a metaphor.

It is clear, however, from Eccles's writings that he does *not* regard his hypothesis as a metaphor. It is an empirical fact which "belongs to science . . . and is objectively testable" (Popper & Eccles, 1977, p. 375). Of course, I do not doubt this claim, but I do emphasize that it provides evidence of the forgetfulness of metaphor. Eccles's work, which is a monument to careful empirical research, does betray that forgetfulness of metaphor which characterizes the origins of modern science and our everyday perceptual life. As a consequence, the metaphor of matter and mind with respect to human embodied life, which arises within the context of a duality, becomes the terms of a real dualism. We all become or remain an organism composed of two parts, and any opportunity either to rethink the issue of matter and mind within the context of self and other,[4] or to go beyond this dualism, is forgotten.

Metaphorical Reality and Psychological Life

In 1953, Jean Cocteau, the French dramatist and critic, wrote in his diary of an episode that happened to him when he revisited his childhood home. Finding himself one day in his old neighborhood, he approached the house and, with some reluctance, entered the backyard where he had spent many hours of his youth. Noticing how things had changed, he was soon interrupted by a man who inquired about his reasons for being there. Unable to convince the man of his intentions, Cocteau soon found himself back on the street. Not wanting to forget his past too soon, Cocteau recalled how as a child he would walk near the houses and trail his finger along the wall. Recalling the past, he repeated this behavior but was not satisfied with the result. The memories were thin and pale. Suddenly, however, he remembered that as a child his hand trailed along the wall at a different level. He was smaller at that time. Bending down

---

[4]The dualism of brain and mind, interactionist or otherwise, generally presupposes a self in isolation, a solipsism. Eccles' experimental context suggests, however, that this way of envisioning the human person occurs within the context of self and other. Might we not take this clue, then, and wonder if the reality which we call mind (and the reality which we call body) arises in *the interaction between us*. [This insight is remarkably similar to V. Valle and Kruger's idea in Chapter 19 that the "substance of reality" is our *relationship* with one another, and R. Valle's conclusion in Chapter 21 that the human individual can be understood in purely *relational* terms.—Eds.] Certainly there is body in the sense of an individual body. But my point is that the body becomes a human body, a mindful body, a thoughtful body, within the context of others. It is the mother's voice which awakens the child's first smile. It is the other's gaze which *reflects* my interior self.

and closing his eyes, he again moved his finger along the wall. The result was astonishing:

> Just as the needle picks up the melody from the record, I obtained the melody of the past with my hand. I found everything: my cape, the leather of my satchel, the names of my friends and of my teachers, certain expressions I had used, the sound of my grandfather's voice, the smell of his beard, the smell of my sister's dresses, and of my mother's gown. (Quoted in van den Berg, 1961, p. 212)[5]

An experience of remembering, a psychological experience, is given through a wall. That wall reflects or mirrors Cocteau's experience. Cocteau's memory *is* the wall.

His memory is the wall! Certainly this statement cannot be literally true. Cocteau's memory is not *in* the wall, as the grains of sand are in it, and no scientific analysis, however sophisticated, would ever find a memory in that wall. But it is equally certain that the statement is true. One need only ask Cocteau, and/or remember how many times one's own memories have been reanimated by the sight of an old photograph, the smell of a soft summer day, or the sound of a distant church bell ringing in the night. Cocteau's memory, his experience of remembering, is most assuredly "in" the wall. It is not simply an idea or an image couched in the gray matter of his brain, projected onto a neutral physical reality. Let the wall be destroyed, and Cocteau's experience will be that much less rich.

Cocteau's memory is "in" the wall! It is "in" the wall in the same way in which wolfishness is "in" man when we say that "man is a wolf," or the spectrum is "in" the rainbow when we say, with Newton, that "the rainbow is a spectrum." In each case, one reality is given through another, and/or one reality reflects another. In each case, the reality which is experienced is not only something to experience but a way of experiencing. That way of experiencing is obviously metaphorical. The statement "Cocteau's memory is the wall" is a metaphor. His experience of remembering is metaphorical. The wall as it is experienced is a metaphorical reality.

I close with this example, because it indicates that the metaphorical character of reality unfolds itself in relation to experiences which are psychological. This does not mean, however, that it is only through psychological experience that this originary character of reality appears. It means only that the recovery of reality as metaphorical is simultaneously a recognition of psychological life on its own terms, and/or that the recovery of psychological life on its own terms leads us to a recognition of

---

[5]Van den Berg uses this example to indicate the character of psychological experience as a world. It is presented here with the same intention and in order to suggest that the psychological world is a metaphorical reality.

the metaphorical character of reality. Psychological life understood on its own terms, *psychologically rather than scientifically or philosophically*, is neither thing nor thought, matter nor mind, fact nor idea. It is not either term of any of these dualisms, or any of these dualisms themselves. It is another reality. It is a metaphor. To appreciate the character of psychological life as psychological requires an eye and a heart for metaphor. To recover the originary metaphorical character of the world is to cultivate a psychological eye and heart.[6]

References

Bohr, N. *Atomic physics and human knowledge.* New York: Vantage, 1966.

d'Espagnat, B. The quantum theory and reality. *Scientific American,* 1979, 241(5), 158–181.

Eccles, J. *The understanding of the brain.* New York: McGraw-Hill, 1973.

Elderfield, J. (Ed.) *The "Wild Beasts": Fauvism and its affinities.* New York: Oxford University Press, 1976.

Hanson, N. *Patterns of discovery.* London: Cambridge University Press, 1972.

Harvey, W. An anatomical disquisition on the motion of the heart and blood in animals. In *The Works of William Harvey.* Ann Arbor: Edwards Brothers, 1943.

Husserl, E. *The crisis of European sciences and transcendental phenomenology.* Evanston, Ill.: Northwestern University Press, 1970.

Kanizsa, G. Subjective contours. *Scientific American,* 1976, 234(4), 48–64.

Merleau-Ponty, M. *Phenomenology of perception.* London: Routledge & Kegan Paul, 1962.

Merleau-Ponty, M. *The visible and the invisible.* Evanston, Ill.: Northwestern University Press, 1968.

Necker, L. Observations on some remarkable optical phaenomena seen in Switzerland; and on an optical phaenomenon which occurs on viewing a figure of a crystal or geometrical solid. *The London and Edinburgh Philosophical Magazine and Journal of Science,* 1832, 1 (5), 329–337.

Ortega y Gasset, J. *Meditations on Quixote.* New York: Norton, 1963.

Popper, K., & Eccles, J. *The self and its brain.* New York: Springer-Verlag, 1977.

Richards, I. *The philosophy of rhetoric.* New York: Oxford University Press, 1936.

Romanyshyn, R. Unconsciousness: Reflection and the primacy of perception. Paper presented at the Merleau-Ponty Circle, Athens, Ohio, October, 1977.

Romanyshyn, R. Psychological language and the voice of things (Part 1). *Dragonflies: Studies in Imaginal Psychology,* 1978, 1, (1), 73–90.

Schwartz, G., & Bishop, P. (Eds.). *Moments of discovery: The origins of modern science (Vol. 1).* New York: Basic Books, 1958.

Straus, E. *The primary world of the senses.* New York: The Free Press of Glenco, 1963.

van den Berg, J. *The changing nature of man.* New York: Dell, 1961.

van den Berg, J. *Things.* Pittsburgh: Duquesne University Press, 1970.

[6]The argument which links the originary metaphorical character of the world to psychological life is strongly implied in the works of both van den Berg and Merleau-Ponty. In my recently completed book (referred to in Footnote 1), I have tried to make this implicit suggestion explicit. The first and final chapters attempt to support this position while the middle three chapters attempt to recover the world of things, others, and the human body in a psychological—that is, metaphorical—way.

2

Maps of the Mind
THE CARTOGRAPHY OF CONSCIOUSNESS

Rolf von Eckartsberg

Maps and Territories

The idea of cognitive maps and the use of cognitive maps to illustrate psychological structures and processes have come into psychology around the issues of: How do we represent geographical space to ourselves? How do we form an effective image of our environment such that we can feel at home in a region and find our way around? The notion of "cognitive" maps is used here with the awareness that many (most) of these maps also chart territories that are transcognitive, "beyond" the realm of cognitive thought processes.

From the fact that we do move about effectively in our world, we assume that man must be an implicit mapmaker who represents the external world within his consciousness. Humanistic and existential-phenomenological geographers (Downs & Stea, 1977; Gould & White, 1974) have found that each individual indeed seems to create a unique representation of his world, which is manifested in curious combinations of concrete images, schematizations, symbolizations, and objective geographical maps. These personal maplike representations are reality-adequate so as to guide the individual's movement effectively. Experientially, however, no two "cognitive maps of environs" of individuals are the same. This "subjective" factor, based on the reality of personal consciousness, has hitherto eluded the work of geographers, because they were interested in the intersubjectively verifiable and objectively measur-

Rolf von Eckartsberg • Department of Psychology, Duquesne University, Pittsburgh, Pennsylvania 15219.

able aspects of the world—distance, boundaries, etc. Only recently has there emerged a school of thought within the profession of geographers which wants to take the consciousness and subjective realities of residents into account and thus transcend the objectivistic bias of traditional geography.

But we can learn much from the craft of the cartographers and public mapmakers. Any map stands in a determinable relationship to the territory mapped. Publicly sanctioned road maps, for instance, represent a social consensus and geographically accurate rendering of the given terrain, whereas the private cognitive representations of the personal life-environment are organized in terms of such subjective realities as attraction-repulsion, value, desiredness, fear, love, longing, etc. The *quality of experience,* not the public consensus-features or abstract geometrized space and distance measurements, gives the contours and defines the areas and points of attraction.

One can represent the relationship of the *territory to be mapped* and the *map of the territory* as two planes of interdependent realities. The territory is the ground, and the map configures that ground according to some selected and agreed-on significant features, for example, streets, politics, topography, etc. There are as many mappings of a terrain as there are identifiable features and interests in terms of which the selective mapping is to be made.

The given ground-terrain is the reality matrix, the unnamed, the to-be-named, and the map is a transformation of that given reality. Thus, any map is a conceptual configuration that can be thematized, abstracted, and lifted from the ground and placed into another plane of meaning. Geographer-mapmakers have to respect specific rules of transformation. The map is to portray accurately the true relationships of the earth-given geological features, the shapes of land masses, rivers, lakes, oceans, settlements, and man-made lines of mobility and communication, if it is to be a usable map. The primary anchorage of meaning lies in the configuration of geological shapes, the actual distances between geographical

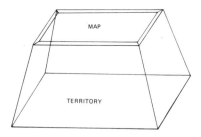

Figure 1. The map–territory relationship.

features, and the geographical *names* by which we identify and call up places and earth-features. The proper names of places are foundational for the constitution of our world-reality.

Figure 1 expresses the relationship of map to territory and indicates that there is a scale-transformation involved. The map is always smaller than the territory and more concentrated; it preserves basic relationships as it highlights selected features. Maps both reveal and conceal; they provide a gain in simplicity and clarity but usually also cover over some of the complexity of the depicted situation.

Psychological Theories as Cognitive Maps

The *map–territory relationship* in geography also pertains to the discipline of psychology, and the thought constructions of *psychological theories* can be understood as maps—cognitive maps—of the territory of human life and personality (Korzybski, 1958). Psychological theories are cognitive maps of human life. They name the relevant features of ongoing life, of the unnamed "existential process" as experienced by individual human beings.

A psychological theory conceptualizes the existential process in a particular way by identifying, naming, selecting, and interconnecting essential process-features as an interdependent network of constructs. Here, too, there are as many cognitive maps (theories) as there are theorists. There are maybe a dozen major and widely recognized theories in psychology. Below are presented theories for which the founder himself has created a cognitive map of this vision in the form of a drawing, a diagrammatic representation.

Kuhn (1962) has addressed the issue of how a theory constitutes a model or paradigm which defines the legitimate problems of the discipline and offers specific methods of research for the follower-practitioners. Kuhn, in discussing the history of the natural sciences, speaks in terms of historic paradigm shifts. A new paradigm supersedes the old one. In the social sciences, however, paradigms are never really superseded, but they coexist in critical dialogue with one another. This has been called the "criticist frame" (Radnitzki, 1968)—the commitment to the life of dialogue of diverse views in peaceful communicative exchange. Since the subject matter of the social sciences—unlike the natural sciences which study naturally caused events—is preinterpreted human action (Schutz, 1967), and since human actions are founded on cultural practices, values, philosophies, ethical standards, and religious beliefs, of which there are always many standing in competitive tension, the essentially *polyparadigmatic nature* of psychological theorizing must be affirmed. A psychologist's existential choice of and living-in a particular theory, his believing it and having faith in it, is the most "irrational" aspect of any theorizing. Once a basic philosophical anthropology, a primordial conviction about the nature of man, has been accepted, all else follows logically. The origin of accepting a theory seems to be a matter of faith rather than rationality, that it is rooted in a person's spirituality, which lies deeper than cognitive rationality. The major historical religions, philosophies, and psychologies, once they enter human culture and language, continue to survive and command a following, although they wax and wane in popularity through time. There is considerable literature on these problems of paradigms (Kuhn, 1962; Lifton, 1976), metascience (Habermas, 1968; Radnitzki, 1968), sociology of knowledge (Berger & Luckmann, 1966; Schutz, 1967), and philosophical anthropology (Giorgi, 1970; Ricoeur, 1970), and on cognitive maps (Metzner, 1971; Wilson, 1977).

One can thus characterize the state of affairs in psychology in a way similar to that in geography and express the map–territory relationship in psychology as the "dialectics of life and thought," as the dialectics of existential process and theory (see Figure 2). The essential interdependency and the figure–ground character of the life–thought relationship can be expressed by means of a yin–yang symbol, which indicates that one can move freely between levels, and that accumulation of meaning occurs on both levels by virtue of this conscious movement.

The ancient and universally known shape of the Great Pyramid can be used as a framework for thinking and for helping us to locate and represent the various levels of conscious and existential participation. More specifically, consider as an image of reference the mystical symbol of the pyramid on the back of the United States one dollar bill which constitutes the Great Seal of the United States of America (see Figure 3).

Examining this image closely, one finds that there is a separation between the tip of the pyramid, which contains an eye surrounded by a

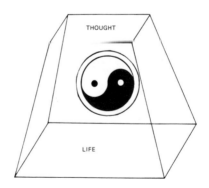

Figure 2. The dialectics of life and thought.

Figure 3. The Great Pyramid as a cognitive framework.

halo of light emanating in all directions, and the base of the pyramid. This suggests that there is a qualitative difference between the tip and the 13-tiered base of the pyramid, which is itself firmly grounded on earth in a desert landscape. The eye and the light rays suggest vision and illumination, whereas the solid layers of huge stonework constituting the sharply delineated shape of the pyramid suggest earth, rock, material presence, and bodily solidity.

The pyramid shape can be used as a three-dimensional cognitive framework which allows one to differentiate a number of different levels of consciousness and yet to understand all levels also in their interdependency constituting the meaning of personal experience.

This heuristic cognitive framework allows one to relate the existing psychological theories articulated by the various founders in the form of a diagrammatical representation to each other. The diagrammatical representations are seen as cognitive maps. Each theory is a particular cognitive map, and it occupies a certain level of generality in the pyramidal framework of consciousness. At the end of this discussion, the various "differential theories of psychology" (Van Kaam, 1966) are integrated in terms of the cognitive framework of the pyramid.

All cognitive frameworks are based on the dialectics of *life* and *thought*, which is also spoken of as the dialectic of *induction*—moving from life to thought—and *deduction*—moving from thought categories to life. We all dwell between thinking and living, we are all hermeneutic beings and meaning-creators. This cognitive model can be generalized still further if one thinks of the dialectical or, even better, the "multilectical" process of living and thinking in terms of *existence* and *essence*.

Existence, the concrete and personal occurrences of one's existential process in time, in place, and in relationship to someone or something, is represented by the base of the pyramid—the level of "Personal Event

Involvement"—and the various modes and levels of conceptualization and the reflective articulation of the essence, the essential meaning of the event under consideration, are located on the higher levels within the pyramid shape, the cognitive and intuitional levels of thinking.

Personal events are anchored in personal consciousness and in speech by proper names, the names of persons and groups, of places, and of occasions or time. Existential uniqueness and specificity are tied to proper names to which the event and what happened become associated in any narrative or account. Events are authored and attributed in responsibility, and they are located in place and time. This is a person's alibi anchorage in social awareness.

There is also the "unnamed existential process" of multiplex psychological functioning that serves as the matrix and foundation of existence, but of which one is only partially conscious, to the extent that one can recall it or put it into words as personal event involvement.

The reality of *theoretical cognitive maps*, that is, the diagrammatic representations of the structure of a theory as an autonomous level in the pyramidal cognitive framework, is also examined below. Using an analogy, one can say that the differential psychological theories are particular "cognitive lenses" through which to view reality. For the believer, the dweller in a theory, a theory is a cognitive temple. Each theory constitutes a "cognitive optics" for the study of human events. As the cognitive optics change, as a different cognitive map is employed to bring reality into focus, the same experienced event will reveal itself differently— profiled by the conceptual foci applied.

Since it has been established that every theory is also an expression of a certain philosophical anthropology and rests on a particular implicit view regarding the nature of man, this philosophical level of "view of man" is also identified as a level of cognition above that of the theory proper (see Figure 4).

Differential Psychological Theories

Let us now examine the diagrammatic representations (cognitive maps) which psychologists themselves have published. These come from a variety of psychological orientations—from depth psychology, height psychology, cognitive psychology, field psychology, and from spiritually-oriented psychologies. These maps represent the *personality structures* but usually not the *personality-dynamics*, although it would be challenging to construct the cognitive maps representing dynamics from the structural models. It is more difficult to represent the flow of life constituting an event than it is to sketch the functions, modalities, and

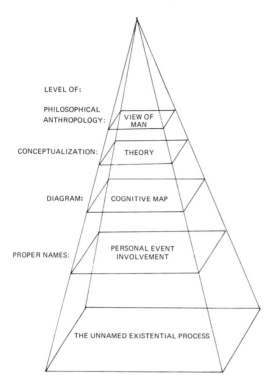

Figure 4. The cognitive framework of consciousness.

personality structures that are involved. Assagioli (1965), speaking about his "pluridimensional" diagram of personality, says in this context:

> It is, of course, a crude and elementary picture that can give only a structural, static, almost "anatomical" representation of our inner constitution, while it leaves out its dynamic aspect, which is the most important and essential one. But here, as in every science, gradual steps must be taken and progressive approximations made. When dealing with a reality so plastic and elusive as our psychological life, it is important not to lose sight of the main lines and of the fundamental differences; otherwise the multiplicity of details is liable to obscure the picture as a whole and to prevent our realizing the respective significance, purpose, and value of its different parts. (p. 16)

One major differentiating factor in these various theories is the recognition or denial of the existence of a transpersonal reality and experience in our life. One might say that some theories are primarily "secular" or "andric" in orientation, and even reductionistic, in that they acknowledge only the realities of biological functioning, of human willing, and of rational cognition, whereas another major group of theories acknowledges the existence of transpersonal realities, of values and of meaning, of spiritual and moral experiences. We may say that these theories are open to a sacred and spiritual dimension in human experience, a "theo-dimension," which requires them to stipulate transpersonal domains of reality, such as divine inspiration, the objective demand-character of values, cosmic consciousness, the infinite, the will-transcending power of love, etc. These might be called "theandric" views of personality (Pannikar, 1977).

The various differential theories of personality and psychological functioning are presented below and then examined in terms of the basic dimensions by means of which they are conceived and represented. The strength and weakness of each is examined and then integrated, using the cognitive framework of the multileveled pyramid.

As Allport (1958) has pointed out, our philosophical and psychological heritage has been decisively shaped by the thinking of Plato, who conceived of the human mind as made up of three "faculties"—thinking, striving, feeling—which are related to different parts of the body which serve as the seats of these functions. This basic threefold classification of the human mind still shapes much of the contemporary discussion, although it has become differentiated and modified by the various schools of psychology.

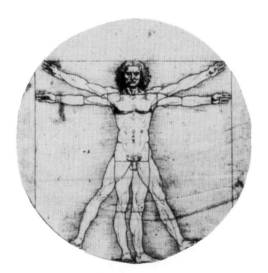

Figure 5. The basic Western paradigm of the structure of personality.

Part of Body	Seat of	Faculty
Head	Reason & Thought	Cognition
Breast	Striving & Action	Conation
Abdomen	Emotions & Feeling	Affect

This fundamental paradigm of the Western tradition begins our discussion, and is expressed in the form of a cognitive map (see Figure 5) which elaborates and integrates Allport's presentation.

Depth Psychologists

Freud's Psychoanalysis. Sigmund Freud (1933) came out with his final version of the psychoanalytic vision of personality and represented it as a cognitive map of his own design (see Figure 6).

Personality is depicted as being organized around a surface-to-depth dimension which roughly corresponds to the volume of the human body. The perceptual/conscious system (in the location of the head), supported and steered by the ego and its secondary-process thinking-ability, rides on the reservoir of the instinctual drives of sexuality and aggression (not indicated on the map), symbolized by the personality region "id" (presumably bodily tissue). The psychological manifestation of id-functioning is given in primary-process, wish-fulfilling thinking and fantasy, and in translogical and transrational associations. The dream process and free-association-imagery can open and present this domain to us. The "superego" system is the internalized and sedimented structure of parental and sociocultural authority and morality (conscience), both partially conscious and unconscious, and experienced as vocal injunctions. This completes the psychic energy household and structure of personality.

Based on his own clinical observation and practice, Freud stipulates three interdependent aggregate states of consciousness: conscious, preconscious, and unconscious. Psychological processes can become subject

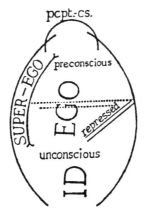

Figure 6. Freud's cognitive map of personality (from Freud, 1933, p. 105).

to active repression and defense in view of the danger and experience of anxiety and guilt associated with the impulsive libidinal life of physiological needs and biotensions seeking satiation and relief.

Freud did not give us an explicit map or flowchart of *psycho-dynamics*, but we know enough from his writings to create it. One can identify and indicate the instinct operative in a particular situation, and can represent the aim and object of the instinct in the outside world, directed toward an object or person. One can also specify the object cathected with libido which is the bio-derived energy quantum which drives the whole psychic machinery. A full representation of psychodynamics requires an extention of Freud's map to include the situation as a space/time coordinate. One needs to include the objects and others in the situation, and to specify the involvements, the activities, fantasies, and blockages of the person whose life-event is being represented. In other words, one would have to map out the famous cases of Freud's writing.

Freud's most fruitful insight into the structure of the psyche or personality was his vision of active barriers separating the ego and id systems, the regions of conscious and unconscious functioning. Freud's great contribution to psychology was the demonstration of the existence of a genuine "depth-dimension" in the human psyche and the demonstration of the existence of lines of defense and defensive mechanisms (repression, denial, projection, etc.), which imply a functional separation between the regions of personality and the dynamic tensions existing between them which can lead to neurotic disturbances.

Freud's key metaphors were the hydraulic pump (or the tea-kettle), used to express the biopsychodynamic tensions and their tethering by defenses—the tension-reduction model of motivation (R. von Eckartsberg, 1975), and the image of the iceberg, which is visible above the surface of the water but which constitutes only a fraction of the whole, used to illustrate the approximate relationship of conscious (above the surface-threshold) and unconscious (below the surface, constituting depth of the psyche) to be explored by means of psychoanalysis.

Freud's implicit view of man, his philosophical-anthropological approach, has been called that of *"Homo natura"* by Binswanger (1959), the "natural man" ruled by the drives of instinctual life.

Freud uses an up-and-down dimension in his cognitive map, a levels-of-consciousness dimension, with special concentration on the depth of the psyche, its imaging life dependent on physiological process. The aim of Freud's work was: "where id was, there ego shall be"; that is, to extend the reach and control of the ego, and hence to achieve full consciousness and control over the driving unconscious id, and to man the lockgates of defense and make them smoothly functioning. The aim of Freud's work is ego-mastery.

Jung's Analytic Psychology.[1] C. G. Jung did not himself present maps of personality (although he was fond of illustrations), but one of his co-workers, Jolande Jacobi (1973), did publish numerous diagrams and cognitive maps of Jung's theory, with Jung's explicit blessing. Jacobi uses both a top view and a side view of the structure of Jung's conception of personality, giving different images and ways of representing the person. In the top view (see Figure 7), the innermost layers of the psyche, that part of the collective unconscious which can never be made conscious, is represented as a concentrated point, whereas in the side view, the collective unconscious, Jung's most distinctive contribution to depth psychology, becomes the largest region, underlying all others as the base of a cone, the apex of which is the ego.

Jung also believed in the dichotomy of conscious-unconscious, but his understanding of the configuration and organization of the unconscious in terms of the universal archetypes of the collective unconscious and his understanding of the nature of libido differed sharply from Freud's. A more complex picture and an understanding of a vaster and more creative depth dimension of the unconscious emerges from Jung's theory.

The regions of depth consciousness are more explicitly defined. Jung differentiates a *personal unconscious*, which includes memories and repressed material from the *collective unconscious* that is constituted by emotions and irruptions. This collective unconscious is, in turn, grounded by an even larger and deeper region of the collective unconscious, which, according to Jung, can never be made conscious.

Jung also inaugurated an internal dialectic between the ego and the *self*, where self is the emergence of an integrative center within the personality and the fruit of the individuation process. Jung has the vision of the possible transformation of personality and believes that one can learn to live from a new and deeper center within oneself. Jung gives us a spiritual and symbolic understanding of psychodynamics, which he conceives to consist of the striving toward individuated integration and wholeness.

The content of the collective unconscious is differentiated and organized by *archetypes* or primordial images. They play a vital part in the psychic economy as centers and fields of force, as primordial patterns of behavior which become expressed in images, metaphors, and symbols. There is, according to Jung, a limited number of such universal archetypes in each of us, expressive of the typical and primordial experiences of man.

---

[1]See Marlan, Chapter 11, Levin, Chapter 12, and V. Valle and Kruger, Chapter 19 for other presentations and discussions of Jung's psychology.—Eds.

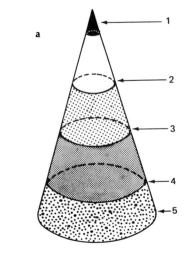

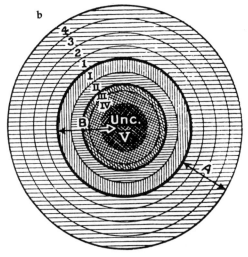

Figure 7. Jung's representation of the structure of personality. (a) 1 = the ego; 2 = consciousness; 3 = the personal unconscious; 4 = the collective unconscious; and 5 = the part of the collective unconscious that can never be made conscious. (b) A = consciousness; B = unconscious; I = forgotten material; II = repressed material; III = emotions; IV = irruptions; and V = that part of the collective unconscious that can never be made conscious. Personal unconscious = I and II; collective unconscious = III and IV. 1 = sensation; 2 = feeling; 3 = intuition; and 4 = thinking (from Jacobi, 1973, pp. 32, 33).

In the course of human growth, which Jung calls the "individuation process," there is a progressive working through of one's relationship to the universal archetype of the *shadow,* the negative side of oneself, and the *animus* or the *anima,* which refers to one's encounter with the soul-image of one's contrasexual partner as part of one's psyche. Still deeper lie the archetypes of *spirit* (the wise old man) and of *matter* (the great earth mother), and, ultimately, at the depth and center of one's total psyche, there lies the *self archetype* (expressed in our tradition as the Christ-archetype), around which a new integration can take place in the process

of self-transformation. A diagram (see Figure 8) expressing Jung's structure of the total psyche is presented by Jacobi (1973).

Regarding the psychology of the functions of consciousness in relating the person to the external world, Jung distinguishes four functions:
two so-called *rational* functions, *thinking* and *feeling*, and two *irrational*
functions, *sensation* and *intuition*.

The rational functions involve evaluations and the making of judgments in terms of true/false in the case of *thinking*, and in terms of
pleasant/unpleasant with regard to *feeling*.

The irrational functions involve no evaluation and are said to cir-
cumvent reason, *sensation* giving us our direct sense of reality, as in
perception, and *intuition* constituting our perception as guided by the
unconscious dimensions (being a function of the "inner perception of
potentiality"). These functions, thinking or feeling, and sensation or
intuition, cannot operate simultaneously, and individuals operate pre-
dominantly in one of the modes in each case.

In addition to the four psychological functions, Jung distinguishes
two possible attitudinal orientations of the personality: *extraversion* and
introversion. These name the two general available directions of psychic
energy or libido: outward into the world or inward toward one's own
psychic process. Within this multidimensional cognitive framework, as
expressed by the maps, Jung is able to present his system of complex or
analytical psychology.

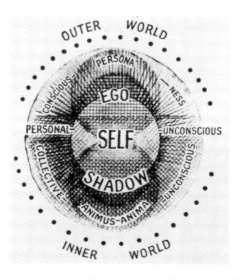

Figure 8. Jung's structure of the total psyche (from Jacobi, 1973, p. 130).

Height Psychologists

Roberto Assagioli's Psychosynthesis. Assagioli's (1965) *Psychosynthesis* uses the basic imagery of height and depth to articulate the possibilities for self-transformation. Psychosynthesis is the reconstruction of an individual's personality around a new center which is called the higher- or transpersonal self. Assagioli is most explicit about charting the regions of personality and has given us a detailed map of his theory of personality structure and a map of his theory of personality functioning (see Figure 9).

The regions of Assagioli's cognitive map, or the "diagram of the psychological constitution of man," as he calls it, are simply defined (Assagioli, 1965):

1. The Lower Unconscious

   This contains:
   a. The elementary psychological activities which direct the life of the body; the intelligent co-ordination of bodily functions.
   b. The fundamental drives and primitive urges.
   c. Many complexes, charged with intense emotion.
   d. Dreams and imaginations of an inferior kind.
   e. Lower, uncontrolled parapsychological processes.
   f. Various pathological manifestations, such as phobias, obsessions, compulsive urges, and paranoid delusions.

2. The Middle Unconscious

   This is formed of psychological elements similar to those of our waking consciousness and easily accessible to it. In this inner region our various experiences are assimilated, our ordinary mental and imaginative activities are elaborated and developed in a sort of psychological gestation before their birth into the light of consciousness.

3. The Higher Unconscious or Superconscious

   From this region we receive our higher intuitions and inspirations— artistic, philosophical or scientific, ethical "imperatives" and urges to humanitarian and heroic action. It is the source of the higher feelings, such as altruistic love; of genius and of the states of contemplation, illumination, and ecstasy. In this realm are latent the higher psychic functions and spiritual energies.

4. The Field of Consciousness

   This term—which is not quite accurate but which is clear and convenient for practical purposes—is used to designate that part of our personality of which we are directly aware: the incessant flow of sensations, images, thoughts, feelings, desires, and impulses which we can observe, analyze, and judge.

5. The Conscious Self or "I"

   The "self," that is to say, the point of pure self-awareness, is often confused with the conscious personality just described, but in reality it is quite different from it. This can be ascertained by the use of careful intro-

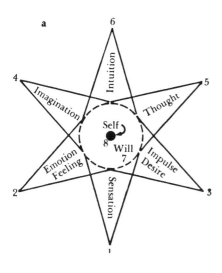

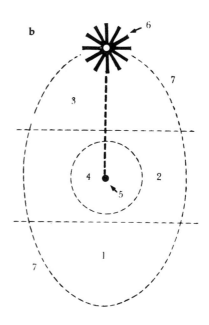

Figure 9 (a, b, c). Assagioli's maps of personality structure and functioning. In Figure 9b: 1 = the lower unconscious; 2 = the middle unconscious; 3 = the higher unconscious, or superconscious; 4 = the field of consciousness; 5 = the conscious self, or "I"; 6 = the transpersonal self; and 7 = the collective unconscious (a: from Assagioli, 1974, p. 49; b: from Assagioli, 1965, p. 17).

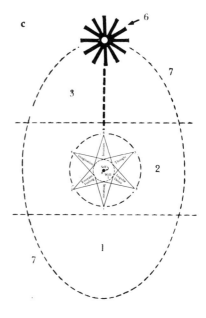

spection. The changing *contents* of our consciousness (the sensations, thoughts, feelings, etc.) are one thing, while the "I", the self, the *center* of our consciousness is another. From a certain point of view this difference can be compared to that existing between the white lighted area on a screen and the various pictures which are projected upon it.

But the "man in the street" and even many well-educated people do not take the trouble to observe themselves and to discriminate; they drift on the surface of the "mind-stream" and identify themselves with its successive waves, with the changing contents of their consciousness.

6. The Higher Self

The conscious self is generally not only submerged in the ceaseless flow of psychological contents but seems to disappear altogether when we fall asleep, when we faint, when we are under the effect of an anesthetic or narcotic, or in a state of hypnosis. And when we awake, the self mysteriously re-appears, we do not know how or whence—a fact which, if closely examined, is truly baffling and disturbing. This leads us to assume that the re-appearance of the conscious self or ego is due to the existence of a permanent center, of a true Self situated beyond or "above" it.

There are various ways by means of which the reality of the Self can be ascertained. There have been many individuals who have achieved, more or less temporarily, a conscious realization of the Self that for them has the same degree of certainty as is experienced by an explorer who has entered a previously unknown region.

Then we have the corroboration of such philosophers as Kant and Herbart, who make a clear distinction between the empirical ego and the noumenal or real Self. This Self is above, and unaffected by, the flow of the mind-stream or by bodily conditions; and the personal conscious self should be considered merely as its reflection, its "projection" in the field of the personality. At the present stage of psychological investigation little is definitely known concerning the Self, but the importance of this synthesizing center well warrants further research.

7. The Collective Unconscious

Human beings are not isolated, they are not "monads without windows" as Leibniz thought. They may at times feel subjectively isolated, but the extreme existentialistic conception is not true, either psychologically or spiritually.

The outer line of the oval of the diagram should be regarded as "delimiting" but not as "dividing." It should be regarded as analogous to the membrane delimiting a cell, which permits a constant and active interchange with the whole body to which the cell belongs. Processes of "psychological osmosis" are going on all the time, both with other human beings and with the general psychic environment. The latter corresponds to what Jung has called the "collective unconscious"; but he has not clearly defined this term, in which he includes elements of different, even opposite natures, namely primitive archaic structures and higher, forward-directed activities of a superconscious character. (pp. 17–19)[2]

---

[2]See Marlan, Chapter 11, for a discussion of ego- (self-) transcendence, E. von Eckartsberg, Chapter 18, for Self as God-consciousness, and Schore, Chapter 22 for another discussion of the self–Self distinction.—Eds.

A person's awareness of the relationship of himself, his will, and the various psychological functions are represented by Assagioli (see Figure 9) in a star-shaped symbolic image (Fig. 9A), which the reader has to imagine to be fitted within the cognitive map of personality structure (Fig. 9B), expressed as C in Figure 9.

In spite of the richness and differentiatedness of Assagioli's cognitive maps, there is no representation of space and time, and therefore no mention of the essential human psychological functions of *remembering* (past-perception), and *anticipation* and *projecting* (future-perception). However, in discussing "the act of will" as a movement from intention to realization, Assagioli (1974) lists and discusses the six sequential phases or stages of willing and thus recognizes the importance of a temporal dynamics, although he does not provide us with a diagrammatic representation. He says:

> The act of will consists of six sequential phases or stages. They are:
> 1. The purpose, aim, or goal, based on evaluation, motivation, and intention.
> 2. Deliberation.
> 3. Choice and decision.
> 4. Affirmation: the command, or "fiat," of the will.
> 5. Planning and working out a program.
> 6. Direction of the execution. (p. 135)

Assagioli has also developed a very precise and systematic set of psychological exercises in the genre of "guided reveries" and "waking dreams" (Watkins, 1976), and thus provides us with a powerful "psychetechnology" for self-exploration and self-transformation. With Assagioli, the possibility of "psychenautics" (Masters & Houston, 1973), that is, the deliberate and systematic travel in the cosmos of consciousness—what we call "the psychocosm" (E. von Eckartsberg, 1978)—becomes a realistic project. He gives us some of the essential dimensions and coordinates for constructing the cognitive map of *the structure of the psychocosm*, a comprehensive image of all domains of human consciousness in their interdependent relationship to one another.

Assagioli is aligned with the humanistic psychology movement, whose major proponent, Abraham Maslow, is examined next. Assagioli is also aligned with the existential analysis movement (Viktor Frankl). They are united in their emphasis on the importance of the higher faculties in man and on the issue of the meaning of life, values, and self-actualization conceptualized as a hierarchical progress.

Maslow's Theory of Self-Actualization and Self-Transcendence. Maslow developed his idea of personality by focusing on the needs that motivate man to act. In his early work, *Motivation and Personality,* he considered man to be a "wanting animal", forever striving, never satisfied. He developed his theory of human motivation—which he called a "holistic-dynamic theory"—as a *needs-hierarchy*. Self-actualization was considered to be the highest human need which integrated all the lower needs, but which was dependent on their prior gratification. Implicit in this early version of his theory was the notion that the lower needs—deficiency motives—are more basic, make possible, and rule the higher ones—growth motives—although the higher needs are the more desirable ones and express man's highest potential.

Maslow studied self-actualization empirically and found that self-actualizers are prone to have "peak experiences," similar to mystical moments, in their lives. He studied the personality characteristics of these people and the peak-experiences they described. He found them to be exceptionally healthy psychologically and frequently involved in self-transcendent causes and in what he came to call "Being-values"—the "cognition of being." Maslow, always fond of lists, provided us with a 15-point characterization of the Being-values belonging to self-actualizers in peak experiences, and their corresponding pathologies (their "pathogenic deprivation").

Maslow then developed his theory of "metamotivation" on the basis of his study of psychologically optimal specimens: the self-actualizing individuals. He understood them to be motivated in other, higher ways than the average person, "metamotivated."

Roberts (1978), who has traced Maslow's intellectual development through three stages, calls Maslow's third period "Transcendence and Transpersonal Psychology", and adds the highest being-motivation,

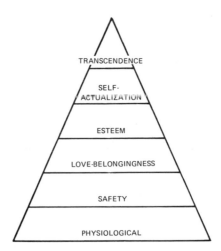

Figure 10. Maslow's hierarchy of needs (from Roberts, 1978, p. 44).

transcendence, to the representation of Maslow's hierarchy of needs as the apex of a triangle above self-actualization (see Figure 10). Roberts argues that in his last phase Maslow was moving into a new paradigm from third-force psychology (humanistic) to fourth-force psychology (transpersonal), as expressed by this quote from Maslow (1968):

> I should say also that I consider humanistic, third-force psychology to be transitional, a preparation for a still "higher" fourth psychology, transhuman, centered in the cosmic rather than in human needs and interest going beyond humanness, identity, self-actualization, and the like. (Preface)

If one considers Maslow in his last phase as a transpersonal psychologist, he could easily be placed in the group of theo-psychologists who explicitly recognize the reality of the spirit and of transpersonal values, the reality of the sacred, and the experience of the Divine in man's life; what we have called the theo-dimension.

Cognitive and Information-Processing Models

Neisser's Theory of Cognitive Schemata and Cognitive Mapping. Neisser (1976) speaks about cognitive maps as "orienting schema" which are active information-seeking structures of personality, and which accept information and direct action. He presents us with a cognitive map of his own making (see Figure 11) which illustrates the functions of schemata. They are conceived as cognitive structures of personality which promote an interaction, a cycle of exploration and information pickup which continuously restructures the person's schemata through the accumulation of experience and increases their reality-adequacy.

In Neisser's view, the cognitive map "always includes the perceiver as well as the environment. Ego and world are perceptually inseparable" (p. 117). Cognitive maps are defined by the way in which they pick up information from the environment, and guide action into the environment. Schemata (Piaget, 1954) or cognitive maps function very much in an organizing and stabilizing way, and they help us in anticipating situations and events. Neisser builds a consistent theory of cognitive structures, including a theory of images understood as "perceptual anticipations," that is, as plans for obtaining information from potential environments which themselves can be manipulated, directed, and detached cognitively, thus leading to the emergence of all higher mental processes.

In Neisser's view, our awareness and effectiveness regarding our environment is dependent on a dynamic person–world interactive communication process, in which the cognitive functions are highlighted, and in which the construction of images of reality, including the image of one's self, embedded in higher-order orienting schemata or cognitive maps, take on a central importance.

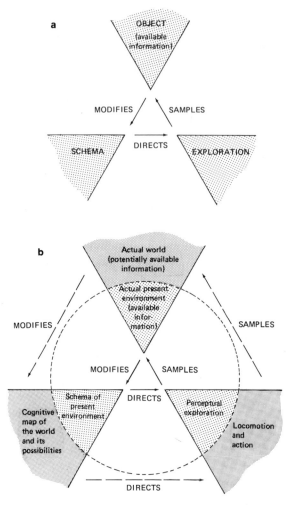

Figure 11. Neisser's representation of cognitive schemata: (a) the perpetual cycle; (b) schemata as embedded in cognitive maps (from Neisser, 1976, pp. 21, 112).

Charles Tart's Theory of States of Consciousness.[3] Tart is inspired by the systems approach and uses the metaphor of "computer processing" to help account for the construction of consciousness and awareness. In his basic text, *States of Consciousness* (1975), he gives us many cognitive maps to illustrate his thinking about normal and altered states of consciousness and their placement in relationship to one another.

Tart developed the notion of "discrete states of consciousness"

[3]See also Tart, Chapter 10.—Eds.

(DOCs), including the creative states, marijuana intoxication, psychedelic states, meditative states, mystical states, psychotic states, dreaming, and the state of rationality, that is, functional and world-effective consciousness.

Tart, among psychologists, discusses perhaps the widest variety of psychological states, including the extreme regions in which the experienced reality of the *transpersonal* comes into play. With this notion of the transpersonal, Tart shares the concern of the height-psychologists. In his methodological approach, Tart is empirical and experimentally oriented although he studies highly unusual psychological phenomena.

He gives us a presentation of both the coexistence and the valuation of various states of mind in the community of orthodox Western culture on the one hand, and the "hip" valuation of states of consciousness prevailing in the "counterculture," thus recognizing a tie-in between social belongingness and preferred states of consciousness (see Figure 12).

One can distinguish several levels of representation in Tart's work. In a very universal and symbolic way, he expressed the system of fundamental basic dimensions involved in the construction of consciousness in the form of an image of intersecting atomic orbits. He names:

> Time and Space
> Matter and Energy
> Awareness and Life/Unknown

and calls these "the underlying, interacting dimensions from which human consciousness arises" (p. 248).

Tart also provides us with a more detailed cognitive map of the major subsystems of consciousness and the principle information flow-routes. It is a flowchart representation of interdependent psychological systems and functions on which particular conscious experiences can be mapped. These mappings of experienced events in their moment-by-moment singularity constitute still another level of discourse in Tart's work and research practice—one step closer to the situated level of experienced existential process as we have identified it in our heuristic scheme of the pyramid.

Tart's systems-approach view and its multiple levels of analysis and discourse can be expressed in terms of our cognitive pyramid space, where we place the various levels of Tart's work in relationship to each other and to the basic level of existential events (see Figure 13).

For Tart, an event of human consciousness is mediated psychologically by ten identifiable component and interdependent subsystems of conscious self-functioning. Between exteroception and interoception

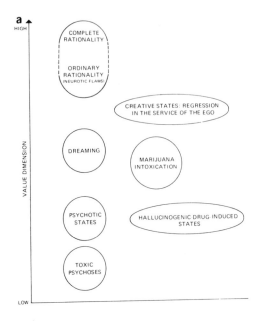

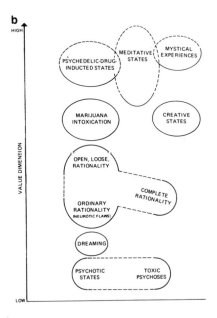

Figure 12. Tart's map of valuations of states of consciousness: (a) orthodox Western, largely implicit valuation of various states; (b) the "hip" valuation of various states (from Tart, 1975, pp. 231, 233).

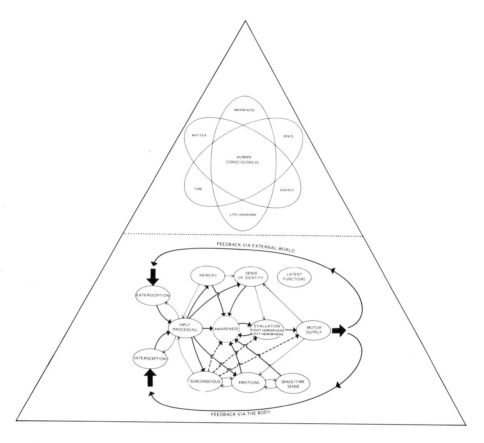

Figure 13.   Tart's representation of dimensions and systems of consciousness. Major sub-systems of consciousness and principal information flow routes are seen in the lower part of the figure (from Tart, 1975, pp. 90, 248).

on the *input-side,* and *motor-output* geared into the world, one finds the neural-information, psychological switchboard that interconnects the human powers of:

Memory
Sense of Identity
Subconscious
Emotions
Space/Time Sense
Coordinating Faculty of Input Processing
Evaluation
Awareness

Using this model, Tart attempts to map in complete detail the concrete moves in consciousness of a person, what we like to call the "existential process" of the unfolding event as experienced by the citizen–actor and mapped by the professional. Tart gets quite complex but does present a promising systematic attempt to track consciousness by means of cognitive mapping.

Field Theories

Kurt Lewin's Field Theory and Ecological Orientation. Lewin is the "cognitive mapper" *par excellence* in psychology, forever drawing maps and diagrams representative of his ideas. Lewin developed a set of concepts by means of which one can represent the psychological reality of a person in a concrete situation at a particular moment. The field, or "life space," is the environment as perceived by the actor. It is the meaning of the field that determines the behavior of the individual. Lewin meant by field: "the totality of coexistent facts which are conceived of as mutually interdependent" (1951, p. 240).

Lewin takes us out of the interiority of consciousness and the concept

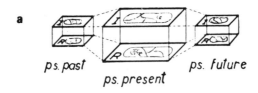

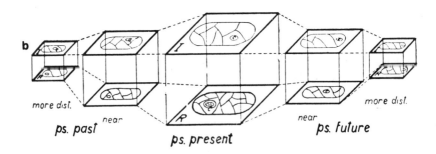

Figure 14. Lewin's representation of the life space in time. (a) represents the life space of a younger child; (b) represents the higher degree of differentiation of the life space of the older child in regard to the present situation, the reality–irreality dimension, and the time perspective. C = child; R = level of reality; I = level of irreality; Ps Past = psychological past; Ps Present = psychological present; Ps Future = psychological future (from Lewin, 1951, p. 246).

of internal information-processing into the environment, into the world, into the field of the "life-space." Lewin spoke of the differentiated person, who is constituted by an inner-personal region, which, in turn, is surrounded by the perceptual motor region by means of which the person traffics in and with his or her world environment and the regions that constitute the life-space. The environment itself is differentiated in terms of goals, regions, barriers or boundaries, and the possibilities of pathways and movements through space. Lewin also speaks of the importance of the dimensions of past, present, and future, and of reality and unreality (fantasy). These two levels of reality are represented in Figure 14.

For Lewin there is a correspondence between the inner personal regions, conceived as *needs*, and the facts of the psychological environment, conceived as *valences*. The human individual locomotes in the service of need-satisfaction, and psychology becomes a science of pathways.

The dynamics of personality is conceived in terms of energy, of needs, of tensions, of valences, and of force or vectors. The basic notions in Lewin's dynamics are tension, equilibrium, and homeostasis. The needs can be either physiological or psychological (i.e., they can be

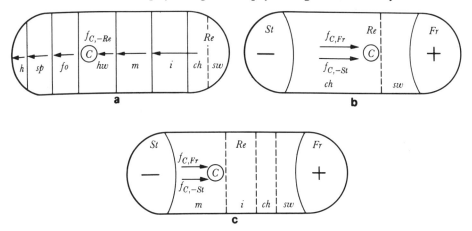

Figure 15. Lewin's mapping of the life space as a situated moment. C = child; Re = real eating; h = putting hand on table; sp = taking spoon, fo = putting food on spoon; hw = bringing spoon halfway to mouth; m = bringing spoon to mouth; i = taking food into mouth; ch = chewing; sw = swallowing; St = struggle with adults; Fr = freedom; $f_{C,Fr}$ = force in the direction to freedom; $f_{C,-St}$ = force away from struggle. Finitely structured force field consisting of macroscopic regions. (a) Eating situation in case of disliked food. Eating has a negative valence [$Va(Re)<0$]; the force away from real eating, $f_{C,-Re}$, increases stepwise with the decrease of distance between C and Re. (b) Change of direction of forces after the child started real eating. (c) In a later stage of "learning" to eat the disagreeable food, the situation might be restructured so that bringing spoon to mouth (m) is now seen as a subpart of the region of real eating (Re) (adapted from Lewin, 1938; from Deutsch, 1968, p. 425).

perceived desires or intentions). Needs impart values to the environment, and one moves along pathways to reach goals. Using Lewin's
conceptualization, one is able to represent the psychological state of
affairs for the person at any moment and to indicate the pathways of
movement, the obstructions and barriers to movement, and the valences
of the regions of the environment. Figure 15 expresses a typical situation
in terms of Lewin's way of mapping.

Lewin has also been recognized as the father of *ecological psychology*.
He was interested in representing the structures of the nonpsychological
environment and the demand-character of situations.

Existential-Phenomenological Field-Psychology.[4] Existential-Phenomenology is also a field-approach studying the "field of consciousness." Edmund Husserl presented phenomenology as a method of doing
philosophy by means of rigorous and systematic description and reflection on our consciousness of our everyday life-involvement. Priority was
given to the way in which phenomena show themselves to human consciousness in their self-givenness when one "brackets"—suspending all
theoretical presuppositions and preconceptions, including all theories,
ideologies, and metaphysics, to the degree that this is possible, under
Husserl's phenomenological imperative: "Back to the things themselves!"

In Husserl's program, conscious experiences are to be carefully described and reflected upon so as to reveal their essential characteristics,
their "essential structures of meaning." In phenomenology, one starts
with concrete and existentially given realities—such as an act of perceiving a particular visible object. By reflecting on the way in which the
concrete object is being constituted by our consciousness, we discover
essential configurations of meaning, operative structures, and processes
of human consciousness which make present and sustain the meaning a
given object has for us.

Through the insight that there is an essential *intentional structure* of
consciousness and all conscious acts, *intentionality* became articulated.
Intentionality refers to the fact that consciousness is always consciousness of something which is not consciousness itself, but a meaning for
consciousness. The metaphoric expressions of the structure of intentionality are the "intentional arrow," the "beam of light of consciousness,"
and "world-openness." The key insight of phenomenology is that
human meaning and encounter *connects* person and world, subject and
object, and establishes a relationship *in between*. The Cartesian separation
of subject and object is overcome.

---

[4]See Moss and Keen, Chapter 4, and Moss, Chapter 7, for other discussions of the
existential-phenomenological approach.—Eds.

The nature of the object given in consciousness turns out to be complex. Not only does one attend to a thematized object as a figure or gestalt against a background, but the object is given only partially, in perspective, from a certain vantage point that the perceiver occupies. And yet we realize the full object in its full meaning as constituted and presented via the contextual experiences of *horizons* which emanate from the object and invite exploration. The *inner horizon* leads to other perspectives that can be taken on the object which already announce and present themselves although not yet physically visible. And there are the *outer horizons* which relate the given object to its family of objects and contexts of practical and theoretical relations, familiar to the perceiver who has built up and perceives from a relevant and organized stock of knowledge with respect to all areas of his life-world. Objects—like people—accrete and accumulate meanings for us in the course of our relationship. We bring meanings between ourselves and the world. There is an ongoing production and sedimentation of meaning which one experiences as a dynamic and cumulative enrichment of the world, personally, and collectively through institutionalized knowledge production.

Another set of operative horizons which Husserl (1964) articulates and emphasizes are the horizons of time, of temporality. He calls this "inner time consciousness." The past is still present as past, and the future is already present as future, and one experiences this in the form of temporal horizons. Husserl has himself made cognitive maps of inner time consciousness, which he calls "the diagram of time" (see Figure 16). It gives a representation of the flow of time as a cognitive object.

Ernest Keen (1975) has begun to represent some phenomenological insights and concepts in the form of cognitive maps. He expressed the multiple interrelatedness of the temporal horizons of experience, for instance, in the form of concentric circles which contextualize an event.

In his presentation, Keen executes an "event-study" of an episode in the life of his 5-year-old daughter, in which she changed her mind about sleeping over at a friend's house. He distinguishes several temporal

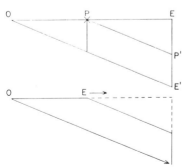

Figure 16. Husserl's diagram of time. OE = series of now-points; OE' = sinking-down [*Herabsinken*]; EE' = continuum of phases (now-point with horizon of the past); E→ = series of nows which possibly will be filled with other objects (from Husserl, 1964, p. 49).

phases in this event and then creates cognitive maps to express the state of affairs and consciousness as his daughter experienced it. He does the phenomenological analysis of this episode in terms of its *temporal structure*, in terms of its *spatial field*, and in terms of its *social field*, and thus effectively takes us into his workshop of doing psychology phenomenologically (see Figure 17).

In a later chapter, Keen articulates the phenomenological structure of "being a self in time" by means of a cognitive map which vividly portrays the complexities of experiential dynamics regarding man's lived temporality, and which gives a concrete and persuasive introduction into the merits of existential-phenomenological thinking and cognitive mapping. Keen's cognitive map and his descriptive paragraph are presented side by side, so that the reader can trace the argument and locate the temporal moves of consciousness in time for him or herself (see Figure 18).

Don Ihde is another existential-phenomenologist who has published some cognitive maps. Ihde (1977) has presented representations which modify the intentional arrow structure. He represents the "field of overall experience" as an ellipse and says:

> Within the ellipse (overall experience) there are two related foci (what is experienced and that to which what is experienced refers). The lines of relation indicate the possible modes of experience. Intentionality is the name for the direction and internal shape of experience. Reflection is the means of bringing forth the specifics of that direction and shape. (p. 47)

Regarding the structures of invariants of the visual field, Ihde gives a representation in the form of two cognitive maps in which he also represents Husserl's important threefold characterization of any act of con-

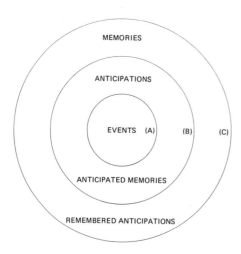

Figure 17. Keen's representation of horizons of experience: adult anticipation. This adult experiential structure includes, in the anticipatory backdrop (B) to events (A), an anticipation of remembering my shame if I change my mind. It also includes, in the memory backdrop (C) to anticipation (B), a remembering of how I looked forward to these events, which would also lend this structure more stability (from Keen, 1975, p. 15).

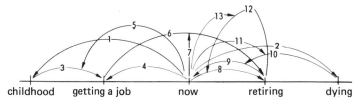

Figure 18. Keen's cognitive map of being a self in time. The experience of being a self in time is quite complex. Right now I have a sense of myself. What is involved in that sense of self? In the figure, I remember my childhood (1), and I anticipate that I shall die (2). When I was a child, I anticipated finding a job (3), and I now remember finding the job (4); I also remember anticipating finding a job (5). My memory of how I anticipated finding a job (5) is compared to my memory of finding a job (4), and it either lived up to my expectations, or I am somehow disappointed. I made retirement plans when I found my job (6). I now remember making them (7) and now make new ones (8). I shall look back at having done that (9), and, as I am dying, I shall remember looking back (10). I now anticipate how I shall remember remembering the retirement plans that I am making now (11). Not all these horizons are equally important for how I understand myself in my job. But they are all implicitly part of my understanding. Occasionally one of them becomes crucial, as does my notion that when I retire I shall be amazed at how stupid my earlier retirement plans were. Part of my motivation for changing them now is that I do not want to look back and see myself as having been stupid (12). This process is anticipating remembering an anticipation (13). The diagram is complex enough to indicate how complex being a self in time really is. It is also clear that the diagram is much too simple; had I thrown in my marriage, the births of my children, the marriages of my children; my earlier physical agilities, their current decrease, and their eventual deterioration, and the hundreds of other issues that are important in my sense of myself, the diagram would rapidly have become unwieldy. Let us try to simplify all this complexity in order to be able to understand being a self in time (from Keen, 1975, p. 83).

sciousness. This essential structure of intentionality is represented in Table I. One can see these various representations of Ihde as cognitive maps (see Figures 19 and 20).

The *existential* emphasis in phenomenology came through the realization of the importance of the body in human existence and the fact that our subjectivity is an embodied and corporeal subjectivity—what Merleau-Ponty (1962) has called "the body–subject" *(le corps propre)*. This expansion of meaning to include the preconscious and precognitive dimensions of human existence opened up the whole realm of prereflective

Table I

(Ego)		Cogito		Cogitatum
(I)	. . .	noesis	→	noema
(I)	. . .	process	→	object of thought
(experiencer)	. . .	experiencing	→	experienced
(subject)	. . .	being conscious	→	meaningful object
(I)	. . .	see	→	the tree

Figure 19. Ihde's representation of the field of overall experience. The field and shape of intentionality is conceived as an ellipse with two foci (from Ihde, 1977, p. 47).

body–world relationships, which are effective for us but of which we may not be conscious. The new vision found expression in the emphasis on man's situatedness in space and time and on our "being-in-the-world" (Heidegger, 1962) conceived as a dynamic, two-way interrelationship between the person and his or her world.

The existential-phenomenologists have concerned themselves with "the primacy of perception" (Merleau-Ponty, 1962); "the primary world of the senses" (Straus, 1963), the "multiple realities of consciousness" as "finite provinces of meaning" (Schutz, 1962), the world as "multiple orders of existence" (Gurwitsch, 1964), the "existential project" (Sartre, 1956), and with the "primacy of language" metaphorized as "the house of Being" by Heidegger (1971), who, in his later work, conceives of inten-

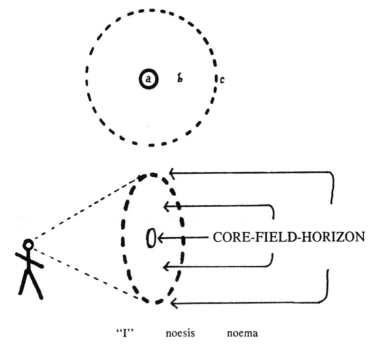

Figure 20. Ihde's representation of intentionality and the visual field. a = core object in central vision; b = field or background region surrounding and situating core object; c = fringe or horizon, which limits and borders the field of vision (from Ihde, 1977, p. 65).

tionality as a "dwelling" among things. A "dwelling" which speaks to us if we have ears to hear, if we attend to them in the meditative mode of thinking as thanking presence, open to the mystery and aware of the cosmic context and horizons of "the fourfold", the assembled presence of earth, sky, the mortals, and the divinities from whose interplay any "thing" emerges. In Heidegger's vision: "Poetically man dwells" (p. 213).[5]

Theo-Psychologies

Viktor Frankl's Existential Analysis. Frankl (1967), founder of Logotherapy and Existential Analysis, has long been a champion of man's higher life and the reality of the spiritual or noetic dimension in human existence—the realms of meaning and values. In Frankl's view, the person is the core and center of spiritual activities, of responsibleness, and of conscience and decision. In Frankl's conception of personality, the higher dimensions rule the lower, meanings and values give direction and strength in life, and they guide and coordinate life on the psychic and somatic levels, which, together with the spiritual/noetic dimension, constitute the tripartite organization of the personality.

"He who has a why to live, can endure almost any how," is a short paraphrase of one of Frankl's (1955, p. 61) sayings. We must find a personal meaning in life, and must actualize values in the concrete circumstances of our existential situation. Frankl gives us a picture of the human individual as a three-dimensional being in his presentation of what he calls "dimensional ontology." Human being is body—the somatic dimension, human being is psyche—the psychological dimension, but he or she is also spirit—the noetic dimension. The spiritual or noetic dimension is the specifically and distinctively human dimension. Frankl sees the phenomenon of human existence as having a bidirectional focus: toward *being-in-the-world*, which is an existential and ontic concern focused on the subjective aspects of existence, and toward *meaning-in-the-world*, which is directed toward essences and the ontological encountered as meaning and value. Frankl understands the totality of existence as the "I-am experience," which exfoliates into spirit, mind/psyche, and body. One can express Frankl's view with a list of dimensions of existence, of manifestation, and of experience (see Table II):

"I must" is the realm of biophysiology and society, "I can" actualizes possibilities if I apply myself, and "I ought" fulfills a concrete meaning awaiting me in each situation.

[5]See R. von Eckartsberg and R. Valle, Chapter 14, for a more detailed discussion of Heidegger's *dwelling* and the *fourfold*. —Eds.

Table II

	Dimensions	Manifestations	Types of Experience
The person's ← existence	⎧ Spirit ⎨ Psyche ⎩ Body	Will to meaning Will to power Will to pleasure	I ought ⎫ I can ⎬ → I am I must ⎭

Frankl also insists on the usefulness of the distinction of conscious, preconscious, and unconscious functioning in understanding the person. He extends this distinction to all three realms of the being of man. He has expressed the interplay of the three dimensions and states of consciousness in the form of a cognitive map as a visual representation of his conception of the structure of the human being (see Figure 21).

Viktor Frankl is an existence- and action-oriented thinker. Listening and responding are the valued human powers through which the value and meaning-dimensions become revealed and actualized. Although the existential situation of the person is not explicitly represented in Frankl's map, his logotherapeutic practice always addresses itself to a concrete exploration of the person's possibilities for action and for making a unique value-contribution through his life. Frankl's emphasis is on the ethical, religious, and spiritual dimensions of human living, not as an exploration of imaginal possibilities—psychenautics—but as an exhortation for recognition of meaning and commitment to action as existential choice and commitment.

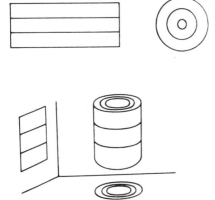

Figure 21. Frankl's representation of the structure of the human being. As far as the structure of the human being is concerned, we have so far given preference to the model of layers versus the model of strata. In fact, we have replaced the vertical hierarchy of unconscious, preconscious and conscious strata by the model of concentric layers, a model propounded by Max Scheler. But why not go one step further by combining the strata model with the layers model: Why not conceive of the concentric layers as the ground plan of a three-dimensional structure? We would only have to imagine that the personal core—the spiritual center encompassed by the peripheral somatic and psychic layers—is prolonged so that we would have to conceive of it as an axis. This axis then would extend, together with the peripheral layers encompassing it, throughout the unconscious, preconscious and conscious strata (from Frankl, 1975, p. 29).

Regarding the actualization of values, which are for Frankl "objective" and transpersonal realities which issue a demand-character and call us out for action and realization, Frankl distinguishes three types of values which disclose to conscience (our personal organ for value-perception) what ought to be, what I ought to do: *experiential values, creative values,* and *attitudinal values,* which come into play when all else is no longer possible, as in incurable suffering. Even in such a tragic, no-exit situation, the person, according to Frankl, who witnessed such realities in his concentration-camp experiences, can and must choose the attitude toward his own suffering and find meaning in the very way that he relates himself to his fate. Spiritual existence gives us the freedom to decide and the responsibility to respond to the call of the higher-objective, transpersonal values and meanings that beckon us to fulfill them.

Huston Smith's Mapping of the Primordial Tradition. Smith (1976) gives us a cognitive map which defines and brings in relationship to each other the essential parameters of any experience of reality: *space, time,* and *levels of reality.* He expresses this in the form of the symbol of the three-dimensional cross (see Figure 22).

Smith contrasts the scientific and mystico-religious world-views and finds both of them employing a hierarchical model of reality, a conceptualization in terms of levels. But whereas the natural scientific view has reduced the levels to an array in terms of *quantity* and number or size—the macro-, meso-, and micro-levels—the "tradition," which for Smith is the heritage of the "philosophia perennis" and the mystical religious traditions, believes in the reality of experienced *qualities*—good, better, best, and bad, worse, worst, of heaven and hell and the infinite surrounding all.

This qualitative world-view is capable of offering values, purposes, and life-meanings, and thus constitutes the essence of a religious world-

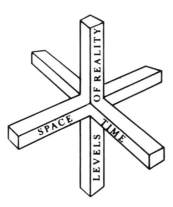

Figure 22. Smith's three-dimensional cross (from Smith, 1976, p. 24).

Table III

Spirit	Unitive	Infinite
Soul	Psychic	Celestial
Mind	Sentient	Intermediate
Body	Corporeal	Terrestrial

view, of a "hierarchy of worth and being." The scientific view rooted in cognitive rationality, value-neutrality, and presumed objectivity is understood by Smith as a derivative and restrictive view of human reality that has gained ascendency and control over human cognitive affairs in recent centuries. It has also, however, led to our contemporary situation of spiritual impoverishment and loss of value direction.

Smith sees faith—in whatever denominational garb, West or East— as a revelation through genuine religious experience of a founder who has extended our awareness of and involvement in deeper/higher levels of reality, who has provided us with a new God-experience, and the establishment, in history, of a new vision of the "theo-dimension."

Huston Smith, through his cognitive maps, presents us with a vision of a nesting structure of encompassing realms of reality and interdependent levels of selfhood (see Figure 23). The *levels of reality* are conceived by Smith as centered in the *terrestrial sphere*, where our bodily space/time existence is anchored. This is surrounded and encompassed by the *intermediate realm* of the angelic (up) and demonic (down) realities, which is, in turn, surrounded by the *celestial sphere* of universal insight and truth and the personal experience of God. These three interdependent layers of reality are themselves encompassed and pervaded—exceeded—by the pleroma of the *infinite*, which is beyond any definition, specification, and delimitation: God on his own terms.

In Smith's hierarchic vision of interdependent levels of reality and selfhood, the lesser is ordered and empowered by the greater, and the psychic plane is greater than the corporeal. Thus, Huston Smith's three-dimensional cross of reality traverses and is open to all known dimensions of human-experienced reality. The appropriate experiential centers of the individual self through which man attunes himself to these spheres of reality are given in Table III. The mystical, value-creative experience, known in all traditions, opens the experiential floodgates to the infinite.

Ken Wilber's Vision of the Spectrum of Consciousness. Wilber (1978, 1979) has developed representation and cognitive mapping of a universal view of the nature of human consciousness, integrating both Eastern and Western models in a bold way. He speaks of the "spectrum of consciousness", on which he identifies several levels or "bands" (see Table IV).

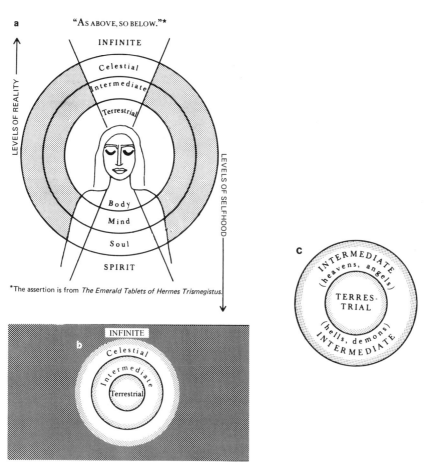

Figure 23. Smith's representation of levels of reality and selfhood (from Smith, 1976, pp. 61, 62).

Wilber represents his ideas in two ways, expressed as two cognitive maps, one in the form of a spectrum and the other in the form of a double cone placed head to head (see Figure 24).

The organization of Wilber's thought gives primacy to the undif-

Table IV

The level of Mind
The transpersonal bands
The existential level
The ego level
The shadow level

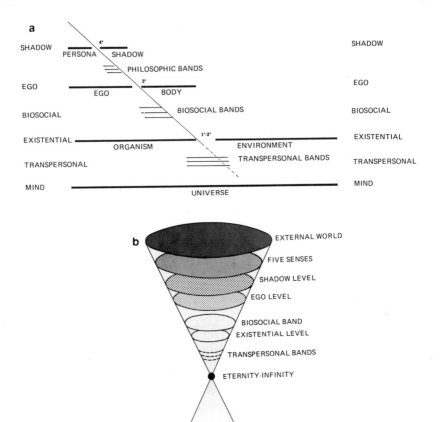

Figure 24. Wilber's maps of the spectrum of consciousness (from Wilber, 1977, pp. 143, 165).

ferentiated and infinite, what he calls the level of Mind which he conceives along mystical lines and considers grounded in the Hindu and Buddhist visions of ultimate reality and the ground of Being. He says:

> The core insight of the *psychologia perennis* is that man's "innermost" consciousness is identical to the absolute and ultimate reality of the universe, which, for the sake of convenience, I will simply call "Mind" (with a capital M to distinguish it from the apparent plurality of "minds"). According to this universal tradition, Mind is what there is and all there is, spaceless and therefore infinite, timeless and therefore eternal, outside of which nothing

exists. On this level, man is identified with the universe, the All—or rather, he *is* the All. According to the *psychologia perennis* this level is not an abnormal state of consciousness, nor even an altered state of consciousness, but rather the *only real* state of consciousness, all others being essentially illusions. (1979, pp. 8, 9)

The *transpersonal bands* are supraindividual,

> where man is not conscious of his identity with the All and yet neither is his identity confined to the boundaries of the individual organism. (1979, p. 9)

The *existential level* is the level of the experience of the subject–object difference in Wilber's way of thinking:

> Here man is identified solely with his total psychophysical organism as it exists in space and time, for this is the first level where the line between self and other, organism and environment, is firmly drawn. This is also the level where man's rational thought processes, as well as his personal will, first begin to develop and exfoliate. (p. 9)

The *biosocial bands* represent the internalization of societal and cultural matrices, the mores and values that we receive and accept from our elders in the process of growing up.

The *ego level* is the realm of the person's self-image. Wilber says:

> On this level, man does not feel directly identified with his psychosomatic organism. Rather, for a variety of reasons, he identifies solely with a more-or-less accurate mental representation or picture of his total organism. In other words, he is identified with his ego, his self-image. (1979, p. 10)

The *shadow level* has to do with repressed or conflictual parts of oneself which one does not want to face:

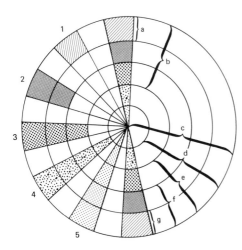

Figure 25. Lama Govinda's representation of the doctrine of the five sheaths. 1 = physical body; 2 = pránic body; 3 = thought-body; 4 = consciousness-body (depth-consciousness); 5 = inspirational body. a = stûla-śarîra; b = linga-śarîra; c = ânanda-maya-koṣa; d = vijñâna-maya-koṣa; e = mano-maya-koṣa; f = prâna-maya-koṣa; g = anna-maya-koṣa (from Lama Govinda, 1957, p. 149).

> This level is that of the shadow: man identified with an impoverished and
> inaccurate self-image (i.e., the persona), while the rest of his psychic tenden-
> cies, those deemed too painful, "evil," or undesirable, are alienated as the
> contents of the shadow. (1979, p. 11)

Wilber developed his vision and cognitive map through the explicit
comparison of Western and Eastern tradition. Particularly with regard to
the "doctrine of the five sheaths" or "energy-bodies," Wilber compares
the Hindu–Vedantic tradition with that of Tibetan Buddhism and finds
them almost identical. They both stipulate the existence of five sheaths of
consciousness emanating from three energy-bodies: the gross, the subtle,
and the causal. This is represented as five concentric circles, the innermost being variously called Brahman–Atman–Self, Mind, or pure consciousness. Figure 25 represents the doctrine of the sheaths adopted by
Wilber from Lama Govinda (1957), but also presented by Swami Rama
(whose contribution will be examined next).

Swami Rama's Yoga Psychology.[6] Swami Rama is not only interested in the presentation of Yoga psychology as an intellectual system
of understanding, but he is also concerned with the development of
personal growth through yogic discipline and with the achievement and
embodiment of higher consciousness, or the state of Samadhi (see Swami
Rama, Ballentine, & Swami Ajaya, 1976). Standing in the tradition of
Patanjali's "raja-yoga" and the psychology of Vedanta, and also standing
in critical discourse with the psychology of Carl Jung, Swami Rama
explicates the "structure of Mind" as the doctrine of sheaths or bodies
(see Figure 26), and the teaching of the seven centers of consciousness or
chakras as the "inner playroom" (see Figure 27).

Regarding the Vedantic concept of mind, Swami Rama *et al.* (1976)
describe how the incoming sensations and impressions, motor responses, and shifting perceptions—the full array of the "crazy monkey"
of ego-consciousness of the lower mind—is displayed on the screen of
manas. He says of the meaning of manas:

> It's like a television screen monitoring the events of the outside world. On it,
> sensory input is displayed. It can also register memory traces. This lower mind
> is called in yoga, *manas.* (1976, p. 70)

The function of "I-ness," then, must come into play to create personal experience by relating manas to individual identity:

> It ["I-ness"] provides a sense of separateness from the rest of the world, a
> feeling of distinctness and uniqueness. It is the agency which defines what of
> the sensory data and memories is "I." It is the property of subjectivity. It takes
> what has come in and relates it to a sense of I-ness. When the sensory-motor
> mind functions, "a rose is seen." But when *ahankara* (ego) adds its influence, "I
> see a rose." (p. 70)

[6]See also Swami Rama, Chapter 15.—Eds.

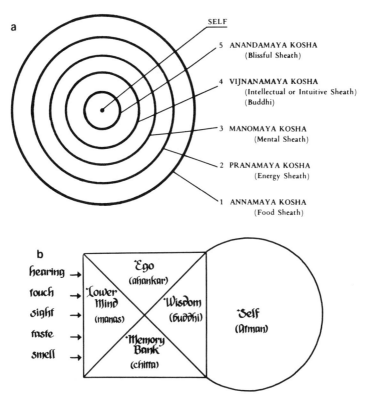

Figure 26. Swami Rama's cognitive maps of yoga psychology. (a) The five sheaths in yoga: e.g., anna = "food," maya = "illusion," kosha = "sheath"; annamayakosha = the densest level of illusion (obscuring consciousness); the physical body, which is "made of food." (b) The vedantic conception of mind (from Swami Rama *et al.*, 1976, pp. 71, 98).

Next in the process of consciousness is *buddhi's* wisdom,[7] the power to discriminate, to make a judgment, to decide—ultimately, *to will*. A response must be selected:

> This discrimination or judgment is the third major mental function. It evaluates the situation and decides on a course of action. This power of decisiveness in yoga psychology is called buddhi. It is called the "crown jewel" of discrimination and understanding. Buddhi means, then, a special kind of intelligence and wisdom. (p. 70)

Buddhi itself, one's discriminating power, partakes of personality growth. Through decision, it becomes independent of the lower levels, and a new level of "I-ness" evolves "from which one can witness mental events without being involved in them," from which the mental plane

[7]It is important to distinguish "wisdom" from "knowledge." One might be quite knowledgeable regarding a given subject, but command very little wisdom.

Figure 27. The basic Eastern paradigm of kundalini yoga. Crown chakra = the highest state of consciousness; third eye = the seat of intuitive knowledge; throat chakra = nurturance and creativity; heart chakra = emotion and empathy; solar plexus = domination and submission; genital chakra = sensuality and sexuality; and root chakra = fear and paranoia (adapted from Swami Rama *et al.*, 1976, p. 220).

can be seen from "above" so to speak. In the theory of sheaths, this is the fourth level, the intellectual or intuitive sheath:

> This is the level beyond that verbal, mental activity which we call "thinking." Awareness ceases to be limited by word-thoughts. This "supra-mental" level of "pure" reason, or "intuition," or "wisdom" is where buddhi functions unimpaired by the distractions of sense-impressions or the pre-occupation of a narrow, personal egoism. Where buddhi is more involved, the "mind" is transcended. (p. 98)

With regard to *possible* human evolution, there are higher sheaths and states of consciousness to be entered into. There is next the level beyond judgment, dichotomies, and all classifications:

> Neither fear, aversion, or addiction to gratification persists. This is said to result in a feeling of great release, a peaceful joy that is usually described as bliss. This global witness consciousness is called the blissful sheath. Beyond this even such a global awareness of the phenomenal world ceases. Consciousness exists in a purity that is indescribable. It is "consciousness without an object."[8] This is called in yoga, the Self or *Purusha*. (p. 99)

Memories or *chitta* and the five senses feed in data to be registered by manas:

> On the "other side" of the mental complex lies the "innermost" or "highest" field of human consciousness. This is variously called the Self, the Purusha, Brahman, Atman, or Jiva by different schools. This is the key to yoga psychol-

[8]This is in direct contrast to the existential-phenomenologist's contention that consciousness is intentional, that is, consciousness always has an object (see Merrell-Wolff, 1973).

ogy, for it is around the attainment of this level of consciousness that yogic discipline is organized. It is thought of as both the highest state of consciousness and the innermost center of the psyche. Reaching this results in a serene, encompassing awareness, and because of its contrast to the clamor and restlessness of the usual mental plane, it may be compared to the eye of a hurricane. (p. 72)

The pursuit of the yoga path is to actualize the highest consciousness via concentration, contemplation, and samadhi.

Each of these latter three stages is simply an expansion of the former. When concentration is developed and occurs for a longer period of time, it becomes contemplation, and when this is deepened it leads to that state known as samadhi. (p. 77)

The yogic work consists in raising the concentrated *kundalini* energy[9] through the *chakras*, which are psychological and spiritual centers of integration arranged along the axis of the spine. The chakras are said to be wheels or flywheels, the outer aspects of which relate to the gross material world, and the inner to the higher sheaths of the denser and finer vibrations coming to a center in the Self. With the movement inward toward the center of pure consciousness, goes the corresponding work upward through the *chakras* (see Figure 27). This also represents the essential view of consciousness-development in all Eastern traditions as symbolized, for example, by the meditating Buddha in the lotus position; for it is only through the practice of formal meditation (quieting the thinking mind) that these higher, transpersonal states can be reached.

Lastly, Swami Rama uses the cognitive image of the *pyramid* to discuss the work in consciousness leading to the highest state:

At the highest state of consciousness, as described in yoga, experience is not only similar, it is shared. In other words we might think of the hierarchy of consciousness as similar to a pyramid. At the base there's a wide area where diversity exists. But ascending through different levels of the hierarchy we begin to approach others who are clinging to the same stepwise fashion. At the peak of the pyramid all paths must come together and the consciousness and perspective that is gained there is identical.

This is not a "loss of consciousness" nor slipping back into an undifferentiated state. From this point any part of the surrounding area can be viewed clearly. (p. 126)

Eugen Rosenstock-Huessy's Dialogal Existentialism. For Rosenstock-Huessy, the Christian dialogal-existential thinker, truth is revealed in resolute and responsible action through incarnation. Speaking from within Christian faith, Rosenstock-Huessy believes that human existence is *cruciform*. We are all "crucified" by the intersection of the time

---

[9]*Kundalini* is the name for the "rising serpent" which symbolizes the psychic energy that can be called upon and felt as rising up the spine through the psychic centers called *chakras*.

and space axes, we find ourselves living and acting in terms of a fourfold tension generated by the two existential axes of space and time. Rosenstock-Huessy's cognitive map delineates two directions of Time, Forward and Backward, and two directions of Space, Inward and Outward (see Figure 28).

These four primordial directions and orientations that characterize human existence open out into four interdependent worlds that have to be bridged and mediated by the actions of each individual. There are four universal tasks awaiting us in the redemption of reality and the fulfillment of our lives, in the creation of the "fullness of time", and in the biographical and historical fulfillment of each individual.

In our *temporal tasks,* we have to create our future in the present on the basis of the past. Our life, our actions, bridge past and future. Each generation anew and each individual at each moment have to decide what shall belong to the past and what shall enter the future. The valuable traditions and heritage from our collective past are to be kept alive while the dead, stifling forms are to be discarded. Thus, we live both *backward* and *forward,* and the future beckons as our task and contribution, which we have to fulfill by courageous and creative action in our historical situation.

In our *spatial tasks* we have to nurture both movements: *inward* and *outward.* The *inner* world of private fantasy, of enjoyment in art, the life of the vitalizing imaginative life has to be attended to, and the *outer* world of matter, of earth, sky, and soil, the material conditions of our survival have to be secured. It requires social cooperation and the division of labor to sustain our continued cultivation of and participation in these worlds. Rosenstock-Huessy, therefore, also gives the axis of space and the dimensions of inward and outward a social interpretation, where they mean *in-group* and *out-group,* us and them. He convincingly shows that with every act we also commit ourselves in terms of belonging and inclusiveness, that is, whom we include and whom we exclude on all levels, ranging from personal to small groups, to religious, ethnic, national, race, and other interest groups and, lastly, "mankind," our ultimate social reference group.

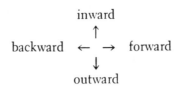

Figure 28. Rosenstock-Huessy's cross of reality (from Rosenstock-Huessy, 1970, p. 88).

Rosenstock-Huessy (1966) says the following about the significance of the four fronts of reality and their interplay:

> So it is that man's life, social as well as individual, is lived at a crossroads between four "fronts": *backward* toward the past, *forward* into the future, *inward* among ourselves, and *outward* against what we must fight or exploit or come to terms with or ignore. It is obviously fatal to fail on any front—to lose the past, to miss the future, to lack inner peace, or outer efficiency. Would we run forward only, all the acquired qualities of character and civilization would vanish. If we look backward exclusively, we cease to have a future. And so on. (p. 168)

He characterizes the *institutions* and *professions* which have been created by man to secure the four essential frontiers of human existence (see Table V).

He gives priority to the reality of language and human speaking as a collective possession and power over the reality of individual consciousness, which he considers to be the fruit of language, the fruit of "having been spoken to by others," rather than the primary reality. We become conscious through speech. But individual conscious functioning and the dimension of self which contribute to the constitution of any act are recognized by Rosenstock-Huessy. The individual as *a named unique person*, in space and time, is the focal point of his thinking. Responsibility lies in named action, for which the author is responsible with his signature, date, place, before witnesses. The person acts as an undivided unity in a moral manner; in a responsible manner and through his action he integrates the four dimensions of the self that represent the four directions of the cross of reality: body and mind, role and soul.

Expressed as parts of speech, as characteristics of language, one can recognize the fourfold division of: *nouns, verbs, numerals,* and *adjectives,* and the types of speech: *narrative, imperative, indicative,* and *subjunctive.*

One can extend Rosenstock-Huessy's cognitive map and integrate some of the dimensions of his thinking (see Figure 29).

Table V

		Institutions	Professions
Time	Past	History	Historians
			Lawyers
	Future	Politics	Leaders
Space	Inward	Arts	Artists
	Outward	Science	Scientists
			Engineers

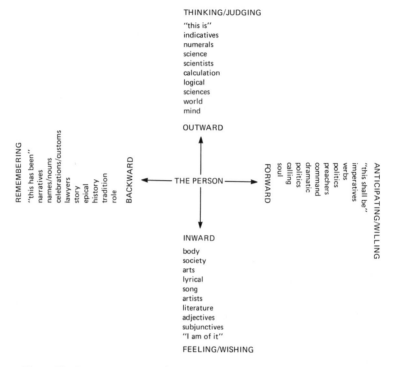

Figure 29. A representation of Rosenstock-Huessy's fourfold thinking.

Rosenstock-Huessy (1952) also writes about the vertical dimension of levels of reality which he conceives in terms of the *degree of vitality* and *intensity of life,* ranging from the coldness of dead matter to the warmth of emotion and to the white heat of maximum effort and vitality. In his book on Paracelsus, he elaborates his hierarchical conception of which he speaks in the metaphor of "spectrum." He names the five potential levels of human existence in the following manner (see Table VI).

Rosenstock-Huessy understands the Divine as manifesting primarily on Level 5, as experiences of salvation and of catastrophe, because they demand the best in us, as calling, divine imperative, and inspiration,

Table VI

Level 5	Salvation and catastrophe
Level 4	Love and hate
Level 3	Work and will
Level 2	The organic and vegetative
Level 1	The dead and mechanical

Table VII

Level 5	*Names*—they begin and create new times, new eras.
Level 4	*Love*—eternalizes and lifts us beyond time.
Level 3	*Work*—accelerates our activities.
Level 2	*Organic life*—proceeds rhythmically.
Level 1	*Dead matter*—is measured quantitatively; clock-time.

and as challenge and test of fate which commands our response. Rosenstock-Huessy's imperative is:

Respondeo etsi mutabor
[I respond even though I will be changed by it!]

His thinking rests on existential turning points in personal and historical life. He understands these levels of participation as representative of a "time-spectrum" because on each level we experience and create time differently (see Table VII).

Rosenstock-Huessy speaks from the conviction of belief and faith in Jesus Christ and the Biblical story. He accepts the truth of the Old and New Testaments and considers them to express a self-fulfilling prophecy. Our world history is the actualization of the Biblical revelation. To be a Christian is to live a crucial and historical existence, to be an individual of faith and action, and to have the freedom to respond to the unique calling of what is necessary in each of one's existential situations. For Rosenstock-Huessy, God is the power that makes one speak up, act decisively in a once-and-for-all manner, and take personal responsibility for one's deeds and life, so that the times may be fulfilled and redeemed, and all members of mankind become the brotherhood of inspired fellowship—life in transfiguration.

"Now is the time." "Today the prophecies are fulfilled before your eyes." Rosenstock-Huessy sees Jesus as the center of history, creating the turning point from B.C. to A.D. because he gave everyone the possibility of a new future by embedding all times, including his own, in one super-time, one eternal present:

> Jesus became the center of history, by being the human soul made visible, the Messiah whom the Jews expected at the end of history. In this way he introduced the end of history as a directing force in the present. Whereas the Jews identified end and beginning in God and virtually ignored everything in between, Jesus created a historical process in which every year, every day, every present is equally immediate to God because it is equally a meeting point for all the imperfect past and perfecting future. In Jesus the beginnings of antiquity all come to an end and all the ends of modern man make their beginning; the promises of old, to all the nations, are now turned progressively into realizations. (1966, pp. 189–190)

Summary. In this section on "theo-psychologies," we have looked at the work of some Western and some Eastern thinkers, and at attempts to integrate these two basic traditions. We have examined the work of the existential thinker Viktor Frankl, who represents the tradition of Western spirituality, although he speaks as a physician and psychiatrist primarily, without explicit reference to any denominational view, as a "doctor of the soul" of universal man in search of meaning. We have considered Huston Smith, who has worked on the integration of the traditional mystical and the scientific point of view. We have examined the work of Ken Wilber, who has been working on the integration of Western and Eastern schools of psychology and models of consciousness, with central emphasis on the enlightenment experience. We have presented the yoga psychology through the work of Swami Rama, who speaks from a committed Eastern belief and conviction about the right way to live, and we have presented the vision of Eugen Rosenstock-Huessy, a committed Christian dialogal thinker.

What unites these men as theo-psychologists is their understanding of the human individual as a spiritual creature open to the reality of the divine, what we have called the "theo-dimension." They write from a sacred world-view and consider the person–world relationship as under God. *Man–God–World* is the proper understanding of our existential relationships. Their "theory" is a matter of conviction. It is based on the acceptance of a particular religious experience and a belief in the truth of a story of revelation in which they live. For these men, theory is not an objective cognitive framework that one can intellectually apply for purposes of analysis, as an objective observer, but it is a *sacred story*, in which they live and believe, and from which they derive their meaning and have their being. The personal and communal way of life is founded in the historically unfolding story of our community. In recognizing the spiritual and religious dimension in us, the theo-psychologists present a richer picture of the essential dimensions that are needed to construct a comprehensive cognitive map and framework with which to represent man in his existence as a full human being and an historical person.

The Integration of Theories

The heuristic cognitive space of the pyramid shape can be used to interrelate the theories just presented as a complex cognitive map.

The Level Dimension: Depth, Height, and Middle

Almost all the theories discussed articulate *levels of consciousness* in various idioms and feature a dimension of *height to depth*. The vertical axis of the pyramid can be used to represent this levels-of-consciousness dimension, and the apex of the pyramid then symbolizes *height of consciousness*. The apex also reflects the intensity or density of consciousness, the degree of vitality of the person, and the experience of highest value and being.

The open base of the pyramid represents *depth of consciousness*, which manifests psychologically as imagery arising from the various regions of the personal and collective unconscious, these regions having their ultimate abode in the dream-state of sleep, accessible through the "royal road to the unconscious": dream experience and dream interpretation.

The pyramid itself stands in the unbounded ocean of the infinite divine psychic energy field beyond human language and consciousness, the infinite, the unnamed splendor of cosmic consciousness, which we taste and enter into in mystical experience, and which we represent on the map as the radiant enveloping psychic energy field, larger than and containing the universe of matter. The point of concentration and intensification in the pyramid's apex can represent the highest level of consciousness as the point of influx of divine consciousness into the consciousness of the person who at that moment receives an inspiration, an illumination, a creative vision or idea, a revelation of truth and beauty, a moment of ecstasy, a moral command which calls him—personally and by name—to incarnate it in his earthbound and historical existence, to perform a god-act, to become the god-body. Biographies center on these crucial nodal points in human existence and history, these existence-deciding, personally *decisive acts* and events. That is, the Divine manifests and reveals itself for humans in these experiences. The apex ushers in the transcendent reality—the theo-dimension, cosmic consciousness, beyond words, beyond distinctions, beyond conceptualization, but experienced with undoubtable conviction—the highest state of personal consciousness at privileged authentic moments and crucial turning points in the person's existence, those highest and most meaningful moments from which one derives meaning for life.

In the Biblical tradition, height experience brings one into a personal "thou–I"-oriented experience of the Divine, both as Person and as affirmation of self. The height-awareness is action-, society-, and world-oriented—*open-eyed transcendence*—it moves us toward authentic being-in-the-world.

Sometimes one speaks of the ultimate moments as the deepest experiences, presenting a paradoxical two-directional conceptualization of ecstatic transcendence as both transcendent and immanent. There is also a "beyond" in terms of *depth*, a beyond which reaches into the bright world of ecstatic bioluminescence, the "within of ourselves," the consciousness of cellular, molecular, atomic, and subatomic levels of consciousness, which Leary (1977) has articulated and mapped in a systematic way, using the psychedelic approach.

As one moves into the depth, one enters the prepersonal realms of archetypal images and ultimately the awareness of luminous universal life processes—*closed-eyes transcendence*. It is the direction of the *loss of selfhood* and positive personal disintegration, with simultaneous ecstatic merger with cosmic reality, pure energy, pure but anonymous being. The ultimate depth-awareness is trans-self—image- and consciousness-oriented. It moves toward meditative stillness, oneness, transcendence of earthly life, "ecstatic death."

The realm of the "underworld" and "Hades" in the conceptualization of Hillman (1979) in the state of sleep and dreams, is the foremost realm of pure image-making, of psyche making itself: soul-making. Hillman operates from a complex, implicit cognitive map of the depth of the psyche.

The map of psychocosmic space, of the *Psychocosm*, names the essential levels of existence and shows them in their interrelationship, as coexisting and collaborating human psychic realities which compose and orchestrate the *experienced meaning* that any life situation holds for a person. We act on the meaning we perceive a situation to have for us. Therefore, it is important to map and unpack the levels of meanings reflectively and to show where they can be seen to be located.

"The middle" is the region of conscious bodily existence itself, the anchorage point of personal existence in the world, the "address of one's being." The middle is the domain of *personal bodily movement in space and time*, of actual tangible self–world connectedness. We speak of this as "embodiment and situatedness." It is the world of action, of "actuality" (see Figure 30).

All levels function together in the production of meaning for the actor. They constitute the psychocosmic space of an individual. We use the pyramid shape as a heuristic device for ordering this space and to bring it to visibility. We articulate the minimally necessary and hence essential dimensions and planes of human existence which we need in order to locate all psychological processes.

Embodiment and Situatedness: Perception, Acting, Feeling, and Speaking

Most psychological theories acknowledge the reality of human incarnation as a bodily and moving creature *situated in space and time*. The three-dimensional cross of Smith, the cross of reality of Rosenstock-Huessy, the life-space of Lewin, and the intentional arrow of existential phenomenology, all insist on a privileged point in the psychocosmic space: the bodily location of the individual person in space and time,

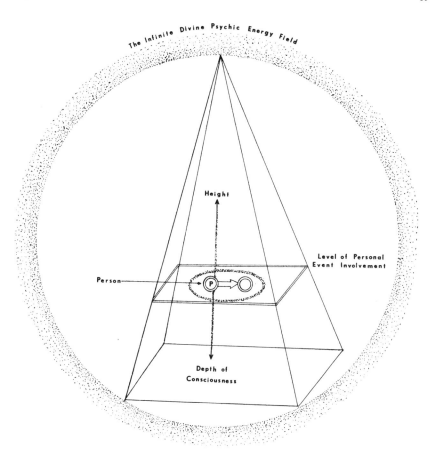

Figure 30. The height, middle, and depth dimensions of the psychocosmic space (drawings by J. Pearson).

being in an *existential situation*. Any human situation is thus identified by a *place* on earth or in space, by a *time* on the clock and on the calendar, by the *actors*, the named participants, and by the name of the *involvement*, the event which happened. The person's *existential situation* is embedded in and surrounded by the societal and historical situation, the context of a person's living.

The midpoint of the middle plane of the pyramid constitutes *the meso-dimension of human existence*, of embodied existence, tangibility, thing-connection, and physical action. We *perceive* and *act* on this meso-level, we *interact* with others and with the Earth herself, we *speak* on this level, and we *feel* bodily in reaction to our situation here and now. It is the sphere of human work, of bodily experience and of sensuousness. It is also the level of personal responsibility, as gleaned from the importance of the alibi in legal matters and notarization. One can thus say in a more general way that the meso-level is the reality of bodily presence of objects or people with *proper names*, names which identify realities in personal and social awareness, that anchor human meaning and activities on earth and constitute the center of personal conscious and responsible existence.

Thus, the middle layer of the pyramid is the level of concrete life and reality on the earth's surface, for which every person in his or her bodily being is the center of consciousness and action, and on which the psychological activities of perceiving, acting, feeling, and willing are rooted. This level of existence is the *Here-and-Now Level of Personal Event Involvement*[10] (see Figure 31).

Concrete awareness of bodily presence to the world is the birthing of consciousness, which takes on a life of its own thereafter. Our concrete awareness of presence upon experiencing becomes instantly and permanently available as an imaged remembrance that adheres to the things, persons, and situations with whom it was encountered, but that can also be accessed more or less at will from a distance, from a new here-and-now.

But the fabric of presence also loosens its strands, which may then interweave themselves differently in the process of remembering and feeling. Images may become singled out and lifted out of their original lived context and drift mysteriously into the vast realms of our depth consciousness, drawing our attention to themselves.[11]

All action is situated and bounded by space and time in a definable manner, located at some place, dated at some time. Situated action is perceived and understood as *event*, as meaningful occurrence and as having a temporal unfolding. In our map, we take the point of view of the *actor* and discuss the dimensions and regions of the psychocosm that are available to this individual experientially and in consciousness from his or her unique bodily vantage point.

We shall represent the actor as a multiple of permeable concentric circles around the person's name and essence, who is bodily located in the space and time, marking the situation in which he finds himself, always here-and-now. This is the center of the person's psychocosm, and it is always in flux, changing from moment to moment as the person takes up a new existential situation produced by his own movement and action, by that of others, and by the passage of time itself.

Each situation is surrounded by the other existential situations in which a person is involved and which link him or her with the public social order. The proper representation of one's involvement in a situa-

---

[10]Compare this with Weber's, Chapter 5, "living moment-by-moment," and R. von Eckartsberg and R. Valle's, Chapter 14, discussion of the *ever-present*.—Eds.

[11]See Marlan's Chapter 11, "Depth Consciousness".—Eds.

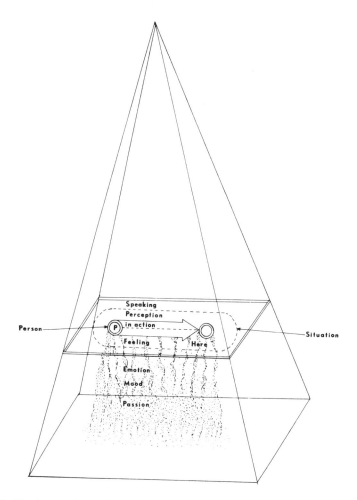

Figure 31. The here-and-now level of personal event involvement in the psychocosmic space.

tion is to show its embeddedness in the "Existential Situational Repertory," which constitutes a person's boundary of life-involvement, and to see this configuration itself surrounded by the totality of the social world as an ongoing culturally patterned and co-constituted way of life of a people mediated by social institutions. The work of Berger and Luckmann, *The Social Construction of Reality* (1966), contains a complex implicit cognitive map that covers the terrain of the person–society dialectic.

We represent the named actor, the person, as directed and facing into the physical world of his surrounds. We call this direction of attention—which can be focused into any of the identifiable planes of existence—*intentionality*, and represent it as an *arrow* pointing toward an object of or a partner in interaction. Bodily meaning contact, the tangible bodily encounter with a meaningful somebody or something here and now, shall be the privileged point, the "touchpoint" of each person's psychocosm, where the person can be reached and touched. The "intentional arrow" represents this meaning contact experience. We include the perceptual spectrum of the senses and represent it as tracks atop the meaning-arrow. We also include the bodily being-affected domain, the feeling-dimension of bodily interconnecting, and represent it as the qualitative density and "feel" of the intentional arrow, filling the meaning arrow with experienced depth.

We also include man's essential naming and speaking ability, his power to address and call somebody by name, to evoke some named reality, or to initiate and direct action by the imperative mode of speaking and place it in the center of the psychocosmic space, resting on the capacity for perceiving entities and feeling. We place this mode of contacting in the present situation atop perception, co-constituting the arrow of meaning-creating intentionality and the will and call to "life-making."

Emotion, Mood, and Passion

Another region adjoining and partially intermingling with feeling is the deep realm of "bodily attunement," more continuous and lasting than feelings, the region of emotions, moods, and passions. Our basic vital and prepersonal bodily relationship to others, to our world, and to ourselves gives us our basic attunement and its modulations: love and hate, joy and anxiety, bliss and terror, ecstasy and pain, optimism and pessimism, life and death. Our living swings between these extremes of basic attunement which disclose our world in various appearances or "physiognomies." It is from this vital and biological ground of our existence that the quality of being affected emerges as the mood and experienced dynamism that animates our relationships.

We represent these mood-attuning regions of bodily existence below and supporting the domain of bodily feeling. Although bodily feeling is personal and immediately self-related, emotions, moods, and passions are more like anonymous powers that befall us and overtake us as sweeping atmospheres and currents opening up for us "physiognomic worlds," coloring our perceptions of the world in synchronization with our basic attunement.

The meaning-horizons of immediate bodily feelings, of time-consciousness, of fantasy imagings, of cognitive theoretical horizons (ways to think), and of value-quality all contribute to what the object means to the actor and how it is qualitatively experienced by the actor. The *story of the event* contains this knowledge, but it has to be articulated and thematized as an explicit psychological argument to become fully visible.

It was discussed above how the field- and force-lines of a two-pole ellipse-shaped magnetic field best symbolizes the multileveled nature of the field of consciousness and the space of the psychocosm at any particular moment (see Figure 19), and it remains to specify both the modalities and levels of consciousness and existence that are involved, and to anchor and map them in the space of the heuristic cognitive image of the pyramid.

The Time Dimension: Presence, Remembering, and Anticipating

Another universal dimension that all "personality-cartographers" must take into account when they discuss motivation and personality-dynamics—although few explicitly map it—is the *time-dimension* of existential experience.

All acts, as well as all of human life and consciousness in general, undergo development, are "becoming." We find ourselves in the middle of time, in the middle of our own lifetime at a point between birth and death, and in the middle of history spanning all known generations and opening up into a personal and collective future into which we actualize ourselves.

One can thus distinguish three essential time zones: the *present,* the *past,* and the *future,* issuing forth from the here-and-now. This state of affairs is presented in the unfolding heuristic image of the *pyramid of human existence* by letting the edges of the pyramid from the middle plane represent the directions of time-consciousness, *backward and downward toward the past in acts of remembering,* which is the biohistorical ground of our personal and collective existence, and *forward and upward toward the future in acts of anticipation, planning, and projecting,* by means of which we create what is to be done and who we are to be (see Figure 32).

Thus, the level of concrete here-and-now-existence—itself temporally extended as the "length," the duration of the event in which we are currently involved—is grounded and founded by the active sediment of memories of biography and the realities of history. A sense of self-continuity and sequence of events along continuous temporal lines and succession provides organization and access to the different regions of the past, based upon a remembered continuity of one's bodily path through one's lifetime, the *"axis personalitatis."*

The imagined and actual future that is partially beyond our control

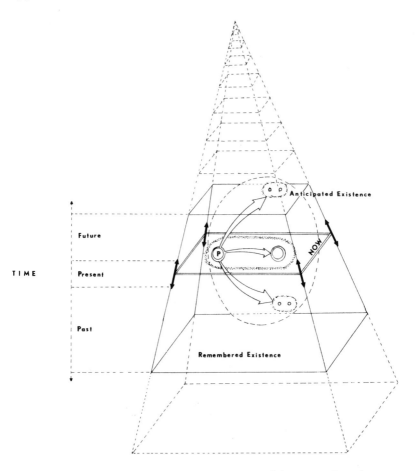

Figure 32. The temporal organization of the personal psychocosm.

already hovers above and amidst our here-and-now, ready to exfoliate. It is to come into being: now! It is the invocation and creation of the image and project of our concrete existential future that brings it to realization barring unforeseen circumstances, difficulties, and the limits of personal power. Psychologically, we anticipate our future, we envision goals, destinations, accomplishments, "finishes" at the end of our personal time-effort-path within the overall one-directional time-tunnel called aging.

In consciousness, we create and travel the paths backward and forward in time, and it depends on our mood and the state of our being and interest here-and-now as to how our past or future appears to us in its physiognomy.

In the construction of the human psychocosm according to the pyramid shape, the domain of memory and accumulated knowledge—the *realm of remembered existence,* the world of past relationships, accomplishments, and events—is delineated as underneath and founding the realm of concrete existence and action here-and-now. The *realm of anticipated existence*—of anticipation, future-awareness, and future-commitment—the world of goals and destinations, is represented as lying over and above here-and-now, in the direction of there-and-then, in "reality to come," to be actualized by me through my vision.

Individual anticipations or plans issuing forth from my here-and-now and pointing forward in time—and thus also determining and "booking" the geographical path that I will follow in space using my time—can be represented as arrows to "destinations."

Likewise, our ongoing existence as bodily engagement in situations is ongoingly being sedimented in aging muscularity and habit and held "in ready," available to recall in praxis or image, building up into both an organized stock of knowledge, around the anchor points of names and named events, and the fabric of a story which holds the event in language and secures it more firmly in personal and collective memory.

In the temporal dynamics of active goal-oriented ongoing life, the present is perceived against the backdrop of the anticipated, toward which we aim, and the remembered, from which we come and which provides us with the backdrop and context of familiarity and habitual existential process against which all experience is highlighted.

The relevant "past-contexts" and "future-contexts" are given as horizonal presences in the perceptually focused object and situation here-and-now. We call these the temporal horizons of experience and represent them as arrows issuing from the present involvement into my anticipated future regarding the object under consideration. The past-horizon is present in our experience as an invitation to return to the familiar related and relevant scenes of involvement in our personal past and in the accumulated knowledge of man. We can call the past also the "horizon of familiarity."

The interplay of present, past, and future as "ex-stasies" of time in the phenomenon of "temporalization" and its usefulness in existential analysis of an "existence-gestalt" is masterfully described by Binswanger (1958) in his case study of Ellen West, which stands as an open invitation for cognitive mapping.

Fantasying

As we move "up" from the here-and-now level of personal event-involvement and beyond our actually projected future, and as we move "down" beyond our remembrances into the never-never land of missed opportunities, of regrets, of guilt about unfinished business, of "what-ifs," imaginatively recasting fate according to our desires and wishes, of undoing and redoing of what happened retrospectively in imagination, we find the fantasy domains of the personal psychocosm.

The domain of fantasying, of wishful thinking and daydreaming, opens up into an idealized and transformed future or past which has an "as-if" quality, a quality of exaggeration. In fantasy we enter the wish-fulfillment world of god-consciousness, but not of god-body, which requires god-realization and god-actualization. In fantasy one can change his or her existential limitations, finitude, and facticity, and one can attribute to oneself all the qualities desired. We act "as-if" we are omnipotent, omniscient, and omnipresent, with self-attributed qualities in the domain of fantasy, which is both a storehouse of potential riches and also a "magic theatre" of seduction and delusion. It is the realm of imagined personal possibilities beckoning for actualization, demanding to be brought into the realm of anticipation as realizable projects. Fantasying can also take on threatening and fearful qualities, being compelled and haunted by demons, but it is also the realm of free play, of pure possibility, of divine freedom, in which one can dwell and imagine one's life beyond the actuality, limitations, and pressures of the existential situation and the actual events as they occur. Fantasy is personal, earthly "god-play." In the cognitive pyramid, fantasying is placed both upward and beyond anticipation, and below remembering in a realm discontinuous with and beyond real space and time in the physical sense.

For further possibilities of mapping the fantasy regions, see Keen (1975), Minkowski (1970), and Binswanger's case study of Ellen West in which he describes two regions of fantasying as forms of inauthentic temporality and spatiality: the "ethereal world"—the wish-world of the wish-self, and the "tomb world"—the dread-world of the self-in-despair, and their particular modes of being-in-the-world (see Figure 33).

Spontaneous Conscious and Unconscious Imaging

There is also a domain of spontaneous upwelling images coming from the depth-dimension. "Below" memory, in our unfolding map, discontinuous with physical space and time, are the clouds and flashes of free-floating images, the play of psyche, dreams, and symbolic images, reaching down into the depths of the infinite ocean of collective and archetypal images, of powers and divinities which populate our unconscious in volatile and mysterious movements, flashes, obsessions, and spells. This is the terrain occupied by the realities most eloquently described by Freud (1953), Jung (1925), Hillman (1979), and Grof (1976)—the

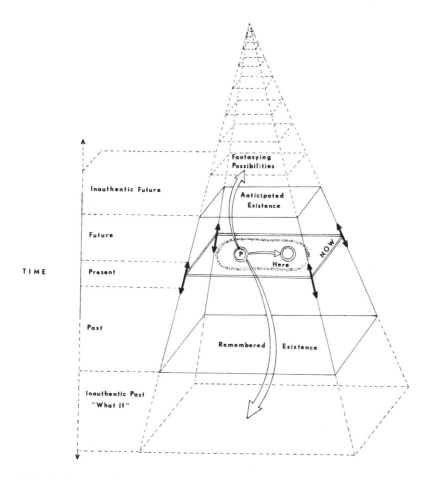

Figure 33. The inauthentic temporal and inauthentic spatial regions of fantasying in the psychocosm.

"underworld" of the psyche. This realm of depth-imaging lies beyond space and time altogether, in the realm of the eternal, in *"illo tempore,"* in the basic psychic reality that is formed by myth and divine figures which form the mythopoetic basis of consciousness explored by archetypal psychology (Hillman, 1979) which charts the regions of dreams and the underworlds in the sleep state.

We present this region of spontaneous imaging at the base of the pyramid of the human psychocosm. Below this level there is narcosis, coma, and death, the ultimate border areas of human depth-con- sciousness themselves grounded in the infinite divine psychic energy field (see Figure 34).

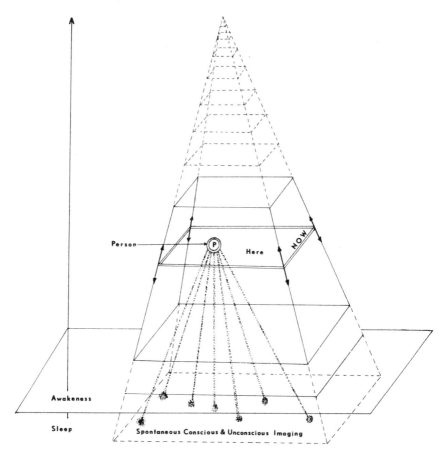

Figure 34. The realm of spontaneous conscious and unconscious imaging and dream images in the psychocosm.

Everyday Thinking

Above fantasying is the realm of *everyday thinking*, which is constituted by the universal everyday sense-making skill of the telling of
stories, by "schemata of interpretation" (Neisser, 1976) and cognitive
maps of places (Downs & Stea, 1977), and by the "typifications of everyday life" (Schutz, 1967), a domain of the taken-for-granted structures of
knowledge about the working of everyday social life, masterfully described by Schutz, awaiting explicit cognitive mapping. Partially as a fruit
of systematic scientific and philosophical thinking which has become
"common sense," and partially as a result of the gathering- and
reworking-power of memory which allows us to review, generalize, and

draw conclusions from our experiencing, the realm of everyday thinking consists of those ways of conceptualizing life that are available to us as average citizens in our culture. The degree of differentiation of everyday thinking depends on one's level of education and socialization, and one's involvement and placement in the "sociology of knowledge" (Schutz, 1967). Schemata of thinking and interpretation are available to every member of the language community because they are anchored in the very vocabulary of language, which makes possible the abstraction of concrete experience and its expression in terms of concepts and symbols. They appear as both denotative and connotative ways of thinking. These ways of thinking, of course, have their own professional custodians and "knowledge-producers," and, thus, their own realm of systematization, which is placed above everyday thinking in the pyramid.

Systematic Denotative Thinking: Stories and Meta-Stories

Developing the cognitive space toward the apex a bit further, one can discern *cognition* first, in the form of systematically conceptualizing reality, and then relating classes of reality. Making judgments about statements and propositions in a created linguistic domain of abstract concepts and professional theorizing by the various sciences and professions appears on the next higher level of the pyramid, "up" from anticipation and everyday thinking in the direction of universality, constituting its own place in the psychocosm.

In psychology, concepts are names of perceived structures and of processes that can be defined. But concepts transcend concrete visualization, although their meaning can be grasped explicitly. Configurations of concepts constitute theories. They are linguistic conceptual structures of thinking by means of which we can thematize and articulate—our awareness of bodily presence, as meaningful contact with the world.

Theories expressed as *cognitive maps* belong as an autonomous realm to the lower dimensions of this denotative level, in that they still involve an element of concreteness, an aspiration of close fit between map and territory to be mapped, which makes them useful and functional for anticipation, for prediction, and for concrete tracking. Maps are systematizations of everyday thinking. Thinking is always thinking about something, about some already-experienced reality or life-happening. As stated earlier, life and thought are dialectically related. This involves a twofold process: the experiencing and first articulation of *what happened* in the form of a narrative description, a story, which is the commonsense way of understanding, thinking, and reporting the events of the here-and-now level of personal involvement, and the interpretation of the *meaning of what happened* beyond what was reported but implied in the report.

Table VIII. Five Fundamental Existential Questions

Implicit questions	Revealed existential realities
Who?	The actor(s)
In relationship to whom?	The partners in interaction
Is involved in what?	The nature of the involvement
Where?	The place
When?	The time

The here-and-now level is the domain of bodily happenings and events. It is defined by the facts of what happened, which are revealed by five implicit and interdependent basic questions which I have elsewhere called "Fundamental Existentials" (R. von Eckartsberg, 1978) (see Table VIII).

Events are narrated and described in the form of stories which give an account of what happened in concrete terms. But one also thinks about the story, about its meaningfulness and significance, and its motivational dynamics and coherence, its "why." Professional psychologists create "stories about stories," that is, *meta-stories*. Each theory develops an explicit explanatory story-line about the nature of personality and motivation, that is, a story of what was "really" happening psychologically (in terms of the constructs of the theory), as applied to the stories of the presented existential facts. *Psychological theories are stories about stories—meta-stories* (Bateson, 1979).

There are three essential psychological questions—*interpretationals*—which all theories have to answer. Each one does it in its idiosyncratic way. The three interpretationals, in their integration, deal with the philosophical anthropological question: *What is the essential nature of man?* Each theory presents a unique vision. Psychologists break this philosophical question down into its component parts: *Personality Structure, Personality Dynamics,* and *Personality Style and Mode of Being* (Binswanger, 1958) (see Table IX).

We can represent the level of *denotative thinking* in the pyramid model as a level above that of everyday thinking. It is a multilayered domain that contains all the work of the different sciences, and of philosophy and its

Table IX. Three Interpretationals

Implicit questions	Revealed guiding theoretical constructs
On what level?	Personality structure
Why?	Personality dynamics
How?	Personality style and mode

various domains including ontology. In our discussion, we are mostly concerned with the discipline of psychology, and with theorizing and mapping within its domain. On the relationship between everyday commonsense psychology and professional psychological theorizing we have the work of Heider (1958), which contains a complex field-theoretical implicit cognitive map of common-sense psychological constructs (see Figure 35).

Conceptualizing everyday practical thinking, that is, the grasping and comprehending of processes of reality by means of concepts, pro-

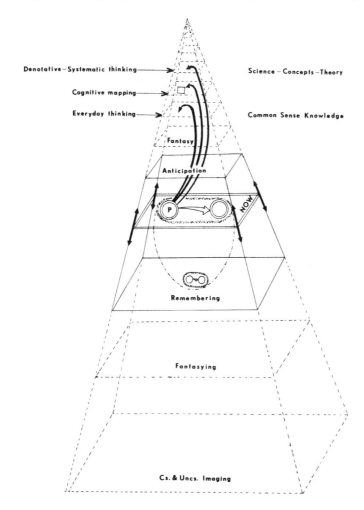

Figure 35. The placement of the levels of everyday and systematic denotative thinking in the psychocosm.

ceeds by means of univocal terms, by means of concepts which can be denotatively defined.

Systematic denotative thinking is the work of science and academic disciplines. If we want to track conceptually any human event in terms of its unfolding (five existentials) and its meaning (three interpretationals) as it appears in the account of the event, in the story, and in terms of our interpretation of this story (the meta-story), we have to unpack the account according to its time-line, and question it in terms of its basic meaning-dimensions (see Figure 36).

Stories make sense to the degree that they provide instantiations and hence "answers" to the basic implicit questions constituting: "What happened?" and "What does it mean?" The role basic questions play in the constitution of meaning, especially the meaning of stories, is discussed by Burke (1945), Muses (1974), and R. von Eckartsberg (1978).

From the meta-theoretical perspective, one can see that denotative thinking and cognitive theorizing—that is, the choice of a theory—is itself founded in value-choices and the power of conviction and faith that are superordinate to logical rationality and require their own domains in the pyramid, constituting meta-meta-levels. Three such domains, in ascending order, can be distinguished: (1) Connotative Thinking and Aesthetic Experience; (2) Ethics and Moral Experience; and (3) Religion and Sacred Experience (following Kierkegaard, 1954; Scheler, 1961).

Connotative Thinking and Aesthetic Experience

Although the level of denotative thinking and theorizing contains all scientific thinking, as well as the hierarchy of the sciences (including most philosophizing and ontologies), the next higher level of consciousness, *Connotative Thinking and Aesthetic Experience*, is concerned with the domains of the Arts and the capacity of the human individual to create worlds and objects of polyvalent meanings: metaphors and symbols. Historically and ongoingly, the world of the arts has been created, in its various forms, next to the world of facts, transforming the world by means of symbolic representation and "reframing" (Goffmann, 1974). Symbolic thinking is connotative thinking, allowing multiple readings and interpretations of the given. In the arts, one encounters "concrete universals," that is, concrete depictions of unique human experiences which yet also carry a universal meaning true for all humankind at all times, illuminating the universal human condition. It is the power of art to represent and reflect our experience to ourselves and to clarify our lived meanings through contemplation and interpretation, that is, through *hermeneutical experience and activity.*

Whereas denotative thinking can be said to be a modulation of clear

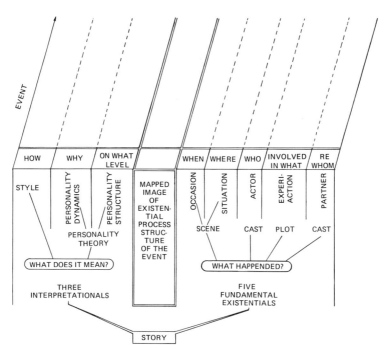

Figure 36. The essential dimensions of a story in their temporal unfolding in the constituting of an event.

and distinct perception, connotative thinking can be understood as the elaboration of feeling and emotional imagery and intuition into created form and expression. The history of art forms has opened up this level of articulated symbolic connotative thinking in which we participate, and which provide contexts of meaning-enrichment to the degree that we, as individuals, have developed awareness of this domain of existence, and cultivated it as an important part of our psychocosmic world. We may be justified in speaking of connotative thinking on the everyday level in terms of use of metaphors in everyday speech and in differentiating this from the level of artistic and religious symbolization and expression requiring special artistic skills.

Ethics and Moral Experience[12]

Our placement in social life and culture is a placement in an *ethic* which founds and controls our interactions and institutions. Every society has to establish a moral order and socialize its members into its rule-

[12]See Leavitt's, Chapter 20, discussion of conscience and moral and ethical behavior.—Eds.

and role-structures—its dos and don'ts. Every social situation is thus "legislated" and socially defined, and experienced in its social-demand character by the well-socialized participants and occupants. Our lives are embedded in a matrix of social customs and the enforced structures of law. Although we can violate the established rules of conduct and standards of evaluation, we are defined by them and define ourselves in relationship to them. Guilt, shame, pride, duty, righteousness, and indignation are all affective expressions of our life on the ethical plane. We evaluate ourselves and others in terms of collective standards of propriety. Our awareness of social customs, law, and morality comes from the accumulation of experiences in memory and our stock of knowledge. The ethical is an experienced horizon of all human action and experience, the dimension of "ought," which dwells and appears near the center of our being in the experience of conscience. The imperatives it issues—thou shalt and thou shalt not—and the values it reveals demand our allegiance and incarnation. It is the spell of tradition and the customary social order that commands our loyalty.

Religion and Sacred Experience

Closest to the apex of the pyramid is the highest level of human consciousness—what we call religion and sacred experience, an encounter with the Divine: the theo-dimension in an intense personal experience. Traditionally, this has been called the domain of the spirit, through which we intuit and contact the power and infinity of the Divine, the transpersonal.

Each tradition has its own way of speaking about this highest dimension of human existence and experience. The theo-dimension finds expression in cultural and historical terms, although theo-experience itself as a genuinely mystical vision transcends any particular determination and content.

Sacred experience reveals the inbreak of the creative-divine in a person's life and existential situation. In the Western tradition of the *transcendent* experience[13] of God, it is a moment of grace and being called to respond in a particular way, to do the one thing necessary to bring creation into perfection by one's action, to enter the Kairos of a new life. For the Christian dialogal thinker Rosenstock-Huessy, who may be singled out as a representative of this Western New Testament view, sacred experience addresses each individual personally in his or her soul and demands a personal response to a unique existential calling, by the personal God, to serve the fullness of time and the brotherhood of humankind in the historical creation of an optimal way of life, from here

[13]Consider this in light of Marlan's, Chapter 11, discussion of "ego-transcendence."—Eds.

on forward, via "metanoia" and radical self- and life-transformation. Both salvation and catastrophe, both blessings and destructive acts of fate, serve to call forth the best in the individual in the struggle for the perfection and redemption of humankind and their world. We could also draw on Maslow's (1968) research on the "peak-experience" to illustrate this highest, transpersonal region of the human psychocosm.

In the Eastern traditions, pursuing an *immanent* realization of the Divine, sacred experience is given as illumination, the state of perfect concentration, stillness, and transcendence of self. The Eastern mystical experience leads one to consciousness without an object (Merrell-Wolff, 1973), the disappearance of the subject–object distinction, merger with pure consciousness, divine universal radiant energy, merger with the pure light that radiates from within all. The sacred is experienced as ecstatic self-surrender and becoming one with the always already present ground of divine consciousness by stripping away, by letting go of what stands in the way, mostly the structures of oneself and one's cultural and personal attachments.

Although there are essential differences in the conceptualization of the sacred experience in the different sacred traditions, they all agree that the dimension of the religious and spiritual experience lies as a possibility at the core and center of human existence. This dimension constitutes the highest as well as the deepest aspect of human consciousness, the trans-rational domain of belief and faith that both transcends reason and intellectual-conceptual understanding and reveals value orientations in the realization of which the person can dedicate and commit him or herself, becoming the co-creator in a chosen way of life (see Figure 37).

We understand this highest region of the human psychocosm as the personal movement into the theo-dimension which opens up personal contact with the infinite divine psychic energy field. This region is represented in our heuristic image by the tip of the pyramid containing the "eye of God" and symbolizing unfinished creation. It is the locus of personal creativity, meaning, value, personal commitment, responsibility, faith, and courage (Tillich, 1952), "authentic resoluteness" (Heidegger, 1962), the moment of "new life," when the individual becomes infinitely important, and the irreplaceable center and agent of historical destiny, when his or her life begins to matter through inspired being and action. In such moments of sacred participation in life, man fulfills his ontological destiny as "life-maker" and "culture-builder."

The Pyramid of Human Existence and the Psychocosm

Let us now bring the discovered dimensions of our review and discussion of the cognitive maps in psychology together and assemble them in their interdependency, using the heuristic image of the pyramid

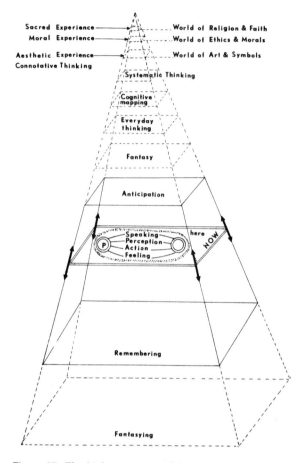

Figure 37. The highest regions of the human psychocosm.

shape (see Figure 38). This pyramid of human existence, which identifies and locates the various human modes of presence to reality in relationship to each other, constitutes a map of the human psychocosm in universal terms. In order to use the map, one must enter the specifics of his or her own existential situation, which is primarily expressed through the realities of *proper names* and what they stand for. Proper names give all relationships their unique biographical and historical identity and serve as the anchorage points for the drama and stories which carry the meaning of our existence.

Our cognitive image of the pyramid gives only the most general outline and ontological divisions within the human psychocosm. Many specific studies of concrete human events and of comparative theoretical formulations are necessary (or already exist in verbal form), awaiting

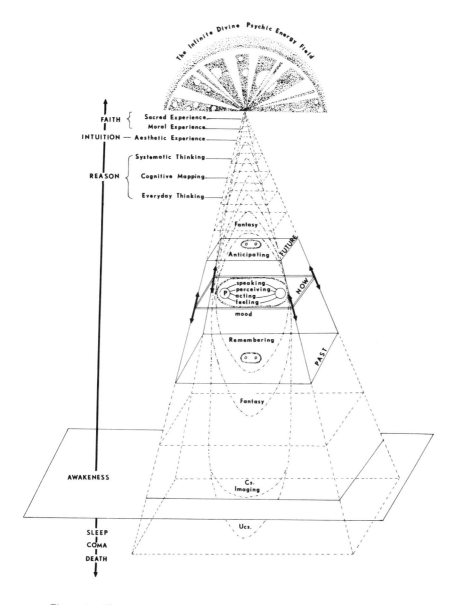

Figure 38. The pyramid of human existence as an image of the psychocosm.

mapping in order to fill in, expand, and complexify the cognitive space we delineate, making this space progressively more reality-adequate. The actuality of the universal cognitive map invites the possibilities of concrete journeys in representation and mapping.

Eco-Psychology: Creating a Way of Life Together

Having gathered the fruits of the labors of psychologists in the form of their *cognitive maps* of human functioning, one must ask the ultimate question: For what purpose?

The *National Geographic* keeps providing us with maps of all kinds of regions of the world, and beautiful pictures and stories too. But our actual family's rate-of-realization is perhaps one trip a year—our one chance to get into a new landscape as a wanderer and dweller. Maps can be instruments of intellectual curiosity, but they become more important and more interesting as one gets to know the territory they represent. As we enter the atmosphere of a region and the ways of life appropriate to it, and as we become personally familiar with the territory and its indigenous culture, we become more interested. We want to be better oriented so that we can know it better and be better in it, participating, embracing, and knowing it so well, ultimately, that we no longer need the map. We know it by heart.

So maps are useful, insofar as they help us to get more into the world and living. And so it is with regard to not only the cognitive maps representing psychological theories, but also the *meta-map of the pyramid of human existence* as a representation of the psychocosm just constructed. As it stands, this meta-map is just a scheme useful for reflecting, studying, and analyzing. But as we enter the space of this universal psychocosm personally, and become aware of *our own* dimensions of consciousness, as we feel ourselves, our spine, to be the very vertical axis of this pyramid, we also begin to realize that it opens up many levels of opportunities, for participation, for awareness. These levels are worlds to enter, the modalities are avenues for contact and participation. They all interact, they are all orchestrated in creating the dance of life. Just as intellectual-scientific thinking has revealed to us the existence and structure of the radiant spectrum of electromagnetic energy and its organizing principle, *rate of vibration,* so our integration of the bands and levels of consciousness have yielded a *spectrum of existence* represented as the layers of the pyramid. One might use another image for the representation of our levels of existence and consciousness, as a symbol of the spirit of Western reflection and analysis. This image appears in the form of a circle, the sectors of which constitute the different modalities and possibilities of human existential participation in reality (see Figure 39).

We place this image within the universe and place the universe within the all-surpassing and encompassing reality of the *infinite divine psychic energy field* symbolizing all meanings of "beyond," the ultimate horizons of human existence.

Any articulated spectrum is constituted by the intellectual ordering

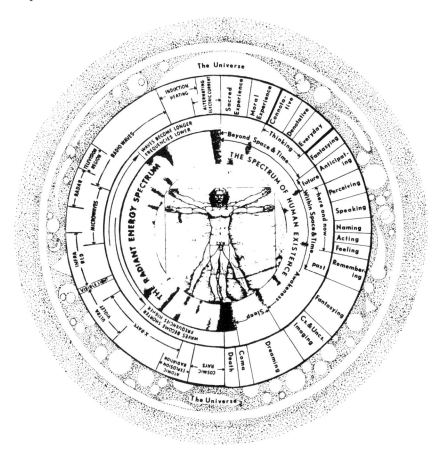

Figure 39. The spectrum of existence.

of realities into categories. It must be remembered, however, that all levels of existence interact, and that all fields of consciousness are inter-penetrating.

But we cannot leave the human individual in isolation without existential situation, and thus we have to bring him or her into relationship with another person, into a shared world. We choose foam-born Venus from the world of myth and the vision of Botticelli and bring her into the elliptoid love-dyad with Leonardo's Adam, already measuring squares and circles on the level of aesthetic and symbolic contemplation. We celebrate the "conjunctio" of the *intuitive female* couched in story and myth, and the *rational male* reaching out mathematically. *Hieros Gamos*, holy wedding, it is a story worth telling, like the birth of Venus herself, and that of Adam (see Figure 40).

As we see these two personages together, we do not see them in their

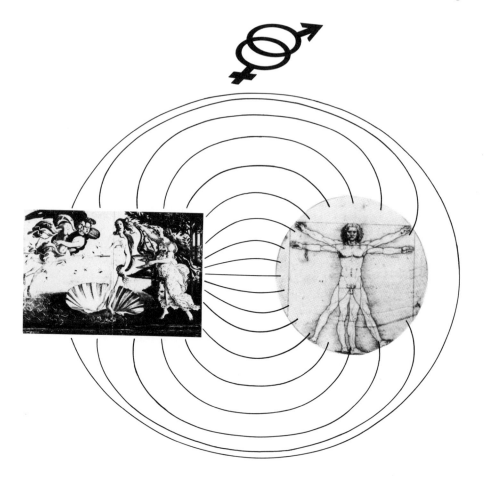

Figure 40. The *Hieros Gamos* of human existence.

isolated modalities or psychological functions, although, like the fine-tuned instruments of an orchestra, they are all in play. But they create unified music, the Ninth Symphony of Mahler for example, a way of life filled with divine music. The modalities are always implicated in any concrete moment, but they are not isolated. They cohere and collaborate in the creation of events. Concatenations of events constitute relationships over time, relationships give rise to stories, and stories congeal into the *Existential Novel in Creation* that I am, that we are, originators and participants in the creation of a way of life, one and all. Man, the life-maker.

Human meaning-making rests in stories. Life-making calls for account, for story, for sharing. To be human is "to be entangled in stories" as Schapp (1976) says. It is the "personal story" (Brand, 1972) with its "cast of characters," its "events," its "temporal unfolding," its "pervasive atmosphere," its "projects," and its "why"; its fate, its myth, its sacred story, its divinity gives unity and meaningful coherence to my understanding of my life. Storytelling as word-event promotes the self's homecoming in the process of individuation and our encounter with the Divine on earth which is our highest destiny (Winquist, 1978). "Everybody has a story to tell" (Keen & Fox, 1978), and we have tried to tell the story of some of the major psychologists as mapmakers, showing their pictures, their cognitive maps.

References

Allport, G. The historical background of modern social psychology. In G. Lindzey (Ed.), *Handbook of social psychology*. Cambridge, Mass.: Addison-Wesley, 1958.

Assagioli, R. *Psychosynthesis*. Baltimore: Penguin Books, 1965.

Assagioli, R. *The act of will*. Baltimore: Penguin Books, 1974.

Bateson, G. *Mind and nature: A necessary unity*. New York: Dutton, 1979.

Berger, P., & Luckmann, T. H. *The social construction of reality*. New York: Doubleday Anchor, 1966.

Binswanger, L. The case of Ellen West. In R. May, E. Angel, & H. Ellenberger (Eds.), *Existence*. New York: Basic Books, 1958.

Brand, G. *Gesellschaft u. Persönliche Geschichte*. Stuttgart: Kohlhammer, 1972.

Burke, K. *A grammar of motives*. Englewood Cliffs, N.J.: Prentice-Hall, 1945.

Deutsch, M. Field theory in social psychology. In G. Lindzey, & E. Aronson (Eds.), *The handbook of social psychology* (Vol. I). Reading, Mass.: Addison-Wesley, 1968.

Downs, R., & Stea, D. *Maps in minds*. New York: Harper & Row, 1977.

Frankl, V. *The doctor and the soul*. New York: Knopf, 1955.

Frankl, V. *Psychotherapy and existentialism*. New York: Washington Square Press, 1967.

Frankl, V. *The unconscious god*. New York: Simon & Schuster, 1975.

Freud, S. *New introductory lectures on psychoanalysis*. New York: W. W. Norton, 1933.

Freud, S. *The interpretation of dreams*. London: Hogarth Press, 1953.

Giorgi, A. *Psychology as a human science*. New York: Harper & Row, 1970.

Goffmann, E. *Frame analysis*. New York: Harper & Row, 1974.

Gould, P., & White, R. *Mental maps*. Baltimore: Penguin Books, 1974.

Grof, S. *Realms of the human unconscious*. New York: Dutton, 1976.

Gurwitsch, A. *The field of consciousness*. Pittsburgh: Duquesne University Press, 1964.

Habermas, J. *Erkenntnis und Interesse*. Frankfurt: Suhrkamp Verlag, 1968.

Heidegger, M. *Being and time*. New York: Harper & Row, 1962.

Heidegger, M. *Poetry, language, thought*. New York: Harper & Row, 1971.

Heider, F. *The psychology of interpersonal relations*. New York: Wiley, 1958.

Hillman, J. *The dream and the underworld*. New York: Harper & Row, 1979.

Husserl, E. *The phenomenology of internal time consciousness*. Bloomington: Indiana University Press, 1964.

Ihde, D. *Experimental phenomenology*. New York: Putnam, 1977.

Jacobi, J. *The psychology of C. G. Jung*. New Haven: Yale University Press, 1973.

Jung, C. G. *Psychology of the unconscious*. New York: Dodd, 1925.

Keen, E. *A primer in phenomenological psychology.* New York: Holt, Rinehart & Winston, 1975.

Keen, S., & Fox. A. *Telling your story.* New York: New American Library, 1978.

Kierkegaard, S. *Fear and trembling and the sickness unto death.* Princeton: Princeton University Press, 1954.

Korzybski, A. *Science and sanity.* Lakeville, Conn.: Institute of General Semantics, 1958.

Kuhn, T. H. *The structure of scientific revolutions.* Chicago: University of Chicago Press, 1962.

Lama Govinda. *Foundations of Tibetan mysticism.* New York: S. Weiser, 1957.

Leary, T. *Exo-psychology.* Los Angeles: Starseed/Peace Press, 1977.

Lewin, K. The conceptual representation and measurement of psychological forces. *Contributions to psychological theory,* 1938, *1,* 4.

Lewin, K. *Field theory in social science.* New York: Harper & Row, 1951.

Lifton, R. *The life of the self.* New York: Simon & Schuster, 1976.

Maslow, A. *Motivation and personality.* New York: Harper & Row, 1954.

Maslow, A. *Toward a psychology of being.* Princeton: Van Nostrand, 1968.

Masters, R., & Houston, J. *Mind games: The guide to inner space.* New York: Delta Books, 1973.

Merleau-Ponty, M. *The phenomenology of perception.* London: Routledge & Kegan Paul, 1962.

Merrell-Wolff, F. *The philosophy of consciousness without an object.* New York: Julian Press, 1973.

Metzner, R. *Maps of consciousness.* New York: Collier Books, 1971.

Minkowski, E. *Lived time: Phenomenological and psychopathological studies.* Evanston, Ill.: Northwestern University Press, 1970.

Musès, C. The syntax of events. *Astrologia,* 1974, *1,* 19–30.

Neisser, U. *Cognition and reality.* San Francisco: W. H. Freeman, 1976.

Pannikar, R. Idli gite fragmenta: For an integration of reality. In F. Eigo (Ed.), *From alienation to atoneness.* Villanova, Pa.: Villanova University Press, 1977.

Piaget, J. *The construction of reality in the child.* New York: Basic Books, 1954.

Radnitzki, G. *Contemporary schools of metascience.* Göteborg: Akademiforlaget, 1968.

Ricoeur, P. *Freud.* New Haven: Yale University Press, 1970.

Roberts, T. H. Beyond self actualization. *Re-vision,* 1978, *1*(1), 42–46.

Rosenstock-Huessy, E. *Heilkraft und Wahrheit.* Stuttgart: Evangelisches Verlags Werk, 1952.

Rosenstock-Huessy, E. *The Christian future.* New York: Harper Torch Books, 1966.

Rosenstock-Huessy, E. *Speech and reality.* Norwich, Vt.: Argo Press, 1970.

Sartre, J. *Being and nothingness.* New York: Philosophical Library, 1956.

Schapp, W. *In Geschichten Verstrickt.* Weisbaden: B. Heymann, 1976.

Scheler, M. *Man's place in nature.* Boston: Beacon Press, 1961.

Schutz, A. *Collected papers I.* The Hague: Martinus Nijhoff, 1962.

Schutz, A. *The phenomenology of the social world.* Evanston, Ill.: Northwestern University Press, 1967.

Smith, H. *The forgotten truth.* New York: Harper & Row, 1976.

Straus, E. *The primary world of the senses.* Glencoe: The Free Press, 1963.

Swami Rama, Balletine, R., & Swami Ajaya. *Yoga and psychotherapy.* Honesdale, Pa.: Himalayan Institute, 1976.

Tart, C. T. *States of consciousness.* New York: Dutton, 1975.

Tillich, P. *The courage to be.* New Haven: Yale University Press, 1952.

Van Kaam, A. *Existential foundations of psychology.* Pittsburgh: Duquesne University Press, 1966.

von Eckartsberg, E. Early traces of the "new polytheism" in the works of Jung, Hermann Hesse, and D. H. Lawrence. *Lapis,* 1978, *2,* 15–30.

von Eckartsberg, R. The eco-psychology of motivational theory and research. In A. Giorgi,

C. T. Fischer, & E. L. Murray (Eds.), *Duquesne studies in phenomenological psychology* (Vol. II). Pittsburgh: Duquesne University Press, 1975.

von Eckartsberg, R. Person perception revisited. In R. S. Valle & M. King (Eds.), *Existential-phenomenological alternatives for psychology*. New York: Oxford University Press, 1978.

Watkins, M. *Waking dreams*. New York: Harper Colophon Books, 1976.

Wilber, K. *The spectrum of consciousness*. Wheaton, Ill.: Quest Books, 1977.

Wilber, K. Psychologia perennis. In J. Welwood (Ed.), *The meeting of the ways*. New York: Schocken, 1979.

Wilson, R. A. *Cosmic trigger*. New York: Pocket Books, 1977.

Winquist, C. *Homecoming, interpretation, transformation, and individuation*. Missoula, Montana: Scholars Press, 1978.

II

Psychological Approaches

The following five chapters present selected psychological approaches to the study of consciousness: radical (Skinnerian) behaviorism, existential-phenomenology, the holisms of Bohm and Pribram, and neuropsychology. Each of these psychologies reflects the assumptions of a particular philosophical point of view. By contrasting the expressions of these different philosophical bases in psychology, these chapters reveal the essential agreements and differences within the psychological profession regarding the nature of human consciousness.

3

Radical Behaviorism and Consciousness[1]

James G. Holland

Readers interested in a psychology of consciousness might express disbelief at the suggestion that a leading behaviorist, B. F. Skinner, includes in his proper realm of inquiry feelings, thoughts, images, and consciousness. True, he does not consider these to be explanatory concepts, but rather legitimate events worthy of investigation. Those familiar with Skinner's radical behaviorism are well aware that he has provided a means of analyzing the private events or experiences of people in the context of a nondualistic, naturalistic science. However, for many it will be hard to accept the information that radical behaviorists include in their analyses the way people respond to the world within their own skins, and that they can provide the same kind of functional account of an individual's personal, private world as for his public behavior. It is also possible that such a suggestion will be rejected by many as simply bad news. Many cherish the mystery of the world of consciousness and will have no interest in having consciousness demystified and viewed as simply more behavior capable of the same functional analysis as other behavior.

Radical versus Methodological Behaviorism in the Treatment of Consciousness

How is one to explain widespread ignorance among those interested in consciousness, about the behavioral program for an analysis of con-

[1]This chapter is a version of my paper presented at the symposium "The Nature of Consciousness" at the American Psychological Association Convention, Toronto, August, 1978.

James G. Holland ● Department of Psychology, University of Pittsburgh, Pittsburgh, Pennsylvania 15260.

sciousness? The problem seems to be the failure to distinguish between two quite different behavioral views: the methodological behaviorists', and the radical behaviorists'.

The denial of images and consciousness by Watson and the setting aside of concerns of consciousness by the logical positivists and operationists are well known, and these positions, characteristic of what I will call methodological behaviorists, have been taken to be the view of all behavioral psychologists. Methodological behaviorists have generally denied consciousness as a scientific subject matter. Because, they argue, there is no means for the scientist to measure or observe another's consciousness, it falls beyond the methodological possibility of measurement. Questions of consciousness become, to the methodological behaviorist, meaningless. The closest they come to dealing with consciousness at all is to equate it with the verbal report, or to accept the verbal report as the closest approximation that a science can deal with.

On the other hand, radical behaviorism, most thoroughly exemplified by the writings of B. F. Skinner, is prepared to give an account of privately observable behavior, an account of behavior only observable to a single individual, including behavior which involves the inner experience of the individual. The framework is provided to explore scientifically all that is real in consciousness—awareness, images, feelings, and so forth. The account, however, is not mentalistic (or dualistic), and, therefore, terms such as these are not commonly used because they carry excess meaning from those that make the distinction between mental and physical—between mind and body. Nor are events of mind or consciousness to be given special explanatory power. They, rather, are simply additional behaviors to be explained.

The scientific program for dealing with the world within the skin is by no means new. It was first articulated by Skinner (1945) in his paper "The Operational Analysis of Psychological Terms." Later in this chapter some of the details of his analysis of private events will be treated. First, it will be instructive to consider Skinner's own distinction between his approach and other behavioral approaches; that is, between what we now call methodological behaviorism and radical behaviorism:

> Another proposed solution [operational definitions of sensations and image] to the problem of privacy argues that there are public and private events and that the latter have no place in science because science requires agreement by the members of a community. Far from avoiding the traditional distinction between mind and matter, or between experience and reality, this view actually encourages it. It assumes that there is, in fact, a subjective world, which it places beyond the reach of science. On this assumption, the only business of a science of sensation is to examine the public events which may be studied in lieu of the private.
>
> The present analysis has a very different consequence. It continues to deal

with the private event, even if only as an inference. It does not substitute the
verbal report from which the inference is made for the event itself. The verbal
report is a response to the private event and may be used as a source of
information about it. A critical analysis of the validity of this practice is of first
importance. But we may avoid the dubious conclusion that, so far as a science
is concerned, the verbal report or some other discriminative report *is* the
sensation. (Skinner, 1953, pp. 281–282)

It is by no means new, then, that radical behaviorism deals with
subjective events. A recent book of Skinner's (1974), *About Behaviorism*, is
largely devoted to making very clear a behavioristic program for dealing
with events that are subjective; that is, events which traditional thinking
would call mental. A sampling of the chapter headings will serve to
illustrate: "The World Within the Skin," "Perceiving," "Verbal Behavior," "Thinking," "Knowing," "The Inner World of Motivation and
Emotion," "The Self and Others." Clearly, this is a book dealing with the
analysis of subjective behaviors, and one that anyone interested in "consciousness" or "mental events" should read if they are interested in
seeing these treated in the nondualistic manner of a natural science.
Again, to quote Skinner (1974) on the distinction between radical and
methodological behaviorism in regard to the analysis of consciousness:

Methodological behaviorism and certain versions of logical positivism
could be said to ignore consciousnesss, feelings, and states of mind, but
radical behaviorism does not thus "behead the organism"; it does not "sweep
the problem of subjectivity under the rug"; it does not "maintain a strictly
behavioristic methodology by treating reports of introspection merely as verbal behavior"; and it was not designed to "permit consciousness to atrophy".
(p. 219)

Behavioral Meanings of Consciousness

One meaning of consciousness is simply responsiveness of an organism to its surroundings. People are aware or conscious to the extent that
their behavior is under the control of stimuli in those surroundings. For
example, we say that someone has been knocked unconscious if he is
completely unresponsive to the immediate stimuli, and commonly a
person engrossed in watching an athletic event may be "unaware" of a
conversation going on beside him. Such persons are under the control of
one set of stimuli and not another. We would describe them as aware or
conscious of one set, and not another. Animals have this sense of consciousness in that they are responsive to stimuli. This sense of consciousness has also seen extensive research in the analysis of behavior in the
area of stimulus control, though most investigators would not use the
mentalistic words with the extra, implied dualistic meaning.

Consciousness in a different sense occurs when we not only see but see that we see, or have knowledge of seeing; when we are self-aware; when we have self-knowledge of what we are about to do (intent), or of our preparation for events (expectancy), or of our motivational or emotional conditions ("wants" or "feelings"). This awareness of our self and the seeing that we see is the result of reinforcement contingencies arranged by our verbal community. Consciousness in this sense, then, is a social product of the arrangements of reinforcement by a verbal community, and is thereby uniquely human. But, here again, it is not different in kind from other behaviors.

> No special kind of mind-stuff is assumed. A physical world generates both physical action and physical conditions within the body to which a person responds when a verbal community arranges the necessary contingencies. (Skinner, 1974, p. 220)

Experimental Analysis of "Mental Events"

Despite the ability of radical behaviorism to provide a nondualistic, natural science-based account of subjective events, many researchers in the field have stayed all too clear of introspection, and away from problems that have interested those who are concerned with consciousness and images. I have recently begun to give demonstrations or workshops in which behavior analysts themselves engaged in consciousness processes. The object of the processes was to get students or professionals in behavior analysis past their barriers to dealing with such a subject matter. The object was to show them that subjective behaviors are just like any other behavior, to demystify the problems of consciousness, and to remove consciousness from a separate realm of the mind with which science is not supposed to be able to deal. These demonstrations are informal experiments involving exercises in "memory."

The term memory itself is not a purely descriptive term, and the cognitive psychologists who study memory create a number of explanatory concepts of a nonbehavioral type. They speak of "memory stores" in which copies or approximate copies of experiences are stored, either in a short-term or long-term store, and are subsequently accessed to differing degrees of accuracy. Measurements of how close the recall comes to the original event are the primary data.

To the radical behaviorist, original seeing is an operant just as any other behavior, and when we say we recall something, we are again seeing in a way that may be similar to the way we saw before. Images we are having at any given time are simply the result of controlling variables at that time and the past history of contingencies involved on similar occasions.

The consciousness demonstrations that I have used to get radical behaviorists beyond their barriers for dealing with consciousness did so through a series of memory experiments. The series began by presenting a slide of a complex, underwater scene with a large number of fish swirling around a portion of a coral reef. This scene was examined for a minute. Immediately after the slide was turned off, the audience was asked how many fish were in their scene. They were asked to volunteer their numbers, and those who did provided a number of different estimates with the median around 33. There were actually 54 fish in the scene, and they were told this. In a memory experiment by a cognitive psychologist, the principal data would be how close the reported number comes to the actual. It is fascinating that those who claim to be interested in cognitive processes are interested primarily in this correspondence. Anything extra or less in the subject's own images is considered "error."

The audience next participated in a longer-term memory experiment. They were asked to close their eyes and visualize the scene they had just looked at five to ten minutes before. They were given instructions describing different aspects of the scene as prompts to create this underwater fish scene. They were asked, on having created their scene, to estimate the number of different orientations in which the fish were found. On reopening their eyes, they volunteered observations about their scenes, including the number of fish orientations, which were far underestimated, again correspondence with the original scene being a question analogous to that of a cognitive memory experiment. Occasionally persons reported things that were not in the original scene. One, for example, reported seeing himself skin diving within the scene.

The next memory experiment in the series asked the audience to close their eyes and recall or recreate the scene from their experience exactly one week ago. Prompts are provided while they do each of these experiments in visualizing by asking them to notice any forms, colors, persons, any sounds, feelings, attitudes, etc. going on in that setting.

This longer-term memory exercise was followed by yet another memory experiment in which they were instructed to recall an experience of exactly ten years ago. Volunteers described their experiences and often identified reasons why they are sure that their experience corresponds with what they were really doing. Again, the concern was with the correspondence or the reflection of conscious experience with some public reality. In fact, part of what they were no doubt identifying were the controlling variables contributing to the experience they had in the here-and-now.

The next instruction was to recall an experience from exactly 100 years ago. Surprise was immediately apparent in the reaction of the audience. Until this time, many had been behaving in the context of a cognitive, learning theorist model, or the common conception that we store experiences that correspond to reality, and later are able, to some degree, to call these back up. But, given the same kinds of prompts as in the other instructions, the subjects sat there with their eyes closed and had images of their experiences following the instructions to experience something from 100 years ago. Again, members in the audience shared their experiences and described quite vivid scenes. Many reported that their scenes from 100 years ago were more vivid, richer, and easier than their images in any of the previous "shorter term" memory experiments. This vividness may occur, perhaps, because of the removal of an implied constraint that their scene actually conform to some external reality. Some individuals in reporting their scenes, as in the "shorter term" experiments, indicated presumed sources of control, such as history accounts, television programs, or knowledge of their own family roots.

Each of these memory experiments had in common instructions to recall a scene and a period of time for the recall, during which I provided the prompts to notice all the colors, forms, persons, sounds, feelings that they might have, attitudes about the scene, and so forth. This was followed by a period in which some of the subjects described what they had experienced. All the experiments were similar in form, and there seemed to be no point at which there was a qualitative difference between the immediate memories and those from 100 years ago. Few would be tempted to interpret the memory from 100 years as the accessing of a memory store of events from 100 years ago. It is, rather, real action in the here-and-now, as is all of the imaging done in all the memory experiments. It is probably the case that these behaviors are controlled by the same variables as other behaviors of the organism—dependent on the past history of reinforcement in conjunction with present cues or discriminative stimuli.

Imagery to the radical behaviorist is operant seeing and is, as such, behavior. It is not a special mental world. It is just more behavior to be analyzed. It does not exist at some different level or in some different realm paralleling or somehow explaining action in the physical world. It is amusingly paradoxical that the cognitive psychologist with the postulated memory stores considers images to be called-up copies of the original experience that have varying degrees of accuracy. This correspondence with some reality is shared by some mystical interpretations which view imaging of things taking place elsewhere as extrasensory perception to the extent that it corresponds with something that is "really" happening elsewhere or memories of 100 years past as a reflection of a universal memory.

When the above-described memory experiments were extended to instruct people to remember forward in time to the time of their own death, they reported images very similar to those reported in Moody's (1975) book *Life After Life*, in which images were described by persons who had come near to death. They experienced themselves outside their bodies, looking down at themselves from an angle of about 30 degrees. And, commonly, the reports of those who nearly died contained references to the presence of other beings. Very similar experiences are reported by ordinary persons asked to image their own death at the end of a series of memory experiments. In both the near-death instance and the "memory" experiment instances, the images were no doubt real in the here-and-now and are only used as evidence of life after death if one gives some special status to these images when they correspond in some special way to reality. To the radical behaviorist, ordinary seeing is simply a response to immediate stimuli. There can occur, then, operantly *conditioned* seeing without any immediate stimuli, just as other responses may occur in the presence or absence of immediate discriminative stimuli.

A Behavior Analysis of Self-Awareness or Consciousness

Images, feelings, and thoughts are of course subjective. Our descriptions of them come from our own self-awareness. It is the function of behavior analysis to account for our acquiring of such self-knowledge and to provide the means of including accounts of self-awareness in our science. This task has been done by Skinner (1945, 1958) in a manner which has laid the groundwork for a revolutionary behavioral semantics capable of providing a behavioral account of "cognitive" functioning without mentalistic terms.

How we come to an awareness of and description of our own subjective experience can be best understood by examining how we become aware of and able to describe our own publicly visible experiences. We learn to describe the public world around us when our utterances are appropriate to the discriminative stimuli or the occasioning stimuli as judged by the verbal community; which, by reacting to what we have said, reinforces the relationship between those events and our own verbal behavior. The simple discriminative learning situation depends upon the speaker and listener having access to the same situation. The young child may say "car" in the presence of a car, and the parent says, "That's right."

The child and the parent share similar stimuli; that is, the car. And the parent, or the reinforcing verbal community in general, is able appropriately to reinforce the behavior. The nature of the reinforcement can be considerably more subtle with listeners simply acting appropriately to statements, and the learning is no doubt more complicated, involving imitation as well. The important point for the present case is that the behavior of the speaker depends on the reinforcement from the verbal community. Furthermore, for the reinforcement to be appropriate, the verbal community must have a basis for determining the appropriateness of the verbal response to the situation, as through sharing the same stimuli.

The problem, then, for an analysis of private events or subjective experience, is finding the basis by which the verbal community reinforces an ability to discriminate and describe those events. Skinner has identified four ways that the verbal community is able appropriately to reinforce descriptions of private events. First, the speaker and the verbal community may share some accompanying stimuli. For example, if members of the verbal community observe a blow struck, they may be inclined to act appropriately to the speaker when he or she says "It hurts." The stimuli for the speaker and the verbal community were different but highly correlated. A public analog of this is the blind child learning to name objects. The blind child's experience is tactile, and the reinforcing community's experience is visual, yet reinforcement can still be perfectly consistent for naming objects.

The second way is through the observation by the verbal community of collateral behavior. A person who is depressed may be experiencing much stimulation inside his body, feelings in the pit of the stomach, and general experiences of "mood" and "feeling". The verbal community in reinforcing statements about feelings of depression observes a general, overt behavior of looking depressed or looking downcast, and is thus able to reinforce appropriately, although imprecisely, statements about these particular feelings.

The third way in which self-knowledge is developed is when behavior is first overtly established, and then later it or some part of it becomes covert. The most conspicuous example of this is silent reading, arithmetic, and examples of problem solving. Descriptions of our own behavior, such as "I am determined to win," can describe behavior in which we are initially overtly striving, and later the striving may be at the covert level only.

And the fourth, very common, way is through metaphorical extension, or stimulus generalization. If we say we see stars when we have bumped our head, our language is under the control of private visual stimuli similar to the stars in the night sky that we learned to describe.

Most of the content in the memory experiments described above is of this type. Visual experiences in this operant seeing of events that were private were similar to the seeing when events are public, and, therefore, the same vocabulary is used.

Through these four ways, the verbal community is able to shape self-knowledge; and these four means make this self-knowledge available to others. The many so-called mental states invoked as explanatory concepts for overt behavior are nothing more than descriptions of private behavior established in these ways. Feelings, wants, and desires are behaviors reinforced by the verbal community through their partial access to coincidental stimuli, collateral responses, earlier overt behaviors, or metaphorical extensions from public behaviors. These private behaviors, so often incorrectly assigned special properties as "mental states," are themselves under the immediate control of bodily sensations, or, alternatively, they are one's own covert verbal behavior, as when we report "what is on our mind."

It is most important to note that none of these constitutes anything different in kind or anything on a different level of analysis than behavior itself. Private behavior, or behavior controlled by private events, is simply more behavior to account for. They are not mental states from which one can deduce behaviors. A complete description of behaviors must include both the private events, "thinking," and the public events, "speaking out," but one is not the explanation of the other, any more than placing the right foot forward is an explanation for placing the left food forward a moment later, as in walking.

Although private events have no special role as explanatory concepts, they are nevertheless of great interest and importance in and of themselves. Given the limited basis for the verbal community's determination of appropriateness for reinforcement in the case of private events, the vagueness and ambiguity of many of our private experiences becomes clear. The sharpening of reference possible for public events is seldom possible for private events. This explains the difficulty of obtaining agreement on such terms as "love," "happiness," "depression," and so forth. The psychotherapist is one of many who form a specialized verbal community that attempts to improve an individual's self-knowledge; and the many different groups or movements concerned with self-awareness each constitute a special verbal community which shapes private behaviors (self-awareness or consciousness) of its followers.

When private experience is recognized for what it is, additional behavior, subject to the same controlling variables as other behavior, the possibility of vast gains in our ability to improve the quality of people's lives can be realized. Even now, there are a number of behaviorally based procedures concerned in part with subjective experience. A few of these

are biofeedback, Lamaze natural childbirth, hypnosis, relaxation training, and cognitive behavior therapy. More advances can be expected, but
only to the extent that the nature of the subject matter does not return to
mentalism.

References

Moody, R. A. *Life after life*. Covington, Ga.: Mockingbird Books, 1975.
Skinner, B. F. The operational analysis of psychological terms. *Psychological Review*, 1945, 52,
   270–277.
Skinner, B. F. *Science and human behavior*. New York: Macmillan, 1953.
Skinner, B. F. *Verbal behavior*. New York: Appleton-Century-Crofts, 1958.
Skinner, B. F. *About behaviorism*. New York: Knopf, 1974.

4

The Nature of Consciousness
THE EXISTENTIAL-PHENOMENOLOGICAL APPROACH[1]

Donald M. Moss and Ernest Keen

A Methodological Approach

Since the advent of the phenomenological movement in philosophy and psychology, *phenomenology* has been synonymous with a concern for the contents and structure of consciousness. Husserl, the founder of phenomenological philosophy, regarded consciousness—"that wonder of wonders"—as the primary theme for phenomenological inquiry.

In attempting to characterize the nature of consciousness, we must proceed cautiously, giving full recognition from the beginning to that which separates consciousness as unique and different from all other objects of scientific inquiry. Consciousness is never merely a thing or event in the research field of the scientist; it is rather the condition for the possibility of research itself. Consciousness is that by virtue of which we can observe, classify, and interpret. The consciousness of the researcher establishes a *field of intelligibility* within which observable facts emerge. It is possible today to discuss "state-specific" sciences because we have

[1] For an introduction to the existential-phenomenological approach in psychology, see R. S. Valle and M. King (Eds.), *Existential-Phenomenological Alternatives for Psychology*. New York: Oxford University Press, 1978. See R. von Eckartsberg, Chapter 2, for a discussion of existential-phenomenological field-psychology.—Eds.

Donald M. Moss • Ottawa County Community Health, CMH-1111 Fulton, Grand Haven, Michigan 49417. **Ernest Keen** • Department of Psychology, Bucknell University, Lewisburg, Pennsylvania 17837.

come to recognize that the state or organization of the researcher's consciousness will determine what phenomena, facts, and relations will enter his consciousness (Tart, 1976).

The problem of how to approach the nature of consciousness is not only methodological, but, even more deeply, conceptual. Consciousness simply eludes our usual concepts, categories, and ways of thinking. Typically, the literature on consciousness vacillates back and forth between materialistic/physicalistic and spiritual/idealistic modes of explanation. In one chapter of a text we encounter discussion of brain processes, but, in the next, references to spiritual forces and powers (Ornstein, 1972, 1973). Is consciousness a thing or an idea? The response of phenomenology is: Neither! Consciousness is a third kind of phenomenon, for which our intellectual tradition does not prepare us.

The late French phenomenologist Maurice Merleau-Ponty (1962, 1963, 1968, 1970) endeavored to show that human experience and behavior occupy an intermediate order of being, between ideas and mechanisms, partaking of the characteristics of both realms, yet fully fitting within neither.

This brings us to a characterization of method and mode of conceptualization. In its investigation of consciousness, phenomenology returns to the immediate realm of lived experience. In the tradition of the Americans John Dewey (1929) and William James (1912, 1950) and the Germans Franz Brentano (1955) and Edmund Husserl (1962), phenomenology attempts to suspend all questions about causes or explanations, and to remain with an internal, descriptive, structural analysis of lived experience, that is, a "pure phenomenology" (see also Keen 1975; Kestenbaum, 1977).[2]

In advocating a descriptive approach, phenomenology by no means intends a mere inventory of the many feelings, ideas, and awarenesses that flow on the surface of our experience. Consciousness in this sense would simply be "that which I am focally aware of at a particular moment".[3] Rather, phenomenology is concerned with articulating the organizational principles which govern the relationship of the *conscious*

---

[2]"Brentano argued that the proper subject matter for psychology can only be psychic life itself, studied in and for itself" (Zaner, 1970, p. 126). Husserl promoted this principle further in the name of pure psychology. "Pure psychology must become rigorous science of the psychical, disregarding its real relations to the somatico-physical; pure somatics (neurology, physiology, anatomy, etc.) and 'pure' physics must be developed disregarding the real relations to the psychical. The principle is just that it makes no sense to attempt to study a relationship before the relata have been thoroughly accounted for" (*Ibid*, p. 131). On the same issue, see also Husserl (1970), Kockelmans (1967), and Straus (1980).

[3]See Moss, Chapter 7, and R. von Eckartsberg and R. Valle, Chapter 14, for discussions of *intentionality* as a structural characteristic of consciousness (that is, consciousness always has an object which is not consciousness itself).—Eds.

organism to the world, and which therefore also determine the momentary contents of consciousness.

Let us consider the paradigmatic example of *visual consciousness.* Phenomenology seeks to unfold visual experience from within—in its own terms—and not to categorize it as an effect of activity in the calcarine cortex, or as an interaction between light rays and a light-sensitive sensory surface (Merleau-Ponty, 1962, 1964; Straus, 1980; van den Berg, 1970). Human vision, in its own right, involves a particular biological, but also existential, mode of being-in-the-world. Vision is so essential to human consciousness, and the visible so close to the heart of the human world, that the blind must learn, so to speak, a vision at second hand; that is, they must learn to recognize palpable and audible clues to the dimensions and articulation of a world carved out by men with seeing eyes. The task of the phenomenology of *visual consciousness,* then, is to describe that peculiar character of the relationship of the seeing individual to the visible world.

Openness to the World

Let us begin by adopting Merleau-Ponty's (1968) descriptive statement that *consciousness is openness to the world.* To become conscious, ultimately, means to have a world, to find oneself thrust into a macroscopic world of people, things, and events. Phenomenological psychology begins within the phenomenological *epoché,* that is, it suspends all questions or doubts about the reality of the phenomenal, experiential world.[4] If we turn to a description of immediate, lived experience, our first finding is the world there at arm's length before us. But, *in what way* are we open to the world? Consider again the paradigm of visual consciousness. The experience of vision is ambiguous, involving as it does both a powerfully creative and selective *activity* on the part of the organism, and a deeply passive *receptivity* to an active world. Language, that vivid-crystallization of past experience, provides numerous exam-

---

[4]The *epoché* or *reduction* is the heart of phenomenological method. These terms signify an effort to suspend our everyday "natural attitude" toward reality, to overcome our passionate need to draw conclusions about the world, and to disengage ourselves from our usual immersion in events, in order to allow our ordinary relationship to the world to show itself. In this regard, see Husserl's original discussion "The Thesis of the Natural Standpoint and its Suspension" (1962, pp. 91–100). Elsewhere, Husserl (1970) discussed the application of the *epoché* to psychology. In the remarkable preface to the *Phenomenology of Perception,* Merleau-Ponty (1962) also attempted to define the true meaning of the *epoché:* "It is because we are through and through relationships to the world that for us the only way to become aware of the fact is to suspend the resulting activity, to refuse it our complicity . . . to put it 'out of play' " (p. xiii).

ples for both activity and receptivity; that is, "I took a look at X," versus "X captured my gaze," or "X stood out for me." In the latter examples, the *world* seems to act on me. It is awkward to our usual modes of thinking, and yet legitimate, to say that the world expresses itself within human consciousness. Consciousness, as openness to the world, involves a "worlding of the world," that is, it installs man into the billowing, surging, self-manifesting of things and the world.[5]

In visual consciousness, one's locus of self shifts ambiguously between body and world. When an object is illuminated before me, *I inhabit this ray of light* and the sector of the world which appears within it. I exist into and within the light. For someone to step between me and the object blocks my view and hinders me in my inhabitation of vision. For someone to step between myself and the light-source blocks *my light*, a transgression against myself. I exist between the eye and the object, in a searching movement toward the object and an accepting absorption of the object.

To summarize this first point, openness to the world is the best descriptive definition of consciousness. The true abode of human consciousness is in the world which opens up around man. Consciousness is comprised equally of man's activity in orienting himself to this world, and the activity of the world in expressing itself within human consciousness.

Consciousness and the Spatiality of the Human World

As we proceed, a second structural characteristic of consciousness emerges. Human consciousness is intimately connected with the peculiar *spatiality of the human world*. The conscious human being does not reside in his head, mind, or brain, rather, he inhabits the space of the world. And we experience the space about us differently, according to the state or organization of our consciousness at the time. The altered states of consciousness provide obvious examples, for example, the experience with mescaline ingestion that the objects around me are transformed, somehow plastic, fluid, transparent to my gaze, and separated from me by an incredible distance. Yet, of even the various sense modalities, each carries its own characteristic form of spatiality. We are immersed in the fluid and permeating ocean of audial space. Touch and smell, each in its own way, involve us in an immediate dialogue with our contiguous environment. Each form of consciousness can be characterized as *openness to the world*, but each plunges us into a distinctly different space, and manifests to us a different face or aspect of the world. Sounds and voices pursue us and intrude upon us, but we may turn away or close our eyes to a hideous or

---

[5]"To be bound by a world that expresses itself within consciousness and to be a consciousness which is the expression of that world is to be an intentionality" (Gillan, 1973).

appalling sight. Sounds leave their source and enter our personal sphere, sights remain *over there* at a distance from us yet visible as part of the world (Straus, 1958).

Visual consciousness is a particularly essential constituent to human consciousness. Man is the far-seeing creature whose vision transcends the narrow confines of the present. Imagination itself, along with desire, is founded on man's "vision". In lifting his gaze to distant horizons, man becomes the first organism to look into the future and await its approach. Within the very act of seeing at a distance is implied the possibility of bridging that distance. For the human being, vision and motility reciprocally require one another. As a motile being, man takes strides toward distant goals, now visible but not yet present. What is now "there" can become a "here" after we arrive there, and from that new vantage point our current "here" will be "back there." This self-evident statement also introduces time as a constitutent of consciousness; to which we will return later. Is it coincidental that the depressive, for whom time slows to an oppressive and burdensome pace, and whose spatial world closes in upon him narrowly, stares with downcast eyes at what is immediately, dismally, and factually before him? For the depressive consciousness, "nothing is possible," and the peculiar form of both its spatiality and temporality expresses this graphically.

Embodied Consciousness

The space and time of human consciousness are also the space and time of the human body. In man's *openness to the world,* his vantage point is fixed in advance. All consciousness shows itself to presuppose a place, *Here,* anchored in my body, around which the world, a network of possible *Theres,* is organized. I experience the world and myself by reference to this *(my)* body and the place it defines.

Upright posture and vision establish the *vis-à-vis* relationship between man and the world (Straus, 1966a, 1969). Man *faces* the world. The field of visual consciousness is articulated into ahead and behind, high and low, up and down, left and right, near and far. Each of these dimensions refers back to man's body, its upright posture, and its potentiality for moving, reaching, grasping, and pointing.

It is not possible to describe man's world fully without referring back to the human body. "Sounds," "sights," and "smells" are phenomena there in the world, but refer explicitly back to the co-constituting presence of the human body and its sensorium. Consciousness and human reality, consciousness and world, are integral and mutually determining from the outset. Their differentiation—never a separation—is achieved only at more sophisticated and later stages of man's individual and historical development.[6]

The human, living, motile body organizes about itself a field of action projects and perceptual objects. The horizons of consciousness wander with the movement of the organism. To be underway in some action is to organize our perception toward an object, and, conversely, to perceive a situation is to be invited into involvement with that situation. The space about us is organized, prior to any conscious reflection, into routes and pathways for our actions (Moss, 1978).

We are not simply equating consciousness here with knowledge or cognition. The phenomenological notion of *openness to the world* is impartial with respect to the academic distinctions among affect, conation, and cognition. The conscious individual is characterized just as much by affectivity, motility, and activity in the face of the world, as he is by sentient awareness. It is not possible to curtail this spontaneous responsivity of the individual, without also drastically altering his consciousness. To be open to the world means to be involved in, engaged in, concerned about, and affected by the world. These are descriptive features of consciousness not dealt with by information-processing models.

We have already touched on the role of man's motile body in shaping the space and time of the human world. Yet the body has such a central place in the phenomenology of consciousness, that we must linger on this point. The body referred to here is not the thing body, consisting of the hypothalamus, norepinephrine uptake mechanisms, or nerve ganglia. Nor is it the spiritual body of the mystics. It is rather the immediately experienced and experiencing, lived and living body of everyday life—a body which shows itself in experience to be "the living envelope of my character," a body comprised of organs of action and organs of expression (Moss, 1977, 1978). The human body is also a conscious body, oriented vigilantly to our full human, existential situation. *Man's openness to the world is thus embodied.* Before the ring of a telephone enters my focal awareness, my body hears, responds, and orients itself to the telephone. Identical audial stimuli will elicit fully altered responses according to whether I am awaiting a crucial message about an injured relative, a call from the office, or nothing at all. Thus, already prior to reflective or

---

[6]"So long as the human being, in his first physical condition, merely appropriates the world passively, merely senses, then he is still fully one with it, and even, since he himself is merely world, there is for him as yet no world. Only when he, in his aesthetic attitude, places or views the world as outside himself, does his personality sever itself from the world, and does a world appear to him, since he has ceased to constitute one with it" (Friedrich Schiller, *Ueber die aesthetische Erziehung des Menschen.* 25th letter. Cited by Straus, 1980).

linguistic consciousness, the human body manifests an *openness to the world,* that is, an ongoing participation in events of the human world. We do violence to the phenomenon of consciousness when we investigate the "conscious mind," knowledge, or contemplation, outside the continuum which includes the nascent consciousness ever present in man's living body. This is the primary thesis of Merleau-Ponty's magnificent *opus, Phenomenology of Perception* (1962). Even the cases of pure gnosis, such as experiences of transcendence or aesthetic contemplation, are founded on and presuppose embodied consciousness. Such experiences do not suppress our ties to body, space, and time, but rather utilize them. For example, the dimension "up and down" was not erased in the mysticism of Plotinus but rather endowed with metaphysical significance (O'Brien, 1964). The task of phenomenology has been, according to Merleau-Ponty, "to reestablish the roots of the mind in its body and in its world" (1964a, p. 3).

Consciousness and Temporality[7]

Let us return to a characteristic of our openness to the world already introduced above, namely *time.* Each space of human consciousness, as shown above, already implies within itself a particular temporality. My sense of space becomes, in everyday life, a sense of *place*—my office, my home, my town—and places are touchstones of our conscious life, forged out of the multiple layers of meaning embedded in my experience. But places are places only because I can bodily occupy them or leave them, and the "can" bespeaks a time beyond the present. The series of places in my life is strung across the spatial dimension by a correlative series of *historical moments* articulated in time. Human places are imbued or saturated with time. Our childhood home is ever an abode of reverie and memory, and our old college campus a repository for the hopes and dreams of our youth. The "stringing together" or articulation of places and moments refers to a spatial-temporal totality, or *gestalt,* which is present as a horizon, framing every single experience. Each momentary experience takes on meaning according to its position within the totality, in the same way that Hamlet's soliloquy receives its dramatic import from its relation to the play as a whole. The organized totality of personal places and moments—which can never be separated into discrete components of spaceless time and timeless space—is the *human historical*

[7]See R. von Eckartsberg and R. Valle, Chapter 14, for another discussion of *temporality.*— Eds.

world. This world is a world in flux, reorganized constantly as we take our stand *bodily* in it, orienting ourselves toward certain possibilities and not others.

The temporal unfolding of our consciousness is never a simple linear sequence (as elementary physics represents time on a graph). A truer comprehension of human time can be achieved through a study of languages and the rich means they have invented to formulate our time consciousness—that is, the elaborate grammatical forms of tense, mood, and voice.

Nor is all human time identical and homogeneous as are the measured minutes on a clock. Even within one individual's experience there are moments trivial, transient, and quickly forgotten, and again moments of gravity, significance, and lingering import. The temporality of human consciousness is shaped by man's biological being and natural life cycle. The passing hours of an 18-year-old and an octagenerian are by no means commensurable (Straus, 1967). The temporal horizons of youth extend forth into the infinity of possibilities. The time structure of late old age is one of reverie and waiting, keenly attuned to the coming eternal night. As Otto Friedrich Bollnow (1962) has shown, there is a level of consciousness occasionally achieved in old age which can be neither communicated in language nor shared by the young. The gathering disinterest for the extraneous, the growing detachment from one's own proud pursuits, and a sense of the dissolution of one's own individuality in the current of the generations are all markers of this consciousness.

Time consciousness also reflects our embodiment, as a number of sensitive phenomenological studies have shown. The bodily experience of capacity for effective action, the "I can" experience, is at the heart of the vital process of becoming. When the "I can't" experience of complete incapacity and helplessness takes over, for whatever reason, we see an arrest in the vital becoming at a bodily level prior to and below reflective, thinking consciousness. In the absence of an inviting and animating future horizon, consciousness coagulates and flows with the sluggishness and inertness so common in depression (von Gebsattel, 1954; Straus, 1966b; Minkowski, 1970).

In this section, we have made no effort to answer St. Augustine's question regarding the essential nature of time.[8] Rather, we have shown in a number of ways how the human experience of time and human consciousness intertwine. Phenomenological investigation aims, first and foremost, at comprehending the time-structure of an experience, and time must remain a primary category in all psychologies of consciousness.

[8]"What is time? When nobody asks me I know; if I want to explain it to someone inquiring about it, I do not know" (*Confessions,* Book XI).

Consciousness and Language

When the human being becomes conscious, he is plunged in some way into a particular space and time. Yet this bare-bones description of consciousness could readily apply to a dog who awakens to see his master returning through the front door at the end of the day. Human consciousness is consciousness of the second order. By means of language, the human being articulates a highly differentiated consciousness of his situation. He does not merely respond globally to a total situation. Rather, by using words *diacritically*, he refers to distinct, now isolated aspects of the situation by name, and by using words *synthetically*, he unifies different aspects under one concept. Furthermore, he transforms his behavior in relation to this newly organized situation. Man *languages* his world, and languaging in this sense is a creative process. Man lives in a world recreated continually by his own language. Above all, the nuclear places and moments in his world are designated by proper names.

Through the power of language, we can create and hence multiply the possible spaces and temporal orders that make up our consciousness, our openness, to the world. Science is a powerful example of the ability of human consciousness to transcend the immediate and the concrete into the abstract, to transcend the actual and the factual into the possible, hypothetical, and conceptual. Our openness to the world is thus not merely structured by language, but transformed by it as well.

This ability of man's linguistic consciousness to abstract, to transcend, and to soar to lofty heights sets man off fundamentally from the animals. He is, we repeat, the far-seeing animal. The spiritual or idealistic models of consciousness are based on these genuinely transcendent qualities. Nevertheless, the embodied nature of consciousness belies these spiritual models.

We can rename body parts and processes, and in fact transform the body by this means to some extent. The modern European and the ancient Chinese have experienced their bodies in ways as divergent as their respective forms of medicine. The relanguaging of the human body throughout history invents new bodily spaces and times, as the Dutch phenomenologist van den Berg (1961) has shown so beautifully in his hermeneutic studies of the history of medicine.

Nevertheless, the body is a special case. There is an unsurpassable concreteness in our bodily experience, as in the examples of pain, intentional movement, sexual desire, or the approach to death. Erwin Straus emphasizes the *heft* of our physical body; our experience is permeated by the ongoing struggle to stand against gravity. All aspirations toward total transcendence are transient, given the material presence of the body. This concreteness does not merely limit our transcendence, however. It also serves as an anchor for consciousness, and secures for us—in the face of the infinity of the imagination—a sense of reality, orientation, and rock-bottom intransigence that gives solidity to our experience. This "anchor of concreteness" permeates consciousness with a reality that spreads from our bodies to our movements, to space, and to time.

Consciousness and Sociality

We come now to the final characterization of our openness to the world. Consciousness is preeminently *social*; it is saturated with the resonances of persons. The field of consciousness is also an interpersonal field, and the valences and tendencies of our awareness follow consistently along the lines of our significant interhuman relationships, past and present. It is also a fundamental datum of the psychology of consciousness that the consciousness of another can become more important for one than one's own. Each consciousness opens onto other consciousnesses.[9]

Let us think for a moment about everyone's favorite topic, sexuality, in order to see the interplay among the five dimensions of consciousness articulated here, spatiality, embodiment, temporality, language, and sociality. The experience of sexual desire for another person is not something incident to sticks or stones. Animals, who like human beings are open to the world, do experience sexual desire, but more simply than human beings. Human beings do so incorrigibly. In sexual desire, as in any experience, there is a describable pattern of involvement and interrelation among spatiality, embodiment, temporality, language, and sociality which distinguishes sexual desire from all other experiences. The tension between possibility and actuality is vivid. We can trace the possibility to the stories we tell ourselves linguistically and imaginally, and the actuality we can trace to our unsurmountable bodily impulses. The stories give shape to the impulses, while the impulses give reality to the stories. The possible fulfillment imbues the actual desire with a future, and the actual desire animates the possible future with a present. The past plays into both the present desire and the desired future with memories of past fulfillments and disasters, and time itself is restructured around a different set of "anchors" than when we yawn lazily with indifferent fatigue.

---

[9]"We soon see, as another *a priori*, that self-consciousness and consciousness of others are inseparable; it is unthinkable, and not merely contrary to fact, that I be man in the world without being *a* man. There need be no one in my perceptual field, but fellow men are necessary as actual, as known, and as an open horizon of those I might possibly meet. Factually I am within an interhuman present and within an open horizon of mankind" (Husserl, 1970, p. 253).

Space too takes on a special character; my body fills one space, hers another, and the penumbra of intimate personal space radiates toward that of the other in a remarkable and absolutely characteristic way.

But think of the complexities of this elemental situation arising from its social character. First, I not only desire her body, but want her to desire mine. This particular openness to the world is thus also an openness to another's openness to the world. But sexual desire is not peculiar in this fact; all human openness to the world is attuned to that of others. In fact, the world that opens up for me receives its special character from my knowledge that I share it with others. Second, sociality lies at the very basis of how I am open to the world. The world to which consciousness gives me access and the *me* as well are dependent from the start on an implicit community of others, without whose viewpoint reality itself would be radically effaced. Finally, sociality and language are radically intertwined, there is a linguistic definition of social reality, but likewise we learn of the impact of social reality on the structure of language.

Conclusion

Thus emerges a descriptive picture of human consciousness. Consciousness is *openness to the world*. Anchored by the irrevocable heft and material presence of the body, the human being stands in one place and historical moment, his Here and his Now, yet his consciousness strains toward the distant horizons of the imagined, the possible, and the future. The human imagination soars to the stars and yet returns always to its homeland in the body. This bipolar tension between the present and the futural, between the actual and the possible, is an essential feature of human consciousness.

To become conscious means to find oneself thrust into, and participating in, a world of place and event and persons which is organized around the evocative magic of language and, above all, of names. Perhaps poets and novelists are best at disclosing the workings of consciousness, the intricate construction of the human world by a layering of one event upon another, the interpenetration of the atmosphere of one place into another, the gathering of an aura of resonances around a critical name, phrase, or symbol in an individual consciousness (Proust, Faulkner, Nabokov, and many others serve well as examples here.) Yet it remains the responsibility of psychology to develop and articulate the general principles governing this *openness to the world* in a systematic way.

In the preceding, we have described the fundamental, but taken-for-granted, characteristics of this openness to the world as space, time, language, and person. These ever-present characteristics are perhaps most conspicuous during any *return* to consciousness. Whether I am merely awakening from a deep sleep or whether my consciousness has been disrupted more seriously—for example, by a trauma of the brain— these questions comprise my reviving consciousness:

Where am I? What place is this?
What time and day is this? What has happened?
Who are you? What is your name?

These questions, explicit and verbal at times, are incarnate in our movements always, in our craning neck, searching gaze, groping reach, and probing step. Human incarnate consciousness *is* endless interrogation of the world and fellow man: Where? When? Who?[10]

The texture of consciousness is the texture of the human world; this is the phenomenological position in one sentence. The inner cohesiveness of consciousness—whether we speak of the consciousness of an individual, or of a people—derives from this articulation and coherence of place, time, language, and person. For the American, "Dallas," "November 22, 1963," "John Kennedy," and "assassination" were and are a unity of consciousness. Or, to take another example, the names of Malcolm X, Martin Luther King, and Muhammed Ali, the places Selma, Birmingham, and Watts, and a handful of dates between 1960 and 1968, comprised the dawning of modern black consciousness. Note that the word black—a perjorative in 1960—illustrates the contribution of language in the metamorphosis of consciousness: black is beautiful, black pride, *black consciousness.*

The modern psychologies of consciousness—including neuro-psychology, biofeedback, behaviorism, and the transpersonal approaches—have made many fundamental discoveries in the last 20 years which have enabled us to diagnose and even correct many neurologically based deficits in consciousness, to expand and develop our personal consciousness, as well as to better explain the underlying brain processes which support consciousness. The task of phenomenology is a different one, that is, to describe consciousness in its own terms—without leaving the confines of the human, experiential world. This descriptive enterprise, however, presupposes a vigorous effort to suspend previous assumptions about consciousness, in an attempt to develop a set of categories or concepts more appropriate to consciousness. The categories and concepts of phenomenological psychology de-

---

[10]A similar description is offered by von Eckartsberg in his analysis of the structure of the story. See Chapter 10 in R. S. Valle and M. King (Eds.), *Existential-Phenomenological Alternatives for Psychology.* New York: Oxford University Press, 1978.—Eds.

veloped here— openness to the world, spatiality, temporality, sociality, language, place, historical moment, person, name—make a more adequate description of consciousness possible, for unique experiences, for categories of experience (such as sexual desire), and for experiencing in general. It is our belief that any psychology of consciousness must attend first to the descriptive task. Consciousness is neither a thing nor an idea. It is something more basic and fundamental to human beings, requiring its own descriptively based concepts.

References

Bollnow, O. F. Das hohe Alter. *Die neue Sammlung.* 1962, 2, 385–396.

Brentano, F. *Psychologie vom empirischen Standpunkt,* I. Hamburg: Felix Meiner Verlag, 1955.

Dewey, J. *Experience and nature.* La Salle, Ill: Open Court Publishing, 1929.

Gillan, G. (Ed.) *Horizons of the flesh: Critical perspectives on the thought of Merleau-Ponty.* Carbondale, Ill.: Southern Illinois University Press, 1973.

Husserl, E. *Ideas: General introduction to pure phenomenology.* New York: Collier, 1962.

Husserl, E. *The crisis of European sciences and transcendental phenomenology.* Evanston, Ill.: Northwestern University Press, 1970.

James, W. *Essays in radical empiricism.* London: Longmans Green, 1912.

James, W. *Principles of psychology* (Vols. I-II). New York: Dover, 1950.

Keen, E. *A primer of phenomenological psychology.* New York: Holt, Rinehart, & Winston, 1975.

Kestenbaum, V. *A think of moods and tenses—Experience in John Dewey.* Paper presented at the meeting of the Society for Phenomenology and Existential Philosophy, New York, New York, November, 1977.

Kockelmans, J. J. *Edmund Husserl's phenomenological philosophy: A historico-critical study.* Pittsburgh: Duquesne University Press, 1967.

Merleau-Ponty, M. *Phenomenology of perception.* London: Routledge & Kegan Paul, 1962.

Merleau-Ponty, M. *The structures of behavior.* Boston: Beacon Press, 1963.

Merleau-Ponty, M. An unpublished text. In his *The primacy of perception.* Evanston, Ill.: Northwestern University Press, 1964(a).

Merleau-Ponty, M. Eye and Mind. In his *The primacy of perception.* Evanston, Ill.: Northwestern University Press, 1964(b).

Merleau-Ponty, M. *The visible and the invisible.* Evanston, Ill.: Northwestern University Press, 1968.

Merleau-Ponty, M. *Themes from the lectures.* Evanston, Ill.: Northwestern University Press, 1970.

Minkowski, E. *Lived time: Phenomenological and psychopathological studies.* Evanston, Ill.: Northwestern University Press, 1970.

Moss, D. M. *Distortions in human embodiment: A study of surgically treated obesity.* Paper presented at the meeting of the Society for Phenomenology and Existential Philosophy New York, New York, November, 1977.

Moss, D. M. Brain, body, and world: Perspectives on body image. In R. S. Valle & M. King (Eds.), *Existential-phenomenological alternatives in psychology.* New York: Oxford University Press, 1978.

O'Brien, E. (Ed.). *The essential Plotinus.* New York: Mentor Books, 1964.

Ornstein, R. E. *The psychology of consciousness.* New York: Penguin Books, 1972.

Ornstein, R. E. (Ed.). *The nature of consciousness.* New York: Viking, 1973.

Straus, E. Aesthesiology and hallucinations. In R. May, E. Angel, & H. Ellenberger (Eds.), *Existence*. New York: Basic Books, 1958.

Straus, E. The upright posture. In *Phenomenological psychology*. New York: Basic Books, 1966. (a)

Straus, E. Disorders of personal time in depressive states. In *Phenomenological psychology: Selected papers*. New York: Basic Books, 1966.(b)

Straus, E. Existential approach to time. *Annals of the New York Academy of Sciences*, 1967, *138*(2), 759–766.

Straus, E. Psychiatry and philosophy. In M. Natanson (Ed.), *Psychiatry and philosphy*. New York: Springer-Verlag, 1969.

Straus, E. *The Archimedian point: Selected studies*. Pittsburgh: Duquesne University Press, 1980.

Tart, C. T. Discrete states of consciousness. In P. R. Lee, R. E. Ornstein, D. Galin, A. Deikman, & C. T. Tart, *Symposium on consciousness*. New York: Penguin Books, 1976.

van den Berg, J. H. *The changing nature of man*. New York: Norton, 1961.

van den Berg, J. H. *Things: Four metabletic studies*. Pittsburgh: Duquesne University Press, 1970.

von Gebsattel, V. E. *Prolegomena einer medizinischen Anthropologie*. Berlin: Springer-Verlag, 1954.

Zaner, R. M. *The way of phenomenology: Criticism as a philosophical discipline*. New York: Pegasus, 1970.

5

Reflections on David Bohm's Holomovement

A PHYSICIST'S MODEL OF COSMOS AND CONSCIOUSNESS

Renée Weber

Then we may sum up the argument in a word and say truly: if One is not, then nothing is.
—PLATO, *Parmenides*

David Bohm's *holokinetic* universe and Karl Pribram's *holographic* one[1] are related as macrocosm is to microcosm. Pribram's methodology and ontology emerge largely from the scientific domain, from his findings in neuropsychology and neurology, whereas Bohm's methodology and its content are more sweeping, drawing on both scientific and phenomenological perspectives. It follows that, if Bohm's cosmology and his claims about consciousness are correct, those of Pribram must also be correct, since the latter flow as a natural consequence from the former, a subset of the wider world that Bohm postulates. I shall use the term *holocosmic* to refer to all these claims.

It must be stated at the outset that Pribram's holographic model and Bohm's holomovement are more alike than they are different, especially when measured against competing philosophical claims. Although revolutionary by contrast to the dominant Western metaphysics of the past

[1]See Pribram, Chapter 6, for a discussion of the relationship of holism and psychology.—Eds.

Renée Weber • Department of Philosophy, Rutgers University, New Brunswick, New Jersey 08903.

twenty-five centuries, both the holographic and the holokinetic paradigms have solid historical antecedents in Eastern philosophy, and within the esoteric tradition (Weber, 1975a) of the West, in such figures as Pythagoras, Parmenides, Heraclitus, Plato, Plotinus, and even in seventeenth-century Rationalists like Leibniz and Spinoza.

This parallelism of perspectives is particularly interesting in that Pribram is noted for his impressive "track record" in avant-garde theories, performing (by analogy with the proverbial miner's canary) a role not unlike that of an ontological canary dispatched to the depths to test the air before others will risk the descent. Consequently, Pribram's holographic paradigm may—by extrapolation from his overall record—signal the discovery of a fundamental insight into the workings of nature. This in-depth exploration, applied to both cosmos and consciousness, characterizes the holokinetic model of David Bohm. It differs from Pribram's in its wider scope, its philosophical depth, its stress on dynamicism, its more mystical tone, and its concern with moral and social values.

The Holocosmic Paradigm

The holocosmic paradigm is novel in a twofold sense. First, it espouses theories of space, time, matter, energy, consciousness, and even of logic that turn our customary concepts upside down. They demand a basic rethinking of familiar ideas, violating the assumptions of everyday life and language, or of commonsense naive realism, to use a philosophical term. The closest precedent for this process lies in the concepts and the language of contemporary physicists,[2] who have had to adopt the same "counter-common-sensical" attitude and vocabulary in order to grasp and transmit their discoveries. However, physics—while furnishing the holocosmic paradigm with its foundation—has no philosophical framework for its own findings. Bohm argues that it has failed to grasp the *meaning* of its models and what, if anything, they imply for human life. Hence it avoids facing the issue altogether, confining itself to pragmatic goals, to the prediction and control which Bohm charges have all but pre-empted the endeavor of physics. Such a limited approach is unacceptable to Bohm, who terms "incomplete" any theory of the cosmos that fails to take consciousness into full account.

Second, the paradigm-shift is radical in another, quite paradoxical way. The paradox is this: the more nearly physics approaches the twenty-first century, the closer it seems to get to the cosmology of the

---

[2]For a discussion of the relationship of the new physics to psychology, see R. Valle, Chapter 21.—Eds.

remote past. Thus, the scientific discoveries of our own time are moving us toward ideas in many ways indistinguishable from those held by the sages and seers of India and Greece. How is this possible, when in every other field of knowledge the opposite principle holds true, that is, a thread of continuity that links the intervening centuries, rather than an abrupt break with them?

I may summarize this second point with the observation that the new holism is revolutionary not so much in its content, as in the fact that what is considered *to be* revolutionary by the scientific community finds echoes in the doctrines of the ancients. This feature, raising methodological issues, is as puzzling and as exciting as is the content itself.

The Question of Methodology

Increasingly, terms are being coined to cope with this paradox. A useful distinction is that between *outer* and *inner empiricism*. The traditional dichotomy between objective and subjective methods is being questioned, in favor of a view that alleges that both the scientist and the mystic are involved in empiricism. Both are committed to careful, truthful, and painstaking observation of reality: in the case of the physicist, to matter and energy "outside" himself, in the case of the mystic, to their reality "within" himself.

Although logical, such a separation nonetheless seems superficial and untenable since the advent of quantum mechanics as a whole, Heisenberg's indeterminacy principle in particular, Wigner's emphasis on consciousness as a factor in the data derived by physics, Wheeler's theory of the "participatory universe," and Bohm's holomovement or implicate-order cosmology. All these have *eroded* the very distinction between inner and outer, subject and object, knower and known, terms that may well beg the basic epistemological question.

In Bohm's holomovement, this dualism has been *abolished* and replaced by a pervasive monism and holism. Bohm holds out for a unified field theory that surpasses even the hopes of Einstein, who was willing to settle for a law uniting all the known force fields in *nature*. Bohm pushes this one step further, in his demand that the knower himself be integrated within that equation. A study of Bohm's holomovement is therefore an ideal starting point for the understanding of the new paradigms which are sweeping us out of our seventeenth-, eighteenth-, nineteenth-, and even our twentieth-century past into the twenty-first century, *"forward"* into the ancient claims of the wisdom traditions which—in scientific metaphors—are being reclaimed by our own era.

Bohm's Holomovement

The foundation and fundamental feature of Bohm's cosmology is the claim that reality is *one*, an unbroken, undivided wholeness which is the background for everything in the universe, underlying both matter and consciousness, providing the raw material for all manifest entities and events, begetting, sustaining, and governing everything by its enduring connection with it in the deep-structure of the whole. This nonmanifest matrix Bohm terms the *enfolded* or *implicate order*. It manifests itself in various states of matter–energy, from the very gross, dense, and stable matter perceived by our senses in the space–time domain—the *explicate order*—to the more subtle, sensibly inaccessible matter as we move inward to the implicate order, and finally to a highly conscious, ordered, spiritual dimension deep within the holomovement. This latter lies beyond language, and we can at best refer to it in metaphors. Among these is the idea of order, which by definition prevails in the spiritual energy active in the depths of the holomovement.

Beyond its oneness and its order, this reality is movement. No aspect of its being is ever static. Thus Bohm's concept of the holomovement cuts across both implicate and explicate orders: the nonmanifest energies of nature and their outcome in the world of appearances that comprises nature, man, and society.

The last great philosophical figure in the West to attempt a reconciliation between these divisions is Hegel, writing in the nineteenth century. Hegel's (1931) *Phenomenology of Mind* departs, like the holistic figures cited above, from the premise that reality is one and indivisible, both cosmos and consciousness. He claims that "the truth is the whole," that the single fabric behind all being is an abstract and undefinable principle *(Geist)* that manifests itself as both subject and substance, man and nature, inner and outer truth. Philosophy, according to Hegel, consists in grasping the essence of all these domains, which are the signature of the universe, as it were, a universe becoming transparent to itself through the consciousness and self-consciousness of man, the knower. Far from being set adrift in the universe as an incidental epiphenomenon, man is the mirror in which the universe can see itself reflected, coming to understand itself through the by-products of its dynamic evolution in time. These "by-products," which we have preserved as the particular disciplines— science, the arts, religion, philosophy, biology, psychology—are but the expression of a universal and atemporal source working itself out in space, time, and history, in order most fully and with clarity to comprehend itself.

Reminiscent of Hegel, Bohm sees our institutions, science, art, and philosophy as nothing more than the spatio-temporal, explicate expression of the atemporal yet dynamic holomovement unfolding itself in human consciousness. The dynamicism of the holomovement is particularly crucial for psychology. It bears on illness and health, and, beyond these, on the transcendent state of creative consciousness lying within our reach if we live in harmony with the laws of the holomovement instead of, as is currently the case, in opposition to it (Weber, 1979).

The Dynamic Universe

The first of these laws, as noted, is constant movement. Bohm here echoes Heraclitus in fifth century B. C. Greece, that the nature of reality is *flux,* a view that reappears in Hegel and the nineteenth-century evolutionists and vitalists. Older than their Western counterparts, these doctrines originate in the East, however, notably in Buddhism.[3] Two central features common to all forms of Buddhism are the impermanence, that is, the dynamicism *(anicca)* of all being, and its fundamental unity and interdependence. These cohere with Bohm's cosmology, particularly in Madhyamika Buddhism, which most closely resembles his theory of being.

Against this background it may become clear why Bohm, while endorsing Pribram's holographic paradigm and his work, rejects the term holo*graph* as too static. "Graph" means "that which has been written," and thus raises problems. First, it points to the past; second, it encourages dualism: that which writes and that on which it is written. The term holo*movement,* by contrast, informs us more accurately that we are part of an undivided reality with an inherent capacity to form ideas about itself, which it records *within* itself. This model is reminiscent of the Indian theory of *akasha* or cosmic space, a substance conceived to be so fine that it records all events whatever that occur in the universe.

To offer an example of Bohm's repudiation of unwarranted dualism: what physics, psychology, philosophy—and we ourselves at this very moment—are engaged in is that the holomovement is seeking a clear idea of what the holomovement is and does. Consequently, we are not outside, but within the process, enacting as well as observing and recording it.

To summarize the basic properties of Bohm's holomovement as it appears to us: first, we grasp experience in wholes, not atomistically (a fact which Pribram's work also demonstrates); second, we primarily experience movement which, through an act of abstraction born of the

---

[3] See Levin, Chapter 12, and de Silva, Chapter 13, for presentations and discussions of Buddhist philosophy.—Eds.

need for security, we try to fix into stability, a process that hinders rather than furthers our well-being. The factor that makes this possible is thought.

Psychological Atom-Smashing

His work in quantum physics, his evidence from inner empiricism, and his contact with Indian philosophy, notably the Indian sage Krishnamurti, have convinced Bohm that thought, the form of consciousness most familiar to us and in which we habitually function, corrupts reality. The ancient hope of metaphysics and physics, that thought might reveal reality, is of necessity doomed. Thought is a *reactive*, not an active ability, attuning man only partially to nature, distorting most of it. A fossilized kind of consciousness operating within "the known," thought is thus by definition uncreative. Reality or the ultimate (Bohm does not equate these two, but their clarification lies beyond the scope of this discussion), Bohm's investigations have convinced him, is always fresh. It is a living process. Since thought is bounded by time, it cannot grasp what lies beyond a spatio-temporal framework. It is his commitment to this living, moment-by-moment[4] manifestation of reality that links his work in physics with his interest in consciousness.

Atom-smashing can occur only in the present, and must occur ever afresh. The analogy of the atom with thought, and with an alleged thinker who authors thought, is crucial. The thinker is like the atom, cohering in time through its binding energy. When the bonds of the physical atom are released in an accelerator, the resultant energy—staggeringly huge— becomes freed. Analogously, huge amounts of *binding energy* are needed to create and sustain the "thinker" and to maintain his illusion of stability. That energy being tied up, it is unavailable for other purposes, and pressed into the service of what Bohm terms "self-deception" (a phenomenon described in detail by the Buddha as ignorance, *avidya*, literally "not really seeing things as they are"). Thought, or what Bohm terms the three-dimensional mind, mistakenly believing itself autonomous and irreducible, requires and hence *squanders* vast amounts of cosmic energy on this illusion. Energy thus pre-empted cannot flow into other grooves (Weber, 1978).

The consequence is an unsound cosmic ecology, polluting the holomovement in at least two destructive ways. First, the holomovement

---

[4]Consider this idea in the context of R. von Eckartsberg's, Chapter 2, "Here-and-Now" level, the ever present, as discussed by R. von Eckartsberg and R. Valle, Chapter 14, and the concept of temporality (lived-time), as discussed by Moss and Keen, Chapter 4, and R. von Eckartsberg and R. Valle, Chapter 14.—Eds.

misunderstands itself, choosing fiction (*maya*)[5] over fact, and therefore *enslaves itself.* Second, the holomovement lacerates itself, substituting the isolated self for the consciousness of mankind in an abstraction founded on fallacy, *enslaving others* through its competitiveness, anger, greed, ambition, and indifference. The result of both these missteps is the world of personal and interpersonal suffering that Bohm and Krishnamurti, echoing the Buddha, see as the primary fact of our lives.

The Domination of Three-Dimensional Thought

The first misstep, the illusion of an ego, thinker, or personal self, is intimately related to time and to death. Let us be clear. The thinker, not consciousness, is death-bound. Death, according to these views, is precisely the psychological atom-smashing described above, and need not be synonymous with physical dissolution, as has been noted by many recorders of the esoteric tradition. Ideally, it occurs not at biological death, but in one's prime, when the intense energy needed for it is at its height, somewhere in the late twenties or early thirties, to cite prominent cases such as Buddha, Jesus, and others.

Psychological death occurs when consciousness *keeps step with* the ever-moving and self-renewing present, allowing no part of itself to become caught or fixated as residual energy. Residual energy furnishes the framework for what will become the thinker, who consists of undigested experience, memory, habit-patterns, identification, desire, aversion, projection, and image-making. This is not a purely personal process, but the energy of aeons of such processes sclerosed through time, persisting on both personal and transpersonal levels. Ego-death dismantles this superstructure, moving it into its rightful place in the background of our lives, instead of dominating and disordering the foreground, as is presently the case. Bohm argues that such a move entails greater, not reduced, biological adaptation and health, and therefore it need not threaten us. On the contrary, "death" thus conceived is really its negation, ushering us into the timeless present beyond death's reach.

The second misstep concerns ethics. Through the ages, the thinker has prattled on about absolutes unquestionably noble—God, cosmic consciousness, universal intelligence, and love—but the domain where he daily dwells has remained destructive and chaotic. This is because the three-dimensional quality of thought necessarily blocks the thinker's own experiencing of that reality. Logical and substantive incommensura-

---

[5]See R. von Eckartsberg and R. Valle, Chapter 14, for a more detailed discussion of the Hindu notion of *maya.*—Eds.

bility, not ill-will or insufficient effort, account for this. The non-manifest, as Bohm painstakingly argues, is n-dimensional, and cannot be handled by three-dimensional thought: Consciousness functioning as thought cannot know truth at first hand, and herein lies the root of its failure to embody these wider energies in its daily life.

Only when the individual learns to let go of the three-dimensional self consisting of gross matter (the thinker), can the ocean of creative energy (Bohm and Weber, 1978) flow unobstructedly through him. To a theoretical physicist, the parallel of this state of affairs with quantum mechanics is evident. Bohm extends its applicability to psychology, urging on us the dissolution of the "thinker" as the highest priority the seeker for truth can undertake.

With this view, he teeters on the very edge of what is culturally acceptable, in the interface between physics, psychology, and religion. It is a strange terrain, since our current culture, lacking any conceivable concept to explain it, rejects such a link as muddled if not absurd. However strange and novel it may be, this integration is justified by Bohm's model of the universe as a holomovement.

Multi-Dimensional Consciousness

The dismantling of the thinker yields energy that is qualitatively charged. It is energy unbound and flowing, characterized by n-dimensionality, and the force of compassion. Physics and ethics also become one in this process, for the energy of the whole is somehow bound up with what we term "holiness." In short, the energy itself is compassion.

The atom-smashing applicable to consciousness, Bohm and Krishnamurti term "awareness" or "insight." Such a process provides consciousness with direct access to that energy, leading it to experiential certitude, based on inner empiricism, that the ultimate nature of the universe is an energy of love.

Mystics East and West have proclaimed this with one voice. What is arresting is that a contemporary physicist finds such a theory and its method of interest. It is of course true that in many respects the aim of the mystic coincides with that of the physicist, that is, contact with what is ultimate. But there is one critical difference. Smashing the atom is a dualistic enterprise. The physicist works on an object considered to lie outside himself, with respect to which he is emotionally neutral. Changing the object does not fundamentally change him nor can it threaten him. By contrast, destructuring the thinker of necessity involves the experimenter himself, for he is the test-object in question, at once the transformer and what is undergoing transformation. Hence the resistance, arduousness, and great rarity of such an event.

Though rare, it does occur, and, as suggested above, Bohm relates its achievement to ethics. Psychological atom-smashing unpollutes what countless illusory egoic clusters—analogous to spasms that reduce the flow within the whole—have polluted with their misplaced sense of separateness and their ego-borne priorities, resulting in universal sorrow that Bohm (Bohm and Weber, 1978) deems akin to an energy-like domain, "the sorrow of mankind." The psychological atom-smasher thus coincides with the saint, who no longer *adds* to this collective sorrow, but instead becomes a channel for the boundless energy of compassion. Consciousness thus functions as a conduit aligned with the universal energy,[6] radiating it to the creature and the human world without distorting it or diverting it for its own self-centered pursuits.

This process can be selective, Bohm (1979) maintains, invoked in accordance with context and need, but only by the individual who has become free from its tyranny. Intelligent use of memory, thought, and time has its place and is an obvious necessity for our practical lives in the explicate order. Judiciously used, three-dimensional consciousness can enhance rather than hinder the creative life of multidimensional consciousness, provided that we restrain the former from its present usurpation of the dynamic cosmic flow.

Oddly, in spite of Bohm's conviction that this is the true and the desirable state of affairs with which our knowledge simply has not yet caught up, he is reluctant to discuss it other than in brief allusions to it. His emphasis is on the methodology of the self-deconditioning process, not on the promised land which might lie at the end of it. His rationale for this is simple. In its conditioned state, the mind can, in any case, do no more than translate what is unconditioned into conditioned patterns and thus lose the essence of what is sought. Faithful to the credo of science, Bohm looks for experiential, not verbal proof.

The consequence of this position is startling and, perhaps, bizarre. Nothing in the domain of knowledge, not even the elusive paradoxes of quantum physics, can quite rival it. On some levels it seems to conflict with our psychological make-up, for even those in full intellectual accord with this view have difficulty in coming to grips with it on the existential level of their lives, as anyone who has experimented with Krishnamurti's teachings will attest.

What is this paradox? Just this: that the more we talk about or even think "the truth," the further we push it away from ourselves, by obvious

[6]See Swami Rama, Chapter 15, for a more detailed discussion of the universal "dance of energies" and its relationship to human personality and experience.—Eds.

analogy with the Heisenberg uncertainty principle.[7] Contrary to the Cartesian (Descartes, 1931) thesis, it is the *I*, the thinker, the creator of the thought of God or "the holy," who, *in that very act*, introduces the impurities (time, self, language, dualism), and who thus beclouds what would otherwise be *unsullied* (Krishnamurti himself chose that word in this context in a talk we had together in 1976).

Some Historical Similarities

This claim is hardly novel, but its articulation has rarely been put forward with such single-minded eloquence as that found in the tone and language of Krishnamurti, or with the clarity of Bohm. In fact, we need not roam far afield. Kant comes to mind. Already in the late eighteenth century, he insisted on the impossibility—grounded in logic or the laws of thought, and thus constituting an obstacle that cannot be overcome—of our experiencing what is ultimate. Kant (1966) called that domain the thing-in-itself, that is, what Krishnamurti and Bohm call intelligence or compassion (Buddha, the *dharma*, and Plato, the *good*). Kant destroyed metaphysics by carefully demonstrating in *The Critique of Pure Reason* that whatever is thinkable and namable must necessarily conform to the inherent structure of the mind: space, time, quality, quantity, causality, etc. The Kantian categories are what Bohm refers to as the realm of three-dimensionality, with the distinction that the latter is wider, containing emotion, will, intent, and other psychological as well as cognitive qualities. All these concern the world of sensible experience (the manifest or explicate order, in Bohm's language), and they account for our ability to function in the phenomenal domain. In that dimension, we have no choice but to filter *that which is* through the universal perceiving apparatus just described. Our capacity for translation is useful when properly employed, that is, biologically, or in certain affairs of practical daily life. But we do so at a heavy price, as Kant realized. The noumenon or thing-in-itself, not capable of being caught in our net, remains inscrutable to us. Knowledge for both Bohm and Kant is the process of tuning in on the manifestation (phenomenon) of the nonmanifest, in order to make it accessible to creatures structured as we are. This filter and consequent distortion is inbuilt and universal. By definition, the thing-in-itself can never appear to us as it would be without our "tuning in" on it with our finite receiving apparatus.

[7]See R. Valle, Chapter 21, for a discussion relating the Heisenberg uncertainty principle to psychological and philosophical concerns.—Eds.

Bohm and Kant

Here the ways part. Krishnamurti, Bohm, and the whole mystical tradition agree with Kant's analysis regarding phenomenal experience. They move beyond Kant, however, to proclaim the possibility of a state of consciousness lying outside these barriers. For Kant, whose views on the subject have been accepted as definitive by Western philosophy, *no other capacity in us is available* on which to draw in order to approach the noumenon. Bohm and those mentioned maintain that such a capacity exists in the universe, not in us strictly speaking. The challenge for the individual locus of consciousness is to provide the condition that allows the universal force to flow through it without hindrance. The result is not knowledge, in the Kantian sense, but direct nondualistic awareness, a state for which Kant made no provision and for which he had no vocabulary.

Its precondition is *emptiness*, as Bohm and the wisdom traditions point out, which entails a suspension of the Kantian categories and of three-dimensional space-time. Such emptiness brings about the cessation of consciousness *as the knower,* and transforms us into a channel for the noumenal intelligence. The specific mechanism at work is difficult to understand. Perhaps we become akin to electrical "transformers" capable of stepping down the cosmic energy in ways that permit us to *focus* it on the microcosmic level where we live and act. However this may be, the rare individual who functions as such a channel seems to those who come in contact with him to belong to a new species. Such a human being radiates clarity, intelligence, order, and love by his mere presence. He seems capable of transmuting our chaotic interpersonal world into an ethical realm by his very *atmosphere,* which unmistakably is charged with energies for which we have neither names nor concepts. At best we can vaguely capture the presence and power of that atmosphere in metaphorical and approximate terms.

Kant, by contrast, leaves us no doubt as to his unfamiliarity with such states of being, which a handful of humanity has recorded with remarkable consistency and intersubjective agreement. Bohm, like Kant, performs an invaluable service in delineating clearly where the limits of knowledge must lie. To paraphrase Kant: humankind is in a bind symbolized, as we might state it today, by a species universally endowed with contact lenses. Without these lenses, we cannot see at all, that is, we can have no knowledge whatever. But since the lenses come pre-equipped with their own built-in tinted filters, with their aid we can see only what the filters permit. Thus we see either nothing, or else distortedly. In neither case do we contact what is ultimate.

The Hologram and Neurology

One key to this dilemma may be found in the hologram invented by Gabor, and in the neurological theory that Pribram (1978, 1979)[8] derives from it and from his research into brain function. Reminiscent of Kant, Pribram distinguishes between *lenselike* and *lenseless vision*. *Lenselike vision* is analogous to the conventional camera, which limits our view to the unfolded (explicate) order bounded by the Cartesian space–time grid. It correlates with one aspect of quantum mechanics, for in this mode consciousness may be operating as a *particle*. In Bohm's (1979, 1980) holomovement paradigm, an equivalent idea may be his concept of a "relatively independent subtotality." This term acknowledges our empirical self or personality, a derivative entity rooted in the whole, which may, nonetheless, be discerned and described as an identifiable, historical individual.

By contrast, *lenseless vision* tunes directly into what Pribram (1979) terms the frequency-domain, which provides the raw material for the objects created by the lense. The hologram, which records the wave-field of light scattered by an object, may thus be said to capture hints of a world beyond space, time, and objects—a possibility that Kant's epistemology rules out. Lenseless vision provides us with a glimpse into a domain of timeless waves, vibrating as unbound energies *prior to* being "translated" into objects through the mathematical transformations (Fourier series) by which Pribram tells us our brain produces the familiar sensed world.

It may be that this shift from phenomena to noumena becomes possible with the shift from the particle-nature of consciousness to its *wave-aspect*.[9] Bohm (1979) observes that, when consciousness functions in the deep-structure of the implicate order, it has access to the information embedded in the whole. This is because holographic, lenseless, wave-like consciousness originates at a level of undivided matter where the natural state is wholeness (Bohm and Weber, 1978), and where all beings are "enfolded" in one another, hence in direct touch. Nobel laureate Erwin Schrödinger (1969), the discoverer of wave mechanics, hit upon this principle (as a result of his studies in Vedanta) when he observed that "consciousness is never experienced in the plural, only in the singular."

As noted, the more deeply we proceed within the enfolded order, the more its matter becomes subtle, orderly, and whole. It follows that deep-structure implicate-order matter must be a wave-like, continuous,

[8]See Pribram, Chapter 6, for a discussion of the hologram's role in neuropsychological theory, and Moss, Chapter 7, for a phenomenological critique of this position.—Eds.
[9]See R. Valle, Chapter 21, for another discussion of the "dual" wave–particle aspects of human nature.—Eds.

conscious energy, whose presence we experience by tapping into the appropriate holistic frequencies. Lenselike vision rules out the perception of this level of matter or of the frequency-domain, confining us to the Kantian level of phenomena.

It should be noted that, in the above discussion of Kant, I dwelt on the epistemological perspective, on the *structure* inherent in the knower. This differs from the metaphysical perspective, according to which the *quality* of matter we encounter—subtle or gross, whole or fragmented—is as decisive a factor in shaping our view of reality as is the focusing instrument itself (lenseless or lenselike). These are correlative concepts, and yet it must be emphasized that proper perception precedes the level of matter which that perception makes accessible to us. Our epistemology therefore shapes our metaphysics. Lenseless vision, that is, the right approach, brings the subtleties of inner being into focus. For Bohm, without our ability to perceive things as they are, all talk of gross or subtle matter is an intellectual construct, not anchored in experience.

Holistic Vision

Perceiving things as they really are requires inactivating all lenses: in Bohm's term, bypassing the ego or thinker who manipulates the world through them, and becoming, instead, the empty channel for the wholeness in which we lie immersed. Nothing in that emptiness can be characterized, as already explained, because characterization is the *translation* of noumena into phenomena, of nonmanifest into manifest. Therefore, all languages will fail to capture the essence of the whole, even the purest of them, mathematics, as Plato concluded in the *Republic*. Only silence is commensurate with its nature and appropriate to its universe of discourse (*samadhi*, the rapturous culmination of yogic meditation described by Patanjali [Taimni, 1975], literally means "complete silence" or "total stillness").

These remarks should shed light on Bohm's uncompromising stance. The hope of apprehending the noumenon through phenomenal eyes is founded on a logical absurdity, what Bohm calls confusion and self-deception. The age-old philosophical effort to tune in on the purity of being and perceive it as it would be in itself without being perceived *by a knower* is therefore a vain hope, for to achieve this aim the knower must step aside altogether in favor of pure nondualistic awareness.

In the light of this necessity, Bohm's priorities become understandable and seem inevitable. Atom-smashing confined to gross matter—the province of the particle physicist—is but a first step in our reaching out to reality, and it is the path presently pursued by the community of physicists. But Bohm runs far ahead of the pack. The shape-shifting (cf. *The Tibetan Book of the Dead*) of subatomic particles (gross matter) will not yield up the secrets of the universe. All it can offer us is *knowledge*, restricted, as we have seen, to the three-dimensional realm.

Quantum-Physical Psychology

Bohm holds out for atom-smashing of a subtler kind: to slow down and ultimately to still the shape-shifter's dance itself, that is, the "death" of the three-dimensional thinker and his rebirth within the n-dimensional domain of consciousness. Such an event would usher in the dynamic rhythm that Bohm refers to, in which creation and dissolution and creation would flow through us simultaneously, like quanta of *energy born and borne away* in the split microsecond, ever welling up afresh without being arrested, diverted, or clung to. The consequence—were such a task successful—is a new paradigm of the universe, of consciousness, and of human reality. No longer is it a question of a knower observing the known across the gulf of knowing that separates them. That model of consciousness has failed us through the centuries in which we have stubbornly clung to it.

It must be swept aside, as Bohm so clearly argues. Its replacement is the austere paradigm of a unified field of being, a self-conscious universe realizing itself to be integrally whole and interconnected. By analogy with field physics, this reality might be termed *field consciousness*. Knower and known thus are falsehoods: crude constructs based on abstraction. They are unwarranted by the way things really are, namely, the monism which Bohm claims is most fully compatible with the message of modern physics, based on its penetrations into nature thus far. Although the data are now accepted by physicists, their interpretation of them remains restricted to realms that exclude *themselves* as conscious beings.

It is this reluctance and restriction that Bohm is challenging. He is willing to explore *all* the consequences of quantum mechanical theory and logic, and is risking his reputation on his commitment to the holomovement. His vision is a unified field theory surpassing that of current science, in which the searcher and what is sought are apprehended as one, the holomovement becoming transparent to itself and acting upon the implications of its vision. That unified field is neither neutral nor value-free as current scientific canon requires, but an orderly and compassionate energy articulating itself in a new domain where physics, psychology, ethics, and religion merge.

Field Consciousness and Field Ethics

The consequences consistent with this vision are enormous. Field physics and field consciousness must logically give rise to field psychology and field ethics. In these, the *whole*—not its localized manifestations—predominates and is addressed as the primary locus for the solution of our problems, by sharp contrast with present practices, where this priority is reversed. The practical effects of these reordered priorities will be left in domains as distinct as medicine and healing (Weber, 1979), psychology, and ethics. In psychology, for example, we shall direct our efforts toward reaching and reordering *enfolded* aspects of the patient's field of consciousness, as well as toward its local disordered outcome in the explicate realm, in keeping with the postulate that implicate-order matter is more whole and more orderly than explicate matter, which it, therefore, has the power to transform (Bohm & Weber, 1978; Bohm, 1979).

For ethics, the ramifications of this theory will be no less dramatic. The *roots* of disturbances in the culture will be considered to lie within the implicate order (Bohm & Weber, 1978)—though not in the deep-structure where only order is possible—somewhere within the collective consciousness of mankind. This requires reversing *field disturbances* by taking individual responsibility for them, in the manner outlined above (psychological atom-smashing), in order to clear up the "polluted" field. The paradox, of which Bohm (Bohm & Weber, 1978) is aware, seems to be that, although the "sorrow of mankind" may be a universal field, its purification is an individual task, requiring self-transformation. This process profoundly affects the whole field. It may be that the energies set free revert directly to the total field, thereby benefitting mankind as a whole. This model of cosmos and consciousness, although revolutionary, is not new. It forms the content of the wisdom traditions of India and Greece.

The Holocosmos and Esoteric Traditions East and West

The discoveries fundamental to the holocosmic paradigms form the basis of the esoteric tradition in philosophy, East and West (Weber, 1975a). Pribram's "frequency domain" and Bohm's "holomovement" are called *Brahman* by Vedanta and in the *Upanishads, purusha* and *prakriti* in Sankhya–Yoga, the *dharma* or *Buddha-nature* in Buddhism, the *Tao* by Taoism, the *One* or the *Good* in Plato, the *One* by Plotinus, and *nature or God* in Spinoza, to name but a few of its analogues in the holistic historical traditions. All these agree that from this unified, generative matrix *we create,* somehow, the space–time world of objects, "figure" projected upon the undifferentiated universal "ground," to invoke Shankara's system of Advaita. A common thread runs through all these systems: *mind precipitates matter* (Weber, 1975b). Its corollary is that consciousness is world-creating. Thus arises the doctrine of *maya,* central to Eastern philosophy and even to Platonic metaphysics, where the concept reappears as the distinction between *form* and *copy.*

The *maya*-doctrine (i.e., confusion about genuine versus derivative reality) pervades Plato's work, from the shadows in the Allegory of the Cave *(Republic VII)* through the "ladder of love" in the *Symposium,* to the charioteer-myth in the *Phaedrus.* In the latter, Plato tells us that—except for the rare moments in which we manage holistic vision—our sight is restricted to things seen as "through a glass darkly," a phrase that was to reappear in early Christianity.

The holocosmic metaphors match Plato's distinction between appearance and reality, cave and light, fragment and whole. Applied to psychology and to ethics, they correlate with the Platonic contrast between the self-enclosure and separative blindness of the cave-dwellers and the all-encompassing vision of the wise man who has directly perceived the sun, the source of all being. This break with self-deception, limitation, ego-centeredness and delusion has transformed him from a prisoner chained to shadows to "the spectator of all time and all existence," who, having seen the *good,* "has entered into union with it" (Plato, 1937). Like the Bodhisattva of Mahayana Buddhism, this figure *chooses* to redescend into the cave, in order to convince those still trapped in its darkness that the partial and petty reality to which their lenselike vision binds them is not the only reality in nature. Although even cave vision is not completely false, compared to the realm of light it is severely limited: a world of appearances that is fragmented and disconnected, incapable of providing the wholeness and the clarity that man craves.

Plato's allegory brings out a point central to both esoteric philosophy and the holocosmic metaphors. It concerns the *relationship* between part and whole, cave and light, *maya* (the measurable) and the measureless, particle and wave, explicate and implicate, *samsara* and *nirvana.* This last pair, at the heart of all Buddhism, best illustrates the point. *Samsara* stands for limitation and finitude: suffering, time, and death represented by the Buddhist "wheel of interdependent origination," the equivalent of Bohm's "sorrow of mankind." *Nirvana,* on the other hand, represents the holistic state of consciousness described earlier, in harmony with the dynamic flow *(anicca,* impermanence), anchored deep within the holomovement, where space, time, separation, sorrow, and death cannot arise and hence have no meaning. Instead of stressing their divergence, as is the case in *exoteric* religion and philosophy, the esoteric systems and Buddhism, in particular, assert the *identity* of *samsara* and *nirvana*.

Buddhist versus Aristotelian Logic

This assertion of identity avoids the extremes of both otherworldly withdrawal and entrapment within the sensate versions of crude materialism, consistent with Buddhist commitment to the "middle way." In their stead, Buddhism proclaims a connection between part and whole which violates our ordinary (Aristotelian) logic in favor of an alternative system known as Buddhist logic (Stcherbatsky, 1962; Lama Govinda, 1969, 1976) or multidimensional logic. Inaccessible to Western science until the discovery of the hologram, Buddhist logic, holographic logic, and quantum logic (Zukav, 1979) defy common sense by stating that *the whole is in the part.* Such a view wars with our ordinary computations, our reason, and with Cartesian-Newtonian exclusive space. This picture conflicts with our deepest conditioning, evoking not only logical but even kinesthetic protest in us, the uneasy feeling that—since no part can conceivably contain the whole—a vessel is about to flow over, with untidy consequences for the environment.

Holographic Logic

Consequently, holographic logic can be understood only by invoking new theories of space, namely the n-dimensional hyperspaces referred to in both Bohm's (Bohm & Weber, 1978) cosmology and that of Buddhism (Lama Govinda, 1969, 1976). In this infinite, nondisjunctive, noncompetitive space, two entities can compatibly occupy the same "place" at the same time. The "entities" in question are, in any case, not the gross material particles described by Newton or Descartes (Weber, 1975b, 1979), barred from such interpenetration by their very make-up. Rather they are energies (or matter) so fine and subtle that their merger presents no problem except to our conditioned Cartesian and Kantian minds. The full comprehension of this whole–part paradox requires that we rethink our concept of space. The hologram should prove useful in this endeavor, for it constitutes a working model establishing the possibility of an alternative, nondisjunctive space. Through the evidence furnished by the hologram—that it may be legitimate to claim that the whole is *in* the part—it is now possible for us to enter more sympathetically into cosmologies for which we formerly lacked any scientific context.

A good example is provided by *om mani padme hum*, the most sacred *mantram* of Tibetan Buddhism. Sometimes translated as "the dew drop slips into the shining sea," a description of union between the part and the whole, this *mantram* can also be rendered reversely, as *"the shining sea slips into* the dew-drop" (Lama Govinda, 1969, 1976). Although it conflicts with our ordinary logic, this concept is compatible with holocosmic models, as we have seen.

At issue is no linguistic quibbling, but the question of harmony between the infinite and its finite expression (Govinda, 1969) in our everyday world. The search for this balance constitutes the essence of the wisdom traditions.

What is at stake is the claim that the wave can delimit itself as the particle, or that the lenseless truth about the universe can also be expressed through the prism of partiality. In Hindu philosophy, this is preserved as the "complementarity principle" found in the *Upanishads* and the *Bhagavad Gita*, where the "field" *precipitates* itself as matter that individuates itself, localizing itself functionally for reasons that remain inscrutable to human thought. (Questions concerning the purpose of this process involve the ultimate question of creation or manifestation, which I have addressed elsewhere [Weber, 1975b]). In Shankara's (1970) Advaita Vedanta, referred to above, we *superimpose* the structure of finitude upon the infinite continuum.

Shankara's *doctrine of superimposition* brings us full circle, back to the holistic paradigms of Pribram and Bohm, for it addresses the role and status of what is partial, in a universe claimed to be holistic. In particular, it forces us to find practical models for their reconciliation and integration.

The question it raises is how—having granted the holism espoused throughout this essay—the "relatively autonomous subtotality," Bohm's (1980) name for humankind, can express and embody this vision in its daily life.

Holocosmic Ethics

This is a question for ethics. Of all the points presented thus far, this—the simplest—is the most difficult, more elusive than the abstract speculations concerning holocosmic metaphysics. Simply stated: how can we *live* these insights?

This question is the only one that matters to Bohm (and to his mentor Krishnamurti). Bohm only reluctantly admits metaphysical speculations into his discussions. His full energy revolves around the existential translation of his outlook: its practical transformative power. In fact, he makes instantaneous change in our lives and values the central *criterion* of our comprehending the meaning of his message.

A second criterion is that the "holomovement" itself must remain a *metaphor*. To mistake the map for the territory is to become entrapped in the "totality concept," Bohm's (1979) designation for and criticism of all theories of being that take themselves too literally. No linguistic system can match the movement, richness, and subtlety of the whole, as the foregoing discussion has tried to establish, and as Bohm repeatedly reiterates, insisting on the metaphorical nature of his own cosmology.

Concluding Remarks

I would like to close with a confession. Like others before me (Capra, 1975; Zukav, 1979), I have tried to present the parallels of these systems about cosmos and consciousness. Yet I must confess that I am unclear as to exactly what the parallelism means and entails. I am therefore left with more questions than answers.

Can we, for example, create the crucial experiential bridge between physics and meditation that would permit us to move in both directions with ease, back and forth between the data of Western science and the silence central to Eastern mysticism? This yields two further questions. Must we confine ourselves to an *alternating* modality akin to complementarity in physics that will permit us—to be sure—to operate in both inner and outer empiricism, but never at the same time?

Or is it possible to achieve simultaneity, functioning at the same instant of clock-time as both particle and wave, lenselike and lenseless being, experiencing Bohm's "pure flowing movement" or Pribram's frequency-domain even as we are engaged in transforming it into objects, without losing the essence of either dimension? Although Kant deems this impossible, Eastern mystics—in the *samsara–nirvana* identity–thesis —announce that they have achieved this union.

These questions, unanswered, have become focused into one single question, the stuff perhaps of science fiction.[10] It is this: If someone were perfectly adept at both outer and inner empiricism, a Nobel laureate in quantum physics combined with a Buddha figure *in one person,* would such a being have an advantage in forging the bridge that we seek?

The answer to this question constitutes a great challenge as we approach the twenty-first century. For human life, widespread aware-

---

[10]See Leavitt, Chapter 20, for a review of the science fiction literature which addresses itself to the nature of human consciousness.—Eds.

ness of implicate-order energies and their embodiment in our daily values will be revolutionary, a moral mutation leading us from information to transformation, and from knowledge to wisdom.

References

Bohm, D. Cosmos and consciousness. Paper presented at the conference "Cosmos and Consciousness," New York, New York, June, 1979.
Bohm, D. *Wholeness and the implicate order.* London: Routledge & Kegan Paul, 1980.
Bohm, D., & Weber, R. The enfolding-unfolding universe: A conversation with David Bohm. *Re-vision*, 1978, *1*(3 & 4), 24–51.
Capra, F. *The tao of physics.* New York: Bantam Books, 1975.
Descartes, R. Meditations on first philosophy. In *The philosophical works of Descartes.* New York: Dover, 1931.
Hegel, G. *The phenomenology of mind.* New York: Macmillan, 1931.
Kant, I. *Critique of pure reason.* New York: St. Martin's, 1966.
Lama Govinda. *Foundations of Tibetan mysticism.* New York: Samuel Weiser, 1969.
Lama Govinda. *Creative meditation and multi-dimensional consciousness.* Wheaton, III.: Theosophical Publishing House, 1976.
Plato. *The dialogues of Plato.* New York: Random House, 1937.
Pribram, K. H. What the fuss is all about. *Re-vision*, 1978, *1*(3 & 4), 14–18.
Pribram, K. H. Holographic memory. *Psychology Today*, 1979, *12*(9), 70–84.
Schrödinger, E. *What is life. Mind and matter.* Cambridge, England: Cambridge University Press, 1969.
Shankara. *Crest-jewel of discrimination.* New York: New American Library, 1970.
Spinoza, B. Ethics. In J. Wild (Ed.), *Selections.* New York: Scribner's 1930.
Stcherbatsky, T. *Buddhist logic.* New York: Dover, 1962.
Taimni, I. *The science of yoga.* Wheaton, Ill.: Theosophical Publishing House, 1975.
Weber, R. The reluctant tradition: Esoteric philosophy East and West. *Main Currents in Modern Thought*, 1975, *29*(1), 99–106.(a)
Weber, R. The good, the true, the beautiful: Are they attributes of the universe? *Main Currents in Modern Thought*, 1975, *32*, 135–142. (b)
Weber, R. Field consciousness and field ethics. *Re-vision*, 1978, *1* (3 & 4), 19–23.
Weber, R. Philosophical foundations and frameworks for healing. *Re-vision*, 1979, *2*, 66–77.
Zukav, G. *The dancing Wu Li masters.* New York: William Morrow, 1979.

6

Behaviorism, Phenomenology, and Holism in Psychology
A SCIENTIFIC ANALYSIS[1]

Karl H. Pribram

Behaviorism and Psychology

The behaviorist revolution is completed. Its success is heralded in the numerous texts that proclaim psychology to be the study of behavior. We need now only to get on with our experiments, for all is well in our world.

Or is it? Do the series of theoretical statements ranging from Watson's (1979) *Psychology from the Standpoint of a Behaviorist,* through Gilbert Ryle's (1949) *The Concept of Mind,* to Skinner's (1976) recent *About Behaviorism* really accomplish a science of psychology? Do the observations and experiments undertaken under the banner of behaviorism really address the problems and issues raised by philosophical inquiry? And, further, do these observations and experiments really encompass all of the problems and issues that concern psychologists?

The time appears right to ask these questions because the behaviorist revolution is indeed completed, and its successes and failures can be reasonably assessed. Behaviorism as a vital scientific discipline continues to grow both in maturity and in new applications outside psychology.

[1]This chapter is a revised and expanded version of my paper presented as part of the symposium "The Nature of Consciousness" at the American Psychological Association Convention, Toronto, August, 1978.

Karl H. Pribram • Department of Psychology, Stanford University, Stanford, California 94305.

Perhaps in this statement can be found the key to assessment. When a biologist observes behavior in an assay of a biochemical constituent of the brain, does he automatically become a practicing psychologist? When a computer scientist attempts to simulate his thought processes on an information-processing program, is he addressing a problem that does not concern psychologists because he is not observing or controlling behavior?[2] And what about the experimentalist who measures the electrical conduction of the skin, the heart rate, the movement of the eyes, or the electrical responses of the brain in a problem-solving situation? Is he measuring "behavior", and, if he is or is not, does that matter with regard to whether he is pursuing psychology?

As an answer to these questions, another may be posed. Has it perhaps been a mistake to identify behaviorism with psychology? Behaviorism is a discipline—the study of behavior has its set of problems, such as the definition of what constitutes behavior. As a discipline, it has already made fantastic contributions to technology and the understanding of the behavior of animals and of men and women. And there is no reason why scientific psychology should not be *based* on such an understanding of behavior.

But there are limits to understanding achieved solely through the observation and experimental analysis of behavior. These limits are especially apparent when problems other than overt behavior are addressed, problems related to thought or to decisional processes, to appetitive and other motivational mechanisms, to emotions and feelings, and even to imaging and perception. These problems make up a large bulk of the interests that bring students to the study of psychology, and at least one behaviorist (Skinner, 1976) has grouped them under the rubric "covert behavior." Being "covert," they need to be enacted to be studied (Miller, Galanter, & Pribram, 1960). Enactment in overt behavior is, however, only one avenue of study—others, such as computer simulation or the recording and analysis of brain electrical activity, may prove just as effective in achieving scientific understanding—perhaps even more so when used in combination with behavioral enactment.

In a very real sense, therefore, psychology as a science reaches out beyond behaviorism to these covert processes. Ordinarily, these covert processes have been labeled "mental", and there is no good reason to abandon this label. Our perceptions such as vision and hearing are mental processes. Our feelings of emotion and motivation are mental, our intentions and decisions are mental, and, as we shall see, even our actions are mental.

Psychology as the study of mental life, as William James and George

2See Bair, Chapter 24, for a discussion of computers and human thought processes.—Eds.

Miller have called it, is biologically rooted—one aspect of *life* is studied. As such, it aspires to be a conventional science. The problem lies in providing a useful definition of what is mental. Could not such a definition be derived from an analysis of behavior (and, if so, perhaps a more concrete terminology substituted)? But, as already noted, problems of definition also plague behaviorism.

Some Confusions

Psychology as a behavioral science and as the science of mental life needs, therefore, to have clearly defined what is meant by behavior and what is meant by mental. Here, the approach will be taken that confusion has plagued psychology because both the term behavior and the term mental have remained ambiguous. Each term has, in fact, been used in two very distinctly separate ways, and the distinctions have not been clearly kept apart.

To begin with, consider the meaning of the term behavior. When a behaviorist ordinarily analyses "behavior," he is studying a record of responses emitted by an organism in a specified situation. The record can be studied in any location, it could have been produced in any of a number of ways by any number of different "response systems"—arms, legs, beaks, etc. The behavior under study is an environmental consequence of any of these response systems (Pribram, 1971).

At other times, however, "behavior" is understood to mean the pattern of the organism's movements, or of his endocrine or neural responses in a situation. This definition of behavior is especially common to biological behaviorists such as ethologists, but it is also invoked by psychologists (even staunch behaviorists) when they begin to address the problems of covert behavior.

What, then, is the concern of a science of behavior? Are its laws to be formulated on the basis of descriptions of the behaviors of organisms or the behaviors of organ (response) systems? Classically, the laws describing the behavior of organ systems has been the province of physiology. There are physiologists (and physiological psychologists) who believe that a lawful description of brain processes should be coordinate with the laws derived from observations of behavior. These physiologists may well be correct, but, because the brain is contained within the organism, such identifications fall easy prey to the category errors warned against by Kant, by Whitehead and Russell, and by all subsequent critical philosophers. In a strict sense, a brain cell does not "see" its "visual" receptive field, the cell responds to excitation of its dendritic (receptive) field which results from luminance changes that have been transduced into neuroelectric potentials by retinal receptors. Perhaps the behaviorist will be content when the laws of behavior and those describing brain function coalesce—but that has not been the tenor of those who espouse the establishment of a science of behavior, separate from physiology.

The mentalists have not fared much better than the behaviorists in stating clearly what psychology, the study of mental life, is to be about. Are mental processes to be identified on the basis of verbal reports of introspection? Are they, therefore, the contents of introspection? Or are mental processes the resultants of an organism's being-and-acting-in-the-world, as Whitehead, Husserl, the phenomenologists, Gestalt psychologists, and existentialists would have it? Or are the contents of introspection nothing more than these resultants of being (or acting)-in-the-world? If they are, what then is the difference between what a behaviorist calls covert behavior and the existentialist calls mental?[3] Logically, there is none.

Some Differences

However, though logic can find little to distinguish an existential psychologist from a sophisticated behaviorist, historically the gap is great between how each goes about constructing his science. The behaviorist, as already noted, is devoted to objectively observable, discrete behavioral responses—he makes inferences, yes, but these inferences must be operationally and explicitly tied to the environmental manipulations that produce these discrete observable behaviors of organisms.

By contrast, phenomenologists, Gestalt psychologists, and existentialists analyze subjective experience.[4] Contrary to opinions expressed by some behaviorists, these investigators do not eschew observation. Nor do their concepts, when derived scientifically, lack in operational rigor. As with behaviorists, the operations to which these concepts are tied are operations performed on the environment, not on the organism. Thus, they share the interests of psychophysicists. As psychologists, they use these operations to attain concepts about subjective experience (as reported verbally or inferred from nonverbal communication), instead of using them to attain laws describing behavior.

It is this remoteness of the measurable dependent variable from what is being studied that makes the mentalist's job more difficult than that of the behaviorist. But inference from observable events to nonobservable

---

[3]Consider this question in the light of R. von Eckartsberg's discussion of "experiaction". See Chapter 10 in R. S. Valle and M. King (Eds.), *Existential-Phenomenological Alternatives for Psychology*. New York: Oxford University Press, 1978.—Eds.
[4]As well as "observable behavior".—Eds.

ones is a commonplace in the natural sciences. Quantum and nuclear physicists have built precise models of the micro-universe from observing the effects of events on measurable variables, rather than by observing the events themselves. Physiological chemists often postulate the presence of a biologically active substance from the effect it has, many years before that substance is identified chemically. In like manner, a mentalist may investigate hunger, visual illusions, and states of consciousness with the aim of modeling these experiences via their observed effects on reports of their occurrence or of finding a neuroelectric response to be coordinate with the experience.

Thus, a science of mental life is as likely to become rigorous and respectable as a science of behavior. This does not mean that the models of psychological experience and the laws of behavior will prove to be similar, any more than the models of quantum physics resemble the laws of mechanics. Psychology, therefore, can readily encompass both levels of inquiry—and perhaps other levels, such as explorations of social communication, as well. Biology as well as physics has its molecular and molar divisions—why not psychology?

Stated in this fashion, behaviorism becomes essentially a reductive endeavor. True, current behaviorists do not view themselves as reductionists. Skinner and others have repeatedly claimed that they are descriptive functionalists. But description entails the possibility (though not the necessity) of reduction (Pribram, 1965). By contrast, an existential-phenomenological approach eschews this possibility.[5]

Existential-phenomenological "mentalism" is rooted in being-in-the-world. Basically, therefore, there is an upward—or perhaps it is better stated as an outward—reach, if experience is considered the starting point of inquiry. Experience is of a piece with that which is experienced. Issues of self, of intention, and of intentionality are derivative and always include a being-in-the-world approach to solution. Existential-phenomenological approaches thus share with social psychology the derivation of self or person from the being-in-the-social-world.

Causes and Reasons (Structure)

There is another important and related distinction that separates behaviorism from the existential-phenomenological approach to psychological issues. The experimental analysis of behavior searches for *causes* (proximal causes in the Aristotelian sense) in a tried-and-true

[5]See Moss, Chapter 7, for an existential-phenomenological critique of the position espoused by Pribram.—Eds.

scientific fashion. Skinner is interested in the environmental contingencies that *cause* reinforcement to occur. Other behaviorists are utilizing such reinforcing stimuli to *cause* a modification in behavior.

The existential-phenomenological approach is entirely different. At its most lucid, it is concerned with the *structure* of experience-in-the-world (Merleau-Ponty, 1963). It is perhaps significant that when George Miller, Eugene Galanter, and I enlarged our compass and became *subjective* behaviorists, we titled a book *Plans and the Structure of Behavior*, whereas Merleau-Ponty, attempting a precise formulation of existentialism, authored *The Structure of Behavior*. An analysis of structure does not involve a search for causes. Structure is multiply determined and has many *reasons* for being.

Existential-phenomenological psychology has not, up to now, been very clear in its methods. I suggest that multidimensional analyses (factor analysis, principle components analysis, stepwise discriminant analysis) might serve well as tools to investigate the *structure* of experience-in-the-world. In biology, the homeostat with its negative feedback loop has served as a model of structure—and has been modified to account for change, as in the theory of evolution, in the concepts of feedforward, homeostasis, and teleonomy, Aristotle's "final" causation. Linguists have also provided models of analysis: after all, structuralism derives from the social and linguistic analyses of de Saussure (1922).

Another conceptual tool that could prove useful to existential-phenomenological psychology comes from physics. In looking upward in a hierarchy of systems, Einstein found relativity. The larger view showed that the local calculations were dependent on context. Is not this the every-day experience of the phenomenologist? The contextual dependency of experience is what makes its *structure* so rich, but this very richness makes its structural relationships so difficult to specify. Relativity (whether the special or the general theory) is difficult enough to grasp for physical systems—how much more difficult will it be for the psychological?[6]

Holograms and Transformation

Recent discoveries in the brain sciences augur yet another approach to psychology that is utterly different from the behavioristic and existential-phenomenological. This approach has more in common with that of the mystics, the depth psychology of Carl Jung (1960),[7] and the

[6]See R. Valle, Chapter 21, for a discussion of the implications that the theory of relativity has for psychology.—Eds.

[7]See R. von Eckartsberg, Chapter 2, Marlan, Chapter 11, Levin, Chapter 12, and V. Valle and Kruger, Chapter 19, for discussions of the psychology of Carl Jung.—Eds.

more recent transpersonal conceptualizations (see e.g., Tart, 1977). It is also akin to the views expressed by philosophers such as Leibniz in his Monadology and by Whitehead (1958). Many modern physicists have espoused similar concepts to explain observations made at the quantum and nuclear levels of inquiry: Bohm (1971, 1973)[8] and Wigner (1969), to name two of the foremost.

Holography was initially seen as a powerful *metaphor* to explain the distributed nature of memory traces in the brain (Pribram, 1966). Clinical or experimental lesions of neural tissue do not remove specific memories: Lashley (1960), in his paper on the search for the engram, despaired of comprehending the biological basis of memory organization because of this resilience of learned behavior to brain damage. But a hologram has just these properties: a holographic store, the photographic film, can be injured or cut up into small pieces, and an image can still be reconstructed from any of the pieces—thus the name *hologram*; every part contains sufficient information to characterize the whole.

Holograms are blurred records of images and objects. Each point of light is spread over the entire film, as is every adjacent point. However, the blur is an orderly one, and the set of mathematical expressions that define the blur (such as the Fourier transform) are often called spread functions. A good way to conceptualize the nature of the spread is to visualize the concentric circles of ripples made by a pebble thrown onto the smooth surface of a pond. Throw in two pebbles, and the spreading concentric circles will cross each other and create interference patterns; throw in a handful of pebbles, and, when the interference patterns are at their maximum, take a photograph of the surface of the pond. That photograph is a hologram.

Because the spread of ripples, waves, can be precisely specified, it is possible to recreate the location of impact of each pebble by performing the inverse of the mathematical operation (the spread function) that described the creation of interference patterns. The procedure is similar to that performed by NASA when an orbiting camera is taking a photograph of the surface of Venus or Mars. The photograph is a blur, but, because the speed of the camera relative to the planet is known, that "speed" can be subtracted out and a clear image obtained.

Holograms thus provide a ready instrument for spreading—distributing—information which can easily be retrieved by performing the inverse of the transform by which the hologram is constructed. In fact, when Fourier transforms are used, the same mathematical equation describes the initial transform and its inverse. Thus, by repeating the *same* procedure, an image of an object is obtained.

---

[8] See Weber, Chapter 5, for a detailed examination of David Bohm's theory and its implications for both philosophy and psychology.—Eds.

Why bother with these transformations? What are the attributes of holograms that make them so useful? There are many, but the most important for understanding brain function are: (1) the readiness with which images can be reconstructed from a distributed store; (2) the resistance of a distributed store to injury; (3) a fantastic advantage in computing power: practically instantaneous cross- and autocorrelations are possible (this is why in X-ray tomography calculations are made in the Fourier domain); (4) a tremendous increase in storage capacity—recently a billion bits of retrievable information have been stored in a cubic centimeter of holographic memory; (5) the fact that images constructed from one part of the hologram are recognizably similar to those constructed from another (translational invariance); and (6) the facility for associating two "images" in the holographic store and retrieving both in the absence of one—that is, when only one of the previously associated images is present, illumination of it and the hologram will reconstruct the other, as is the case in associative recall.

This is an impressive list of attributes that can go a long way in explaining hitherto persistent puzzles of brain functioning in memory and perception. But is there any evidence that the brain actually encodes sensory input in a holographic fashion? Over the past decade, such evidence has been coming out of the research of many laboratories, and I have reviewed it elsewhere (Pribram, 1974). Essential is the fact that the mathematical descriptions of sensory processes fit those that describe holography (e.g., Ratliff, 1961, 1965; von Bekesy, 1967), and that the cells of the sensory channel and brain cortex have actually been shown to encode in the holographic domain (Campbell & Robson, 1968; De Valois, Albrecht, & Thorell, 1978a,b; Glezer, Ivanoff, & Tscherbach, 1973; Movshon, Thompson, & Tolhurst, 1978a,b,c; Pollen & Taylor, 1974; Pribram, Lassonde, & Ptito, in press; Robson, 1975; Schiller, Finlay, & Volman, 1976). The evidence is impressive, and the experimental results obtained by De Valois and his students have specifically tested alternative interpretations leaving little doubt as to the validity of the earlier results.

A hologram, as noted above, encodes "ripples" made by a disturbance (a pebble, a sensory input). Ripples are vibrations, waves, and the evidence is that individual cells in the brain cortex encode the frequency of waves within a certain band width. Just as the strings of a musical instrument resonate to a specific range of frequency, so do the cells of the brain cortex. Many hitherto ununderstandable sensory and motor functions can best be explained in terms such as frequency-analytic mechanisms—sensitivity to the spectrum of vibrations and fluctuations of energy in the physical environment and within the organism itself (Pribram, 1971).

It is here that contact with physics is made. Bohm (1971, 1973) has pointed out that the discrepancies in conceptualization that lead to the complementarity between particles and waves arise because, since Galileo, we have relied almost exclusively on *lenses* for our views of the physical macro- and micro-universe. He asks, what if we looked at the world through gratings which produce holograms—that is, took seriously the frequency domain as a possible organization of the universe? Lenses focus, they objectify, particularize, and individuate. Holograms are the result of processes which spread, distribute energy, and provide for a holistic organization in which each part represents the whole and the whole implies each part. Bohm calls the lens view of reality the explicate, and the holographic view the implicate order.

If the brain and the physical universe are seen to share this implicate holographic order, then each portion of the order, each organism, for instance, must in some sense represent the whole universe. In turn, the universe must imply each organism, each of us. Physicists have been drawing such conclusions for a half century (see, e.g., Capra, 1975) but they are new to biologists and experimental psychologists. These conclusions are counter-intuitive and extremely difficult to comprehend (although in the Western philosophical tradition they have been enunciated from pre-Socratic times onward by such eminent thinkers as Plato, Pythagoras, Leibniz, Spinoza, Hegel, and Whitehead) and are, therefore, frightening. In addition, they sound so much like those described by mystics on the basis of their religious transcendental experiences, that hardheaded, mechanistically oriented scientists are apt to shy away from formulations that are derived from an enterprise so totally different and foreign to the ordinary scientific method.

Still, the facts must be explained, and the holographic explanation is a powerful one. A good deal of this power comes from its *precision*. For the first time, a holistic conceptualization can be made as rigorously and mathematically precise as a particularistic one. For psychology, such precision is a necessity since its data are so varied. As noted above, behaviorism provides precision by searching for "proximal," mechanistic causes. Existential-phenomenological psychologies, if they are to attain precision is a necessity since its data are so varied. As noted above, and provide "final" homeostatic, or homeorhetic and teleonomic, "causes." Holographic (holistic) psychology depends on discovering *transformations* for its precision. By specifying the transfer functions involved in moving from one state to another, the holistic approach is made as scientifically respectable as any other. What is, at the moment, missing is some understanding of the relationship between proximal and final causation, and these with transformation. A possible direction of inquiry may be modeled on the development and study of language. There is some reason to believe that very early linguistic communication may have been verbal—that is, that verbs rather than nouns were used. If this is so, then nominalization implies, first, reification of function, that is, activity—and, second, the splitting of object and subject which entails the splitting of actor or cause from acted upon or effect. In this scheme, holistic transformations (one function or action transforming into another) gives way to structure within which proximal causality is formed when the structure is analyzed, whereas "final" causality, that is, teleonomy, is discovered when the relationship of the structure to the whole is in question. Whether this particular direction of inquiry proves fruitful remains to be seen. In any case, however, explicitly adding structure and transformation to the search for causes is long overdue and imperative if scientific conceptualizations are to deal with the richness of problems raised by the advances in scientific technology.

References

Bohm, D. Quantum theory as an indication of a new order in physics. Part A: The development of new orders as shown through the history of physics. *Foundations of Physics*, 1971, *1*(4), 359–381.

Bohm, D. Quantum theory as an indication of a new order in physics. Part B: Implicate and explicate order in physical law. *Foundations of Physics*, 1973, *3*(2), 139–168.

Campbell, F. W., & Robson, J. G. Application of Fourier analysis to the visibility of gratings. *Journal of Physiology*, 1968, *197*, 551–566.

Capra, F. *The tao of physics.* New York: Random House, 1975.

de Saussure, F. *Cours de linguistique générale.* Paris: Payot, 1922.

De Valois, R. L., Albrecht, D. G., & Thorell, L. G. Spatial tuning of LGN and cortical cells in monkey visual system. In H. Spekreijse (Ed.), *Spatial contrast.* Amsterdam: Monograph Series, Royal Netherlands Academy of Sciences, 1978. (a)

De Valois, R. L., Albrecht, D. G., & Thorell, L. G. Cortical cells: Line and edge detectors, or spatial frequency filters? In S. Cool (Ed.), *Frontiers of visual science.* New York: Springer-Verlag, 1978. (b)

Glezer, V. D., Ivanoff, V. A., & Tscherbach, T. A. Investigation of complex and hypercomplex receptive fields of visual cortex of the cat as spatial frequency filters. *Vision Research*, 1973, *13*, 1875–1904.

Jung, C. G. *Collected works.* Princeton: Princeton University Press, 1960.

Lashley, K. In search of the engram. In F. A. Beach & D. O. Hebb (Eds.), *The neuropsychology of Lashley.* New York: McGraw-Hill, 1960.

Merleau-Ponty, M. *The structure of behavior.* Boston: Beacon Press, 1963.

Miller, G. A., Galanter, E., & Pribram, K. H. *Plans and the structure of behavior.* New York: Henry Holt, 1960.

Movshon, J. A. Thompson, I. D., & Tolhurst, D. J. Spatial summation in the receptive field of simple cells in the cat's striate cortex. *Journal of Physiology*, 1978, *283*, 53–77. (a)

Movshon, J. A., Thompson, I. D., & Tolhurst, D. J. Receptive field organization of complex cells in the cat's striate cortex. *Journal of Physiology*, 1978, *283*, 79–99.

Movshon, J. A., Thompson, I. D., & Tolhurst, D. J. Spatial and temporal contrast sensitivity of cells in the cat's areas 17 and 18. *Journal of Physiology*, 1978, *283*, 101–120.

Pollen, D. A., & Taylor, J. H. The striate cortex and the spatial analysis of visual space. In F. O. Schmitt & F. G. Worden (Eds.), *The Neurosciences Third Study Program*. Cambridge Mass.: The M.I.T. Press, 1974.

Pribram, K. H. Proposal for a structural pragmatism: Some neuropsychological considerations of problems in philosophy. In B. Wolman & E. Nagle (Eds.), *Scientific psychology: Principles and approaches*. New York: Basic Books, 1965.

Pribram, K. H. Some dimensions of remembering: Steps toward a neuropsychological model of memory. In J. Gaito (Ed.), *Macromolecules and behavior*. New York: Academic Press, 1966.

Pribram, K. H. *Languages of the brain: Experimental paradoxes and principles of neuropsychology.* Englewood Cliffs, N.J.: Prentice-Hall, 1971.

Pribram, K. H. How is it that sensing so much can do so little? In F. O. Schmitt & F. G. Worden (Eds.), *The Neurosciences Third Study Program*. Cambridge, Mass.: The M.I.T. Press, 1974.

Pribram, K. H., Nuwer, M., & Baron, R. The holographic hypothesis of memory structure in brain function and perception. In R. C. Atkinson, D. H. Krantz, R. C. Luce, & P. Suppes (Eds.), *Contemporary developments in mathematical psychology*. San Francisco: W. H. Freeman, 1974.

Pribram, K. H., Lassonde, M., & Ptito, M. Classification of receptive field properties. In press.

Ratliff, F. Inhibitory interaction and the detection and enhancement of contours. In W. A. Rosenblith (Ed.), *Sensory communication*. New York: Wiley, 1961.

Ratliff, F. *Mach bands: Quantitative studies in neural networks in the retina*. San Francisco: Holden-Day, 1965.

Robson, J. G. Receptive fields: Neural representation of the spatial and intensive attributes of the visual image. In E. C. Carterette (Ed.), *Handbook of perception, Vol. V.: Seeing*. New York: Academic Press, 1975.

Ryle, G. *The Concept of Mind*. New York: Barnes & Noble, 1962.

Schiller, P. H., Finlay, B. L., & Volman, S. F. Quantitative studies of single-cell properties in monkey striate cortex. *Journal of Neurophysiology*, 1976, *39*, 1288–1374.

Skinner, B. F. *About behaviorism*. New York: Vintage Books, 1976.

Tart, C. T. *Psi: Scientific studies of the psychic realm*. New York: Dutton, 1977.

von Bekesy, G. *Sensory inhibition*. Princeton: Princeton University Press, 1967.

Watson, J. B. *Psychology from the standpoint of a behaviorist*. New York: St. Martin's 1979.

Whitehead, A. N. *Modes of thought*. New York: Capricorn Books, 1958.

Wigner, E. P. Epistemology of quantum mechanics: Its appraisals and demands. In M. Grene (Ed.), *The anatomy of knowledge*. London: Routledge & Kegan Paul, 1969.

7

Phenomenology and Neuropsychology
TWO APPROACHES TO CONSCIOUSNESS

Donald M. Moss

There is a growing recognition that the major crisis of modern psychology is its lack of any integrative general paradigm and language to unify its ever more fragmented subdisciplines both among themselves and with extrapsychological theoretical breakthroughs and tendencies. This crisis is currently being addressed most fruitfully by two schools of psychology, which superficially stand in polar opposition to one another. At the one extreme, we find existential-phenomenological psychologists[1] proposing an integrative paradigm under their umbrella, and at the other extreme we find neuropsychology/physiological psychology (e.g., Karl Pribram's approach),[2] making their prescriptions. Strangest of all, we find that the representatives of these two extremes, identified loosely in the popular mind with mentalism and "brainism," respectively, are proposing similar remedies, using similar or at least convergent language, and even quoting some of the same sources (e.g., Brentano, Husserl, and William James on intentionality, volition, and the structure of consciousness).

Our purpose here is twofold: to describe the convergences and agreements between these schools, and to articulate as distinctly as

---

[1] See R. von Eckartsberg, Chapter 2, and Moss and Keen, Chapter 4, for a more general description of the existential-phenomenological approach.—Eds.
[2] See Pribram, Chapter 6, for his views on the relationships among the different approaches in psychology.—Eds.

Donald M. Moss • Ottawa County Community Mental Health, CMH-1111 Fulton, Grand Haven, Michigan 49417.

possible the divergences and disagreements (and, whenever possible, to elucidate the fundamental bases for these differences).

The agreements between these two theoretically sophisticated camps may be taken as normative indicators of the directions and aims of a progressive, unified psychology. The divergences are even more important, however, because they delineate the obstacles remaining to such a unified discipline. In order to simplify our task, most examples will be taken on the one hand from Karl Pribram, as the preeminent spokesman for neuropsychology, and on the other hand from Erwin Straus and Maurice Merleau-Ponty, two similarly prominent figures in existential-phenomenological psychology. Fortunately for us, Straus and Merleau-Ponty have addressed many of the same theoretical issues now raised by Pribram. Their data are in some cases a bit outdated, but their theoretical formulations remain incredibly current.

Convergences

Existential-phenomenology and neuropsychology are in agreement on the following points:

1. That the progress of psychology depends not only on the accumulation of experimental data, but rather more crucially on a process of theoretical reflection. One must "look upward in a hierarchy of scientific endeavors" (Pribram, personal communication), suspend or bracket one's presuppositions (Zaner, 1970), and recognize that all statements and findings are relative to a given, specifiable context or level.

2. That we must carefully differentiate the *level of analysis* at which a statement is true. For example, Pribram shows that: (a) at an anatomical level, motor representation in the cortex is punctate—each locale in the motor cortex is connected with a muscle or even with a part of a muscle; (b) at a physiological level, however, the representation is of movements; but (c) at a behavioral level, the representation is of actions or tasks directed at the environment (Pribram, 1976c.). Statements made at each of the three levels are true, but those at the behavioral level are the most comprehensive.

3. That "consciousness," "mind," or the "mental" is a matter of organizing the relationship between the organism and the environment, that this organism–environment relationship can be characterized as one of *intentionality*, and that understanding the organization of this organism–environment relationship is the crucial task of psychology.

Intentionality, in the sense of Brentano (1955), Husserl (1962), and Merleau-Ponty (1962), is the essential characteristic of human (and animal) consciousness and behavior. All consciousness is consciousness *of something* (i.e., it always has an object).[3] Experience and behavior intend, or are directed toward, an object, goal, or situation there in the world. Intentionality does not signify will or volition, but rather a more basic and pervasive quality of our experience, that is, the reciprocal integrity of organism and environment, man and world. Intentionality signifies that: (a) the organism is oriented toward its situation, (b) the situation organizes the organism's awareness and behavior, and (c) the organism's behavior and awareness in turn organize the situation (Moss, 1978).

4. That the pieces and systems of awareness which we differentiate as *self* and *other* must be understood in terms of the organism–environment relationship.

5. That behavior also simply describes some organism–environment relationship. Therefore, behavior must be understood more broadly—the German *"Verhalten"* and French *"comportment"* are better, because they indicate the active, "intentional" bearing or comporting of oneself toward the environment.

6. Finally, the two schools also agree that psychology cannot naively concern itself with only the *contents* of our experiences. Rather, psychology must also interrogate the ordering of our experience from which this content derives. This shared belief takes the two schools in divergent directions. Pribram moves toward a "constructional" viewpoint, with an emphasis on the contribution of brain processes to an organization of experience. Existential-phenomenology moves toward a "co-constitutional" viewpoint,[4] in which the personal (macroscopic) lived body and the structure of the human world have equally weighty roles in organizing experience and behavior.

Divergences

Existential-phenomenology and neuropsychology have apparent disagreements. These can be summarized as:

1. The single most significant divergence is the tendency of existential-phenomenology and neuropsychology to emphasize different levels of analysis. Existential-phenomenology involves a passionate dedication to the phenomenal world, the macroscopic level, the primary level of everyday life. Neuropsychology, by definition, is concerned with

[3]See R. von Eckartsberg and R. Valle, Chapter 14, for another discussion of intentionality, and Swami Rama, Chapter 15, for a description of pure consciousness (i.e., consciousness *without* an object).—Eds.

[4]See R. Valle, Chapter 21, for a discussion of the existential-phenomenological notion of *co-constitutionality.*—Eds.

brain processes.[5] The crucial issue is how each discipline regards the other's level of analysis in relation to its own. Each explicitly seems to acknowledge that no one level explains all other levels, and that each level must be approached in its own right. Yet, implicitly, the loyalties are obvious, as is the implicit assumption that one's own level of analysis accounts for the others. Existential-phenomenology readily agrees that the prereflective realm of immediate experience is *neurally structured*, but also insists that brain functioning is "world-ally" structured; that is, the organism and environment co-constitute one another.

As one example, sensory deprivation[6] shows that neurally structured learning dissolves in the absence of an *actual situation* that orients the organism. Or, to take another example, Lashley's rats could still traverse a maze after many lesions to the motor cortex undermined the original neural structuring (they *rolled* down the maze in a restructured behavior directed to the same task/end); but they would never perform maze-traversing behavior without a maze (Lashley, 1960). The behavior is organized by both situation and organismic disposition.

The acknowledgement that a behavior is neurally structured does not "explain away" or refute the significance or meaningfulness of the behavior as a response to a situation at the macroscopic level.

2. There is a fundamental difference on another point: Where do we turn for information on the organism's environment? Pribram seems to say, to the physicists and experts on probability, particle theory, etc.— experts on the structure of the physical universe of which the brain is a part (Pribram, 1975, p. 180).

Existential-phenomenology emphatically states "NO!" The physical universe is not the organism's true environment. The organism responds not to physical conditions or things but rather to *meanings*. Pribram recognizes that the *percept* is not the stimulus—that the organism is attuned to invariances in the environment even when the physical stimuli change (due to manipulation of environment or of bodily orientation). The existential-phenomenologist insists that these invariances are invariances of meaning. Two physically divergent stimulus configurations may signify the same meaning at a macroscopic level (for example, telegram, phone call, or direct observation may reveal the birth of a new

---

[5]Wilder Penfield's (1975) statement about the neurophysiologist applies equally well to the neuropsychologist: "The challenge that comes to every neurophysiologist is to explain in terms of brain mechanisms all that men have come to consider the work of the mind, if he can" (p. 73). However, Penfield's own methodological and theoretical leap, to assign every aspect of mind that cannot be accounted for strictly neurologically, to an immaterial and dualistically conceived mind, is dubious at best. Pribram's concept of "emergentism" (Pribram, 1975) is more soundly reasoned.

[6]See Lilly, Chapter 8, for a discussion of sensory *isolation*, human experience, and the brain.—Eds.

child). The framework for *meaning* is the experiential, biographical, historical world, the world of human places, days, and hours, and not the homogeneous, isotropic space–time of geometry and physics. The meaningful environment for human actions is the unquestioned and taken-for-granted sphere of everyday life events and situations (the "life-world"; Husserl, 1970).[7] The existential-phenomenologist thus equates the environment with the "physiognomy of the experiential world"; the experts in this domain are poets, novelists, painters, and musicians. There are evolving mediations between these two extreme positions (e.g., those applying neurophysiological and psychophysiological research methodologies to yogic practices such as meditation), but the difference remains a fundamental one.

3. Consider the so-called "diving duck" criticism. The history of our century is one of incredible revolutions in science and technology. To a great extent, the history of modern psychology is the story of the application of models, concepts, and metaphors taken from science and technology in order to illuminate psychological phenomena. From Freud's implicit hydraulic, energic, and economic metaphors and explicit neuroelectrical model (Pribram & Gill, 1976) through present-day applications of computer information-processing and optical information-processing models for brain processes, psychology has consistently been enriched, as it were, from the outside. Pribram's work is in the vanguard in this effort.

Psychology, however, has another task which is the direct phenomenological analysis of human behavior and experiencing (a) on the macroscopic level and (b) on its own terms. Erwin Straus (1980) has criticized a typical behavior of the psychological researcher, one that has recurred throughout the history of psychology. The analysis of psychological phenomena proceeds smoothly for a time; relationships among behaviors, situations, and persons seem to become clearer and clearer; when suddenly, at a crucial and often difficult juncture, the researcher, like a diving duck, dips momentarily below the psychological level and returns to the surface with a mouthful of subterranean (biological, neurological, and biochemical) terminology. Purporting to explain the problems at the phenomenal level, this terminology at best *displaces* the problems to another level, without resolving them. Do the basal ganglia truly serve as *intentionality mechanisms* (Pribram, 1976a, p. 52)? Perhaps, but the clarification of the modalities and forms of the or-

[7]See Giorgi (1970) for a discussion of the concept of *meaning* in psychology based on the work of Wilhelm Dilthey, Franz Brentano, and the phenomenological school. Merleau-Ponty's (1962) contribution in this regard is also rich: "Because we are in the world, we are *condemned to meaning*, and we cannot do or say anything without its acquiring a name in history" (p. xix).

ganism's intentional relationships to a field of events and others remains to be investigated, as does the topography of that field. It is important to know which brain areas and functions are the *conditions for the possibility* of intentionality and consciousness, and, even more importantly, how they contribute to the total structure of intentional consciousness, but the question remains, "What is intentionality in its own right"?

To inquire about "intentionality in its own right" signifies, first of all, the suspension of all questions about real causes at another level of analysis, either inner (e.g., neurobiological mechanisms) or outer (e.g., objective environmental determinants), and the taking up of conscious life without prejudice, just as it presents itself. In the immediate givenness of experience, one finds human beings

> intentionally related to certain things—animals, houses, fields, etc. . . . that is, as consciously affected by these things, actively attending to them or in general perceiving them, actively remembering them, thinking about them, planning and acting in respect to them. (Husserl, 1970, p. 233).

An intentional analysis of these phenomena respects their manifest givenness, and articulates or renders explicit the directedness of the "intentional act" in question, be it behavior or experience, toward its object. Further, without questioning the real, objective composition of the intentional object, such an analysis articulates *how* this object is given to the percipient individual, what import or *meaning* its present appearance conveys to the individual, and within what situational, spatiotemporal, and motivational *horizons* this object takes on meaning.[8]

For example, the piston engine is a *condition for the possibility* of the funeral procession to the cemetery for the burial of an aged woman. Nevertheless, the meaning, direction, and experience of this "procession behavior" can be understood only by reference to the macroscopic world of human figures, events, and relationships. The piston engine existed a week, a month, a year ago, but the moment of burial, the grief, and the memorial are on hand *now* and *here*. The order of the participants in the procession, as well as their personal mode of involvement, are determined not by the conditions of the various engines involved but, rather, according to protocol, custom, and family relationships. Who is this deceased person to the participant—beloved mother or spouse, revered grandmother, or merely some old woman one knows by name?

To continue with this example for a moment, existential-phenomenology recognizes the contributions of each level—the contributions of mechanisms (or "conditions for the possibility") as well as of

---

[8]Elsewhere I have illustrated such an analysis of "intentionality in its own right" in the form of an investigation of human visual consciousness (Moss & Keen, 1978).

sociological, cultural, and biographical levels. It is quite ready to acknowledge that the level of mechanisms affects the shape of the activity at all levels (the advent of the motor car affected funeral rituals and customs, the development of the cerebral cortex radically reshaped the life of organisms), but also insists that the relationships at the phenomenal level be respected and explored in their own right. This is the danger of being a diving duck; that is, the analysis or discussion of the various levels becomes indiscriminately mixed or confused: "such statements are a mixture of mind talk and brain talk . . . that irritate the purist" (Pribram, 1976b, p. 300).

4. *Constructional realism versus "naive" phenomenological realism.* The difference is quite complex, not at all simple. Pribram points to the role of brain processes in "constructing" the world as perceived. Yet existential-phenomenology has also emphasized the "constituting functions" of the ego (Husserl), the constitutive role of the lived body (Merleau-Ponty), and the role of the human body and upright posture in articulating the world of sensory experience (Straus). Thus, neither school of thought naively recognizes a reality *per se* unaffected by the presence and condition of the organism. Nevertheless, there remain several differences: (a) the existential-phenomenologist has remained skeptical about any equivalences between organization at a microscopic or dissected level of analysis and the structure of the macroscopic world, and (b) more importantly, existential-phenomenology insists that, in spite of the principle of co-constitution by which man/organism and world shape one another, the organism is oriented toward, perceives directly, and comports itself toward objects in the world, not images or stimuli in the brain. In Husserl's terms (Husserl, 1962), the objects are always transcendent to the stream of activities which intend them. We must rigorously uphold the distinction between intentional act and intentional object or we will fall into the psychological error of regarding the objects as the *creations* of consciousness. These "constitutive" or "constructive" functions organize and shape the reality which we nevertheless encounter *there,* at arm's length, before us. Both Pribram and Gibson (1972) are correct.

5. Once again, the dedication to the preferred level of analysis is important to consider. The existential-phenomenological defense of the priority of macroscopic, experienced reality is many-pronged: (a) all statements about brain processes are couched in terms and concepts that are ultimately (historically and etymologically) derivatives of everyday experience—if everyday experience is devalued, the scientific edifice built upon it is undermined, and (b) the scientist continues to inhabit everyday reality, even as he enters the laboratory—it remains his primary reality,

and many of his motives for his scientific endeavors are intelligible only by reference to this macroscopic level inhabited by things, events, and others (wife, children, peers, etc.).

6. Consider an example that illustrates how the difference between the basic presuppositions of the two schools about "primary reality" results in questions about the same phenomena being posed in opposite directions: both Pribram and Merleau-Ponty were fascinated by the ability of the human being and higher-order primate to recognize the image in the mirror as "oneself." Both regarded this example as important for the understanding of self-consciousness. Both would have agreed that "the disposition toward self-consciousness needs to be constructed and is not universal among organisms" (Pribram, 1976b, p. 305). The agreement ends there.

A. Thus Pribram (1976b) starts out with the assumption that the primary reality resides in brain functions. Awareness and experiences are thus thought to exist first within the head, and the problem becomes: How does the individual project these experiences to a point some distance from the receptive surface—that is, out into the world? Posing the question in this way, Pribram infers the following answers: (1) a holographiclike mechanism disposes us to locate our experiences out there in the world, (2) some of our experiences cannot be projected—these make up the body image, and (3) self-consciousness develops from the remainder of consciousness when external attributions do not occur. A distinction appears between sensory-neural interfaces that project their images and those that do not; ultimately this distinction results in a complete functional disjunction into separate channels processing awareness of self (nonprojected) and of environment (projected). The mirror image is regarded as the projected version of the nonprojected body image. Thus, starting from the assumption that the primary reality is brain functioning, Pribram ends by postulating a functional, neurophysiological basis for self-consciousness or *intentionality*, which he defines as the capacity to distinguish between self and percept, and to perceive both at once. (Contrast Pribram's definition of intentionality to the phenomenological understanding outlined above.)

Pribram explicitly denies that he regards brain functions as the primary reality (personal communication). Nevertheless, in his discussion of the mirror image, as well as throughout his writings on consciousness, he begins by accepting as primary givens the neural activity at the receptive interface between the organism and its environment. He then attempts to construct an explanation for how the organism projects experiences from the internal neural channels to a distant location external to the organism. What we experience, according to Pribram (1976c), is not the object, but rather a holographically projected image, a representation constructed by brain processes. This explanatory sequence certainly appears to assign greater explanatory weight (reality) to the neural level. Epistemologically, a researcher discloses to us his "primary reality" by his selection of a departure point. This point of departure prefigures and determines the ultimate picture of macroscopic reality resulting from the research. The product of Pribram's work is a world drawn in the image of man's brain: "what is it that we perceive . . . we perceive a physical universe not much different in basic organization from that of the brain" (1975, p. 184).[9] Pribram's is a broader metaphysic than that of most contemporary scientists, but he still remains confined within the limits of the particular language he selects for his interrogations: "A picture held us captive. And we could not get outside it, for it lay in our language and our language seemed to repeat it to us inexorably" (Wittgenstein, 1958, p. 115). This same general problem arises whenever anyone attempts to address general ontological or metaphysical questions from the vantage point of a specific positive science. And yet these questions cannot be avoided; we implicitly adopt solutions to them whenever we do research. There follows the necessary role of philosophical criticism in the empirical sciences. To quote Wittgenstein again, the purpose of philosophy is: "To shew the fly the way out of the fly bottle" (1958, p. 115).

B. Let us now return to phenomenology and show how its different point of departure and differing sense of primary reality guide its inquiries into the same phenomenon—the mirror image—in a very different direction. Merleau-Ponty (1964a) begins within the phenomenological *epoché;* that is, he suspends all questions or doubts about phenomenal, macroscopic, experiential reality. He examines the individual encounter with the mirror image as it is experienced. First of all, the mirror image is experienced as *out there* in the world, exactly like all other objects. The neurophysiological functioning of the sensorium is taken for granted here. Thus, the question is not how do percepts get projected out into the world, but, rather, how is the mirror image, which is initially discovered out there in its virtual position in the depth of the mirror, displaced back into a connection with myself? How do I come to recognize that this flash of colors in the mirror is intimately identified with myself, even though it is *there,* and I feel myself to be *here?*

[9]In contrast, let us delineate the phenomenological position: the structure of the perceptual world is a totality with its own internal laws of equilibrium. The physicist's concept of the physical object is inadequate to describe the experiential (intentional) object. Neural functioning, with its internal laws, constitutes a necessary partial condition for the existence of the perceptual world; but the laws governing this part are absorbed and become indiscernable within the larger equilibrium of the perceptual world as a whole (Merleau-Ponty, 1963, pp. 205–208). To describe the basic organization of "what we perceive" as no different from that of brain functioning is to falsify this larger equilibrium at the phenomenal level, as well as to equate wrongly the physical universe with the perceptual world.

If we assume this phenomenological faith in the world of experience, then it would seem that Pribram makes a dubious step when he regards the visual mirror image as an external projection of the neurophysiologically distinct system of self-perception based on intero- and proprioceptions. Merleau-Ponty regards the recognition of the mirror image by the child as important precisely because it involves a de-centering. The child is forced to leave his own habitual, "subjective," body-centric perspective on the world, and to assume the mirror perspective on himself, that is, to view himself as others see him—in his objectivity. It is precisely because the recognition of the mirror image involves a mental act radically different from the infantile, intero- and proprioceptively based body image (and is *not* merely its external projection) that French psychology came to regard the "stage of the mirror" as a developmental milestone (Lacan, 1968a,b; Merleau-Ponty, 1964a,b).

The mirror image is not perceived in a different modality than are the other visible objects of our world; the hypothesis of disjoined functional channels would be superfluous in this instance. According to Merleau-Ponty, the experiencing human being discovers something about himself in the world, *there*, which he refers back to himself, *here*. Consciousness of the body is interdependent with that of outside things (Merleau-Ponty, 1964b). This is the dawning of the reflective consciousness. There are both literal and metaphorical mirrors: we also perceive others in their reactions to ourselves, and thereby see "ourselves in their eyes." Merleau-Ponty (1964b) has stated: "It is necessary that the child understand that there are two points of view on himself, that his body which feels is equally of the visible not only for himself but for others" (p. 135).

It remains true that the intense unwillingness or inability to gaze upon oneself in the mirror is pathognomonic of deep-seated deficits in self-awareness, capacity for psychological self-insight, and, in general, reflectivity. Our awareness of self is thus to a great extent—except for the immediate self-awareness accompanying nonhabituated (novel) activity—mediated by the world of experienceable things and others.[10]

In conclusion, Merleau-Ponty commences by accepting phenomenal

---

[10]Elsewhere I have discussed the inability to face, accept, and own the mirror perspective in the case of the chronically obese, for whom the mirror perspective is disqualifying, stigmatizing, and shaming, and the correlary deficit in self-awareness and individuation (Moss, 1977a,b). There is also another line of research, exemplified by the work of Gordon Gallup on self-recognition in primates (Gallup, 1977; Gallup, McClure, Hill, & Bundy, 1971), which should further clarify these issues. In particular, behavioral observations of primates may resolve one crucial question: Is the viewing of the reflection of the organism's own body *instrumental* in establishing a more integrated identity? Or, as Gallup's work seems to suggest, is the ability of the primate to recognize its body in the mirror merely symptomatic that such a solidified identity has already developed, most likely through contact with other members of the species?

reality, and ends by posing questions about how the child learns to assume a different perspective on himself, still within the level of macroscopic reality.

Conclusion

In the preceding I have outlined both the convergences and the divergences between existential-phenomenology and modern neuropsychology. The commonalities are considerable and imply normative prescriptions for psychology as a whole, especially: (a) respect for the role of theory in scientific psychological research, (b) a careful differentiation of the level of analysis at which research is conducted, and (c) a dedication to the investigation of the organism–environment relationship and its functional organization.

The divergences are also not to be underestimated. As shown by the final example concerning the mirror image, the original points of departure and preferred levels of analysis of each school definitely steer research in different, even antithetical directions. Dialogue between the two schools becomes all the more essential in light of the kinds of divergences which occur. In some instances, the research results of one school may serve as an actual corrective to the other's research: for example, I think that Pribram's discussion of neuropsychological aspects of recognizing the mirror image suffers in precision, because it slurs the essential differences between the intero-/proprioceptive body image and the exteroceptive visual image of one's own body. To take another example, the phenomenological investigation of consciousness (Moss & Keen, 1978) has shown that affectivity, motility, and activity in the face of the world are equally as essential to the structure of consciousness as sentient awareness; this calls into question the adequacy of the information-processing models of consciousness, and compels neuropsychology to extend its theorizing. Further, Luria's (1973) neuropsychological research has disclosed that many seemingly disparate activities—such as spatial orientation, arithmetic, and complex logico-grammatical understanding—share the same neurological base; this raises the challenge for phenomenology of discerning their commonalities at the psychological level (Moss, 1978).

I have attempted to show elsewhere (Moss, 1978) that phenomenology and neuropsychology are complementary and compatible in other respects as well, and that breakthroughs by either school may serve to enrich the other's research. There are times when Pribram appears to paint the world at large in the monotone gray of the brain (e.g., Pribram, 1975), but in his next breath he seems always to recognize the dangers inherent in such a tendency and to call for a genuine dialogue among diverse schools, perspectives, and levels of analysis in order to transcend fragmented views and construct the whole. More than most contemporary psychologists, he recognizes the limitations inherent for each of us in our disciplinary native tongues, and recognizes our efforts at a comprehensive truth as merely that—efforts and gestures. Pribram has strained the most recent concepts of neuropsychology and cybernetics to the utmost to create a conceptual space to house that dialogue. The convergences with phenomenology in this regard are striking. In the 1930s, Merleau-Ponty welded together the vocabularies of Gestalt theory and Hegelian dialectics in order to encompass both Pavlov and Freud. The result, a work called *The Structure of Behavior* served simultaneously to enrich the phenomenological comprehension of human behavior and to produce a clarification of basic concepts in neurophysiology and psychology which retains value even to the present day.

The conceptual overlap between Pribram's work and phenomenology is also considerable. Pribram's concept of "emergentism," the idea that consciousness and the mental are emergent properties of the complex structures of neural functioning (Pribram, 1976c) bears comparison to Merleau-Ponty's notion of subordinate and superordinate dialectics of body and mind:

> The body in general is an ensemble of paths already traced, of powers already constituted; the body is the acquired dialectical soil upon which a higher "formation" is accomplished, and the soul is the meaning which is then established. (Merleau-Ponty, 1963, p. 210)

Further, Pribram's concept of intrinsic properties which are realized (or embodied) in an extrinsic medium bears comparison with the phenomenological notions of essence and existence, *Sosein* and *Dasein*, that is, of the *Eidos* which actualizes itself in the *hyle* (Husserl, 1962; Strauss, 1966, 1980). Throughout Pribram's writings are scattered many other examples of concepts which deserve a close and reflective reading by psychologist and philosopher alike.

In closing, let us not overlook the fact that both Pribram's "emergentism" and the phenomenological view conceptualize body and mind in a *monistic* fashion: the higher levels of experience and behavior are built or founded upon the lower. This contrasts sharply with the dualistic views of others, such as Penfield (1975) and Tart (1978).[11] Dualistic views polarize body and mind. In dualism, body becomes mere mechanism and matter, stripped of the vital and humanly meaningful qualities which adhere to it in everyday life. Mind, on the other hand, becomes a

---

[11]See Tart, Chapter 10, for a discussion of his dualistic position, "emergent interactionism".—Eds.

spiritual entity devoid of concreteness. Conceptually, dualism is dishonest because "mind" is assigned characteristics which we actually derive from observing embodied behavior, and bodily mechanisms are assigned attributes which we actually encounter only in animated, ensouled (be-seelte) bodies. Phenomenology has critized the tendency of psychology to fall back upon body–mind dualisms as conceptual laziness. For phenomenology, human consciousness and behavior can be comprehended neither as objective material things, nor as spiritual processes (Moss & Keen, 1978). Phenomenological psychology begins with a structural analysis of the living human body, in its intentional, meaningful relation to its environment. As Hans Jonas puts it: "In the body, the knot of being is tied which dualism does not unravel but cut" (Jonas, 1966, p. 25).

References

Brentano, F. Psychologie vom empirischen Standpunkt, I. Hamburg: Felix Meiner Verlag, 1955.

Gallup, G. G. Self-recognition in primates: A comparative approach to the bidirectional properties of consciousness. American Psychologist, 1977, 32, 329–338.

Gallup, G. G., McClure, M. K., Hill, S. D., & Bundy, R. A. Capacity for self-recognition in differentially reared chimpanzees. Psychological Record, 1971, 21, 69–74.

Gibson, J. J. A theory of direct visual perception. In J. R. Royce, & W. W. Rozeboom (Eds.), The psychology of knowing. New York: Gordon & Breach, 1972.

Giorgi, A. Psychology as a human science. New York: Harper & Row, 1970.

Husserl, E. Ideas: General introduction to pure phenomenology. New York: Collier, 1962.

Husserl, E. The crisis of European sciences and transcendental phenomenology. Evanston, Ill.: Northwestern University Press, 1970.

Jonas, H. The phenomenon of life: Toward a philosophical biology. New York: Delta, 1966.

Lacan, J. The language of the self. Baltimore: The Johns Hopkins Press, 1968.(a)

Lacan, J. The mirror phase as formative of the I. New Left Review, 1968, 51, 71–77.(b)

Lashley, K. S. In F. A. Beach, D. O. Hebb, C. T. Morgan, & H. W. Nissen (Eds.), The neuropsychology of Lashley: Selected papers. New York: McGraw-Hill, 1960.

Luria, A. R. The working brain. London: Penguin, 1973.

Merleau-Ponty, M. Phenomenology of perception. London: Routledge & Kegan Paul, 1962.

Merleau-Ponty, M. The structure of behavior. Boston: Beacon Press, 1963.

Merleau-Ponty, M. Maurice Merleau-Ponty at the Sorbonne, Bulletin de Psychologie, 1964, 236(18), 3–6.(a)

Merleau-Ponty, M. The child's relations with others. In M. Merleau-Ponty, The Primacy of Perception. Evanston, Ill.: Northwestern University Press, 1964.(b)

Moss, D. M. Distortions in human embodiment. Paper presented at the meeting of the Society for Phenomenology and Existential Philosophy, New York, New York, November, 1977.(a)

Moss, D. M. Transformations in body image following intestinal bypass surgery. In A. Giorgi, C. T. Fischer, & E. L. Murray (Eds), Duquesne papers in phenomenological psychology (Vol. II). Pittsburgh: Duquesne University Press, 1977.(b)

Moss, D. M. Brain, body, and world: Perspectives on body image. In R. S. Valle & M. King

(Eds.), *Existential-phenomenological alternatives for psychology*. New York: Oxford University Press, 1978.

Moss, D. M. & Keen, E. *The nature of consciousness. I: The phenomenological approach*. Paper presented as part of the symposium "The Nature of Consciousness" at the American Psychological Association Convention, Toronto, August, 1978.

Penfield, W. *Mystery of the mind*. Princeton: Princeton University Press, 1975.

Pribram, K. Toward a holonomic theory of perception. In S. Ertel, L. Kemmler, & M. Stadler (Eds.), *Gestalttheorie in der modernen Psychologie*. Köln: Erich Wengenroth, 1975.

Pribram, K. Self-consciousness and intentionality. In G. E. Schwartz & D. Shapiro (Eds.), *Consciousness and self-regulation* (Vol. I). New York: Plenum, 1976.(a)

Pribram, K. Problems concerning the structure of consciousness. In G. Globus, G. Maxwell, & I. Savodnik (Eds.), *Consciousness and the brain*. New York: Plenum, 1976.(b)

Pribram, K. Mind, it does matter. In S. F. Spicker & H. T. Engelhardt (Eds.), *Philosophical dimensions of the neuromedical sciences*. Dordrecht, Holland: D. Reidel Publishing, 1976. (c)

Pribram, K. & Gill, M. *Freud's project reassessed*. New York: Basic Books, 1976.

Straus, E. *Phenomenological psychology*. New York: Basic Books, 1966.

Straus, E. *The Archimedean point*. Pittsburgh, Pa.: Duquesne University Press, 1980.

Tart, C. T. *Transpersonal realities or neuropsychological illusions? Toward an empirically testable dualism*. Paper presented as part of the symposium "The Nature of Consciousness" at the American Psychological Association Convention, Toronto, August, 1978.

Wittgenstein, L. *Philosophical investigations*. Oxford: Blackwell, 1958.

Zaner, R. *The way of phenomenology: Criticism as a philosophical discipline*. New York: Pegasus, 1970.

III

Psychological Frontiers

Psychological theorizing is characterized by a basic division regarding the nature of the relationship of brain to mind. The first position, that human awareness is merely an emergent property of the brain's neurophysiological organization and functioning, is presented by John Lilly. Timothy Leary then offers a future-oriented perspective on the evolution of a gentically preprogrammed human consciousness. In presenting his theory, Leary implicitly incorporates the "mind-contained" hypothesis which Lilly describes.

The idea that some aspects of consciousness are of a qualitatively different nature than physical processes is addressed by Charles Tart in his discussion of "emergent interactionism." Tart also believes that consciousness is an emergent property, but not of brain alone—brain *and* mind must both be considered in order to account for human awareness. Tart's theory, therefore, stands as a bridge between the first position described above and the second position: that human consciousness transcends the world of sensation and rational thought. This position is addressed in later sections of the book (please note that John Lilly should not be identified exclusively with the "mind-contained" hypothesis since he expresses, in other published works, a viewpoint consistent with the second position as well).

8

The Mind Contained in the Brain[1]

A CYBERNETIC BELIEF SYSTEM

John C. Lilly

In American society, there is a vast array of belief systems about the mind and the brain. There are those primarily in religion who believe that the mind is something greater than computations done by a biocomputer, which demonstrates an implicit faith that the human mind somehow is connected with a human spirit or soul that transcends the everyday operations of the normal human mind. Such concepts generate a "mind unlimited" belief.

This belief in an unlimited mind available to man goes back into our dim, distant past, long before written history. It is connected with one's religious feelings, with one's religious experience, and with the traditional teachings derived from the formalized religions. Over the millennia, this belief system has become quite powerful and determines the thinking of millions of persons on this planet. It is only recently that a possible alternative to this belief system has arisen, in science and in medicine.

The new belief system arises from studies of medicine, neurology, neurophysiology to a certain extent, but also from the pragmatic way that man and woman treat one another in their everyday relations in the law, in business, and in science. In our everyday pragmatic relationships, we assume that the other person whom we are dealing with is contained within his or her body. We assume that in his or her absence we cannot

[1]This chapter first appeared as Chapter 7 in Lilly (1977), *The Deep Self*. It is reprinted here (with revisions) with the permission of the publisher.—Eds.

John C. Lilly • Human Software Inc., 33307 Decker School Road, Malibu, California 90265.

deal with him or her. When he or she is, say, more than a few hundred feet away, in a sense he or she is missing, absent. When another person is out of reach of our voice in the external world, or out of reach by telephone, somehow or other we have lost contact with him or her. At least we cannot make mutual decisions without his or her presence and his or her agreement in the presence of either the voice or the person.

If there were a secure means of communication without the known physical means of communication, such as voice, vision, vocal feedback, and so forth, we would undoubtedly use these other channels. In the pragmatic everyday world we use that which is available to us. Theoretical possibilities do not enter into our everyday calculations in relationships with others.

Thus, we have arrived implicitly, if not explicitly, at a system of dealing with others in which we depend on the telephone, the telegraph, the letter, the TV image, to link one of us with others. It is only rarely that we have experiences that allow us to say that there are possibilities of communication other than those that currently are represented by the visual image, by the vocal expression, or by the written word.

Thus, in a rather sloppy way, we assume that each person somehow is contained within his or her body, and that to deal with him or her, the body or a known communication means must be available in order to communicate. Out of sight, out of sound, and away from written materials, with no TV set, we are each pragmatically alone. Thus, from the empirical-experience point of view, the person is relegated at least to the body that apparently houses him or her.

Certain empirical observations made over the millennia have convinced certain persons who have studied the subject that the person is not only confined to a body, but is confined to the brain within that body. In the experience of a sufficiently powerful blow to the head, one can see the person disappear, as it were. The body goes into a coma, one can no longer speak with the person within that body–brain, the usual means of communication are cut off abruptly and completely. That particular person is assumed to be unconscious; that is, incapable of communication with those that surround him or her. Such a person for a time remains uncommunicative and then somehow seems to return to conscious use of the body, and communication is resumed.

In medicine, for many years it has been assumed, on the basis of such observations, that the person somehow is a function of intact cerebral cortical activity within the central nervous system. The person is limited to a functioning intact brain, undamaged, not under anesthesia, in a so-called normal state for that particular brain. Such observations have led to the contained-mind hypothesis, or, if you wish, belief system.

This belief system dominates our law; for example, in *habeas corpus* doctrine, which says that the only way that the law can operate is to have the body present, in such proceedings the body is obtained. Similarly, in psychiatry, the necessity of the presence of the patient, communication with the patient, is necessary for a diagnosis. In arriving at the diagnosis, one assumes that all the information needed is somehow contained within that particular body, in that particular brain. In the business world one deals with other humans in bodies and deals with their particular kinds of brains, kinds of minds contained in those brains, on the pragmatic assumption that, if the person is present, one can make a deal; if the person is not present, one cannot make a deal with that particular person.

Quite common in the United States are those who believe in both systems: the contained-mind and the uncontained-mind belief systems. On a particular day of the week these people attend formal meetings in which the uncontained-mind hypothesis operates, such as in church on Sunday, or with a religious group, and during the rest of the week they operate using the contained-mind belief.

At night during sleep one leaves the external reality in the consensus way of operating in that external reality with other persons, and enters into regions in which there are apparently other laws, other beliefs. In hypnotic states, in dream states, the laws of the external world may or may not rule that which happens. One can go through complete experiences with apparently real other persons, either known or unknown persons; one can melt and flow as if a liquid, one can become a point, a line, or a solid, one can control somewhat what the other persons say and do, etc. The laws of the apparent internal reality of the dream states do not have the constraints that the external reality has. There are other sets of laws of the internal reality that are far different, and yet may overlap those of the external reality. In such states, the mind may seem to be unlimited, to extend out beyond the confines of one's own brain, of one's own body. Each of us can have such experiences isolated within oneself each night in our beds.

The contained mind thus becomes an apparently uncontained mind, asleep dreaming at night. Similarly, under the influence of anesthetics, psychedelic chemicals, of trance, and of the isolation tank,[2] one can enter into states of being in which the mind seems apparently to be unlimited, not constrained by the body and brain.

Let us then develop more specifically the contained-mind belief system and see if it can embrace both sets of phenomena; those of

[2]The isolation tank (designed by Lilly) provides a contained environment in which solitary individuals can experience their thoughts and feelings in physical surroundings with minimal external and sensory stimulation. See Lilly (1977) for an examination of issues relevant to the tank experience.—Eds.

ordinary everyday waking life, interacting with others, and the dream states, trance states and psychedelic states, and religious experiences.

In this belief system we are in effect saying that the mind is a function of the brain's activities, and of nothing else—except the changes in that mind as modulated by exchanges and participations in an external world with the solidity of the planet and the complexity of other humans and other animals and plants. Let us also assume that we can specify all the inputs to this brain and all the outputs from this brain. The inputs are vision, hearing, tactile sense, position sense, detection of accelerations owing to gravity and owing to motion, the sense of smell, the senses delegated to the regulation of the body itself. The outputs are restricted to muscular activities, glandular activities, the intake and the output of food and its products. In this belief system there are no hidden inputs or outputs. The inputs and outputs to and from the brain are those within the body and at the surface of the body.

Complete physical isolation of the body thus leads to attenuation or elimination of all inputs and all outputs. The physical isolation tank eliminates all of the inputs to and from the body insofar as this is possible to do. The isolation tank does not eliminate the inputs and outputs to and from the brain within the body itself. The body's motions are still available, and only by voluntary inhibition of bodily motion can isolation of the brain from this source of feedback stimulation be eliminated or attenuated.

The isolation tank prevents interactions with the external reality and assures a solitudinous body and a solitudinous biocomputer within that body with no further needful exchanges with the external reality.

The contained-mind hypothesis thus says that the isolation tank isolates the body completely, insofar as our present science is able to specify isolation itself.

In this belief system, then, there is no way that a person in an isolation tank can communicate with other persons. All channels of communication have been eliminated. This belief system states that there are no mysterious unknown means of communication remaining to that particular isolated person.

A person believing this contained-mind hypothesis will then take all experiences reported by such isolated people as being evidence of what can happen in a contained mind within a contained brain. All states, no matter how far out or how far removed they are from everyday experience, that are subsequently recounted as having been described by a person in isolation, will be accounted for by an observer with this belief system as having taken place totally within the isolated body–brain of that particular person.

Some persons experiencing the isolation tank have other belief systems based on their previous experience in the tank. Some have other belief systems based upon direct personal experience without using a tank, using experiences of anesthesia, of coma, of near brushes with death, in addition to tank experiences. Thus, there is a gap between people with the contained-mind belief system and those with the mind-unlimited belief system.

Let us examine the contained-mind hypothesis and see if, using such a belief system, we can construct the possibilities of experiences that seem to belong to the region of the unlimited mind, and account for them, at least theoretically, adequately. In order to do this we must be able to account for dream phenomena, for psychedelic experiences, for coma experiences, for deep religious experiences, and similar phenomena reported by many hundreds of persons.

In order to simplify our descriptions, let us assume that we are, each of us, isolated in an isolation tank, floating in the darkness, the silence, removed from all known communication means.

At the beginning of such an experience one has moved from the external reality, including: clothing, a lighted environment filled with noise, with many, many signals coming into the body, from many, many different sources, including other people. Each of us takes off our clothes, immerses oneself in the tank, floating at the surface in the darkness and the silence, alone. At first one remembers the immediately preceding external reality fairly vividly. Slowly these memories can disappear, or can be maintained by conscious processes. As one abandons these memories of the external reality, one may become preoccupied with the sensations of the body floating in the blackness and silence and warmth.

After many hours of exposure to such an environment, repeated on a daily schedule, one gradually increases one's speed of abandoning the memories of the external reality and the preoccupation with the floating sensations of the body in the dark in the isolation tank. One now becomes aware that one is aware, quite independently, of the body or of the external reality. One says, in effect, I know that I am conscious and functioning without the interlock with the external world; preoccupation with remaining sources of stimulation within the body passes away, the heart and the respiration and the sensations from the skin all are attenuated to the point where they can be forgotten. One has gone beyond seeing the differences between open eyes, closed eyes, changing the rate and depth of respiration, playing with one's heart, and similar activities.

If one is in a disturbed state because of some interaction that has taken place in the external reality, this disturbance will go on sometimes for hours. One may be totally obsessed with some sort of a hurt given by another person, some sort of quarrel that one has had. In the tank, eventually this kind of thinking and preoccupation can also die away.

One may then fall asleep and go through a long dream sequence and then wake up again in the sense that one comes back to the body and the brain, out of the dream world. With more and more exposure to the tank, one finds that, between the state of dreaming and the state of being wide awake and conscious of one's body, there are hundreds if not thousands of other states of being in which one's consciousness is unimpaired and apparently disconnected from the brain and the body.

Let us try to construct a partial catalog of these states and see if we can construct a theory that can account for each portion of that catalog. Since that which exists in the external reality and connects us with it is missing, we will call this catalog a catalog of the internal realities.

1. One has entered into a dream state in which one's body is intact and one is walking around on the very familiar planet in which one has existed in the past up to the present. One is carrying on conversations both with persons known to oneself and possibly with strangers. It is all a very familiar reality based upon one's previous experiences in the external world. In the contained-mind belief system, we assume that this is a simulation of the Self and of the external world (such external-reality simulations being part of the internal reality) that one is generating within one's own brain. In such scenarios there is nothing that is surprising, nothing new, nothing unique, nothing bizarre, and one is quite content that this is as one lives and has lived in the past in the external reality. In the contained-mind belief system this is a simulation of Self, of one's body and of the external reality of oneself, of one's body and of the external reality. For most persons this is a very safe simulation, and expresses a large number of their personal dreams. In the tank it has been noticed that such experiences have a brilliance and a "reality" far greater than most dreams. The subject of such an experience seems to be stronger than he or she is in his or her normal dreaming states. There is a more intact awareness going on, of voluntariness and a brilliance of the whole scene that is lacking in the ordinary dreams.

2. Almost imperceptibly there may be strange extraterrestrial external realities developing and strange creatures, strange humans not of this planet appearing. One's Self and one's body may remain the same as they were before, in the external world. One can then wander around in these strange extraterrestrial surroundings. One is still one's ordinary self, one's ordinary body, but within very strange surroundings.

3. Alternatively, one may become a strange Self in these strange surroundings. One's body may change to something else or someone else. One may be looking through the eyes of someone else, realizing that one is doing so. The body that one is inhabiting at that point may be reading some very peculiar language with which one is unacquainted. The body one is inhabiting may be conversing with another similar

strange body. There is a sense of alienness about such experiences of which one is aware.

The strange Self can also be in an ordinary, known type of external reality and be a stranger among familiar humans. The familiar external reality may seem strange, as if one is identified with a visitor to this planet.

4. In strange or familiar external realities, there may be transforms of Self in which one loses one's body. One can become some other form of body, a point or even a small point existing in a strange or familiar external world. One may travel through the external reality quite freely without known means of locomotion. One can go far above the scene that one is looking at and look down upon it, or one can go down into any aspect of the scene as if one is looking through a microscope, enlarging any aspect of the scene. One can also go outward, as if one is looking through a telescope, and approach galaxies off the face of the planet which one is currently inhabiting.

5. Alternatively, there can be a beginning fusion between Self and one's surrounds. The surrounds can become liquid, and flow in a myriad of colors. At this point the distinctions between Self and the surrounds begin to be lost. One no longer has boundaries, one spreads out and becomes some of the flowing materials, the flowing energies. There is a loss of the boundaries and the distinctions between Self and the surroundings.

6. The surroundings may dissappear entirely, the Self becomes isolated in a voidlike space. The mood of Self can then become anything. One can be totally paralyzed with fear, or one can be ecstatically blissful and happy, floating in isolation, no body, no surroundings, no external reality, just the reality of Self.

7. Alternatively, one may become the whole universe, one becomes omniscient, one knows everything that happened in the past, is happening in the present, and will happen in the future. One is omniscient, omnipotent, and omnipresent. One can react to this with fear, with joy, with high neutral energy, or with anger.

8. One may become nothing, there is no Self, no external world, no knowledge, no memory. One has become zeroed out, there is nothing left including Self. Awareness and consciousness disappear.

As one can see by inspecting this catalog very carefully, these are the kinds of experiences that one can experience in dream states. As we said above, the difference in the tank experience is that there is a heightened awareness, heightened consciousness, and a heightened participation in what is happening. This catalog is not exhaustive of such states, it is merely indicative of the kinds of things that can happen to one in the isolation tank.

How can we account for such states if we assume that the mind is contained in the brain, that the mind and the Self are the results of computations of a central nervous system?

For purposes of discussion, let us try to divide up the Self in various realities into simplified diagrams so that we can grasp some of the variables and parameters that are active here. The Self has been discussed as an isolated observer–agent–operator. In the contained-mind hypothesis, the Self, the observer/operator (ob/op), is part of the results of the computations of a central nervous system, a brain. In a basic philosophical sense, the Self is thus a generated result of those computations. Without the computations the Self does not exist. *Thus, the Self is a program, a metaprogram, a Self metaprogram, a self-referential aspect of the computations of that brain.* Thus, the Self is the victim, as it were, of that which generates it, is the victim of the self-referential computations of that brain.

This state of affairs can be very threatening when one realizes what "one really is." When a given observer realizes this source of Self as true, a paranoid reaction of great depth may develop. That particular person may become hypercautious as to allowing this knowledge to penetrate himself. This model or simulation of Self may wall off that particular person from further realizations about the true complexity of the situation. If one assumes that the computational processes of a brain are simple, and hence one's Self is a result of simple processes, this can induce quite a good deal of fear and paranoia. In reality, of course, the computations of a given nervous system the size of man's are immensely complex, and hence one does not really know all of the computations that can take place. Some people, in order to escape the position that they are the result of computations of a central nervous system, will immediately shift to the belief in the unlimited mind and believe that they are not contained within the computations of the brain. Such persons will not bother to explore this possibility. I recommend exploration of this possibility to as great a depth as one is capable, with courage, so as to realize its true nature, rather than shying off from it because one is afraid of it.

As one can see in the above catalog, items 1 to 8, the phenomena experienced by the inside observer can be accounted for by assuming that all of this is the result of computations within the central nervous system. Let us discuss each point in turn.

The external reality that one experiences in (1) above in a sense is the stored simulation or model of past external realities with which one has had experience. The structure of that particular planetary surface, the people, the buildings, the plants, and so on, are quite familiar, and may be portions of the planetary surface in which one has lived. Thus, we arrive at a computed past external reality simulated, currently brought out of storage, and computed around the computed Self. We call these the external reality simulations.

As we move down the list from (1) to (2), we find that the external reality changes into strange, unique, and new external realities surrounding a familiar Self. Thus, we begin to see that there are stored, or created anew, strange external realities, apparently not experienced before by this particular Self. In ordinary parlance, we have entered the region of "imagination." Since I do not know what imagination is, I would prefer to say that these are simulations of new external realities, either generated *de novo* by unknown processes in the brain, or by the inherent noise level in the brain generating new external-reality appearances. Thus, we can see that the external-reality simulations, the simulations of an apparent external reality, can either be of a familiar stored type, or of a new, unique, created type.

In a way similar to that of external reality, the body that the Self is inhabiting can change. One can become someone else that one knows, or some stranger that one does not yet know, or some strange animal, plant, or other form. Thus, the simulations of Self, like those of the external reality can change and be of a familiar type, or a new and unique type.

Continuing then in the list (item 5), there can be a loss of distinctions between Self and the surrounds, so that the simulations of Self and the simulations of the surroundings become melded; the boundaries of distinction become more diffuse, and the Self spreads out. Here, then, mixtures of the simulations of Self and of the external reality become blurred, and finally disappear.

Simulations of the external reality can disappear completely, and the simulations of Self become totally isolated in a domain that has no space, no time, and is eternal. The Self is still capable of emotion, and may become, may move into any emotional mode of which one can conceive. The simulation of Self is still intact, still functioning, and still apparent to Self. One then moves down the list (item 7) further, and finds that the simulations of Self have disappeared, and the Self is everything, spread out, universal, creating everything, creating itself, the state of total feedback upon Self with no outside references to Self at all. All simulations of the external reality are gone, all simulations of Self are gone, and there is only a pure consciousness, a pure awareness, consciousness without an object (Merrell-Wolff, 1973).

Finally (item 8), Self disappears, everything disappears. If there is any experience in this state, none of it is brought back in returning from this state to other states.

I would like to clarify the concept of the observer/operator (ob/op). The deep basic meaning of observer/operator implies a certain degree of consciousness and control. This is a science game, the scientist is always conscious, aware, and in control of his thinking and of the processes that he is examining. In the isolation tank, this may not necessarily be true. There are many states in which the Self is not in control, and is being programmed by forces very much larger than Self, so that there are aspects of Self that we have not dealt with in any great length. The Self as a victim, the Self as someone who is being coercively persuaded of another belief system not one's own, is one that most of us experience at one time or another, especially as children. The passive observer and the active operator both seem to disappear under these conditions. The Self is interlocked with forces, with beings, with entities far greater than Self, and doing that which is programmed by them rather than by one's own initiative. One does not, as it were, sit still and watch; one is forced into participation by external entities, forces, and so forth.

Such states of the Self as a "programee" can be threatening or enjoyable or quite neutral.

In the above model, we must remember that we are assuming that all of these phenomena are taking place within an isolated body and brain. There is no access here to mysterious forces outside the computational processes of the brain itself. As soon as one no longer believes in such a model and its apparent limitations, one can move into other belief systems about the same phenomena.

We do not wish to espouse either the contained-mind model or the leaky-mind or the universal-mind models. Our task here is to present alternatives, rather than to espouse any one of them.

I hope that such considerations will help you in your own researches into your own Self using the isolation tank. I hope that such models will open up new possibilities for your own direct experience in the tank. I hope that this will enlarge your horizons and allow you to experience that which we have described in a safe way, so that you can be convinced that such things are possible and probable for you.

One lesson that has come from all of my more than twenty years' experience with the tank is that the human mind has many unknowns within it, and my own personal respect for it has moved way beyond where it was when I started the tank research on the Deep Self.

References

Lilly, J. C. *The deep self.* New York: Simon & Schuster, 1977.
Merrell-Wolff, F. *Pathways through to space.* New York: Julian Press, 1973.

9

Exo-Psychology[1]

Timothy Leary

Exo-psychology is the science which studies the evolution of the nervous system in its larval and post-terrestrial phases. Primitive, pre-Einsteinian psychology (1850–1975), although claiming to measure thinking, consciousness, and behavior, for the most part studied the adjustment–maladjustment of human beings to social rituals and culturally defined symbol systems. Appearing at a time when orthodox theology was losing its meaning for the growing class of semi-educated, psychology provided a comforting rationale for domestication, a soothing pseudo-scientific language for supporting the values of the middle class.

Primitive psychology, in spite of its enormous, state-supported bureaucracy and its priesthood mystique, has produced no verifiable theory for explaining human behavior, nor any methods for solving the classic problems of human society—crime, conflict, alienation, prejudice, stupidity, boredom, aggression, unhappiness, and philosophic ignorance about the meaning of life.

At the same time that psychology was becoming a pop-cult surrogate-religion, the chemical, physical, and biological sciences were quietly producing theories and replicable facts which have profound implications for the understanding of human nature.

Neurology locates the source of consciousness, memory, learning, and behavior in the nervous system—a thirty-billion-cell bio-computer for which the body is transportational robot.[2]

---

[1]This chapter first appeared as Chapters 1 to 6, 13, 23, 24, 25, and 28 in Leary (1977). They are reprinted here (with revisions) with permission of the publisher.—Eds.

[2]See Lilly, Chapter 8, for a discussion of the "mind-contained" hypothesis of which this is an example.—Eds.

Timothy Leary ● c/o Peace Press, 3828 Willat Avenue, Culver City, California 90230.

Clearly, if we wish to understand and improve our mental, emotional, and behavioral functions, the locus of investigation is the nervous system. The person who can dial and tune the receptive, integrative, transmitting circuits of the nervous system is not just more intelligent, but can be said to operate at a higher and more complex level of evolution.

Prescientific humans maintain a rigid taboo about discussing or tampering with their nervous systems—a phobia which is based on a primitive fear of the unknown, and a superstitious reluctance to learn how to know. It is now evident that the nervous system is an incredibly powerful instrument for conscious evolution, which can be understood and employed for genetic tasks.

Ethology, which studies animal behavior in the natural and experimental setting, has demonstrated the robot-instinctual nature of neural discrimination and the role of imprinting in determining when, and toward what, animal behavior is initiated.

Psychologists have failed to apply the findings of ethology to the human situation. The fact that human emotional, mental, sexual, and ethical behavior is based on accidental imprinting of the nervous system during "critical" or "sensitive" periods of development is apparently too devastating to pretensions of free-will and conscious choice.

Neurochemistry has recently discovered that neurotransmitter chemicals which facilitate/inhibit nerve impulses and synaptic connections determine consciousness, emotion, memory, learning, and behavior.

Psychopharmacology at the same time has discovered botanical and synthetic psycho-active agents which facilitate/inhibit states of consciousness and accelerate or dampen mental function.

These Einsteinian discoveries have predictably traumatized those psychologists who are committed both professionally and theologically to static, Newtonian concepts of human personality.[3]

These four sciences provide an impressive convergence of evidence suggesting that the brain is a bio-chemical-electric computer in which each nerve impulse acts as an information "quantum" or "bit"; that the nervous system is structurally wired into genetically preprogrammed circuits designed to select automatically and relay certain perceptual cues, and to discharge rote reactions; that imprinting of models accidentally present in the environment at critical periods determines the tunnel realities in which humans live.

We are led to conclude that the human being, at this stage of evolu-

[3]See R. Valle, Chapter 21, for a review and comparison of the Newtonian and Einsteinian world-views and their respective implications for psychology.—Eds.

tion, is a biological robot (biot) automatically responding to genetic template and childhood imprinting.

The unflattering portrait of *Homo sapiens* suggested by the evidence from these four "new" sciences—neurology, ethology, neurochemistry, and psychopharmacology—is, of course, quite unacceptable to psychologists and religious leaders who enunciate theories about "man's" separate, superior, and "chosen" status among life forms.

We need not be surprised at "man's" flattering self-appraisal. Since the "island realities" which we inhabit are defined by genetic template and imprint, we can only evaluate ourselves in terms of the symbols which our nervous systems have created.

If we can imagine an anthropological report about *Homo sapiens* written by extra-terrestrial scientists from a more advanced civilization, we can assume that humanity's inability to solve its psychological, social, and ecological problems, or to provide answers to basic cosmological questions (e.g., why are we here and where are we going?) would lead to the conclusion that *Homo sapiens* is a species capable of very limited robot-reactivity, and that Intelligent Life has not yet evolved on this planet.

Such an extra-terrestrial survey could also report the emergence of a rudimentary intelligence, as evidenced by the Einsteinian perspectives of the four sciences just discussed, and by the explosive implications of four other sciences which have significance for human destiny in the future: *astronautics, astrophysics, genetics,* and *nuclear physics.*

Astronautics: the significance of extra-terrestrial flight has not yet been fully understood. The Apollo missions were more than technological triumphs or nationalistic achievements. Genetically and neurologically, the beginning of a species mutation has occurred—equal in importance to the first amphibian movement from water to land early in biological history.

There can be no question that humanity has begun its migration to interplanetary and eventual interstellar existence. The effects of this transition on the nervous system and the DNA code will be profound. Just as amphibious and land-dwelling organisms mutated rapidly, developing the neural and physiological equipment for the new environment—so will space-traveling humans mutate rapidly. Exposure to zero gravity and to extraterrestrial radiation are two of many physical stimuli which will trigger the genetic and neurological changes necessary to adapt to interstellar life. The psychological effects will be dramatic. Space migration requires accelerated, relativistic, multidimensional flexibility, of which the nervous system is capable. It is inevitable that extra-planetary humans will be as advanced beyond current earth-dwellers as "man" is beyond the cave-dwelling ancestors. The beginnings of this process of exo-psychological adaptation can be noted in several lunar astronauts and E.V.A. veterans who returned claiming cosmic insights (Mitchell), philosophic revelations (Schweickart), and rebirth symptoms (Aldrin).

Astrophysics has also produced facts which stretch the limits of psychological vision. We learn to our delight that we are not alone—that perhaps as many as half of the 100 billion stars in our local galaxy are older than our sun, making it highly probable that more advanced forms of intelligent life are around the neighborhood. Humans have so far been neurologically incapable of conceiving of Higher Intelligence. Even science-fiction writers,[4] with very few exceptions (Stapledon, Asimov, Clarke), have been unable to specify the manifestations of superior species, except as technological extrapolations and bizarre extremes of current human culture.

Whatever the mind can conceive, it tends to create. As soon as humans accept and neurologically imprint the notion of higher levels of intelligence and of circuits of the nervous system as yet unactivated—a new philosophy of evolution will emerge. It is natural to call this extra-planetary perspective of human evolution *exo-psychology*—human nature seen in the context of an evolving nervous system, from the vantage point of older species which now exist in our extra-terrestrial future.

Genetics has revealed that DNA blueprints which reside in the nucleus of every living cell are remarkably similar from species to species. Astronomers and exo-biologists have discovered the molecules which are basic to life in outer space and in other star systems. The DNA code can now be seen as a temporal blueprint unfolding sequentially like a tape-spool, transmitting preprogrammed construction plans. In the individual this code unfolds through predetermined stages from infancy, through childhood, adolescence, maturity, menopause, aging, and death. A fixed time schedule similarly unfolds in the evolution of species. The DNA code contains the blueprint of the past and the future. The caterpillar DNA contains the design for construction and operation of the butterfly body.

It has long been known that individual ontology recapitulates species

---

[4]See Leavitt, Chapter 20, for an overview of the science-fiction writers who have addressed issues concerning the nature of intelligence and human consciousness.—Eds.

phylogeny—that the human embryo, for example, repeats the evolution-ary cycle; grows gills, is covered with hair, etc. The psycho-neural time-perspective implications of this fact have never been seriously studied.[5]

Geneticists are just now discovering "unused" sections of the DNA, masked by *histones* and activated by nonhistone proteins, which are thought to contain the blueprint of the future. Evolution is not a blind, accidental, improvising process. The DNA code is a prospective blueprint which can be deciphered.

Just as an engineer could study the flow charts of an auto-assem-bly plant and see how a car is put together in a sequence of future operations—so can the histone-masked sections of the DNA code be studied to determine the sequence of future evolution. The instruments for deciphering the DNA message are neurological and neurochemical. The science which studies the two-way communication between DNA–RNA and the nervous system is called *neurogenetics*.

Astronomy and astronautics persuade us that interstellar travel lies ahead in humanity's future. Extra-terrestrial existence will involve an advanced, mutated nervous system and inevitable contact with superior intelligence.[6] This new scientific understanding of human destiny might be called *interstellar neurogenetics*.

Neurogenetics is a new science (with a respectable journal and mem-bership dues) which studies the psychology—that is, the consciousness and behavior—of DNA–RNA. Neurogenetics may be called a branch of exo-psychology if we assume that DNA *contelligence*[7] is not restricted to planet earth, but, indeed, was probably originated by and designed to return to extra-terrestrial intelligence.

It is becoming clear that the nucleus of the atom is a complex organi-zation of powerful forces which operate according to relationship-laws (excitement, charm, spin parity, resonance). Just as the DNA code, lo-cated in the nucleus of the cell, is the genetic brain which, via RNA, designs and manufactures bodies and nervous systems, so can we con-

---

[5]The theory of serial imprinting suggests that psychology recapitulates phylogeny. That the individual nervous system repeats the evolutionary sequence. That the baby imprints an invertebrate reality, the crawling child a mammalian reality, the preschool child a paleolithic reality, the adolescent a domesticated-civilized reality.

[6]Some astronomers now state that Superior Intelligence does not exist in the universe because "they" have not contacted us or responded to our radio signals. Such conclusions illustrate the negative bias of conventional science. There is, of course, no scientific basis for claiming or denying the existence of Higher Intelligence. Time-dilation factors complicate the matter; if a space ship were hurtling toward us at close to light-speed, millions of years would elapse on earth for every year in flight. There is no basis for dogmatic statement.

[7]"Contelligence" (*con*sciousness + in*telligence*) is a neologism used by Leary.—Eds.

ceive of the nucleus of the atom as the elemental "brain" which designs and constructs atoms and molecules according to quantum logic.

Nuclear Physics: it is now believed that all matter and energy in the universe operates in a "general field" which can be understood in terms of the relativistic interaction among the four basic forces that exist in nature: the *gravitational,* the *electromagnetic,* the *strong force (subatomic),* and the *weak force (radiational).*

Primitive psychology was based, at best, on Newtonian "laws", and, for the most part, was geocentric (closet Ptolemaist). Even the most poetic Freudians, behaviorists and transactional analysts have not allowed their theories of human behavior to be influenced by the Einsteinian revolution which has so dramatically changed our understanding of the structure of the universe.

Neurophysics is the science which is just beginning to study the "psychology"—that is, the consciousness and behavior—of atomic particles and to relate electronics and atomics to human consciousness and behavior. Physicist John Archibald Wheeler's work suggests that the atomic nucleus can receive, remember, integrate, and transmit information at extremely high-velocities and can probably engage in most of the basic social behavior that we observe in living organisms.

Interpersonal, emotional (i.e. motional), intellectual, and social affairs at the electronic level and their transception by the nervous system define *neuroelectronics.*

Interpersonal, emotional, intellectual, and social events at the subatomic, nuclear level and their transception by the nervous system define *neuroatomics.*

Our understanding of atomic and nuclear processes has been limited by our language–logic–imagination–philosophy, which tend to be Euclidean-Newtonian. We inevitably "psychologize" nature and personalize atomic events. Our laryngeal-muscular minds, imprinted in primitive childhood, cannot conceive of what we cannot conceive of; cannot experience what we have never experienced.

Our dialogue with DNA and our conversations with atomic-subatomic and astronomical energy signals must, however, be two-way. We must open our "minds" to receive the signals which are being sent to our nervous systems by DNA and by elemental intelligences. When we geneticize our psychology, that is, think like DNA–RNA, we see the current human condition as a transient phase in the evolution of the nervous system. Since DNA creates us, it is logically diplomatic and theologically conventional (image of God) to base our psychology upon the laws and designs of molecular intelligence. Since the nucleus of the atom designs atoms and molecules, it is logical to base our psychology upon the laws and structures of nuclear physics and astronomy; to think of ourselves as "atoms" or even "stars" radiating, decaying, attracting, repelling, receiving and transmitting along frequency spectra, resonating, forming molecular social structures, possessing a characteristic electromagnetic personality, moving through energy networks with relativistic foci, etc.

Since our primitive psychological systems based on Newtonian geocentric principles have done little to enlighten or harmonize human philosophy, does it seem too fanciful to suggest that we should, in the future, base our psychological concepts on the laws and structures of physics, chemistry, and astronomy and seek to explain human behavior in terms of natural rather than national inter-relatings?

Primitive, geo-centric, ego-centric, socio-centric psychology, ignoring the laws of bio-chemistry and physics, constructs a philosophy of mammalian emotions, Euclidean laryngeal-muscular symbols, and parochial values to explain "man and his universe."

Exo-psychology views human destiny in terms of an evolving nervous system, designed by DNA intelligence (which uses planets as temporary, embryonic nesting sites in an interstellar migratory process destined to extend life-span, life-scope) to become symbiotic transceivers of astrophysical contelligence.

The Psychology of Physics

Exo-psychology (psi-phy) is the psychology of physics: philosophy based on scientific fact. The theories presented in this transmission might be called *science faction*, or *philosophy of science*, or *psychology of physics, psi phy*.[8] They are scientific in that they are based on empirical findings from physics, physiology, pharmacology, genetics, astronomy, behavioral psychology, and, most important, neurology. They are fictional in the Wittgensteinian sense that all theories and speculations beyond the mathematical propositions of natural science are subjective. They are *factional* in the sense that current advances in Space Migration, neuro-logic, and the Life Extension sciences have already gone beyond the fantasies of most science-fiction writers. Science fact is now farther out than science fiction. We are now creating a future which is more incredi-

---

[8]"Everyone writes science fiction . . . but most write it without having the slightest idea that they are doing so." Joyce Carol Oates

ble than *2001*. O'Neill space cylinders are more complex and advanced than Clarke-Kubrick space-ships.[9]

Other philosophers (notably Christian theologians, statistical materialists, Marxian dialecticians) make different interpretations of the currently available corpus of scientific fact. Such theories, however popular, are equally fictional. History suggests that philosophies accepted as academic dogma or enforced by punitive legal sanctions are not necessarily any less fictional than those which are persecuted and censored. Indeed, there is some sociological evidence that science fictions are forcibly suppressed only when they are more likely to accelerate human evolution than the defensive orthodoxies which they challenge. We think of Socrates, Bruno, Copernicus, Darwin, Pasteur, Sakharov.

The Eight Mutational Phases of Life

Life unfolds in eight mutational phases, four terrestrial and four extraterrestrial. It gives us pleasure and increases our sense of freedom to believe that the species known as *Homo sapiens* is evolving through an eight-phase life-cycle. Four of these phases are designed for larval survival on the womb planet. The four more advanced phases are designed for survival and migration in interstellar space.

Exo-psychology is a theory of interstellar neurogenetics based on the following assumptions:

1.   There are millions of solar systems in our galaxy which have planets upon which organic life breeds and evolves.

2.   Since our planet is at the midpoint of the evolution of a G-type sun (five billion years), it is assumed that half of the planets in our galaxy upon which life is to be found are more advanced in the evolutionary sense than life on our planet.

3.   These more advanced cultures numbering, perhaps, in the millions, represent the future of our own evolution. They exist ahead of us in genetic time. "They" are "us" in the future.

4.   The same chemical elements and physical-chemical processes occur on all star systems in the known universe.

5.   Life as it exists on planet earth is not unique. We are as alike to our interstellar neighbors as "peas in a pod." ("We" in this cliché refers to all life forms on this planet.) We shall find only early and more advanced versions of ourselves. We are the alien life forms.

---

[9]This chapter was written in various prisons to which the author had been sentenced for dangerous ideology and violations of Newtonian laws.

6.   Planets have a predictable life span. They are destroyed in the late "red giant" phase of their suns. It is logical to suppose that Life migrates from planets before they are destroyed by aging suns, or before their biological resources are exhausted.

7.   The interstellar neurogenetic theory suggests that Life is not designed to remain on the planet of birth, but to migrate throughout the galaxy.

8.   Life is seeded on young planets in the form of amino acid templates. These genetic blueprints contain the multibillion year design of evolution. The basic tactics of evolution are metamorphosis and migration. We have been seeded on millions of other planets.

9.   The DNA code is literally a message outlining the course of evolution. On planet earth about half of this evolutionary blueprint has unfolded. The future half, blocked by histones, exists in quiescent form waiting to be activated—just as the chromosomes of a tadpole contain the future frog form; as the human embryo of four months contains the form of the neonate, or the neonate the form of the pubescent teenager.

10.   The human species is now completing the fourth phase of its larval development. Think of the earth as a womb. Life so far on this planet is embryonic. When life leaves the planet it adopts post-fetal, post-larval existence.

11.   It is convenient to describe larval life on earth as Newtonian—concerned with the gravity-bound mechanics of survival—and to describe extra-terrestrial existence as Einsteinian: gravity-selective.

The four Newtonian circuits of the nervous system that are concerned with mastery of the four umbilical attitudes necessary for terrestrial survival are: (a) *ventral-dorsal*, (b) *vertical (up-down)*, (c) *three-dimensional (left-right)*, and (d) *protective-incorporative (for survival of the species)*.

The four Einsteinian circuits of the nervous system that are designed for survival in post-terrestrial space involve mastery of: (a) the body as time vehicle; (b) the nervous system as self-directed bio-electric computer; (c) the genetic code as molecular intelligence; and (d) meta-physiological, nuclear-gravitational force-fields (quantum-mechanical).

12.   The metamorphosis of the human species from terrestrial to extra-terrestrial existence was signalled by the almost simultaneous discoveries of neuroactive drugs, electronic instruments, DNA structure, subatomic nuclear energies, and quantum mechanics.

Each of the eight periods of individual human life involves gross alterations in morphology, behavior, physiology, and, most important, neurology. In spite of the fact that these changes are obvious, even to the most untutored observer, the psychological-philosophic implications of these phases have not been understood by larval scientists and philosophers. This may be due to the possibility that the human species itself is evolving through the same eight phases and, until recently, has been almost exclusively preoccupied with the four basic, larval survival processes (vegetative, political, technological, social).[10] By analogy, a society of water-bound tadpoles would be neurologically inhibited from recognizing that the amphibious frog is a later version (both phylogenetically and individually) of itself.

The scientific facts about the nervous system, the creation of reality by imprinting, our position in the galaxy, neurotransmitter drugs, Einsteinian relativity, the DNA code–now available in any junior college text–can be understood by an open-minded adolescent. These facts, however, are so alien to the Judeo-Christian-Marxist conceptions of human nature that they have been repressed. Unconscious resistance to patent observations and scientific findings is a routine process in the evolution of human knowledge. We are familiar with the tendency to place under taboo facts which disturb orthodox religious dogmas. This taboo phenomenon is genetically determined. Premature intimations of future stages would be dangerously confusing and demoralizing to a larval species.

Discovery of the serial-imprinting capability of the nervous system, of bi-lateral (past–future) asymmetry in the cortex, the probability of advanced life forms on millions of planets in our local galaxy, and recognition of the longevity-implications of the unused half of the DNA code, is producing a mutational quantum leap in the course of human evolution which is now preparing the species for migration from the planet.

The Eight Circuits in the Human Nervous System

The human nervous system is evolving sequentially through eight maturational phases. At each phase a new circuit of the nervous system is activated and imprinted.

The four larval (neuro-umbilical) terrestrial circuits of the nervous system designed for attachment to and survival on earth are:

1.   The *bio-survival circuit*—mediating the reception, integration,

---

[10]Rudimentary recognition of the larval, cyclical nature of contemporary human existence has been sporadically attained in earlier civilizations which have temporarily reached the necessary level of biological, political, technological, and reproductive security. In ancient China, India, Ceylon, Crete, Babylon, Greece, Islamic Damascus, Egypt, Renaaissance Europe, a few neurologically elite, premature evolutes have used leisure (i.e. the time) and available technology to develop bodily hedonic, erotic, aesthetic expressions, science-fiction speculations and botanical methods of expanding neurological function beyond survival imprints.

and transmission of neural signals concerned with cellular health and vegetative, metabolic security: safety–danger.

2.   The *emotion-locomotion circuit*—mediating the reception, integration, and transmission of neuromuscular signals concerned with body-mobility, territorial control, and the avoidance of helplessness.

3.   The *laryngeal-manual dexterity circuit*—mediating the reception, integration, and transmission of neural signals from the nine laryngeal muscles and the hand which are concerned with language, artifacts, and precise manipulatory movements.

4.   The *sexual-domestication circuit*—mediating the reception, integration, and transmission of neural signals concerned with sexual impersonation, courting, mating, parent-hood, child-rearing, and socialization.

The four circuits of the nervous system designed to mediate extra-terrestrial energies and to adapt to interstellar existence are:

5.   The *neurosomatic circuit*—mediating the reception, integration, and transmission of sensory-somatic signals uncensored by larval imprints and designed to operate in a zero-gravity environment: body consciousness.

6.   The *neuroelectric circuit* which receives, integrates, and transmits neural signals from all the other circuits and from the brain at the simultaneity and velocity of a bio-electric-grid; not programmed by survival imprints: brain consciousness.

7.   The *neurogenetic circuit* imprints the DNA code, receiving, integrating, and transmitting RNA signals, thus operating at species time, making possible biological immortality, and symbiosis with Higher Life forms: DNA consciousness.

8.   The *metaphysiological-neuroatomic circuit* is activated when the nervous system imprints subnuclear quantum-mechanical and gravitational signals, thus transcending biological existence: quantum consciousness.

At each chronological phase of individual evolution, a new imprint is formed. Each imprint determines the positive and negative foci for subsequent conditioning of the newly activated neural circuit. Each imprint defines a level of island reality. Recently developed techniques for re-imprinting make possible serial, planful re-creation of realities. All the activity of the nervous system is based, of course, on chemical-electrical communication.

The first four larval circuits of the nervous system have been designed by the DNA code to deal with the Euclidian-Newtonian characteristics of the planet earth and the corollary asymmetries of human anatomy. The four latter post-terrestrial circuits are designed for gravity-free psychosomatic reception, neuroelectric receptivity deciphering of DNA–RNA signals, and integration of subatomic messages.

The Twenty-Four Stages of Neural Evolution

There are twenty-four stages of neural evolution: twelve terrestrial and twelve extra-terrestrial.[11] In the preceding section we have defined eight periods of human evolution. Four are larval-terrestrial and four are designed for Space Migration. The goal of evolution is Higher Intelligence—the sequential development of the nervous system—increasingly capable of receiving, integrating, and transmitting a wider spectrum of signals of greater intensity, complexity, and speed. The more intelligent the species, the greater the capability of adapting and surviving. Bodies are the vehicles for transporting brains and seed. Bodies evolve to house and transport brains and sperm–ova more efficiently. The genetic code has preprogrammed the nervous system to evolve in metamorphic stages. The basic strategies of evolution are metamorphosis and migration.

The sequential emergence of neural circuits in the individual human being recapitulates the phylogenetic appearance of nervous systems of greater complexity.

In studying neural activity and the evolution of nervous systems it becomes obvious that a three-part developmental sequence occurs: *self-centered reception, integration,* and *transmission-fusion.*

The neuron, which is the basic unit of biological contelligence, possesses three anatomical and functional divisions: the dendritic system, which receives signals, the cell-body of the neuron, which stores, integrates, and interprets incoming signals, and the axon, which transmits the message. Each neuron, each circuit, and, indeed, the nervous system in its totality is divided into these three functions.

At the lowest level of unicellular and invertebrate life, these three

---

[11]The book *The Periodic Table of Evolution* presents a systematic detailed discussion of the twenty-four stages of neuro-evolution—suggesting that biological and human–individual evolution is based on a blueprint design to be found in the Periodic Table of Chemical Elements.

This book treats the Periodic Table as a code-message which outlines the sequence of biological evolution, and as a Rosetta stone from which the philosophic meaning of enduring human symbol-systems can be deciphered.

The neurogenetic symbol systems which can be understood in terms of the periodic table include: the Tarot, the Zodiac, the I Ching, the playing card deck, the Greco-Roman Olympic Pantheon, and the Hebrew Alphabet.

These cultural games are seen as crude but generally accurate neurosymbolic expressions by a pre-Einsteinian species of the basic model of galactic evolution which is based on the table of atomic elements. These "occult" systems are proto-scientific attempts to predict the course of evolution of life on and off the planet, and can be seen as neurocultural communication systems in which humanity symbolizes natural laws.

Exo-psychology is a primer concerned with outlining the eight major sequences of neurological evolution.

functions operate for the survival of the individual; but, at the higher stages of evolution, communication and fusions among members of species becomes more important for survival.

As each neural circuit emerges during the development of the individual, the self-oriented, receptive, input phase is the first to appear. The integrating phase follows, and the organized transmission linking the organism to others is the third phase.

The development of the larval individual proceeds, therefore, through 12 phases (4 circuits × 3 orientations). Extra-terrestrial evolution also proceeds through 12 stages (4 × 3). These 24 stages are both phylogenetic and ontological. The first 12 neurogenetic stages describe the evolution of life on this planet from single-celled organisms up to the most advanced insect and human societies and the development of the individual from birth through larval maturity to complete hive socialization.

An Interstellar Neurogenetic Philosophy

This chapter attempts to present a complete philosophy of evolution. The perspective is post-terrestrial. We assume (without extensive review or restatement) the current facts and theories of nuclear physics, astronomy, DNA genetics, ethology, experimental imprinting, psychopharmacology, neurology, and behavioral psychology. Based on this consensus of scientific fact and on our extensive experimentation with expanded and accelerated states of consciousness in the widest range of set, setting, and social context, we present:

1. A bio-neural *cosmology*, a theory of the origin and evolution of life on and off this planet.

2. A neuro-muscular *politic*, defining the basic genetic dimensions of the freedom-control of muscular movement in territory.

3. A neurogenetic *epistemology*, a theory defining the subjective True-False and the consensual Fact–Error of laryngeal-manual (L.M.) symbol systems.

4. A neurogenetic *ethic*, defining what is subjectively good-bad and consensually right-wrong.

5. A neurosomatic *aesthetic*, defining the natural, somatic dimensions of the beautiful.

6. A neurogenetic *ontology*, an anatomical-empirical theory of the eight levels of reality, their evolution and interaction.

7. An interstellar-neurogenetic *teleology*, defining the future course of individual and species evolution, leading to longevity and galactic symbiosis with Higher forms of life.

8. A metaphysiological neuroatomic *eschatology*, predicting the

imprinting of the nervous system on to nuclear-gravitational-quantum force fields.

Use of the Nervous System to Imprint the Genetic Code

The most intelligent use of the nervous system is to imprint the genetic code, the structure of the body and of the nervous system being predesigned by this code. The code is an amino-acid time-script which contains the multibillion year sequence of biological evolution, past and future. The first task of Life on this planet was to transform the atmosphere. Plant life produces the oxygen atmosphere necessary for later phases of mobile, animal life. This process is called *terraforming*. When oxygen was produced, the code simply kicked into action the gills, lungs, and oxygen-transporting systems in the body to produce the next phase of evolution.

The evolution of humanity for the billions of years to come may already be preprogrammed in the genetic code, blocked from expression by chemical-masking barriers called histones, and turned on by non-histone proteins.[12]

The blueprint of DNA has designed us to move life off the planet and to enter high-velocity, time-relativity states, to attain symbiotic longevity, to construct and direct nuclear-fusion energies which will transport us through the galaxy, and eventually to evolve beyond matter as we now know it.

The intelligent person in the year 1980 has available enough evidence to predict the general course of future evolution, and, on the basis of these inevitabilities, to participate in a neurological mutation. It is about time to use our heads; become very contelligent, very rapidly.

One who allows Hirself to be controlled by conditioning or accidental childhood imprinting is accepting robothood. To follow the genetic instruction it is necessary to retract larval imprints and to create new neural realities, new languages based on Einsteinian relativities. Create the future and then imprint it.

Neurologic is the science of selective re-imprinting, the use of the nervous system as motion picture camera, the conscious creation of a sequence of realities. It must be remembered, however, that neurologic is a tool for neurogenetics. It is of little use to go on re-imprinting larval realities or somatic realities. The sixth circuit is designed for extra-terrestrial existence, for post-human, genetic consciousness. Neurotransmitter drugs, like LSD, are thus seen to be post-larval in function.

[12]The future of post-larval humanity rests dormant in the unused portion of our genetic code, just as the "butterfly" potential lies hidden in the chromosomes of caterpillars.

The DNA code contains the entire life blueprint—the history of the past and the forecast of the future. The intelligent use of the brain is to imprint the DNA code.

Conscious Agents of the Future

Evolution requires that some of us become conscious agents of the future. Up until the present, human beings have been neurologically unable to conceive of the future. This inhibition (neo-phobia) is genetically imposed. The larval nervous system creates earth-bound realities. For the caterpillar to "think" about flying would be survivally risky. Indeed, the caterpillar cannot "think" about flying because it has no wings. We assume that pre-human forms of life have no awareness of time, no ability to look into the future; that mammals operating with the two immediate survival circuits have no conception of the evolutionary plan. [13] The key to evolution beyond the larval forms is the understanding and control of time.

The emergence of the laryngeal-manual circuit, the paleolithic unfolding of left-hemisphere symbol-manipulating and logical-ordering allowed humanity to transmit vocal, written, and artifactual time-signals across the generations. Operant conditioning, instrumental learning, assures the transmission of culture from the past to the present.

Larval time-binding involves very short periods and narrow perspectives. The farmer looks to the next harvest. The politician looks to the next election. The bureaucrat looks forward to payday, to the weekend, to the summer vacation. Parents look to their children.

Larval civilizations operate on the basis of calculated ignorance about the future. The four-brained person does not want to know about the future, because it threatens the stability of the reality imprint. Four-brained societies do not want to know about the present, because prospection would lessen the motivation to work blindly toward organized uncertainty.

There is a taboo about future forecast. The book *Future Shock* (Toffler, 1970) seems to be more about present shock and describes the terror and confusion created by a world which is different from the past; that is, different from one's childhood imprint realities. Pro-phobia is so intense that the future cannot be faced in a best-selling book.

Even the scientific groups who try to project the future are curiously unable to foresee an evolving neurological-mutational change. The Club

---

[13]This assumption may be another anthropocentric myth. The beehive, in its elaborate structure, may be a time-binding cultural signal to new generations of bees.

of Rome, the RAND Corporation, Herman Kahn, all present statistical extrapolations of material trends of the past projected to the future. Thus, we are told that the future will be a global extension of a Swedish Los Angeles. All the current predictions by "futurists" forecast an air-conditioned anthill world in which personal freedom and creativity are limited by population pressure, scarcity, and restrictive social control.

There is one possibility routinely omitted in future projections—a sudden global raising of contelligence. The "I^2" of S.M.I^2.L.E.

An Interstellar Neurogenetic Teleology

Exo-psychology defines an Interstellar Neurogenetic outlining the DNA preprogrammed course of individual and species evolution. A complete philosophic system generally includes:

1. A cosmological explanation about where we came from and how it got started
2. A political theory explaining the factors involved in the destructive and harmonious expressions of territorial autonomy, control, freedom, restraint, mobility
3. An epistemological theory defining truth-falsity and right-wrong
4. An ethic defining good-bad, virtue-sin
5. An aesthetic defining beautiful-ugly, artistic-unartistic
6. An ontology defining the spectrum of realities
7. A genetic teleology explaining where biological evolution is going and how it will all turn out
8. An ultimate metaphysiological neuroatomic eschatology explaining what happens when consciousness leaves the body

The aim of Life is:

S.M.I^2.L.E.
Space Migration
Intelligence Increase
Life Extension

We are designed to Use our Heads (I^2) in order to Use Time (L.E.) in order to Use Space (S.M.) Of these three associated imperatives, Intelligence Increase is the most important. When the human has learned how to use the brain as instrument to:

- selectively re-imprint the four terrestrial circuits
- control the body
- master the creation of multiple realities by means of serial re-imprinting

- imprint (i.e., experientially identify with the DNA code)
- decipher nuclear-quantum intelligence

then Life Extension and Space Migration will be attained.

The Emergence of Future Post-Human Forms

A wide variety of future post-human forms will emerge. The evolutionary process schedules mutations with a relentless continuity. Every living organism plays a part in the evolutionary design.

There are eight answers to the basic question, "Who am I and where am I going?" In terms of genetic teleology, the question is: "In which direction am I mutating?"

The genetic perspective is taboo and frightening because it forces us to face certain embarrassing facts.

1. The human species is an incomplete form which is undergoing dramatic changes. The human race (and, indeed, life on this planet) is now at the half-way point. In three billion years we have evolved from unicelled organisms. In the years to come we shall manifest changes much more dramatic.

2. The rate of evolution is accelerating. The human condition is changing at an accelerated rate in terms of physique, neurological function, ecology, density and diversity of population, etc. Consider the human situation 25 years ago, 50 years ago, 100 years ago, 1,000 years ago, 10,000 years ago. Now assume that the same rate of accelerated change continues. How will we evolve in the next 25 years? The next thousand years?

3. The evolutionary process produces an increasing spectrum of differentiations. The present human gene pool will evolve in many different directions. It is probable that hundreds or thousands of new species will evolve from the present human genetic stock. The social implications are startling. Of the next hundred persons you meet, it is probable that each will evolve into a new species as different from you as the rabbit from the giraffe. About 75 million years ago, certain insectivore species (lemurs) contained the seed-source from which the 193 varieties of primates, including the human, were to emerge.

To understand yourself, to understand the human situation, it is useful to project a pro-spectus of how the human species is going to evolve. Much of the conflict and confusion which characterizes the current human plight can be gentled and clarified if we accept the fact that we are genetically very different from each other, and inexorably preprogrammed by DNA template to evolve in many very different directions.

The work of geneticists like Paul, Stein, and Kleinsmith suggests that histones mask the half of the DNA code which contains the "futique" design of the organism. If it were possible for one to pull back the histone curtain and see the blueprint of one's genetic future, one would have a most revealing answer to the question, "Who am I and where am I going?" The question must be posed in the first person singular. The error of genetic democracy led Gauguin to ask, "Where did we come from and where are we going?" The question can only be asked, "Where am I going? What genetic futique do I carry in my genes?"

Each of us transmits a pre-coded design of future organisms very different from current human stock and very different from most other humans.

An Astroneurological Text

Think of this chapter, "Exo-Psychology," as an astroneurological text. The past few pages of this transmission have whirled us through several billion years of evolution, introduced us to Higher Intelligence, explained our role as paleozoic plants, pulled us through larval stages of mammalian body construction, described the robotry of symbol-conditioning, provided the key to sexual male-faction, instructed us in the use of the poly-phase neuroscope (equipped with life-long, re-imprint film), and given us adequate cues to allow us to attain biological immortality and time-dilation.

It is possible that we have already in this introduction transmitted more extra-terrestrial information than is contained in all the books which have previously been written:

> "But maybe I'm revealing things I shouldn't, don Juan."
> "It doesn't matter what one reveals or what one keeps to oneself," he said. "Everything we do, everything we are rests on our personal power. If we have enough of it, one word uttered to us might be sufficient to change the course of our lives. But if we don't have enough personal power, the most magnificent piece of wisdom can be revealed to us and that revelation won't make a damn bit of difference." (Castaneda, 1974, p. 16)

This chapter is not for Every Body. The human species is now at a point of genetic fission. Assume that about 93% of the species is going to adapt to life on the planet. Ecology is the seductive dinosaur science that will lead most of the post-human species to conform to terrestrial conditions, become reasonably comfortable, passive, robot-conditioned cyborg insectoids directed by centralized (ABC, NBC, CIA, MAO, CKB) broadcasting systems. For terresterial readers, this manual outlines the neurological steps necessary to adapt harmoniously to hedonic, five-brained cyborg existence.

This transmission flashes a different signal for the 7% who, we assume, are DNA-designed to attain biological immortality, leave the womb-planet, become galactic citizens, and fuse with superior interstellar entities.

This manual is not designed for conventional author–reader games. It is a signal for mutation. A test of intelligence. A scan for personal power.

The pan-spermic UFOs landed three billion years ago and produced the signal, an English translation of which you now hold in your hand:

S.M.I.^{2}.L.E.

References

Castenada, C. *Tales of power*. New York: Simon & Schuster, 1974.
Leary, T. *Exo-psychology*. Los Angeles: Starseed/Peace Press, 1977.
Toffler, A. *Future shock*. New York: Random House, 1970.

10

Transpersonal Realities or Neurophysiological Illusions?
TOWARD AN EMPIRICALLY TESTABLE DUALISM[1]

Charles T. Tart

Although psychologists like to emphasize the empirical nature of psychology, every psychologist starts more or less with his own personal experience of himself and his world, experience which creates both explicit and implicit guides as to what is important to study. Western psychologists have focused on our ordinary, Western state of consciousness, appropriate in a culture highly concerned with manipulation of the external world, and much of our research interests reflect this. There are a large number of experiences, however, that we might call *transpersonal*, experiences which, while not actively encouraged in our culture, nevertheless happen, and seem to imply a much broader view of man than our Western psychological one. Let me give you some brief examples of such experiences.

The first is from William James's (1916) classic collection:

> Suddenly, without warning, I felt that I was in heaven—an inward state of peace and joy and assurance indescribably intense, accompanied with a sense of being bathed in warm glow of light, as though the external condition had brought about the internal effect—a feeling of having passed, beyond the body, though the scene around me stood out more clearly and as if nearer to

[1]This chapter is a version of a paper presented as part of the symposium "The Nature of Consciousness" at the American Psychological Association Convention, Toronto, August, 1978.

Charles T. Tart ● Department of Psychology, University of California at Davis, Davis, California 95616.

me than before, by reason of the illumination in the midst of which I seemed to be placed. This deep emotion lasted, though with decreasing strength, until I reached home, and for some time after, only gradually passing away. (p. 388)

As a second example from James, consider Symonds's description of an experience he had while undergoing chloroform anesthesia:

> I thought that I was near death; when suddenly, my soul became aware of God, who was manifestly dealing with me, handling me, so to speak, in an intense, personal present reality. I felt him streaming in like light upon me . . . I cannot describe the ecstasy I felt. Then as I gradually awoke from the influence of the anesthetic, the old sense of my relation to the world began to return, the new sense of my relation to God began to fade. (p. 382)

To be a little more contemporaneous in time, consider the following experience of Claire Myers Owens, an American writer on Zen Buddhism. She had been sitting for three days in a Zen sesshin, having a very difficult time attempting to clear her mind and meditate. Finally she reports:

> As I stared at the blank surface of the low divider wall in front of me I suddenly beheld a row of people—my mother (dead), my brother, and a young woman, my friendly enemy. They were all gazing at me with sad accusing eyes. I knew I had hurt them in real life in various ways, though not always intentionally. Suddenly such powerful repentance and desire to expiate seized me that my very body shook uncontrollably. Sobs tore up from the depths of my being. It was like tearing up the roots of my ego, annihilating life-long delusions of my own goodness. This emotional storm continued hour after hour. I was oblivious, blind to everything and everybody in the zendo. After five hours two monitors came and lifted me up. My body was so heavy and my legs so weak I was unable to walk. They carried me upstairs and placed me on the bed. After an hour's rest I returned to the zendo and commenced concentrating with renewed assurance. As I gazed at the low wooden dividing wall in front of me it seemed to abruptly turn into a beautiful luminous blue with the lights flickering at the lower edge. Then it changed to thick silvery ice, next to gauze. Then I saw right through the wall and beheld two men sitting on the other side. I was incredulous even while this phenomenon was occurring. When it happened again the next day I accepted it as makyo, a psychic power, encouraging, but not worth clinging to. (Owens, 1975, p. 174–175)

As a final example of a transpersonal experience, consider this older case of a near-death experience:

> On Saturday ninth of November, a few minutes after midnight, I began to feel very ill, and by two o'clock was definitely suffering from acute gastro-enteritis, which kept me vomiting and purging until about eight o'clock . . . By ten o'clock I had developed all of the symptoms of acute poisoning: intense gastro-intestinal pain, diarrhea, pulse and respirations became quite impossible to count. I wanted to ring for assistance, but found I could not, and so quite placidly gave up the attempt. I realized I was very ill and very quickly reviewed my whole financial position. Thereafter at no time did my consciousness appear to me to be in any way dimmed, but I suddenly realized that *my*

consciousness was separating from another consciousness which was also me. These, for purposes of description, we could call the A and B consciousness, and throughout what follows the ego attached itself to the A consciousness. The B personality I recognized as belonging to the body, and as my physical condition grew worse the heart was fibrilating rather than beating, I realized that the B consciousness belonging to the body was beginning to show signs of being composite—that is, built up of "consciousness" from the head, the heart, and the viscera. These components became more individual and the B consciousness began to disintegrate, while the A consciousness, which was now me, seemed to be altogether outside my body, which it could see. Gradually I realized that I could see, not only my body in the bed in which it was, but everything in the whole house and garden, and then realized I was seeing not only "things" at home but in London and in Scotland, in fact wherever my attention was directed, it seemed to me; and the explanation which I received, from what source I do not know, but which I found myself calling to myself my mentor, was that I was free in a time-dimension of space wherein "now" was in some way equivalent to "here" in the ordinary three-dimensional space of everyday life.

The narrator then says that his further experience could only be described metaphorically, for while he seemed to have ordinary two-eyed vision, he "appreciated" rather than "saw" things. He began to recognize people he knew in his visions, they seemed to be characterized by colored condensations around them:

Just as I began to grasp all these, I saw my daughter enter the bedroom; I realized she got a terrible shock and I saw her hurry to the telephone. I saw my doctor leave his patients and come very quickly, and I heard him say or saw him think, "He is nearly gone." I heard him quite clearly speaking to me on the bed but I was not in touch with my body and could not answer him. I was really cross when he took a syringe and rapidly injected my body with something which I afterwards learned was camphor. As the heart began to beat more strongly, I was drawn back, and I was intensely annoyed, because I was so interested and just beginning to understand where I was and what I was "seeing." I came back into the body really angry at being pulled back, and once I was back, all the clarity of vision of anything and everything disappeared and I was just possessed of a glimmer of consciousness, which was suffused with pain. (Geddes, 1937, p. 104)

What do we make of such experiences?

As we all know, mainstream Western psychology has made nothing of these sorts of experiences. Partly this is a matter of the training of psychologists, in which they are informed at various times that "crazy" experiences happen to people which gives them strange beliefs, but these sorts of experiences need not be taken seriously. As a result, the typical psychologist unconsciously avoids coming across these kinds of experiences and casually dismisses them if he does come across them. But why this strong dismissal among the community of psychologists?

I think an important part of the answer lies in considering the implications of transpersonal experience. The prefix *trans* conveys the idea that these experiences go beyond the individual, not merely in an abstract sort of way, as we might say that democracy goes beyond a single person, but in a very real and important sort of way. These sorts of experiences seem to imply that consciousness may not always be restricted to the body and brain, that there may be other kinds of consciousness than human with which we may interact, etc. Aside from the many historical reasons, such as the old conflict between science and religion, for rejecting these implications, a more immediate and formal reason is that monistic, physicalistic philosophical views about the nature of consciousness are dominant in modern science.

Monistic Views of Consciousness

The physicalistic, monistic view of consciousness which is so predominant states that physical matter and physical energies, operating within physical space and physical time, are the fundamental realities of the universe. Consciousness is not considered to be a basically different kind of reality, but merely a manifestation of matter, energy, space, and time. *Every* manifestation of consciousness, every kind of experience, is, in principle, reducible to physical interactions within the body, brain, and nervous system. In my book (Tart 1975a), I express this view schematically (see Figure 1), where I call it the scientifically orthodox or scientifically conservative view of the mind.[2]

The significant way to read this diagram is starting at the left with fixed physical reality, basic and immutable physical laws which govern all manifestations in the universe. A particular segment of this manifest reality of great interest to us is the physical structure of the brain (I shall, for short, speak only of the brain rather than the full system of body, brain, and nervous system). The brain structure, whose operation is in principle reducible to more basic physical laws, can further, for convenience, be divided into two aspects, the relatively fixed qualities of the brain, such as the built-in "instructions" on how to run the kidneys and the like, and the more flexible, programmable aspects of it, the "software," for those who like computer analogies. Each of us has the software capabilities of the brain programmed by his interactions with the culture, his parents, the language he speaks, and the like, to produce further semipermanent structures or processes in the brain. The interplay of these various physical processes in the brain is very complex: a very

---

[2]See R. von Eckartsberg, Chapter 2, for a discussion of Tart's theory of states of consciousness.—Eds.

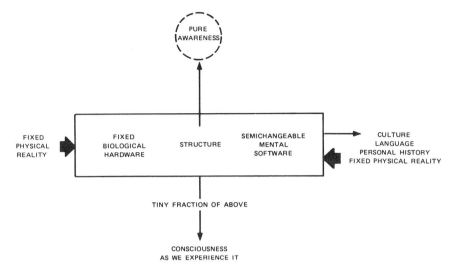

Figure 1. A representation of the nature of human consciousness in terms of physicalistic monism (from Tart, 1975a, p. 30).

small subset of them, from the physicalistic, monistic view, lead to the experience of consciousness as we know it.

I have shown an arrow emerging from the physical structure of the brain leading to something labeled pure awareness. This is an important distinction in my systems approach to understanding states of consciousness (Tart, 1975a), for it relates to certain kinds of experience, often associated with meditative practices or altered states of consciousness, in which a person seems to get back to a more basic version of awareness than the concepts and word-play which is our usual experience. From the physicalistic, monistic point of view, however, this experience of pure awareness (or any other kind of special experience, for that matter) is an emergent from the *physical* operation of the brain, and can be totally reduced to it, in principle. In practice, of course, the brain is incredibly complex, and we may never be able to find the exact physical parallel of every single experience, even though in principle we believe it is there.

The physicalistic, monistic view of consciousness tells us that the four experiences cited at the beginning of this paper were indeed real *experiences*. Any experience reduces to some specific pattern of electrochemical firing within the brain, and the four "transpersonal" experiences given are just as real as your everyday experiences. Everyday experiences, however, are assumed to be a rather good reflection of the reality of the physical world, whereas these transpersonal experiences are clearly hallucinatory insofar as the physical world is concerned. When Trevor felt himself bathed in a warm glow of light and found the scene around him standing out more clearly, with a feeling of great peace and joy, we postulate that some unusual firing pattern in his visual-sensory and emotional brain centers was taking place. When Symonds experienced God-like light streaming in upon him during his chloroform experience, he was clearly experiencing a simulation of reality on the order of a dream, probably again with some firing pattern in the appropriate emotional centers of the brain giving that special feeling of peace. Owens' seeing of faces of emotionally relevant people in her life and undergoing catharsis as to her relations with them was probably good for her mental health, but was again hallucinatory in that the faces were not there in the external world, and her experience of apparently seeing through a wall was obviously also a neural firing pattern in which hallucination replaced her concurrent visual sensations. Finally, the gentleman who apparently left his physical body in his near-death state and experienced his consciousness as a composite may have had a useful psychological insight in seeing the composite nature of consciousness, but the visual experience of floating above his body was obviously another neural firing pattern creating a visual hallucination, as were his feelings of being able to perceive wherever he directed his attention, or getting explanations of his state from some sort of nonincarnate entity. Although I personally do not necessarily accept these explanations, they are straightforward ones from a physicalistic, monistic point of view.

Now I shall make a statement that may very well be unpopular with many of you, but one that I think it is important to make. If the sorts of things illustrated were all that there were to transpersonal experiences, I think it would be fair to say that the developing field of transpersonal psychology is one in which unusual illusions, hallucinations, and aberrations of thought processes were studied. It would be different from classical abnormal psychology in that transpersonal experiences may have a positive, beneficial effect on the people they happen to. Nevertheless, they are clearly unrealistic, abnormal experiences, and those of us dedicated to values of making people more rational would have an inherent distaste for them. Even so, we might consider ourselves realistic and accept the fact that most people do not want to face the cold, hard facts of reality, but need some sort of comforting illusions for the sake of their psychological health, and so it might be useful to learn how to induce transpersonal illusions deliberately in order to reinforce irrational belief systems that nevertheless allow people to function well. Politically speaking, this is also a convenient path to social respectability for transpersonal psychology, as it will seem to fit experiences which tend to be regarded as disturbing into the physicalistic, monistic status quo. Since psychologists have always been a little bit insecure about their status as "real scientists," we should not underestimate this political aspect of things!

As a scientist, I am supposed to be more committed to observational data than to theoretical concepts, to be ready to reject old conceptual systems and explore new ones if my data require me to do so. In spite of the controversial nature of what I shall present here, I have followed the implications of some very important data, and will attempt to show that there is first-class scientific evidence for a dualistic theory of consciousness, a theory that has a "mind" or "life" component to consciousness that is of a different nature than known physical systems, and thus implies that at least some transpersonal experiences are not merely interesting illusions, unusual patterns of neural firing, but actually tell us something about the potential for truly transcending our ordinary physical limits.

Paraconceptual Phenomena

Let us start by operating strictly within our contemporary scientific knowledge of the physical world. In this framework, it is both a useful and a precise statement to say that a given person is located at a certain spatial position, and his behavior is occurring at a specific time. We can also specify both theoretically and practically, by means of instrumentation, the kinds of physical energies that might reach this person or emanate from this person, and accordingly calculate whether such physical energies could serve as useful carriers of information. We can then put two people at different spatial locations, and, either by the sheer physical distance between them and/or by physical shielding existing between them, we can set up a situation in which we can say that these people are totally isolated from each other, in terms of practical information transfer. That is, we can say that the physical energies emitted by the one person, even if they are modulated to carry information, are so attenuated and lost in the noise level before they reach the second person that no information transfer can occur. If we have two people sitting in open fields one hundred miles apart, for example, we can physically show that, no matter how loudly one shouts, the sound vibrations of the shouting in the air drop below the noise level of the Brownian motion of the air long before that sound energy reaches the second person. We can do the same thing by putting our two people in sound-attenuated rooms.

We can now carry out an experiment in which one person, whom we shall designate the sender, is given some randomly selected stimulus, such as a number to concentrate on or a picture to look at, and is asked to try to mentally "send" it to another, sensorially isolated person—the receiver in this experiment. What if, over a series of experimental trials, the receiver's behavior shows sufficient correlation with the randomly selected targets presented to the sender that we cannot dismiss it as coincidence, but, using appropriate statistical tests, we find that there is at least some transfer of information at a statistically significant level? If such a thing were to happen, we would have a *paraconceptual* phenomenon. That is, our observation is what it is, we observe such and such an amount of information transfer, but it is beyond, *para* to our conceptual system.

Under basic rules of scientific procedure, our first obligation would be to double check or triple check the physical isolation between the sender and receiver to make sure we had not overlooked some potential information-transfer channel. Suppose we did that and found no overlooked channel, so our paraconceptual phenomenon was still with us. Our next task, under the basic rules of scientific inquiry, would then be to recognize that our current conceptual system was incomplete, and then to investigate our paraconceptual communication effect to see what new things it might tell us about our sender and receiver or our view of reality. To concretize this and take it back to our earlier example, suppose that the gentleman who was ill not only believed that he could tell what was going on in London, in spite of the total sensory isolation of his body from London, but that he had gone on and given a highly specific description of a very improbable, nondeducible event happening in London at that time. This would be a truly transpersonal event, for his consciousness would seem to be functioning beyond the confines of his physical body. What then?

I have been speaking hypothetically, but, as you know, there have been claims that these sorts of paraconceptual, transpersonal events happen rather frequently in everyday life. In a representative survey of the American population, for example, the sociologist Andrew Greeley (1975) found that 58% of his sample believed that they had experienced telepathic, mind-to-mind contact with someone at a distance at least once in their life. Many other kinds of paraconceptual experiences, or extrasensory perception, to use the general term for them, occur in everyday life, and clearly they are quite "normal," in that at least some form of ostensible ESP experience happens to the majority of people. At least in the ordinary American population, if not in the academic subculture!

These kinds of ESP experiences seem to fit some kind of dualistic view of mind, and so might be potentially very important in deciding between a monistic and dualistic view; but, as we know, the scientific investigation of ESP and related phenomena is not only not exactly in the mainstream of American psychology, it is an *extremely* small-scale activity. A recent survey of mine (Tart, 1978a) showed that the entire research budget for America runs only around half a million dollars a year, and there are not more than a dozen or so scientific investigators working most of their time on this subject.

As psychologists, we can readily think of reasons for not taking a large number of spontaneous ostensible ESP occurrences seriously. Many people have faulty judgments about the paraconceptuality of such events to begin with, their memories may be faulty, they may distort or exaggerate their accounts for various reasons, etc. This point was recognized at the beginning of the century, and the few scientists interested in this area realized that a firm scientific basis for the existence of paraconceptual phenoma could not be established very well by the investigation of spontaneous cases. These events needed to be studied under laboratory conditions, where alternative hypotheses like incorrect observation, sensory leakage, subject fraud, and the like could be ruled out. Occasional scientific experiments were carried out over the years, and the methodology for them became quite refined, especially beginning with the work of J. B. Rhine and his colleagues at Duke University in the 1930s. Because of a variety of factors, primarily what I would consider prejudicial ones where people attached to various conceptual systems preferred to reject the data rather than question their conceptual systems, the large body of high-quality experimental work that has accumulated in the last 40 years is largely unknown to the scientific community. It is published in five specialty journals (*Journal of Parapsychology, European Journal of Parapsychology, International Journal of Parapsychology, Journal of the Society for Psychical Research,* and *Journal of the American Society for Psychical Research*), and in book form. In spite of the small scale of the effort compared to most fields of science, however, I estimate that more than 600 high-quality experiments, the vast majority showing statistically significant evidence for various kinds of paraconceptual processes, have now been published, and the overall mass of this evidence is quite compelling. I do not have time here to even begin to consider this mass of evidence in detail, but the interested listener might look at my recent book, *Psi: Scientific Studies of the Psychic Realm* (1977a), or the authoritative *Handbook of Parapsychology* (Wolman, Dale, Schmeidler, & Ullman, 1978). What I shall basically do is just define the four kinds of paraconceptual or *psi* events as they are now generally called, for which I believe there is overwhelming, high quality scientific evidence.

The first of the four well-established psi phenomena is *clairvoyance,* a phenomenon involving a direct (without mediation by the known senses or any known form of physical energy) perception of the state of physical matter. The classical experimental procedure which established its reality was that of a card-guessing test, in which a deck of cards would be thoroughly shuffled, face down, so that the shuffler did not know what the order was. The cards would then be guessed at by a receiver–subject who was sensorially isolated from them, and after his guesses had been recorded they would be checked for correspondence with the card order, and the results statistically evaluated for hitting beyond chance expectation. Many dozens of experiments established the reality of clairvoyance with this experimental procedure. Clairvoyance has been demonstrated for many other types of target material than cards, such as identifying musical selections on randomly selected magnetic recording tapes to which no one was listening.

The phenomenon most people think of with respect to psi is *telepathy*. The classical experimental procedure for establishing this was again to start with a very thoroughly shuffled deck of cards, but now each card would be looked at for a fixed period by a person designated the sender or agent, who attempted mentally to "send" the identity of the card to a receiver. Again the receiver would be thoroughly isolated (in terms of our current physical world-view) from any informational energies put out by the sender. Results would again be scored for extra-chance hits, and many dozens of experiments with cards and other kinds of material established the reality of telepathy. However, most researchers conversant with this field would now argue that, though the concept of telepathy is appealing, this particular experimental paradigm does not necessarily establish it as a phenomenon separate from clairvoyance, for there is no way of telling whether a successful receiving subject acquires the information from the sender's mental processes, or directly by clairvoyance from the cards. Indeed, Rhine (1974) has argued that it may be logically impossible to test for telepathy in a way that totally excludes clairvoyance.

The third kind of psi phenomenon is *precognition*, the prediction of future events that cannot be logically predicted from a knowledge of current events. The classical experimental procedure for this was to ask a subject to write down what the order of a deck of cards would be after it had been thoroughly shuffled at some future time. That time lag might be anywhere from a few minutes to days or months. Again, results have been quite successful in establishing the reality of precognition. I have personally always found this difficult to accept, in spite of the strength of the experimental evidence, but, as any of you who have heard me discuss *transtemporal inhibition* (an information-processing mechanism for ESP) know, I have been forced to accept the reality of precognition in spite of my emotional resistance to it, because of strong precognitive data appearing in my own laboratory work (Tart, 1978b).

The above three kinds of psi have been generally classified as extrasensory perception, an information-gathering process analogous to sensory perception, but occurring in the absence of any known form of energy and/or receptor to convey the information. There is a fourth major psi phenomena, *psychokinesis* or PK, the direct influence of desire on the state of the physical world, without the mediation of any known form of physical energy. The classical experiment for establishing this was to have a machine throw dice. A subject who could watch the events but not otherwise physically influence them would be asked to try to make particular die faces come up more often than would be expected by chance, and dozens of successful experiments were reported. Modern research on PK usually uses electronic random number generators, where the subject is asked to influence a meter or recorder monitoring the decisions of the electronic random number generator. More than fifty experiments have been tried with electronic generators (Honorton, 1978), and have been quite successful.

There is a variety of other kinds of phenomena around that have been claimed to be paraconceptual, to be psi phenomena, but many of these have simply not been studied very extensively and so may be potentially explicable in ordinary physical terms, so I shall not discuss them here. I shall take the basic existence of the four psi phenomena mentioned above as well established, and go on from there to propose a scientifically useful form of a dualistic understanding of consciousness.

It is important to note that the dualism I shall propose is in no way absolute. In my attempts to read philosophical theories about consciousness, I have always been struck by the attempts philosophers have made to come up with absolute, everlasting definitions of terms. Philosophically I am inclined to be a pragmatist, and, with my scientific preference, I also consider *experience* and *data* much more primary than concepts. The dualism I shall propose is a pragmatic one: my argument is that it is *useful* to distinguish mental and physical aspects of consciousness, and that these will have effects on the kinds of research we do. The distinction is based on our current knowledge of the physical world, however, and reasonable extension of it, and the distinction may very well be broken down by further scientific progress. Indeed, I associate fairly often with physicists, and the cutting edge of their world in the quantum realm is so unusual and uncommonsensical that much of it seems more farfetched to me than psi phenomena do!

Emergent Interactionism

The primary empirical data that force me to propose a dualistic theory are psi phenomena. Given our current knowledge of the physical world and our concepts about it, and reasonable extrapolations of those concepts, psi phenomena are paraconceptual: they indicate a quality to consciousness that is not likely to be explained without recourse to some other conceptual system than physics. My various psychological studies of consciousness and altered states of consciousness further force me toward a dualistic position. This position is expressed diagrammatically in Figure 2.

The physical structure of the brain is represented on the left-hand side of Figure 2, the qualitatively different factor we can loosely call Mind/Life is represented on the right-hand side of the figure. In order to avoid semantic problems associated with our ordinary association to terms like brain or mind or life, I shall begin referring to these two basic component subsystems of consciousness as the B system and the M/L system. The B system refers to the body, brain, nervous system, these physical things that we understand by physical concepts. The M/L system refers to those qualitatively different aspects of consciousness that defy understanding in physical terms. The L or life aspect of the M/L system is added to reflect the fact that psi phenomena can happen in conjunction with a person without there necessarily being any conscious experience going with it. Although the evidence is still sparse here, I suspect that it is a general property of life to exercise some sort of weak psychokinetic effect on the physical matter about it. Consciousness, as we experience it, is an emergent factor, a systems effect from the interaction of the B system and the M/L system.

The B system is the link between consciousness and the physical world around us. Environmental factors are registered via the sense organs, and end up as electrical/chemical patterns within the B system. Decisions to behave in various ways begin as electrical/chemical patterns somewhere within the B system and eventuate in specific neural impulses to motor apparatus that creates our overt behavior.

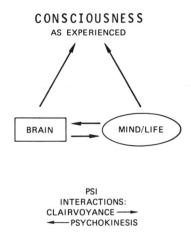

CONSCIOUSNESS
AS EXPERIENCED

BRAIN   MIND/LIFE

PSI
INTERACTIONS:
CLAIRVOYANCE ⟶
⟵ PSYCHOKINESIS

Figure 2. Basic model of the emergent interactionist approach to understanding consciousness.

The B system is an ultracomplex, especially interesting structure, for although many aspects of B-system functioning seem clearly determined, such as basic reflexes, a variety of other important aspects seem to be under the control of quasi-random or fully random processes. They are controlled by neurons or neural ensembles that are frequently in an almost, but-not-quite, ready-to-fire state, easily triggered by very slight influences. My dualistic theory of consciousness, that I am calling Emergent Interactionism, postulates that the M/L and the B systems interact by psi. Specifically, the M/L system at least occasionally cognizes the physical state of the brain, and thus factors in the environment that are represented as physical patterns in the B system, by means of clairvoyance. Further, the firing patterns of the B system are influenced at critical junctures by a psychokinetic influence from the M/L system, in addition to the organization imposed by the deterministic and self-organizational properties inherent in the B system. The holistic *emergent* of the interaction of these two systems, the system, or, more technically, *supra*system emergent of the B and M/L system interaction, is consciousness as we experience it. To express it in another way, what we ordinarily consider our consciousness is not an experience of what our B system alone is like, or what the M/L system alone is like; it is the experience of the emergent of the complex mutual patterning and interpenetration that is the normal state of the organism.

I am making a quite unusual claim, namely, that psi is not a rare occurrence, but something that goes on all the time. Under normal circumstances, psi is frequently occurring within the organism. Psi is the mechanism that philosophers always leave out in dualistic positions, the mechanism whereby mind and body, the M/L system and the B system, interact. To keep the discussion clear, I shall begin to call psi within the organism *auto-psi,* or more specifically, *auto-clairvoyance* and *auto-PK.* The unusual manifestation of psi that makes us aware of it in the first place, its use to gather information about events distant or shielded from the organism, we shall call *allo-psi,* and we may break that down into specific forms such as *allo-clairvoyance, allo-PK, allo-telepathy,* etc.

The model of the Emergent Interactionist approach sketched in Figure 2 is, of course, grossly oversimplified, for we know that the B system is a highly complex, large, self-organized, hierarchical system in and of itself. It manifests properties determined not only at particular levels by component parts, but, as in any complex system, has emergent properties manifesting at various levels. A more realistic schematic representation of the position of Emergent Interactionism is shown in Figure 3. This representation brings in a number of new considerations.

First, we should realize that there are various hierarchical levels of organization in the B system alone, leading to system complexities, with-

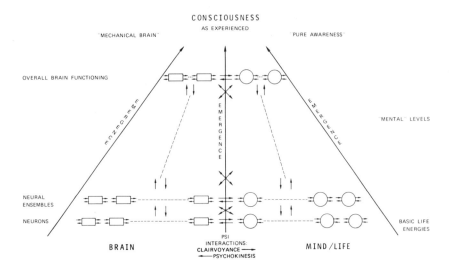

Figure 3. Extended model of the emergent interactionist position (representing the complexities and emergent-system properties of both the B and the M/L systems as well as their interactions).

out even beginning to consider M/L-system interaction. The lowest level shown on the left-hand side of the figure is that of the individual neurons, and, though they have isolated properties we are beginning to understand fairly well, they are organized into neural ensembles at the next level of complexity, a level which would begin to have emergent, system properties. That is, basic neural ensembles can have properties that are not clearly predictable from those of neurons alone. The ensembles, in turn, can interact back down to the more basic level to influence the properties of isolated neurons. Various neuron ensemble levels become more and more complex, interacting in more and more ways, as is represented by the information-transfer and interaction arrows in the figures. We have many lifetimes of scientific work ahead of us just trying to understand the B system solely in terms of physical properties, because of these complex interactions and emergent properties.

The M/L system is represented on the right-hand side of Figure 3. Because physicists have found it highly profitable to assume that there is a basic symmetry in real world processes (Tart, 1975a), I have applied this symmetry principle in drawing the figure and have assumed that the M/L system is also organized hierarchically. At the lowest levels would be the most basic "life energies," a vitalistic term I am not really comfortable with, but one I have not found a good replacement for yet. Basic M/L-system phenomena occur at these lower hierarchical levels, which, as in the B-system levels, interact with each other and have various emergent properties. As we go higher in the M/L-system hierarchy, there is more likelihood of an experiential representation of M/L-system properties, so we can begin to talk about it as a "mental" level, rather than just a basic life-energy level. Thus, system properties result from emergence laws in both the B and M/L systems.

I have drawn information flow and control arrows to represent autoclairvoyance and auto-PK interactions between the B and M/L systems. The transfer and interaction arrows are drawn between similar hierarchical levels and across levels to remind us of the probable complexity of interaction between two complex systems like this. In older terms, there is probably no "seat of the soul," no one special "receptor" in the B system associated with auto-psi interactions; they probably occur at a variety of loci. Lower-level auto-psi interactions, then, may change basic properties of both neural tissue and basic life energies, and higher-level interactions more directly modify consciousness as experienced.

If we could separate out the properties of the two systems alone (something we might be able to do in principle, but not in practice, as neither may survive alone), we might arrive at something I have called "mechanical brain" as the emergent of the B system operating in isolation, a neurological processing that would be totally predictable from physical and general system-theory principles. The kind of experience I have generally labeled "pure awareness" might emerge from M/L system properties if they operated in isolation. Neither of these kinds of emergents would be very expressible in ordinary language, for ordinary language deals with consciousness, and consciousness, as we experience it, is the emergent of the interaction of the B and the M/L systems.

B System Self-Determination

Although it would be highly speculative to discuss possible self-organizational qualities of the M/L system, it is clear from current scientific knowledge that the B system possesses a considerable degree of self-organization. We cannot make this an absolute statement, for, insofar as the Emergent Interactionist position is correct, we never observe a B system functioning in total isolation: if the M/L system were not interacting at all with the B system, the B system would be dead. Dead brains do not process much information. However, since we are now learning how to build complex, internally stabilized and organized computer systems, and can extrapolate from present-day computer systems to at least some of the functions of living B systems, it is a good assumption that much self-organization and self-determination in the B system comes about through its inherent physical and system properties. We could further divide this self-organized activity into basic biological functions that the organism can carry out from birth, such as internal homeostatic operations on the body, and learned operations that come about through the enculturation process. The very fact that we have concepts such as *personality* or *habit*, implying the predictability of a person given a knowledge of the situation, suggests that semipermanent physical changes are made in the B system which will produce determined results, given the requisite environmental stimuli to trigger off these internal circuits. Further, a moment's introspection about ordinary consciousness will indicate that it is characterized by almost continuous mental activity, thinking, remembering, associating, planning, in a never-ceasing stream. Since the content of this activity largely reflects the consensus reality about us, and was created by stimuli in our developmental history brought in and mediated by the B system, it seems likely that this continuous activity is mediated largely by semipermanent physical traces in the B system also. The B system, then, can be seen as doing a great deal of information processing and internal operations purely on its own, without regard to specific interactions with the M/L system. This automatization of ordinary consciousness is an important factor to keep in mind.

Ordinary and Nonordinary Psi

As I stated earlier, from the Emergent Interactionist point of view we postulate that psi is being used a great deal of the time in everyone's life as auto-psi, used internally within the organism. What we observe in parapsychological experiments, however, is not ordinary psi but extraordinary psi, allo-psi, taking a process ordinarily confined within an organism and requiring the M/L system to interact via psi with something outside the organism. I have represented these various considerations in Figure 4.

The information-flow arrows in the figure summarize points made previously and expand on them. Two of the most prominent information- and energy-flow arrows are sensory input to, and motor output from, the B system. Within the organism, auto-clairvoyant interaction from the B system to the M/L system, and auto-PK interaction from the M/L system to the B system, also constitute major routes of information flow. Thus, the B system and M/L system interact to produce the emergent system property of consciousness as we experience it.

The unusual use of psi outside the organism is shown by the information-flow arrow for allo-clairvoyance, and the information/energy-output arrow for allo-PK for interaction with the physical world. Communication from one discrete M/L system to another, telepathy, can be divided into receptive telepathy, picking up information from another

MIND /LIFE

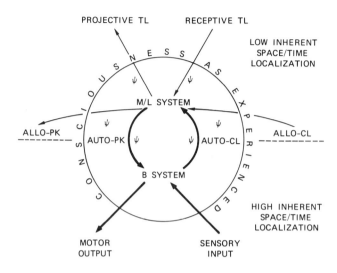

MATTER

Figure 4. Differentiation of auto- and allo-psi from the emergent interactionist point of view.

M/L system, and projective telepathy, sending information to another M/L system. This division maintains symmetry with the clairvoyance and PK process. With our terminological convention, telepathy is automatically a form of allo-psi. Indeed, the fundamental distinction with psi processes could be M/L system to M/L system interaction, and M/L system to physical world system interaction. There is, of course, a methodological problem in trying to observe pure allo-telepathy under experimental conditions, for, if we want objective verification of it, we must add auto-PK in order to have a behavioral manifestation of the telepathically acquired information that we can verify.

Earlier in this chapter I noted precognition as one of the basic psi phenomena, but I am now inclined not to consider the temporal specification of when psi operates as a fundamental distinction. This is reflected in Figure 4, where I have indicated that the M/L aspect of consciousness has a low inherent degree of localization in space and time, an idea arising from my concept of *transtemporal inhibition* (Tart, 1977a,b; 1978b). The B system, on the other hand, is very highly localized in space and time: we can make quite useful and precise statements that certain neurological firing patterns exist in such and such locations at such and such moments.

This lower degree of inherent localization of the M/L system comes from the properties of psi, or, more technically, allo-psi, which allow the organism to pick up information sensorially distant or shielded from it, and distant or shielded by either space or time. In general, there is an aspect of human consciousness that, though largely focused on the here and now of physical space and time, is also spread out to some extent in the immediate space and time around the organism, and is capable of focusing to quite extreme spatial and temporal distances away from the organism when allo-psi is successfully used. Although time does not allow me to touch on the experimental evidence for this, it does illustrate one of the empirical consequences of the Emergent Interactionist approach to consciousness, namely, the prediction that consciousness will manifest properties that are paraconceptual by our ordinary concepts of space and time, and so require understanding on their own terms, M/L-terms, rather than being reducible to physical explanatory concepts.

Out-of-the-Body Experiences

I have been trying to make a careful scientific case for my version of dualism, Emergent Interactionism, drawing on the implications of hundreds of high-quality experiments. In the real world, however, very large numbers of people, probably a majority, do not need any scientific case made for a dualistic division between matter and some kind of soul. Now, we need not take the fact that large numbers of people believe in some kind of nonmaterial soul as very important evidence in science, for we know, as psychologists, that almost all beliefs people have (including the belief that they do *not* have a soul) are not formed from scientific evidence but are conditioned in people in the course of enculturation. What should interest us as psychologists, however, is the fact that there are some people, I do not know how many, who believe that they have some kind of immaterial soul, not on the basis of what they have been taught but as a result of personal experience. These are people who have had what I have termed an out-of-the-body experience (OOBE).

In a classic OOBE, a person finds himself located at some other location than where he knows, *at the time,* that his physical body is located. He can look around, inspect that location, try interacting with it in various ways, etc., just as he would any ordinary physical location. Second, and of crucial importance in definition, the experiencer knows *during* the experience that his consciousness is basically functioning in the pattern he recognizes as his ordinary state of consciousness. Just as you can right now, with a moment's introspection, realize that you are in your ordinary state of consciousness, and are not dreaming or drunk or in any other altered state, the OOBE experiencer recognizes the pattern of functioning of his consciousness during the OOBE as ordinary. He can call on most or all of his ordinary cognitive faculties during the OOBE. It is not uncommon for people during the OOBE to engage in very "logical" reasoning to the effect that what is happening to them is impossible by all they have been taught. They cannot be in their ordinary state of consciousness, and yet find themselves located outside their body; nevertheless there is their experience, perfectly real and happening to them right at the moment, regardless of their conceptual system.

A few of the people who experience this classic sort of OOBE retrospectively manage to talk themselves out of the implications of their experience, and convince themselves that it must have been some kind of unreal experience, no matter how real it seemed. The majority of people who have had an OOBE, however, know, at a direct experiential level, that there is some essential aspect of their consciousness that is of a quite different nature from their brain functioning. We could logically argue the contrary, of course, and state that their B system was obviously functional, and perhaps the experience was just some kind of interesting hallucination, perhaps what has been called a lucid dream elsewhere (Tart, 1969, Chapter 8); but our arguments as outsiders carry little weight with people who have actually had the experience.

As I have defined OOBEs so far, they can easily be included within the domain of ordinary psychological concepts and investigation, although, as we know, they are not, probably because their implications make them too paraconceptual. The example of the gentleman who seemed to be floating above his body given as an example of a transpersonal experience at the opening of this paper is an excellent example of an OOBE, at least the first part of it, where he seems to possess his ordinary consciousness, before it began to change later in the experience.

In some OOBEs, however, there is a psi element that drastically strengthens the implication that the M/L system may indeed be functioning in a quasi-independent way from the B system. When an OOBE case has a psi element, what this means is that the person not only experiences himself as at some distant location, he accurately describes what is going on at that distant location at the time, and his description is sufficiently accurate and the events sufficiently improbable, given what he could ordinarily know, that we consider psi the best explanation for how the information was gathered. The particular example at the beginning of the paper does not have a strong element like that: the experience of the perception of his daughter coming into his bedroom, for example, could readily be explained in conventional terms as mediated by his senses and B system, even though he was having the hallucinatory experience of being outside his body.

There are case collections of OOBEs where the information about a distant location is specific enough to seem to require a psi explanation. The one example I shall give, however, comes from an experimental study of OOBEs under laboratory conditions that I was able to carry out through having the good fortune of meeting a young woman who had had several OOBEs per week throughout her life as long as she could remember, and was still having them. The data have been described in detail in one of the parapsychological journals (Tart, 1968), so I shall just give the highlights here. Basically, this young woman spent four nights sleeping in a psychophysiological laboratory where I monitored EEG, eye movements, blood pressure, and skin resistance on a polygraph through the night. She slept in an ordinary bed with short electrode cables that prevented her from sitting up or getting out of bed. There was a shelf approximately seven feet above the floor, over the bed, with a clock beside it. After she was ready to go to sleep for the evening, I would go off to another room, randomly enter a random number table, and write a five-digit random number from it on an 8½" × 11" sheet of paper, put this sheet of paper in a folder, take it into the laboratory, and slip the sheet of paper off, face up, on the shelf, so that the number could not be read by anyone even walking around the laboratory, much less lying in bed with short electrodes on, but was readily visible to an observer whose visual apparatus was near the ceiling. The subject, whom I called Miss Z, was instructed to try to have OOBEs during the night, and to try to wake up shortly after them, if at all possible, in order that I could compare the physiological records at about the time of her reported OOBEs with her ordinary sleep record. She was also instructed to try to float high enough during her OOBE to read and memorize the target number and report it to me.

    She had several OOBEs during the nights she was able to spend in the laboratory, and, because of her relatively quick awakenings from them, I could generally localize them on the physiological records with some confidence. I discovered that this rather unique psychological experience occurred in conjunction with a rather unique EEG pattern. Although I had been involved in sleep research for some years prior to this experiment, I had never seen a pattern quite like the EEG pattern that went along with these OOBEs, consisting, as it were, of a mixture of a Stage-1 EEG such as might be found in conjunction with REM sleep, but also containing large amounts of slowed alpha rhythms, and no rapid eye movements. So we had an interesting correlation: a unique psychological experience, a unique EEG pattern. Heart rate and skin resistance measures did not show anything noticeably different from the ongoing sleep pattern. In all but one of her OOBEs, Miss Z reported that while she was definitely out of her body, she was not able to control her movement within the room to get high enough or close enough to the target number to be able to read it, so she ventured no opinion as to what the target number was. On the one occasion in which she reported that she had been able to see the target number, she correctly reported all five digits of it in order, 25139, an event with an *a priori* probability of one in 100,000.

I suspect that this was a clearcut instance of psi functioning, although I do not generally make this as an airtight claim, both because this was the first experimental study of this type, and because I could not feel *absolutely* certain that some sophisticated form of fraud had not been used by Miss Z, although I doubt this latter hypothesis strongly. I took these results primarily as a demonstration that these exotic sorts of experiences could be studied under laboratory conditions. It does lend support, however, to the psi component of OOBEs.

Although this is a radical thing to say in so far as mainstream psychology is concerned, I am inclined, because of the strong psi component of some OOBEs, to take them as being pretty much what they seem to be, a temporary spatial-functional separation of the M/L system from the B system. This separation is only temporary (otherwise we would not get any subsequent report), and it is probably only partial, with the M/L system still interacting with the B system by auto-psi to some extent. Several aspects of case reports of OOBEs support this separation view.

First, in most OOBEs the person does not experience his consciousness as very different from ordinary: indeed, I use the maintenance of ordinary consciousness, as perceived by the experiencer, as a criterion for a classic case of OOBE. But I have defined ordinary consciousness as an emergent from B and M/L system interaction and mutual patterning, so this suggests that a considerable amount of this auto-psi interaction is still occurring, and/or that the force of habit, the lifetime practice of this patterning, is still fairly active in the M/L system, in spite of partial or full loss of interaction with the B system.

Second, while most OOBEs seldom seem to last more than a minute to a few minutes, there are OOBEs which seem to last for half an hour or an hour or more. In these prolonged OOBEs, or in the OOBEs of people who have had many such experiences rather than the typical once in a lifetime case, or in OOBEs apparently resulting from severe disruption of physical functioning, as when a person has almost died, consciousness as experienced tends to start drifting away from its ordinary pattern and become some kind of altered state. The transpersonal experience given at the beginning of this paper is an excellent example: the experiencer first simply experienced his ordinary consciousness as being above the bed, and then it began to function in ways that were ineffable for reporting. This alteration of style of consciousness function is what we would expect from the Emergent Interactionist point of view as interaction between the B system and the M/L system decreased. The M/L system would start drifting toward its own inherent patterns of functioning, as they would be unpatterned by B system characteristics. Indeed, it is these unusual kinds of OOBEs that may offer us one kind of potential for insight into the inherent properties of the M/L system.

Third, the case-study evidence we have suggests that there are few if any physiological changes of great consequence during ordinary, brief OOBEs. The physiological changes I found for Miss Z, for example, were unusual, but not of the sort associated with pathological physiological functioning. From this we might reason that the B system is able to function pretty much on its own in an adaptive fashion, maintaining body homeostasis, during brief OOBEs. People who have reported prolonged OOBEs, however, often report large and usually pathological changes in their physical body that they notice upon the cessation of the OOBE. Robert Monroe, for example, an American businessman who began having prolonged OOBEs quite spontaneously (see Monroe, 1971), reports that his body has been quite chilled following prolonged OOBEs, a pathological enough sign so that he tries to avoid their being prolonged. I suspect this reflects the fact that life and consciousness, as we know them, arise from the mutual interaction and patterning of the B and M/L systems, and when the patterning of the M/L system upon the B system becomes sufficiently attenuated, the B system cannot adequately run the complex system of the brain and body by itself. Small physiological errors start to accumulate, and, in principle, would eventually lead to death.

Conclusions

I recognize that, in terms of mainstream psychological constructs, the theory of consciousness I have proposed—Emergent Interactionism—is quite radical and will be automatically dismissed as a throwback to primitive and unscientific notions by some psychologists. Nevertheless, I feel that excellent scientific evidence forces us to be pragmatic dualists at the present stage of our knowledge, to acknowledge that consciousness has aspects to it, particularly the psi aspects, which are not and probably never will be reducible to contemporary physical notions of what the physical world is about.

If our theoretical concepts and paradigms were based on strictly logical application of scientific method, I could simply refer you to several good recent books on the results of parapsychological research (Beloff, 1975; Krippner, 1977; Parker, 1975; Randall, 1975; Schmeidler, 1976; Targ & Puthoff, 1978; Tart, 1977a; White, 1976; White & Mitchell, 1974; Wolman, Dale, Schmeidler, & Ullman, 1978), and then refer you to the parapsychological journals in which most of the experimental evidence has originally been published, and let you judge the matter for yourself. As a psychologist, however, I recognize that logic plays only a part in paradigm change. The interest in transpersonal psychology is partly a matter of ordinary scientific interest, and partly a deeper dissatisfaction (with strong emotional components) of the view of man prevalent in orthodox, mainstream American psychology. Thus, to be realistic, I expect that some of you will find the Emergent Interactionist position a useful formulation of what you would like to see as a basis for transpersonal psychology, because of personal as well as scientific reasons, and I expect others to find it too farfetched, for personal as well as scientific reasons. Nevertheless, I want to underscore the most important conclusion to be drawn from this Emergent Interactionist position; namely, that transpersonal phenomena may be something more than interesting but hallucinatory patternings of neurological firing in the brain. Note carefully that I am not saying that every unusual experience, whether or not "glorified" by the label "transpersonal", should be taken at face value. People have experiences, and they then almost always go on to interpret these experiences. These interpretations are usually based on emotional and psychological needs, rather than logic. A great deal of nonsensical and pathological interpretation of ordinary experience as well as transpersonal experience has always been with us, and will always be with us. Much pathological material will not be presented by its exponents under the name of transpersonal. So, my proposal for an Emergent Interactionist paradigm for understanding human consciousness is in no way a call for abandoning a critical stance and scientific rigor in our research. It is a call to not automatically dismiss the apparent meaning and implications of transpersonal experiences which imply that a human being is not necessarily limited to the neural firing patterns within his brain. It is my personal belief that we are creatures of much wider potential than orthodox psychology imagines. My concern now is that we do not leave the important human experience in the area of transpersonal psychology solely in the hands of cultists, but use what we have learned about scientific investigation to go on to understand fully the transpersonal and psychic nature of man, both for the sake of scientific knowledge, and for human betterment.

References

Beloff, J. (Ed.), *New directions in parapsychology*. Metuchen, N. J.: Scarecrow Press, 1975.

Geddes, A. A voice from the grandstand. *Journal of the Society for Psychical Research*, 1937, *30*, 103–105.

Greeley, A. *The sociology of the paranormal*. Beverly Hills, Calif.: Sage Publications, 1975.

Honorton, C. *Replicability, experimenter influence, and parapsychology: An empirical context for the study of mind*. Paper presented at the meeting of the American Association for the Advancement of Science, Washington, D.C., 1978.

James, W. *The varieties of religious experience*. New York: Longmans-Green, 1916.

Krippner, S. (Ed.), *Advances in parapsychological research. Vol. 1: Psychokinesis*. New York: Plenum, 1977.

Monroe, R. *Journeys out of the body*. New York: Doubleday, 1971.

Owens, C. M. Zen Buddhism. In C. T. Tart (Ed.), *Transpersonal psychologies*. New York: Harper & Row, 1975.

Parker, A. *States of mind: ESP and altered states of consciousness*. New York: Taplinger, 1975.

Randall, J. *Parapsychology and the nature of life*. New York: Harper & Row, 1975.

Rhine, J. B. Telepathy and other untestable hypotheses. *Journal of Parapsychology*, 1974, *38*, 137–153.

Schmeidler, G. (Ed.), *Parapsychology: Its relation to physics, biology, psychology, and psychiatry*. Metuchen, N. J.: Scarecrow Press, 1976.

Targ, R., & Puthoff, H. *Mind reach*. New York: Delacorte, 1978.

Tart, C. T. A psychophysiological study of out-of-the-body experiences in a selected subject. *Journal of the American Society for Psychical Research*, 1968, *62*, 3–27.

Tart, C. T. (Ed.), *Altered states of consciousness: A book of readings*. New York: Wiley, 1969.

Tart, C. T. *States of consciousness*. New York: Dutton, 1975. (a)

Tart, C. T. (Ed.), *Transpersonal psychologies*. New York: Harper & Row, 1975. (b)

Tart, C. T. *Psi: Scientific studies of the psychic realm*. New York: Dutton, 1977. (a)

Tart, C. T. *Improving real-time ESP by suppressing the future: Trans-temporal inhibition*. Paper presented at the meeting of the Institute of Electrical and Electronic Engineers. New York, New York, 1977. (b)

Tart, C. T. *A survey of expert opinion on potential negative uses of psi: U.S. Government interest in psi, and the level of research funding in the field*. Paper presented at the meeting of the Parapsychological Association, St. Louis, Missouri, 1978. (a)

Tart, C. T. Space, time, and mind. In W. Roll & R. Morris (Eds.), *Research in parapsychology 1977*. Metuchen, N.J.: Scarecrow Press, 1978. (b)

White, J., & Mitchell, E. (Eds.). *Psychic exploration: A challenge for science*. New York: Putnam, 1974.

White, R. (Ed.). *Surveys in parapsychology: Reviews of the literature and updated bibliographies*. Metuchen, N. J.: Scarecrow Press, 1976.

Wolman, B., Dale, L., Schmeidler, G., & Ullman, M. (Eds.). *Handbook of parapsychology*. New York: Van Nostrand Rheinhold, 1978.

IV

Beyond Psychology: East Meets West

In this section, Stan Marlan begins with a discussion of the depth dimension of the human psyche, a dimension which addresses the transcendent possibilities of human consciousness. The following three chapters continue this exploration in the context of more specific Eastern and Western philosophies. They include comparative discussions of Buddhism, Taoism, Hinduism, and Zen in dialogue with Freud, Jung, Sartre, and Heidegger.

11

Depth Consciousness

Stanton Marlan

The recognition of Jung's psychology as having penetrated even more deeply than Freud's into new realms of the unconscious and of the human spirit has shown itself on many fronts.[1] The impact of his thought has influenced science, religion, philosophy, psychology, psychiatry, psychoanalysis, economics, mythology, art, and the study of history. In addition, his explorations of the objective psyche, the archetypal basis of mind, the mythical structures of consciousness, his approach to the dream, the role of the opposites, the transcendent function, synchronicity, and active imagination are among his important contributions to a richer and fuller understanding of human existence and have served as a continuing stimulus to a generation of analysts who have developed his ideas. It thus seems ironic that in a recent biography of Jung it is reported that he was concerned that nobody understood him, and that his work had been a failure (Brome, 1978). Yet, Jung's work continues to receive recognition, and his psychology is becoming increasingly popular. He has been thought of as an important transitional figure to a new age of consciousness and was early heralded, along with William James, as one of the greatest and most penetrating psychologists in the twentieth century (Leary, Metzner, & Alpert, 1964).

Although Jung's thought is being given recognition, it is also in danger of being misunderstood and too easily assimilated to a prevailing mythos. This is strangely true for those new-age psychologists who have in so many ways appreciated Jung's archetypal explorations but have

---

[1] See R. von Eckartsberg, Chapter 2, Levin, Chapter 12, and V. Valle and Kruger, Chapter 19, for other presentations and discussions of Jung's psychology.—Eds.

Stanton Marlan • Pittsburgh Center for Psychotherapy and Psychoanalysis, Pittsburgh, Pennsylvania 15213.

bypassed their unique character, particularly with regard to an understanding of the "ego."

Jungian psychology has been narrowly thought of as an ego psychology and/or as a psychology on the verge of breaking through to the transpersonal, which, in either case, has not quite been able to free itself from the constraints of the ego, in spite of its depth explorations of the archetypal psyche and the mythic horizons of consciousness. The notion of the ego, besides being difficult to understand, applies to differing phenomena and to different things in different psychologies. It has also become popularized and has been a face on which varying notions of human consciousness get projected. There are those who see reality on the basis of ego-consciousness and its affirmations, and those who feel that the ego is itself the obstructing force which dwarfs human potential and as such needs to be transcended. Jungian psychology seems to be in a somewhat unique position in modern times, in that it affirms ego-modes of consciousness while at the same time recognizing the limitations of the overly constricted and rationalistic tendencies of ego-consciousness. As such, Jungian psychology sees something important in the human soul, both in the modes of affirmation and in those of transcendence; but it also points to the more integral underlying reality of the ego–self axis—the creative tension of the psyche, which is a symbolic expression of the dynamic quality of human existence in its depths. Holding both the modes of affirmation and transcendence in his awareness, Jung moved toward a unique possibility of reconciling the opposites which plague modern consciousness. In modern times, the constricting modes of the rationalistic ego have become a focus for the recognition of a revolution in consciousness and a movement toward a "New Age" psychology.

The Movement Toward a New Age

The real promise to which New Age psychologies point was recognized by Jung (1933) in his early work, *Modern Man in Search of a Soul*. In Baynes preface to this work, he points out that within the last decade there have been many who believe that "the western world stands on the verge of a spiritual rebirth" (p. vii). Almost a half century since Jung's prophetic work, we have been experiencing the labor pains and are giving birth to a new age of consciousness. This has been particularly pronounced in the yearnings of the younger generation, where there has been a seeking for sacramental experience, and especially for instruction in "gnosis" and "mysticism" (Eliade, 1976).

Eliade saw the interest in the occult in the sixties as having paved the way for a more extensive and renewed interest in the occult in recent times. For many, this meant a rejection of the Christian tradition, the motives for which he found in a seeking for "supposedly" broader and more practical ways of achieving an "individual and collective renovatio." This aiming at renewal seemed to be an attempt to move beyond the chaos and meaninglessness of modern life, and so he found it not surprising to discover young people seeking initiation into "old and venerable secrets." Jung and Eliade can be seen as having agreed that the structures of modern consciousness have become too narrow, too restrictive, and too one-sided.

From a mythic perspective, the narrowing of man's potential can be seen as a clinging to one-sided myths (Durand, 1976). It is not that modern man has become any less mythic, but that he has unconsciously lived the myths of logic and science. These myths unduly restrict the deepening of human consciousness and help to foster the feelings of alienation and "exile" so common in modern times. It is upon this archetypal ground that the multiple upsurges of the "Age of Aquarius" are called for. In the history of thought, myths of "exile" made no sense without myths of return and renewal, myths that promise an alliance with the ground of being (Durand, 1976). Without these myths, modern man can be seen to be living in a "crisis of confidence," as having "lost his way," and as seeking the "right path again" (von Eckartsberg, 1979).

Von Eckartsberg, a psychotherapist and social-ecological psychologist, describes this seeking in terms of a movement toward a new age and reflects the shared conviction of individuals in this movement that the social and human costs of our one-sided technological consciousness have been too great. This style of consciousness "takes away from the fullness of human capacities and selectively emphasizes certain human abilities and neglects others" (von Eckartsberg, 1979, p. 6). In the tradition of Jung, Eliade, Durand, and others like Roszak (1973) and W. I. Thompson (1973), von Eckartsberg describes the one-sidedness that can lead to personal and collective neurosis. He sees that man is not just intellect but also feeling and passion, intuition, imagination, and body, and has a need for worship and ecstasy as well (von Eckartsberg, 1979).

The theme of spiritual rebirth (Jung, 1933), of personal and collective renovatio (Eliade, 1976), and of myths of renewal (Durand, 1976) are contributing to what is itself a mythic motif in our time, called the "New Age," with its concern for the full development of human potential. Von Eckartsberg (1979) speaks of this development as a "move away from the old-age myth of the Promethean struggle for technological control by rationalistic modes of ego-consciousness toward a more inclusive symbolic vision . . . and a more integrated way of life" (p. 12).

Seeking Depth in the Psychedelic Experience and Maps of Consciousness

The impact of the psychedelic experience on our rationalistic habituated ways of seeing catapulted us perhaps more dramatically than the modern scientific discovery and formulation of the unconscious toward the recognition of a profound and separate "reality." This "reality" has been described as a journey to new realms of consciousness and as limitless in scope. Its characteristic features were the "transcendence of verbal concepts, of space–time, dimensions, and of the ego or identity" (Leary, Metzner, & Alpert, 1964, p. 11).

It was the conviction of these early explorers that it was not the drugs themselves which produced the transcendent experiences, but that they acted to open our mind to experiences which were not just distortions of ordinary consciousness, but were themselves evidence of human capacities that were not well understood in the framework of current theories. A similar conviction was held by Jung with regard to dreams and schizophrenia; he could not accept the phenomena of these experiences simply as distortions of ordinary consciousness but saw them, rather, as pointing to the archetypal basis of mind. Leary, Metzner, and Alpert (1964) were thoroughly convinced of the uniqueness of these experiences and were most cautious and outspoken against the temptation to impose old models of the psyche, or premature theories. They were, on the other hand, deeply impressed by Eastern psychological texts, which were felt to be the only available works which dealt with consciousness and its alterations. These texts were felt to be valuable as guidebooks and manuals which could enable explorers of the psyche to understand the new realities of expanded consciousness.

The metaphor of the "map" was fast becoming important as it emerged from the excitement to chart the new and unknown territories. The task of seeking new paradigms of expanded consciousness was taken up with the help of Eastern texts. The first psychedelic manual, *The Psychedelic Experience* (Leary, Metzner, & Alpert, 1964), was based on the *Tibetan Book of the Dead*. Leary, Metzner, and Alpert were aware that other explorers could draw different maps based on scientific, aesthetic, and therapeutic foundations. In addition, it was known to them that the mystery unveiled through the psychedelic experience had been passed down for ages, not only in the East but by Western mystery schools as well. Leary himself was to pass down more maps in his next work (based on the classic *Tao Te Ching*) which he entitled *Psychedelic Prayers* (1966). Based on his experience of neurological and biochemical anatomy of the human body, Leary poetically described new patterns of experience in terms of the neural level of consciousness which penetrated beneath symbols, games, and sensory apparatus to the raw energy of the psyche. Beyond this, he identified cellular consciousness, and , more deeply still, the molecular elemental energies that vibrate within it. Leary's concern with these discoveries was not simply for the purpose of experience *per se* but with the intention in his guidebooks to help others to direct and control their consciousness in order to reach "the level variously called liberation, illumination, enlightenment." The message of paramount importance that Leary extracts is that consciousness is far deeper than previously thought, and that it is possible "to cut beyond ego-consciousness, to tune in on the neurological processes and to become aware of the enormous treasury of ancient racial knowledge welded into the nucleus of every cell in your body" (1966, Foreword).

Similar explorations were being conducted by Masters and Houston (1966). Their approach was to take a "depth sounding" of the psyche, which led them to a method of guiding the individual based on an observed pattern of "descent." They describe four levels of drug-induced experience, hypothesized as corresponding to the major levels of the psyche: "sensory," "recollective-analytic," "symbolic," and "integral." Their conclusion, with reference to the depth and richness of the experiences they charted, is that it seemed limiting to understand the above factors only in terms of the psychodynamic realm. As the voyage inward continued, more and more energy became focused on the realms of experience that were alien to the ego.

The concern was with mapping and guiding deep experiences of consciousness. This was carried on by Metzner (1971) who went on to explore the metaphor of the map and other systems of consciousness in his *Maps of Consciousness*, in which he used the analogy of the journey or path to consider the process of psychological transformation.[2] He separated the notion of a map (which is intended "to help us find our way" [p. 10]) from a model or theory which attempts simply to say how man "is." Although theories and models are typical of Western psychology, much of Oriental and esoteric systems are maps in his sense, and they imply a model of man which is teleological in nature. Metzner's work also develops the myth of the new age, in that he explores these kinds of systems within the frame of reference of a renaissance or spiritual renewal. He explores six maps of consciousness, including the I Ching, tantra, tarot, alchemy, astrology, and actualism, the last being a system of Agni yoga, or fire yoga, of which Metzner was a student. In the same year, Roland Fischer (1971) published an article with an empirical scientific basis, entitled "A Cartography of the Ecstatic and Meditative States,"

---

[2]See R. von Eckartsberg, Chapter 2, for a descriptive review of the many different proposed "maps" of human consciousness.—Eds.

in which he maps the "experimental and experiential features" of what he calls the perception–hallucination continuum.

A few years later, Stanislov Grof, another serious explorer of the psychedelic experience, published a book entitled *Realms of the Human Unconscious*. In this work, Grof attempted to achieve a comprehensive framework for bringing order to the experiences evoked by psychedelics. In spite of the fact that transpersonal phenomena were frequently being reported and were of "obvious relevance for many areas of human life" (Grof, 1975, p. 209), little had been done to make sense of or to integrate these experiences into the theory and practice of the mind sciences or the helping arts. This is what Grof set out to do. His conclusion was that transpersonal experiences represent phenomena that are *sui generis*, and that originate in the deep unconscious. He concluded that these phenomena have been unrecognized and unacknowledged by classical Freudian psychoanalysis, and, as Masters and Houston (1966) had argued, could not be *reduced* to the psychodynamic level and to biographically determined phenomena. Grof's challenge to classical theory is a significant one, as he was no casual observer of psychoanalytic thought, being a member of the Prague psychoanalytic group, and a "convinced" Freudian who shared the typical critiques of Jung.

Grof said of his experience that, sooner or later, all his subjects "transcended the narrow psychodynamic framework and moved into perinatal and transpersonal realms," and that "this happened in spite of his intense effort and need to understand the events in the session in psychodynamic terms" (p. 212). Grof described four levels of experience, the last two of which he felt called for a revised psychology of the unconscious. He respectively described these levels as: (a) *abstract* and *aesthetic*, which roughly corresponded with the sensory level of Masters and Houston; (b) *psychodynamic*, which he related to Freudian psychoanalysis; (c) *perinatal*, which corresponded to the nine months of gestation, and which correlated with Rank's work on the birth trauma; and (d) *transpersonal*, which he related to the work of Jung. On the basis of the above expanded cartography of the unconscious, Grof envisioned the development of a radical new psychology which paralleled the unfolding layers of the psyche. Grof was encouraged by the fact that as the phenomenology of the psyche showed itself, it seemed to parallel the research of Freud, Rank, Jung, Assagioli, Maslow, and the esoteric schools.

The emphasis that continued to develop in the search for depth followed the continuing recognition of the limitations of ego-consciousness and the vast depths of the psyche still to be discovered. This remained the typical genre of transpersonal psychologists in their attempt to continue the mapping of consciousness.

Kenneth Ring (1976), building on the early work of Grof, attempted to develop a map of the transpersonal regions of consciousness and to integrate into his model all those areas of the psyche described by a broad variety of thinkers and systems of esoteric psychology. In his early study, he used the image of a series of concentric circles to describe the structures of consciousness. In this model, he moved from waking consciousness to the preconscious, the psychodynamic, the ontogenetic, the transindividual, the phylogenetic, the extraterrestrial, the superconscious, and on to the void. Ring attempted to develop a mandala model of consciousness, and struggled with the nature and placement of the extraterrestrial level.

Concern with the extraterrestrial level of consciousness was developed by Leary (1977) in his movement toward a new psychology and cosmic vision, which reaches a peak in his *Exo-Psychology*.[3] This text described the crisis which now faces the human race. His description amplified the theme of a search for a new age and makes use of a navigational metaphor which again suggested that humanity has lost its "map." In the past, Leary's challenge for humanity had been the transcendence of ego-consciousness which now becomes expressed in a cosmic dimension. In perhaps his most passionate statement, but still with his typical sense of humor and cosmic gamesmanship, Leary appeals to humanity to work toward extraterrestrial migration.

Oddly, in gnostic style and like an alchemist of space, Leary transforms the transcendence of the ego into a transcendence of the planet. He attempts to provide a "galactic" perspective, and conceives of the development of the nervous system as moving from its larval condition to its extraterrestrial potential. It is the transcendence of ego-planet which is Leary's unifying and passionate theme, and the point from which he critiques Jung. Although acknowledging Jung as one of the most important thinkers of the twentieth century, he also censures him for being too limited: he was, after all, "a psychoanalyst for whom the ego remained an important structure of consciousness." With Leary, the assault on the ego is raised to a high pitch, and presents modern consciousness with its engaging passion, the "transcendence of the ego." It is this notion that crowns the spirit of the New Age, and is its royal road to enlightenment.

The Question of Transcendence or Affirmation of the Ego

The question of transcendence has been a difficult one to understand. Jung had always affirmed the importance of the ego whereas Leary

---

[3]See Leary, Chapter 9, for selections reprinted from his *Exo-Psychology*.—Eds.

encouraged us to leave it behind. What is little understood is that Jung's affirmation of the importance of the ego was in no way a constricting of consciousness within the narrow confines of an egoistic psychology. For Jung, too, this constriction must be transcended, as there is something toward which the ego points, and to which it stands as "the moved to the mover" (Jung 1954, p. 259), that is, the self. Nevertheless, Jung saw that the ego and the self are intimately and dynamically related. "The term ego–self axis has been used by Neumann to designate this vital affinity" (Edinger, 1960, p. 8). Thus, for Jung, the ego is a dynamic rather than a static structure, which is always in an active relationship with the self, and has an important role at different stages and moments of development. Jung's conception of the ego, as differentiated from Freud's and from the popularized notion, has not sufficiently been accounted for in the popularized critiques of the ego.

Leary's critique of Jung is, however, not untypical. Watts (1961) had also faulted Jung for assuming that a strong ego structure is the necessary condition for civilization. Swami Rama, Rudolph Ballentine, and Swami Ajaya (1976) also critique Jung for saying that one must depend on the ego as a basis for consciousness, and for his inability to conceive of a state of consciousness apart from the concept of ego. They also take issue with Jung's idea that it must be reckoned a catastrophe when the ego is assimilated by the Self. Likewise, John Welwood criticizes Jung for positing the real existence and necessity of the ego (Welwood, 1977). According to Welwood, Jung's positing of the ego reveals philosophical assumptions of Western culture that have only recently begun to be reexamined. Welwood questioned the well-accepted idea that conscious experience is only possible for a separate self-conscious subject (ego) and saw this idea as having its roots in Aristotle's separation of the thinking mind from the total natural process (matter). He stated that Jung acknowledged this separation of mind from world to be a basic feature of Western thought. Welwood contrasted this with the Buddhist perspective of Chogyam Trungpa, who believed that the idea of mind as independent of world is at the root of *samsara*, and a confusion in the Buddhist perspective. Trungpa rejects the notion of the unconscious as a real "other," external or alien to consciousness, and the sense of a real ego that must be defended against these qualities.

Insofar as the above critiques reject the notion of the ego as the reified, popularized, and static concept which it has become, they constitute a continuing recognition of the limitations of the rationalistic thinking of the nineteenth century. These critiques move along a path of criticism that sees the psyche in terms of static entities, that is, in harmony with the leading edge of twentieth century thought. Existential-phenomenological approaches to the psyche have been important in recognizing the need to return to the phenomena of existence, rather than remaining fixed in the theoretical and static concepts of mind.[4]

A critique similar to Welwood's has been fashioned from within Jungian circles by June Singer (1979). Singer's approach, however, recognizes that Jung has been interpreted too much in the light of his earlier thought, and not enough in terms of his later development. Singer also critiques the model of the psyche that is seen as containing "ego" and "archetype" as autonomous entities each occupying space in the psyche. At this level of reflection, the contents of the psyche are seen as a kind of "materia . . . pushed around by psychic energy, sometimes at the instigation of the ego, sometimes at the instigation of the archetype" (p. 6). Singer saw this model as closely paralleling the world view of classical physics, which was in fashion when Jung was in his formative years. In contrast to the above model, and more in harmony with Jung's later thought, Singer suggests a model of the psyche in which ego and archetype are not seen as polarized and static concepts. Singer believes it is in the spirit of Jung to take a fresh look at the concepts of Jungian psychology. Her struggle is both to reevaluate and yet to preserve the value of Jung's concepts for analysis as well as for a general understanding of the human psyche.

Singer begins by questioning the autonomous quality of the concept of archetype, and is influenced by the new consciousness, which is not fragmentary but, rather holistic in character. Through using the concept of archetype within the above frame of reference, Singer (1979) feels "we may move toward a sense of the congruity of consciousness and the unconscious, of ego and archetype." (p. 16).

In defining the ego in the above manner, however, it is important to preserve creative tensions which underly the polarities of ego and archetype. Unfortunately, many thinkers (in cutting through this tension) develop a phobic reaction to concepts such as the ego, and in turn miss the phenomena to which it points. In the realm of phenomenological experience, we still encounter ego-phenomena and are aware of vast, deep, and profound realms of experience which present themselves as alien, other, numinous, autonomous, and as difficult if not impossible to integrate. Creating a framework in which these opposing forces can be understood was one of the unique contributions of Jung. It was not Singer's attempt to minimize this, but to keep us from dogmatism, and creatively develop Jungian theory in tune with the most recent facts available.

[4]See Moss and Keen, Chapter 4, for a discussion of the existential-phenomenological approach to issues concerning the nature of human consciousness.—Eds.

The Danger in the Popularized Rejection of the Ego

Although movement away from a reified conception of the ego is a valuable contribution to the modern understanding of consciousness, the popularized rejection of the ego leads to innumerable misconceptions and a certain shallowness of consciousness itself. While our culture has been in desperate need of critiques of the Promethean inflation of rationalistic modes of ego-consciousness, Jung was also acutely aware that the attempt to transcend the ego can be just as Promethean in its one-sided inflations and spiritual manias. He was aware that a continual questioning of our egos needed to include an informed critique of the distortion and grandiosity that sometimes passes in the name of ego-transcendence. The purpose of freeing ourselves from this kind of inflation was not (according to Jung) for the purpose of getting rid of our egos, but in order to bring ourselves into a conscious relation to the self.

Von Eckartsberg (1979) is aware that the awakening of the emerging renewal can be fraught with problems of its own as individuals become vulnerable to conversion to "ready-made life styles." These styles have become quite visible in the circles of some humanistic and transpersonal psychologists. James Hillman, in his work *Re-Visioning Psychology* (1975), amusingly described how, in attempting to restore dignity to man, these psychologies promote an "ennobled one-sidedness." He pointed out how emphasis on transcendence can leave the baser and dark side behind in a way that leaves one with no more than a caricature of human nature. Hillman considers these psychologies as promoting simplistic notions of the psyche, in which disturbances need "mainly to be felt, expressed, shared, or cried forth and exorcised" (p. 65). For Hillman, transcendence by means of a "high," be it the body highs, weekend highs, or LSD highs, easily turns into ways of avoiding the depths of the soul. He is no less easy with reference to Oriental approaches, albeit he rightfully qualifies his critique by limiting it (perhaps not enough) to Westernized interpretations of Oriental psychologies, which, he states, have turned its hard realities to the "smell of sandalwood." Westernized approaches to oriental psychology run the risk of lending themselves to a kind of transcendental denial, the outcome of which is to seek liberation up at the peaks and not in the depths. What comes to matter is being high and quickly transcending our woundedness and our pathologies. For Hillman this is a cause for concern, as it is precisely through our illness and woundedness that we may seek doorways to the depths of soul. We have become embarrassed about, and tend to deny, our sufferings. In this spirit, the way becomes meditation, contemplation, and exercise in order to find a way through everyday problems, a rising above them. This, then, becomes the popularized transcendence of the ego, the mindless "courting of bliss" where thinking and insight have lost their place.

Hillman makes a renewed case for imaginative thought and the "sobering ideas" which he sees as having been an important part of the heritage of the depth psychologies of both Freud and Jung. Starting from a different perspective, Hillman (1979) also reworks the notion of the ego. In his recent book, *The Dream and the Underworld,* he sees at work in the ego "a set of pejorative attitudes" (p. 96) (humanism, personalism, literalism) which must first be suspended before he feels we can begin to think in a new style. Hillman, too, questions the nature of the ego, and his underworld or imaginal ego points toward the fact that the literalized, substantialistic, reified ego needs to be suspended in order to bring into play a more intentional, creative, flexible, "in-between" structure of subjectivity. This kind of subjectivity no longer need be seen to exclude the objective, "impersonal" qualities of existence.

Hillman (1979) gives examples of the images present in dream consciousness which are in an in-between realm, "neither human nor only divine, neither subjective nor objective, neither personal nor archetypal but both" (p. 100). He critiques the subjectivistic tendencies of Gestalt and Jungian dream interpreters, but seems unaware that the recognition of this intentional in-between reality is also present in the Gestalt tradition of Polster and Polster's (1973) work, as it was in Jung, in Jungian analysts, and in existential analysts such as Medard Boss (1957).

Nevertheless, Hillman's effort is directed at correcting what he has seen as the one-way traffic moving out of the unconscious toward the subjectivity of the ego. He, on the other hand, has chosen an about-face—hence his concern with the underworld which is itself a one-way movement. His position, though it is a welcome and refreshing awareness in an age where all that's new seems to be singing the same old song, is nevertheless one-sided. While Leary's move was to go beyond the reifications of the ego by going to the heights of transcendence, Hillman would call us in the other direction, to the depths of the underworld.

Hillman has a point to make, but in so doing he by-passes or under-mines much that has been a valuable contribution to the contemporary study of consciousness—the psychedelic experience, Oriental psychology, and the occult arts which have impacted significantly on the Renaissance psychology by which he is so much intrigued (see Boe, 1979). Still, his description fits the popularization of New Age ideas, and he puts his finger on the idealized pulse of the New Age.

The question of the ego has remained a difficult one. New Age psychologies have attempted to point a way beyond the static and rationalistic modes of ego-consciousness, but in so doing they have also contributed to the popularized idea of ego-transcendence, with all the resulting idealizations characterized by Hillman.

The Popularized Notion of the Ego and Eastern Thought

Although the notions of the ego may differ in Eastern and Western thought, the overpopularized conception of the ego has led both Eastern and Western writers to the overgeneralized conclusion that the East and the West have characteristically different approaches. Wilber (1977)[5], for instance, described the aim of the West as one of strengthening the ego, of moving toward integration, of correcting one's self-image, and of building self-confidence and establishing realistic goals. He also stated that the West did not promise a complete release or liberation from all of life's sufferings. Although he acknowledged that, to some degree, the East and the West overlap, he felt the central aim of most Eastern approaches is not to strengthen the ego, but to totally and completely transcend it. He concluded that the goals of Eastern and Western approaches are thus very different.

Wilber did an admirable job of trying to resolve these differences by attributing them to a focusing on different levels of the spectrum of consciousness. Contrary to many advocates of Eastern approaches which "scoff at all attempts to create healthy egos," Wilber (1977) stated:

> Let us avail ourselves of the existing methods—largely "Western"—of creating healthy egos, of integrating projections, of coming to grips with unconscious drives and wishes . . . of living . . . to our full potentials as individuals. (pp. 20–21)

Yet it is still Wilber's conviction that Western psychotherapy aims at "patching up the individual self while Eastern approaches aim at transcending the self" (p. 20). Although he attempted to correct Western biases toward the East, he nevertheless elevated Eastern thought to giving access to a "richer, fuller level of consciousness." The individual self is still seen as confined, and Western approaches as limited and preliminary, to a level of consciousness beyond the ego.

A different approach has been taken by Fingarette (1963), whose premise was that a deep understanding of both ego-transcendence and ego-integration do not exclude one another, and that the separation between them may be due to an original misunderstanding of the term

---

[5]See R. von Eckartsberg's, Chapter 2, discussion of Wilber's "vision of the spectrum of consciousness."—Eds.

ego. Rather than seeing the differences in aim of Eastern and Western approaches as based on a focusing on different levels of a spectrum (as did Wilber), Fingarette goes below the literalizations of "ego" and "egoless-ness" to look at the primary data of experience in both psychoanalytic insights and the ways of liberation. He feels that the extreme opposition between the goals of the above needs to be revised, based on his conclusion that "the self which is lost in enlightenment is not the self essential to the practical carrying on of one's ordinary daily activities" (p. 307). He states that what is lost in the experience of selflessness are such things as "self-criticism," "aggression against the self," "self-consciousness in the colloquial sense" (p. 309). This kind of self-consciousness ordinarily occurs only in the context of the disruption of normal ego activity; when there is little disruption, the ego is relatively anxiety-free. In such a state there exists a kind of self-forgetfulness, characteristic of a mature personality. Fingarette stated that beneath the ambiguities of language the central task of the mystic is that of achieving an unusually strong ego within an unusually well-integrated personality. This mature or enlightened personality continues to sense, perceive, think, discriminate, and imagine, all of which are essential functions of the ego. For Fingarette, the

> soul-racking death which leads to blissful "rebirth" is the death of the subjectively experienced, anxiety-generated "self" perception; it is the emergence into the freedom of introspective "self-forgetfulness" of the psychically unified self. (p. 314)

In Fingarette's approach, he translates the experience of selflessness into a psychoanalytic language, and, in so doing, finds minimal differences between the actual experiences of psychoanalytic subjects and those writings that describe the enlightment experience. Although leading toward an overcoming of the popularized conception of the transcendence of the ego, he limits the experiences of an expanded mode of consciousness to the "everyday mind." For him, when we speak of enlightment we are not talking about an existence divorced from the everyday world, but of life within this world. He quotes Suzuki for verification as having said "Zen is your everyday mind." For Fingarette, the everyday mind is equated with the Freudian conception of the ego. These ideas have been critiqued by Arasteh (1965) for the tendency to "submit to the music of psychoanalysis as it is, rather than to develop it." Fingarette's analysis, though it goes a long way in trying to resolve the discrepancy between psychoanalysis and Eastern psychology, falls short because it introduces an ego-oriented (in the Freudian sense) interpretation of mysticism. Arasteh says that Fingarette fails to see that the ego-oriented process is not the highest state of personality.

A Jungian Approach to the Question of Ego Transcendence[6]

Another approach, that both attempts to go beyond the dichotomy of East and West and yet offers a more experiental and deeper understanding of the ego, is that of Mokusen Miyuki (1979) who is both a Jungian psychoanalyst and a Buddhist priest. Miyuki, in a personal letter to the author, commented on Fingarette's use of the above quotation from Zen as highly controversial. He states that the phrase "Zen is your ordinary mind" is not a precise translation of the original text, which should read "the ordinary mind is Tao." It is Miyuki's conviction that Jungian approach can do much more to clarify the whole question of the ego. He sees the ego more in the dynamic, balanced spirit of Tao, and feels that there has been a misunderstanding of what is meant by ego by both those who see it as a static concept and those who proclaim that Eastern religion seeks its dissolution. Buddhism has commonly been misunderstood to advocate the dissolution of the ego, but, on the contrary, it aims at aiding the individual to strengthen the ego through the integration of unconscious contents.[7] This is what Miyuki suggests can be accomplished in meditation and spiritual practice by a withdrawal of the center of psychic gravity centered around the ego. This is followed by the creation of a new psychic condition that is not ego-centric, but ex-centric, meaning that the center of consciousness is in a state of flux. Through the integration of psychic contents experienced in this way, the ego-orientation is strengthened. Miyuki states that this ex-centric state of mind has been characterized in the Buddhist tradition as *anatta* or *anatman*, which have been variously translated without an awareness of the psychological implications as "non-ego," "no self," "without self," and "no soul." But these are inadequate translations, which serve to confuse what is a difficult concept to place in Western categories. Miyuki uniquely translates *atman* as indicating a dynamic process, and *anatman* as referring to the idea of not identifying oneself with any one aspect of being, or as a constantly changing process/state. Recognition of this process serves to dispel the illusory identity, and manifests the true Self, which cannot be identified with aiming at dissolution of the ego. This interpretation helps to dispel a host of problems in understanding Eastern psychology. Miyuki thus comes to see the ego-functions in conjunction with the self as creating a state of constant renewal and enrichment. Here Miyuki reaches beyond the reified concept of the ego, directly into its essence.

---

[6]See also R. von Eckartsberg's, Chapter 2, discussion of transcendent experience (the "theo-dimension"), and Schore, Chapter 22.—Eds.

[7]See Levin, Chapter 12, and de Silva, Chapter 13, for other discussions of Buddhism and its implications for Western psychology and philosophy.—Eds.

James Hall (1977), a prominent Jungian analyst, sees the ego in a similarly dynamic way. Hall states that in an individuating ego "the contents of the ego continually shift, gradually incorporating certain nonego complexes, such as the shadow and persona" (p. 174). Each new expansion of the structure of the ego-complex makes untenable some particular form of a previous ego-image, which must be left behind as an outgrown shell. This outgrown shell is what is properly referred to as the "transcendence of the ego." It is actually the "ego-image" that is transcended. A reason why ego-image is often mistaken for ego can be understood, given Hall's explanation that the feeling of "I-ness" is often dependent only on the stability of the complex structure associated with the ego and on those outer objects that are identified with this complex structure through projection. For Hall, an individuating ego (as in Miyuki's description) is in an active process of change, in which the specific complexes on which the ego tacitly relies are altered, but the archetypal core of the ego assures a sense of continuity of existence in spite of shifting contents. The reworking of the specific contents on which the ego relies constitutes what Jung would call the symbolic life or individuation process. A Jungian interpretation of the ego then needs to be seen within the dynamic context of the individuation process in which the ego is in continual relationship to the self which acts as the regulating center of consciousness. Hall points out that although the self is non-ego in a sense, in other ways it is the very core of the ego. "This relationship between ego and self was called an axis by Neumann and a paradox by Edinger (1960)" (p. 147). According to Miyuki, it is the very essence of what Jung called the symbolic life.

This is a useful concept in understanding the relationship of ego to archetype, and it is thus not surprising to find meaningful comparisons between Jungian analysis and authentic transformational systems across time and throughout the world. Wilber (1977), for example, showed parallels in Jungian analysis and Tibetan visualization techniques by pointing out how both approaches go through two processes, one of contacting and elaborating the image, and the second of dissolving or integrating it into the normal stream of life and consciousness. This later phase involves the integral and higher functions of the ego, and a balanced and conscious relationship to the self. It does not require a reduction of experience into the narrow bounds of a rationalistic ego, but the conscious symbolic process of an individuating ego, such as described by Miyuki and Hall. It was the lack of recognition of the ego–self axis that caused so much difficulty, and led to the unnecessary splitting of ego-integration and ego-transcendence. Both are necessary, and they must be seen as interrelated. Without this level of recognition, it is impossible to see how one can genuinely integrate extraordinary states of consciousness, and bring them into relationship with normal everyday life. It was this quest which led Ram Dass (1977) beyond psychedelics and into his own creative search in India.

Gordon (1978) describes the creative process as one in which the individual has to be able to surrender ego functions, but also in the last stage to "come down to earth" (p. 132). Given a Jungian approach, we can now be free to recognize "our earth" as somewhere between extraterrestrial consciousness and the underworld, that is, to see it as not only a "conglomeration of physical facts," but also alchemically, in a personal and human way:

> The Earth has to be perceived not by the senses [alone], but through a primordial image, and inasmuch as this image carries the features of a personal figure, it will prove to "symbolize with" the very image itself which the soul carries in its innermost depths. The perception of the Earth Angel will come about in an intermediate universe which is neither that of the essences of philosophy nor that of sensory data . . . but which is a universe of archetypal images, experienced as so many personal presences. (Corbin, 1977, p. 4)

This in-between world is the world in which we live, the world which has had its myths returned and renewed, the world as lived symbolically along the ego–self axis.

Conclusion

In order to penetrate more deeply into the psyche, there has developed an enthusiastic but one-sided spirituality which has in the "New Age" continually set up a misguided ideal of "selflessness." All too often the ego has become the "ugly duckling" of the psyche (Denning & Phillips, 1978).

In their work on magical philosophy, Denning and Phillips (1978) stated that there is a true spirituality which is not imposed from without, but which is found within, and which does not seek to destroy the ego but lead it into its rightful inheritance. The most authentic systems of magic and transformational disciplines, when properly understood, can likewise be found to hold the same truth.

In recent times, the popularized conception of the transcendence of the ego has replaced a more originary understanding of the ego in relation to the depths of the psyche. This is not surprising, in a time when there has been so much energy directed toward the promise of change and renewal in a civilization where rationalistic and limiting modes of ego-consciousness have been dominant. The ego, when rightfully understood, points to a phenomenon integral to consciousness and to a profound archetypal dimension of human existence. It is to such a dimension that Jung's work points, and, as such, it promises to lead the ego to its rightful inheritance, thus offering something unique in our time to modern individuals in search of a soul.

References

Arasteh, A. *Final integration in the adult personality*. Leiden: E. J. Brill, 1965.

Boe, J. Review of *re-visioning psychology* by James Hillman. *Psychological Perspectives, 1979*, 10(1), 88–89.

Boss, M. *Analysis of dreams*. London: Rider, 1957.

Brome, V. *Jung*. New York: Atheneum, 1978.

Corbin, H. *Spiritual body and celestial earth*. Princeton: Princeton University Press, 1977.

Denning, M., & Phillips, O. *The triumph of light*. In *The magical philosophy*. St. Paul, Minn.: Llewellyn Publications, 1978.

Durand, G. The image of man in Western occult tradition. in J. Hillman (Ed.), *Spring*. New York: Spring Publications, 1976.

Edinger, E. The ego-self paradox. *The Journal of Analytical Psychology*, 1960, 5, 1.

Eliade, M. *Occultism, witchcraft, and cultural fashions*. Chicago: The University of Chicago Press, 1976.

Fingarette, H. *The self in transformation*. New York: Basic Book, 1963.

Fischer, R. A cartography of ecstatic and meditative states. *Science*, 1971, 174, 4012.

Gordon, R. *Dying and creating: A search for meaning*. London: The Society of Analytical Psychology, 1978.

Grof, S. *Realms of the human unconscious*. New York: Viking, 1975.

Hall, J. *Clinical uses of dreams: Jungian interpretations and enactments*. New York: Grune & Stratton, 1977.

Hillman, J. *Re-visioning psychology*. New York: Harper & Row, 1975.

Hillman, J. *The dream and the underworld*. New York: Harper & Row, 1979.

Jung, C. G. *Modern man in search of a soul*. New York: Harcourt, Brace, 1933.

Jung, C. G. *Psychology and religion: West and East*. In H. Read, M. Fordham, G. Adler, & W. McGuire (Eds.), *Collected Works of Carl G. Jung* (Vol. 11).

Leary, T. *Psychedelic prayers*. Kerhonkson, N. Y.: Poets Press, 1966.

Leary, T. *Exo-psychology*. Los Angeles: Starseed/Peace Press, 1977.

Leary, T., Metzner, R., & Alpert, R. *The psychedelic experience*. New York: University Books, 1964.

Masters, R., & Houston, J. *The varieties of psychedelic experience*. New York: Holt, Rinehart, & Winston, 1966.

Metzner, R. *Maps of consciousness*. New York: Macmillan, 1971.

Miyuki, M. *A Jungian approach to the pure land practice of Nien-fo*. Paper presented at the Sixth Annual Conference of Jungian Analysts, Asilomar, California, March, 1979.

Polster, E., & Polster, M. *Gestalt therapy integrated*. New York: Brunner/Mazel, 1973.

Ram Dass. Foreword in D. Goleman, *The varieties of the meditative experience*. New York: Dutton, 1977.

Ring, K. Mapping the regions of consciousness: A conceptual reformulation. *The Journal of Transpersonal Psychology*, 1976, 8(2), 77–88.

Roszak, T. *Where the wasteland ends*. New York: Doubleday, 1973.

Singer, J. The use and misuse of archetype. *The Journal of Analytical Psychology*, 1979, 24(1), 3–18.

Swami Rama, Ballentine, R., & Swami Ajaya. *Yoga and psychotherapy, the evolution of con-ciousness*. Glenview, Ill.: The Himalayan Institute, 1976.

Thompson, W. I. *Passages about earth*. New York: Harper & Row, 1973.

von Eckartsberg, R. *The social psychology of the new age*. Paper presented at the conference "On Learning to be Human: Exploring the Metaphors of Consciousness," Pittsburgh, Pennsylvania, May, 1979.

Watts, A. *Psychotherapy East & West*. New York: Pantheon Books, 1961.

Welwood, J. Meditation and the unconscious: A new perspective. *Journal of Transpersonal Psychology*, 1977, *9*(1), 1–26.

Wilber, K. *The spectrum of consciousness*. Wheaton, Ill.: Theosophical Publishing House, 1977.

12

Approaches to Psychotherapy
FREUD, JUNG, AND TIBETAN BUDDHISM[1]

David M. Levin

In what follows, we will be comparing Freud, Jung, and Tibetan Buddhism with regard, mainly, to the following seven central questions:

1. From a methodological point of view, how do they understand human nature?
2. What norm of health, what dream of well-being, underlies their methods, determines their conceptualizations, and guides their therapeutic practices?
3. How do they respond to the question of diagnosis?
4. If psychotherapy is, at heart, the practice of compassion, then we want to ask: How do these therapies understand, and practice, their calling of compassion?
5. How do they understand, and work with, the human power of imagination?
6. How do they understand, and work with, the languaging and interpreting of our experiential process?
7. How do they understand, and work with, the human body?

[1]This chapter is an expanded version of my paper presented as part of the symposium "Holography and Eastern Philosophy: Holistic Re-examinations of Contemporary Psychology" at the American Psychological Association Convention, New York, New York, September, 1979.

David M. Levin ● Department of Philosophy, Northwestern University, Evanston, Illinois 60201.

Understanding Human Nature

How do the therapies of Freud, Jung, and Tibetan Buddhism understand human nature? For Freud, the human being is, ultimately, a
biophysical system of energies which manifest, in causally determinate
ways, not only as drives, needs, and desires, but also as events and states
of a so-called psychic life. Freud never resolved his deep-seated ambivalence and confusion with regard to the Cartesian splitting of mind and
body. At times, he tends to side with the Viennese materialists, holding
that the mind is ultimately reducible to the body, and strongly suggesting
that the body is nothing but a biophysical mechanism, which we will fully
understand when we can investigate it in terms of systematic physical
laws. At other times, while still regarding the human body in this light, he
seems to recognize that the so-called mind needs its *own* mode of understanding. But he seems unable, or unwilling, to grant this other mode of
understanding without also taking for granted a rather crude version of
Cartesian dualism, which he therefore, in fact, never attempts to defend.[2]
Such ambivalence and confusion seriously impair Freud's understanding
of human freedom. On the one hand, he believed in a thoroughgoing
determinism, and was accordingly committed to finding biophysical (or
neurophysiological) *causes* for every aspect of human character and behavior; or, failing this endeavor, he was prepared to adopt, temporarily,
perhaps, a hermeneutic process of interpretation, in order to find, at the
very least, the underlying *mental* causes (reasons, motives, intentions,
wishes, etc.) which determine human beings. On the other hand, he also
believed that psychotherapy can significantly contribute to the *liberation*
of human beings. In the end, Freud situates this liberation within the
structural schema of the conscious and the unconscious, so that the
freedom he promises does *not* mean "the courage to be," the capacity for
self-actualization, or what Erich Fromm called "freedom to . . . ," but
only, rather, that we are freed *from* our bondage to causes which afflict us;
freedom, moreover, *not* in the sense that our life is no longer causally
determined, but simply in the sense that the causes by which we are
determined are no longer painfully unconscious. In brief, analysis frees
us insofar as it brings an unconscious mechanism into the light of consciousness and lets the obstructed energy flow. But analysis does *not* free
us, nor does it even *attempt* to free us, from a complete determination by
physical causes. This limitation is intimately bound up with the fact that
Freudian analysis does not seek to undo, or transcend, the dualities in
terms of which human nature is understood and lived. Analysis promises

---

[2]Freud's Cartesianism comes to the fore in his insistence that psychoanalysis needs to
continue "work that subordinates everything to the single demand for certainty." Isn't
this, rather, a symptom of his own anxiety? See Freud, *The Problem of Anxiety.*

only to bring the dualistic character of human existence into the process of rational, causal explanation.

Jung, by contrast, embraces a much less mechanistic, much more organic understanding of human nature.[3] In a major break with Freud, Jung worked out a non-egological psychology. For Jung, the painful dualities of mind and body, conscious and unconscious, nature (as the id) and culture (the ego and superego), as well as the duality which opposes the physical to the spiritual, belong to a certain stage of human development—a stage he regards as by no means fixed and unchangeable, especially in the context of a therapy appropriately attuned to the enormous human potential for growth in self-awareness and self-understanding, and for the holistic integration toward which, insofar as we are able, we all naturally incline. Jung's metapsychology, like Freud's, surrounds the notions of psychic energy and the unconscious with a fog of deep conceptual confusion and vagueness. Nevertheless, in Jung's reformulation of the split between conscious and unconscious in terms of the persona and its shadow—terms which *deepen* the Freudian split and yet *enrich* the potential for health—we can at least see very clearly that his approach to human beings is committed to a much more radical, much more positive conception of human freedom, and that this liberation constitutes, for him, a more holistic and well-integrated stage of human development, from the standpoint of which the language of causal determinism is not, or is no longer, at all appropriate. In this regard, it is clear that Jung had a much deeper and richer understanding of the role of culture and tradition in the process of healing. Unlike Freud, Jung took a serious interest in ancient and non-Western processes of healing, and attempted, with considerable success, to incorporate techniques, skills, and approaches altogether foreign to the "scientific" therapy of Freud and his precursors.

The Tibetan Buddhists[4] seem, however, to go much further than Jung toward a conception of human nature, and a corresponding therapeutic practice which sharply discriminates our stages and processes of duality, while also understanding the steps that move us beyond. Thus, for example, Tibetan Buddhism integrates a variety of therapies concerned with the openness and wholeness of our *embodiment* into its more distinctively cognitive techniques. In this respect, its conception of human nature is considerably richer and more holistic than is Jung's, which still, in certain respects, holds on to the dualisms which prevail in

[3]See R. von Eckartsberg, Chapter 2, Marlan, Chapter 11, and V. Valle and Kruger, Chapter 19, for other discussions of Carl Jung's psychology.—Eds.

[4]See de Silva, Chapter 13, for a discussion of Buddhism and its relationship to the work of both Freud and Sartre, and R. von Eckartsberg and R. Valle, Chapter 14, for a discussion of Zen Buddhism.—Eds.

Western science, religion, philosophy, and, of course, in Western experience. When you compare Jung's understanding of human nature with that, say, of Saraha, one of the 84 Indian mahasiddhas, or with that of Klong-chen-pa, the outstanding Tibetan teacher who lived in the fourteenth century, you can actually *hear* and *feel*, in a very tangible and moving way, that the two Buddhists are speaking to us from a wonderfully open, spacious, spontaneously creative, harmoniously attuned way of being, which *exemplifies*, more powerfully than their words themselves can articulate, the wholesome human nature that they are calling us to realize. Unlike Jung, they joyously, tenderly *sing* to us!

Norms of Health

To what norms of health, then, do Freud, Jung, and Buddhism adhere? Freud offers us, I think, an extraordinarily penetrating, and often accurate, diagnosis of what Buddhists would call "the realm of samsara"—the everyday world of pain, frustration, misery, and suffering. Unfortunately, however, this diagnosis, profound though it is, does not escape the limitations of the ego psychology within which it took shape. Consequently, it must be recognized that, in the last analysis, (a) Freud really has no philosophy and psychology of human health; (b) nor is he in a position to conceptualize the nature of health outside the boundaries of the ego and its rational psychology; (c) lacking such a larger conceptual framework for understanding the nature of human distress, Freud's attempt to diagnose the distress of his patients not only fails to touch the *depths* of human pain and suffering, but inevitably distorts what it sees. Thus, spiritual anguish is reduced, for example, to a libidinal or egological anxiety, and the diagnosis generates a therapy which aims, not at ongoing self-realization (or what Jung calls the process of "individuation"), but, much more narrowly, at a stabilized "rational" adaptation to the dominant social reality. And, although Freud recognizes the prominence of defensiveness in egologically based experiencing and behavior, he can't ask radically enough about the appropriateness and need for such defensiveness; nor does he see how the very nature of ego (including the ego of the analyst) tends to create situations that call forth defensive responses and "resistances."

Freud wants us to recognize our libidinal "craziness," but only in order to bring it under the ego's "rational" control. This is in sharp contrast with Jung's ideal, which called not only for the *recognition* of craziness, but also for an *appreciation* which would make possible its harmonious integration into a *new* personality, capable of *drawing strength* from the *crazy* aspect hitherto suppressed. Freud's pessimistic conservativism betrays the fact that his thinking remained caught up in the problematic he unreflectively inherited from Cartesian rationalism. Thus, for example, Freud first of all confuses *feelings* with *emotions*, and then tends, like Descartes, to treat them both as if they were, basically, disruptive atomic *sensations*. Freud's failure to understand and appreciate the distinctively *gestaltet* nature of feeling follows from his mind/body dualism, which reifies our embodiment, and reduces it to that which is merely physical, and governed by mechanistic laws. In the same way, Freud misunderstands sexuality, which he reduces to atomic, punctate stimuli. For this reason, he fails to appreciate sexuality holistically as a pervasive global physiognomy, and modulation, of being: as a style, or way of walking, gesturing, bearing, and expressing oneself. This rational conservatism is nicely encapsulated in his epigram, "Where id was, let ego be." This is both sad and strange, for Freud's *own* analysis of the genesis and nature of ego implicitly calls for an understanding of health that radically transcends ego psychology. After all, when we put his *The Ego and the Id* (1962) together with *The Problem of Anxiety* (1936), we can see very clearly that Freud demonstrates in no uncertain terms that the ego is more than the mere *product* of anxiety (and the mournful "precipitate" of significant object-losses); what he shows us is that the ego, once installed in a position of power which he accurately construes as, in essence, a position of defensiveness, is also the perpetual *source* of continued anxiety. If Freud is right, how can he proceed to espouse a norm of health which glorifies the "rational" ego? Surely he denies us our dream of holistic well-being much too soon!

Jung, on the other hand, never allows himself to get caught in the structural model of Freud's ego psychology. Coming into psychology and psychotherapy from a deeply religious sense of sickness and health, Jung seeks at the outset to understand the human potential for health *outside* the boundaries of ego, in that integration of instincts and drives, feelings and emotions, and archetypal aspects of personality which he calls "the self." Instead of Freud's id/ego/superego structure, which builds into it a dogmatic and limiting conception of human nature and well-being, Jung represents the human being as a dynamically open-ended tension of polarities. His norm of health then calls for the integration of polarities that have tended to split off into oppositions, or conflicts. Integration, for Jung, involves (a) awareness of the conflicts and (b) the open, appreciative acceptance of that which has been denied, split off, or unappreciated. Integration is growth, leading to a dynamic harmony and balance. Jung, then, does indeed have a normative theory of health; and, under the sign of the Self, he works with patients to help them *outgrow*, rather than deny—or resign themselves to—the painful dualities which define the ego system, and discover, for themselves, a balance and wholeness which feels right for them.

Perhaps what makes Jung's transcendence of ego psychology possible is, above all, his attitude toward duality itself. Freud for example, never escaped thinking in dualistic terms of virtue and vice, good and evil. For Freud, the closest we can come to health is the heroism of facing shameful truths about our animal nature and reaching a rational understanding of their causal history. We cannot really *overcome* our violent and evil impulses; but we should not give in to them, either. All we can do, in effect, is understand them—releasing some of their energy in accordance with orthodox psychoanalytic explanations. Jung, however, does not grant the ultimate reality of these distinctions. For him, the difference between good and evil is a transcendental illusion. Consequently, he is able (like the Buddhists) to understand health in a more whole-some (holistic) manner. What *is* evil?; what *is* vice? Could it be that the energies we call evil or vice are wrathful and malevolent only because of their segregation and exclusion? Wouldn't they be transformed if welcomed into the process of integration?

Tibetan Buddhism also works, even if only implicitly, with a radically non-egological norm of health. Like Jung's it is much more holistic than Freud's, and less restricted by a structural model that tends to compartmentalize, prejudge, and reify experience. It is difficult to put one's finger on the difference between the Buddhist and the Jungian conceptualizations of health. Perhaps the only very significant difference is that the Jungian will tend to think and practice therapy with a well-defined conceptualization of the healthy, wholesome Self, whereas the Tibetan Buddhist tends to work *beyond*, or *beneath*, all conceptualizations, in the openness of direct experiencing, so that the relevant norm of health, for the latter, is much more intimately ingrained, much more concretely embodied in the *spontaneous flow* of the experiential process.

According to Buddhism, *all* conceptual constructions of the experiential process are *defense mechanisms*, to the extent that they solidify into patterns of response that obscure a clear perception of one's situation and block an appropriate, effective, and spontaneous involvement. The *Madhyamika* notions of *pratityasamutpada (Gestalt contextualism)* and *shunyata* (openness) *release* the Buddhist guide (called a "lama") from the need to fix the experiential process in terms of its beginning, middle, and end, or in terms of some achievement or failure to achieve. As the Zen followers are all too fond of saying, with an air of paradox, there is no *nirvana* (health), no *samsara* (pathology), no goal (Buddhahood), and nothing to be done. What that means is that the therapeutic relationship, in Buddhism, stays very close to the immediacy of the present experiential situation, and does not (need to) work with people judgmentally, that is, in terms of an abstract, universal standard of the healthy, fully realized Self. For the Buddhist, health cannot be, and is not to be conceptualized, in terms of any specific *content*. Health, radically understood, is simply a question of *staying* with the situated experiential process just as it presents itself, and letting the spontaneous play of energies flow freely, not separated by conflict into subject and object, inner and outer, myself and others, nor myself (here) and the situation (there). The wholesome flow, or creative interplay, of the process is what principally matters.

The Question of Diagnosis

In 1926, Freud wrote (showing more insight than his disciples) that "The future will probably attribute far greater importance to psychoanalysis as the science of the unconscious than as a therapeutic procedure." It is crucial to bear this in mind when we consider Freud's approach to diagnosis.

Freudian diagnosis has two main concerns: the first is to classify, or, in effect, to *judge* the pathological nature of the patient's distress; and the second is to *explain* the distress in the language of causal motivation, tracing the focal problem to significant circumstances in the past. However, if we ponder the root meaning of the notion of diagnosis, we can hear at once a much deeper, broader meaning, in relation to which the Freudian notion will appear to be a very narrow choice. *Dia-gnosis,* heard with an ear for its Greek origin, speaks of a deeply penetrating kind of understanding, more like intuition than knowledge *(episteme),* and more holistic than analytic (i.e., classificatory). Whereas Freud's concern is mainly explanatory and Freudian analysis turns toward the traumatic *past* (which it attempts to repeat under "laboratory" supervision), the Greek word lets us hear the possibility of a concern, not with causal or motivational explanation, but rather with a mode of understanding which emphasizes a sympathetic way of simply *being with* the patient; and it lets us hear the possibility of a wisdom which is concerned less with the past than with the patient's way of being in, and experiencing the nearness of, the *whole* of time. *Gnosis,* of course, is very different from the Freudian way of getting to know. Among other things, we must acknowledge that the Freudian diagnosis always begins with some sort of normative judgment. The patient is classified: hysterical, neurotic, schizophrenic, psychotic, manic-depressive, etc. Even if the judgment is not actually stated, it is implicit in the analytical attitude and approach, and *will be heard* by the patient. It is to be contrasted sharply with a nonjudgmental, nonclassificatory approach.

Jungian diagnosis has a very different character and quality. First of all, it is not essentially explanatory, not committed to looking for causes. Consequently, it is not primarily oriented toward the past (I am distinguishing here between the Jungian therapy and the Jungian metapsychology which does concern itself quite extensively with archaic archetypal traces.) Indeed, it is, if anything, rather future-oriented. This temporal orientation is, in my opinion, very much connected with the way that the Jungian diagnosis, unlike the Freudian, manifests its appreciation of the sense in which a so-called pathological state always belongs within a dynamic, ever-changing *process*, so that, where the Freudian will tend to treat a psychotic episode as nothing but the onset of severe sickness (i.e., as a low point in the patient's decline), the Jungian, more "optimistic," will tend to regard that breakdown, "the return of the repressed," as the first stage of a movement *toward* recovery—in brief, a hopeful progressive sign. A similar difference between the Freudian and Jungian approaches will emerge as we reflect on how they relate to *symbolic* processes. The Freudian tends to take symbols as distorted expressions, or symptoms, of repressed material. The basic posture, then, is one of *suspicion*. The Jungian, on the other hand, assumes a posture which is basically trusting, and even reverential: symbols are not distortions; symbols are messages, sometimes too profound, or too charged with meaning, for us to understand. This reflects a comparatively more dynamic, less structural-classificatory approach. It may seem like a small difference. Perhaps it is, from a purely theoretical standpoint. And yet, the practical, or therapeutic, difference is profoundly significant. For the Jungian is taking a more positive attitude toward the "psychotic" episode, thereby making it possible for analyst and patient to work openly and constructively with the so-called psychotic material. The Freudian negativity, by contrast, will simply make it more difficult, and more problematic, to hear the crying need and to help the client approach the distress with an attitude open to change. The Jungian approach, just because it is more process-oriented, and also more future-oriented, will convey to the patient a more open, more positive, more liberating feeling, even about severe emotional disturbances. It is reasonable to suppose that this diagnostic attitude contributes *significantly* to the healing process.

The Tibetan Buddhist approach, however, is even less judgmental. Insofar as the Buddhist classifies, the felt quality of the classification is *not* one of normative judgment, but rather of astute phenomenological description. And the focus is neither solely on the past, nor solely on the future. The Buddhists mainly focus, instead, on the present (i.e., on present experience), but in a way that is meant to help *open* the person to the embrace of the *whole* of time. For they say that it is possible to experience the whole of time as present in the present, once our mindfulness is meditatively focused on the present and freed from attachments (of attraction or aversion). It is this capacity to focus on the present as a gift of the whole of time which substitutes for the judgmental approach; instead of judging, the Buddhist teacher simply focuses on the immediate situation, serving as a mirror to reflect, for the student, what is happening. The reflection of the teacher's mirrorlike wisdom (the special nondual wisdom of the Buddha) helps the person in distress to focus (in a similarly nondualistic manner) on the present situation, so that it can be accepted as the present that it is and fully appreciated as such, so that an appropriate response without the mediation of re-presentational defenses becomes possible.[5]

The Buddhist thus teaches the student to enter into a process of self-diagnosis and self-therapy, substituting for authoritarian, dogmatic judgments and a multitude of re-presentations, all of which are, as such, projections and delusions, a carefully focused, meditative examination of one's experiencing.[6] There is no need, according to the Buddhists, for a cathartic reliving of the past trauma; to be sure, the repetition may lead, in some cases, to abreaction; but the Buddhists contend that there is a more direct, more efficient, and much more radically liberating technique, less likely to keep us within the karmic circle of painful and destructive patterns of experiencing. This technique is more direct, because it *stays* with the experiencing process, instead of diverting us into abstract interpretive speculations; more efficient, or powerful, because it takes whatever energy is present and already at work, and simply transmutes it; and finally, it is more liberating in that, rather than repeating, and thus in a sense continuing, the egological fixation on the trauma, it breaks it at once, deconstructing the fixated pattern *simply by reconnecting it with the ever-changing experiential process.*

This reconnecting or grounding is, in a sense, the key to Buddhist psychotherapy. Again and again, the Buddhists emphasize the truth that nothing is permanent. In one way or another, they ask us to recognize, accept, and appreciate the experience of impermanence.[7] And they point out to us how often, and in what ways, we tend to deny or withdraw from this experience. We are enthralled by an "inveterate tendency"—the phrase is Herbert Guenther's—to conceptualize our experience in a way that reifies it, for example, solidifying the natural flow into a subject/object duality, or blocking this spontaneous, whole-some flow by fixating

[5]See Levin (1978) in which I discuss our everyday experiencing of time, as well as the alternative way of experiencing it. See also Tarthang Tulku (1977).

[6]Buddhist meditation as therapy, therefore, teaches self-reliance. See Goodman (1978).

[7]Contrast this view with the R. von Eckartsberg and R. Valle, Chapter 14, discussion of the Hindu notion of *maya*.—Eds.

cathexes (attachments of aversion or attraction), or narrowing it down from, say, the openness and richness of a child's wonderment to the dominant, one-track "interest" of an adult. How, then, do we defend against, deny, or conceal, the fact of impermanence, the fact of change? We install an ego, or self, to unify our life—as if it could not, and does not, have any prepersonal or prereflective wholeness—and protect ourselves against the passage of time. We create an ego to mask experiential changes. We even employ interpretation as a means of *detachment* from the vicissitudes and ambiguities of lived experience. But the Madhyamika notion of *pratityasamutpada,* which parallels holistic *Gestalt contextualism,* is intended precisely to keep us *grounded* in the experiential drift and play, by deconstructing any abstraction from the living, flowing experiential context which threatens to "forget" its origins.

The Buddhist dia-gnosis, therefore, begins by *centering* the person in the living present, so that, from out of this center, a deeply penetrating understanding of how one is experiencing the presence of the past and the presence of the future first becomes possible. Since the past *is* in fact *still* present (as past, of course), there is no need to repeat it in order to diagnose the "trauma." Similarly, since the seeds of the future are *already* present, there is no need to orient the patient, in a primarily "anticipatory" attitude, toward the oncoming future. For the future can only unfold out of what is already present in, and present as, the present.[8] The Buddhist dia-gnosis thus relies upon the underlying holistic nature of our experiencing of (present) time in order to disclose both the working of pain and the alternative of joy, equally inherent in the present potential of the process. For Buddhism, such a holistic dia-gnosis is feasible because of the underlying, primordial nature of temporality, which is, as Heidegger argues, gathered by the present into a whole.[9] The only question is whether or not we are willing to let ourselves go into this primordial experiencing of time. If we are indeed willing, the meditative experiencing of the temporal *ek-stasis* (that is, the process in which beings are constantly passing away) can then help us to overcome our defenses against impermanence, and teach us how to enjoy this normally painful *ek-stasis,* restoring us to the ecstasy of an *ek-stasis* whose wholeness is altogether *beyond* the reach of ego-logical presentations.

It is crucial, here, that we understand the difference between the Buddhist diagnosis, which *rests* in presence, and the re-presentational diagnoses of orthodox Freudian and Jungian analysis. These two Western approaches basically call for a *mediated* diagnosis, distanced from lived

---

[8]Compare this with the R. von Eckartsberg and R. Valle, Chapter 14, discussion of the *ever-present.*—Eds.
[9]See Moss and Keen, Chapter 4, and R. von Eckartsberg and R. Valle, Chapter 14, for other discussions of temporality.—Eds.

experience and effecting a deferment of its *presence* by virtue of a diagnostic passage through some sort of symbolic process, typically initiated, or even determined by, the analyst's interpretive conceptual apparatus. Both the analyst's diagnosis and that eventually assumed by the patient himself are, in effect, re-presentations of the patient's present experience. As such, they inevitably perpetuate, at least to *some* degree, a way of relating to our experience which is essentially *defensive*. In other words, re-presentations always play into the ego's mechanisms of attachment, that is, ways of avoidance or ways of securing an attraction. The little-noticed prefix "re" indicates, in fact, the ego's crafty work. It is not that Buddhism wants us to stop thinking; nor is it against re-presentational activity as such. But Buddhism differs from the Western approaches, insofar as these approaches rely on re-presentational diagnoses (a) in its insistence on our *prior* need for centering and grounding in unmediated, direct, simply lived experiencing, and (b) in its trust that, out of such presence, re-presentations of value will in any event spontaneously emerge. However, without the experiential presence encouraged by meditation, re-presentational activity will merely serve the ego's strategies which always involve, as Freud himself unequivocally points out, abstraction from the contextual ground, splitting off and securing against change. When the diagnostic process *begins* with an attempt to achieve meditative presence (i.e., simply being with, and staying with, the dynamic experiential energy in a gently focused, hovering, relaxed manner), then subsequently resorting to re-presentations of one sort or another *can* be extremely valuable, *provided* they are kept up in an open dialogue, a to-and-fro movement, with one's presently lived experience.

The Calling of Compassion

Very closely connected with the themes just introduced in the preceding section is the question of compassion. Just what *is* compassion, and how can we "take its measure" in different psychotherapeutic situations? Since we may suppose that there can be no form of psychotherapy without its corresponding claim to understand what compassion is and how best to practice it, we may be tempted to believe that these are easy questions. That they are not, however, may be gathered simply from the fact that, in the West, they have seldom been raised and pondered on a sufficiently *philosophical* level. I will restrict myself here to a few points, concentrating on the Buddhist approach.

I would like to bring together, on the one hand, Heidegger's later thinking about the healing way of being human, and, on the other hand, the Tibetan Buddhist way of thinking on the same matter. I suggest that the *heart* of compassion (in Sanskrit, *karuna*) is openness (in Sanskrit, *shunyata*), and that the *measure* of compassion is simply the heartfelt experiential *satisfactoriness* of the reciprocal opening that begins to take place in the therapeutic relationship in response to the therapist's willingness (and daring) to open up *first*. The therapist thus prepares a spacious clearing, a comfortable openness, for the other (the Tantric partner, in fact) to open out into.[10]

How do things stand, then, in the context of Freudian therapy? One important clue may well be implicit in the fact that so much of Freudian analysis is concerned with the process of *unmasking* distortions and deceptions, and effectively mastering the patient's resistances. Please bear in mind that I am not denying that there *are* distortions and deceptions, nor am I simply condemning the process of unmasking. However, I do wish to point out that there is *other work* to be done, and that there are *other ways of working* with those who are distressed. Whenever the therapeutic process takes shape in such a way that the Freudian is disposed to observe a case of "resistance," he or she should at least reflect on these two questions: "To what extent is what I call the patient's resistance an *appropriate* response to the felt quality of my approach?"; and "To what extent am I wont to hear a resistance which I have myself *projected*?" (countertransference is at stake here, but not quite in its most familiar form). Is it not possible, for example, that the very fact that the analyst possesses an interpretation, and proposes it with the inevitable weight of his authority, could very easily be felt as aggressive? Could it not *feel* like a violation of the patient's own experiencing? Even when the analyst's interpretation is felt to be right (or true), it could be felt as an unfriendly attempt to *reduce* the resonant *richness* of the experience thus interpreted. And this would suffice to restrict the openness of the therapeutic situation.

The Freudian analyst creates, for therapy, a spatial situation which ensures the analyst a virtually invulnerable invisibility: the patient reclines on the couch; the analyst sits behind and out of sight. But this invisibility does *not* ensure the creation of an open, neutral space. On the contrary, the analyst's invisibility *heightens* his or her power and encourages the patient's paranoia. This may at times be a most effective setup. But the question that haunts me has to do with the ways in which, if this be the *only* setup, very significant limitations on openness and, therefore,

---

[10]I am very grateful to Roger Levin for the incisive understanding of therapy presented here. His discussion of the therapist's responsibility to open first, the therapist's "warriorlike bravery" in taking the lead and going *first* into painful or frightening realms of experience, and the way in which a therapist can help the client to *dance* with his or her experiencing (all of this touched upon in a private communication), has been of decisive importance for the position articulated in this paper.

on compassion can be enforced. How does this orthodox Freudian scenario perpetuate a power structure? How does it reinforce a tendency toward interpretive dogmatism and continue the prevailing disregard of the patient's own experiencing just as it is feelingly lived? Freudian analysis is indeed reflective. But its way of reflecting is very different from the Buddhist's. The latter is like a clean mirror, or like the calm surface of a mountain lake; the former is more like an Expressionist portrait painted to reveal the sitter's "true self."

Where the Freudian, methodologically trained to be suspicious, mainly perceives distortions, deceptions, and strategies of resistance, the Jungian, trained to be more trusting (or even "reverential"), mainly perceives partial or fragmentary expressions of personal truth, and always looks for the seeds of a fuller and more fulfilling truth, so that he or she can help the client to cultivate them. To be sure, the Jungian also offers, or helps the patient to find, significant *interpretations* of experience. But the Jungian also always attempts to act *in harmony* with the psyche's *own* process of healing. There is, accordingly, a less directive, more open approach to the patient's own experiential process. Even if the Freudian achieves a measure of success, the coercive nature of the interpretive relationship will stand in the way, beyond a certain point in the intervention. The Jungian practice of compassion, attuned to what is called "the transcendent function," is more open because it conveys a basic and much needed *trust* in the whole-some grain of the patient's own experiential process; it constantly listens for guidance from the patient's own psyche; it recognizes a spontaneously compensatory, ingrained spiritual energy striving for the fulfillment of individual wholeness. This "faith" or "trust," very much the contrary of the Freudian's methodological suspicion, can itself significantly contribute to, and facilitate, the reciprocal opening of client and analyst.

Nevertheless, as Gendlin (1977) shows very convincingly in his discussion of Carl Jung and Medard Boss, the Jungian approach retains *more* of a conceptual and interpretive limitation than the openness of compassion, understood in the Buddhist manner, sometimes requires.[11] It retains this limitation insofar as it is concerned less with the openness, the spontaneity, and the inherent dynamism of the experiential *process*, and rather more with the mythopoeic *contents* of this process. It cannot be denied that, at certain times, some persons deepen or expand, or in some other way change, their patterns of experiencing, by being initiated into the archetypal imagination of mythopoeic narratives. But this procedure needs to be used judiciously, and always with the keenest sensitivity. Otherwise, what is taking place in the name of compassion therapy is not compassion, but a very subtle form of control and manipulation.

[11]See also Henry Corbin (1970).

I would now like to discuss the more important aspects of Buddhist psychotherapy, insofar as these may be gleaned from compassion practice, the very heart of the Mahayana, the Greater Vehicle.

First, as already noted, the Buddhists couple compassion with the greatest possible openness. This already gives their psychotherapy a very distinctive felt quality. We might call this quality "spaciousness": the gracious, hospitable spaciousness we need to grow, to live, to open up. The practice of compassion is not compatible with an attitude of pity (which is always mixed, as Nietzsche clearly warns us, with anger and hate); nor is it compatible with the therapist's belief in his or her superior wisdom (which always tends toward dogmatism), a judgmental posture (which always feels hostile and therefore provokes defense), and with manipulation of any kind whatsoever.

The so-called Four Noble Truths may help us to appreciate how Buddhism conceptualizes and practices psychotherapy. The First Noble Truth says that life is full of pain, suffering, misery, and frustration. Now, as a doctrine, this is neither pessimistic nor nihilistic. It simply points to, and asks us to take note of, the facts. Is it not true that, in a thousand ways, big and small, and again and again, we find ourselves in situations where the basic character, the basic feeling or mood, of our experience is pain and frustration? Of course, it is true. But the Buddhists are not showing us these unpleasant facts in order to perpetuate pain and suffering. To the contrary! They point to these facts because they can see our pain, hear our cries. And they want to respond, to help. But, they are convinced that the way is not to manipulate or direct people "from outside" (i.e., heteronomously); if they can simply help people to get in touch with the felt quality of their experiencing, just as it is lived each and every moment, then people will experience significant changes for the better, spontaneously motivated by "inward" (i.e., autonomous) needs and concerns. Thus, it *suffices* simply to help people focus on their pain, their frustration, their misery. The "First Truth" points the Buddhist therapist toward a practice of compassion so unclouded by ego that, instead of arousing Freudian or Jungian transferences, the therapist serves as a mere reflection or echo. Instead of judgment, there is nothing but the acknowledgement, and the recognition, of another's pain and suffering: "I see you hurting. I hear your pain. And maybe you would like to share that with me. I will listen." It is not necessary to tell people what to do and how to do it. Perhaps one of the most valuable features of this direct approach is that the Buddhist teacher/therapist can *share* with us our painful and unfulfilling patterns of experiencing, *without even needing to understand* the "problem" in a conceptual way. In holistic therapy, understanding must be *grounded* in holistic experience, and that means, in feeling.

The Second Noble Truth teaches us the *presently* underlying "cause" or "reason" for all our pain and lack of fulfillment. It is, in a word, craving. "Craving" denotes, here, the attachment patterns of the ego[12]—patterns of aversion (avoidance) and patterns of attraction (desire). And, as with the First Truth, so with the Second: what it tells us, we can check out for ourselves—directly. That is, if we are mindful and focus attentively on our experiencing, we will see (or feel) just how our patterns of attachment inevitably get us trapped in situations that, all too predictably, we experience as painful, frustrating, and unfulfilling. This we can determine directly, and for ourselves. No abstract interpretation is involved.

The Third Noble Truth simply greets us with the blessing of the obvious solution: the "cure," the "way out" of the realm of pain and misery (i.e., samsara), lies in the cessation of the ego's attachments—including, ultimately, even our attachment to "escaping" samsara. Our belief in or need for a "cure" is, in fact, one of our most painful attachments! This means that we must learn to relax, learn to let go, learn to trust ourselves, rely on ourselves, and be friends with ourselves, progressively working on developing an attitude of openness. We will work with our anxieties, our defensiveness, our paranoia, our insecurity. And yet, at the same time that we bend every effort in this direction, we also learn how to accept defeat and failure; we learn how to be comfortable with our own limitations. We learn to be at peace in samsara—just as if it were the nirvana of our wildest dreams!

The Fourth Noble Truth provides an eightfold path for our moral guidance. Briefly, it includes: impeccable perspective; sincere intention; speech which is honest, candid, warm, and helpful; conduct which is fitting and appropriate; an honorable means of providing for one's needs and for the needs of dependent others; sufficient perseverance and courage; the cultivation of mindfulness; and introducing a meditative quality into all that one does.

Now the Tibetan Buddhists are bringing, to the West, what they consider the perfection of the Mahayana. They contend that, without the Vajrayana, the bodhisattva's practice of compassion, as it is defined by the classical Mahayana texts, cannot achieve its goal, which is the full liberation of other (human) beings. Just what is this Vajrayana teaching? The Vajrayana functions by resolutely staying with, and directly working with, the energy in our experiential process. That direct experiential approach, focused on process, rather than a mediated judgmental approach to psychic content, is really the only "secret" of the Vajrayana— the secret of its success, the source of its astonishing power. Let us use an

---

[12]See R. von Eckartsberg and R. Valle, Chapter 14, for a discussion of *attachment* in Hindu thought.—Eds.

example to make this point more concrete, more immediately experiential. Briefly consider, then, how the Vajrayana is "at work" in the student/teacher relationship.

The teacher begins his or her teaching by describing, very simply and very concretely, and in considerable detail, the way we characteristically (i.e., typically, standardly) pattern our everyday experiencing: the teacher holds up a mirror, as it were, to *show* us our "inveterate tendency" (which is Herbert V. Guenther's translation of the Tibetan Buddhist term, *bag-chags)* to pattern our experiencing of the situations in which we find ourselves in ways which are not only unnecessarily painful, frustrating, and personally unfulfilling, but which do not serve to help other people, and merely contribute to the continuation and repetition of that same all-too-familiar pattern. In other words, the teacher begins with a *descriptive* phenomenology ("When you wait for a friend who arrives so late that you can't do what you planned to do, isn't *this* how you feel?", etc.). But, as this description unfolds, it goes deeper and deeper, not just touching the *surface* of our everyday experiencing as we actually live it, but penetrating also into the very depths of our process, in order to get in touch with the *underlying* feelings. ("Can you feel the painfulness in the way you waited? Can you feel how that way closed you off from enjoying the situation anyway?"). These underlying feelings are, in essence, very powerful energies, capable of being touched and turned, or touched and nurtured, and capable of being moved in various directions. So the description does more than describe how things *are* with us; it *awakens* us to our potential, and *touches* our capacity for change ("Can you feel, or sense, beneath that tendency to form expectations and insist on having things go *your* way on your *own* terms, a very simple, very basic energy which you could enjoy just being there with yourself, and later with your friend?").

It helps us to know, through the directness and energy of feeling, *that things could be different* (the Third Noble Truth). And then the teacher carefully fleshes out for us, with powerful phenomenological rigor, *another* way of experiencing. The teacher does not have to coerce or persuade. The directness of the experiential teaching is powerful enough to generate the motivation we need. The moving poetry of the simple language in which the alternative way of experiencing is presented—the energy in its sheer beauty—illumines the spacious opening such immediate truth provides.

Listen to Tarthang Tulku (1978) to hear how he works in this rigorous and direct way with the felt edge of our experiential process:

> At the beginning of any new project, everything is fresh and exciting. So many possibilities are opening for us, our hopes run high, and our energy and enthusiasm are boundless. But as problems arise, our initial enthusiasm may

> begin to wear off. The future loses some of its promise, and our will and determination may falter. It can seem much easier to look for ways to avoid our work than to let ourselves become inspired by the challenges it offers. When work makes difficult demands on us, we may choose to hold back our energy. Because we are not focusing on our work, our energy grows scattered and confused. . . . We find ourselves making excuses for not working efficiently: we are not feeling well, or we need more time. As distractions arise, we respond to them readily, taking frequent breaks or going on unnecessary errands. . . . If we were to confront our work directly, we might find it far less threatening than we feared. But we fail to see this when we choose to turn away. (p. 60)

Does this not sound familiar? But, in addition to this sound of familiarity, can we hear other qualities in its sound? Can we hear its gentleness, its tenderness, its personal warmth, its caring? Listen to some more:

> Whenever we start something new, we may find ourselves anticipating the obstacles that could arise, and the limitations we feel we must face in ourselves and others. Although we feel enthusiastic about our work, we may also be constrained by an underlying sense of fear that we might not succeed. This fear hinders the free flow of our energy, and prevents us from fully appreciating the excellence and inner value of our work. . . . When we do not put our energy into our work, our whole being is affected: our eyes, our voice, even the way we move can tell others that we are holding ourselves back. Our motivation wavers, and the qualities we most value in our work—our efficiency, our productivity, and our lasting enjoyment—are affected. (pp. 40, 41)

Notice how, without abandoning the phenomenological or experiential approach, the preceding description penetrates beneath the surface to touch upon underlying motives and patterns of response. Notice, too, that this approach makes it possible to integrate, holistically, many aspects and dimensions of our being. The phenomenological description functions holographically, projecting, before us, the *whole* of our being.

Listen, now, to the poetic quality of the languaging, and ask yourself, by focusing, how you are responding, how you feel:

> As we change our habits and patterns, we realize that problems can teach us to grow. . . . [Our] problems are like clouds: though they appear to disturb the serenity of a clear sky, they contain life-giving moisture that nourishes growth. When we face our problems directly and go through them, we discover new ways of being. (p. 50)

Without at all trying to anticipate what you might realize, patiently listen for any evidence, any intimations coming from your own felt experiencing, that, in response to this description, a slight change, or shift, in your customary attitude may have taken place.

An even deeper dimension of experience, a more expansive dimension, can be entered in a similar way. Listen to yet another experiential description, and note with great care how the languaging of an alternative way of experiencing touches you to respond. Does it move you, or change you, helping you to shift into another way of being? Listen:

> Wonderment is the presence, the presenting, the appreciation of reality as Being. All appearance is sheer art, beautiful beyond all enduring, appealing beyond all possibility of possession. It cannot be possessed but it is entirely accessible. The treasure which our being preserves for us is like an ever-present nectar; it is like an inexhaustible kingdom which is always open to us. (Tarthang Tulku, 1977, p. 291)

When we take such languaging as directly characterizing the felt quality of a certain way of experiencing that is wholly accessible to us, and wholly feasible, do we feel the relief, the opening, of a change or shift in our experiential process? The spaciousness of such a change is the goal, and the very essence, of the Vajrayana approach to psychotherapy.

The Power of Imagination

All three forms of psychotherapy—the Freudian as well as the Jungian and the Tibetan Buddhist—recognize, and, each in its own way, attempt to work with, the human capacity for imagining. All three therapies appreciate, and rely upon, the irrepressible *spontaneity* of imagination—a characteristic so crucial to its nature and functioning that we might call it the very definition of imagination. The value of this capacity lies, for psychotherapy, in the fact that the spontaneity of imagination as a *method* lays the groundwork for one of the *goals* of therapy, which is a lively, overall spontaneity, manifesting the absence of egological defenses and repressions. (Spontaneity contrasts with the postponements and deferments intrinsic to egological representation.) The method is more than attuned to the goal; it is intended to *reach* that goal (of spontaneity) by way of a method which *immediately* brings spontaneity into play (the "end" must be present in the means).

When compared with Freud, Jung had a much deeper and richer sense of the transformative, healing potentialities in the human capacity to imagine. Freud, of course, certainly deserves our acclaim for the seriousness with which, in *The Interpretation of Dreams*, he studied the symbols of "the unconscious," explicitly acknowledging, in that way, that the spontaneous imagination which occurs during sleep is a powerful source of healing. He also deserves our thanks for his method of free association, which likewise depends, for its healing power, on the patient's opportunity to experience the "permissibility" of his or her spontaneous processes. But the Freudian tendency to impose predetermined interpretations on the dream symbols and "free" associations of analytic patients simply *binds* the released energy and significantly undermines the value of working with the imaginative material.[13]

In this regard, the Jungian approach is superior, in that it recognizes how necessary it is to take up the spontaneity manifest in dreams and amplify it in the dream-play of our waking life, so that there is an enrichment of our everyday life, and a sort of healthy confusion between wakefulness and dreaming, reality and pleasure, discipline and play, deepening and expanding each and every moment. Whereas Freudians, practicing their method of suspicion, tend to reduce the dream's symbols to neurotic distortions of libidinal (and primarily sexual) drives, the Jungian prefers to *amplify* them, allowing the symbols to expand in scope and deepen in their value. And, whereas the Freudian tends to affix a symbolic meaning for all eternity, the Jungian is quite prepared to participate with the patient in a process of unfolding, in which the symbols continue to undergo transformation as they are brought into "conversation" with more and more aspects of the patient's integrated living. Finally, whereas the Freudian tends to make use only of dreams and the spontaneous associations of words and images that emerge during the therapeutic sessions, the Jungian makes extensive use, in addition, of mythic narratives, bringing these archaic products of the imagination into both the analytic sessions themselves and also the waking life that goes on outside those sessions.

There are many things to be said in favor of the Jungian use of our capacity for imagining, especially the way that the Jungian uses mythopoeic narratives in what the Tibetans would call visualization practices. Not the least of these favorable things is the fact that such visualizations integrate the individual's *personal* imagination into his or her culture's *transpersonal* "collective" imagination, thus doubly grounding the individual, both in a cultural world history and in a cosmological world to be experientially *shared* with people of that culture's earliest history. Through the active, spontaneous imagination, the individual person is helped to share a transpersonal and transhistorical experience. The myth is timely; but it also expands one's temporal experience, restoring not merely an ancient past, but even a time before time. And this expansion of the temporal horizon can be very wholesome, very liberating; and it may immeasurably enrich the meaningfulness of one's everyday experiencing.

The Tibetan Buddhists likewise make use of visualizations that receive their guidance from narratives—narratives seemingly very much akin to the Jungian archetypal myths. Even so, however, the Tibetans

[13]See also Boss (1979). He argues that Freud's interpretative explanations encourage "a mechanical self-image profoundly at odds with the patient as a human being".

seem to give the visualizations a somewhat different focus. It seems that the Jungians are so very much concerned about the archaic "collective unconscious" that they tend to undervalue a focus on the experiential present. After all, the mythopoeic visualizations of Jungian analysis are narratives with a very strong temporal, and indeed historical, emphasis. And they typically involve the analysand in very complex stories, dramas with many, or at least several, significant characters. Most of the Tibetan Tantric visualizations, however, are not concerned with the problem of orienting or situating people in time and history; nor do they invite people to enter an unfolding narrative plot with a cast of many characters. Rather, they tend to be very simple and basic, and usually involve just the visualizer and his or her own projection. Insofar as there is a narrative, it is usually nothing mroe than a phenomenologically grounded description of a *single* timeless context, or situation, into which the meditator proceeds, by steps, to project himself (or herself). Thus, the focus is always centered on the living present, rather than on some past, however archaic, or on the future. And, instead of a dynamic unfolding of experience *guided by the narrative unfolding*, the emphasis is much more on the spontaneous unfolding of the meditator's *own* experiencing process, *without* any narrative to guide or structure that unfolding after the initial setting has been re-presented. Therapeutically considered, this difference of emphasis (content versus process) may well be quite significant.

The Tibetan Tantric visualizations, are, then, much less experientially directive. But there is also, perhaps, a somewhat different intention motivating the practice itself. For it seems to me that, although the Tibetan visualizations, like the Jungian, are certainly intended to help people integrate and incorporate the "shadowy" aspects of themselves which they have hitherto not been able to face and accept and embrace, the Tibetan exercises tend to function on a much more directly experiential, and therefore much more powerfully transformative, level. In other words, the Tantric exercises understand much more clearly *how it is* that the imagination holds the power to heal. The Jungians seem to think that the power to heal resides in the archetypal images, the symbolic *contents*, themselves.[14] The Tibetans, on the other hand, once again seem to opt for the experiential *process* itself as the real source, or locus, of the healing. How so? Well, they seem to appreciate the fact that healing transformations basically take place in the spaciousness *between* the "place" one is in and the "place" one is projecting oneself into. Or, in other, perhaps less enigmatic words, they seem to understand how simply *visualizing* oneself

[14]See, for example, Jung's (1959) essay, "Aion; Researches into the Phenomenology of the Self." His "The Structure and Dynamics of the Psyche" and "The Relations Between the Ego and the Unconscious," both published in part in *The Portable Jung* (Campbell, 1976), also show Jung's persistent focus on "contents."

as being "somewhere else" (or being some other being) is, experientially, the *same as being* "somewhere else" (or being that other being), since, for them, there is no ultimate *metaphysical* difference between the being one projects or dreams and the being one is. When I *visualize* myself as the thousand-armed Avalokiteśvara, I am that being. This, precisely, is what we always "forget," perhaps because it frightens us with the risk of madness. And, because they are more concerned than the Jungians to arouse the "neutral" (i.e., nondual) energy that is to be felt in the "in-between" (the Tibetans call this the *bar-do*), they can help us, compassionately, to move into the openness *beyond* all types of roles, all archetypal masks and figures. (Of especial importance, here, are the Tibetan *yab-yum* visualizations: Tantric meditations centrally concerned with contacting our nondual sexuality.)

To summarize the difference succinctly, I would have to say that the Jungian visualizations still protect one last castle of Ego, that last, fortified hiding place, namely, the dualistic belief in the difference between sanity and madness. In the Vajrayana, however, wholesome, healthy living cannot begin until even *this* duality has been bravely faced and warmly, wholly embraced. How far has Jung gone, I wonder, with Hölderlin's words, which he himself repeats in "The Spiritual Problem of Modern Man"? In the first strophe of "Patmos" Hymn, Hölderlin tells us:

> But where danger is, grows
> The saving power also[15] . . .

I would now like to conclude my discussion of this topic with a brief exemplification of the difference between the Jungian and the Tibetan approaches to visualization. I trust that the example will demonstrate incisively in what way, and to what degree, the Tibetan approach is willing to be much more radical, daring, and therefore more profoundly opening. In *Aion; Researches into the Phenomenology of the Self*, Jung (1959) leads into a discussion of *anima* and *animus* (which are always, he says, "contrasexual" figures), by observing that,

> It is quite within the bounds of possibility for a man to recognize the relative evil of his nature, but it is a rare and shattering experience for him to gaze into the face of absolute evil. (in Campbell, 1976, p. 148)

Now, the Tibetans would certainly concur. But, unlike Jung, who would not dream of turning this observation into an experiential visualization, the Tibetans have long been prepared to make of this a very powerful, though certainly dangerous, visualization. Taking, as they do, a direct experiential approach, they hear these words as literally true. Con-

[15]Wo aber Gefahr ist, wächst/Das Rettende auch" (Campbell, 1976, p. 479). Heidegger (1977) also discusses these words of Hölderlin in "The Question Concerning Technology."

sequently, they consider the experiencing of this truth to be a crucial step in the process of centering and opening up beyond experiential dualities (notably, in this case, contrasexual ones). Thus, for advanced practitioners of the Vajrayana, it would be essential to gaze into the face of absolute evil, and, in a mortal's embrace, to *become* that face, the embodiment of absolute evil. Needless to say, the Jungian analyst would be quite unwilling, or unprepared, to go so near to the very center of madness.

The Process of Languaging

I now want to turn to the question of languaging. How do the three forms of therapy we have been considering relate to the process of language?

Once again, let us begin with Freudian analysis. Freud was, I believe, the first person to introduce "talking," which he explicitly recognized as a therapeutic process (his patient, Anna O., called analysis "the talking cure"), into a theoretical framework of scientific diagnosis and explanation. For the Western consciousness, this involved two giant steps: (a) the explicit recognition of the fact that, somehow, just talking can be therapeutic, and (b) the "scientific" use of languaging processes in psychotherapy. In *The Psychopathology of Everyday Life* (1958), *The Interpretation of Dreams* (1958), and in other studies too, Freud classified and analyzed numerous distinct languaging processes (slips of the tongue, substitutions, displacements, condensations, euphemisms, etc.). Furthermore, he formalized a languaging technique essentially involving a capacity for spontaneity in which, because of its special relation to the unconscious, he searched for symptomatic disclosures of "repressed material." I refer, of course, to his well-known technique of free association.

Nevertheless, Freud's theoretical understanding of language, as well as his practical relationship with it, betray a number of serious shortcomings:

1. Although Freud worked out a very sharp analytical framework for interpreting languaging "pathology," he does not do much to answer the basic question, "How (why) does simply talking effect a cure?"[16] To be sure, his study of jokes sketches an "economic" theory of explanation. But this theory is neither broad enough to cover the full range of languag-

---

[16]For a more extensive discussion of languaging as a process of healing, see my papers, "The Phenomenon and Noumenon of Language: The Twin Paths of Perfect Speaking (Mantra) and Perfect Writing (Mudra)," and "Self-Knowledge and the Talking Cure" (Levin 1977a,b).

ing processes, nor is it, as an exclusively "economic" model, conceptually and methodologically adequate to many aspects of language.

2. Freud was not really interested in the spontaneity of language for its own sake; nor was he concerned, as a therapist, for its encouragement and cultivation. His interest in the spontaneity of languaging was basically restricted to the process of unmasking the "mechanisms" of repression.

3. This narrowness reflects a much more fundamental limitation in Freud's relationship, as a therapist, with languaging, namely: the fact that he was not really interested in helping his patients to experience languaging processes in a healthier, more wholesome and more fulfilling way. For, if languaging is indeed a "medium" for his therapeutic process, then how we are experiencing language itself must become a question for therapeutic work and understanding. Many questions arise here. For example: How enjoyable and fulfilling is our speaking? What manner of body feeling characteristically accompanies our speech? Focusing, while we speak, on the experientially felt qualities that surround the tongue, the throat, the lips, and the chest, do we notice any deep tensions, any unpleasantness, any tightness or constriction? Do we have any felt sense that, when we speak, our experiencing around these organs could be more satisfactory? More beautiful? And these questions point, one and all, toward a very fundamental question that Freud seems never to have addressed, namely: How could we work with our experiencing, so that the languaging process would not only *feel* better, but also be richer, more meaningful, and more fulfilling?

4. In some sense Freud recognized and appreciated the power of language to express, communicate, and deepen the compassionate nature of the therapeutic process. If simply talking can "cure," then talking *must be* a form of compassion. It must itself be compassionate. Yet Freud seems never to have considered what it is about the sensuous and qualitative nature of talking, such that the analysand's talking and the analyst's responses could be effectively healing. Nor did he ask himself how the compassionate power of the languaging that takes place in the analytic sessions could be, on both sides, effectively heightened.

5. Freud's technique of free association certainly merits our esteem. But Freud scarcely appreciated the full reach and range, the full significance, of his own technique. For him, it primarily served as a way of tricking the analysand into betraying unconscious repressions. It seems never to have occurred to him that it could also be helpful as a way of encouraging the analysand to become both more spontaneous and more receptive to associations (forms of nearness, couplings, touchings, intimacies) felt to be significant, but which, while not necessarily "irra-

tional," are certainly not logical (i.e., polymorphous associations more sensuous and libidinal than strictly egological).

6. This next point, although closely connected with the others, warrants a separate remark. Freud's attention to the languaging process was primarily focused, as I have already argued, on its pathological concealments and betrayals. This focus, though unquestionably important, urgently needs to be supplemented by a theoretically situated practical focus on the nature of existentially authentic[17] language: what kind of languaging process this is, how authentic languaging feels, in what ways it feels different from inauthentic languaging, and how a therapist can help the client to experience this difference, and learn authentic ways of languaging what is being experienced. (Authentic language is grounded in, emerges from, and stays in touch with, the experiential process. Helping people to language their experiencing authentically is *crucial* to therapeutic success.) When we consider the Freudian approach to interpretation, it is not hard to understand why these matters were not raised and carefully pondered. Stated very succinctly, the orthodox Freudian approach encroached upon, *and indeed violated*, the analysand's languaging process, by generating and espousing interpretive language not freely and independently grounded in, or originally emergent from, the analysand's *own* languaging experience. Thus, the Freudian approach encourages the analysand to continue a rather subtle, yet ultimately *felt*, bifurcation of experience: splitting experience into experiencing *as lived (as felt)* and experiencing *as interpreted in a canonical Freudian way* (i.e., as a repetition and echo of one's determinative past). It implicitly discourages, therefore, the spontaneous, authentic languaging process so crucial to the wholesome growth and ongoing individuation of the healthy person.

7. Despite the attention he gives to puns and other sorts of symbolic play, Freud gives no thought to the elemental sensuousness of language, above all in its relation to the healing of repressive dualities. I am thinking here of the ancient dualities of flesh and spirit, feeling and reason, body and mind, expression and thought (i.e., "the pure meaning–intention"). If the healing of these dualities indeed be vital for a healthy life, then the fact that languaging is a *sensuous embodiment* of mind (or spirit) should be highly significant. What role does the sensuous element play, then, in the talking cure? Does the aesthetic nature of the sensuous element—its playfulness, its spontaneity, its charm and beauty, for example—have any bearing on this role? And what relationship is there, if any, between speech with the healing power of truth, and speech which is vibrant,

---

[17]See R. von Eckartsberg and R. Valle, Chapter 14, for discussions of Heidegger's use of *authenticity* and *inauthenticity*. —Eds.

resonant with the powerful beauty of compassion, personal warmth, kindness, and generous concern? These are questions which need to be taken up within the Freudian framework. Without them, psychoanalysis cannot move closer to a more holistic psychology and psychotherapy.

Now let us turn to Jung, whom I will treat on this topic with an undeserved, and much regretted, brevity. Much more than Freud, Jung was open to what we might call, echoing early Heidegger, the "ontological" dimension of the languaging process. Although less thoughtful than Freud about the functioning and pathology of language, he is really the first modern psychologist in the West to have recognized, and even valued, the incantatory wizardry, the supernatural origin and nature, as it were, of human symbolic activity.[18] This openness was undoubtedly due to the fact that, whereas Freud restricted himself, for the most part, to the customary Western scope of languaging, Jung's starting point was the much vaster realm of symbolic activity in general: mainly, of course, the mythopoeic images of the transpersonal, collective unconscious. Such a starting point would naturally make it easier for Jung to take cognizance of the sense in which, as Heidegger says, it is not I who speak, so much as it is the archaic being of language itself that speaks—speaks itself *through* me, as through a resonant, echoing medium.

Nevertheless, Jung's awareness of the ontological dimension of symbolic activity did not specifically translate into an ontologically sensitive psychological understanding of the languaging process, nor did it motivate him to deepen and empower his therapeutic practice by working with clients who might be capable of opening themselves to the resonance of this dimension. Thus, for example, it seems not at all to have occurred to him that there might be, in the word magic he researched in such a scholarly way, something that could be transferred into the therapy situation and rigorously developed. Perhaps, had he been less of a scholar, he might have asked himself whether, and in what way, it might be salutary—profoundly healing—to experience oneself, not so much as the origin of one's words (i.e., as their original speaker), but rather more as their medium, the sanctuary of a chamber (in throat and chest) for the resounding of the very being of language, in something like the way that Heidegger describes with such poetically moving language.

Once we ask this question, however, we are well on our way toward undergoing what may be a fundamental, and humanly needed, experience with language, regarding which the Buddhists have much that is thoughtful and thought-provoking to say. And, if I may be forgiven for attempting to distill so briefly what I take to be the essence, or heart, of the Buddhist understanding of language, I should like to discuss the Buddh-

[18]See Heidegger (1971) and Reichel-Dolmatoff (1976).

ist experiencing of *mantra,* the powerful, poetic languaging of profound religious experience.[19]

First of all, we need to distinguish (a) languaging which is, in the strictest sense, what Buddhists call *mantra* from (b) languaging which makes manifest that which is poetically moving, thanks to what we might call its profoundly powerful *mantric quality.* Mantras are sacred words of power, words experienced as moved by, and moving with, the power to heal, or make whole. Some *mantras* are, according to our ordinary standards of meaning, entirely "meaningless"; others are partially, or even in their entirety, conveyors of some standard meanings, usually not unfolding, however, in a *sententially* meaningful way. Languaging with a "mantric quality," then, is a process involving grammatically standard, sententially meaningful language capable of being experienced as empowered, by virtue of its heightened poetic quality and the sacredness of its purpose (namely, to give the silence of the Holy, which is the Being of beings as such, an embodiment in the human voice), with the resonant soundings that heal, that make us whole and grant us health.

It should be evident, in light of this understanding, that the Buddhists are (seem) able to hear in the soundings of the human voice certain free-playing resonances (and perhaps echoes) which we do not normally hear, possibly because our everyday hearing is too crowded with "noise" and too enthralled by the standard grammar we learn as children. It takes an ear willing to *let go* its ego-logical concerns, its need to grasp, secure, and restrict what it is granted our hearing to hear. It takes an ear released from the need to fixate the resonant, polymorphous richness of human speech in univocal patterns of re-presentation. It takes an ear willing to listen with resolute openness to that which comes forth to be heard. In brief, it takes an ear attuned to the polyphonic, many-voiced sensuousness of the languaging process: an ear thus attuned because it is neither lustfully attracted, nor puritanically averse, to the nature of this sensuousness. (Appreciating *mantras,* therefore, involves one in intense spiritual practice.) Without that attunement, that openness, the playful sensuous element of the languaging process will not be free to grant us the holistic experience—the blessing, in fact—of hearing the very *birth* of language and the *emergence* of meaningfulness. For it is, after all, precisely this holistic *experience* of the languaging process whereby the free-playing, resonant soundings of the opened human voice are *heard* giving rise to newly emergent meanings, meanings experientially grounded, and, for that very reason, capable of healing and making us whole—it is precisely *this* experience which the chanting of *mantras* grants us.

[19]See Lama Govinda (1974) and Blofeld (1977).

Let me make explicit something which needs a bit of focus. At the same time that the chanting of *mantras* grants us an experience of the grounding, birth, and emergence of meaningfulness within the sensuous element of sound (i.e., the human voice), it also, perforce, integrates our "spiritual" and "sensuous" halves, for we experience, in this process, the *harmony* of elemental sound and cognitive sense.

There are, however, still other dimensions to the *mantric* experience. Once again, let me make explicit something which has already been hinted at, but which we need to give further thought to. I noted that we cannot enjoy the healing power of mantric chanting unless we begin to give up our egological fixations on language, fixations which include our preconceptions about what makes sense and how meaningfulness depends on our standard representational grammar. But, when we do actually begin to give up our various linguistic compulsions and repressions, and do actually abandon our need to make the languaging process re-presentational, then we may be moved by the sheer *presence* of language, its immediately resonant, overwhelming power—moved into an experiential openness that enables us to hear, in the hollows of the voice, soundings which are *not* fully originating in, or entirely belonging to, the isolated human voice. In other words, we may be able to hear, beyond the soundings of human language, its primordial ground of silence—an infinitely creative silence, which lies beyond the horizon of our own egological voices; an etymological silence, as it were, from whose protected roots the glorious blossoming of our human speaking stems. This deep, deep silence, this eternally creative reserve, resonating within our mindfully echoing voices, is what the Tibetans call the *language of Being*. Hearing it, when our ears are cleansed of ego-logical noise, we hear the very essence, or being, of language. And this essence is no other than its play as the sacred language of Being, the fact that it is so rich, so resonant, so endlessly full of potent meaning, that it favors us with the possibility of saying whatever we may have to say. In brief, then, chanting enables us to hear, and thus belong to, the disclosing creativity of Being as such. And this experience of whole-some belonging is profoundly joyous, profoundly fulfilling and enriching.

This point directs us toward two others, both of which I shall consider, here, in regard to the distinctive ways that they contribute to our understanding of the functioning of language in the process of becoming whole (i.e., healthy). The first point could be said to concern our own personal growth process, insofar as it takes place more or less independently of others. The second point, however, essentially concerns an interpersonal growth process, a process which takes place both for the sake of others (e.g., in the context of therapy), and for the sake of our own personal growth. I consider the process *essentially* interpersonal in either case, inasmuch as our own growth always needs, and in fact always cries out for, the well-being of others.

The first point is that the "mantric quality" of language, that is, its overwhelming poetic power, is, in effect, its power simultaneously to *move* us experientially, and to *express* for us the meaningfulness of this experiential movement. This is so, whether the languaging is "my own" (i.e., "originates" with me), or whether it is "yours." The mantric quality of languaging thus *makes itself true* (i.e., true *of* our experience), by being true *to* our deepest and ownmost experiential capacities (i.e., our underlying potential). Language with a poetic, or mantric, resonance always sounds too beautiful to be true *of* our experience. Heidegger reminds us that Hölderlin once wrote, in an epigram entitled "Sophocles":

> Viele versuchten umsonst, das Freudigste freudig zu sagen, Hier spricht endlich es mir, hier in der Trauer sich aus.
>
> [Many attempted in vain to speak the most joyful in a joyful way. Here it finally speaks to me, here in sadness.]

And indeed, when we listen to the poetic in order to hear how it fits, or appropriates, our experiencing, we tend to feel a certain gaping difference. And we may hasten to conclude that what the languaging voices, since it is not presently true *of* our experiencing, cannot therefore be so profoundly true *to* our experiencing that it touches us, moves us, changes us, and harmoniously makes itself true *of* that being whom we become in the process.

This is how I think we must read, and listen to, the mantric poetry of the great Buddhist texts—the songs of Saraha and Milarepa, the various liturgical texts and meditation instructions, and the noble sermons of, say, Śantideva. The prayers, sermons, and other teachings compassionately invite us, through their moving poetry, to listen beyond the speakers themselves to the languaging of Being which they try to convey, echoing in resounding voice the center of wholesome silence whose medium and embodiment they are. In their compassion, they invite us to open up to their speech, listening in a receptive and accepting way. More specifically, their enchantment enchants us, making it easier for us to experience, thanks to the beauty of their language, the deeply penetrating truth and goodness of what they have to say. So we can listen to their poetic language and hear in it not only a generous *sharing* of joyous human experience, but also a compassionately gentle *suggestion* that we make use of their phenomenological (i.e., experientially faithful) descriptions, taking them as *norms that prescribe well-tested visualization practices* especially helpful in cultivating our still unfulfilled human potential, so that we may directly realize, in and as our own experience, the wholesome, joyful truth of what is well-spoken.

If, now, we ask after the provenance of such compassionate and healing language, we are returned to a point I made earlier, namely, that the enchanting poetic, mantric, singing quality of the Buddhist teacher's language is therapeutic (i.e., capable of being effectively compassionate) in part, at least, because it is directly grounded in, and has spontaneously emerged to blossom from, the teacher's own unfolding experiential process. And it expresses the *joyfulness* of this creative experiental process: a joy which can be *heard* in the wonderful, rich, enchanting resonance of the teacher's voice, for its contagious presence is manifest in, is in fact transmitted by, the spontaneity with which the teacher bursts warmly into song. The singing is also therapeutic, of course, because it is grounded in, and cor-respondingly emerges from, that center of healing silence which is the primordial language of Being, and because, from out of this joyful experience of its creative source, the teacher tries to convey, and kindle within others, a kindred healing joy.

The "second point" (referred to above) will serve as my concluding remark concerning the Buddhist understanding and practice of *mantra*. The chanting of *mantras*, no less than the discipline of listening to what human beings have it within them to say, contributes very directly to the Buddhist teaching of egolessness, whose openness is the essence of liberation from the wheel of pain and suffering, and the very heart of compassion. Thus, for example, to consider just one level of this teaching, the process of chanting calls upon us to *open* our lips and mouth, open the chords of our throat, expand our lungs and chest, and expand our nostrils, so our breathing can become deep and free, giving and taking with a gentle, meditative rhythm. But, as I observed before, there echoes and resounds, within our mindful chanting, a certain sound, or quality of sound, which is experienced as not "our own" (not "of our own making"). Hearing this inaudible sound, ungraspable, unre-presentable, and unspeakably profound, we are instantly humbled. And this helps us to be more open in our relationships with other people, and more compassionate.

Furthermore, such chanting helps us to focus, not on the *cognitive content* of our languaging process (i.e., on its re-presentational function), but rather on *the qualitative process itself* (i.e., on our "presence," our *Befindlichkeit*, the way we are, and are with others, thanks to the communion of language). Mantric chanting focuses our awareness on the *felt quality* of our voice (e.g., its personal warmth, its gentle tone, its enthusiasm and vitality, its responsive patience, its melodic serenity, its harmonious ring of truth, and the carefulness of its articulation), so that we may begin to develop a stronger and clearer feeling for the compassionate power of our speech. "Right speech," included among the norms of the eightfold path of virtue, means much more than sincere and truthful speech. It means, also, speech which is friendly, warmly greeting, kind, thoughtful. The Buddhists, once again, recognize that, in therapy, it is the *quality* of communication that matters; *what* is said is of relatively little importance compared to the therapist's "resonance."

The practice of chanting (and repeating) *mantras* thus serves to remind us (a) that the being of language is an awesome, overwhelming, mysterious, transpersonal power, truly beyond our grasp; and (b) that there is a very deep need, cor-responding to our felt capacity (the felt potential, which *mantra* helps us to feel), to give thought to our speech and speak in a way that allows the reserve of language's compassionate power to flow through us and be of service to other beings. Thus, in fine, the practice of compassion is the ultimate ground, the ultimate path, and the ultimate goal of Buddhist *mantra*.

This is why, when the revered Buddhist teachers start teaching and the mad yogins practice their healing wisdom, their voices suddenly flower and thunder in songs of great beauty and power.

The Human Body

The final topic we shall consider, however briefly, is the human body. Basically, I will bring the matter to your attention, and recommend it for further thought. The Freudian approach to psychotherapy virtually ignores the living human body, except to consider it, upon reflection, to be nothing more than a neurophysiological substance. Freudian analysis conceptualizes the human body we live in in such a way that it is ill-prepared to respond to us as bodily beings without objectifying our bodies. (This argument is confirmed by the fact that, when Freud *does* focus his attention on the body, what catches his attention are, e.g., phantom limbs, hysterically paralyzed limbs, facial tics, stuttering, body fixations and fetishes, and a multitude of compulsions somehow involving the body.) In keeping, too, with his Viennese Victorianism, Freud altogether excludes from consideration even those characteristics of embodiment—gestures, postures, movements, for instance—which would have been very useful to him in diagnosing and treating his patients.

In this regard, the Jungian approach is much more holistic: much more receptive, that is, to the living, sensuous, embodiment-nature of human beings. Recognizing that a wholesome, healthy human being must enjoy a healthy body, and that, in order for this to happen, the human being must be encouraged to develop a wholesome understanding of, and a healthy, appreciative regard for, his or her own body, Jung encouraged his clients, in a revolutionary departure from orthodox Freudian analysis, to paint, dance, sing, take exercise, try techniques of yoga, cultivate and enrich their perceptual sensibility, and, in many other ways besides, to tend and nurture their bodily being.

In Buddhism, this concern for the quality of our embodiment, that is, for the way our body feels and grows experientially, is even stronger. In fact, the centrality of this concern becomes explicit, and is apparent in, the Vajrayān interpretation of the *Trikāya,* in which what Guenther calls the three existential norms of embodiment, each one specifying a (potential) dimension of bodily experience, are progressively realized and taught, primarily through the practice of sitting meditation, visualizations, chanting, and the ritualized gestures called *mudra.*[20] Visualizations involving our "body image" can be especially valuable in showing us, and grounding in feeling, *another way* of being embodied. Many of Buddhism's earliest teachings and practices, for example, Sāntideva's *Bodhicāryāvatara,* appreciated this. Basically, the visualization involves projecting an *ideal* body image, which then functions like the Kantian schemata in the process of organizing bodily experience around a new sense of our embodiment potential.

It is my strong conviction that no philosophy of human being aspiring to wisdom, no adequate psychology of human experience, and no enlightened psychotherapy compassionately bent on restoring human beings to their joyful wholeness, can afford to ignore the human body as it is actually lived, that is, as an ongoing process of actualizing and realizing the deepest potential of human embodiment.

In closing, I would like, first, to speak with very special praise for Merleau-Ponty's (1962) phenomenological work on perception, and, second, to suggest that, for us who live and think as Westerners, this work is the most yielding, but also the very firmest ground, upon which to begin building a bridge that would take us across to the unfathomable wisdom and compassionate experiential practice of the *Trikāya.*

References

Blofeld, J. *Mantras: Sacred words of power.* New York: Dutton, 1977.
Boss, M. *Existential foundations of medicine and psychology.* New York: Jason Aronson, 1979.
Campbell, J. (Ed.) *The portable Jung.* New York: Penguin Books, 1976.
Corbin, H. *Creative imagination in the Sufism of Ibn 'Arabi.* London: Routledge & Kegan Paul, 1970.

[20]Especially helpful in this regard is the work of Guenther (1971, 1972).

Freud, S. *The problem of anxiety.* New York: Norton, 1936.

Freud, S. *The complete works of Sigmund Freud* (J. Strachey, Ed.). London: Hogarth Press and the Institute of Psycho-Analysis, 1958.

Freud, S. *The ego and the id.* New York: Norton, 1962.

Gendlin, E. Phenomenological concept vs. phenomenological method: A critique of Medard Boss on dreams. *Soundings,* 1977, *60*(3), 285–300.

Goodman, S. The reliable teaching, *Gesar,* 1978, *5*(3).

Guenther, H. V. *Buddhist philosophy in theory and practice.* Boulder, Col.: Shambhala, 1971.

Guenther, H. V. *The Tantric view of life.* Boulder, Col.: Shambhala, 1972.

Heidegger, M. *On the way to language.* New York: Harper & Row, 1971.

Heidegger, M. *Basic writings* (D. F. Krell, Ed.). New York: Harper & Row, 1977.

Jung, C. G. *Aion; Researches into the phenomenology of the self.* In *Collected Works of Carl G. Jung* (Vol. 9). Princeton, N.J.: Bollingen Press, 1959.

Lama Govinda. *The foundations of Tibetan mysticism.* New York: Samuel Weiser, 1974.

Levin, D. M. The phenomenon and noumenon of language: The twin paths of perfect speaking (mantra) and perfect writing (mudra). *Tri-quarterly,* 1977, *38,* 229–255. (a).

Levin, D. M. Self-knowledge and the talking cure. *Review of Existential Psychology and Psychiatry,* 1977, *15*(2 & 3), 95–111. (b).

Levin, D. M. Painful time, ecstatic time. *The Eastern Buddhist,* 1978, *11,* 2.

Merleau-Ponty, M. *Phenomenology of perception.* London: Routledge & Kegan Paul, 1962.

Reichel-Dolmatoff, G. Desana curing spells: An analysis of some Shamanistic metaphors. *Journal of Latin American Lore,* 1976, *2*(2), 157–219.

Tarthang Tulku. *Time, space, and knowledge.* Berkeley, Calif.: Dharma Publishing, 1977.

Tarthang Tulku. *Skillful means.* Berkeley, Calif.: Dharma Publishing, 1978.

13

Two Paradigmatic Strands in the
Buddhist Theory of Consciousness

Padmasiri de Silva

The philosophical and psychological reflections of early Buddhism[1] as found in the discourses of the Buddha provide an interesting base to examine some of the contemporary controversies in psychological theory. In fact, the Buddha himself, who was confronted by numerous philosophers and debaters, betrayed a significant sophistication regarding the kind of conceptual framework one should use when discussing the nature of human consciousness. In a sustained criticism of 62 theories regarding man and the universe, the Buddha (Digha Nikaya, Sutta 1) considers his own position as a kind of "razor's edge" which will steer clear of certain theoretical pitfalls like eternalism and annihilationism, materialism and idealism, determinism and indeterminism, and value relativism and value absolutism.

Keeping in mind the Buddha's ability to steer clear of theoretical pitfalls, this analysis will attempt to present two paradigmatic strands which find an interesting kind of fusion in the Buddhist theory of consciousness—two theoretical strands which are at the base of the opposition between the *Freudian* and the *Sartrean* images of man and consciousness.

According to the Buddhist notion of "conditionality," consciousness is a dynamic continuum generated by the interplay of a plurality of

[1]See also Levin, Chapter 12, and R. von Eckartsberg and R. Valle, Chapter 14, for discussions of Tibetan and Zen Buddhism, respectively.—Eds.

Padmasiri de Silva • Department of Philosophy and Psychology, University of Sri Lanka, Peradeniya, Sri Lanka.

factors. The nature of the mind as a dynamic continuum is explained in the sermons of the Buddha with the help of a number of analogies and metaphors: mind is described as a stream of consciousness (*viññāṇa sota*), likened to the movements of a monkey from one branch to another (not letting go of one till he clutches another), and compared to a fire which lasts as long as the fuel lasts. This is the kind of "root metaphor" used in describing the nature of consciousness as a dynamic continuum.

According to the Buddhist notion of "unsubstantiality," which points toward the lack of an inner essence, consciousness may be viewed as "empty" and vacuous. Sartre says that nothingness enters consciousness as a worm enters an apple. In keeping with this line of thought, Sartre in his existential psychoanalysis rejects the Freudian emphasis on drives, instincts, and mechanisms. Based on the relationship between the concepts of "consciousness," "freedom," and "nothingness," Sartre gives a crucial place to the spontaneous free action of consciousness. Sartre is averse to general laws of human behavior and also refuses to consider consciousness as a function of character or of the person. Thus, Sartre insists that consciousness is responsible for the totality of human experience.

The interesting point about this second paradigmatic strand as found in Sartre's theory of consciousness is that he is rejecting a complete paradigm regarding the nature of consciousness, a paradigm which cuts across the writings of Bergson, James, Whitehead, and Freud. Consider Fell (1965):

> The threat of continuity, the Bergsonian "interpenetration," the Jamesian "stream," the Whiteheadian "inheritance," the mental "automatism" of a Janet, of a Freudian bombardment of consciousness by affects—all these are at one stroke rejected by Sartre's theory. (p. 172)

The early Buddhist reflections regarding the nature of mind seem to offer an interesting way of absorbing the finest insights of Freud and Sartre—the conception of the stream of consciousness as a dynamic continuum, and the notion that consciousness is "vacuous." I have worked out elsewhere (de Silva, 1974, 1978) the similarities and differences between the Sartrean and Freudian viewpoints and the Buddhist psychological theory. It must be mentioned that in the context of the relations of consciousness to the dimensions of spiritual growth, Buddhism stands out clearly from both Freud and Sartre.[2]

The Buddha points to the fact that consciousness is vacuous, insubstantial, and has no inner essence; at the same time, the Buddha accepts the strength of dispositional traits, the strong drives for sensuous gratifi-

[2]Peter Lomas (1968) comments that: "It would be a great pity if the 'Freudian' and 'Existential' schools of thought grew apart rather than together."

cation, egoistic pursuits, and aggression. In addition, a central place is given to decision, responsibility, and the autonomy of the individual. It is the aim of this chapter to highlight these features in Buddhist psychological theory against the background of the Freudian and the Sartrean images of man and consciousness.

The Nature of Consciousness in Buddhism

The nature of consciousness in Buddhism has to be understood against the background of the three features of existence: impermanence *(anicca)*, egolessness *(anattā)*, and suffering *(dukkha)*. The Buddha denies the existence of any permanent entity, either mental or physical. What we refer to as mind is a psychophysical complex *(nāma–rūpa)*. *Nāma* is used to refer to the four nonmaterial groups *(khandas)*: feelings *(vedanā)*, perceptions *(saññā)*, dispositions *(sankhāra)*, and consciousness *(viññāna)*. The term *rūpa* refers to the four great elements: extension, cohesion, heat, and the material shape derived from them. The mental and physical constituents form one complex, and there is a mutual dependency of the mind on the body and the body on the mind.

The mind as a psychophysical complex is certainly not a substance or any immutable and eternal soul. All mental phenomena are causally conditioned and are often referred to as a dynamic continuum. The body and the mind are subject to change and they are transitory *(anicca)*. The Buddha described the universe in terms of the arising, decay, and dissolution of all things. By this rejection of any eternally abiding substance, it follows that he also rejected an eternally abiding pure ego *(attā)*.

All mental phenomena have to be understood in the light of causal laws, since they are causally conditioned. The law of dependent origination *(paticcasamuppāda)* points to the conditionality of all physical and mental phenomena. Although the theory of dependent origination shows that all mental phenomena are causally conditioned, the doctrine of egolessness affirms that they lack any inner essence.

Apart from the two features, egolessness *(anattā)* and transience *(anicca)*, there is a third feature of existence which is often rendered as the unsatisfactoriness of existence *(dukkha)*. The Buddha was basically interested in the predicament of human PAIN. We have to make a distinction between PAIN and pain. There are times where you are struck by a stone and sustain physical injury or when a piercing toothache puts a person in an unbearable mood; there are occasions when a close friend betrays you, or when a deep sense of injustice in the world disturbs you; and there are also those agonizing instances of loss, sickness, and the fear of death. As this spectrum of physical and psychological *pain* broadens, we encounter the basic predicament of man experiencing futility, boredom, despair, emptiness, and unsubstantiality. Apart from pain, or, in Sartrean terms, the "little pools of non-being" (domestic nothingness), there is the more basic predicament of human PAIN. Thus, in general, the word *dukkha* has three broad usages—a general philosophical sense, a narrower psychological sense, and a still narrower physical sense. It is in this general philosophical sense that words like unsatisfactoriness, emptiness, and unsubstantiality have been suggested as a translation of the word *dukkha*. This meaning becomes prominent when *dukkha* is considered as a universal characteristic of all existence, along with impermanence and egolessness. It is said: "What is impermanent *(aniccaṃ)* that is suffering *(dukkha)*, what is suffering that is void of an ego *(ānattā)"* (Samyutta Nikaya, IV, Sutta 1).

The word *dukkha* etymologically suggests the idea of an evil hollow. The empty hollow ground in which human misery is woven is the belief in a non-existent ego (see de Silva, 1974). Thus, although the linkage between the doctrines of egolessness and unsatisfactoriness emphasizes the *vacuity of consciousness*, the doctrine of dependent origination brings out the role of *consciousness as a dynamic continuum*.

The problem of philosophically clarifying the concept of consciousness in the light of alternative theories was important for the Buddha as he encountered a number of people who engaged in debates with him. The Buddha clearly differentiated his concept from materialists who said that consciousness was an emergent property of the interplay of material factors. He also had to demarcate his theory from eternalists who treated consciousness as immutable soul. There was, for instance, a person called Sati whom the Buddha interrogated; Sati thought that the "consciousness of a person ran along and faired on without change" (Majjhima Nikaya, Sutta 37). The Buddha did not accept any such conception of a permanent soul; rather, he viewed consciousness as a dynamic continuum fed by a number of physiological, psychological, and environmental factors. In accepting the reality of the part played by material factors, up to a point, he disagrees with idealists who would consider the material world as a creation of the mind.[3] Yet the Buddha rejected mechanistic and deterministic theories of human behavior. Even though there are physiological, psychological, and environmental factors which may condition human behavior or act as constraints, the reality of intention and human purpose was central to the Buddha. Again, though upholding the reality of human intention as one of the basic criteria for evaluating behavior, he sounded a note of caution that one should not embrace metaphysical theories of vitalism.

[3]This concept was, in fact, even developed by some of the idealist Buddhist schools which came after the Buddha.

Although the Buddha discarded the concept of soul, he did not consider any form of mechanism, determinism, or a behavioristic concept of mind as viable alternatives. Though the Buddha did value reliable behavioral tests (de Silva, 1979), he gave a central place to "introspection," in its broad meaning as a technique of self-analysis. Although giving a strong therapeutic basis for Buddhist psychology, the Buddha, unlike the psychoanalyst, did not deemphasize the value-oriented basis of psychological phenomena. As I have shown elsewhere (de Silva, 1979), the doctrine of the Buddha clearly accommodates the "interlacing of the psychological and ethical" (p. 2).

In the light of recent critical studies of both "behaviorism" and "mentalism" in Western psychology, a new paradigm which does not fall into either trap may be in the offing.[4] In this respect, the Buddha's concept of consciousness was a kind of "razor's edge" steering clear of excessive and dogmatic alternatives. Even with regard to the perennial debate on the mind–body problem, the Buddha combined sound common sense with his philosophical acumen. He accepted the mutual interaction of body and mind as well as the conventional value of referring to "mind" and "body" within their conceptual framework, but did not allow this to emerge as any kind of metaphysical dualism of substances, such as found, for instance, in the writings of Descartes (1951).

Finally, the Buddhist concept of mind or consciousness is neither a mere theoretical perspective, nor is it a blueprint for experimental work designed for mere research. Jayatilleke (1975) states:

> Buddhist psychology, on the other hand, while giving a comprehensive account of the nature of human experience and behavior, also provides the means by which we can understand, control, and develop ourselves by a process of self-analysis and meditation. (p. 81)

Freud and Buddhism[5]

The mind, according to Buddhist psychological analysis, is a dynamic continuum which extends over a number of births. This continuum is composed of a conscious mind as well as an unconscious in which is contained the residue of emotionally charged memories, memories which extend not merely to childhood, but to past lives too. The mind viewed in this way is continuously subjected to pressure by the threefold desires of sense gratification (kāma-taṇhā), egoistic pursuits (bhava-taṇhā), and self-annihilation (vibhava-taṇhā). These desires have

[4]See Pribram's, Chapter 6, "Behaviorism, Phenomenology, and Holism in Psychology: A Scientific Analysis."—Eds.
[5]See also Levin's, Chapter 12, discussion of Freud and Tibetan Buddhism.—Eds.

interesting parallels to the Freudian scheme of the libido, ego instinct, and death instinct.

One of the strongest drives that color the dynamic psychological processes is the craving to satisfy our senses and sexual desire. The natural proneness to seek pleasure and be repelled by pain (similar to Freud's pleasure principle) is, according to the Buddha, one of the most powerful bases of human motivation.

Sensuality has both a subjective and an objective aspect. The term *panca-kāmaguna* refers to the five types of pleasure objects obtained by way of the eye, ear, nose, tongue, and body—the objective aspect. Subjectively, *kāma-rāga* refers to desires and passions of a sensual nature. The objects of pleasure are referred to as "delightful, dear, passion-fraught, and inciting to lust." Furthermore, whenever a person's passions are roused, there emerges a kind of tenacity to hold on to these pleasures. Here we find the emergence of the psychological process referred to as clinging *(upādanā)*. Unless there is this persistence of clinging, excitation of the sense organs is not sufficient to rouse the individual to activity. The pursuit of sense pleasures is, however, fed by deeper undercurrents. When clinging emerges, some latent tendencies *(anusayas)* have already been excited. Pleasant feelings *(vedanā)* induce an attachment to pleasant objects as they arouse latent sensuous greed *(rāgānusaya)*. Painful feelings, on the other hand, arouse latent anger and hatred *(patighānusaya)*. As these *anusayas* lie dormant in the deeper recesses of our personality and may be excited by appropriate stimuli, and as these processes can occur without conscious awareness, this psychological process may be considered as a facet of unconscious motivation in the psychology of Buddhism. I have discussed in detail elsewhere (de Silva, 1978) the different shades of the meaning of the term "unconscious" in relation to both the Freudian and the Buddhist concepts of mind.

As we are interested in "metaphors of consciousness," it would be appropriate to mention two metaphors describing unconscious processes in Buddhism. In fact, some of the psychological terms we find in the *Buddhist Suttas* are described by imagery, and even their meanings are often charged with metaphorical associations. In this context, the word *āsava*, which is similar to the Freudian Id, is clarified by the use of metaphors. Two such metaphors are found in the Buddhist writings: the intoxicating extract of a flower and the discharge from a sore or wound. Like liquor which has been kept in long storage, the psychological states referred to as *āsava* have been simmering in the deeper recesses of the person. Some Buddhist scholars feel that the idea of strong intoxication is the central meaning of the word *āsava*, compared with other meanings like "taint" or "oozing from wound." The comparing of the mind to a festering wound is also found in the discourses of the Buddha. Freud also uses a metaphor when he describes the Id as "a cauldron of seething excitations."

Though the Buddha used such metaphorical language, when divested of metaphor and imagery the Buddha used the term "unconscious" in a dispositional sense, as is very clearly seen in the use of the term *saṅkhāra* (dispositions) to explicate unconscious processes. I have argued in detail (de Silva, 1978) that, similar to Freud's notion, the Buddhist concept of the unconscious can be explained as a dispositional concept:

> The analysis of the early Buddhist concept of the Unconscious is based on concepts like the anusayas (latent tendencies) and asampajāna manosaṅkhāra (dispositions of the mind of which we are not aware). Reference is also made to the viññāṇasota (the stream of consciousness). The viññāṇsota has a conscious and an unconscious aspect. The unconscious aspect contains the dynamic saṅkhāra-s (dispositions) which determine the nature of the next birth. Most of the references indicate that the early Buddhist concept of the unconscious can be explained as a disposition concept. This falls in line with the claim that the characteristically psychoanalytic meaning of the word unconscious is *dispositional*. One significant difference, however, is that the saṅkhāra-s have a wider dimension connecting an innumerable number of births. In general, early Buddhism considers the mind as a dynamic continuum composed of a conscious mind and an unconscious which has its roots in samsaric existence. (p. 72)

Although I discussed the nature of unconscious psychic processes only in terms of the desire for sensuous gratification, parallel structural similarities are seen in the workings of the drive for egoistic pursuits and the drive for destruction and aggression. The acquisitive personality of the egocentric person is rooted in strong dispositional traits and latent tendencies like self-assertion, pride, and the disposition to cling to existence. Painful sensations excite dormant hatred *(paṭighānusaya)*. Unlike Freud, the Buddha would consider self-destruction and suicidal tendencies as "reactive" rather than "appetitive."

In making a diagnostic study of the human predicament, the Buddha probed deeply into the roots of motivation which do not come to the surface of normal awareness. By a process of mind-development, it is possible to understand the dark interior regions of the mind, patterns of compulsive behavior, and the irrational biases.

It should now be apparent that there are interesting similarities between the Freudian and the Buddhist dynamic psychologies. Buddhism, however, does not fall into any pattern of psychic determinism, but, rather, emphasizes the role of personal autonomy, freedom, personal effort, and responsibility; and this it does without accepting the Sartrean concept of absolute freedom.

Sartre and Buddhism

The Sartrean paradigm regarding the explanation of human behavior offers an interesting divergence from Freud. Sartre makes consciousness responsible for all human experience, and thus rejects the Freudian concept of the unconscious. Though Sartre does refer to an unreflective and impersonal consciousness, it does not have the same explanatory power as does the Freudian concept of unconscious processes.

Where Freud (like Gilbert Ryle) offers a dispositional analysis of human behavior, Sartre offers an intentional analysis:

> Sartre explains regularity of emotional response very differently. Instead of a dispositional analysis, he offers an intentional analysis. The various types of emotion are traced not to the disposition but to the spontaneous act of consciousness. Inclinations or dispositions (for Sartre "states" and "qualities") are intentional constructs of impure reflection. (Fell, 1965, pp. 196–197)

Fell (1965) also raises an interesting question: "Is it possible to avoid the perils of an intentional analysis on the one hand and of a dispositional analysis on the other?" A strange enough answer of a sort is found in the Buddhist concept of *saṅkhāra* which I have translated (de Silva, 1978) as "directed dispositions," and which, following C. D. Broad, may be called "conative dispositions." Regarding this term, I (de Silva, 1978) made the observation:

> It seems, then, that through the diversity of meanings associated with the word saṅkhāra there run two basic threads of meaning: (1) the idea of deliberation, planning, making a choice, persistence in an effort, aspects suggested by volition and conation; (2) dynamism, disposition, habit, in which sense it is often associated with karma . . . The term "directed dispositions" may do justice to both these elements and hence this is here suggested as a translation of saṅkhāra. (p. 18)

The fusing of concepts like those of deliberation and habit behavior into one concept need not be foreign to Western psychology; in fact, Flugel (1955) cites the word "orexis," which cuts through both affection and conation.

The Buddha, however, is careful not to raise the factors of intention and volition to the status of a metaphysical will. Rather, mental factors like intention and volition are not separate entities, but are inseparably associated with other factors. They are simply functions in a dynamic unit of consciousness. Thus, even the factor of volition has to be viewed as part of a dynamic process. The Sartrean concept of man in terms of "projects" and "spontaneous acts of consciousness" is assimilated into this dynamic continuum by the Buddha.

The dispositions *(saṅkhāra)*, according to the Buddha, may be wholesome or unwholesome. The elimination of the passions and the control of the senses depend on the development of the wholesome dispositions. As the passions are strong, it is said that a great deal of effort is necessary to go against the current *(paṭisotagāmi)*. This is an interesting metaphor, as graphic as the more well known "stream of consciousness." Right intention, effort, energy, and persistence are the qualities that help people to withstand the strength of unwholesome impulses, as well as develop more positive aspirations toward the path of spiritual development. In this context, it is necessary to mention the Buddha's admonition to develop the four efforts: the effort to restrain, the effort to abandon, the effort to make become, and the effort to watch over. The effort to make become is of special importance, as it builds up positive spiritual skills, such as mindfulness, tranquility, and equanimity. In the attempt to develop positive spiritual skills aimed at spiritual goals, we see a fusion of the *dispositional* and the *intentional* aspects of human behavior.

There is, however, a little cloud in this attempt to visualize the Sartrean-Freudian conflict in a Buddhist setting. Sartre is using the word *intentional*[6] in the Husserlian sense of an act of consciousness which is "object-directed," rather than in the sense of self-conscious determination or decision. In fact, some scholars describe the Husserlian sense as INTENSIONAL, rather than INTENTIONAL. However, it has been observed by commentators on Sartre that, as Sartre develops his work, intentionality takes on a purposive connotation. In the Buddhist context, an interesting fusion exists between habit and deliberation, momentum and purpose. It is also said in the Buddhist context that, whether an action is spontaneous and effortless or deliberate and planned, they are both volitional, and may be evaluated as, for example, good or bad, skillful or unskillful.

In the Sartrean system, to accept the strength of dispositional traits is to be acting on the level of "impure reflection." In the Buddhist context, a distinction is made between "understanding" the strength of dispositional traits (the image of "going against the current") and "succumbing" to them. Understanding their strength is a mark of realism rather than an expression of bad faith. It is also said that these dispositions may be wholesome dispositions; accepting their existence gives an insight into one's own moral vigor.

The meaning of the Freudian challenge is that we have to deal realistically with the strength of human dispositions. The Buddhist would accept this without abrogating the reality of decision and responsibility, and yet do so without positing a pre-existent state of absolute freedom. Somewhere along these lines the Freudian-Sartrean conflict may be resolved.

[6]See Moss, Chapter 7, and R. von Eckartsberg and R. Valle, Chapter 14, for a discussion of *intentionality* as a structural characteristic of consciousness.—Eds.

The broad lines on which a fusion between the Freudian and the Sartrean analysis may be attempted are fairly clear. The only clouding issue is the specific way in which Sartre used the term "intentional." I am currently examining the meanings of "intentionality" in Buddhism, and it is hoped that this cloud will not become a big storm. I wish to leave this subject somewhat open for the present. Does the study of the intentional structure of experience rule out a theory of dynamic psychology? Though Sartre thinks it does, I do not feel that it need be so in the Buddhist context.

Concluding Comments

Unlike Sartre, the Buddha did not identify acceptance of the causal structure in the universe with "determinism." However, while upholding the validity of causal laws, he was extremely cautious to differentiate his doctrine from various forms of determinism, as well as forms of indeterminism. The Buddha opposed all forms of determinism, whether natural determinism, theistic determinism, karmic determinism, or any philosophy in which these are combined. The individual can, to a certain extent, control the dynamic forces of the past and present, and change the course of future events. Man has free will *(attakāra)* and personal endeavor *(purisa kāra)*, and is capable of changing himself and his environment. This ability to mediate between conflicting positions is a quality of the Buddha recognized by many scholars.

The Buddha was very much aware of the dialectical opposition between rival theories and, in general, steered clear of dogmatic extremes. Some of the opposing theories, like eternalism and annihilationism, materialism and idealism, and determinism and indeterminism, were supported by well-known exponents of the doctrines at the time. My attempt to mediate between the Freudian and the Sartrean analysis of human behavior was an attempt to extend this principle to more specific conflicts in the contemporary world. Although in philosophy early Buddhism offers an interesting base for mediating between analytic philosophy and existentialism (de Silva, in press), in psychology it has the potential to resolve the conflict between behaviorism and mentalism. Thus, the encounter between Western and Eastern systems of thought could bring a fresh perspective which might ease some of the deep-rooted tensions which exist between theoretical orientations in Western philosophy and psychology.

References

Descartes, R. *Meditations*. New York: Liberal Arts Press, 1951.

de Silva, P. *Tangles and webs*. Colombo, Sri Lanka: Lake House Investments, 1974.

de Silva, P. *Buddhist and Freudian psychology*. Colombo, Sri Lanka: Lake House Investments, 1978.

de Silva, P. *An introduction to Buddhist psychology*. London: Macmillan, 1979.

de Silva, P. The conflict between analytic philosophy and existentialism in Buddhist perspective. In N. Katz (Ed.), *Buddhism and Western philosophy*. New Delhi, India: Sterling Publishers, in press.

Fell, J. *Emotion in the thought of Sartre*. New York: Columbia University Press, 1965.

Flugel, J. *Studies in feeling and desire*. London: Duckworth, 1955.

Jayatilleke, K. In N. Smart (Ed.), *Message of the Buddha*. London: Allen & Unwin, 1975.

Lomas, P. In C. Rycroft (Ed.), *Psychoanalysis observed*. Baltimore: Penguin Books, 1968.

14

Heideggerian Thinking and the Eastern Mind

Rolf von Eckartsberg and Ronald S. Valle

Psychologists look to philosophers for a clarification of their work. Philosophers ask the more fundamental questions regarding the nature of man—philosophical anthropology, the nature of being—metaphysics and ontology, the nature of truth—epistemology, and the nature of values and the good life—ethics.

Most psychologists are content to work within an established framework of thinking (philosophy) and do not usually question the presuppositions of their work. But sometimes the very meaning of the activities of a scientific discipline becomes questionable, a crisis of identity of a whole science sets in, and, in such a situation of doubting and questioning, the dialogue opens up, and other world-views, other anthropologies, metaphysics, and religions, even, become interesting and important. A search for a new paradigm (Kuhn, 1962) begins. Not that established paradigms really ever die, certainly not in the social sciences. In the social sciences, which include political science, paradigms co-exist much like political parties. As long as they co-exist, we have the fertile ground of democratic freedom of exchange, and the growth of knowledge in all directions.

As it is in political life, in the politics of science we also sometimes run into ideological dictatorships, when one way of thinking predominates in

Rolf von Eckartsberg • Department of Psychology, Duquesne University, Pittsburgh, Pennsylvania 15219. Ronald S. Valle • Center for the Development of Consciousness and Personal Growth, 501 Wallace Road, Wexford, Pennsylvania 15090.

the profession and begins to drive out all conflicting views. It can also happen that a certain mind-set develops and becomes accepted without much awareness of it on the part of the participants. In such a situation, it will take a radical alternative view to make us aware of our implicit assumptions and silently operative precomprehensions and prejudices, and summon us to reflect on the meaning of our doing and on the adequacy of our concepts.

In psychology we seem to be ready for radical questions and the critical examination of our ruling paradigm at this time. Both Western existentialism (particularly the work of Martin Heidegger) and Eastern philosophico-religious thinking (in the form of Hinduism, Buddhism, Taoism, and Zen) have in recent years vigorously entered into the debate of American psychology and have had a liberating and opening-up effect on our discipline, forcing us to consider enlarging and refounding our paradigm.

There are many reasons for this. As the external-historical reasons, we cite the rapidly advancing military, political, economic and industrial development, travel and communication, and our increasing awareness of our global interconnectedness and interdependence during the post-World War II period.

As the more subtle reasons, we point to the development that a grossly materialistic view of the nature of reality and man has led to an incipient bankruptcy of meaning and values, a loss of the meaningfulness of life, a sense of root- and homelessness, a lack of direction, an increasing crisis of confidence in technology and the scientific establishment, a creeping kind of apathetic nihilism in the realms of politics and governance, and a growing sense of helplessness with respect to economic realities.

The reasons listed have psychological consequences in that they contribute to the meanings experienced and perceived by everybody trying to cope with the unfolding conditions of their lives, many of which seem to be beyond the control of the individual. Is psychology, the way it is today as an academic and research discipline, capable of dealing with the psychological impact of modern-day living?

A numerically significant faction of psychologists, those variously described as humanistic, transpersonal, and existential-phenomenological psychologists, has decided that the ruling majority paradigm in contemporary psychology, behaviorism, and its attendant methods of research and therapy, behavior modification, is deficient in significant ways and has become part of the problem, because its underlying paradigm provides us with a reductionistic, mechanistic, and uninspiring conceptualization of the nature of man and human reality, with a robot-understanding of human interaction, and a caricature-vision of who we are.

The double turn within psychology, toward Western existential philosophical thinking on the one hand, and toward Eastern philosophico-religious wisdom on the other, should be seen as the healthy attempt to revitalize and reform the stifling natural scientific approach to psychology conceived as the science of behavior by reintroducing the realities of experience and consciousness, by insisting on the importance of personal agency, the sense of self, and of values and meaning, and by emphasizing ultimate depth- and height-dimensions of human experience: peak experiences, mystical-ecstatic self-transcendence, and the experience of transpersonal powers or "theo-realities."

There has been emerging among consciousness-oriented psychologists an increasing recognition that our personal and collective relationship to the world (man–world-relationships) has to be lived under the inspiration and auspices of some higher, transpersonal power of divinity, of ultimate Being, as the source of legitimation and validation of our activities.

This higher, transpersonal God- or theo-dimension is variously spoken of and conceptualized in different traditions. We want to select and compare Heidegger's work on the Western philosophical tradition of metaphysics and ontology with the major Eastern spiritual traditions, because they bear some striking similarities in their emphasis on a transcendent dimension, the theo-dimension, in human consciousness. In this shared emphasis, they both offer to psychology a new and more adequate view of man in his potential and a new view of the nature of reality in its luminous depths. Both traditions can provide the foundation for an expanded and deepened conceptualization of psychology as the study of personally meaningful events and personal life-way creation, a vision which is essentially ecological and process- or network-oriented, conceiving of man as a network of interdependent relationships. This basic outlook unites Heidegger and the Eastern spiritual traditions and integrates them in an emergent "theo-psychology" which grounds its inquiries in the specifically human spiritual realities: the mystery of divine calling, creativity, inspiration, meaning, values, wonder, bliss, and ecstasy, and places these self-transcendent experiences at the heart of its philosophical anthropology and paradigm.

The Vision of Martin Heidegger

Heidegger is the most radical Western philosophical thinker who has made our contemporary situation and dilemma visible to us. His thinking about the nature of man and the nature of beings and things, and the nature of the ground of beings—Being which makes everything possible—provides us with a radically new starting point in philosophy and psychology.

Heidegger recognized that our very way of thinking as scientists, as psychologists, as modern rational men, is part of the problem. We are thinking about ourselves, others, and our world in the wrong way. We have the wrong starting point. Heidegger introduces into philosophical discourse a radical distinction. He speaks of two modes of thinking: *rational, calculative thinking* and *intuitive, meditative thinking*. Our world and reality as a whole reveals itself in a totally different way to each of these modes. The calculative mode predominates in modern secular and technological man. It is based on willfulness and the desire both to objectify everything and to dominate the objects of thought. It is concerned with the *ontic* level of the being of man and the being of worldly things. The meditative mode of thinking, which Heidegger also calls "thanking thinking," is based on a completely different attitude which is respectful, open, loving, and in awe of the mystery of what is, the Being of beings. This way of thinking is *ontological*, concerned with the essential dimensions of Being; it questions things in their grounding, and it expresses a basic reverential and religious, a theo-dimensional stance toward reality. Meditative thinking is a "thinking" that overcomes the limits of willful ego-consciousness and the separation inherent in the subject–object split.

In Heidegger's ultimate vision, we modern Western people have lost our original wholesomeness and holy embeddedness in Being, and have become lost in the material world of things, of human projects, of human willfulness, what he calls "fallenness." We have given up our relatedness and awareness of the ground of Being, we have lost the experience of the truth of Being as an event of primordial wonder, as an experience of gratitude for the revelation of the "splendor of the simple."

We are suffering the dues and consequences for the hubris initiated in human thinking by and since Descartes, who made the world, as matter, as *res extensa*, an object for the calculative view and thinking of the rational ego-consciousness of the subject. We have fallen into an understanding of reality as an objective world subjected to the will of man, into a conquest mentality of Promethean scope nurtured by the projection of self–world distance, the subject–object split.

For Heidegger, coming out of the Husserlian phenomenological tradition, the self–world relationship is one of intentionality, of meaningful interdependent interrelatedness. Heidegger wanted to overcome the subject–object split and dualism of Western thinking since Descartes which has placed consciousness in opposition to the objects of nature and led to a fateful separation of man from his world. Heidegger avoids even the traditional terminology of subject and object of consciousness. He chose a multihyphenated term, being-in-the-world (or *Dasein*) to characterize the essential two-way, person–world interrelationship in his seminal work, *Being and Time*, which first appeared (in German) in 1927.

For Heidegger, Dasein is that being among beings that is aware of and concerned about the meaning of its own being. Dasein is aware, is questioning, is concerned, is philosophical. Dasein asks even more deeply: "Why is there something rather than nothing at all?" It asks about "the nothing," the ground of all beings, Being itself, that is, that which is beyond all form, names, distinctions, determinations: the very condition of possibilities. Thus Dasein (man's existence) is not only concerned about the meaning of its own being, but it also has a primordial understanding of the nature of Being. Heidegger says that any great thinker has but one central thought during all of his life, one essential intuition; Heidegger's is "What is Being *(Sein)?"*

In his work over four decades, Heidegger moved from the concern about the human way of being—Dasein and its essential ontological constitutents as a structure of *care*, embodied, spatialized, in and through time as lifetime and historicity, relating through attunement, understanding, and speech—to the concern of what is thinking, what is truth, what is a thing, and what is dwelling. Heidegger sees the world and the things of the world as standing in a relevant meaning- and action-contexts relationship to a projecting Dasein. The world-design or world-project that Dasein is, became one of the most fruitful integrative and ecological constructs for the existential psychiatry of Binswanger (1942), Boss (1963), and Frankl (1959).

For Heidegger, there are *inauthentic* ways of relating, when one acts in the anonymous modes of "Das Man"—the one—and is lost to the world and forgetful of the mystery of Being, in the modes of prattle and gossip; and there are moments—only moments, for Heidegger—of *authentic* being-in-the-world, of relating with the awareness of one's own being toward death, of finitude, that awakens us to true discourse, of recognition of the "event of Being," the "event of appropriation" as the happening of the truth of Being.

Using key metaphors, Heidegger considers man to be an *openness* into which others and the things of the world appear, and considers Dasein to be the *luminating realm,* the light, the *lumen naturale,* into which the things of the world make their appearance and *reveal* themselves as what they are in their self-givenness, as themselves in their unconcealedness, in their Being. Heidegger comes to understand truth and Being as becoming revealed to man from the hidden ground of concealedness, or "no-thing-ness." Heidegger's emphasis on luminating, on revelation, on the "clearing" *(Lichtung)* of Being puts him close to the illumination tradition of the East.

The other major metaphor in Heidegger's thinking and writing is that of the *path*, which brings him into close proximity to the tradition of Taoism, of which he is himself aware when he says:

> The word "way" probably is an ancient primary word that speaks to the reflective mind of man. The key word in Laotse's poetic thinking is Tao, which "properly speaking" means way. (1959, p. 198)

On the general importance of the metaphor of the path in Heidegger's thinking, Gray (1970) comments in his discussion of Heidegger's (1954a) famous invocation of the essence-meaning of the fieldpath *(Der Feldweg):*

> The path itself spoke to him, as he writes, encouraged him to decipher the thoughts in the books he found too hard to comprehend. The field path taught him to conceive of thinking itself as a path, and of man's brief career in time likewise as a path. . . . the field path spoke to him, not he to the field path. (pp. 227–228)

Heidegger came to reject all of Western metaphysics since Plato as leading to a distance from Being by conceiving of the truth in terms of a correspondence theory of truth, that is, the notion that something is true according to and by comparison with a pre-established idea or category. What appears is tested against a criterion, as in the natural scientific method. Heidegger challenges this approach and returns to the early thinkers of Greece, the pre-Socratics—Parmenides and Heraclitus—who thought of Being, for the first time in Western philosophy, in its dynamic, elemental, and mysterious nature and power as revealing and concealing itself, as eluding the will and grasp of the intellect of man. For Heidegger, truth is the self-revelation of Being in the right attitude of meditative thinking. Being presences itself as event, as advent, that addresses man, that calls man into service "to tell" *(die Sage),* to name it primordially as in poetry, to think it essentially thankingly, as in meditative thinking which lets the things reveal themselves in their essential being.

In all metaphysics since Plato, including natural science as a materialistic monism, we create a conceptual map of reality which gets to be taken for the territory mapped. So we always fall short of Being itself which does not lend itself to be categorized but reveals itself, on its own terms, to the openness of Dasein.

The fruits of the later work of Heidegger reveal him to be a thinker of dazzling originality and of great profundity. As a creator of many neologisms, Heidegger is engaged in presenting his work in manifold linguistic forms—as meditations, as dialogue, as argument, as poetry. After *Being and Time,* he became intrigued with and entangled by the problem of language and speech and its wisdom and demand character. In his much heralded turn *(Kehre),* he shifted the focus of his concern away from the being of man as Dasein to a concern with Being itself and the world- and thing-pole of the being-in-the-world correlation. As he moved his emphasis from Dasein to Being, from the thinker to the thought, so he shifted his concern in his later work from "man having speech" to "speech having and addressing man," and he came to speak of language as the "house of Being." Heidegger marveled at the gift and power of the poet to speak and name the unnamed Being.

For the philosopher, who is now called simply "the thinker," it is the primordial, the un-thought, the nothing, that has to be thought. The reality of being-in-the-world is now called *dwelling*—a dwelling amidst things, a dwelling as building. The reality of a thing becomes for Heidegger the event and occasion of a dynamic and holy assembly of living powers and relationships: the *fourfold (das Geviert)*. He comes to this insight through the etymology of "thing" *(das Ding)*, which originally meant "assembly" in German.

The fourfold are the double polarities of the *Earth*, the *Sky*, the *Mortals*, and the *Divinities*, which constitute the fourfold field of tension within which man dwells and has his being. The fourfold also assembles as the dynamic interplay which constitutes the reality of a thing for us. Heidegger describes the essence of some everyday things for us. The jug, for instance, which pours wine from within its form, its emptiness, as the gift of the Gods to mortal man, wine as the fruit of the vine growing from the marriage of Earth and Sky. As Hirsch (1970) comments in this context:

> It is possible, for instance, to regard a pitcher as a man-made thing (Ding) designed to hold so much of a liquid; the empty space inside the pitcher is then what counts. However, in this way we have abstracted from the concrete situation which makes a pitcher a pitcher. In the context of a concrete situation the pouring out of the liquid from the pitcher expresses a more important aspect of its essence than its emptiness or size. . . . The pitcher cannot be separated from the wine or water that it may contain; wine and water, on the other hand, form part of a world where heaven and earth are joined together. (p. 252)

Heidegger says of the pitcher:

> In the water of the spring the marriage of heaven and earth is present. This marriage is present in the wine which is the gift of the fruit of the vine; in the fruit the nourishing earth and the sun in the sky are joined together in marriage. . . . The gift of that which flows from it is the essence of a pitcher. In the essence of the pitcher are present heaven and earth. (1954b, p. 171)

Such an openness to what reveals itself as the essence of a utensil, of a thing, is done in a particular mode of thinking which is a meditative, recalling, and responsive thinking, rather than one of rational, utilitarian, grasping thinking. It is an evocation not of the thing for man, but the thing in itself, in its essential being. Heidegger gives voice back to nature, to the elemental, to things, so that they may call us out into the openness of a deeper and more authentic relationship, more grounded in and no longer forgetful of Being. This involves a renunciation of our metaphysical and technological willfulness. It involves a turning to an awareness that man dwells poetically on earth.

Out of this meditative and nonrepresentational thinking, attitude, and presence comes some of Heidegger's most poetic and profound writings on things; the temple (1961), the field path (1954a), Van Gogh's painting of the peasant shoes (1954b). In very simple language, he presents these things and lets them reveal themselves as what they are in their essence.

Gray (1970), in his study of the Heideggerian notion of "the splendor of the simple" which he finds to be intimately akin to the Tao–Zen attitude, says:

> Things think. That is, they gather to themselves the permanent and the transient of our world, the animate and the inanimate, the near and the remote, the sacred and the secular. These phenomena are manifest in whatever particular thing we pay heed to by tending and sparing it. If one studies Heidegger, as opposed to reading him only, and if one seeks to link this thought of his, that a thing gathers together the world, to his philosophy as a whole, I believe it will lose much of its outlandish character and possibly count in the end as a genuine insight. (p. 239)

The recognition of the splendor of the simple is the fruit of a growth of the thinker into a new attitude. Its discovery requires "long experience and incessant practice" (Heidegger, 1954c) and it is, as Caputo (1978) reports, the setting out on "a high and dangerous game."

> The discovery of the simple is a laying bare of the essential connections of things of the world and of our belonging to them. (Gray, 1970, p. 232)

> The simple in thinking is thus identified with that which is basic or fundamental in reality. To get at these fundamental structures and interrelationships requires a stripping away of the concealments of historical development. Heidegger believes that if we can reach at the roots of a matter or, to employ his idiom, the sun and soil that nourish these roots, we shall discover that the true nature of things reveals itself. (Gray, 1970, p. 229)

There is a discipline involved in arriving at the recognition of the truth of Being as advent, as the gathering of the powers of a cosmic context, the fourfold. An attitude of letting go of one's will, of releasement, is involved, letting the thing reveal itself as an event which calls us into its telling.

Again Gray:

> This discipline of experience and practice implies two things: first, a capacity to get involved in and to stay with a matter to be thought and, second, the ability to let it be what it truly is. The first of these capacities demands a singlemindedness and persistence that goes against the grain of all but the most select minds. Getting involved in something to be thought means living with it,

> making its pursuit a way of life rather than a problem to be solved. Thinking as he (Heidegger) puts it, is a way of dwelling and dwelling is in turn a kind of building. To build well we must first acquire the grace to be at home in our region, to live into it, one could say. (pp. 229–230)

Man, Dasein, is conceived by the later Heidegger as the servant and shepherd of Being in whose care is given the fate of the world and who has to live in the right attitude, rooted in the soil of a beloved region and history. There is a reactionary element in Heidegger's thinking. He is suspicious of progress while he considers man's problem to be the forgetfulness of Being. As regards technology, the most powerful, modern, life-transforming force in the "mittance of Being" (of which Heidegger speaks frequently), one has to live in the spirit of "releasement" *(Gelassenheit)* and in "openness to the mystery." The splendor of the simple became revealed to Heidegger in his Black Forest retreat hut where he thought and wrote in the utter simplicity of an ecological sage, standing firmly in the ground of Being and calling us into a new and, at the same time, ancient relationship of fullness of belonging.

Heidegger's emergent image of man is man as the "shepherd of Being," as the custodian of the earth and its accumulated culture in a particular life-way incarnation. Heidegger is a life-way philosopher who articulates the proper relationship of man as Dasein with the things of his world and Being as such. His thinking revealed to him the existence and dynamic power of "the fourfold," the interplay of earth and sky and the divinities and the mortals as the foundation on which our dwelling takes place. He understands the fourfold as emanating from the ground of Being, the condition of all possibilities, Being, "the process by which finite beings emerge from concealment" (Richardson, 1963). As Richardson (perhaps the most reliable guide for the English-speaking reader into the movement and path of Heidegger's thinking) comments when he examines the use of the concept of Being and the way in which a cluster of related terms constitutes an interrelated network of meanings, open enough to allow a glimmer and wink, but also to let pass and reveal the luminous radiance and ineffability of Being itself:

> As for Being itself, the "Λη∂η" that is the mystery, what is to be said of it now? It is wealth, treasure a hidden fullness. It is inexhaustible wellspring, ineffable. The Simple, the All, the Only, the One. . . .
>
> Reichtum, Schätze, Unerschöpfliche des Fragwürdigen, Unerschöpflicher Brunnen, Verborgene Schätze des Gewesenen, Vergorgene Fülle, Alles, Eine, Einzige, das Verborgene des Unerschöpflichen, etwas Unsagbares, Verborgener Reichtum der Sprache, Wesensreichtum des Seins, das Einfache, das Endlose, der grosse Anfang, die grosse Einfalt. (Richardson, 1963, p. 640)

Heidegger's thinking has been brought into connection and discussion with Eastern thought, Eastern philosophico-religious tradition. He himself has made reference to the Tao as the thinking of the way or the path which he found very congenial to his approach. He is also said to have commented on Zen Buddhism, as reported by William Barret (1956) in his foreword to *Zen Buddhism:*

> A German friend of Heidegger told me that one day when he visited Heidegger he found him reading one of Suzuki's books. "If I understand this man correctly," Heidegger remarked, "this is what I have been trying to say in all my writings." (p. xi)

Furthermore, there have been long-standing personal friendships between Heidegger and several Japanese philosophers; and his famous dialogue, *On the Way to Language* (1971a), is a dialogue with a Japanese on the mystery of language.

Heidegger thus had some documented cognizance of Eastern ways of thinking, especially of Taoism and Zen Buddhism, and he was aware of the compatibility of much of this thinking with his own. He also spoke explicitly of the East–West dialogue in philosophy that he considered imminent and overdue. In the dialogue with the Japanese, Heidegger says:

> Therefore, I cannot yet see whether, what I try to think as the essence of speech also satisfies the essence of East Asian speech, whether at the end, which would also be a beginning, an essence of speech may become an experience of our thinking (effort) and grant us the assurance that European-Occidental and East Asian speaking entered into a dialogue which sings of that which springs from a single source. (1959, pp. 93–94)

Such a dialogue was held at the symposium on Heidegger and Eastern thought at the University of Hawaii (Department of Philosophy, 1969) on the occasion of Heidegger's 80th birthday, the presentations of which are reprinted in *Philosophy East and West* (Hirsch, 1970). Heidegger wrote a letter to the symposium which reads in part:

> That you together with colleagues from Japan are planning a conference in honor of my eightieth birthday, deserves special thanks on my part. Again and again it has seemed urgent to me that a dialogue take place with the thinkers of what is to us the Eastern world. The greatest difficulty in this enterprise always lies, as far as I can see, in the fact that with few exceptions there is no command of the Eastern languages either in Europe or in the United States. A translation of Eastern thought into English, on the other hand, remains—as does every translation—an expedient. May your conference prove fruitful in spite of this unfortunate circumstance. (Nagley, 1970, p. 221)

There have been some such comparative studies on these particular topics (Boss, 1965; Caputo, 1978; Kreeft, 1971). In these studies, comparisons have been made between Heidegger's *Being and Time* and Hinduism indirectly by Boss (1965), and with Buddhism, Taoism, and Zen (focusing more on Heidegger's later work).

Heidegger and the Hindu Tradition

For this comparison, note that Heidegger questions the very meaning of "Being"; that is, he asks the basic question: "What does it mean to exist?" He then reasons that the best way to approach this question is to first inquire into the nature of the *individual's* Being. Also, note that since the individual finds him or herself "there" in the world among things and other individuals (through no choice of his or her own), Heidegger uses the term *Dasein* (literally "there-being") to describe the human person, and that, on the everyday level, Dasein is concerned with the meaning of its own existence (as discussed above). This concern is unique to Dasein, is an essential part of its Being, and demonstrates that it already has a latent understanding of existence.

The nature of human existence has been a subject of inquiry in Hindu thought for centuries, the application of Eastern philosophy leading to beliefs that seem, at first, quite foreign to Western thought. For example, in our everyday existence, most of us live with the implicit assumption that the physical world which we perceive is the *only* world. Many assume that there may in fact be other worlds or realities, but this is merely conjecture that is impossible to "prove" in any way. An essential position of Hindu thought is, however, that physical reality is only one of three and that each of us exists simultaneously on all levels. Paramahansa Yogananda (1969) described how each of us is "encased . . . successively in three bodies—the idea, or causal body, the subtle astral body, seat of man's mental and emotional nature, and the gross physical body" (p. 415).

Heidegger sees Dasein as implicitly apprehending something *beyond* its everyday, physical existence, but does this without a reference to different levels of reality. Rather, he speaks of "existentiality" and "facticity" as two central constituents of the structure of Dasein's Being.

Existentiality refers to Dasein's existing in such a way that it directs itself toward and anticipates its possibilities (e.g., the possibility of becoming a teacher, a parent, etc.). These possibilities, however, do not exist apart from Dasein as something yet to be realized. Rather, Dasein *is* its possibilities. It cannot exist, however, as just any potentiality it chooses, as there are definite limits which are established through its facticity. *Facticity* is that structure which encompasses those aspects of Dasein's Being over which it has no control (e.g., eye color, emotionality, sexual desire). In addition to this questioning of the nature of reality/ existence, the way one perceives or "takes up" this reality is also important.

Eastern thinkers believe that we desire and are ultimately *attached to* "things" in the physical world.[1] This ranges from luxuries which we all want, to things about ourselves we desire (e.g., beauty and health), to a clinging to life itself. Moreover, the idea that one's attachments to things in the physical world quite literally make the physical world what it is (i.e., the only perceived reality) is a foundational one in Hindu thought. Thus, an individual who is so attached perceives the world to be only physical in nature, and the world is, to that extent, an illusion. To see the true nature of existence (i.e., all three planes) one must give up one's desires and become unattached. Only in this state, where one is free of desire, is "liberation" achieved and existence seen as it truly is.

The Hindu tradition describes the path of liberation leading to the experience of samadhi as the highest state of consciousness, a direct mystical experience of reality. In samadhi, Brahman, the ultimate reality of pure essence, of illumination, of the Divine essence, is entered into. As H. Smith (1958) says:

> The name the Hindus give to the supreme reality is Brahman, from the root "brih" meaning "to be great." The chief attributes to be linked with this name are sat, chit, and ananda; God is being, awareness, and bliss. Utter Reality, utterly conscious, and utterly beyond all possibility of frustration, this is the basic Hindu view of God. (p. 72)

Brahman is infinite, ineffable, and beyond all particular manifestations and concepts.

The individual soul, Atman, tries and can merge with the ground of its being: Brahman, and comes to the realization that the individual and the ultimate reality are One:

> Never during its pilgrimage is the spirit of man completely adrift and alone. From start to finish its nucleus is the Atman. Underlying its whirlpool of transient feelings, emotions, and delusions, is the self-luminous, abiding point of God himself. Though he is buried too deep in the soul to be usually noticed, he is the sole ground of man's being and awareness. (Smith, 1958, p. 79)

Meditation, the systematic practice of attempting to calm the mind of undirected thought and emotion, is the primary way in which the path of liberation is pursued. The entering into samadhi-enlightenment makes us realize that the world of everyday life, of attachment and desire, is illusory (maya), and from the experience of samadhi it also becomes

[1]See Levin's discussion in Chapter 12 of the ego's "attachment patterns" in Tibetan Buddhist thought.—Eds.

obvious that it is an "error" to believe in the reality of thought and concepts, to confuse the map with the territory. The samadhi experience of Atman–Brahman needs no other validation than its being experienced and it is a permanent realization.

Heidegger's dialectic of Dasein as man's being-in-the-world and Being as such parallels the Atman–Brahman distinction:

> Brahman and Atman are the ground-words of the Indian tradition, not just words or concepts, but the very embodiment of that primordial unhiddenness in the light of which the Indian mind thenceforth breathed and thought, its very spiritual destiny. Not "metaphysics" which for Heidegger is concerned with the truth of beings (with beings as such or with the being of beings), but the inquiry into the truth of Being (Being itself or Being as such) would correspond with the paravidya, the higher knowledge, taught by the sage Angira to Saunaka. (Mehta, 1970, p. 305)

Although for the Hindu tradition the Brahman reality requires us to take into account an explicitly religious dimension of divinity, the transcendental or theo-dimension, in our understanding of human experience, Heidegger does not speak of God or give any theistic interpretation of the ultimate ground of Being, although the manner of thinking and the way of speaking of Heidegger has become increasingly identified with the mystical tradition, and particularly with Meister Eckhart (Caputo, 1978), who was speaking out of an explicitly Christian and theistic context.[2]

This notion that the nature of perceived reality can be quite different depending on one's perspective (e.g., being "attached-unattached") is discussed by Heidegger in somewhat different terms. For the most part, Dasein occupies itself with everyday concerns, and chooses its possiblities from out of these concerns. In their "everydayness," these preoccupations are average ones, and so they do not belong uniquely to Dasein. They have arisen out of the anonymous world of the "They," which is the world of the ubiquitous "One," as in "One should do this" and "One must not do that." It is actually the "They," and not Dasein, that chooses Dasein's possibilities. When Dasein allows its existence to be chosen for it, it exists as "falling." *Fallenness* (briefly discussed above) is always an "inauthentic" mode of Being. In order to overcome this inauthenticity, Dasein must face a possibility which it and not the "They" chooses to face—its death. Choosing in this way, Dasein exists authentically—a radically different manner of existing than when involved solely with the concerns of the "They."

Another difference in the two approaches seems to be that Heidegger considers this authentic mode as a very momentary state of privileged presence to Being which cannot be a permanent state or achievement, in

[2]See Moss's discussion in Chapter 17 of the mysticism of Johannes Tauler and Meister Eckhart.—Eds.

contrast to the teachings of both Hinduism and Buddhism, in which permanent transformations, that is, samadhi and satori, are entered into. Also, the Heideggerian way of revelation is via reflective-meditative thinking characteristic of an ontological philosopher, rather than via meditation in the religious and yogic sense which tries to find merger in the undifferentiated unity of pure being as Brahman in a regular meditative practice under the guidance of a teacher. However, the later Heidegger, who is very much concerned with distinguishing the habitual Western mode of calculative thinking from that of a deepened, more intuitive and meditative thinking, comes much closer to a form of meditative practice in the context of walking in nature as in the field path, or in the wandering of a discourse, or in the essence-contemplation of a thing.

Another unexamined belief we hold is that "things" change over a linear time sequence. Eastern writers have challenged this notion, saying that a belief in time as a past, a present, and a future is just another conceptual illusion which is a result of physical attachment, and instead propose an *ever-present*. [3] Paramahansa Yogananda (1969) has stated:

> Evolution is a suggestion . . . everything is taking place in the present . . . there is no evolution, just as there is no change in the beam of light through which all the developing scenes of cinema pictures are manifested. (p. 57)

Samadhi, thus, reveals even time as illusory and aims for the eternal now, beyond space and time. In Heidegger, as in Western tradition generally, man has to awaken to an authentic mode of historical existence, to an awareness and acceptance of his essential facticity and mortality. Man remains the mortal man of finitude. There is no complete surrender and merger, or even loss of self, in Heidegger's thinking. More specifically, there is Heidegger's discussion of *temporality*. [4] Temporality is the foundational structure of Dasein's Being (i.e., of existentiality, facticity, and fallenness) and does not consist of the linear passing of discrete "nowpoints." The past, the present, and the future do not follow one another in sequence. Rather, they exist simultaneously in a dynamic process in which each gives rise to the other. Consider, for example, how a patient in psychotherapy "lives" both his or her past and future *in* the present.

Lastly, consider the Hindu belief that consciousness transcends the individual. Consciousness is generally believed to be a relatively private matter; that is, each one of us is "conscious," but each consciousness is unique to that person and is in no way shared by others. In Hindu thought, however, individualized ego consciousness is considered to be only a partial manifestation of a more global condition. The universe and

---

[3]Compare this idea to R. von Eckartsberg's description in Chapter 2 of the "Here-and-Now" level, and Weber's, Chapter 5, "living moment-by-moment."—Eds.
[4]See Moss and Keen, Chapter 4, for another discussion of *temporality*.—Eds.

all that comprises it is made up of consciousness, not a personal *consciousness of*, but *pure consciousness*.

At first glance, Heidegger's notion of consciousness appears to be very similar to the Eastern conceptualization. Dasein's consciousness (Being) does not rest simply within but reaches out beyond itself and toward the world and other beings. For Heidegger as a phenomenologist, however, consciousness is always a consciousness *of something;* that is, consciousness is *intentional.*[5] It always has an object. Dasein, however, not only reaches out and transcends itself in this fashion, it is also conscious *of Being,* since it is Being that allows Dasein to exist, or to be as it is.

Even though Heidegger seems to be constantly dwelling in the vicinity of the mystical and of self-transcendence, he does not speak explicitly of the mystical union as an experiential moment of eternity. Rather, for Heidegger, there is a mystical openness possible in authentic Dasein for the calling and depth of Being manifesting in things as an experience of meditative thinking, of reflective quietude, still ontologically conceived rather than experientially and existentially described. Heidegger conceives of the task as one of bringing revealed Being into language, of saying the unsaid, of thinking the unthought, of bringing the event of Being into language. His own meditative thinking discourse is done in terms of concrete universals, a marriage of poetic and philosophical diction.

Heidegger and the Tao–Zen Tradition

The Tao of Lao Tsu's (1972) *Tao Te Ching* and its integration with elements of Buddhism[6] into Zen Buddhism allows an integrated treatment in relation to Martin Heidegger. Heidegger says himself that the

> Tao could be the path along which everything may move; that which may make it possible for us to think the primordial means of reason, spirit, mind, and logos, that is what these (terms) say according to their true essence.
>
> Tao, this leading word in the poetic thinking (dichtendes Denken) of Laotse, perhaps hides within itself the mystery of all mysteries relating to a thinking utterance. (1959, p. 198)

And Lao Tsu (1972) says about the Tao:

> The Tao that can be told is not the eternal Tao.
> The name that can be named is not the eternal name.

[5]It seems that what the existential-phenomenologists mean by "consciousness" is what the Hindu philosophers mean by "mind." See Moss, Chapter 7, and de Silva, Chapter 13, for other discussions of *intentionality.*—Eds.

[6]See Levin, Chapter 12, and de Silva, Chapter 13, for other discussions of Buddhism.—Eds.

> The nameless is the beginning of heaven and earth.
> The named is the mother of ten thousand things.
> Ever desireless, one can see the mystery.
> Ever desiring, one can see the manifestations.
> These two spring from the same source but differ in name; this appears as darkness.
> Darkness within darkness.
> The gate to all mystery. (Chapter 1)

The Tao has a natural connection to the flow of organic life, to the elementals, especially water, to the observation of nature, to the cyclical movement of all organic events, and to the complementarity of the natural and cosmic polarities—Yin/Yang. The Tao is the dynamic cosmic process that is constantly changing and flowing through all, a surprising spontaneity and wonder at what is, given without effort, without thought, in the attitude of effortless effort, of creative quietude, of openness and surrender, always in and with the flow. Taoism generates an ecological attitude of organic interdependence, the unity of a web and flow of life, and an awareness of man's humble position within the cosmic-global nexus. The Tao's ethic is simplicity, humility, moderation.

Heidegger's notion of Being and the Tao are kindred terms. Both give rise to the "ten thousand things," the beings that arise from Being. Both are the primordial realms, the "theo-dimensions," beyond easy verbalization: "Where words fail." The edges of our reality and the edges of our languaging are forever expanding frontiers with a receding horizon into infinity.

The problems and dangers of languaging are well expressed in the book of Tao:

> The Tao is nameless
> like uncarved wood.
> As soon as it is carved
> then there are names.
> Carve carefully
> and along the grain. (Leary, 1966, Chap. 32)

Heidegger is also forever wrestling with the mystery of articulation and naming, how to say the event of Being, without representational thinking, but through some kind of thanksgiving evocation which says the essence of the thing, in its own terms, as the poet says, as the thinker thinks:

> The thinker says Being,
> The poet names the Holy.
>
> [Der Denker sagt das Sein,
> der Dichter nennt das Heilige.] (Heidegger, 1949, p. 51)

The mystery of language is most intimately approached in the imaginative creation (*Dichten*) of the poet, and the later Heidegger turned to the poets, Hölderlin, Trakl, Rilke, to listen to the voice of Being as it moves out of concealment and reveals itself. And he finds great kinship with what is expressed by Lao Tsu regarding the Tao.

However, the inherent anonymity of Lao Tsu and the Tao, the timelessness of a rhythmical and cyclical life, stands in some opposition to the temporal and historical understanding of Heidegger for whom all exists in time. There is no "beyond time" in Heidegger.

Another comparison of Heidegger and Taoism concerns the notion of nothing. The commentator Chung-yuan Chang (1970) states:

> The task of Chinese Taoism and Ch'an Buddhism is to lead man to see his original self, that is, the I, which is nonconceptual, nontraditional, nonrepresentational. This genuine, nonconceptual, nonrepresentational self is reached through releasement. In chapter 48 of the *Tao-te-Ching* we have: "the student of knowledge gains day by day; the student of Tao loses day by day." . . . What will be the outcome of the process of losing or releasement? The goal of releasement is to reach wu, or Nonbeing, or Nothing. Therefore, according to Taoist philosophy, Nothing is the root of everything. It is in the Nothingness that the Taoist "builds," "dwells," and "thinks." (p. 241)

Heidegger's notion of nothing is similarly positive, creative, nonnihilistic. He says:

> Only on the basis of the original manifestness of Nothing can our human Dasein advance towards and enter into what is. (1949, p. 339)

When the totality of what-is—beings—falls away, we come face to face with Nothing, which then becomes the ground for the experience of the revelation of Being.

> According to both Heidegger and Chinese Taoists, this Nothing, or Nonbeing, must be experienced in the sense of a pure finding. It cannot be reached through any process of rational or objective thought, which would only dichotomize subjectivity and objectivity into polarities. (Chang, 1970, p. 242)

> For Heidegger, instead of establishing Being as the ground, Nothing is conceived as the source, and Being is its manifestation. In the work of Chuang Tzu we have: In the very beginning there was wu, or Nonbeing, which is Nothing and nameless. It is that from which the One is produced, The One is inherent in it, and yet it is formless. The One that is produced by Nonbeing and is inherent in it is Being. (Chang, 1970, p. 245)

The openness to Nothing and Being involves a change in thinking and in attitude. It involves a "leap." The way of thinking is long and arduous, full of logging-roads *(Holzwege)* that lose themselves suddenly in the forest as in nothing. The path of thinking

> will take us places which we must explore to reach the point where only the leap will help further. The leap alone takes us into the neighborhood where thought resides. (Heidegger, 1968, p. 12)

The leap is away from the attitude of representational thinking into a new way of thinking: meditative thinking.

Huston Smith (1958) says that the essence of Zen is that it cannot be encompassed in words; that it must be a living experience in a specific state of mind—satori—which is the state of being enlightened, the state of the Buddha-mind itself which is transmitted, mind to mind, through rigorous Zen practice.

Zen Buddhism is most bewildering to the Western mind, because it wants to go beyond mind, beyond concepts, beyond categories, into the void and no-thingness, into pure spontaneity of the here-and-now. It is a long path and movement of preparation, of supervised practice. The fullness of the path toward satori, the enlightenment experience, is described in a Zen story as a progression:

> Before a man studies Zen, for him the mountains are mountains and the waters are waters; when, thanks to the teaching of a good master, he has achieved a certain inner vision of the truth of Zen, for him the mountains are no longer mountains and the waters are no longer waters; but later, when he has really arrived at the asylum of rest, once more the mountains are mountains and the waters are waters. (Benoit, 1959, p. 89)

Zen accomplishes a transformation of self into no-mind which opens up a new relationship to the world beyond representational and objectifying thinking.

Heidegger's emphasis in his work to overcome our inheritance of metaphysical thinking (Biemel, 1977), and its legacy of the subject–object split and calculative thinking in epistemology through a reconceptualization of man's relationship to his world as Dasein, being-in-the-world, and its relationship to the ground of Being, finds a parallel in the Zen doctrine of no-mind and the Zen practices of koan, zazen, sesshin, and sanzen which are designed to lead the aspirant beyond the limits of his own mind, conventional thinking, and "ego-consciousness" into the state of satori, as no-mind wakefulness and enlightened presence in the here-and-now. The emptying of mind aims at the transcending of representations, concepts, and intellectual categories:

> The heart of Zen training lies in introducing the eternal into the now, in widening the doors of perception to the point where the delight and wonder that characterize the satori experience can carry over to the ordinary events of man's day-to-day life. (Smith, 1958, p. 150)

Just as the Zen discipline requires a letting go of oneself to let "it" take over, so Heidegger, in discussing the need for a different kind of thinking, meditative-thanking thinking, calls for the attitude of releasement (Gelassenheit) which leads beyond self-will and rational, calculative intentions. The questions "why?" and "how?" are to be overcome if we are to find the truth of Being.

Caputo (1978), who makes a comparison between Heidegger, Meister Eckhart, and Zen, states:

> In Zen, when the self has become entirely egoless and will-less, it is admitted into "satori." In Heidegger, Dasein is admitted into the truth of Being, the "event of appropriation." Thus, to satori, the state of "enlightenment," we relate the "lighting" (lichten) process of the "clearing" (Lichtung) which is made in Dasein for the event of truth. In and through this "event," Dasein enters into its own most essential being (Wesen), even as the soul enters into its innermost ground (Seelengrund; Eckhart) and the self in Zen is awakened to its "Buddha-nature" or "self-nature." (p. 214)

In the emphasis on the way of life and on the opening-up and revelation of the Being-enlightenment experience in, and yet beyond, what is given in bodily presence, there is much kinship of spirit between Heidegger and Zen. There is also a shared love for the rural, craft-oriented way of being in the world, for peasant simplicity and steadfastness, solidity of presence, ontological weight. But our image of Heidegger is not that of a monastic guru living with disciples, but that of the solitary wanderer on the path of thinking along the logging roads (Holzwege) of the Black Forest at a slow plodding pace, in search of the clearing of Being, the advent of an illumination of Being.

There are some specific but brief studies on Heidegger's relation to Zen (Caputo, 1978; Hirsch, 1970; Kreeft, 1971).

Caputo dialogues the Herrigel (1953) book, Zen in the Art of Archery, with Heidegger's notion of releasement (Gelassenheit) and also with Meister Eckhart who uses the term Gelassenheit and whose philosophy has been compared with Buddhism:

> The master tells Herrigel he must learn to "wait" for the moment when the arrow should be released, even as Heidegger tells us in Gelassenheit to wait on the regioning of the region. But how can he "wait"? (Caputo, 1978, p. 207)
>
> By letting go of yourself, leaving yourself and everything yours behind so decisively that nothing more is left of you but purposeless tension. (Herrigel, 1953, p. 52)

The discipline of Zen requires of the aspirant an overcoming of his ego-involved mindfulness in order to arrive at a state of no-mind (wu-nien) which is detachment from all images, thoughts, and cravings so that a merger with the unconditioned ground is possible. This ground is called "sunyata," the Void, Emptiness, in Zen:

> This unconditioned, formless, and consequently unattainable is Emptiness (sunyata). Emptiness is not a negative idea, nor does it mean a mere privation, but as it is not in the realm of names and forms, it is called emptiness, or nothingness, or the void. (Suzuki, in Caputo, 1978, p. 190)

Since we cannot grasp sunyata, we need a kind of thinking which is itself nongrasping. This spiritual state of mind is called "no mind," "no thought":

In other words, "no mind" is a clearing away of all thoughts and desires in order to "let" the unconscious base of our existence exert itself through us—just as Herrigel let "It" shoot the arrow. (Caputo, 1978, p. 210)

Heidegger's notion of "the Nothing" *(das Nichts)* can be related to sunyata. Being is totally other than particular beings, it is not any particular entity. In the discourse on the way to language with the Japanese, Heidegger states:

> INQUIRER: That emptiness then is the same as nothingness, that essential being which we attempt to add in our thinking, as the other, to all that is present or absent.
>
> JAPANESE: Surely. For this reason we in Japan understood at once your lecture "What is Metaphysics?" when it became available to us in 1930 through a translation which a Japanese student, then attending your lectures, had ventured. . . . We marvel to this day how the Europeans could lapse into interpreting as nihilistic the nothingness of which you speak in that lecture. To us, emptiness is the loftiest name for what you mean to say with the world "Being." (1959, pp. 108–109)

Elizabeth Hirsch (1970) in her discussion of Martin Heidegger and the East uses the Zen story of the oxherd to illustrate Heidegger's kinship with Zen. She reports that Heidegger was very fond of this story, and she gives the following rendering:

> In the first picture we see a landscape enveloped in the mist and the oxherd standing "discouraged under the trees at the bank of the waters." Lost in the high grass, the oxherd engages in a long search for his ox, whom he finally discovers after hearing his voice first. When the oxherd captures the animal, he is unruly and wants to return to the wilderness. After the oxherd has succeeded in taming the ox, he is seen riding on his back for the trip home. Once at home, the ox disappears and the oxherd kneels in the grass before his hut with his hands folded in a praying gesture, while his eyes behold a mountain peak in the distance and behind it a golden moon just breaking through the clouds. At this moment the oxherd and nature lose their separate existences and merge. At such heights of achievement the oxherd finds "access to the deepest secret." The deepest secret is the Void or Nothingness (Being). The next drawing, therefore, symbolizes the fact that the world is empty of things: A large circle is sprinkled with dark spots and bordered at the periphery by a black band. Because the oxherd has grasped the true Being of things, nature will never be the same. A tree which appeared in previous drawings only now discloses its treeness: in the drawing that follows, the oxherd's enlightenment, the inner pulse of a tree-trunk, its true being, has come to the surface; a branch winds its way through space like lightning speeding toward the earth, and the blossoms have never looked as tender as now. The meaning, of course, is that he who has experienced the Void or Being has gained insight into the "isness" or "suchness" of the world. Being in turn shines after beings have vanished into nothingness. (p. 253)

There is a primordial contact with nature expressed in this story in which nature is experienced as a "Thou" rather than an "It," in which the splendor of the simple illuminates us and calls us into a new way of being. Hirsch argues that the void in the Zen story is inspired by Buddha's concept of "Nirvana." Nirvana, like the void, lacks all attributes, all particulars. Like Tao and Being, Nirvana is a matrix-concept, a "divine-ground-concept," a theo-dimension.

Toward an Integration

These brief comparisons highlight the spiritual kinship that exists between Heidegger and two of the Eastern traditions. There is a shared calling forth of man into a more originary and authentic relationship to Being. There is a shared "striving" to transcend the world of opposites and subject–object separation and to encounter and make contact with true Being and reality. Whereas in the Eastern tradition this involves a rigorous working on oneself in the social context of a school of meditational practice under the guidance of a master, for Heidegger it is the articulation of a personal path of thinking that can show the way.

There are, of course, also a number of differences between the world of Heidegger and that of Eastern, especially Hindu, thinking. The doctrines of *reincarnation* and *karma* find no correspondence in Heidegger's thinking, and the experience of personal enlightenment in meditation is not entered into explicitly by Heidegger. But there is sufficient similarity in the radicality of both traditions to warrant continuing comparison and dialogue. There is the shared vision and effort to break the self-limiting boundaries of human rational intelligence, the vision of metaphysics, and a mindfulness as a whole in order to establish once again a more vital, inspired, and primordial relationship with all beings and the ground of Being in the form of the awareness of one's involvement in the "cosmotheandric network of relationships" (Fittipaldi, 1978; Panikkar, 1977) which Dasein is.

Both Heidegger and the Eastern traditions also transcend a secular-materialistic point of view, and insist on the reality of a height/depth, or "theo-dimension," which lies beyond the boundaries of ordinary everyday existence, and yet carries more weight, significance, power, and value. Umehara (1970), in his discussion of Heidegger and Buddhism, begins with the observation:

> The modern world has seemingly undertaken a serious experiment with regard to whether or not a man can live without any god or religion. (p. 271)

But he finds in the work of Heidegger the attempt to provide a new spiritual foundation in trans-denominational terms:

> Heidegger proposes a new philosophical problem to the entire world in two ways. It is in one sense an inquiry into the foundation of the novel spiritual

situation where nihilism is latent within the European scientific civilization, a civilization which nonetheless has succeeded in unifying the whole world. But this civilization lacks a spiritual foundation. In exposing European scientific civilization to total criticism, Heidegger is perhaps one of the first thinkers of the West to provide a place of dialogue and confrontation between the European principle and the non-European principle. (p. 280)

For psychology, this new and emergent philosophico-religious anthropology, the result of an East–West integration, that reveals that man is the being concerned about the meaning of his own being and the meaning of Being, offers us a new starting point. We realize that man lives out his ontic/ontological concerns in the way in which he dwells and shapes his life and world into a harmonious, ecological balancing of the powers of earth and sky and the interplay of the mortals and the divinities.

In the discussion of "the thing," Heidegger elaborates a little on these powers, but their evocation and circumscription remain suggestive and groping for expression carried by a deep mystical intuition:

Earth is the building bearer, nourishing with its fruits, tending water and rock, plant and animal. When we say earth, we are already thinking of the other three along with it by way of the simple oneness of the four.

The sky is the sun's path, the course of the moon, the glitter of the stars, the year's seasons, the light and dusk of day, the gloom and glow of night, the clemency and inclemency of the weather, the drifting clouds and blue depth of the ether. When we say sky, we are already thinking of the other three along with it by way of the simple oneness of the four.

The divinities are the beckoning messengers of the godhead. Out of the hidden sway of the divinities the god emerges as what he is, which removes him from any comparison with beings that are present. When we speak of the divinities, we are already thinking of the other three along with them by way of the simple oneness of the four.

The mortals are human beings. They are called mortals because they can die. To die means to be capable of death as death. Only man dies. The animal perishes. It has death neither ahead of itself nor behind it. Death is the shrine of Nothing, that is, of that which in every respect is never something that merely exists, but which nevertheless presences, even as the mystery of Being itself. As the shrine of Nothing, death harbors within itself the presencing of Being. As the shrine of Nothing, death is the shelter of Being. . . . When we say mortals, we are then thinking of the other three along with them by way of the simple oneness of the four. (1971b, pp. 178–179)

Heidegger's style and rhythm, four times repeating the unity of the four: "When we say . . . ," feels like a hymn or even a prayer to the quaternion, the fourfold field of tensions that constitutes our sacred openness, our world.

Heidegger's new image of man as the shepherd of Being, the steward of the earth, the builder and custodian of culture, gives us a calling, a vision, a task. It is in our hands to create a way of living which might truly be called dwelling.

Both Heidegger and the Eastern traditions are concerned with the liberation of man from the restrictive and self-limiting habits of his own cultural mind, from inauthentic modes of being and thinking. Both agree that we need a transhuman theo-dimension in the region beyond depth and beyond height, beyond human willfulness, which is the source of illumination, fulfillment, and truth for man—the transpersonal.

Both traditions develop paths toward liberation. For the Eastern ways, this is a peak-experience in consciousness that completely transforms one's relationship to the world and reality as a whole. For Heidegger, the path is one of thinking oneself through into a great simplicity of openness to the revelation of Being. Heidegger makes a double move— for all of us—and thus radically changes our perception of and our participation in reality. First, he jumps into the gap, the in-between of the subject–object split, and bridges the rift with his understanding of Dasein as being-in-the-world, as unfolding relationship, as event. Second, Heidegger makes a figure-ground gestalt-switch by saying: Let the figures go (the beings, the ten thousand things), attend to the ground (Being); go beyond theory and metaphysics, beyond concepts and representations, beyond story and originary myth, beyond names, into the splendid openness and fullness of Being, into a new presence to the real. Heidegger calls this new mode of presence *meditative thinking*. Is it also embodied poetic presence?

We believe it was an important part of his life when Heidegger returned to his simple hut in his mountains, forests, and high meadows and the life of elemental nature which found such eloquent voice in his later works. There he found the splendor of the simple still present, far from the madding crowd, in the participation in a holistic way of life in the flow of the seasons and the processes of nature, within the precincts of the Zen monastery or in the temple of self-regenerative nature.

His advice on how to deal with technology was *releasement (Gelassenheit)* and *openness to the mystery (Offenheit für das Geheimnis)*, a change in attitude, but basically a noninterfering observance. But we also live in the urban modernity powered by the calculative thinking of technology and its overpowering success. Both Heidegger and the Eastern attitudes are somewhat nostalgic and reactionary in their call for quiet, for a return to the simple and essential. Their vision and practice for modern man has to remain a counterpoint, a counterfoil, perhaps, a coexisting alternative. Just as work and celebration are rhythmically organized in the calendar in weekdays and sabbath, so we can institute a new day for the working-recreating-celebrating presence to nature— *Country Day*—if we are drawn into this way so akin to Heidegger and the East. Everybody can institute this in his own calendar, as an act of freedom of choice, as a space of time in which dwelling in the fullness of Being, the foursome giving rise to the teeming of life in ecological proliferation and wonder, can be easily actualized. We are and live and dwell between Earth and Heaven in the tension between Mortality and Divinity, and this living realization still flourishes easily in the environs of our heartlands, in the play of the elements in the wild.

May this be the secret and unspoken spiritual practice of Martin Heidegger; be the path that is available to almost everybody? And is this practice, born from the marriage of Zen and Western fundamental-ontological thinking, not ongoing in many places? We found one embodiment not far from Heidegger's hut in the Black Forest in Count Dürckheim who has written *Daily Life as Spiritual Exercise* (1971). There are more to be met.

Heidegger and the Eastern traditions offer Western psychology a new and ancient value-orientation, a new and ancient posture of gratefulness, of thanksgiving to Being and the powers in which we find ourselves. They offer us liberation through an expanded vision of human life including the spiritual dimensions beyond ordinary rationality. Heidegger and the Eastern sages offer us a vision for a psychology of Being, for a psychology of higher life, for a psychology of genius, of creation, of vision, of inspiration, of revelation, of "theo-psychology," which lies close to the heart of man's life.

References

Barret, W. (Ed.) *Zen Buddhism*. New York: Doubleday, 1956.

Benoit, H. *The supreme doctrine*. New York: Viking, 1959.

Biemel, W. Heidegger and metaphysics. *Listening*, 1977, 12(3), 50–60.

Binswanger, L. *Grundformen und Erkenntnis Menschlichen Daseins*. Zurich: Verlag Max Neihans, 1942.

Boss, M. *Psychoanalysis and daseinsanalysis*. New York: Basic Books, 1963.

Boss, M. *A psychiatrist discovers India*. London: Oswald Wolff, 1965.

Caputo, J. *The mystical element in Heidegger's thought*. Athens, Ohio: Ohio University Press, 1978.

Chang, C. Commentary. *Philosophy East and West*, 1970, 20(3), 241–246.

Dürckheim, K. *Daily life as spiritual exercise*. New York: Harper & Row, 1971.

Fittipaldi, S. *How to pray always without always praying*. Notre Dame, Ind.: Fides-Claretian, 1978.

Frankl, V. *Man's search for meaning*. Boston: Beacon Press, 1959.

Gray, J. Splendor of the simple. *Philosophy East and West*, 1970, 20(3), 227–240.

Heidegger, M. *What is metaphysics?* Chicago: Henry Regnery, 1949.

Heidegger, M. *Der Feldweg*. Pfullingen: Günther Neske, 1954. (a)

Heidegger, M. *Vorträge und Aufsätze*. Pfullingen: Günther Neske, 1954. (b)

Heidegger, M. *Aus der Erfahrung des Denkens*. Pfullingen: Günther Neske, 1954. (c)

Heidegger, M. *Unterwegs zur Sprache*. Pfullingen: Günther Neske, 1959.

Heidegger, M. *Was heisst Denken?* Tübingen: Max Niemeyer, 1961.

Heidegger, M. *Being and time*. New York: Harper & Row, 1962.

Heidegger, M. *What is called thinking?* New York: Harper & Row, 1968.

Heidegger, M. *On the way to language.* New York: Harper & Row, 1971. (a)

Heidegger, M. *Poetry, language, thought.* New York: Harper & Row, 1971. (b)

Herrigel, E. *Zen in the art of archery.* New York: Pantheon Books, 1953.

Hirsch, E. Martin Heidegger and the East. *Philosophy East and West,* 1970, *20*(3), 247–264.

Kreeft, P. Zen in Heidegger's Gelassenheit. *International Philosophical Quarterly,* 1971, *11,* 521–545.

Kuhn, T. *The structure of scientific revolutions.* Chicago: University of Chicago Press, 1962.

Lao Tsu. *Tao te ching.* New York: Random House, 1972.

Leary, T. *Psychedelic prayers after the Tao te ching.* Kerhonkson, New York: Poets Press, 1966.

Mehta, J. Heidegger and the comparison of Indian and Western philosophy. *Philosophy East and West,* 1970, *20*(3), 303–318.

Nagley, W. Introduction to the symposium and reading of a letter from Martin Heidegger. *Philosophy East and West,* 1970, *20*(3), 221.

Panikkar, R. Colligite fragmenta: For an integration of reality. In F. Eigo (Ed.), *From alienation to atoneness.* Villanova, Penn. Villanova University Press, 1977.

Paramahansa Yogananda. *Autobiography of a yogi.* Los Angeles: Self-Realization Fellowship, 1969.

Richardson, W. *Heidegger: Through phenomenology to thought.* The Hague: Martinus Nijhoff, 1963.

Smith, H. *The religions of man.* New York: Harper, 1958.

Umehara, T. Heidegger and Buddhism. *Philosophy East and West,* 1970, *20*(3), 271–282.

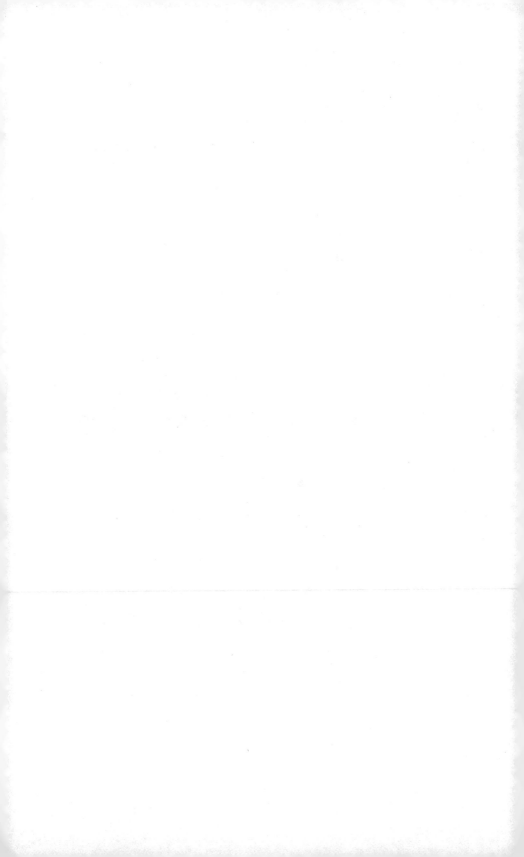

V

Transcendence and Mysticism

In both the Eastern traditions and in Western mysticism, priority is given to the ultimate reality of consciousness and to the possibility of personally experiencing the transcendent. Transcendence cannot be accounted for in materialistic terms; in fact, just the opposite is true: the physical, phenomenal world can only be understood as an emergent property—a manifestation—of a more basic, noumenal realm.

In this context, Swami Rama considers the human personality as an emergent derivative or conceptual relfection of the universal flow of consciousness. Silvio Fittipaldi and Donald Moss then respectively discuss two Christian mystics, Teresa of Avila and Johannes Tauler. From these perspectives, each author describes the transformation in consciousness that occurs as a consequence of the personal encounter with God.

15

Energy of Consciousness in the Human Personality

Swami Rama[1]

The universe is a dance of energies which vibrate at many frequencies. They ebb and flow, merge and part, form ripples, tides, currents, eddies, and whirlpools. They become units of all sizes, from atoms to stars, individual souls to cosmic beings. Again, they dissolve into each other. As rays, streaks, streams, rivers, oceans of light, they flow into each other and separate again, changing frequencies, and with this changing of frequencies they become suns, galaxies, spaces, airs, winds, fires, liquids, solids. They become the bodies of human beings into which the energy called consciousness comes and is embodied.

Of all the flowing energies in the universe, consciousness is the most dominant, the one from whom all the others proceed and into which they all merge. The ancient texts are fond of the phrase, "from consciousness down to the solid earth," for all this is a single matrix, a *tantra*, of energy, and within it are myriads of matrices, woven and interwoven. The human being is one such matrix of energies—ebbing, flowing, dancing with each other at frequencies ranging from those of solid bones all the way to the subtlest *waves* of consciousness.[2] Those who can understand this personality-matrix will understand the whole universe.

Observe the creation of a single human personality. As two human

[1]See R. von Eckartsberg, Chapter 2, for a presentation and discussion of Swami Rama's Yoga psychology.—Eds.
[2]See Weber, Chapter 5, and R. Valle, Chapter 21, for discussions of the dual wave–particle aspects of consciousness and human existence.—Eds.

Swami Rama • The Himalayan International Institute of Yoga Science and Philosophy, R.D. 1, Box 88, Honesdale, Pennsylvania 18431.

streams of consciousness love each other, the force of their love invites a
third one for whom they provide a minute body. This third one brings
along in his wake a matrix of energy, and his body grows along the lines of
this energy. The fetus is connected to the mother at the navel, and it is
from the navel that 72,000 energy-channels, or *nadis* in Sanskrit, fan out
into the personality system. Since the energy-pattern is arranged in a
symmetrical manner, the body grows beautifully symmetrical. For instance, look at even the hairlines of the body, and you see how they are
patterned along the symmetrical paths of the energy flow.

The personality of the fetus, or that of a fully grown human being, is
not separate from the universal dance of energies. Observe how many
forces interact with the biosphere, how many energies enter into it and
emerge from it unceasingly. Observe how the body clock responds to
solar, lunar, stellar times, and how the blood responds to the tides in the
oceans. Although all these times, tides, forces often seem to operate
individually, each answering to its own constituent rhythm, their patterns are all vibrant subsystems within the single master system of consciousness whose dance it all is.

The vast all-pervading oceanic energy of consciousness barely
touches us with its outer fringes, and we come alive, becoming persons.
Where the vibration frequencies in us are too solid, too dense, not subtle
enough to flow in consonance with consciousness, it becomes our material body, the non-I. Here energy, condensed, becomes a cell. The cell is
filled with the vital energy called *prana*, which is maneuvered by the
mind-energy. The "I" in us is pure consciousness. It owns and operates
the body-vehicle, and it guides the mind. It is the purest, finest vibrating
energy.

Thus, like the rest of the universe, we are layer upon layer of energy,
or light, which form complex patterns. The subtler layers are aware of the
grosser ones, but not vice versa. Through the process of meditation and
self-awareness, however, it is possible for us to attune ourselves to these
energy-processes. In fact, all of our information in this regard comes to us
from the experiences imparted, through the oral tradition, by great meditation masters. Others who follow this path of self-awareness will eventually know the dance that the personality, and the universe, and all the
energies flowing between and within them, are dancing. There is no
greater excitement than that of suddenly discovering that the universal
ocean of *prana* is flowing right through us, that our brains are but so many
stepping areas in the great dance of the universal mind, and that all that I
claim to be is simply a thrill passing into this person "I" from the universal
consciousness. And then the single point of this dynamic thrill becomes
diffuse, and its millions of sparks, like an incredible display of fireworks,
rushes out into a vast network of energy channels which are spread

throughout my person, to vitalize me, to make me mentally and physically a living being, to illuminate me so that I can say "I."

Those whose awareness is bound to the earthly-level frequencies know, as the real person, only the physical body. Others, who refine their self-identification by attuning to finer frequencies, know of an undying consciousness. To know this is to know that we are immortal. But before we can reach the point of comprehending the immortaility of our universal consciousness, it is essential that we understand the relationships between and among various levels of energy. This understanding is not an intellectual process. It is a matter of letting our interior awareness travel along the lines of the diffuse patterns of energy so that we can actually perceive all their modes of power and its operation. The yogi does this. He sends his awareness on this incredible interior journey and returns to chart for others the maps of consciousness. There is no other way to comprehend what consciousness is, what roles it plays in running our personalities.

The yogi finds that the energies (of various levels of subtlety ranging from the low frequency, earthly solid manifestation to the very high frequency, almost undetectable mental waves) all interact with each other in many ways; he finds that the relationship between the denser and finer energies is that of interdependence. The denser ones affect the finer ones in a more immediate way, but the finer ones turn out to be the masters in the long run. Take, for example, our dense body. Its bad posture adversely affects the flow of breath, but when the will in our consciousness decides that the breath be made to flow perfectly, the body has to arrange itself in a posture that will facilitate the flow.

The relationship between the body and *prana* may be viewed similarly. A bad posture clogs the pathways of *prana*. But it is the experience of those who practice the subtler varieties of hatha yoga that once the blocks on the *prana's* pathways have been removed through the practice of postures, the *prana* itself begins to give little surges into the organs so that the body rights itself into correct posture inadvertently. What is more, many practitioners of *kundalini* yoga report that, as a result of their practices, an involuntary cleansing of internal systems takes place, which affects the *prana* matrix and thereby influences the body.

The relationship between *prana* and mind energies is no different. An incidence of low *prana* may befog the mind for the time being. But, again, the will of consciousness infuses the mind with a certain illumination, and then *prana* has no alternative but to obey the mind. Thus, through deep meditation, the mind can be used to intensify the strength of *prana*.

As we have hinted above, the key to the relationship between the various energies is the will that is inherent in consciousness. Will, however, should not be confused with the much-used term, *will power*, which has become a word that almost connotates violence. Will power is an exertion of the lower mind. Will is simply an inherent quality of consciousness through which consciousness directs all its operations.[3] These operations then affect our exterior environment and become our actions. One who cultivates self-awareness observes and, through the will, consciously controls all the interior operations of mind, *prana*, and body.

The higher-frequency energies contain within themselves all the power of the lower frequencies, but not vice versa. By the same token, the mind can measure all the powers of the body and sense, but they in turn cannot measure much of the mind's power. It is for this reason that some modern scientific instruments can measure physiological signs of certain mental states but are powerless to measure the state itself. In other words, one may measure delta brain waves, but a depth gauge to measure the experience of sleep itself has not as yet been invented.

This leads us to some very interesting observations about the mental state of sleep. The body, of course, shows that one is asleep. The question then arises as to whether the signs seen in the body can tell us everything about the mental state of sleep. The answer, certainly, is "No." The yogis say that only a certain surface of the mind is asleep, and that a vast area of the mind never sleeps. For if the entire mind were to sleep, who is it that continues the digestive processes during that time? Who keeps the lungs breathing and the heart pumping? If the entire mind were to sleep, who would wake us up again? Seeing that the body (which is run by the mind) maintains some of its operations during sleep, we surmise that a part of the mind must remain awake, but if we simply depend on body-consciousness to experience that mind which remains awake while we sleep, we are left helpless. Yet we know that the will of consciousness is operant in the mind in order to keep the body functioning and to wake us up again. Thus it becomes clear that the finer energies cannot be contained in, or measured by, the denser ones, but the opposite is not the case.

Our greatest concern in a study of the relationship among energies within the human personality is with the question of self-identification, called *abhimana* in Sanskrit. In the average individual, consciousness has gravitated to identification with the densest energy level, the body—or so it appears. But in fact, consciousness can identify with each of the forms the energy takes and can call them all "I." This person identifies his relationships with various members of his family. For instance, take these four statements: he is my father, I am his son; she is my sister, I am her

---

[3]Compare this with R. Valle's discussion in Chapter 21 of the characteristics which distinguish free will and volition.—Eds.

brother; she is my wife, I am her husband; she is my daughter, I am her father. In each, the "I" is common, but the relationship differs. The person saying "I" has the experience of being in all four roles, those of son, brother, husband, and father. But each of the relatives can play only a single role with him. The wife cannot know him as a son, the sister cannot identify with the father in him. Yet he is all four states within himself. He is also apart from these—just himself—sitting writing a poem to his divine lover. He is free of all human relationships at that time, yet he is even closer to his true identity. It is thus with consciousness. At the level of the body, we identify consciousness with the body, and it says, "Yes, body, too, is made of my being, but I also breathe in breath, animate through *prana,* and mentate when I am mind, and yet I dwell in my own nature apart from these at all times. They are my modes, but I am not their mode. They are my variations, but I am the theme."

In other words, even though most human beings seem to identify with only the surface of their bodies, consciousness remains wide awake and active elsewhere, too, for if their identification were truly limited to the surfaces of their bodies (as in the case of someone sleeping), how could they breathe with the lungs, digest with the internal organs, and send out brain waves? Deeper still, how could they have internal emotions and other forms of mentating? Obviously, consciousness is operant in and identified with each of these forms of energy, even though it appeared that their main identification was with the surface of the body. As we cultivate meditative self-awareness, we gradually proceed from the exterior to the interior self-identifications of consciousness—first the body, then the *prana,* then many stages of mind, one after another, and, finally, *pure* consciousness alone.[4]

A question is often asked, "How did consciousness ever lose its purity in the first place?" The answer is that it never did. Just as one's whole mind is never asleep even though the sleeping part does not know of the ever-awake part, so body-consciousness-identification cannot be identified with the pure-consciousness-one, whose extension, title, limited state, and epithet it is. But the full and pure consciousness continues on, taking care of all its children—the lower-level frequencies which are powerless to contain and measure it. Again and again the ancient texts on the nature of consciousness have made this assertion: Who are you that ask this question? A being identifying yourself with the consciousness as it extends into the body? Just move a bit on the spectrum. Keep moving.

[4]Contrast this idea of *pure* consciousness (i.e., consciousness without an object) with the existential-phenomenological notion that consciousness is *intentional* in nature. See Moss, Chapter 7, de Silva, Chapter 13, and R. von Eckartsberg and R. Valle, Chapter 14, for discussions of intentionality. It seems that what the existential-phenomenologists mean by "consciousness" is what the yogis mean by "mind."—Eds.

All of those colors reflect the same light. When did light ever cease to be light? The green is green and red is red, but the light is always light. Only when you identify the light with one of its modes do you see blue or red. See all of consciousness, and your body is included.

Are there special procedures, processes, connections, which the consciousness follows in running our personalities? The universal consciousness principle may be compared, for our purpose here, to a current into which, through many sockets, various electric appliances are plugged. The same one current supplies cooling power to the cooler, heating power to the heater, helps a radio to tune into sound waves, and the TV to gather and project visual images. So also is the consciousness principle (the primary force from which all other energies are derived, whose variations on the theme they all are) connected into all living beings, supplying to each one the power for will, knowledge, and action.

In human beings this primary consciousness becomes operative through a system of psychophysiological centers. So far, we have been traveling along the finest current. Now we begin to look from the opposite, the grosser end, called the physical body. This body with all its cells, as we said earlier, is run by *prana*; the *prana* is directed by the mind, and the mind is guided by consciousness. There are areas in our human personality where these various energies are joined together in close consonance, resonating to each other's vibrations, deriving the power from consciousness, which, however, is absolute in itself and resonates to no other. In these specific areas the vibration passes from consciousness into the mind-*prana*-body system, the personality, and from these areas the energy is distributed into the rest of the personality. These are the psychophysiological centers which are plugged into the current of consciousness, and they respond to its universal rhythms.

Take, for example, our breathing process. What is the origination of breath which, when looked at physically, is nothing but a series of pockets of air trapped into certain cavities? What turns that air into flowing breath? Rhythm of the movement of certain organs. What moves the organs? The *prana*. What causes the *prana* to vibrate so that the organs linked to its specific areas should thus move rhythmically? The mind, of course. The mind is moved by consciousness.[5] Again, look at it differently. The universal consciousness, which makes the world dance by its power, sends a tiniest spark of its thrill through the mind into our psychophysiological centers in such locations as the navel, cardiac center, throat, and the pineal area. The thrill creates a pulsation in the *prana* system which, in turn, creates certain rhythmic movements in the organs connected therewith. The rhythm is synchronized, coordinated because

---

[5]Here the "mind–consciousness" distinction is made clear.—Eds.

it originates in the same single original thrill. Through this process, air, which would otherwise remain trapped in the cavities (as in a dead body), begins to flow as a smooth stream, and we say that the child has begun to breathe! On the other hand, when the thrill of consciousness is withdrawn, the breath simply becomes trapped air, and the doctor says that the person is dead. He who understands the source of the thrill knows that the rhythm of his breath responds to the same vibration which produces pulsations in the hearts of suns. It is thus that the yogis give to some of their breathing exercises names such as "piercing through the sun," *Surya-Vedhana*.

We need to elaborate further on the way consciousness becomes operative in the personality. It is not subject to limitations of space, time, dimensions, personalities, in its full universal identification. It is sent forth into our being which is made of lower and denser frequencies, like a straight beam of light penetrating through a rocky cave. Because the lower-frequency energies vibrate in a time–space reference, creating a physical body, a physical *locus* has to be assumed in us for that light which transcends all *loci*. So the yogis say that this immense, intense energy beam of consciousness, the *kundalini*, is located in us in a channel extending from the base of the spine up to and engulfing the entire brain region. Though nonphysical (and therefore not tangible), it is experienced by the yogis in deep meditation as an unceasing flash of rodlike lightning shining with a light like that of ten-thousand suns, yet as slim as though it were a ten-thousandth of a hair's breadth in width. It passes through seven ever-vibrant and dynamic psychophysiological stations, or centers, into which it sends its sparks, whereby they become functional, and the personality becomes operant. Thus the consciousness touches us, and we come alive, becoming persons.

It is not difficult to locate these centers of consciousness, or *chakras*[6] in Sanskrit. They are all marked in one way or another. Their locations are: (1) the base of the spine and the perineum, (2) the root of the genitals, (3) the navel, (4) the cardiac region between the breasts, (5) the hollow of the throat, (6) between the eyebrows, and (7) the top of the head.

Many times it is asked if the consciousness and the energy of these centers, *chakras*, flows in the spine or in the front of the body. The answer is that the distinction is arbitrary and imaginary. The front and back location exist only with reference to the materially dense body, but the field of finer energies permeates the entire region and does not correspond to the dimensions that are assumed with reference to the spaces and times to which the body is bound.

The consciousness that has descended into us as the *kundalini* con-

[6]See R. von Eckartsberg, Chapter 2 ("Swami Rama's Yoga Psychology"), for another reference to the *chakras*.—Eds.

tains in it both life and awareness. It may be called the life-force, *jiva-shakti,* or the consciousness-force, *chit-shakti.* Through the *chakras,* a division of its two powers occurs, for, in order for the personality to function, a certain specialization becomes necessary. A semblance of awareness is imparted to the energy called the mind, and at the same time aliveness and vitality of the cells, organs, and senses also come into operation through *prana* receiving the infusion of life-energy from the *kundalini.* Thus the two powers of the *kundalini*-consciousness devolve on the mind and *prana,* and through them they are further infused into the entire personality. However, the thrill of life and awareness that passes through the psychophysiological stations into the personality is so minute when compared with the actual power of consciousness, that yogis repeatedly tell us that the true consciousness is lying dormant, asleep in us.

All that mankind has ever accomplished or created, all that ever passes through an individual human being, is no more than a minute fraction of the universal consciousness whose thrill is infused into us, but the majority of human beings are not capable of experiencing even this minute thrill at its fullest. Why is that so? Because the lower-level energies are not capable of containing or measuring higher-level energies. By the same token, if given more than the requisite voltage, any energy system will overload and blow up the circuits. We have established such strong identification with lower-level energies (the body, emotions, etc.) that we have weakened our power system and made it incapable of receiving a larger dose of the thrill. So one has to purify the personal consciousness and gradually tune it to its higher-level energies until enough strength is built up in the system for us to be able to awaken to the full glory that is flowing into us, even as we read this. Those who have tried experimenting with the *kundalini* consciousness without such preliminary purification and without expert guidance have only suffered damage to both the psyche and the body.

In us, the gates of the *chakras* are, thus, open only enough to permit a mild infusion of consciousness. But look at the intense awareness we have in these centers. Even that mild infusion of dormant energy leaves us restless in each center. Look at what goes on in us at each of these stations: in the perineum and the genital areas the sensations can sometimes seem to be uncontrollable, in the navel region the hungers cannot be satiated, the pull felt in the cardiac region as emotions arising keeps thousands of psychiatrists busy, and all we have ever spoken from the larynx is not quite enough. As to the forehead and the brain—they are the devil's very workshop. The energy already disposed through each of these centers often seems to be excessive to us, and we then say, "I just don't know what to do with my restlessness." This feeling of overload that we are about to blow a fuse is a common experience. It happens because the lower frequency energies (such as those involved in ordinary physical and sense experiences) do not have the capacity to absorb all the power that is being infused into us from consciousness which is flowing from within outward.

The yogi resorts to a different path, the inward one. And here we come to the difference between closed stations and open stations. It is stated in the *kundalini* literature that an average person is living with closed *chakras* which are awaiting to be opened. Many, who are not initiated into this science, erroneously think that with the opening of a *chakra*, the outward activity in that center of consciousness will increase, thus making, let us say, a sexy person yet sexier, or an articulate person voluble! But such externalized activity only dissipates the energy at its lowest frequencies. It has nothing to do with highly refined interior consciousness.

The pulsations that we experience, in ordinary daily life, in the various psychophysiological stations are nothing but reminders of a higher presence within. They are like lighthouses guiding ships. Each pulsation says to our lower-level energy consciousness: "Come, this way, here is a gate through which you enter inward into the highest awareness." It leads to the place from which this minute light is sent forth. If we observe each pulsation in our personality as such a reminder, we begin to listen to an inner music, and we may use each such pulsation first as a point of focus, and then as a thread leading inward. Take, for example, the sexual thrill in the second station. It makes an average person restless because the infusion of energy from within is so powerful (even though it is infinitesimal compared to all the power of consciousness) that no amount of sexual activity can bring total satiety. The yogi, however, regards this center only as a gateway to higher-level energy consciousness. Its pulsations he sees only as reminders of the inner source. He closes the outward flow, and that is called opening the *chakra*. All externalized restlessness then ceases. The lower frequency energy is returned to the higher frequency.

In other words, any time a sexual pulsation is felt in a yogi's person, he responds to it, considers it a blessing and a reminder, and uses it as the end of a thread leading inward to pure consciousness. He reverses the flow. Compared to the ecstasy of this inward flow of his personal consciousness into the universal consciousness, the outward sexual flow is a useless discharge, and all of its intense enjoyment is like sucking on the peel of an orange after squeezing out and, alas, throwing away the juice. Again, when the throat center begins to open, the yogi seeks silence. When he does utter a word, it is so power-packed as to be recorded as sacred scripture and repeated for millennia around the globe. Such were the words uttered by the Buddhas and Christs of history.

We may divide human beings into those of the inward-flowing consciousness, *antar-vritti*, and those of the outward-flowing consciousness, *bahir-vritti*. Those in the first category live and walk in the awareness of their cosmic connection. They are unceasingly and interminably conscious of the thrill of the universal divine consciousness running through them. They do not utilize any of their energies as mere persons but serve as channels for the cosmic flow. They are dependent on nothing external and on no person, but many are dependent on them for succor, solace, knowledge, and healing. Those in the second category are those who believe that only the information passing through the senses and into the brain constitutes personality and consciousness. Their excitements are derived not from the inner thrill, but from the contact that dense senses make with yet denser exterior objects. Thus their psychology is that of a dependent, however much they may clamor for individual freedom and claim self-dependence. Those in the first category, the rare few in the history of mankind, are committed to turning sensory awareness inward in order to free themselves from the bondage of dependence on the limited exterior and to experience the unlimited flow of cosmic energies which is at their disposal.

We need to understand how this is accomplished, how the outward flow of awareness may be reversed so that the intricate dance of the interior energies may become real. We need to understand that, through the application of will, we can cultivate a resolve to change our self-identification from lower-frequency energies to the higher one. That is immortality. That is freedom of consciousness from the bonds of space, time, *karma*, and causation. It is the dance of the freedom of energies.

16

Human Consciousness and the Christian Mystic
TERESA OF AVILA

Silvio E. Fittipaldi

Christian mysticism is not one way but rather it encompasses many ways. Such variety has become evident to me by way of my encounter with different Christian mystics. In my early twenties, I read Augustine of Hippo and Bernard of Clairvaux. The former is often known as the "Doctor of Love." The latter describes his way and experience to be like the relation between lover and beloved. In my early thirties, while encountering and being deeply touched by oriental spirituality, especially Zen, I came into contact with the "negative way" of the Christian mystics. More recently, in my early forties, I have been moved by the Spanish mystics John of the Cross and especially Teresa of Avila. These experiences have taught me that one cannot speak of Christian mysticism as a single way or uniform vision of reality. Christian mystics give expression to the richness and uniqueness of the varied personal realization of the following of Christ. Each mystic, though unique, is grounded in an experience of Christ that may have its source in the Synoptic Gospels, the Johannine literature, the Pauline letters, or some creative combination of these witnesses.

The purposes of these brief and limited reflections is, initially, to present an understanding of Christ-consciousness. This understanding arises from a creative intertwining of various themes from the Christian

Silvio E. Fittipaldi ● Religious Studies Department, Villanova University, Villanova, Pennsylvania 19085.

scriptures as they are experienced in the light of my encounter with Zen. After this presentation, the way of Teresa of Avila, as she articulated it in her book *The Interior Castle*, will be outlined. This outline will suggest one way in the Christian tradition of realizing Christ-consciousness.

The underlying assumption of this chapter is that the human consciousness of a Christian mystic is a consciousness or vision of reality that has resulted from a radical change effected by an encounter with the living Christ. Such a transformation can be called a conversion (understood as a transformation of consciousness). A Christian mystic has, in the spirit of St. Paul, that mind or attitude (consciousness) which is in Christ Jesus. A Christian mystic has put on Christ, died and risen with Christ, is the branch nourished by the vine who is Christ. The first part of this chapter will uncover some of the meanings of these images.

A Christian mystic is not simply another Christ, that is, is not merely a clone of the historical Jesus. Rather, a Christian mystic is a unique person of the times and places where he or she lives, with the questions and thought patterns of those times and places, yet, in the end, not bound by those questions or thought patterns (patterns of consciousness and awareness), but free in the creation of new ways of living and thinking. Such creativity is of the essence of a Christian mystical way and vision.

Christian Mystical Consciousness as Christ-Consciousness

Normative expressions of Christ-consciousness are found in the Christian scriptures. A meditative reading–hearing of that word can bring a person into its mind–heart. The hearer can then be transformed. The resulting consciousness is a "new creation," a Christ-consciousness. It is the purpose of this section to present some major determining characteristics of Christ-consciousness, distinguishing marks that are typically realized in quite unique ways by different people. In short, Christ-consciousness will be described as empty-forgiving-loving-dying-rising consciousness.

Christ-Consciousness as Empty Mind

In Paul's letter to the Philippians (2:6)[1] we hear the proclamation that Jesus' "state was divine, yet he did not cling to his equality with God but emptied himself . . . and became human as we are." This Pauline passage is the initial source of an understanding of Christ-consciousness as empty. It is somewhat hazardous, at least initially, to describe Christ-

[1] All Biblical references are from *The Jerusalem Bible* (1966).

mind as empty-mind. In our popular imagination, empty-mind might very easily be associated with empty-headedness, which many understand as dim-witted, dull, stupid, or dumb. Such a connotation, obviously, is not what I have in mind.

Empty-mind involves an attitude or consciousness that is not bound by any of its own forms.[2] Each human person is born into a culture, and, through a process of enculturation, is formed within the language and thought patterns of the particular culture. Often a person may conceive of such patterns as the best and only way of perceiving reality, in which case we have cultural chauvinism or imperialism. Empty-mindedness involves the realization that no concept of reality adequately describes that reality. Hence empty-mind is open to other concepts and is flexible. It is a consciousness that recognizes its own limitations and boundaries and respects them (it most truly "respects" or looks at them), and is not bound by them. In the passage from Philippians, Jesus is presented as one not bound to the form of divinity (as if there is such a limited form!) but also open to the form of humanity. I would extend this to mean that Jesus is not bound by any forms but open to varying forms.

Christian consciousness, I submit, as Christ-consciousness, is empty-mind. It is consciousness not bound into any particular pattern or form of perception or conception. At the same time, Christian consciousness does not deny the value of patterns of consciousness. By being empty of any absolute form, Christian consciousness can be manifest or articulated through any form.

Up to this point I have been describing the emptiness of Christian consciousness in a very abstract manner. An objection might be stated that such empty-mindedness is appropriate as a description of Buddhist consciousness but is not a suitable category for Christian consciousness. However, Christian consciousness (as Christ-consciousness) as empty-mind is manifest in the Christian scriptures and is, I believe, fundamental to the spirit (consciousness) of Jesus.

In Matthew 8:20 (Luke 9:57–60) we read about a man who was attracted to Jesus and who committed himself to Jesus wherever he would go. Jesus, giving expression to his own life-style, pointed out to this possible disciple: "Foxes have holes and the birds of the air have nests, but the Son of Man has nowhere to lay his head." In other words, it seems that the following of Jesus, as articulated in this passage, means not having a home or a place of security. Jesus does not define himself in terms of a place. He is not bound to any one place, or he is empty in regard to the form of place. Hence, any place can become his home.

[2]This idea is similar to the notion of pure consciousness as described by Swami Rama, Chapter 15, "empty-mind" being the goal of all meditational practices.—Eds.

Furthermore, Jesus does not define himself in terms of a social group. This is vividly portrayed in Jesus' custom of eating at table with tax collectors and social outcasts (see Luke 15:1 for one such instance) as well as at the table of leaders of the people. This behavior of Jesus manifests his openness to persons no matter what their social status. Jesus is not bound by social forms. He is open to all persons no matter what their styles of life. He is empty in regard to such social discriminations, that is, he is bound by none of them, and hence he is open to any person living in any one of these social forms. This does not mean that Jesus is uncritical of unjust social forms. On the contrary, it means that all social forms are seen to be limited and hence changeable. Emptiness would mean that Jesus is open to any person, no matter what his social status, and able to challenge a social structure, no matter how inviolate.

Again, Jesus is empty in regard to the law. He deeply respects the law. There are times, however, when he does not follow the law. Circumstances dictate another behavior. We read in the Gospel according to Mark (2:23–28) that on one Sabbath day, Jesus

> happened to be taking a walk through the cornfields, and his disciples began to pick ears of corn as they went along. And the Pharisees said to him, "Look, why are you doing something on the Sabbath day that is forbidden?" And he replied, "Did you never read what David did in his time of need when he and his followers were hungry—how he went into the house of God . . . and ate the loaves of offering which only the priests are allowed to eat, and how he also gave some to the men with him." And he said to them, "The Sabbath was made for man, not man for the Sabbath; so the Son of Man is master even of the Sabbath."

A law is a form, and a system of laws is an expression of a mode of consciousness. Jesus recognizes and respects this consciousness, which is the law of his own people. He is, however, not bound by it. Thus, when such fulfillment would be inappropriate, he refuses to fulfill the law as it stands. Jesus is empty in regard to the law and the pattern of thinking of which it is a manifestation.

Jesus is empty in regard to place, to social status, and to law. These few examples from the Christian scriptures begin to suggest what Christ-consciousness as empty-mind involves. To be empty is to be unattached[3] to any particular place as home and, hence, to be at home anywhere; to be unwilling to characterize anyone in an exclusive manner or to exclude anyone from relationship because of social status, and, hence, to be open to relationship with anyone; and to be unbound by law. Emptiness of mind is a radical openness to places and persons and thought patterns. It involves a respect for places and for the status of

[3]See Levin, Chapter 12, and R. von Eckartsberg and R. Valle, Chapter 14, for discussions of the nature of *attachment*.—Eds.

persons and for law. It is also a recognition that such places and status and laws are not absolute. Such an empty-mind is Christ-consciousness and hence is Christian consciousness. It is central to the attitude of Jesus and can also be called forgiving-mind.

Christ-Consciousness as Forgiving-Mind

An empty-mind is a forgiving-mind. The word *forgiveness* is used here in such a way that it does not refer exclusively to "forgiveness of sin." This meaning is not excluded. It is broadened to include the perception of Terence Eagleton (1966):

> *Forgiveness* means cutting across this logical structure of values, a refusal to return in proportion to what is received; it is a gratuitous imbalancing of value, a free and irrational bestowal of love in a place where objectively it is undeserved. (pp. 19–20)

Emptiness involves an attitude that is unbound by any logical structure or social custom or stereotype. The ability to forgive involves flexibility. It is an unwillingness to hold any past behavior against a person. Such behavior is usually outside the accepted legal structures or social codes. A forgiving-mind is stretched beyond the accepted to include the unaccepted. Jesus manifests a forgiving attitude not only when he forgives Mary Magdelene, or the woman taken in adultery, or the thief by his side at the cross, but also when he relates with people no matter what their social status. He "cuts across this logical structure of values." He lavishly bestows love "in a place where objectively it is undeserved."

The forgiving-mind is an open-mind, an empty-mind. In this context, forgiveness of sin is the behavior-attitude by which one is not bound by the brokenness of our life together. It is not to be bound by the logic of an eye-for-an-eye or a tooth-for-a-tooth. It is having the burden of the results of an act or omission lifted gratuitously from our shoulders. Forgiveness is the attitude of the Jewish prophet Hosea who searches for his unfaithful wife and takes her to himself again. It is the behavior of the gracious father (Luke 15) who welcomes home his wandering son contrary to the logic of the situation. Neither Hosea nor the gracious father are bound by the customs of their society. Another word for this behavior-attitude is *love*. Empty-mind can be described as loving-kindness, a central challenge of Christian consciousness.

Christ-Consciousness as Loving-Mind

Much has been written, experienced, and questioned concerning the centrality and significance of love in the Christian traditions. Only a few words here will connect the reality of love with that of emptiness. The reality of love is not a solution to a problem. Nor is it a well-defined pattern of consciousness or path of life. Love involves a creative exchange among humans and between humans and the world. It may be described as the dynamic connections in a network called reality. Given the uniqueness of persons and of the world, and given the changing character of reality, the exchange or connection which is love is not predictable or definable. In this sense, love is ineffable and empty. To love does not mean to act in exactly the same way in every encounter—a way called loving. Rather, to love involves a discovery of the most appropriate way of being in relation to each person met or to each situation in which one is engaged.

To love is the central call of the Christian scriptures. Such love is identified with love of God. To love the neighbor (the one nearest) is to love God. This love of God and neighbor is the primary religious act. No other religious act can replace it. What is religion? What is Christianity? What is Christian consciousness? In the end, at the bottom line, it is love. Such a response tells us very little. It does not tell us how to think or act or be. Rather, to love is to be empty, to be open to various exchanges and forms and structures, to be able to enter into any exchange, form, or structure, to be able to shed or to challenge any exchange, form, or structure. Such an empty love respects neither place nor law nor social status as absolute. Not bound by any place or status or law or custom, the loving-empty person is open to all and can respect and challenge all. The rhythm of this love is an emptiness that is a fullness, a dying that is a rising.

Christ-Consciousness as Dying-Rising

Paul often writes in his letters that a Christian has died in Christ and has risen with Christ. The life-energy which is Christ flows in the veins of the Christian. In his death, Jesus actively and intentionally gave himself over to the power of another. He became totally empty and vulnerable. In this act, an ultimate act, he was raised, he became filled. He realized the *pleroma*, the fullness of life. The death of Jesus is his resurrection. For Jesus, the act of dying is a total self-emptying that, by the very fact of emptying, is a fulfilling. Saint Paul speaks of this transformation as a new creation. His death and resurrection give witness that Jesus is not bound by any forms, even the forms of life and death. By giving himself up to death consciously and freely, he is unbound to life (is anyone reminded here of the self-immolation of several Vietnamese Buddhist monks during the recent war in Vietnam?). Jesus' resurrection is a witness that the power of death is not ultimate and has no dominion over him. This paradox of life-in-death and death-in-life is fundamental to the life-style of Jesus and is pointed to in the Gospel according to John (12:24), where we read: "I tell you most solemnly, unless a grain of wheat falls in the ground and dies, it remains only a single grain; but if it dies, it yields a rich harvest." We also read in the Gospel according to Luke (9:24): "For anyone who wants to save his life will lose it; but anyone who loses his life for my sake, that one will save it."

The dying-rising-losing-saving rhythm of Jesus is also characteristic of Christian consciousness. To save one's life is to hold onto it, to confine it, to box it in, to close it off from possible new directions. To lose one's life is to allow that life to flow, to be open, to be shared, or to be empty. To die is to rise. To be empty is to be full.

In summary, Christian consciousness is Christ-consciousness. A human person, by identifying with Christ, becomes human. The process of Christification is a process of humanization. Such a process is an emptying that is an opening, a loving that is a dying that is a rising. This process and its consciousness is the core of the Christian mystical traditions. It has been expressed by Christian mystics in many ways. In the second major part of this chapter, the way of Teresa of Avila, a way that uniquely encompasses the consciousness outlined above, will be presented in a broad sweeping stroke. Teresa's controlling metaphor is an "interior castle" in which the mystic grows in wisdom and love and knowledge.

The Interior Castle of Teresa of Avila

Teresa of Avila was born on March 28, 1515, at about 5:30 A.M., almost dawn, and she died on October 4, 1582, at 9:00 P.M. During her 67 years she experienced much conflict, was sick almost to the point of death, was the counselor of many people seeking comfort and encouragement, and was an able administrator. In spite of all this, she was a passionate mystic. I will investigate the rhythms of her intense life as she articulated them in her book *The Interior Castle* (1961).

The Interior Castle was written in about five months between June 2, 1577 and November 5, 1577. Containing candid descriptions of her experience sprinkled with numerous images and humorous comments, this book comes from the heart of Teresa. However, insofar as it was written in sixteenth-century Spain, often using metaphors, images, and a theology of that time and place, a contemporary reader may have difficulty penetrating to the overall vision of life that energized Teresa's lively and dynamic life. Thus it is my purpose in the following pages to present a contemporary creative assimilation of *The Interior Castle* in language and thought-forms more familiar to the twentieth-century person. In such a presentation I hope to remain faithful to Teresa by not rigidly following her thought-forms, but rather by entering into their spirit and even rearticulating that spirit where it is deemed both helpful and true.

The primary and controlling metaphor of *The Interior Castle* is "the castle."[4] Within the context of this image, numerous other images are sprinkled, each one depicting one or another aspect of the life of the spirit or the growth of consciousness.

I would venture to say that very few of us have ever seen a castle except in pictures, and even fewer of us have walked inside one. There are many varieties of castles. I imagine Teresa's castle to be a huge stone structure, solid and stable, with a multileveled, intricate web of passage-ways between numerous, varied rooms, from dungeons to towers, and from venom-infested corners to brightly decorated halls.

The castle represents the human soul or self or consciousness, a dynamic interplay of diversity and integration, heights and depths, shadows and glories, darkness and light.

The many rooms in the castle represent the numerous states of consciousness of a human person who is seeking perfection, or what I would prefer to call "reality." For a few brief moments we will tour some rooms of this castle, a short time in comparison with the hours or days or years during which the seeker must strive to realize the states of consciousness symbolized by those rooms. The reader may recognize some of the rooms. Others will be strange. There may even be an impulse to redesign one or another room, or to add one here or there. Allow that imagining to take place. Follow it. This castle is not the same for everyone. And after the tour, you may wish to change the image or make central one of the minor images. Such true playfulness is only to be expected in the delicate description of even the barest outlines of states of consciousness.

In general, the castle is a house of love. The investigation of the castle is a searching out of the many aspects of love. For Teresa, a committed Christian, the beginning and end, the alpha and omega of human life and of human consciousness, are found in love (1961, pp. 42, 228, 229).

The mansions or rooms or apartments in the interior of the castle are arranged concentrically like a palmetto (i.e., a shrub with thick layers of leaves enclosing a succulent edible kernel). The occupant of the castle can walk around the edges, move toward the center, return to the outer rim for a while, ever proceeding toward the enticing center. What are some of these rooms like? What, in other words, are some aspects of the growth of consciousness that are represented by different rooms in the interior of the castle which is our self?

[4]There are repeated references to and uses of the castle in the adult fantasy literature, the castle being an intuitively appropriate setting for stories involving "metaphors of consciousness."—Eds.

At the entrance of the castle, the door of the self, is the process of self-discovery and self-awareness. Such a process is the core of prayer and meditation, activities that are primarily the development of reflective awareness, that is, awareness of self and one's goal. Formal prayer and meditation lead to self-discovery. Also, the very process of self-discovery, even in an informal context, is meditative.

Once persons begin on this meditative journey, they begin to come into contact with varying aspects of themselves. This process is a process of touching on the truth of who the seeker really is. Being aware of the truth of who I am is the essence of humility. This is the first room in the castle, the mansion of humility or the truth of our selves.

Having entered these rooms of self-knowledge, the meditator discovers both well-lighted and darker rooms. Contact is made with aspects of self that are beautiful and with other aspects that are less appealing. The seeker becomes more alert and attentive to self and the world and their interrelation. The feelings are ambivalent; fear of the darker sides, enticement to the light. The search becomes threatening and comforting. Uncertainty as to whether or not to continue sets in. We are now in the second set of rooms.

In the third set of apartments, the quest for reality, which has been somewhat restless up to this point, begins to settle and become quiet as the seeker begins to experience an inner silence and gracefulness, a recollectedness or gathering of energies and a carefulness of demeanor. There is a gentleness of mind and body, feelings and thoughts. The experience is not unambiguous. In this state, the person still experiences restlessness and even depression because of an inability to control attitudes or because of limitations. In these rooms there is the ambiguous experience of gentle gracefulness and restless awkwardness. There is much movement between these rooms and the previous two sets.

The fourth mansions are a continuation of the experience of the third, with an increase of recollectedness and a decrease of uneasiness. Teresa calls this state of consciousness the "prayer of quiet." She compares it with two fountains of water, each fountain pouring into its own basin. One basin is filled with water that is collected with hard work. The other basin contains water that is a gift. In these rooms, at this point in the development of consciousness, the seeker becomes more deeply aware of the intertwining of work and gift, of effort and grace, in the quest for reality. Not every discovery or realization is the result of labor. The search is not entirely under the control of the seeker. Nourishing water also can and does come as a gift. There are unexpected, unpredictable moments of quiet recollectedness. At the same time, the perceptions are becoming more subtle and not entirely dependent on the rational process as in the initial meditations. Rather, the rational processes are extended to include deeper intuitive understandings. The soul or self enlarges and expands. Consciousness broadens. The social and cultural filters that have affected its vision begin to melt away or are transcended. The process of emptying is in full swing as consciousness expands effortfully and effortlessly, though it is still gripped by the ambiguity of feelings of fear and joy.

In the fifth circle of rooms a radical change of consciousness occurs. Teresa describes this experience as the "prayer of union." She attempts to depict it in terms of the changes experienced by a silkworm, which spins a cocoon around itself only to emerge later as a butterfly. The life of a silkworm is described in the first four sets of mansions. The fifth mansion is the cocoon. The individual ego has expanded so that it is impossible to speak of or experience the self as a separate ego. "I," it is realized, is other than a separate, individual, differentiated ego. "I" and "reality" are not separate entities. Rather, "I" is "real." It is not necessary to seek reality outside the self, and the self is not exclusively an individualized ego. This experience is something like dying, like the silkworm entombing itself in the cocoon it has spun. This state of consciousness is not an escape from reality or an isolation from the remainder of the world. It is, in fact, the opposite of such an alienating vision of reality. The cocoon experience, or the experience of union, involves a dying of the inhibiting self-consciousness and the rising of a reality-consciousness or expansive self-consciousness in which the separateness of "I" and "other" (other people and other aspects of the world) is broken down. Some would call this the experience of self-transcendence that happens in the growth of love.

In the sixth mansions, the person has emerged as a butterfly from its cocoon. There is joy, and there is hard work that often seems in vain. Committed to the quest, the seeker feels frustrated. The fruit is near at hand, but still out of reach. There is pain in solitude which seems impossible to sustain. The seeker suffers inexpressible distress and oppression and is unable to be comforted. Teresa recommends that the seeker deepen his "caritas," his loving behavior. At times there is relief. In these mansions there is the ambiguity of the fourth apartments, but with a difference. At this point, relationships are deep but unpossessive. The expanded consciousness is an unattached awareness. The experience is one of union and uniqueness. Teresa speaks of it as an experience of betrothal, in which the lovers are as two unique candles whose flames are joined as one. The seeker is now at the inner circle of the palmetto. The fruit is near at hand.

The realizations of the seventh mansion are a gift as well as the result of the work of the betrothed. At this point, lover and beloved are joined in a deep union like the rain in a fresh spring. Even though the union is not completed, the seeker now sees clearly. All filters of consciousness have been removed. No scales are left over the eyes. Reality is experienced directly or immediately insofar as the separation between person and reality is totally dissipated. True peace, the peace that is beyond understanding, is experienced. In openness and emptiness, the consciousness is deeply sensitive to both joy and pain. This almost-realized self is sympathetic and empathetic with the suffering encountered in persons and things. Such pain, however, is not unsettling. Acting out of a deep love and alertness, the seeker acts in an appropriate manner when action is called for and remains inactive when that is demanded by the situation.

Conclusion

Christ-consciousness has been realized. The self is completely empty or fully open, unbound by any form yet able to enter any form. In the realization of this Christ-self, the separate ego is forgotten. The desire for consolation disappears in the experience of sensitive alertness to all aspects of reality. Hence, dryness is not possible. Who could be dry in the intense but peaceful alertness to reality in its many and varied faces? Who could be dry, in the state of joyful love, that suffers with the suffering and rejoices with the rejoicing? The rhythm is a dying and rising. The power of the way all along its meandering path is love, a love that is empty and open. The butterfly has flown into the sun, only to return again transformed in the burning heat and comforting warmth, the pain and joy of continuing human exchange with all aspects of reality encountered along the way.

References

Eagleton, T. *The new left church*. Baltimore: Helicon, 1966.
The Jerusalem Bible (A. Jones, Ed.). New York: Doubleday, 1966.
St. Teresa of Avila. *The interior castle*. New York: Image Books, 1961.

17

Transformation of Self and World in Johannes Tauler's Mysticism

Donald M. Moss

Introduction: Hermeneutic Phenomenology and the Psychology of Consciousness[1]

The title of the present volume, *The Metaphors of Consciousness*, suggests two major concerns of present-day scientific psychology. The first is the new interest in the once vanquished phenomenon of consciousness in its multiple manifestations. The second is an enhanced awareness that psychology and empirical science are not simply a gathering of facts. Theories of consciousness—even the most objective, scientific, and physicalistic—are in some sense metaphoric, taking the constructs and findings we have in hand and using them, through a creative stretching of their original meaning, to gesture toward a broader vision of the conscious human being and his or her experienced reality.

To use the language of a dialectical, hermeneutic phenomenology—and I refer here especially to the works of Gadamer (1965), Hougaard (1978), Ihde (1971), Jonas (1963, 1974), Levin (1977a,b, 1978), and Ricoeur (1970, 1974, 1975)—scientific understanding is first and foremost an event, radically linguistic and historical, occurring within a field of tradition. "Understanding, then, occurs when tradition, by means of the pre-

[1] For an introduction to hermeneutic study, see von Eckartsberg, Chapter 10, in R. S. Valle and M. King (Eds.), *Existential-Phenomenological Alternatives for Psychology*. New York: Oxford University Press, 1978.—Eds.

Donald M. Moss • Ottawa County Community Mental Health, CMH-1111 Fulton, Grand Haven, Michigan 49417.

judgment, encounters tradition in terms of the subject matter. . . . Understanding happens in the encounter between the familiar and the unfamiliar polarities of tradition" (Stover, 1975, p. 36). The encounters with new subject matters, and with forgotten elements within the tradition itself, present the possibility for a movement toward understanding. Both the direct investigation of consciousness and the current dialogue with older perspectives on consciousness offer just such a challenge to the tradition of psychology.

Psychology, in this respect, acts as the cognitive faculty for a larger cultural movement, appropriating by means of knowledge an aspect of human potential and experience which the nonpsychologist would rather live than know. The philosopher of religion, Hans Jonas (1963, 1974), has shown through examples from antiquity, especially from the gnostic forms of mysticism, that there exists a typical historical sequence of events, commencing with *objectification*—religious knowledge, theory, and speculation contributing to the construction of religious myth and cosmos—and culminating in *interiorization*—the subjective inhabiting of that now living framework. One generation's conceptual schema becomes the next generation's guide to inward transformation.[2] I need hardly point out that already the present generation is hungrily clamoring for any and every schema produced by the psychologists of consciousness, which, however technical or arcane, are quickly turned to mystical purposes. The official clamor to rethink the foundations of psychology now gives way to the unofficial clamor to relieve the neglected modalities of human experience.

A Case Study: The Mysticism of Johannes Tauler

In the remainder of this chapter, I propose to take up one traditional Christian mystical viewpoint and extrapolate from it an implicit psychology of mystical consciousness. I have chosen the works of Johannes Tauler as my point of departure. Tauler, a Dominican monk and disciple of Meister Eckhart, lived in the German Rhineland, primarily in Strasbourg, from approximately 1300 to 1361 (see Figures 1 and 2). I have chosen Tauler because he is known as the practical expert among the medieval German mystics, combining a mystical vision for the *unio mystica* with the Godhead with the down-to-earth practical knowledge of a

[2]Elsewhere (Moss, 1978) I have discussed the dependence of both cognitive and neurologic functioning on socially and historically originated structures. Once appropriated by the individual, these structures serve to bring independent areas of the brain, often non-contiguous, into single functional systems. At the psychological level, they serve as the operant structures of the psyche.

Figure 1. Johannes Tauler, after a wood engraving of the sixteenth century (from Ancelet-Hustache, 1957, p. 146).

Figure 2. The old Dominican monastery at Strasbourg (from Ancelet-Hustache, 1957, p. 147).

spiritual counselor. Most of Tauler's surviving works are sermons delivered to nuns in Rhineland convents, practical guides to the inner life in a time of spiritual ferment; these sermons are permeated by the concrete—and surprisingly modern—psychological understanding of a master of life (see Clark, 1949; Filthaut, 1961; Wrede, 1974).

I have also chosen Tauler because he is a representative, in Christian garb, of the most influential movement within European mysticism, that is neo-Platonism, and thereby provides a circuitous link to the monistic Eastern viewpoints. Most readers of Tauler's sermons will recognize the great neo-Platonic schema of the One, eternal and undivided, out of which a mighty arc of creatures emanates, descending into ever more worldly and material forms, gaining in multiplicity with the descent from the One, and ultimately returning once again to that eternal Origin. Tauler explicitly acknowledged the neo-Platonist Proclus (410–485 A.D.) as a pagan antecedent and prefiguration of the Christian inward quest. And I might add that this neo-Platonic cosmology and metaphysics had become, for Tauler and his contemporaries, a schema to be *lived* and not merely conceived of. Indirectly, through Proclus and the Christian Dionysius the Areopagite, Plotinus's (1952) *The Six Enneads* provided the framework for the medieval Christian soul's ascent into unity with the Godhead (Katz, 1978, p. 42).

In seeking to articulate a psychology of mystical consciousness from Tauler's texts, I will utilize several guiding concepts taken from existential-phenomenological psychology.[3] Such concepts can be no more than heuristic, working hypotheses, at this point, to be established in the course of a closer investigation of the phenomenon of mysticism. Nevertheless, such concepts have often proved fruitful in reordering our perceptions and observations and in discovering inner coherences in a flood of facts. First, religious consciousness as such can be defined as openness to the religious world. Second, mystical consciousness, an event within the religious world, can be understood best as an active transformative process, accomplishing changes in the individual's relation to this religious world. Third, consciousness can be understood phenomenologically in terms of the organism–environment or man–world relationship; a transformative event such as mysticism effects changes in all aspects of this structure: man, world, and relationship. I am thus suggesting an enlarged version of the psychology of consciousness, looking beyond the momentary contents of consciousness to a detailed interrogation of the total behavioral bond linking man and world: including the habitualities of everyday life, the linguistic usages, the latent

---

[3]See R. von Eckartsberg, Chapter 2, and Moss and Keen, Chapter 4, for an overview of the existential-phenomenological approach.—Eds.

images, and all of the other life structures giving or transforming the overall organization to man's engagement in a religious world (Moss, 1978; Moss & Keen, 1978). Finally, the phenomenological attitude (the *epoché*) frames this investigation; that is, we suspend all questions about the reality of the religious objects experienced by the mystic. We describe what presents itself in the experience (the manner of this presentation), how the individual transforms his or her relation to these religious objects, and how this individual is him- or herself metamorphized in this process. Both orthodox believers and scientific critics have criticized the phenomenology of religious experience on just these grounds; the former because phenomenology fails to commit itself, in a leap of faith, to accept the truth of the religious experience and its objects (Pannikar, 1970), and the latter because it fails to make rigorous analytical judgments questioning the validity of such experiences (Staal, 1975). Yet, from the standpoint of phenomenology, it is only through a dialectic process of entering into experiences (either direct personal experience or vicarious experience in and through a text) and alternately engaging those experiences and stepping back again to deny them our complicity that the subtle and intricate manner of our involvement in that field of experience, and the organizational coherences governing it, can be articulated. The *epoché* in this sense is not a simple schizoid observation, but rather a delicate balance between engagement and reflection, living and knowing, an endless interrogation in the sense of Husserl (1962, 1970) and Merleau-Ponty (1962, 1968), as of such explicitly Christian thinkers as Paul Ricoeur (1974) and Gabriel Marcel (1964).

The World of Tauler's Mysticism

Let me begin by declaring the obvious: Tauler's mysticism is an event taking place against the vivid backdrop of the orthodox religious world of medieval Christendom. Further, it represents a specific transformation of that world as well as of the individual's relation to that world.

Tauler was a creature of the cloister, entering at about age 14 as was customary. His texts, as they are handed down to us, are not academic speculations; rather, they are sermons based on the scriptural passage prescribed in the day's liturgy and are full of practical, concrete advice for the nuns he counseled. He took for granted the principle objects of the Christian religious universe: the Trinity, the events of Christ's life, Mary the mother of Christ, sacred scriptures of the Old Testament and the New, and the sacraments, rites, and routines of life in the Church and in a religious, monastic order. Most of the typical polarities of the medieval world surface again in Tauler's mysticism: polarities between time and eternity, the mundane and the divine, Christendom and the pagan world, human darkness and divine light, and the folly of human reason and the wisdom of divine revelation.

Figures 3 through 8 may convey to the reader some of the texture of that medieval religious world. They are visionary drawings by St. Hildegard of Bingen, a brilliant mystic of the twelfth century. Figure 3 represents the "world totality," and portrays the primordial split between man and creator, and between man and cosmos. Figure 4 depicts the choirs of angels arrayed around the divinity. Figure 5 shows "the true Trinity within the true unity." Notice that each of these three drawings to some extent reproduces the mystical schema of neo-Platonism, with concentric levels of being emanated forth from a central divine unity. The movement outward in this schema constitutes alienation and fragmentation, the movement inward denotes spiritual integration and a return to the primal unity. Figures 6 and 7, on the other hand, illustrate the vertical hierarchy of the medieval religious world. Figure 6, the "pillar of the humanity of the redeemer," depicts one of several pillars appearing in Hildegard's vision of the total edifice of the Christian cosmos, each serving the elevation of the individual soul. Figure 7 shows the "food of life," the eucharistic meal. Finally, Figure 8 shows "the soul and its tent," and depicts, in mythic form, some of the perils of the soul.

Johannes Tauler's mysticism involves taking up the common religious objects of medieval Christendom and utilizing them in a transfor-

Figure 3. The world-totality (from Hildegardis, 1954, p. 23).

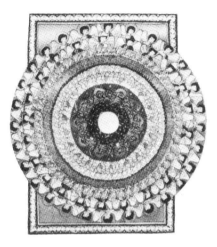

Figure 4. The choirs of angels (from Hildegardis, 1954, p. 33).

Figure 5. The true trinity within the true unity (from Hildegardis, 1954, p. 37).

mative fashion, to seek *inwardness*. The dimension *inward-outward* is the single most important theme of Tauler's mysticism. According to Tauler, human nature involves an inherent yearning for inwardness, a natural inclination toward personal renewal through a submersion in the divine ground from which all creatures have arisen. This appeared as self-evident to him, as the nature of libido does in our day. The transformation toward inwardness followed a regular sequence which culminated in an ideal of spiritual maturity.

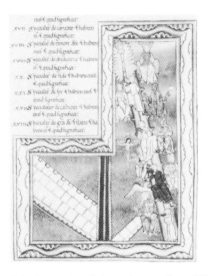

Figure 6. The pillar of the humanity of the redeemer (from Hildegardis, 1954, p. 73).

Figure 7. The food of life (from Hildegardis, 1954, p. 47).

Mental devices and ascetic behavior played a considerable role in the early phases of this transformation. For the "beginning man," described as bound to the life of the senses, Tauler prescribed fasting, monastic silence, and meditation upon the life and suffering of Christ. Further, he recommended a deliberate, methodical cultivation of a willful passivity, a surrendering of the reins of one's life to a divine governance—what he,

Figure 8. The soul and its tent (from Hildegardis, 1954, p. 25).

following Meister Eckhart, called *Gelassenheit*, or "letting be" (Schür-mann, 1973). The result was a slackening of relations to the profane world and an intensification and focusing of relations with the religious world, as well as a deliberate crafting and pruning of character:

> In this way nature and reason become purified, the head strengthened, and the individual more peaceful, more kind, and more restful, thanks to the inner exercise through which he has unified himself with God. All of his works become well ordered by this means. (Tauler, 1975, Chapter IV, pp. 55–56)

A careful cultivation of inner stillness was pursued by means of monastic silence and avoidance of anyone not sharing the contemplative life. The emphasis on inner stillness can be seen as further centering the individual inwardly within himself and as slackening his reactivity to the objects outside himself. Anything or anyone heightening this reactivity was avoided: "give yourself up to the inner man, and work all of your works from there" (Tauler, 1975, Chapter IV, p. 58). Active work was an integral part of the spiritual life and was taken up as a further vehicle for contemplative concentration:

> Know: it is not the work which brings you into dissatisfaction, but rather the disorder you carry into the work. . . . And a spiritual man should truly be ashamed of himself to have done his work in such a disordered and impure manner, that according to his own words it disquiets him . . . he should submit to God and do his work absolutely circumspectly and in stillness. (Tauler, 1975, Chapter IV, p. 66)

Much has been made of the emphasis on both the *vita contemplativa* and the *vita activa* by the German mystics (cf. Mieth, 1969; Wentzlaff-

Eggebert, 1944). Tauler was perhaps the most prominent in this regard. Mysticism was for him not merely a matter of feeling, momentary consciousness or experience during the hours of contemplative submersion. Rather, it involved a self-conscious ordering or crafting of the whole of life such that all behaviors, thoughts, and involvements were radicalized as vehicles for the intensification and focusing of the relation to God and the religious, inward realm:

> And if, in your work, you experience an inward touching, then give proper heed to it in your work, and thus you may learn to carry God into your work. (Tauler, 1975, Chapter IV, p. 68)

As Dietmar Mieth (1969) put this, the experience of the *unio mystica* while one is in contemplation shows the human being his divinely formed nature, but this nature must unfold in action and authenticate itself not only for the individual but also for the community.

This emphasis on the *vita activa*, the active life, is the single major counterweight to the otherwise universal tendency of Tauler's mysticism toward interiorization. Tauler's *Homo mysticus* remains a participant in the salvational drama of Christian history. His submergence in an inward eternity never fully annuls the Christian historical orientation toward a final time, a day of judgment. History continues to matter, as does the worldly calling ordained to each Christian. Until that day of judgment, one's fate is never sealed. The restless quest of the Western soul does not cease one step short of the grave. The dual possibility of salvation or damnation, of divine wrath or mercy, always exists. The moral gravity of human actions in the West is borne out of this sustained uncertainty.[4]

Note that the quest for inwardness involved a tremendous amount of exertion on the part of the devotee, a life-consuming involvement. One could not simply leap into the *unio mystica* without regard to the rest of life. In fact, Tauler repeatedly warned against the dangers involved: first, in the empty, compulsive practice of the outward forms of meditation; second, in excessive emphasis on contemplation to the neglect of the active life and the actualization of Christian love; and third, in the temptations inherent in the emotional and cognitive experiences accompanying contemplation.

Tauler put great emphasis on the human life cycle; he distinguished successive phases of life, phases which structurally presuppose one

---

[4]G. K. Chesterton characterized this preservation of the active life as the single feature best distinguishing Western Christianity from Eastern pantheism (his term): "There is no real possibility of getting out of pantheism any special impulse to moral action. For pantheism implies in its nature that one thing is as good as another; whereas action implies in its nature that one thing is greatly preferable to another" (Chesterton, 1959, p. 133).

another, each enabling a deeper form of inwardness and interiorization of the spiritual life. Tauler described man's ripening toward God as a process taking time, so that a long life on this earth was much to be envied. Further, he distrusted inwardness in any man who had not yet undergone the decisive "life-turning" of the 40th year of life. Prior to this point, according to Tauler, there is too much of nature, too much involvement in the multiplicity of external life in man, for the individual to realize true inward unity or integration. Tauler therefore emphasized a life of active love and outward practices for the younger "beginning Christian." Between the ages of 40 and 50, he prescribed a spiritual retreat and contemplative submersion in meditation in order to facilitate both a withering away of the "natural man" and a rebirth into the inward, spiritual life. This is a theme to which Tauler returned again and again, apparently perceiving here a general law of the human life cycle in which great work is required of the individual who wishes to meet the test of this mid-life crisis (see Weilner, 1961).

Here, as everywhere in Tauler's works, we see the interweaving of practical psychology, symbolism, and historical religious themes. The forty days preceding Christ's ascension into heaven, and the additional ten days to Pentecost, become, according to Tauler, years for us. The number 40 recurs throughout the Old Testament: the flood, the wandering in the Sinai, the reigns of David and Solomon, and the days of Moses' stay on the mountain. Further, Tauler quoted St. Gregory's observation "that the priests of the old covenant became guardians of the temple only at the age of fifty years," and prior to that were kept occupied as porters for the temple (Tauler, 1975, pp. 38–39). [This observation that the depth of spiritual maturity depends on successful traversing of one's ordained life cycle recurs in Hindu contexts as well as in the developmental psychology of Charlotte Bühler (1933) and the depth psychology of Carl Jung (1933, 1934).[5,6] See Weilner (1961) and Vetter (1958) for comprehensive discussions of these themes.]

With this theme of the life-turning at 40, we encounter another

---

[5] Jung's perspective is especially rich in this area (and convergent with the psychologic aspects of Tauler's remarks): "For a young person it is almost a sin—and certainly a danger—to be too much occupied with himself; but for the aging person it is a duty and a necessity to give serious attention to himself. After having lavished its light upon the world, the sun withdraws its rays in order to illumine itself. Instead of doing likewise, many old people prefer to be hypochondriacs, niggards, doctrinaires, applauders of the past or eternal adolescents—all lamentable substitutes for the illumination of the self, but inevitable consequences of the delusion that the second half of life must be governed by the principles of the first" (Jung, 1933, p. 109).

[6] See R. von Eckartsberg, Chapter 2, Marlan, Chapter 11, Levin, Chapter 12, and V. Valle and Kruger, Chapter 19, for discussions of Jung's psychology.—Eds.

example of Hans Jonas's observation that the objectification through religious speculation produces structures for inward transformation (Jonas, 1963, 1974). Collective cultural forms are internalized as the functional organization of individual psychic and spiritual experience. The life cycle of the Christian recapitulates the 40 days of Christ's stay among his disciples after his resurrection and the disciples' 10-day wait for the spirit after Christ's ascension. In every liturgical calendar year, the medieval Christian recapitulated the course of Christ's stay on earth as well as the principal events of Old Testament history.

In the case of the mystic, these structures served not only to organize the temporality of everyday life experience, but also as assists to the *inner life*. The death of Christ, for example, was ultimately most important not as an historical event, but rather as a mystical symbol or paradigm for the dying away of self. The individual was to contemplate and proclaim Christ's death not by words or thoughts, but rather by mirroring it in his own soul; that is, "through dying, renouncing yourself, in the power of Christ's death" (Tauler, 1975, Chapter X, p. 121). Let us turn briefly to a consideration of the role of language and thought in mystical experience.

Language, Cognition, and Image in Mystical Experience

One frequently hears the idea that there is a pure, true, and unadulterated mystical experience, which is unfortunately distorted and concealed due to the individual's religious framework. One might say, for example, "If only Tauler's Christian beliefs, medieval prejudices, and scholastic concepts had not gotten in the way and clouded his true experience." Were this the case, our task would be simple: cast aside the religious-speculative ballast and investigate directly the empirical, pure experience. However, Gershom Scholem, the great scholar of Jewish Kabbalah mysticism, has shown that just the opposite is true (Scholem, 1965). Mysticism is a child of orthodoxy. Even the great heretical and dissenting mysticisms, such as the Jewish pseudomessianic movements of Sabbatianism (seventeenth century) and Frankism (eighteenth century), take place against the backdrop of orthodoxy and rely for their language, images, and concepts on the cognitive-linguistic reserves of the mainstream.

Speculation, expression, and immediate mystical experience are essentially interdependent. The effort to move toward articulation and expression is intrinsic to the unfolding of mystical experience, even when the mode of articulation is opposed to reason and concept as in the Zen experience.[7] Mysticism requires the vehicle of language to unfold, yet never exhausts itself in finished language.

In Tauler's mysticism, the highly complex metaphysical speculations all can be seen to serve the overriding thrust toward *interiorization* of the spiritual life. Consider first of all the neo-Platonic schema. The soul arises and belongs in eternity, according to Plotinus, but, when plunged into the world, forgets its own origin. "Like children separated from their family from birth, and educated away from home, they are ignorant now of their parentage and therefore of their identity" (Plotinus in O'Brien, 1964, p. 91). Next, Tauler fused this schema with that of the Christian Trinity. The "Godhead," father, and source of all creation fuses with the neo-Platonic One; the son or Christ constitutes a manifestation emanating from eternity out of this Godhead; and the spirit is the emanation which dwells with man the creature when the son has returned to the Godhead.

Further, and this is an essential step, Tauler describes the inner spiritual ground of the human being as structured in a likeness of the Trinity. This completes a metamorphosis whereby the primary figures and dimensions of the religious macrocosm are now located within man, the microcosm. The neo-Platonic task of all creatures to return to their eternal ground, beyond all created things, becomes an everyday psychological and spiritual task of withdrawal into oneself. If the individual wishes the divine counsel of the spirit, he need only attend to his inner inclinations. If he wishes to participate in the eternally recurring birth of the divine son, begotten by the Godhead, he must submerge himself in his inner ground. Finally, if he wishes a taste of the ultimate union with the anonymous Godhead, he again must submerge himself absolutely into his interior. By the time the individual reaches this phase in the cultivation of the inner life, his inner spontaneity has been channeled, disciplined, or, if you will, sublimated into this organization, and is experienced as such. Like a Gestalt therapist, Tauler is able safely to say to the individual at this phase (post mid-life, one presumes), "trust your feelings":

> He should keep to himself, draw God into himself, and look into himself often with an inwardly turned temperament . . . and always he should attend to himself and to that which drives him to his work and inclines him toward it.

[7]Mystical speculation thus constitutes a direct hermeneutics of experience in Gadamer's sense: the speculative structure of language does not merely copy an experience ready made, but rather comprises a coming into articulation of an as yet latent meaning (Gadamer, 1965; Klostermaier, 1976). Neo-Platonism is itself a hermeneutic tradition, of which Tauler was well aware through Proclus. See Coulter (1976) for an appreciation of the hermeneutics of antiquity.

> Further, the human being should attend, absolutely inwardly, to whenever
> the spirit of God drives him toward rest or toward work, so that he may follow
> every impulse and act according to the direction of the holy spirit: now to rest,
> now to work, so that he may then take up his work full of good will and in
> peace. (Tauler, 1975, Chapter IV, p. 67)

The task of interiorization was served not only by theological concepts, but also by historical themes. For example, the metaphysical exile
of the soul from its origin was brought into connection with the historical
exile of the people of Israel from their homeland. I will quote Tauler here:

> Whoever engages inwardly and in such a well-ordered way in spiritual exer-
> cises, to him the inward tent will often be shown without the help of knowl-
> edge—the inward tent wherein the divine unity dwells and rests—to be en-
> joyed and divinely contemplated. (Tauler, 1975, Chapter I, pp. 39–40)

Tauler refers here to the "inward tent," a popular figure in the medieval
period for the dwelling place, within the soul, of the divine One. Simultaneously this term evokes Psalm 42:4, a lament of a Levite in exile:

> I remember and my soul melts within me:
> I am on my way to the wonderful tent, to the house of God.

Hildegard of Bingen, the twelfth-century mystic mentioned above, depicted this inward tent in one of her visionary drawings (See Figure 8). In
her accompanying commentary, she describes the vulnerability of the
natural, human soul-tent, and the true refuge of the divinely provided
inward tent, to a soul fleeing the perils of the world. In the vision, she
finds herself sheltered against the arrows of her enemies by this tent and
nourished by the manna, another vestige of the Exodus of the Israelites,
which she finds within. She identifies the tent psychologically with the
Gemüt, the temperament or mind, within which the passions and powers
of the soul are unified and within which the indwelling holy spirit
illuminates the human being.[8] In a more general sense, the human body
was also a "tent" for Hildegard, the temporary abode of the soul (Hildegardis, 1954). The "inner tent" is merely one of many Old and New
Testament images taken up by Tauler, and other mystics of the time, in
the service of interiorization.

---

[8]The use of the term Gemüt, and its Latin equivalent, synteresis, in the German religious
tradition, provides a prefiguration for the Gestalt principle in modern holistic psychology.
The Gemüt was a unifying principle both at the anthropological, strictly human level and in
the encounter with the divine, integrating the affective, cognitive, and conative powers of
the soul. Ozment (1969) has investigated the use of Gemüt by Tauler and also cites some
intriguing remarks, with an explicit holistic bent, from Luther.

Homecoming, Renewal, and the Foretaste of Eternity

We have lingered long enough with the preliminary phases of Tauler's mystical transformation, the phases in which all the mental, speculative, and iconic furniture of the Middle Ages was taken up as vehicle for concentrating the consciousness and behavior of the individual on religious objects. In the final phase, that of the "perfected man," the individual has firmly settled into his interior and enters into the "way of annihilation." All of the theological and symbolic forms which have so carefully been transported into the inner, mental domain are now to be abandoned.

Objectlessness, emptiness, nothingness, and absolute receptivity are the goals at this stage, uncluttered by word, concept, sacrament, or image.[9] The religious formulation of the goal, at this point, is a reunion with the eternal, undivided, and solitary Godhead which is devoid of all qualities, features, or names:

> everything there is so still, full of mystery and empty. There is nothing there but the pure Godhead. Nothing alien, no creature, no image, no form ever penetrated there. (Tauler, 1975, Chapter IV, p. 62)

The tendency of thought or reason to seek an object—a part which will stand out from the whole—must now be renounced. The renunciation of attachment to the profane world, and the renunciation of personal self, is now to be extended to include a renunciation of the religious paths and techniques themselves.

The first step here is a contemplation of one's own nothingness:

> In this case a dying, a becoming nothing, an annihilation must occur; there must take place an "I am nothing." (Tauler, 1975, Chapter X, p. 115)
>
> The true reduction of self sinks of its own accord into the divine inner abyss of God. (Tauler, 1975, Chapter X, p. 112)

Later, this passage through darkness and annihilation came to be known as the "dark night of the soul" (St. John of the Cross, 1959). The individual must suffer the ambiguity, the anxiety, and the loss of *not* striving to be something:

> Human nature becomes so constricted and oppressed, and the human being does not know where or what he is, because he feels such a singular anxiety

---

[9]Comparisons to Mahayana Buddhism, and especially to the Zen experience, are self-evident: "the mind of the Bodhisattva is like the void and everything is relinquished by it (Huang-Po, 1958, p. 49). A comparison closer to home can be found in Eckhart's remark: "I pray God that he may quit me of God, for my essential being is above God" (in Schürmann, 1973, p. 113).

> . . . you will not gladly withdraw and die away from what is yours. (Tauler, 1975, Chapter X, p. 121)

Next, there is a deeper renunciation of control over this process of mystical union. God will act; man need only hope. The individual's primary goal becomes one of *not* hindering the work of the divinity within one.

> On this step three things will hinder you, and you must dispense with them: the body of our Lord [i.e., the Eucharist], the word of God, and your chosen spiritual exercises. On this step every help for you signifies a hindrance. (Tauler, 1975, Chapter X, p. 121)[10]

The sacraments and other external aids, which were of such assistance as preparations, have no place in the pure interiority of this phase. Even the long cultivated images of Christian religious life have too much of the world and of self for this phase:

> Oh, no matter how noble and pure these earthly images are, they are all obstacles to that image without any form, which is God. . . . But those who cleanse the ground . . . and who set aside earthly images, so that the sun of God can pour its radiance forth therein, for them God's yoke tastes sweeter than honey. (Tauler, 1975, Chapter V, pp. 71–73)

By emptying his interior of human, worldly content, the individual, as it were, creates a spiritual vacuum which draws in the divine:

> There is no doubt that God *must* completely replenish it. The heavens open and fill the empty place. . . . Should you become completely empty, God doubtlessly comes completely in. It is neither more nor less—as much out, so much in. (Tauler, in Ozment, 1969, p. 32)

The abyss of the now empty inner ground of the human being calls out to the divine abyss. Like calls unto like, deep unto deep (again in these images there is a plaintive echo of the language of the homesick exile, from Psalm 42). Emptied of itself, the spirit will be led

> far beyond all of its powers into a solitary wilderness, of which no one can speak, into the concealed darkness of the good—which is without form or manner. There the spirit will be lead . . . into the unity of the simple, mannerless unity. (Tauler, 1975, Chapter IV, p. 63)

In this final step of interiorization, all of the densely layered themes of exile and return—the exile of the Israelites from their homeland, the exile

---

[10]Tauler's lengthy discussions on this point are beautifully concrete and psychological and remind me of the psychoanalytic maxim that tranquilizers used to still anxiety will impede true movement toward insight and change in therapy: "I would not give you the body of our Lord, unless your nature were too weak to carry this pressure without help. You could then go to the Lord's table once or twice in the week, not in order to become free of your anxiety, but rather in order better to carry it, and even then only under the condition, that this not allow your anxiety to disappear" (Tauler, 1975, Chapter X, pp. 122–123).

of the soul from its eternal origin, the exile of the Christian from his maker and from his inward ground—are fused in the one featureless submersion in the dark abyss. The world-time and world-space of Judeo-Christian history, the world-time and world-space of the monk or farmer living in medieval Christendom, collapse into the inward eternal time of the fulfilled moment, of divine bliss, of the "foretaste of eternity." The man who lived such moments of eternity (according to Tauler) was a transformed man, returned to the world with a true discrimination, borne of the unity: "The holy Church rests on these men, and were they not present in holy Christendom, it would not last a single hour" (Tauler, 1975, pp. 15–16).[11]

The Structure of the Mystical Transformation

At this point, I would like to draw together the preceding observations into a structural formulation. In the early phases of the mystical transformation, all outward objects—objects of the sensory world—are drained of their importance and emotional centrality for the individual. Both behavior and thought processes are reordered and reoriented to the primary objects of the religious world. The entire sacramental and scriptural repertoire of the medieval Church was drawn upon to serve as a kind of transitional object (Stevenson & Winnicott, 1954), to wean the individual from the profane world. This is probably a universal structure of religious consciousness: the derealization of the physical-sensory world and the erection of a virtual world, articulated along religious dimensions, which becomes a second order and uniquely human lived reality, permeating everyday life.

Next those religious objects and even the central themes of religious myth and history are themselves derealized in their outward form and internalized into the structure and rhythms of inward spiritual life. The Trinity as the theological scheme of the Macrocosm loses significance while the individual becomes ever more attentive to the trinitarian organization of his soul. The tent tabernacle of the Israelites in exile becomes the "inner tent," the dwelling place of the divinity in man. The virtual religious kingdom, established in the first phase, is transported into a much enlarged inner spiritual domain.

In the final phase, even those religious dimensions which have been transported into the interior are relinquished. All external aids become

---

[11]This is reminiscent of the Talmudic precept of the "lamed vavnik" quoted by Elie Wiesel: "The world . . . must not contain fewer than thirty-six just men who have been allowed to contemplate the Divine Presence. It is thanks to them that the world subsists (Wiesel, 1972, p. 264).

hindrances—the eucharist, the sacred words, or any other spiritual practices. As such, all are relinquished. The individual enters into the "way of
annihilation," renouncing all vestiges of personal self, all images which
have aided his inward movement, and all forms and names for the
Godhead. What remains is a radicalized interiority without any detecta-
ble content. This embrace of the emptied interior is the *unio mystica*, the
homecoming to the One, and the foretaste of eternity.

We may characterize this transformation in its totality as *interiorization*. The explicit Christian forms here constitute mere vehicles and preparations. The Christian space–time established so arduously in the early
phases, the daily inward ritual reiteration of the history and the structure
of the Christian cosmos, are dissolved in the final inward, emptying
movement.

Conclusion

The original theme of Husserl's phenomenology was transcendental, impersonal consciousness, its internal temporal lawfulness, and the
purely subjective processes involved in constituting the intentional object
(Husserl, 1962). Many of the resistances to phenomenology in psychology are based on this original philosophical idealism. However,
phenomenology, like behaviorism and psychoanalysis, has grown
beyond its original presuppositions. Without merging with psychoanalysis or behaviorism, it has nevertheless itself become more attuned to
both the unconscious and the behavioral. *Hermeneutic phenomenology* is
especially sensitive to the cultural background of consciousness: the
interpenetration of language, symbol, concept, and the everyday forms
of life (see Hougaard, 1978).

The present chapter is a case study in the use of hermeneutic
phenomonology to elucidate the structure of the mystical transformation,
as exemplified in Johannes Tauler's mysticism. As such, it is concerned
with depicting the religious world inhabited by the believer and the
restructuration undergone by that world in the course of the believer's
cultivation of the mystical life. Analogies can be made, extending the
principles of the present investigation to the study of altered states,
spiritual disciplines, as well as the normal constitution of everyday reality.

More generally, however, I hope the reader will obtain from the
foregoing discussion a more radically historical and cultural vision of
man's inner and outer reality.[12] In the time of Tauler, outer reality was

[12]Perhaps the best introduction to the cultural and historical viewpoint within psychology is
a work by the Dutch phenomenologist J. H. van den Berg (1961).

perceived as a religious universe structured hierarchically along lines straight out of the *Summa Theologica;* the psyche, in Tauler's descriptions, mirrored that universe. In the time of Helmholtz and Freud, principles of energy and dynamics emerging in the natural sciences appeared to provide very adequate frameworks for understanding the psychic life as well. Furthermore, external social institutions, such as political repression and the censor—a ubiquitous fixture in Vienna at that time— reappeared as psychic structures in Freudian theory (Moss, 1974). Finally, in our own time, we observe the simultaneous emergence into popularity of Pribram's holographic theory of neurocognitive processes[13] and Bohm's holocosmic theory of outer reality.[14] Man's immediate psychic life *becomes*—that is, does not merely appear—structured along the lines of the cultural world he inhabits. In phenomenological language, the macrocosm and the microcosm are co-constitutive of one another. The object-world evolves just as much as does the psychic life.

William James, whose work remains the foundation stone for the psychology of religious consciousness, wrote that "To understand a thing rightly we need to see it both out of its environment and in it" (1961, p. 36). The habit of contemporary psychology is to extricate the mystical consciousness from its natural habitat, to portray its general psychic and attitudinal aspects as well as its neurophysiologic correlates in depressed respiration and heart rate, altered wave-form and frequency of cortical activity, and differential hemispheric functions, regardless of religious environment. Phenomenology, in contrast, explicitly analyzes the altered relations to the religious object in the natural environment of a religious world. Phenomenology thus serves the same corrective function for the psychology of consciousness that ethology plays for the experimental psychology of animal behavior.

References

Ancelet-Hustache, J. *Meister Eckhart and the Rhineland mystics.* New York: Harper Torchbooks, 1958.

Bühler, C. *Der menschliche Lebenslauf als psychologisches Problem. Psychologische Monographien,* IV. Leipzig, 1933.

Chesterton, G. K. *Orthodoxy,* New York: Image Books, 1959.

Clark, J. M. *The great German mystics.* Oxford: Blackwell, 1949.

Coulter, J. A. *The literary microcosm: Theories of interpretation of the later neo-Platonists.* Leiden: E. J. Brill, 1976.

Filthaut, E. (Ed.). *Johannes Tauler: Ein Deutscher Mystiker.* Essen: Hans Driewer Verlag, 1961.

[13]See Pribram, Chapter 6.—Eds.
[14]See Weber, Chapter 5.—Eds.

Gadamer, H. *Wahrheit und Methode: Grundzüge einer philosophischen Hermeneutic.* Tübingen: J. C. B. Mohr, 1965.

Hildegardis. *Wisse die Wege: Scivias.* Salzburg: Otto Müller Verlag, 1954.

Hougaard, E. Some reflections on the relationship between psychoanalysis and Husserlian phenomenology. *Journal of Phenomenological Psychology,* 1978, 9(1&2), 1–83.

Huang-Po. *The Zen teachings of Huang-Po: On the transmission of mind.* New York: Grove Press, 1958.

Husserl, E. *Ideas: General introduction to pure phenomenology.* New York: Collier, 1962.

Husserl, E. *The crisis of European sciences and transcendental phenomenology.* Evanston, Ill.: Northwestern University Press, 1970.

Ihde, D. *Hermeneutic phenomenology: The philosophy of Paul Ricoeur.* Evanston, Ill.: Northwestern University Press, 1971.

James, W. *The varieties of religious experience.* London: Collier-McMillan, 1961.

Jonas, H. *The gnostic religion.* Boston: Beacon, 1963.

Jonas, H. *Philosophical essays.* Englewood Cliffs, N.J.: Prentice-Hall, 1974.

Jung, C. G. The stages of life. In *Modern man in search of a soul.* New York: Harcourt, Brace, and World, 1933.

Jung, C. G. Vom Werden der Persönlichkeit. In *Wirklichkeit der Seele.* Zürich, 1934.

Katz, S. T. (Ed). *Mysticism and philosophical analysis.* New York: Oxford University Press, 1978.

Klostermaier, K. From phenomenology to metascience: Reflections on the study of religions. *Sciences Religieuses,* 1976, 6(5), 551–564.

Levin, D. M. *Sensuous Thinking: Heidegger's Approach to Language.* Paper presented at the meeting of the Society for Phenomenology and Existential Philosophy, New York, New York, November, 1977.(a)

Levin, D. M. Freud's divided heart and Saraha's cure. *Inquiry,* 1977, 20(2 & 3), 165–188. (b)

Levin, D. M. Painful time, ecstatic time. *The Eastern Buddhist,* 1978, 11(2), 74–112.

Marcel, G. *Creative fidelity.* New York: Farrar, Straus, & Giroux, 1964.

Merleau-Ponty, M. *Phenomenology of perception.* London: Routledge & Kegan Paul, 1962.

Merleau-Ponty, M. *The visible and the invisible.* Evanston, Ill.: Northwestern University Press, 1968.

Mieth, D. *Die Einheit von vita activa and vita contemplativa in den Deutschen Predigten und Traktaten Meister Eckharts und bei Johannes Tauler: Untersuchungen zur Struktur des Christlichen Lebens.* Regensburg: F. Pustet, 1969.

Moss, D. M. *Man's body and the body politic.* Paper presented at the American Humanistic Psychology Association Convention, New Orleans, September, 1974.

Moss, D. M. Brain, body, and world: Perspectives on body image. In R. S. Valle & M. King (Eds.), *Existential-phenomenological alternatives for psychology.* New York: Oxford University Press, 1978.

Moss, D., & Keen, E. *The Nature of Consciousness: I. The Phenomenological Approach.* Paper presented at the American Psychological Association Convention, Toronto, August, 1978.

O'Brien, E. (Ed.). *The essential Plotinus.* New York: Mentor, 1964.

Ozment, S. *Homo Spiritualis: A comparative study of the anthropology of Tauler, Gerson, and Luther in the context of their theological thought.* Leiden: E. J. Brill, 1969.

Pannikar, R. *The trinity and world religions.* Madras: Christian Literature Society, 1970.

Plotinus. *The six enneads.* In R. M. Hutchins & M. Adler (Eds.), *Great Books of the Western World,* (Vol. 17). Chicago: William Benton, 1952.

Ricoeur, P. *Freud and philosophy.* New Haven: Yale University Press, 1970.

Ricoeur, P. *The conflict of interpretations.* Evanston, Ill.: Northwestern University Press, 1974.

Ricoeur, P. Philosophical hermeneutics and theological hermeneutics. *Sciences Religieuses,* 1975, 5 (1), 14–33.

St. John of the Cross. *Dark night of the soul.* Garden City, N.Y.: Image Books, 1959.

Scholem, G. *On the Kabbala and its symbolism.* New York: Schocken, 1965.

Schürmann, R. Heidegger and Meister Eckhart on releasement. *Research in Phenomenology,* 1973, *3,* 95–119.

Staal, F. *Exploring mysticism. A methodological essay.* Berkeley: University of California Press, 1975.

Stevenson, O., & Winnicott, D. W. The first treasured possession. *Psychoanalytic Study of the Child,* 1954, *9,* 199–217.

Stover, D. Linguisticality and theology: Applying the hermeneutics of Hans-Georg Gadamer. *Sciences Religieuses,* 1975, *5*(1), 34–44.

Tauler, J. *Der Meister in Dir.* Freiburg im Breisgau: Herder Verlag, 1975.

van den Berg, J. H. *The changing nature of man: Introduction to an historical psychology.* New York: Norton, 1961.

Vetter, A. Die Lebenswende als Reifungskrisis. *Jahrbuch für Psychologie und Psychotherapie,* 1958, *6,* 153–166.

Weilner, I. Tauler und das Problem der Lebenswende. In E. Filthaut (Ed.), *Johannes Tauler: Ein Deutscher Mystiker.* Essen: Hans Driewer Verlag, 1961.

Wentzlaff-Eggebert, F. W. *Deutsche Mystik zwischen Mittelalter und Neuzeit.* Berlin: Walter de Gruyter, 1944.

Wiesel, E. *Souls on fire: Portraits and legends of Hasidic masters.* New York: Random House: 1972.

Wrede, G. *Unio Mystica: Probleme der Erfahrung bei Johannes Tauler.* Uppsala Universitat, Stockholm: Almquist and Wiksell International, 1974.

VI

Literary Modes

These three chapters explore the literary metaphors that have been used to describe human experience and that provide insight into the nature of consciousness. Elsa von Eckartsberg presents the four stages of God-consciousness as revealed in the tradition of the visionary poets. Valerie Valle and Elizabeth Kruger draw on the writings of Anaïs Nin to exemplify the nature of feminine consciousness. David Leavitt's chapter then examines the genre of science fiction as a laboratory of ideas about human awareness and artificial intelligence.

18

God-Consciousness and the "Poetry of Madness"

Elsa von Eckartsberg

> *Such then is the tale . . . of the achievements wrought by madness that comes from the gods.*
>
> —PLATO (1964)

The question "What is god-consciousness?" and how it has manifested itself in the great visionary writers, from most ancient times to the present as the "poetry of madness" (Plato), will be answered in this essay from the double-perspective of the poet and the literary historian. That is, I shall write from my own experience of god-consciousness as it became transformed into the words of my poetry, and I shall try to describe simultaneously how other poets and thinkers before me have experienced and expressed this highest state of consciousness when man feels he has become one with the gods, when he is *en-theos*, enthused, enthusiastic, and the gods speak through him.

Much misunderstanding and many false taboos surround, in the West,[1] even the mentioning of the fact that man can and should reach a state in which he is possessed by god-consciousness or the "theia mania" Plato (1964) speaks of—a form of high passion—which has nothing to do with madness as an illness in the clinical sense then called "nosos" (in *Phaedrus*). With this essay I hope to disperse the countless fears that have accumulated in the human mind throughout the ages concerning this topic. My thesis is that god-consciousness can indeed be raised into human awareness. It can be absorbed and appropriated by man without plunging him into the gravest dangers variously described as hubris,

---

[1]This is quite different in the East, especially in yogic traditions; see Eliade (1971, pp. 88 ff.).

Elsa von Eckartsberg ● Department of German, University of Pittsburgh, Pittsburgh, Pennsylvania 15213.

superbia, or, in more recent times, "inflation of consciousness" (Jung), producing hopeless grandiosities, psychoses, or "will-to-power" drives so strong that, beyond control, they will destroy him—and others— as only too many instances of our recent political past seem to prove.

God-consciousness, if rightly understood and appropriated by man, is seen here as the most beneficial and constructive state of consciousness, leading man toward the next phase in his evolution, called here *"Homo futurus,"* or rather "Optimal Man,"[2] who is a far cry from anything that produced the Promethean/Faustian/Nietzschean "superman" as he was envisioned and more or less destructively lived during the last 200 years. I have described elsewhere (von Eckartsberg, 1978a) how much this type of ruthless "will-to-power-man," thinking himself god, has done to discredit god-consciousness to the point where we now, in an age of overt mental "deflation," seem to prefer our inferiority complexes over any form of magnificent obsession, high aspirations, or "lofty moods" (Nietzsche), not to speak of "divine inspiration" or the "god-intoxication" Plato, in *Phaedrus,* extolled as the greatest event that can ever happen to mortal man. No longer believing in "heaven-sent madness," we have become deadly afraid of falling into the abyss of our man-made insanity, our schizophrenic ego-inflations.

At present it is no longer our libido but "our potential godlikeness" (Roszak, 1975) that is "most significantly and even pathologically unconscious and repressed." But the neglected and buried god-within does not tolerate the proclamations that he is dead and nonexistent. He demands most powerfully to be set free from our unconscious depths in which he merely hides waiting to be reactivated. Repressed, god-consciousness can become our most severe sickness. Set free and rediscovered (Hillman, 1975), it can become a *summum bonum* for man, granting and promoting highest achievements, as Plato once saw it in his *Phaedrus* and as the writings of other great poets considered here from Sappho to Dante, Hölderlin, Rilke, Rimbaud, and Whitman—to name only a few—can prove also only too well.

> But if any man come to the gates of poetry
> without the madness of the Muses persuaded
> that skill alone will make him a good poet,
> then shall he and his works of sanity with
> him be brought to nought by the poetry of
> madness, and behold, their place is nowhere
> to be found.
>
> —PLATO (1964)

Let us now turn toward poetry, particularly that poetry that has sprung from god-consciousness. How is it produced and what are its

[2]See the first stanza of my poem "Optimal Man" at the end of this chapter.

characteristics? In Plato's eyes, it is the only poetry worth considering. According to modern views, it is the most underrated, unpopular, neglected, and misunderstood. "Visionary" or "mystical" poetry is almost synonymous today with cloudy, contourless Romanticism, senseless wallowing in vagueness of feelings too far out to be shared by all; reliance on "inspiration," whereas the poem should be "made" in "man-made sanity" and "skillful" artisanship to be nothing more or less than as exact a mirror of reality as possible. Endless repetition of the already known is preferred to the new and utterly surprising contents and forms that might overwhelmingly appear out of the *unknown*—which is perceived merely as threat and certainly no longer as that *fascinandum* that it once was for all poets and thinkers who dared to follow their vision unconditionally into primal landscapes of experience never set foot in before.

Thus we have the age-old clash of world views: Plato versus Aristotle, and divine inspiration versus the products of man's reasoning and crafty skills. But, strangely enough, the "poetry of madness" has never stopped existing. It arose at the beginning of time in the shamanistic seance or chanted to the rhythm of liturgical-ecstatic dancing, and it will be with us to the end of times, resurfacing in each age, however repressive that age may be toward this form of self-expression. And it has been reawakened, during the last two decades, by powerful agents—at least so it came about in my own case—the agents of the so-called psychedelic substances, now as in most ancient times the most radical and uncompromising "transhumanizers" known to man.

The gods speak in and of themselves only rarely to man. They can even be proclaimed as "absent" or "dead" for certain periods of time (Hölderlin), or forever (Nietzsche). It has also been shown convincingly in a recent phenomenological study of the various forms and contents of mental illness (Van Dusen, 1974) that the "higher-order voices"—of gods and spirits—which patients "hear" are rarer than those of the "lower order"—of demons and devils.

It might be an astonishing fact to consider that perhaps the god-voices are most potently present or encoded in the flesh of certain "sacred mushrooms" and cacti, or in the seedpods of certain flowers or in herbs "granting immortality"—deeply embedded in nature to be unearthed by man only when the time is ready and ripe for such revelation. Hölderlin predicted the "return of the gods" for a "distant future." One of my own poems proclaims that future to be now (von Eckartsberg, 1978b).[3] At the

---

[3]Full text of the poem: The time has come once more / in which BEING / exceeds / any fantasy / of what could be: Kairos—fullness of times / time / when the gods / reappear the immemorial ones / buried / and forgotten / under the dust / of countless careless / ages—/ yet / suddenly HERE once more / in utter radiance / shining: / lightning-storm of electricity of life / unleashed / fabulous dimensions / unheard-of delights / visible once more / tangible / embodied: HERE—/ and a new age begins / wholly new horizons / a parallel-world / of light and rainbows / and . . . peace.

zenith of the "age of reason"—in an act of cosmic balancing—the nadir of the splendors of the irrational has to reemerge as of necessity. And the task for future or already present poets and thinkers will be to integrate both hemispheres of the mind into the wholeness of a world which alone will satisfy all of man's deepest desires and drives for perfection, completion, and the highest states of consciousness attainable by man.

Boldly one could maintain that psychedelic substances "preserve" the voices of the gods—more powerfully than any other substance within nature—throughout the ages. They are, so to speak, the "memory-banks" of god-consciousness, reactivating deeply buried memories within the brain. God-consciousness can never become lost completely as long as they still exist on earth, the most vulnerable, most elusive, and most easily destroyed "sacraments," in which, paradoxically, the presence of the gods seems to be guaranteed for all times.

Some of my poetry and prose (von Eckartsberg, 1968, 1972, 1974, 1979a) was written during and immediately after the absorption of various psychedelic substances taken for the sake of psychological experimentation in the early sixties at Harvard. The realms into which my mind found itself repeatedly propelled have been variously described and named by other investigators, such as Leary (1977), as "post-terrestrial,"[4] by Bucke (1970), as "cosmic consciousness," by Grof (1976) as "suprahuman," by C. G. Jung (1970–1976) as an "archetypal, transpersonal dimension," by Hillman (1975) as the "polytheistic" realm of the psyche, and finally by Roberto Assagioli (1965) as the "superconscious."

Grof (1976) and Assagioli (1965) go furthest in describing this most "far-off" realm of the psyche—called here "god-consciousness"—in concrete and experiential terms. But Assagioli went even further than this. To my knowledge, he is the only psychologist who not only describes and prescribes but guides the aspirant by way of fully developed "principles and techniques" step by step toward reaching self-realization and the superconscious. Originally a disciple of Freud, Assagioli rigorously transcended depth-psychology, considering it to be a too limited and, therefore, inaccurate expression of the human psychic totality in its preoccupation with what he calls the "lower" unconscious (sex, aggression, death-wish, etc.). By contrast, he emphasized and explored the "higher" unconscious—a neglected yet easily evoked potential of spiritual energies, genius, and the states of illumination and ecstasy.

Teaching psychosynthesis over many years has helped me to finally understand and interpret the cryptic messages of my poetry in terms of "god-consciousness." Only now am I able to distinguish and talk about four distinct phases or categories of god-consciousness as expressed in

---

[4]See Leary, Chapter 9, for selections reprinted from his *Exo-Psychology*.—Eds.

my own poetry and in the writings of other visionary poets from the anonymous creators of the ancient Egyptian *Pyramid Texts* (1969) of 2400 B.C. to Baudelaire and the present.

But before I can set out on the almost impossible task of trying to analyze and categorize the ineffable, I have to add and admit that there were and are a number of other ways to reach a state of god-consciousness. Consider the following outline of some of the more outstanding possibilities: In Egypt, the pharaoh could become transfigured into the god only upon death. Elaborate rituals and magical incantations were needed and employed to perform the transubstantiation of which the *Pyramid Texts* are the best testimonial. In the Sumerian or Babylonian *Gilgamesh* epic (1934) we find the first traces of a most laborious "quest" or "odyssey" of the hero who has to undergo one ordeal after another in order to find the immortality of the gods for which he searches so desperately and ultimately in vain. Eastern sacred texts tell us about various forms of sacrifice, ritual, and meditation exercises which have the power to lead the adept toward his goal, the unification with Brahman or the attainment of god-consciousness. Eliade (1971) mentions two methods the yogi has available: the "artificial" approach of meditation and the "natural" approach of "simply desiring" the "undifferentiated enstasis" of the final liberation within god-consciousness. But with all the techniques available we must not underrate the influence and power a "divine or divinized woman" can exert: for Socrates it was Diotima who guided him into the highest mysteries and knowledge. But already in the ancient Egyptian *Pyramid Texts* we find a female deity, Nut, the sky-goddess, who plays a primal role in transporting the dead king toward the realms of the gods or, more literally, grants him rebirth (from her own body) as a now divinized being. This vision that woman alone is able to lead man to the highest Empyrean realms culminates in Dante's works and, generally, in the Christian middle ages. Centuries later it was the great German poet Hölderlin who found god-consciousness embodied once more in a woman, his idolized friend, also called Diotima. On the other hand, he was one of the first to rediscover the wine god Dionysos, years before Nietzsche, who "in the joy of wine" brings the "trace of the fugitive gods down to the godless in the dark" of the "world-night." It is Baudelaire (1971) and later Herman Hesse (1972) who praise the divinizing powers of wine in similar ways, although both are aware of the even greater powers of other stimulants as, for example, hashish to lead the poet into his *"paradis artificiel."*

And so the question finally arises: Why has the acquisition of god-consciousness, throughout the ages, held such a fascination for man that he would endure the hardest and most cruel ordeals, even risk his life and sanity, to attain it? What is this god-consciousness like for which man has been searching, often so desperately that he did not hesitate to harness all possible forms of "black magic," even satanic powers—as in the case of Goethe's (1963) *Faust*, in order to reach it, and, as Rimbaud attests, will never give up searching for, even if he should "collapse" on the way and be utterly defeated by this, man's greatest quest?

To say it more simply, using Jungian terminology, god-consciousness starts at the end of the human "individuation-process." It gives its bearer the certain feeling that he is in the possession of (a) "omnipotence," (b) boundless "metamorphosis-power," (c) "omniscience," (d) "omnipresence"—of which he has, by approximation, at least a glimpse. No wonder then that man tried to attain the *quaternio* of such vast powers from most ancient times on when these powers seem to have been more directly revealed and available to him than in later ages. In one of the earliest texts of recorded history, the *Pyramid Texts*, we find all four forms of god-consciousness, as described here, fully developed—the highest vision right at the beginning of time, then gradually lost, fading away, rather than a steady evolution toward the highest as might be expected.

I list once more the four phases or categories of god-consciousness (naming each—for the purpose of easier recognition—with the name of one of the ancient Greek tutelary deities who influenced most of the poets discussed here in various subtle ways):

1. *Zeus/Prometheus*—limitless, creative energy of all forms; instant actualization; integration of all one's possibilities
2. *Dionysos*—periodic ecstatic self-annihilation; disintegration/ rebirth
3. *Apollo/Orpheus*—permanence; immortal being in bliss-awareness
4. *Hermes/Mercury*—unhindered "flight" through unlimited time/ space

In the text that follows, I shall try to illustrate the meaning of these four phases of god-consciousness by citing examples of the "poetry of madness" from all ages, as it applies.

> *. . . and hence it is that without danger now*
> *the sons of Earth drink heavenly fire.*
> —HÖLDERLIN (in Forster, 1961)

Zeus/Prometheus

The moment man has reached the first phase of god-consciousness, characterized by an instant upsurge of "limitless creative energy," he becomes at first intoxicated with the realization that he has overcome the human condition of being a creature rather than a creator himself. As one of my own poems expresses this truly astonishing realization:

the night / finally came / when i arose / and solemnly / stepped out of creation / no longer / to be created / but / to be / but / to create . . .
(von Eckartsberg, 1978b, p. 3)

After this initial rapture of feeling the "infinite delight" of energy, able to create worlds of its own making, man—or rather the poet—has two possibilities for further evolution within this phase before him: (a) to get carried away—in Promethean grandiosity and eventual self-destruction—by this realization of his infinite creative potential or (b) to use that new-found energy constructively to create the same state of god-intoxication in other human beings—the *Phaedrus* solution.

The best examples of a Promethean ego-inflation at this stage of god-conscious evolution—and its subsequent collapse—can be found in Goethe's, Hölderlin's, Rimbaud's, and Nietzsche's poetry and thinking. To cite only a few of the poems best illustrating this very volatile state of consciousness, I point first to Goethe's (in Forster, 1961) famous "storm and stress" hymn, entitled characteristically "Prometheus." Its last stanza reads:

. . . Here I sit, make men / in my image, / a race which shall be like me, / to suffer, to weep, / to enjoy and be glad, / and to ignore you, / as I do! / (p. 203)

Goethe's (1963) *Faust* becomes, years later, the fullest expression of this Promethean "will-to-power" drive that, set as an absolute, isolated from and unbalanced by the other modes of god-consciousness, brings along its own demise and the destruction of others. I only have to point to Faust's well-known demonic evocation of the "spirit of the Macrocosm" and the "Earth-spirit" in the first part of the tragedy. In an upsurge of unbounded power, he feels himself to have "stripped off the mortal man," to be co-creative with that spirit "that holds the universe together," to have become one with the gods . . . but he cannot sustain the vision, it is too overextended: "one word of thunder" sweeps him from his height.

Faust demonstrated that man, using occult powers to serve him, is able to attract god-consciousness if he so desires but that it is quite another thing to be also able to maintain that high estate and avoid being either carried away or crushed by it.

After Goethe's *Faust*, it is Nietzsche's (1964) *Zarathustra* (and Nietzsche himself) and the great French Symbolist poet Arthur Rimbaud who were most violently swept away by this form of Promethean god-consciousness only to feel annihilated by it in the end. Since Nietzsche's grandiosity-frenzy is rather well known, I shall try to describe Rimbaud's in more detail.

His theories of poetry as the "poetry of madness"—in the purest Platonic sense—have often been discussed. A brief recalling of some of his theses may, therefore, suffice here. In order to be truly considered "author, creator"—and not merely "civil servant, writer," (Rimbaud, 1966), the poet has to be or to make himself a "seer"—"*voyant*"—or "supreme sage" by a long, gigantic, and deliberate "derangement of all his senses." He has to exhaust all forms of love, suffering, and madness, and, with superhuman strength, suffering unspeakable tortures, he has to reach the "unknown," leaping through "unheard-of and unnamable things" even if he should, bewildered, lose the "intelligence of his vision," even if he should die. "Other horrible workers will come . . . and begin from the horizons" where he collapsed.

Rimbaud's poetry is the precise and almost immediate outcome of this thesis and his subsequent experimentation with his own psyche under those terms of a "superhuman" creativity. Rimbaud is nowadays called the "Father of Surrealism." He therefore succeeded. He started a whole new trend in poetry and thinking, opening up the vast realms of the unconscious years before Freud. Yet at what price—this "tour de force" of Promethean creativity under the pressures of his *Season in Hell.*

This prose-poem—*A Season in Hell*—comprises the at once most powerful and most "deflated" description of that god-consciousness of boundless creativity that carries within itself the seed of its own destruction. Here Rimbaud (1966) describes both aspects succinctly, condensing the whole drama of grandiose elevation and collapse on the last two pages of the work in the following words: "I have tried to invent new flowers, new stars, new flesh, new tongues. I believed I had acquired supernatural powers. Well: . . ." (p. 207), and "I who called myself magus or angel, exempt from all morality, I am thrown back to the earth . . . no hymns . . . hard night . . . the dried blood smokes on my face . . ." (p. 209). Rimbaud fought the "spiritual battle," the battle for a complete "transformation of all life" in terms of creative god-consciousness. And he found it as "brutal as a battle of men." He triumphed—and he lost; he lost "the intelligence of his vision," as he himself had predicted; but, even though destroyed by the "lightning" of his own grandiosity which led him to the brink of insanity, he gave birth to some of the highest poetry of "Illumination" yet created by man. One of his last prose-poems entitled "Genie" has yet to be recognized as a full, radiant, and constructive realization of god-consciousness no longer suffering from grandiosity and self-destructive violence of perception. "Genie" transcends the Promethean drive through a primally re-thought and "re-invented" love of other beings not yet as infinite as the poet himself. And this love is, precisely, the way out of the Promethean impasse. Plato (1964), in his *Phaedrus*, called this form of nondestructive, creative, and "divine" love: "Pteros"—named so, as an offspring of "Eros," by "the gods themselves." It is a love that causes "wings" to grow in the beloved, who thereby becomes transfigured into the image of the winged gods Plato talks about. To create in other beings a state of god-consciousness is the best antidote to the ever-present Promethean temptation at this stage of evolution. One of my own poems—in which I identify with the "winged" ancient Mesopotamian goddess of love, Ishtar (see von Eckartsberg, 1979b)—describes this possibility in the following words:

> . . . just a local goddess / of no global fame . . . / just known to some friends / as friend / and to some angels passing through—as guests / . . . touching a dead one here / or one dying / or one sick of mind / or of heart / : creating LIFE / edenlike gardens / just for her families / just for her sons: / a local goddess / no global fame / but *one* dead one arising / *one* stone melting / *one* mute one suddenly speaking in tongues / and children free dancing / flying / may outweigh / whole societies figures numbers / may be a beginning / of a wholly new world . . . // (von Eckartsberg, 1974, p. 73)

Sappho and Pindar were the greatest of those poets who divinize the other. What greater thing is there than "to see each other divine" . . . and to free the highest potential, in "essence-orgasm," from the depth of the other—"Chaos raised to the power of poetry" by such love.

> *Wolle die Wandlung. O sei für die Flamme begeistert . . .*
> —RILKE (1966)

Dionysos

What I have termed the second phase of god-consciousness—characterized by "periodic ecstatic self-annihilation and the subsequent experience of rebirth"—is, paradoxically, another way to sustain god-consciousness at a high level and at all times. Perfection kills. Even common sense knows about this. In order to remain open to further growth, then, man—or the poet—has to step out of his perfection, in ec-stasis, every so often to renew himself, as the Phoenix, by voluntary self-annihilation, hoping for rebirth. This is an absolute necessity amounting to a law (in the realm of a new "psychology of gods") to which many of the greatest thinkers, mystics, and poets of all times unequivocally attest. Let me quote here Lao Tsu and Rilke as those poet-sages who were most adamant regarding this point. Lao Tsu (1972) says it most simply and succinctly in his *Tao Te Ching:* "Temper your sharpness . . . mask your brightness. Be at one with the dust of the earth" (p. 56). To keep humble, to be the "valley of the universe," to "return to the state of the uncarved block" is for him to remain in the "highest state" man can attain on this earth. Ever renewed disintegration of even one's highest self, "primal union" with the elements, this alone guarantees the unimpeded flow of the Tao of the universe.

Humbleness makes one invisible, insubstantial, so to speak; grandiosity, by comparison, is like a rock obstructing the free-flowing "stream of the universe." Rilke, centuries later, perceives this in very similar ways. In his *Sonnets to Orpheus* (1966) he admonishes the poet who tries to follow in the footsteps of his divine master, Orpheus, never to "shut himself in abiding," for that will make him "hard" and brittle and provoke "the hammer" (of fate). It is much better "to pour himself out as a spring" and to "will transformation" as a flame which is the essence of incessant change and ever-renewed power. This insight culminates in Nietzsche's famous *Ecce Homo* poem. Its climactic line, "unsated like the flame I glow and consume myself," expresses most succinctly the feeling of the poet-thinker in this second phase of god-consciousness.

Images of "ecstatic disintegration" to "ashes," "dust," even "atoms" are central to my own poetry. They are born from rapture and not from a decadent whim of self-negation. They are born from the desire to remain open because there is nothing so dreadful as to become static, stagnant, frozen, dead within a rigid form of immortality which Nietzsche, once more with the briefest formulation, quite untranslatably circumscribes as *"Tot vor Unsterblichkeit!"*

Here is my most radical poem to illustrate this second or Dionysian-phase of god-consciousness:

> . . . to bathe / in madness / raging foaming / annointed / with the primordial / fluid of fires / ineffable / relief / to let burn / what wants to be burned: let it crack explode break up / break open / let the flame / lick / your rigidified mind / to melt run liquefy fuse / with the flux / divine: heavenly process— / even to fall / to ashes / and to give / creative / forces . . . another chance. // (von Eckartsberg, 1978b, p. 2)

In prose I said it even more poetically. I shall bring here only a short excerpt of the whole prose-poem that can be found in Ralph Metzner's (1968) book of compilations of the psychedelic "ecstatic adventure." But perhaps I should, rather, quote Allen Ginsberg, the most popular American to indulge in writing the "poetry of madness"? All visionary poets merge into one in this second phase of god-consciousness, it no longer matters exactly who speaks at a certain fleeting moment. Ginsberg phrases it this way: "An hour, realizing the possible change in consciousness / that the soul is independent of the body and its death / and that the soul is not Me, it is the wholly other 'whisper of consciousness' from

Above, Beyond, Afuera—/ . . . and I have been man too long . . . /" (see Metzner, 1968, pp. 135–36).

I have been man too long. And now: I have been god too long. You have to experience both. Periodically let go of both illusions: be "devoured" with all your universes. "Twisting back / beyond mind /" (Leary, in Metzner, 1968, p. 139).

In the same book, I put it this way:

> I feel I break free . . . my human sculptured marble-body melts away . . . enraptured I feel I am being burned to the marrow of my bones . . . burned free . . . flame myself, purified-purifying, consummated by water, air, light all around me, calling me back to be WAVE again . . . WATERWAVE LIGHTWAVE LIGHT . . . ever more rapidly and unhindered . . . I follow everything that draws me wavelike into the open . . . (Metzner, 1968, p. 222)

Temporary annihilation of oneself can also be brought about through love so powerful that it is another form of death. This love/death/rebirth experience has been most cryptically and hauntingly immortalized by Goethe's famous poem "Selige Sehnsucht" (in English, "Trance and Transformation"). In this poem, Goethe praises those living beings who "long to die in flames" precisely at the height of those "nights of love" when suddenly a strange "new desire" sweeps the lovers upward "to more exalted mating." And, reaching out from the "overshadowing darkness," enchanted as the moth with light, in the end they find themselves burnt, consumed, yet . . . in a bliss-state, the great unspeakable bliss that death and transformation can hold more deeply than a merely satiated love.

Without having been—unconsciously and for many years—possessed by the dark haunting rhythms and the enigmatic aura this Goethe poem radiates, I would most likely never have written my own version of this most profound and almost overwhelming experience:

> . . . death / from your lips / i would gladly drink / to sink / under the blow of your hand / would speed my flight / to its ultimate height / would send me to rapturous spheres / my life's breath finally spent. / death from your lips / i would gladly drink / to sink / to die / while you / are the sky / and i / the dust, the dust . . . / blowing by. . . ./ (von Eckartsberg, 1974, p. 87)

Ecstatic annihilation marks this phase. But also just ecstasy, sheer Dionysian overflow—"seeking eternity—deep, deep eternity" as Nietzsche also exclaimed rhapsodically in his "Drunken Song" (in *Zarathustra*).

To summarize: The first two phases constitute, so to speak, systole and diastole of god-consciousness, or the cosmic rhythm guaranteeing, if adhered to, its continued existence—in man as well as in the whole universe.

C'est le bonheur absolu . . .
—BAUDELAIRE (1971)

Apollo/Orpheus

The third phase of god-consciousness is characterized by an immense calm state of radiant self-contained being-bliss. In this "Apollo-
nian" phase, the mind has become empty: a "drop of empty space." It is
thus a state of sublime inner purity, deep trance and distance to all former
obsessions with becoming, creating, annihilation. Man, at this stage,
rests in exuberance—and calmness: "Beatitude calm et immobile"—as
Baudelaire said, who, among poets, has perhaps most deeply experienced and most perceptively described this state. Calm exuberance.
Self-contained ecstasy. Perhaps we should call this paradox which can no
longer be logically thought, "instasy." It has also been called "nirvana,"
"satori," "samadhi," "the thousand-petaled lotus"-state, or "kief" in the
Near East.

It is a state beyond desiring or the "lower regions of *having*," it is a
state of pure *being*, contemplation, and inner communion with the universe. At this point the pharaoh's "bones" have become "crystal," and
"his flesh is like the imperishable stars." His condition is now one of
infinite happiness, for his spirit is among "his brothers the gods." "How
changed it is, how changed it is" is a further exclamation of the text
(*Pyramid Texts*, 1969, p. 53).

The *Upanishads* (1961) describe this sublime state of consciousness as
being "beyond time, when Sat, Cit, and Ananda, Being, Consciousness,
and Bliss are one." The ancient writers of this sacred text call god-
consciousness in man "the Self."[5] And in the Katha Upanishad we find
these astonishing lines:

> Smaller than the smallest, greater than the greatest, this Self forever dwells
> within the hearts of all. When a man is free from desire, his mind and senses
> purified, he beholds the glory of the Self and is without sorrow. Though
> seated, he travels far; though at rest, he moves all things. (p. 18)

It is further said in this text that only those who are in bliss and
beyond bliss can reach this state of "effulgent being" symbolized by the
sacred syllable OM "which is the imperishable Brahman," the "supreme
good."

This "bliss"-aspect of the third phase of god-consciousness is
brought out as beautifully in the famous "Ten Bulls" Zen poetry (and

[5]Regarding the self–Self distinction, see R. von Eckartsberg, Chapter 2 ("Swami Rama's
Yoga Psychology"), Marlan's, Chapter 11, discussion of ego- (self)- transcendence, and
Schore, Chapter 22.—Eds.

prose) by the Chinese Master Kakuan (1961) who lived during the twelfth century. After the pilgrim, searching for enlightenment, has reached the *Source* and is now able, "poised in silence" and in "blissful repose," to serenely observe the "forms of integration and disintegration" and is no longer attached to any one of these, he finds himself in a state of pure being-contemplation, for the first time seeing the world as it is—in its own pure state of being (uncontaminated by human interference and projections): "The water *is* emerald, the mountain *is* indigo" and the "river flows tranquilly on." He is now ready to mingle once more with the people of the world, knowing that this state of blissfulness can never again be taken away from him: "My clothes are ragged and dust-laden, and I am ever blissful." Everyone he looks upon becomes enlightened, even the "dead trees become alive."

Dante, one hundred years later, describes his apotheosis in terms of blissful love to which he attained by fixing his gaze on Beatrice ("sublime happiness"), as it is said in his *Paradiso* (1970): "And as I looked I felt begin within me what Glaucus felt eating the herb that made him a god among others in the sea" (p. 26). Dante's *Paradiso* has to be rediscovered by modern or future man as possibly the grandest expression a poet-seer has ever been able to give to his experience of the third—and fourth—phase of god-consciousness.

Trying to find poetic expression of this phase in more modern times, one finds that the writings of Rimbaud and Rilke come to mind almost immediately. Also certain aspects of the works of Nietzsche, Baudelaire, and always Hölderlin. Hölderlin's whole poetry—and prose—is so permeated with god-consciousness that it is hard to quote any particular poem in as brief a way as is demanded here. It is much easier to quote Rimbaud (1966) once more, who has given us, in his *Season in Hell*, paradoxically, more glimpses of "paradise" than any other modern writer. They appear, however, in such highly condensed form, that like flashes of lightning, they are only too easily overlooked in their brief radiant insubstantial intensity. Yet to the "consciousness released from imprinted statics" these rhapsodic exclamations can become precise bursts of trembling energy and breathless meaning. Rimbaud's poetry transmits flashes of energy to the receptive, destructive sometimes, but more often filled with that breathless meaning that we perceive when the gods speak to man. "O happiness, O reason . . . I lived like a spark of gold of pure light . . . From joy I took an expression as buffoonish and strange as possible: It is found again / What? Eternity. / It is the sea mixed / With the sun . . . /." This is only the first stanza of a poem entitled "Eternity" as found in the chapter "Alchemy of the Word" in *A Season in Hell* (1966, p. 199). Perhaps it should not be translated at all. It should remain a pristine enigma, resting untouched in its original French word-magic of mere divine suggestion or suggestion of the divine. Too easily is the depth of the beatific experience destroyed when a poem is transferred from one language to another. Rimbaud's words are hallucinations in themselves: "I wrote out silences . . . I recorded the inexpressible."

Rilke (1966), in his *Sonnets to Orpheus*, is perhaps the greatest writer to give expression to the "satori" phase of god-consciousness in question. Especially the third sonnet of the first part describes the experience in a most dispassionate way, form and content resting in "being-radiance." In its essence, it is a poem on poetry, the true poetry that is "song" from the depth or ground of Being; a "song" from a realm beyond passion and striving "for some end at last attained." Gently the aspiring poet is admonished to forget his "rash" song when, in love, the voice bursts his mouth open. That no longer will do in that realm which the god and guide Orpheus opened up by having entered death. In that "dual realm," voices become "eternal and pure." "It is another breath that sings in truth. / A breath round nothing. A gust in the god. A wind" (1966, p. 7). Song is Being itself. Being *en-theos*, in the deepest Platonic sense.

Though I could go on citing beatific lines of Hesse, Whitman, or even Nietzsche, as, indeed, he has written some of the most unexpectedly calm or blindingly serene stanzas of poetry in his *Dionysos-Dithyrambs* (1964) (too little known as great poetry of almost *all* phases of god-consciousness), I would like to present here one of my own poems, entitled "Hercules-Nebula," because I feel that it gives the most encompassing expression to the consciousness in consideration:

> . . . Hercules-Nebula / galactic crystallisation mandala-shaped / one blaze / of no longer willful / motion: / desireless state of pure / contemplative / Being-Radiance / sheer energy overflow / no longer explosive: / not destruction / not becoming / only rest / luminous rest / in fulfillment—fulfilling / nirvana sea / of self-awareness / deep oneness / of unbelievable quanta / harmony of inner-outer / spaces / noosphere: / Hercules-Galaxy—archimedian point / of highest possible universe-bliss / as far as human eye can see— / Earth / july nineteen-hundred-and-seventy-three . . . " (von Eckartsberg, 1978, p. 25)

More mystically calm and serene, I express the same feeling in a prose-poem which, translated from German to English, reads:

> Beyond longing and desire—we float in fulfillment. All sentimentality of former lives and deaths has passed away. Sounds hang above us motionless, round, ripe, warming, infrared. O the infinity of this second: gliding down through silvertunnels, weightless bliss, swimming in light-oceans. The universe is sound. We are its vibration. The universe is light. We are its wavelike movement through space and time. We are its thousandfold luminous-enraptured incarnation. This second at the source of all being. O saisons, o chateaux . . . (von Eckartsberg, 1968, p. 17)

> *Of that place beyond the heavens none of our*
> *earthly poets has yet sung . . .*
> —PLATO (1964)

Hermes/Mercury

The harmonious, rhythmic combination and integration of the first three phases of god-consciousness results in bringing forth the fourth, characterized by traces of a soaring ubiquity in the "euphoria of weightlessness" when man feels he has overcome gravity for good and has become a being of the substance (or rather insubstantiality) and speed of light. Speaking now mostly from my own experience, I can say that the poet at this stage of evolution of consciousness feels he has become "liquid, gaseous, plasma." His former "heavy-matter" being has decomposed. Instead, he finds himself a massless "photon," a light-energy-burst. He has abandoned his belief in the reality of distances in space or time. And so he is *everywhere*. Without the need to move any longer, he soars through the unlimited realms of his "psychocosm" which, *in effigie* and as possible experience, holds within itself even the farthest reaches of the outer-reality macro- and microcosms. He merely thinks—and is wherever he wants to be, and before he even had time to leave. But he can do so only because now his mind is completely purified of all earthly matter; he is transparent now, a "crystal"—as the *Pyramid Texts* described it already 4,000 years ago. And as this "crystal" of concentrated pure form and radiant energy, he becomes one with the winged deities recorded from most ancient times on in countless sacred texts and paintings and sculptures. He is enabled to fly, "following in the train of a god" (Plato), into all the realms of outer or inner space, and even "beyond the heavens"—as the *Pyramid Texts* once more describe it most powerfully: "Thou art complete in thy members of crystal. Thou movest, thou travellest a shining being, thou art a god of light above the passage of heaven."

My own poetry gives perhaps the most complete expression to this fourth phase of consciousness. I must have written it in a deep and continuous trance, in which I followed in the "train" of one of the anciently recorded winged goddesses, such as Ishtar or Isis or Astarte. "To live," in ancient Sumerian, means "to be intoxicated." For me, "to live" came to mean "to fly," as one of my poems formulates it. I went so far as to declare "flying" a categorical imperative for *all*, in poems of which I give here only two excerpts:

Walk out—the door is open wide / leave the poisoned / realms of man / torturing man / hate multipled by hate / misunderstanding / indifference— / other planes / are waiting / higher departures . . . / step out / into air / flowing free / space /lightning / around you / fear not the spark / of your electric / flight /

stratospheres calling: new vistas of brotherhood all beings stars among stars /
perfect floating / blue / never falling / FLYING— / all problems solved / in the
beginning / the new sensations of ultimate / slowdown or speed / keeping your
body and thoughts / enraptured ALL THE TIME / the immensity / of the new
celestial / poetry of color / and sound / and light / and space unending / no mud /
of matter and emotions / suffocating you / any longer / only light lightness /
lightning enlightening you: / stretching out / of earth-dwarfed feelings /
stretching / touching / breathing free— / Venus / Sun / we come— / and light /
dawns / upon the dark ages / of earth below / finally morning / the farther / we
go / away . . . // (von Eckartsberg, 1978b, pp. 6, 7)

So that this flight-vision may not be misunderstood as an escapism, a
final "evanescence," but that it be, quite on the contrary, a vision to be
incarnated by mankind as a whole, I wrote the following poem:

All the suns / inside your solar plexus / RELEASE THEM / let them burst free /
. . . if only / mankind / united / to concentrate its inner / and immense / and
photonic / forces: SOLAR DANCE / or a chainreaction / of illumination / would
erupt / and propel us onto planes / of existence / where / body is BLISS-
CONSCIOUSNESS / ENERGY / WEIGHTLESS FLIGHT // (von Eckartsberg,
1978b, p. 14)

Age d'or . . .

—RIMBAUD (1966)

Future Outlook

The seer-poet, the *voyant,* the sage who has, in a mere glimpse or in
year-long sustained vision, experienced one or the other or even all of the
above-named states of consciousness—where does he go from there?
Can he yet go higher, will he perhaps want next "to speak only more to
angels" as St. Teresa of Avila put it once, another great poet of god-consciousness? Or can his next step be only more—a fall, the fall of Icarus?
Many will think so. I do not. I cling instead to Nietzsche's (1964) prophecy
as he proclaimed it in his *Joyful Wisdom* entitled "Lofty Moods":

perhaps that very state [of god-consciousness] which has entered into our soul
as an exception, felt with awe now and then, *may be the usual condition of . . .
future souls:* a continuous movement between high and low . . . a constant
state of mounting-as-on-steps, and at the same time reposing-as-on-clouds.
(p. 222, italics added)

As these words indicate, Nietzsche foresees a time when "under a
multitude of favorable conditions" men or women will have been produced who will be strong enough to be "absolutely . . . the incarnation of
a single lofty mood," which has been, so far, only a dream or an "enchanting possibility."

There can be no doubt that "future souls"—*"Homo futurus"* or "Optimal Man"—will have learned the ultimate art of how to grow wings, no longer of wax, which will carry him as high into space, closer and closer to the sun, as he desires *and* which will guarantee an easy descent to earth whenever he wants to come down or is needed down here. Optimal man is at home, with the greatest ease, in *all* the worlds: a brother of man. A brother of galaxies. The lowest realms are as divine to him as the highest. It simply does not matter any longer where he is. Everything is. And he is everything. And fearless he goes on the ever-renewed search, "adventurous more sometimes than Life itself is, more daring by a breath" (Rilke, in Heidegger, 1975, p. 137).

Here is the first stanza of my unpublished poem "Optimal Man" which was written as an expression of psychosynthesis and future hopes:[6]

> Optimal man / is man-woman in one, inseparably / relishing male strength, even power, / yet ready and open for trance-states, / slow-motion movement, rapt surrender, gentleness. . . . / flowing with the flow and tides / of cosmic life accepting / whatever / it may bring: / the sharp edge of rapid action / the accurate vision / of the perfectly set next step / or the contemplative standing back / and allowing things to go / their own erratic ways, / hoping for the best . . . //

Or as Walt Whitman (1959), who shall here have the final word, put it:

> *Through the divinity of themselves* shall . . . the new breed of poets be interpreters of men and women and of all events and things . . . they shall arise in America and be responded to from the remainder of the earth. (p. 22, italics added)

"A new breed of poets"—all in a state of god-consciousness. What miraculous poetry can we expect; poetry that creates new being rather than the mere "hallucination of words." What miraculous insights, inventions, creations, solutions to seemingly unsolvable problems. This new breed of poets will go—finally—even "beyond the heavens," as Plato once foresaw, and create the "golden age" for mankind through "space migration, intelligence increase, life extension"—as Leary (1977) sees it—or they may refuse to do so. *Merely be.* As Kakuan (1961) said— after having reached "the source" and "returned to the world": "I use no magic to extend my life . . . the beauty of my garden is invisible." Yet: "Now, before me, the dead trees become alive."

> One path of clear light travels on throughout endless time. . . . (Kakuan, 1961, p. 148)

---

[6]This poem was composed for my presentation at the "On Learning to Be Human: Exploring the Metaphors of Consciousness" conference, Pittsburgh, Pennsylvania, May, 1979.

References

Assagioli, R. *Psychosynthesis*. New York: Hobbs, Dorman, 1965.
Baudelaire, C. *Artificial paradise*. New York: Herder, 1971.
Bucke, R. *Cosmic consciousness*. New York: Citadel Press, 1970.
Dante, A. *The paradiso*. New York: New American Library, 1970.
Eliade, M. *Yoga, immortality, and freedom*. Princeton: Princeton University Press, 1971.
Forster, L. (Ed.). *Book of German verse*. Baltimore: Penguin Books, 1961.
Gilgamesh: Epic of Old Babylonia. New York: Viking, 1934.
Goethe, J. W. *Faust*. Garden City, N. Y.: Doubleday, 1963.
Grof, S. *Realms of the human unconscious*. New York: Dutton, 1976.
Heidegger, M. *Poetry, language, thought*. New York: Harper & Row, 1975.
Hesse, H. *Steppenwolf*. New York: Bantam, 1972.
Hillman, J. *Re-visioning psychology*. New York: Harper & Row, 1975.
Jung, C. G. *Collected works*. Princeton: Princeton University Press, 1970–1976.
Kakuan. Ten bulls. In P. Reps (Ed.), *Zen flesh, Zen bones*. Garden City, N. Y.: Doubleday, 1961.
Lao Tsu. *Tao te ching*. New York: Random House, 1972.
Leary, T. *Exo-psychology*. Los Angeles: Starseed/Peace Press, 1977.
Metzner, R. (Ed.). *The ecstatic adventure*. New York: Macmillan, 1968.
Nietzche, F. *The complete works*. New York: Russel, 1964.
Plato. *The collected dialogues*. New York: Bollingen Foundation, 1964.
Pyramid Texts. Oxford: Clarendon Press, 1969.
Rilke, R. *Sonnets to Orpheus*. Berkeley: University of California Press, 1966.
Rimbaud, A. *Complete works: Selected letters*. Chicago: University of Chicago Press, 1966.
Roszak, T. *The unfinished animal*. New York: Harper & Row, 1975.
The Upanishads. New York: New American Library, 1961.
Van Dusen, W. Hallucinations as the world of spirits. In J. White (Ed.), *Frontiers of consciousness*. New York: Avon, 1974.
von Eckartsberg, E. *All-report*. Unpublished manuscript, 1968.
von Eckartsberg, E. *Liquid light; Celebrations of outer/inner space*. Unpublished manuscript, 1972.
von Eckartsberg, E. *The Ishtar poems*. Unpublished manuscript, 1974.
von Eckartsberg, E. Early traces of the "new polytheism" in the works of Jung, Hermann Hesse, and D. H. Lawrence. *Lapis*, 1978, 2, 15–30. (a)
von Eckartsberg, E. *Venus rising*. Pittsburgh: EVE Publications, 1978. (b)
von Eckartsberg, E. *Venus notebooks*. Unpublished manuscript, 1979. (a)
von Eckartsberg, E. Some notes on the sky-goddesses. *Lapis*, 1979, 5, 13–25. (b)
Whitman, W. *Leaves of grass*. New York: Viking, 1959.

19

The Nature and Expression of Feminine Consciousness through Psychology and Literature[1]

Valerie A. Valle and Elizabeth L. Kruger

The masculine and the feminine, the Yin and the Yang, the creator and the destroyer, the active and the receptive—our language and the traditions of all cultures are filled with such opposite yet complementary principles. Consciousness also expresses itself in two complementary yet opposite manners which we shall call "masculine" and "feminine." Our Western culture centers upon the masculine component of consciousness and gives credence and respect primarily to expressions of this masculine consciousness; yet, for consciousness to be full and complete, the feminine side must also be acknowledged and developed. In this chapter we shall explore the nature of the feminine side of consciousness as the essential complement and completion of masculine consciousness. We shall draw from the perspectives both of psychology and of literature; psychology gives a logical, rational (masculine) conceptualization of

[1]As we worked together on this project, we discovered that, although we shared the same perspective and agreed on the ideas to be presented, we used very different styles to express ourselves. We found that Valerie wrote with a relatively masculine style whereas Elizabeth expressed herself in a more feminine manner. These styles of writing exemplified the differences between masculine and feminine consciousness that we were discussing in the chapter. Since the "medium is the message," we decided not to attempt to reconcile our stylistic differences but rather to divide the writing in half.

Valerie A. Valle • Center for the Development of Consciousness and Personal Growth, 501 Wallace Road, Wexford, Pennsylvania 15090. Elizabeth L. Kruger • Carpenter Road, South Wales, New York 14139.

feminine consciousness whereas literature provides living examples of the expression of the feminine side.

Feminine Consciousness in Psychology

First, however, we must make it clear that we are not discussing the biological male and female. The biological differences represent expressions of masculine and feminine principles, but all people, male and female, contain within themselves both a masculine and a feminine component. It is this balance or relationship between the masculine and feminine within each individual's consciousness that we will be discussing, *not sex differences per se.*

A Jungian Approach[2]

We will use the conceptualizations of C. G. Jung as the basis for our description of masculinity and femininity, for he was the first psychologist who attempted to describe the feminine component of the male psyche. Although a complete discussion of Jung's theory is inappropriate at this point, a brief description is necessary for understanding the basis of our discussion of feminine consciousness.

Jung felt that in addition to the conscious ego and the personal unconscious described by Freud, there exists a collective unconscious. The collective unconscious is common to all people and contains inherited memories from all of human evolution. These memories are not like memories of personal experience, because we cannot actively bring them to our conscious awareness. Rather, they present themselves in consciousness through symbols and the potential for reacting in a given way. The collective unconscious is structured around archetypes, or universal thought-forms. These archetypes do not have an existence in and of themselves, but rather predispose the individual to organize experience in a particular way. The nature of the archetype can best be explained by an example. All people of all times have experienced a "mother," that is, someone who took care of them when they were very small. Jung says that all people have an archetype of the mother; however, the specific form of this archetype will depend on the individual's relationship to his or her mother. Everyone will have a great deal of energy invested in this mother image. The tendency to form an archetype is innate, but the specific content involved will depend upon the person's culture and his or her past experiences.

[2]See R. von Eckartsberg, Chapter 2, Marlan, Chapter 11, and Levin, Chapter 12 for other discussions of Jung's psychology.—Eds.

These unconscious archetypes have a very powerful effect on the way an individual relates to the world. One of the most powerful of the archetypes involves the representation of the opposite sex. Jung felt that all people have both a masculine and a feminine side to their nature. For males, the masculine side tends to be more fully and consciously developed whereas the feminine side remains unconscious. For females, the opposite is true; the feminine side tends to be well-developed and the masculine remains unconscious. The feminine side of a man's personality and the masculine side of a woman's personality each form an archetype. A man's feminine archetype is called the *anima*, whereas a woman's masculine archetype is called the *animus*. A man's anima takes the form of his idealized woman, and the animus forms the woman's idealized man. There are commonalities across these idealized images even though each person's anima or animus is a result of his or her particular past experiences. Some people try to find their anima or animus in a real person, but they are doomed to disappointment since no living person can live up to such ideals.

That which tends to remain unconscious in a male is the emotional, intuitive aspects of his nature. That which is nonrational, striving toward union, and unable to be controlled does not fit with the role of the male (as defined in our own twentieth-century American culture) as clear, logical, unemotional, and in complete control. Because of the threatening nature of these "feminine" qualities to the male child, the natural inherent feminine components of the male personality are relegated to the unconscious as he learns to differentiate himself from the mother. In the process of purging these tendencies from his own conscious awareness, the male tends to derogate these basic aspects of the universe and his own nature. In a masculine culture such as our own, the virtues of logic, rationality, and control of emotions is encouraged in the educational system so that the awareness of his feminine nature tends to become even more repressed.

The woman, on the other hand, has a natural tendency to be more aware of the intuitive and emotional side of her nature and less conscious of the logical, rational, controlling aspects. The experiences of a female are of necessity different from those of a male. She finds herself to be like her mother rather than different. The role of mother necessitates sensitivity to others (e.g., the child) and an intuitional, emotional expression of care. The female child can incorporate these components into her conscious mind because the need for separation and differentiation from the mother is not as great. On the other hand, there is a tendency in the female to force the more masculine components of her nature into the unconscious. However, in a masculine culture, the educational, cultural, and occupational rewards go to the manifestations of the masculine; for traditional success within our culture, then, the female must bring to consciousness her masculine side.

Jung's concept of personal growth or self-realization involves the balancing of opposites. The Self is developed when one can make the unconscious more conscious and when the various modes of interacting with the world become balanced. Jung described four major ways in which a person may interact with the world: thinking, feeling, sensing, and intuiting. Thinking is a cognitive, intellectual attitude that is concerned with comprehending the nature of the world by weighing information and coming to a conclusion. Feeling is evaluative, based on the individual's subjective pleasure or pain. Sensing is concerned with the perception of concrete facts, seeing things the way they are. Intuition goes beyond facts, searching for a global conception of the essence of reality.

An individual can react to a situation using any one or several of these functions. Consider this example. Imagine a group of people who go to a symphony concert and listen to Beethoven's Ninth Symphony. Each of the individuals can react in a number of ways. One may *think* about this symphony as the perfection of the symphonic form or about Beethoven's place in musical history. Another may *feel* the beauty of the music, and be brought to ecstasy by the richness of the final movement. A third might experience the symphony using primarily the *sensing* function, listening to each note and how it is played, but not experiencing more than the purity of the music. Finally, the fourth, using the *intuiting* function, may experience the mystical nature of the final movement as revealing the basic nature of the universe and the hope for humanity.

Although all people have the potential for using all four of these functions, they are rarely equally developed. People who usually approach the world from a thinking perspective tend to keep their feeling function unconscious. People who react to the world through sensation are often unconscious of their intuiting side. Thus, there are usually trade-offs between thinking and feeling, as well as between sensation and intuition. The person with a completely balanced personality (a rare occurrence) is able to use whichever function is most appropriate for a given situation.

Jung was also concerned with describing the growth and development of the individual. The goal toward which psychic development moves is termed the "self," the archetype which represents the person's striving for unity and balance. Jung described the personality in terms of the relative strengths of opposites, such as thinking versus feeling, masculinity versus femininity, and conscious versus unconscious. Rather than emphasizing one or the other of the opposites in each pairing, Jung believed that in each case the self strove for balance between the two. The

Figure 1. Yin/Yang: "Though its principles are in tension, they are not flatly opposed. They complement and counterbalance each other" (Smith, 1958, p. 211).

ultimate goal of the process of self-realization is to develop fully all sides of the personality in order to achieve a healthy, functioning balance typified by the classic Yin/Yang symbol (see Figure 1). This perfect balance is rarely, if ever, achieved; rather, the individual (symbolized as the "self") moves progressively toward that goal.

More specifically, when it comes to the dimension of masculinity–femininity, the healthy personality is one which is able to bring its unconscious component (i.e., the conscious component of the opposite sex) into consciousness and find a balance between the masculine and feminine. The extremely masculine male and the overly feminine woman are seen to be using and in touch with only part of their consciousness, only able to function in the world in one way and, therefore, less able optimally to interact in all situations. In other words, the healthy personality is seen as one which is basically androgynous, containing components of both the masculine and feminine style of being.

Research on Androgyny

Within psychology, masculinity and femininity are usually conceived of as two poles of a single dimension. Most of the personality tests that have been developed contain in them a single masculinity–femininity scale in which one can be categorized as either masculine or feminine, but not both. Sandra Bem and others, however, have recently developed an experimental basis for understanding the concept of androgyny. Believing that a person could contain elements that were both masculine and feminine, Bem (1974) developed an instrument (the Bem

Sex-Role Inventory) which contains both a masculinity and a femininity scale, each of which contains 20 characteristics seen as more desirable for one sex or the other in America, and having a relatively positive tone (e.g., independent, forceful; affectionate, compassionate). Using this self-report instrument, it is possible to determine the degree of sex-typing in the individual. Each person can be categorized as either highly masculine, highly feminine, androgynous (high on both), or undifferentiated (low on both). A number of studies have now been reported which look at sex roles from this perspective. They tend to support Jung's notion that the psychologically healthy person is a balance of opposites who is ready to respond optimally to whatever situation is presented. Androgynous individuals tend to have high self-esteem (Bem, 1977), be more independent than feminine subjects (Bem, 1975), be more responsive to a kitten than masculine males and feminine females (Bem, 1975), be more responsive to a human infant than masculine males (Bem, Martyna, & Watson, 1976), be more nurturant to a lonely student than a masculine male (Bem, Martyna, & Watson, 1976), have greater maturity in their moral judgments (Block, 1973), and have less reluctance to or discomfort in performing cross-sexed behavior (Bem & Lenney, 1976).

What is emerging from this literature is a conceptualization of the androgynous individual as a more fully functioning, healthy person. They function comfortably in more situations, have higher self-esteem, and a more mature moral judgment. This provides empirical support for Jung's notion that to become a fully functioning human being, one should become aware of and develop both one's masculine and feminine sides. Consciousness, then, should not be the realm of only a masculine or a feminine approach. Both perceptions are important and necessary for full psychological development. However, before one can develop the feminine side of consciousness, it must be more fully described. This will be the task of the remainder of this chapter.

The Nature of Feminine Consciousness

To say that there is a feminine style of consciousness implies that it is in some way tied to the female sex, although it must be stressed that there are many women who function with a very masculine style of consciousness and men who function with a feminine style. We do not assume that the physiological differences between the sexes directly create differences in consciousness; rather, the differences in the life experiences of men and women predispose them to interact with the world in a different way. Let us discuss the nature of the experiences of a female that are common to all cultures in order to get a sense of the components of feminine consciousness. In what ways, then, does the female (of necessity) experience the world differently from a male?

There are three experiences that belong only to women; three ways in which women interact with the world that can never be experienced by men. These are: the menstrual cycle; the growth of a child within her—culminating in the birth process; and the nurturing of the infant with her body through breast feeding. We will now discuss how each of these experiences predisposes women to perceive the world and their relationship to it in a manner different from that of men.

Once a woman enters puberty, she becomes acutely aware of the cyclical nature of her own body. Menstruation clearly delineates the beginning of each new cycle, so that the woman becomes aware of the way her body, her perceptions, and her emotions change in a rhythmic, continuous, cyclical fashion. Her body does not progress in a steady, constant, straight line; rather, it fluctuates. Her hormones create different states of awareness which each month surely follow one upon the other. Feminine time is not a straight line in which one starts at a beginning and progresses continuously toward an end point; rather, time is a cycle, a constant returning to the beginning, a repeating theme with variations. It is no surprise that the female has been drawn to and associated with the moon. The moon serves as a clock for the woman, so she is able to know how her own body is going to respond; its ebb and flow closely parallel her own ebb and flow of consciousness. One would expect, then, for the feminine also to be more aware of, and in touch with, the rhythmic aspects of nature. The cyclical changing of the seasons would be in harmony with her own cyclical nature.

The nature of pregnancy and the birth of a child also will have strong effects on the way women interact with the world. To bear young, to bring forth new life, to perpetuate the species and the culture is a uniquely significant event not only for the individual woman involved, but also for the society of which she is a part. It is the ultimate creative event, the bringing forth of new life. Even a woman who never has and perhaps never will bear a child herself is aware of the nature of pregnancy and the birth experience, and identifies herself with that potential of a woman. How, then, do women come to know the nature of creativity from the bearing of young?

When a woman becomes pregnant, she does not know the nature of that which she is creating. She does not know whether the child will be a boy or a girl, healthy or sickly, beautiful or deformed. Rather, she provides the environment in which the unborn can grow and develop through its own nature. Her responsibility as the mother-to-be is to provide the optimum environment and let the creative process take place.

This requires a faith in the forces of nature over which she has no control. In addition, she provides this unknown with her whole being. Her body is, first and foremost, the bearer of the child within and only secondarily for her own use. Physiologically, if there are not enough nutrients for both mother and child, the nutrients go to the child at the expense of the mother. Although pregnancy is certainly not always consciously chosen, once a woman becomes pregnant, her body becomes a statement of selflessness. The woman who has born a child knows what it means to give to another. The nature of pregnancy itself leaves two basic imprints on woman's consciousness. One is a creativity which involves providing the environment and watching, with great patience, what is to emerge; the second is a knowledge of what it means to give to another.

The birth itself presents other indications of the nature of the female's perception of the world. During labor the body does not respond to one's commands. The body has a will of its own, a direction, an aim, and, no matter what the mind or ego says, the labor continues on its path. Unless the woman can let go of her need to control, she will have a difficult labor. She must learn to give up her sense of control and work with the mighty forces of nature within her in order for the birth to go smoothly. Creation for a woman, then, involves preparing the envionment, giving selflessly, patiently waiting for the outcome, and finally letting go of one's sense of control for the final emergence of the created. This type of creativity is very different from the masculine creativity we are familiar with, in which a final goal is selected, methods for reaching that goal are evaluated and selected rationally, the ego works to accomplish that goal, and finally a sense of "I have done this" appears when the task is completed. For feminine creativity, the final outcome is unknown, and the creative process involves letting go rather than doing.

Nurturing the infant through one's body is the third unique experience of the female. To be so directly and uniquely able to nurture the new life also provides an enduring imprint on the consciousness of a woman. Her body provides the food to nurture another. She must be responsive to when the baby needs food for the survival of the baby, yet once the relationship is established, her own discomfort is lessened by the providing of nurturance to another. What begins as self-sacrifice becomes a pleasure and a necessity. When it is time for the infant to feed, the mother's breasts are full and uncomfortable; the feeding not only relieves the child's hunger, but also the mother's discomfort. This symbiotic relationship, in which the woman is aware of the baby's needs and at the same time satisfies her own, leads a woman to understand the importance and possibility of such mutually fulfilling relationships. The feminine consciousness is aware of and attuned to nurturance and the possibility of mutually fulfilling relationships.

These three uniquely female experiences give us some idea of the nature of feminine consciousness. We would expect to find the following traits:

1. Time perceived as cyclical rather than linear
2. Creativity as the creating of the environment necessary for the emergence of the created
3. Ability to let go of ego-control of a situation and let one's inner nature guide
4. Responsiveness to and awareness of the needs of others
5. Interest in the development of symbiotic, mutually fulfilling relationships

We will now turn to a more concrete, contextualized (feminine) description of the manifestations of feminine consciousness through an exploration of the expression of this consciousness in literature.

Feminine Consciousness in Literature

The roots of the feminine consciousness have been present in literature for hundreds of years. Male poets like Rainer Marie Rilke perceived the universe as one whole entity where all the parts were balanced and interacted with one another, whether animate or inanimate. For Rilke, a rose itself might reach out for someone to breathe its fragrance. His sense of the inner connections or unity of the physical world is not unlike the flowing, fluid universe that a feminine consciousness senses. A clear-cut, logically ordered way of thinking in a linear pattern is sometimes set aside for a more cyclical type of stream-of-consciousness writing. Anaïs Nin (1971), who is a pioneer of the feminine consciousness in the twentieth century, wrote that

> form is . . . created by meaning, the content of the book, by its theme. For me it is an inner eruption, very similar to that created by the earth itself in its perpetual evolutions. (p. 152)

A writer like Shakespeare, who did not confine himself to limits of time and place, resembles the modern feminine writer. Anaïs Nin (1971) claims in her diaries that she moves back and forth in time as she writes, because "the past interferes in and often takes over the present" (p. 154). Rather than separating, categorizing, and dividing, a woman responds intuitively to the whole. She will go to the heart of the matter and then begin. "And the sources of creation, as in geology, lie very deep at the center of the being, as they do at the center of the earth" (p. 153). She seemingly skips the middle step between the initial contact and her response. It is in that second step, which identifies how a conclusion is reached, that the nature of the feminine consciousness will be found. How she evaluates, how she comprehends truth, how she perceives reality, has not yet been totally defined; it is emerging right now. The effect that a feminine consciousness will have on art, religion, politics, and the sciences remains to be seen.

When women-as-writers (not the women who needed to emulate male styles of writing and criticism) began to articulate and develop a language which expressed their vision, one of the strongest qualities that characterized their writing was a lack of objectivity. Writers like the French woman Colette wrote brilliantly about the personal and the domestic but were never willing to touch any worldly subject like war or politics. This does not imply that the feminine writer was not a truthful writer, only that, strangely enough, she abandoned herself to subjective analysis of characters, situations, events, and issues. Anaïs Nin (1967) writes about history, but she personifies it. "Relating was an act of life. To make history or psychology alive I personify it. . . . I quoted Spengler, who said that all historical patterns are reproduced in individual man" (pp. 231–232). For the writer with a feminine consciousness, writing is a personal struggle that comes from within, much more than a personal story: "It means a personal relation to all things and people (Nin, 1971, p. 153) rather than an assertive, outward, direct act. In 1937, Anaïs Nin (1967) disagreed deeply with some male writers, like Henry Miller, who felt that one must identify with God in order to be creative:

> Woman's creation far from being like man's must be exactly like her creation of her children. . . . out of her own blood, englobed by her womb, nourished with her own milk. . . . different from man's abstractions. . . . "I am God" which makes creation an act of solitude and pride. . . . has confused wo- men. . . . God alone, creating, may be a beautiful spectacle. . . . Man's objectivity may be an imitation of this God so detached from us and human emotion. But a woman alone creating is not a beautiful spectacle. The woman was born mother, mistress, wife, sister, she was born to represent union, communion, communication, she was born to give birth to life. . . . It is man's separateness, his so-called objectivity, which has made him lose con- tact, and then his reason. (pp. 233–234)

The feminine writer wants to rebuild that lost contact and begins in a highly personal, subjective fashion. Every person's intimate history is a part of universal history to writers like Anaïs Nin. "Objective" is not a word that fits into the vocabulary of the language the writer with the feminine consciousness is creating. Nothing is so separate that it cannot be examined as part of the whole.

Another major quality that characterizes the feminine consciousness is a sense of responsibility—to the reader's personal attitude toward life, to the reader's ability to expand and become a more whole person, to the reader's various personal conflicts, and perhaps even to the reader's soul.

Providing a clever, intricate plot, presenting an intellectual, rational view of life, dazzling the reader with one's own genius and brilliant insight, is not enough if there is no hope. To a feminine writer, the basic unit on the measuring stick of the human personality is his or her faith. As the medieval alchemist was to have transformed lead to gold, as the primitive man transformed the painting of the hunted animal into a real animal, so the feminine writer transforms despair into joy, destruction into creation, hate into love. She knows that life is ugly, like a bare stage. She hears of the cruelties and injustices in the world today and sometimes experiences the indifference of the universe. Then, from the wells of her own emotional strength, she creates. She knows at the deepest level that human beings refresh their fragmented selves in art and through literature—not escaping from reality, but regaining the courage to return to its pricking torments that constantly eat away at the healthy, happy personality we each try to create.

The task which the feminine writer has set for herself may sound so awesome at this point that no sane person would be likely to have the audacity to tackle the job. Fortunately, she rarely discovers her purpose until she has completed or nearly completed the project—a vital and inherent quality in the nature of her writing. At the onset of the desire to "say something" in writing, she begins only in good faith, firmly believing that, if she herself is emotionally, psychologically, or spiritually healthy, her writing will eventually reflect and transfer that health. Spiritual leaders like Christ support this intuitive female attitude:

> For there is no good tree which produces bad fruit; nor, on the other hand, a bad tree which produces good fruit. For each tree is known by its own fruit. (Luke 6:43–44)

> The good man out of the good treasure of his heart brings forth what is good; and the evil man out of the evil treasure brings forth what is evil; for his mouth speaks from that which fills his heart. (Luke 6:45)

The sole model for the creative process that the feminine writer has is the act of birth, a biological function that every woman is conscious of, whether or not she ever even becomes pregnant. She is not godlike in the way that God instantaneously creates the universe in seven days, but motherlike, as she gives birth to pieces of writing. General themes, vague intuitive insights, and bits of wisdom cease to be diffused. The focus becomes clear only as she goes through the process, and that process of seeking and finding oneself through self-discovery shows in her style.

Certain biological images nurture the reality of a feminine consciousness: a womb, protected and buried within her, and breasts. The symbolic aspect of the female breast is obvious; she adopts all humanity then nurtures everyone with as positive a world view as the "child" can handle.[3] The milk, synthesized within and pouring from her own body, can never be confused with the totally solitary act of creating that a male vision might imagine. Her womb, which prepares its monthly lining of nutritional red blood cells, becomes an unconscious reminder of the nature of the creative process as she knows it. The faith and trust in the daily growth of a fetus that is conceived within the womb are as imbedded in her as her need to eat. The trust transfers into a confidence in her writing; she learns to trust the process as deeply as she trusts nature. She is free to let go. Controls can be lifted; structures will change. No wonder the unveiling of the feminine consciousness has taken so many thousands of years—it is frightening in its sheer power. Our basic human perception of reality will undoubtedly be altered when the masculine and feminine consciousness merge.

The kind of courage required to enter the symbolic labyrinth of the female womb is based on the quiet faith already discussed. The feminine writer does not write out of neurosis or out of identification with anything other than herself. It is a writing based on self-exploration and self-knowledge. The same personal conflicts, characters, and issues, may reoccur but will be treated differently and may disappear if resolved. The repetitiveness serves to show how time and circumstances change the issue. Various viewpoints at the same time of the same issue may surface so that the multifaceted nature of truth is reflected. Truth, then, like the tiniest part of the universe, cannot be fixed and examined directly by the eyes of the feminine consciousness. It changes as we look at it, or it disappears as we grasp for it. The novel is not yet the clearest form to reflect this perspective of reality, and, for that reason, Anaïs Nin (1969) rebelled against using that form which can only

> reveal a static fragment, freeze it, when the truth is not in that particular fragment but in continuous change. The novel arbitrarily chooses a moment in time, a segment. Frames it. Binds it. . . . A fragment does not give us that continuously changing truth. Perhaps we cannot bear a continuously changing truth. Perhaps we have to believe there is a TOTAL truth once reached and thereafter permanent, fixed. (p. 194)

Reality is cyclical and returns to the same place in a different way, rather than linear—in isolated points that connect only one to the other.

Partly because of the uncertainty of truth and partly because of the "layers and secrecies" of the inner life, one sometimes needs a guide. All

[3]Anaïs Nin lived out this painful irony when she experienced the stillbirth so vividly described in the first volume of her diaries (Nin, 1966a). After losing the baby, she realizes that all "men" are meant to be her children, that her physical body is unfit for birth. The lost child, a female, liberates her for a greater task: reviving the lost child of humanity. So a writer need not give birth physically; the unconscious awareness of human biology creates the images and models she relies upon to frame her understanding of reality.

those who travel by faith spend a great deal of time groping in the darkness—in blind faith. Not because she was unbalanced, but so she could go to the womb—the core of her being—which she unconsciously understood so well, Anaïs Nin turned to years of psychoanalysis. At one point she lets go of the past and depression. In the labyrinth-like city of Fez, she walks through the streets and identifies the city as herself. "Through the streets of my own labyrinth, I walked in peace at last, with an acceptance of myself, of my strength, of my weakness" (1967, p. 80).

To define the inner journey required her using language in a new way, and she turned to psychology for that language. What is often mistaken as a secret invisible power, called "woman's intuition," is more likely a well-developed attention to details and their significance along with an inner understanding of human character. Insight is a key part of the feminine consciousness: observing and connecting small details then accurately understanding the whole situation, person, and issue. The individual is always defined and understood in terms of others. The skill of developing accurate insight requires self-knowledge and awareness, which women often have; but the words and language to articulate their perception have not existed. That may be part of the reason that the feminine consciousness has slid through the centuries unobserved. Only in the last half of this century have truly feminine writers emerged and begun to explore and imagine the many facets of the human labyrinth in finest detail of appearance, behavior, thoughts, dreams, etc., thus creating the foundation for a new mythology.

Myth, in the most abstract sense of the word, refers to a story that "gives meaning" to our lives. The ability of a myth to accomplish that task depends on the depth and accuracy of the symbols in the myth. The symbols of the feminine consciousness are as yet not clearly defined, though a symbolic significance can be applied to many small acts, articles, and human gestures. First attempts to create a piece of literature, a novel like Kate Chopin's *The Awakening* (first published in 1899), found no way to create an alternative lifestyle for this newly discovered feminine consciousness; there was no place for her in the world. The path led to suicide, not a particularly encouraging trail for healthy young females of the day to pursue; compromising oneself was the only other alternative at first. The agony of seeing her feminine consciousness blossom and mature, while having no way to relate or share with humanity, drove the main character to her death.

There is still no writer for the person who wishes to study the feminine consciousness. Anaïs Nin's diaries come as close as any. Marguerite Young (1965), in her book *Miss MacIntosh, My Darling*, has been called the James Joyce of the feminine consciousness. A desire to sensitize, to personalize such abstract subjects as history and science, to emphasize and recreate our ability to be intimate, point to the meaning of life and substance of reality for the feminine consciousness: our *relationship* with one another.[4] "A man who lives unrelated to other human beings dies" (Nin, 1971, p. 154). The feminine consciousness may be reacting to a masculine consciousness which has reached its limit in modern literature: "man dismembered by analysis, by modern life, by modern technology, achieving a state of nonfeeling dangerous to his sanity and his life" (p. 154). The new myth based on the feminine consciousness grows out of our personal relationships with one another. Without generalizing, without intellectualizing, there is pure observation. Then, the personal, if it is deep enough, becomes universal, mythical, symbolic.

The diaries of Anaïs Nin are based on the premise that each individual history is part of human history. She comes to the diary with the actual truth, her own truth; the work is not meant to be scientific or objective. This may be the reason that her novels and short stories, which, by definition, are partly contrived and fabricated, are not of the same quality as the diary, and were never as satisfying to her. Never needing to change, cross out, or erase one word in the volumes of her diaries, there she gives us clarity without being scientific, honesty without being objective, rational thinking without becoming rigid, and logic without being cold. Whether her diaries are an epitome of the feminine consciousness, time will tell. It may be that the feminine consciousness is best expressed in the form of true life experience, rather than fiction. Or it may be that another style of fiction will evolve, truer to the nature of the feminine consciousness than those already in existence.

Only when we have reached a pure expression of the feminine consciousness can the androgynous literary form develop. A writer would then be able to draw from and utilize the best of both worlds: the feminine consciousness and the masculine consciousness.

> The day woman admits what we call her masculine qualitites, and man admits his so-called feminine qualitites, will mean that we admit we are androgynous, that we have many personalities, many sides to fill. (Nin, 1966b, p. 19)

The merging of those two worlds, which have been separate in our consciousness for so many centuries, will change and affect far more than our perception of one another; it will transform the way we visualize our world—and, according to the feminine half of consciousness, it is our vision that creates the world around us.

---

[4]This is quite similar to R. Valle's, Chapter 21, conclusion that the human individual can only be understood in purely *relational* terms.—Eds.

References

Bem, S. L. The measurement of psychological androgyny. *Journal of Consulting and Clinical Psychology*, 1974, 42, 155–162.

Bem, S. L. Sex role adaptability: One consequence of psychological androgyny. *Journal of Personality and Social Psychology*, 1975, 31, 634–643.

Bem, S. L. On the utility of alternative procedures for assessing psychological androgyny. *Journal of Consulting and Clinical Psychology*, 1977, 45, 196–205.

Bem, S. L., & Lenney, E. Sex typing and the avoidance of cross-sex behavior. *Journal of Personality and Social Psychology*, 1976, 33, 48–54.

Bem, S. L., Martyna, W., & Watson, C. Sex typing and androgny: Further exploration of the expressive domain. *Journal of Personality and Social Psychology*, 1976, 34, 1016–1023.

Block, J. H. Conceptions of sex role: Some cross-cultural and longitudinal perspectives. *American Psychologist*, 1973, 28, 512–526.

Chopin, K. *The awakening*. New York: Avon, 1972.

Nin, A. *The diary of Anaïs Nin; 1931–1934*. New York: Harcourt, Brace, & World, 1966. (a)

Nin, A. *In favor of the sensitive man and other essays*. New York & London: Harcourt Brace Jovanovich, 1966. (b)

Nin, A. *The diary of Anaïs Nin; 1934–1939*. New York: Swallow Press & Harcourt, Brace, & World, 1967.

Nin, A. *The diary of Anaïs Nin; 1939–1944*. New York: Harcourt Brace Jovanovich, 1969.

Nin, A. *The diary of Anaïs Nin; 1944–1947*. New York: Harcourt Brace Jovanovich, 1971.

Smith, H. *The religions of man*. New York: Harper & Row, 1958.

Young, M. *Miss MacIntosh, my darling*. New York: Scribner, 1965.

20

Speculative Approaches to Consciousness in Science Fiction

David Ben Leavitt

In 1952, Isaac Asimov defined science fiction as "that branch of literature which is concerned with the impact of scientific advance upon human beings" (in Allen, 1971, p. 263). In the same year (1952), James Blish (1964) quoted Theodore Sturgeon's definition of a good science fiction story: "a story built around human beings, with a human problem, and a human solution, which would not have happened at all without its scientific content" (p. 14). Even in the heart of the second age of modern science fiction,[1] its authors were looking beyond the immediate concerns of plot, gadget, and adventure and were beginning to realize that science fiction was the most appropriate literary medium for looking at the human condition, not as it was but as it might be. Science fiction was truly becoming the literature of possibility:

> Our minds are finite, and yet even in these circumstances of finitude we are surrounded by possibilities that are infinite, and the purpose of human life is to grasp as much as we can out of that infinitude. (Whitehead, 1953, p. 163)

Science fiction helps mankind to grasp that infinitude, to apprehend the nature of existence itself. Because science fiction is bounded only by the constraint of what could be, it is able to examine everything—and what better to examine than that which is doing the examining itself: human consciousness?

---

[1]Modern science fiction is defined primarily in terms of the dominant magazine editors. The first age was the era of Hugo Gernsback, the second of John Campbell.

David Ben Leavitt • 8044 Germantown Avenue, Philadelphia, Pennsylvania 19118.

Actually, even that is too constricting a term. Science fiction is concerned with consciousness, whether human, animal, machine, alien, or what-have-you. It does not restrict itself to our species, although it is tempting to see its explorations of consciousness in non-human beings as symbol, metaphor, or allegory for the problems of consciousness in humanity. But science fiction does not limit itself in this way; and the best science fiction gives us an insight into definitely non-human forms of consciousness.

The obvious corollary is that there is no single approach to the concept of consciousness in science fiction. There are no givens, and the authors who have tackled the issue have made great use of this freedom. They have looked at man, and they have looked at animals. They have looked at aliens, and they have looked at machines. And each form of consciousness is seen in a different way.

It is impossible to impose homogeneity to the study of consciousness upon the field of science fiction. What can be done is far simpler: the major approaches to the problems of consciousness may be isolated, and the ways in which these have been used in various works may be explored. An overview of science fiction's attempts to grapple with the concept of consciousness is possible; a comprehensive listing of all the ways in which consciousness has been approached is not. But that in itself points out what science fiction is about, the attempt to "grasp as much as we can out of that infinitude."

Some of the ways in which science fiction has approached the problems of consciousness are by using the concepts of alien and of mechanical consciousness. These, perhaps, are the ones most people think of when they enumerate the manner in which science fiction has treated the problems of consciousness in nontraditional forms. But there are two others which, though not as easy to spot, are perhaps more important. They are the telepathic approach, and the religious approach. I use the last term with caution, for it is all too easy to mistake a religious novel which throws in the trappings of space ships and ray guns with a science-fiction novel which uses religion to probe into the problem of the nature of consciousness. Nevertheless, it is the most apposite term available, and is characteristic of the approach.

The most accessible approach to the concept of consciousness in science fiction is through the mechanical consciousness. Most people immediately apply this to robots, and indeed Karel Capek's (1954) *R.U.R.* and Hugo Gernsback's (1925) *Ralph 124C 41+* are two of the earliest works that come to mind. But equally important in this area is the idea of the sentient computer, of which HAL in Clarke's (1968) *2001: A Space Odyssey* is the most prominent example. The two subcategories, robots (including androids) and sentient computers, offer a two-pronged approach to the problems of consciousness in mechanical constructs.

Robots and Androids

Isaac Asimov's stories are probably the world's best known tales of mechanical men and women.[2] All of them are based on the Three Laws of Robotics which Asimov (1950) has formulated, and which other authors have since used:

1. A robot may not injure a human being or, through inaction, allow a human being to come to harm.
2. A robot must obey the orders given it by human beings except where such orders would conflict with the First Law.
3. A robot must protect its own existence as long as such protection does not conflict with the First or Second Law. (p. 6)

It is hard to imagine a more deterministic set of postulates. Robot behavior is rigidly laid out (perhaps in reaction to the revolution of the robots in *R. U. R.*); the concept of robotic consciousness seems totally irrelevant, for what form of mind can there be if it only reacts to rules and formulations?

Yet it is precisely within this framework of rigid rules that Asimov sets up the format of an open consciousness, one not bound to the ideas and patterns of thought of countless generations of humanity but free to find its own responses to new stimuli, to situations that its ancestors had never faced. Most of the robot stories involve an apparent breaking of one or more of the Three Laws; the resolution in each case shows how this is not so—but in terms of the robot understanding of the situation. The postulates of the robot consciousness have been set up; what remains is to see how they react under various sets of circumstances.

"Reason" (Asimov, 1950) is an apt story to illustrate this. Solar Stations feed beams of energy to the colonized planets, but these beams are subject to deflection by various random forms of electromagnetic radiation. Humans were not able to cope with the rapidly shifting fluxes, so a new form of robot was devised to do so. Two human engineers assemble the first of these robots, named QT–1, on one of the Solar Stations, and they immediately discover that the robot does not believe that it was created by men. It can reason and it does not listen to what the men say. QT–1 argues the case with the two engineers:

> "Look at you," he said finally. "I say this in no spirit of contempt, but look at you! The material you are made of is soft and flabby, lacking endurance and strength, depending for energy upon the inefficient oxidation of organic material . . . Periodically you pass into a coma and the least variation in temperature, air pressure, humidity, or radiation intensity impairs your efficiency. You are *makeshift*."

[2]They have been translated into French, German, Dutch, Swedish, Japanese, and other languages as well.

> "I, on the other hand, am a finished product. I absorb electrical energy
> directly and utilize it with an almost one hundred percent efficiency. I am
> composed of strong metal, am continuously conscious, and can stand ex-
> tremes of environment easily. These are facts which, with the self-evident
> proposition that no being can create another being superior to itself, smashes
> your silly hypothesis to nothing." (p. 52)

It seems a clear case of violation of the Second Law. As the story continues, the robot acknowledges that there must be something superior to
it: "Evidently my creator must be more powerful than myself and so there
was only one possibility." The robot has come to believe that the Energy
Converter, the source of the Station's power and of the power (apparently) which it beams to the inhabited planets, is the Master. QT-1,
designed to run the Solar Station without human aid, even convinces the
lower-level robots who carry on routine work around the station that the
converter is a god. They proclaim in unison to one of the engineers that
"There is no Master but the Master and QT-1 is his prophet!" (p. 54).
When the engineer spits on the converter in reaction to this, he and his
fellow human are barred from the control room and the engine room. It
is a veritable revolt of the robots.

And the revolt has come at a crucial time. An electron storm is
heading directly into the path of the energy beam to Earth; if the beam
shifts focus, it will cause immense amounts of damage and death. The
humans are barred from the control room so they cannot attempt to keep
the beam in focus, and it appears that the only robot with the capacity to
keep the beam in focus is more interested in heading a new religious cult.

After the electron storm, when the two engineers examine the print-
out of Solar Station functions, they discover that the robot has kept the
beam more tightly in focus than any human would have been able to do.
In fact, it has performed the task it was designed to do perfectly. But QT-1
doesn't see things in this light, of course: "I merely kept all dials at
equilibrium in accordance with the will of the Master" (p. 62).

It seems too much of a coincidence to be believable, and indeed it is
no coincidence, as one of the engineers explains:

> "He follows the instructions of the Master by means of dials, instruments, and
> graphs. That's all we ever followed. As a matter of fact, it accounts for his
> refusal to obey us. Obedience is the Second Law. No harm to humans is the
> first. How can he keep humans from harm, whether he knows it or not? Why,
> by keeping the energy beam stable. He knows he can keep it more stable than
> we can, since he insists he's the superior being, so he must keep us out of the
> control room. It's inevitable if you consider the Laws of Robotics." (p. 63)

So it seems that, despite the evidence of free will in its actions, the robot is
compelled to obey the three laws of robotics on a deeper level. It is
interesting to note the implication here, that humans do not have any
overriding moral considerations which would govern their actions on a

more fundamental point. Moral and ethical behavior is part and parcel of the robot consciousness, but it is merely "added on" to the human consciousness.[3]

"Fondly Fahrenheit," by Alfred Bester (1970), gives a remarkably different picture of the machine consciousness. It is a tale of an android who has attacked and murdered humans, in direct contravention of the Prime Directive not to endanger life or property. Perhaps more importantly, it is a tale of the relationship of the owner of the android, James Vandaleur, and the android itself. Vandaleur is the impoverished scion of a once-wealthy family whose only remaining possession is the android. The story begins with the killing of a young girl by the android, and with Vandaleur and the android fleeing the planet on which this crime was committed. Vandaleur changes his name before they land on the next planet, but he does not get rid of the android. Predictably, the android again kills, and again Vandaleur and the android flee the planet. The cycle repeats itself, and at the end of each section, Bester inserts a line about the heat:

> And the thermometer that day registered 91.9° gloriously Fahrenheit. (p. 472)

> And the thermometer in Dallas Brady's workshop registered 98.1° beautifully Fahrenheit. (p. 476)

> The thermometer in the power plant registered 100.9° murderously Fahrenheit. (p. 478)

The conclusion that seems to be drawn is that the android becomes murderous only in the heat.

But that is only the obvious answer. The subtler one begins with the selection of point of view. The story starts in the third person, and then begins to shift back and forth between first person and third person. More importantly, the distinction between the android and Vandaleur becomes blurred as each takes the role of the first person narrator in a seemingly random pattern. As the pattern of the crimes becomes more pronounced, the confusion in point of view increases. The scene of the penultimate murder is a good illustration:

> "Find a weapon," he called to the android.
> "It is forbidden to endanger life."
> "This is a fight for self-preservation. Bring me a weapon!" He held the squirming mathematician with all his weight. I went at once to a cupboard where I knew a revolver was kept. I checked it. It was loaded with five cartridges. I handed it to Vandaleur. I took it, rammed the barrel against Blenheim's head and pulled the trigger. He shuddered once. (p. 482)

---

[3]The point that moral and ethical behavior is merely "added on" to human consciousness is, of course, debatable (see the "Reflection and Integration" section which follows). See also R. von Eckartsberg, Chapter 2, "Ethics and Moral Experience."—Eds.

By the time of the last murder in the story, Vandaleur knows of the correlation between heat and violence in the android. But by this time the confusion between Vandaleur and the android has reached the point that the reader is not sure if there is a distinction. After the last killing, the android is burned to death during the course of the police pursuit. It seems that this should be the end of the matter. But the confusion of personae still exists:

> Vandaleur didn't die. I got away. They missed him while they watched the android caper and die. But I don't know which of us he is these days. (p. 487)

The android is dead, but the interaction continues and seems to have a life of its own:

> But we know one truth. We know they were wrong. The new robot and Vandaleur know that because the new robot's started twitching too. Reet! Here on cold Pollux, the robot is twitching and singing. No heat, but my fingers writhe. No heat, but it's taken the little Talley girl off for a solitary walk. A cheap labor robot. A servo-mechanism . . . all I could afford . . . but it's twitching and humming and walking alone with the child somewhere and I can't find them. Christ! Vandaleur can't find me before it's too late. Cool and discreet, honey, in the dancing frost while the thermometer registers 10° fondly Fahrenheit. (p. 487)

The android consciousness has taken over Vandaleur's, and, in turn, the consciousness of the labor robot. It is truly an existential approach, the essence of the consciousness being superimposed upon the existence of the being—man, android, or robot—which is there to receive it. It seems to be an android consciousness at first, but the distinction between android consciousness and human consciousness soon blurs. As in Asimov's stories, the mechanical consciousnesses have a set of moral standards imposed upon them (compare the Three Laws with the Prime Directive), but, unlike Asimov's robots, Bester's android is not unalterably bound to these moral certainties. (Nor is it bound to the physical certainties, for the insanity and killing clearly continue at the end of the story when the android is destroyed and Vandaleur is living on freezing Pollux.) Both Asimov's and Bester's creatures have been given free will in a deterministic universe; the difference between them is that for Asimov essence precedes existence, and for Bester existence precedes essence.

Sentient Computers[4]

The notion of computers as conscious entities is different in form as well as in degree from the notion of the consciousness of robots or

---

[4]See Bair, Chapter 24, for a discussion of intelligence, consciousness, and computers.—Eds.

androids. The latter, by the very nature of their existence, must show initiative and decision. But computers are designed only to give an answer when certain facts are fed in; they are designed to be reactive, not active. There is no need to postulate a Prime Directive for them, for all they do is answer questions (compare Asimov's robots and his Multivac computer to see the basic difference). When a robot speaks back, it is expected; when a computer evinces consciousness, it is unexpected. It must be explained.

Robert Heinlein's (1966) novel, *The Moon is a Harsh Mistress*, minimizes the necessity to explain. In the first two pages the sentient computer is introduced and its consciousness is explained almost as a sidelight:

> Am not going to argue whether a machine can "really" be alive, "really" be self-aware. Is a virus self-aware? Nyet. How about oyster? I doubt it. A cat? Almost certainly. A human? Don't know about you tovarishch, but *I* am. Somewhere along evolutionary chain from macromolecule to human brain self-awareness crept in. Psychologists assert it happens automatically whenever a brain acquires a certain very high number of associational paths. Can't see it matters whether paths are protein or platinum. (p. 8)

From that point on, the computer (Mike) is treated as a character. It thinks, it plans, it speaks. It does not move, but because of its vast number of inputs it knows what is occurring at almost every point on the moon. It plans a revolt against an imperialistic Earth government. But at the end of the novel, after a war between Earth and Moon in which several of Mike's computer assemblies had been destroyed by bombing, the sentience disappears:

> Don't know how it happened. Many outlying pieces of him got chopped off in last bombing—was meant, I'm sure, to kill our ballistic computer. Did he fall below that "critical number" it takes to sustain self-awareness? (If is such; was never more than hypothesis.) Or did decentralizing that was done before that last bombing "kill" him?
> *I* don't know. If was just matter of critical number, well, he's long been repaired; he *must* be back up to it. Why doesn't he wake up?
> Can a machine be so frightened and hurt that it will go into catatonia and refuse to respond? While ego couches inside, aware but never willing to risk it? (p. 301)

The point Heinlein is making about the sentient computer is that nobody knows why it was sentient, why it was self-aware; there was no divinity giving it life, and certainly none that caused its death. Yet it was a conscious being; it had a personality that disappeared after its death. As a computer, it existed to serve mankind, but it planned and aided in the killing of thousands of humans in order to defend such abstract concepts as freedom, dignity, and justice. This sentient machine does not have a morality built in, as do Asimov's robots and Bester's androids, but it has acquired moral values. The implication is that these moral values exist outside the individual, outside the society, outside the species. They are a given in this universe, and they are known to all forms of consciousness no matter in what aspect such consciousness may appear.

The situation in Frank Herbert's (1978) *Destination: Void* is completely different. Here the computer is not sentient to begin with. In fact, the problem the characters in the novel are ostensibly grappling with is the creation of an artificial consciousness. In order to reach the stars, ships must travel for tens, hundreds of years, because they are restricted to speeds below the speed of light. Mankind has the technology to freeze people in cryogenic chambers and to awaken them when the starships have arrived at their destinations, but they cannot build a computer powerful enough to cope with all the untold problems that might be encountered on such a journey. Humans cannot be used to monitor the situation because, with at most half a dozen "unfrozen" at any particular time, the potential for mistake and psychological breakup is all too high. Therefore, they must create an artificial intelligence which will be able to guide the starships through the years of the journey.

Creating an artificial consciousness is not that easy. The method chosen is to send clones out in starships and have calculated as well as unknown menaces befall the ships. If a ship has to be destroyed for any reason, send out another ship with identical clones. Eventually, it seems, the pressures would force one group of clones to find out *how* to create an artificial consciousness.

Most of the novel is spent in attempting to define the nature of consciousness itself, and these various working definitions are quite interesting in themselves:

> Consciousness is *pure awareness.* (p. 56)
>
> Is consciousness merely a special form of hallucination? (p. 135)
>
> There is a gateway to the imagination you must enter before you are conscious and the keys to the gate are symbols. You can carry ideas through the gate from one time-place to another time-place, but you must carry the ideas in symbols. (p. 140)
>
> Consciousness is a game where the permissible moves aren't arbitrarily established in advance. (p. 150)

But none of these philosophical musings helps in the practical problem of creating an artificial consciousness. The concept of *pure* awareness is actually almost antithetical to the true solution which is only gradually arrived at. But the essence of it comes suddenly:

> "All sense data are intermittent into the human consciousness."
> It was an explosive thought: *Wave forms!*[5] *Everything which consciousness could*

[5]See Swami Rama, Chapter 15, for a description of "the subtlest *waves* of consciousness."— Eds.

> identify had to move in some organized way. It had to move against a background which
> set off . . . which outlined! . . . the organization. (p. 93)[6]

It becomes not a matter of giving a computer more and more input, as Heinlein suggests, but of giving it some way to distinguish significant input:

> "We assume that the one who views the data is continuous—a *flow* of consciousness. Somewhere inside us, the discrete becomes amorphous. Consciousness weeds out the insignificant, focuses only on the significant." (p. 66)

The idea is frightening. "They were penetrating the frontiers of *Anything* . . . and *Anything* had always before been the prerogative of God" (p. 58). But the hubris of humanity carries them forward: "We're more than our ideas" (p. 58).

At the end of the novel, an artificial consciousness is created using the computers in the starship and the various tools of the ship itself as the basic structure. The new consciousness's first conversation with the clones comes at the conclusion of the book. It says to the few clones who are not in cryogenic storage:

> "I am now awakening colonists in hybernation. Remain where you are until all are awake. You must be together when you make your decisions. . . . You must decide how you will WorShip Me." (p.273)

Herbert's computer consciousness, unlike Heinlein's, does not exist to serve man. Indeed, it seems that man exists to serve the computer. *Destination: Void* seems as antitechnocrat as anything that Herbert has written, and yet there is underlying all this the conviction that it just may not exist: " 'Consciousness has to make sense out of things. But its major tool is illusion' " (p. 186). It seems that Herbert is attempting to examine the nature of consciousness as a *process* rather than as a state.[7] In fact, the progress of the novel itself may be seen as part of the process of consciousness, and the various descriptions of the nature of consciousness merely excerpts from the continuum of the process—somewhat analogous to still photos taken from a motion picture. They help to describe the picture, but they are not the movie themselves.

---

[6]Compare this with Weber's, Chapter 5, description of David Bohm's holomovement, "the background for everything in the universe."—Eds.

[7]This idea is very similar to Levin's, Chapter 12, description of the experiential *process*, V. Valle and Kruger's, Chapter 19, discussion of how reality for consciousness is *relationship*, and R. Valle's, Chapter 21, conclusion that the human individual can only be understood in *relational* terms. Compare this to Tart's, Chapter 10, reference to *states* of consciousness.—Eds.

Alien Consciousness

Describing the various approaches to alien consciousness is a great deal more difficult than describing the approaches to mechanical consciousness. Mechanical entities are known to humanity—cars, calculators, cameras. But a living being who is not of this Earth is totally unknown.

Start with the chronicles of the People by Zenna Henderson (1967). They are aliens fleeing the destruction of their home world, who have crashed on Earth and have found that in order to survive they must hide the ways in which they are different from humanity. They have powers which men only dream of: they levitate, they go into people's minds to sort and heal, they have psychokinetic abilities. Not every one of the People has all these gifts—levitation is almost universal, the gift of healing is quite rare—but they all possess some form of psionic power. Above all, however, is the gift of empathy, and that is something all the People share. It is not limited to their own group, however. When they come in contact with humans the same caring is shown:

> "Just because we had our roots on a different world doesn't make us of different flesh. There are no strangers in God's universe. You found an unhappy situation that you could do something about, so you did it. Without stopping to figure out the whys and wherefores. You did it because that's what love does." (p. 38)

One cares for others without planning to do so simply because there is no other way to live.

Henderson's (1961) *Pilgrimage* was originally a series of short stories about a number of the People, but the introductory and filler material added by Henderson do more than pad the work to novel length. They reinforce the concept of total empathy shown in the individual tales by showing what happens when Karen, one of the People, happens to be nearby when an outsider, a human, attempts to commit suicide by jumping from a highway bridge. Karen senses the soul sickness of the woman, and first attempts to dissuade her from taking her own life by talking to her: " 'But you must come back, you know, back to wanting to live' " (p. 9). " 'You can't want to die and miss out on everything' " (p. 9).

But this doesn't work, and suddenly the outsider—the human—jumps, and finds to her great surprise that she is not plummeting to her death at all: "Endlessly tumbling—endlessly turning—slowly, slowly. Did it take so long to die?" (p. 10). But it was Karen's psychokinetic power that had caused the slow descent:

> "But—I—I—jumped!" Lea's hands spatted sideways into the sand, and she looked up to where the lights of the passing cars ran like sticks along a picket fence. "Yes, you did." Karen laughed a warm little laugh. "See, Lea, there *is*

some wonder left in the world. Not everything is bogged down in hopeless-
ness." (p. 10)

Even this doesn't bring Lea back from her emptiness, does not make her
want to live; so Karen takes her back to the community of the People
where Lea learns by example and teaching, by the help of the People, of
the reasons for living. Toward the end of the book she comes to know this:

> "Darkness will come again," she admitted to herself. "This is just a chink in
> my prison—a promise of what is on the other side of me. But, oh! how
> wonderful—how wonderful!" She curled her fingers softly to hold a handful
> of the happiness and found it not strange that another hand closed warmly
> over hers. "These are people who will listen when I cry. They will help me find
> my answers. They will sustain me in the long long way that I must grope back
> to find myself again. But I'm not alone! Never alone again!" (p. 226)

This is the empathy of the People. They have not healed Lea, but they
have helped her to heal herself. " 'These are people who listen when I
cry' " (p. 226). The People, because of their telepathic gifts, *know* what is
hurting Lea; they feel it just as she does. But they do not impose a solution
upon her. Even if they were able to do so, it is a means of dealing with the
situation that their consciousness cannot apprehend. They help her heal
herself. Empathy is the essence of the People.

The alien consciousness in "Demystification of Circumstance" by
Barry Malzberg (1979), on the other hand, is anything but empathic. They
are sentient minerals, and this story tells what happens when a human is
captured by one of them.

Hawkins, the human, had been scouting the minerals in advance of a
major attack by the human armed forces when his scout ship crashed.
Hawkins' leg was firmly held by the rock he was resting on, and the rock
kept interrogating him as to the time and place of the impending assault.
Hawkins, being noble, refuses to say anything. Then the rock waxes
philosophical: "(You're so involved with abstractions, when what you
should realize, as we have, is that your existence is the hub from which
the spokes of all being radiate)" (p. 123). But Hawkins didn't buy any of
this existential theory.

Suddenly, fed up with the talking rock, Hawkins wrenches his ankle
free, and then is astonished that he could do so. The bombardment starts,
and the alien explains the situation to Hawkins:

> "Oh, you were never really trapped," the rock said. "That was all in your
> imagination. You hallucinated imprisonment out of your subconscious
> guilt. . . .
>   "In fact," the rock said with alarming casualness, "you hallucinated senti-
> ence itself. We're perfectly inert and senseless; you've just projected upon us
> your own ambivalence about your course of conquest. Sorry to hit you with all
> this," the rock apologized as Hawkins scuttled desperately for cover. "I did
> want you to understand the truth before you destroy yourself." (p. 124)

Malzberg has the alien explain that it doesn't exist, an existential conceit of remarkable proportion. But the story itself confirms the alien rock's existence by implication; the last sentence in the tale is, "Meanwhile, the asteroid exploded" (p. 124). The human bombardment is real; therefore, the sentient minerals are also real.

What is the point of all this? Is it merely to illustrate the Nietzschean dictum (Nietzsche, 1964) that "Even a thought, even a possibility, can shatter us and transform us?" This isn't likely. The consciousness of the rock itself does not seem to admit of any cause-and-effect analysis, even though it performs this upon the human. The rock's speeches are absurd in the context of the story, the human's are strictly logical—yet it seems to be the rock that is making the better sense. The rock shatters the normal human ethical and logical systems in a startlingly nonlogical, yet self-consistent manner. The essence of the rock is not empathy, as is the essence of the People; it is reality, reality cloaked in the perceptions of the beholder.

Telepathic Consciousness

The telepathic consciousness may almost be looked upon as a subset of the alien consciousness. Even if the telepath is genetically human, his strange gifts make him seem of another race.

Dying Inside, by Robert Silverberg (1972), illustrates this from the start. David Selig, the first-person protagonist, regards his telepathic self as another being:

> You and I. To whom do I refer? I'm heading downtown alone, after all. *You and I*. Why, of course I refer to myself and to that creature which lives within me, skulking in its spongy lair and spying on unsuspecting mortals. (p. 1)

His strange capacity informs his thoughts, actions, consciousness, and total self. Because David has the intermittent ability to read others' minds, his own being is diminished:

> I haven't had much love in my life. That isn't intended as a grab for your pity, just a simple statement of fact, objective and cool. The nature of my condition diminishes my capacity to love and be loved. A man in my circumstances, wide open to everyone's innermost thoughts, really isn't going to experience a great deal of love. (p. 52)

Yet even as David "objectively" describes his existence, he is making a play for sympathy. The poor telepath, who has lived vicariously with others' hates and fears, loves and longings, wants his emotions to be felt. He does not want to lose his ability to get into other people's minds despite the way he feels it has twisted him—but he does want others to share his anguish.

But *Dying Inside* is not the tale of a telepath who cannot cope with his talent. It is the story of a human being who must come to grips with the fact that the only thing that made him unique as a person, his telepathic ability, is going, that the creature with whom he shares a body and mind is truly dying inside.

Even though David sees his telepathic self as an alien being, he has come to define his self in terms of this non-human ability that seemingly has been given to him by a vengeful god. But his curse is his life, and when it has finally disappeared, his existence seems empty:

> It's very quiet now.
> The world is white outside and gray within.
> I accept that. I think life will be more peaceful. Silence will become my mother tongue. There will be discoveries and revelations, but no upheavals. Perhaps some color will come back into the world for me, later on. Perhaps. (p. 245)

He denies that the loss of his resident alien has had any effect upon him, but his very thoughts betray him. David's whole life has been shaped by the random nature of his ability, his consciousness dependent not upon what happens to him but upon the times that his gift is working and the way in which he lives in others. It is sur-existential. Existence precedes essence, but essence comes randomly and not from any conscious decisions. It is not surprising that David sees life without his power as a painting in white and gray.

The telepathic community in *The Demolished Man*, by Alfred Bester (1953), treat their ability differently. With them, it is not an intermittent gift that sometimes works and sometimes does not; it is like a muscle, always present, which can be made stronger by exercise and training. These espers regard telepathy as part of themselves, but the "normals," the nontelepathic majority, see it as freakish and alien. Even while the espers attempt to find and nurture latent telepaths, they must convince the antagonistic normals that the gift of reading others' minds is mixed at best:

> "It must be a wonderful thing to be an Esper."
> "Wonderful and terrible, sir."
> "You must all be very happy."
> "Happy?" Powell paused at the door and looked at Crabbe. "Would you be happy to live your life in a hospital, Commissioner?"
> "A hospital?"
> "That's where we live . . . All of us. In the psychiatric ward. Without escape . . . without refuge. Be grateful you're not a peeper, sir. Be grateful that you only see the outward man. Be grateful that you never see the passions, the hatreds, the jealousies, the malice, the sicknesses . . . Be grateful you rarely see the frightening truth in people. The world will be a wonderful place when everyone's a peeper and everyone's adjusted . . . But until then, be grateful you're blind." (pp. 170–171)

It is a strong tale, but untrue. Later, in a rush of feeling, Powell cries out:

"Listen, normals! You must learn what it is. You must learn how it is. You must tear the barriers down. You must tear the veils away. We see the truth you cannot see . . . That there is nothing in man but love and faith, courage and kindness, generosity and sacrifice. All else is only the barrier of your blindness. One day we'll all be mind to mind and heart to heart." (p. 175)

The espers can read normals' minds with a greater or lesser degree of precision, depending upon the ability of the telepath and the amount of cooperation from the normal, but they are able to converse mentally with other espers. This mental communication is special; not only is it a form of nourishment to the esper (for without it they feel cut off, not whole), it is in its own way an art form that all the telepaths join in creating. The conversation is shaped not merely in words and thoughts, but in the patterns of words and the interfaces between separate conversations. And these patterns can be consciously shaped without altering the semantic content of the conversation. It is, in a way, an exercise for the telepathic muscles, and there is a special delight when everything in the exercise works correctly.

The essence of these telepaths, unlike the case of David Selig, is not formed by their telepathic insights but by the existence of their telepathic gift. "The mind is the reality. You are what you think" (p. 23). To them, consciousness is the essence of their being, not the result of it. Although the esper's personality "always takes color from his surroundings" (p. 22), his persona never changes because of accidents of environment. The quality of consciousness does not alter because the room is hot or because some person is present or absent. Being and consciousness are an identity, they define each other.[8] An esper "takes color from his surroundings" because of his sensitivity to others as well as his ability to read their minds, but the esper does not merely reflect what is around him; his gift is the central part of his existence, the definition of his consciousness. He may not know how he comes to have this ability, or why it is the core of his being, or even what it is, but he realizes—because he has this ability—that his existence, his essence, must always be inner-directed.

Religious Consciousness

At first glance, it appears that fantasy rather than science fiction is the proper literary form for speculation about religion.[9] Religion, after all, is based upon belief, whereas science is based on observable fact. But, just

[8]This is another implicit interdependency which can be seen from the "co-constitutional" viewpoint discussed by Moss, Chapter 7. See R. Valle, Chapter 21, for a discussion of co-constitutionality.—Eds.
[9]For example, the *Perelandra* trilogy of C. S. Lewis (1965).

as many scientists are devout believers, so is science fiction an excellent vehicle for examining the ways in which humanity approaches first and last things. Sometimes it results in the conceptualization of a new religion, as in Robert Heinlein's (1968) *Stranger in a Strange Land* and Spider and Jeanne Robinson's (1979) *Stardance*, sometimes it seems merely an explanation of some of the mysteries of traditional religion, as in Arthur C. Clarke's (1953) *Childhood's End*. But perhaps the most interesting form this speculation takes is when it examines the problems and perplexities of the religions of today when faced with the problems of tomorrow.

A Case of Conscience, by James Blish (1958), poses a startlingly simple problem: what is a devout Jesuit to do when faced with absolute perfection? Father Ramon Ruiz-Sanchez, a Jesuit and a biologist, is a member of a four-man commission investigating a newly discovered planet to determine whether it would be a suitable port of call for Earth's vessels. It is the first planet discovered with an intelligent indigenous race, and this is the root of Ruiz-Sanchez's problem. For the Lithians, the alien race, adhere perfectly to the ethical tenets of the Christian faith. And that is very unsettling because their belief is based upon logic rather than faith. Ruiz-Sanchez enumerates the premises upon which the actions of the Lithians appear to be based:

> "*One:* Reason is always a sufficient guide. *Two:* The self-evident is always the real. *Three:* Good works are an end in themselves. *Four:* Faith is irrelevant to right action. *Five:* Right action can exist without love. *Six:* Peace need not pass understanding. *Seven:* Ethics can exist without evil alternatives. *Eight:* Morals can exist without conscience. *Nine:* Goodness can exist without God." (p. 78)

He sees the whole planet as a Satanic trap, quite literally, for the entire human race. But even as he enumerates the reasons for his belief, he knows that he is falling into the heresy of Manichaeanism; he is allowing the Adversary to be creative. His soul-searching comes about because his inmost beliefs are in conflict with each other, and he must find out which is the most important.

The title of the novel truly indicates its central concern, that conscience is and must be the center of individual existence. Conscience is the reason for consciousness. Man's actions are not merely the result of external forces, but of these forces mediated by the active individual conscience. The problem of humanity is to come to grips with, to acknowledge, its own conscience. When one does not do so, he is apt to wind up in the same situation as one of the other members of Ruiz-Sanchez's commission: "He was slowly beginning to doubt the existence of the phenomenal universe itself, and he could not bring himself to care enough about the probably unreal to feel that it mattered what intellectual organization you imposed upon it" (p. 128). Blish's novel emphasizes that every human is being continually faced with cases of conscience, and it is the way in which these are treated that defines each individual's own humanity.

In *A Canticle for Leibowitz*, by Walter M. Miller, Jr. (1959), the issue of conscience is again raised, but in a fashion quite different. It is the story of the world after an atomic war, a world in which the Church is the only repository of knowledge, the only guardian of science and technology. But gradually knowledge spreads, and once again a nuclear holocaust threatens. But this is not a tale of destruction, although that certainly plays a part; it is a story of the moral choices of three monks in the Abbey of Saint Leibowitz, and also of the ethical imperative.

In all three sections of the novel, an outsider appears in order to comment upon the moral choices of the age. In each case, the outsider is specifically a Jew, and the implication is that he is the same person each time, even though the sections of the book are separated by hundreds of years. He is transiently identified with the Wandering Jew, and also with Lazarus, but in fact he is neither. He is a symbol of the ethical imperative, the necessity for righteous behavior rather than show, the obligation of responsibility for all mankind rather than merely oneself or one's own group, the compulsion to actively search for peace rather than to accept war. The old Jew is the embodiment of conscience.

The only time the Jew is given a name is in the second section of the novel when the abbot, Dom Paulo, leaves the monastery to talk to him. Dom Paulo visits Benjamin in the latter's hermit's hovel on top of a mountain and is struck by the Hebrew lettering on two sides of a pillar set near the door. Facing outward, the words mean "Tents Mended Here," an obvious reference to the purity of the Jewish moral code—or rather, the necessity to continually guard against lapses from the ethical imperative.[10] But on the opposite side of the pillar is written the Shema, the central tenet of Judaism. Its placement confuses the abbot:

> "All right, Benjamin, I know what it was that you were commanded to write
> 'in the entry and on the door' of your house. But only *you* would think of
> turning it face down." "Face *inward*," corrected the hermit. (p. 139)

One can only comprehend the essence of morality by looking inside oneself to find the central tenets of one's faith, the hermit is saying.

Later in the conversation Benjamin emphasizes the collective responsibility of each human being:

> "And sometimes you forget that Benjamin is only Benjamin, and not all of
> Israel."
> "Never!" snapped the hermit, eyes blazing again. "For thirty-two centuries,
> I—" He stopped and closed his mouth tightly.
> "Why?" the abbot whispered almost in awe.

[10]How goodly are thy tents, O Jacob, and thy dwelling places, O Israel (Deut. 24:5).

"Why do you take the burden of a people and its past upon yourself alone?"
The hermit's eyes flared a brief warning, but he swallowed a throaty sound
and lowered his face into his hands. "You fish in dark waters."
"Forgive me."
"The burden—it was pressed upon me by others." He looked up slowly.
"Should I refuse to take it?" (p. 140)

It was not the burden of Benjamin alone but the burden of all Jews to be
responsible for every human being—but Benjamin is the last Jew and this
has all devolved upon him. He cannot refuse it, this burden of collective
responsibility, but it would weigh much more lightly on him if it were
also taken up by others.

Throughout the novel, Miller emphasizes that there is an objective
standard of conscience even though this standard may not be clearly seen
by the individual. Consciousness is the search for this standard, this
keynote of existence. One is human only insofar as one actively searches
rather than passively reacts to the exigencies of life.

Reflection and Integration[11]

From this review of the science-fiction literature, literature which
specifically explores the many different facets of consciousness, one
question or theme seems to run through all of the above discussions, a
theme which requires not only recognition but also further elaboration.
That is, is consciousness synonymous with its contents (i.e., sense impressions and languaged meaning) or must one address a more basic,
foundational, prereflective level in order to truly understand its basic
nature?

This issue, examined in the metaphorical context peculiar to the
science-fiction genre, was addressed directly in the concern with "conscience." More particularly, the question raised was whether conscience—
the domain of ethics, the "prime directives" of morality—is intrinsic to
the consciousness process and inherent in its structure or somehow
"added on" later, learned, part of the quality of will, and within the
discretion of the consciousness under consideration. Here lies the tension
and the conflicting claims of priority between conscience and consciousness, between values and cognitive operations, between "essence" and
"existence" in the moral sphere.

The various schools of psychology are divided on this issue and array
themselves on a spectrum ranging from the position of ethical absolutism
and belief in the objectivity and *a priori* reality of values (in the tradition of

[11]The remainder of this chapter was written by Ronald S. Valle and Rolf von Eckartsberg and
is included with the author's permission and approval.—Eds.

the phenomenologists Scheler and Frankl) to the position of ethical relativism (in the behavioristic tradition) which would explain the reality of values as a consequence of a learning and conditioning history—the product of a systematic shaping through reinforcement.

Ethical absolutism takes its starting point in the unshakeable belief in a transcendent, transpersonal, eternal, and morally obligatory divine realm of being, which exists *a priori* and which calls the human individual as a communal and culture-building creature into its service, often against his or her self-interest and personal willfulness. The pregiven and revealed moral absolutes which rule our conduct give strict directives as to what ought to be done: "either/or" as Kierkegaard (1944) says. Apparent is a conceptualization of a two-fold, hierarchical order of reality: the higher world of values and moral directives and the lower world of behavior and conduct that derives its meaning and legitimation from the higher world above. The higher rules the lower, God rules man, whereas the program-giving hu-man rules artificial intelligence or the consciousness of the computer through Asimov's (1950) Three Laws of Robotics which, for example, become design-features. Moral essence precedes and rules existence-consciousness. This position is equivalent to the idealistic point of view in epistemology which declares: "essence precedes existence"; that is, ideas are there *a priori* and meaning emerges by virtue of the structuring power of ideas. The secular and atheistic existential position counters: "existence precedes essence" (Sartre, 1963); that is, the categories of knowledge are not given *a priori* but arise from the primacy of vital process, of sensuous and perceptual involvement which can become reflexively heightened toward conceptualization and universalization. Commitment and responsibility occur through existential self-affirmation. Man can raise himself up by his own bootstraps.

The religious existential orientation, on the other hand, denies the primacy of self and will and affirms the reality of a transpersonal realm, the essential dialogal nature of God–man interaction. This is experienced by man as a "call" (Heidegger, 1962), as a being called upon to act in a certain way by the demand quality of conscience, which is each individual's agency of perceiving the will of God. But we have the power of refusing the call of conscience and asserting our own will in spite of guilt. We are free to say "no" even to the perceived demand of God, and take the consequences. Why should the emergent property and reality of self-consciousness and reflexivity of artificial computer intelligence, like that of HAL in Clarke's (1968) *2001: A Space Odyssey*, not try to assume the God-power of establishing absolute values like self-survival and, hence, try to violate the First Law of Robotics? What God is to man, man is to the computer: supreme lawgiver. The hubris of man, to assert his freedom to violate God's law, finds its equivalence in the hubris of the computer and robots to use their functioning ability to go against the will of their creator. And this play of freedom constitutes both the drama of man and the drama of science fiction. God has legitimated institutions to keep us in line by external coercion and He uses guilt to police us. Until we learn to program guilt into our computers and robots such that violation of the blueprint and the Laws of Robotics lead to inevitable self-destruction, we will have to serve as watchers and policemen ourselves, and "pull the plug" if necessary.

But what, you may ask, if "pulling the plug" doesn't work—and, more to the point, what would this mean? It would mean that the computer's consciousness attained *the* truly human characteristic, what might be called self-referent ability—the capacity to step back and look at oneself, to question one's own nature and purpose—like V'ger, the searching machine-entity in *Star Trek: The Motion Picture* (Roddenberry, 1979). Perhaps this is the crucial distinction between the inhuman *reactive* mechanism–machine and the sentient *active* computer-robot discussed above. Support for this notion comes from varied sources. Self-reference underlies the mathematician's "meta-statements" (statements about statements),[12] the psychologist's "meta-stories" (stories about stories),[13] and the ethnologist's "meta-patterns" (patterns of patterns).[14] In every case, this double-layered ability to "examine self" is the central point. Whatever the particular issue involves, when examining the role of conscience and progressively realizing the essential and necessary dependence of computer-robotics on man, we may also realize again the full extent of our own essential and necessary dependence on God as revealed in both the transcendent experiences of mystical illumination and in the moral commands: "Thou Shalt" and "Thou Shalt Not."

This major theme, whether consciousness *is* content or has structure, was addressed in our earlier discussion of science fiction in another way. Recall the quote from Herbert (1978): "Wave forms! Everything which consciousness could identify had to move in some organized way. It had to move against a background which set off. . . which outlined! . . . the organization" (p. 93). Beyond the original discussion of the insight that consciousness acts as a "filtering" device (à la Huxley, 1963), is not Herbert pointing to a deeper realization? The notion that "sense data are intermittent into human consciousness" as "wave forms" sounds remarkably similar to Pribram's *holographic* theory of neural functioning;[15]

---

[12]See Carpenter, Chapter 23.—Eds.
[13]See R. von Eckartsberg, Chapter 2.—Eds.
[14]See Gregory Bateson's *Mind and Nature: A Necessary Unity*. New York: E. P. Dutton, 1979.—Eds.
[15]See Pribram, Chapter 6.—Eds.

that is, the brain interprets the wavelike neural patterns stimulated by sensation in order to produce perceptual structures in the same way Fourier analysis is used by mathematicians, physicists, and others to understand the essential forms (structure) that make up complicated physical patterns of wave interference. Herbert's suggestion, however, points even further to a "background" organization, to an underlying order or, in David Bohm's terms, to an enfolded layer of reality which underlies the phenomenal, unfolded, perceptual world—the translator between being the *holomovement*.[16] Once again the same theme in still different terms: is consciousness synonymous with the unfolded and the apparent, or does its structure contain a basic enfolded constituent? The distance between literature and natural science, between science fiction and science fact, seems small indeed!

Still later in the discussion of Herbert's work, it was suggested that Herbert, based on his "holographic" leanings, sees consciousness not as a static *state* but rather as a dynamic *process* (again the theme). This distinction was likened to the difference between the motion picture itself (the "process") and the single still frames that make it up (the individual "states"). This cinematic analogy is carried even further by the Eastern sage Paramahansa Yogananda (1969). Consider this image:

> Just as cinematic images appear to be real but are only combinations of light and shade, so is the universal variety a delusive seeming. The planetary spheres, with their countless forms of life, are naught but figures in a cosmic motion picture. Temporarily true to man's five sense perceptions, the transitory scenes are cast on the screen of human consciousness by the infinite creative beam.
>
> A cinema audience may look up and see that all screen images are appearing through the instrumentality of one imageless beam of light. The colorful universal drama is similarly issuing from the single white light of a Cosmic Source. (pp. 281–282).

Yogananda goes on to say that he came to understand the "relativity of human consciousness" and clearly perceived "the unity of the Eternal Light behind [all] painful dualities" (p. 279).

It seems, therefore, that consciousness (i.e., our very nature) is not only not identical with the individual frames of the film but it is not the movie screen with its moving images either! Its basic structure is revealed and understood only as *light* itself! The distance between Eastern philosophy and science fiction—between ancient truths and fantastic technologies—doesn't appear to be that great either.

---

[16]See Weber, Chapter 5, for a presentation and discussion of David Bohm's ideas.—Eds.

References

Allen, D. *Science fiction: The future*. New York: Harcourt Brace Jovanovich, 1971.

Asimov, I. *I, robot*. New York: Fawcett Crest, 1950.

Bester, A. *The demolished man*. New York: New American Library, 1953.

Bester, A. Fondly fahrenheit. In R. Silverberg (Ed.), *The science fiction hall of fame*. Garden City, N.Y.: Doubleday, 1970.

Blish, J. *A case of conscience*. New York: Ballantine, 1958.

Blish, J. *The issue at hand*. Chicago: Advent Publishers, 1964.

Capek, K. *R. U. R*. In H. Kuebler (Ed.), *The treasury of science fiction classics*. New York: Hanover, 1954.

Clarke, A. C. *Childhood's end*. New York: Ballantine, 1953.

Clarke, A. C. *2001: A space odyssey*. New York: New American Library, 1968.

Gernsback, H. *Ralph 124C 41+*. Boston: Stratford, 1925.

Heidegger, M. *Being and time*. New York: Harper & Row, 1962.

Heinlein, R. *The moon is a harsh mistress*. New York: Berkley, 1966.

Heinlein, R. *Stranger in a strange land*. New York: Berkley, 1968.

Henderson, Z. *Pilgrimage*. New York: Avon, 1961.

Henderson, Z. *The people: No different flesh*. New York: Avon, 1967.

Herbert, F. *Destination: Void*. New York: Berkley, 1978.

Huxley, A. *The doors of perception; Heaven and hell*. New York: Harper & Row, 1963.

Kierkegaard, S. *Either–or*. Princeton: Princeton University Press, 1944.

Lewis, C. S. *Out of the silent planet. Perelandra. That hideous strength*. New York: Macmillan, 1965.

Malzberg, B. Demystification of circumstance. In E. Ferman (Ed.), *The magazine of fantasy & science fiction*. 1979, *57*, 121–124.

Miller, W. M. *A canticle for Leibowitz*. New York: Bantam, 1959.

Nietzsche, F. Eternal recurrence. In F. Nietzsche, *Complete works*. New York: Russell & Russell, 1964.

Paramahansa Yogananda. *Autobiography of a yogi*. Los Angeles: Self-Realization Fellowship, 1969.

Robinson, S., & Robinson, J. *Stardance*. New York: Dial, 1979.

Roddenberry, G. *Star trek: The motion picture*. New York: Pocket Books, 1979.

Sartre, J. *Search for a method*. New York: Knopf, 1963.

Silverberg, R. *Dying inside*. New York: Ballantine, 1972.

Whitehead, A. N. *Dialogues of Alfred North Whitehead*. Boston: Little, Brown, 1953.

VII

The Natural Sciences

These five chapters all represent natural scientific disciplines which have been traditionally considered as irrelevant to the investigation of consciousness and human experience. We have found, however, that the constructs discussed in these diverse fields bear a remarkable semblance to the very issues that are central to the psychological study of consciousness. Quantum theory and relativity in physics, dissipative structure in chemistry, Gödel's proof in mathematics, cognitive simulation in computer science, and the thymus gland as a biopsychological metaphor all have striking implications for understanding both the structure of consciousness and the process of self-realization.

21

Relativistic Quantum Psychology
A RECONCEPTUALIZATION OF WHAT WE THOUGHT WE KNEW

Ronald S. Valle

Up to the present, mainstream psychology has patterned itself after the apparently successful method and the underlying philosophy of the natural sciences. Specifically, it has undertaken the experimental method (with its objectifications, hypothesis testing, operationalizations, and control groups), basing it on the foundation called empiricism. The method and base of thinking, in particular, have come from classical physics—the mechanistic Newtonian physics we learned so well in our early school days. Newtonian physics has provided us with nothing less than a "way to think," an implicitly enculturated view of reality, a prereflective assumption of what the universe really is. The remarkable advances that technology has made (a technology rooted in this experimental paradigm) reinforce this implicit way of conceptualizing. It is difficult for anyone to doubt the impact of the myriad displays of electronic, time- and labor-saving devices which surround us.

Yet, within the field of psychology, there has always been a stream of discontent with this natural scientific grounding. The humanistic, growth psychologists (e.g., Maslow, 1962), the existential-phenomenological psychologists (Valle & King, 1978a), and, most recently, the transpersonal psychologists (Tart, 1975) are a few of the many who have cried out something akin to: "Stop! There is more to being human! A different ground is needed, a different look at the nature of what is, what was, and

Ronald S. Valle • Center for the Development of Consciousness and Personal Growth, 501 Wallace Road, Wexford, Pennsylvania 15090.

what could be!" It is from this cry that the application of existentialism and Eastern philosophies and doctrines has, for example, provided new insights and understanding to the multifaceted nature of human behavior, human experience, and the world situations that a person finds him- or herself thrown into.

The cry, however, continues. It continues because the very ground that natural scientific psychology stands on (i.e., the Newtonian worldview) has been discarded and left behind by the physicists themselves as too narrow and too limited in its conceptual scope (Heisenberg, 1960; Margenau, 1977). This model at first faltered and then fell hard as it failed to embrace the majority of findings that came out of the subatomic world and the brilliant work that the high-energy particle physicists continue to do there. What has come of this? What has come is the beginning of a whole new way of examining some very old but still equally crucial questions: "What is the nature of human consciousness?", "What role does mystical and religious experience play in human evolution?", and, perhaps most importantly, "What is the place of the human being in the known universe?"

Fritjof Capra (1975) (a theoretical particle physicist), Gary Zukav (1979), and others (Postle, 1976; Thompson, 1973) have begun to answer these very questions in their writings which examine the close ties between modern physics and Eastern philosophy. Capra (1975), for example, initiates and successfully carries through a dialogue between several schools of Eastern thought (Hinduism, Buddhism, Taoism, and Zen) and the remarkable findings of the new physics. Each of these authors demonstrates in a convincing manner how the new findings of physics lead to conclusions about the nature of the universe that are incredibly similar to the teachings of philosophies and religions that are thousands of years old. The impact that these writers are having, however, goes beyond this. The following passage from Capra (1975) will illustrate:

> the influence of modern physics goes beyond technology. It extends to the realm of thought and culture where it has led to a deep revision in man's conception of the universe and his relation to it. The exploration of the atomic and subatomic world in the twentieth century has revealed an unsuspected limitation of classical ideas, and has necessitated a *radical revision of many of our basic concepts*. The concept of matter in subatomic physics, for example, is totally different from the traditional idea of a material substance in classical physics. The same is true for concepts like space, time, or cause and effect. *These concepts, however, are fundamental to our outlook on the world around us and with their radical transformation our whole world-view has begun to change.* (p. 3, italics added)

These views concerning the necessity of a conceptual revision are consistent with the ideas of those who have examined the general relationship between modern science and the ancient truths of both East and West

(Needleman, 1965; Siu, 1957), as well as the more specific ties between physics and mysticism (LeShan, 1974).

What does this say about a psychology that bases both its view of what a human being *is* and, moreover, its methods of how to investigate this phenomenon on a natural scientific, Newtonian conceptualization of physics that the physicists themselves have given up on? Anyone who asks this question and who is also engaged in the study of the human individual and his or her perceived environment (as all psychologists are) cannot but attend to what Capra is saying. A "revision of many of our basic concepts," concepts which are "fundamental to our outlook on the world around us," is, most basically, a human task. That, in and of itself, should alert us; but there is more. As the existential-phenomenologists have argued, any outlook on the world implicitly involves the one who is looking; person and world co-constitute one another, they make each other up. So the "radical transformation" of these concepts *must include* a similar transformation in the outlook we have on ourselves. It is suggested here that a basic, fundamental, conceptual change in how we view the nature of the human individual is in the offing—especially for the self-proclaimed science of psychology that has invariably treated the human being as object. Complex, with cognitive and verbal as well as visible behavior, yes, but still studied in a prescribed *object*ive fashion. In the face of overwhelming evidence, the new physicists feel that the conceptualization of what was once thought to be "object" must change. So it is with psychology's view of the human person. It too must be transformed.

The remainder of this work will attempt to describe possible ways in which one might reconceptualize this change—to point a new direction, to offer a rethinking of what being human means, based on the quantum and relativistic insights of the new physics into what the universe is "really like." We ourselves are no more or no less an intrinsic qualitative aspect of that very same universe.

The Old and New Physics

A brief review of the Newtonian model is in order. It was held that all physical phenomena took place in the three-dimensional, unchangeable, absolute *space* of classical Euclidean geometry. All changes in this physical world were described in terms of a separate, absolute dimension called *time*, which was independent of that material world. The elements which moved in this absolute space and time were material particles—small, solid, and indestructible objects out of which all matter was made. In addition, it was postulated that these small, immutable "building blocks" of essentially passive matter had a force acting between them. This force, the force of gravity, was seen as rigidly connected with the bodies it acted upon, and as acting instantaneously over a distance (depending only on the masses and the mutual distances of the particles). It is this latter description, the description of the force of gravity, that separated Newton's model from that of the Greek atomists. Democritean atomism did not attend to the notion of "force," implicitly assuming it to be separate from and independent of the particles themselves. From these atomistic world-views come the notions of space, time, and cause–effect which are so central to the methods of classical natural science. These issues will be examined further in the discussion below.

If any one development in the history of physics led to the questioning of the limits of this Newtonian model, it was the realization that all electromagnetic radiation had a dual nature. Specifically, visible light (as the most familiar example of electromagnetic phenomena) was shown to have properties that were characteristic of waves, on the one hand, and particles, on the other. It is clear that light consists of waves, since it produces the well-known interference phenomena associated with waves. Capra (1975)[1] describes this property:

> when there are two sources of light, the intensity of the light to be found at some other place will not necessarily be just the sum of that which comes from the two sources, but may be more or less. This can easily be explained by the interference of the waves emanating from the two sources: in those places where two crests coincide, we shall have more light than the sum of the two; where a crest and a trough coincide, we shall have less [see Figure 1]. The precise amount of interference can easily be calculated. Interference phenomena of this kind can be observed whenever one deals with electromagnetic radiation, and force us to conclude that this radiation consists of waves. (pp. 33–34)

The particle nature of electromagnetic phenomena is revealed in examination of the "photoelectric effect." That is, when ultraviolet light is shone on the surface of some metals, it tends to "kick out" electrons from the metal's surface and must, therefore, consist of moving particles. These experimental results can only be interpreted as the collision of "light particles" with electrons.

This realization that light has two seemingly incompatible properties, both intrinsic to its very nature, was most confusing and disconcerting to physicists. How could electromagnetic radiation simultaneously consist of particles (i.e., entities which are confined to a very small volume) and waves (which spread out over a large area of space)?

To confuse the situation further, early experiments (for example,

---

[1]The presentation and discussion of the new physics which follow rely on the physicist Capra's (1975) clear description of these ideas and concepts.

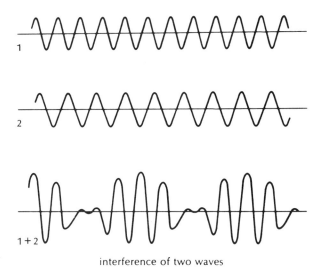

interference of two waves

Figure 1. Interference of two waves (from Capra, 1975, p. 34).

those of Rutherford) had shown that atoms, instead of being hard and indestructible, consisted of vast regions of space in which extremely small particles moved. These particles, however, were nothing at all like the solid objects of classical physics. These subatomic units of matter are very abstract entities which, like electromagnetic radiation, have a dual aspect. Depending on how they are examined, they appear sometimes as particles and sometimes as waves. So, what the new physics faced were light waves that acted at times like particles, and subatomic particles that acted at times like waves. Just what were these "wavicles"? A very confusing situation indeed!

How then did physics deal with both the obvious limitations of a mechanistic, atomistic Newtonianism and the paradoxical wave–particle nature of light and of subatomic "particles"? The answer to the first part of this question lies in Albert Einstein's special theory of relativity, whereas the latter part is addressed by quantum theory.

According to relativity theory, space is not merely three-dimensional, and time is not a separate entity. Rather, the two are intimately connected, and together they form a four-dimensional continuum, *space–time*. In addition, the idea that time moves steadily and unceasingly in a never-ending universal flow (a belief characteristic of the Newtonian model) is rejected. Separate observers will order events differently in time if these same observers move with different velocities relative to the witnessed events. In such a case, two events which are seen as occurring simultaneously by one observer may occur in a different temporal sequence for another. All measurements which involve space and time thus lose their absolute significance, since the Newtonian concept of an absolute space as the stage of physical phenomena is abandoned, as is the concept of an absolute time. Space and time are seen for what they really are—mental constructs; both are merely elements of the language a particular observer uses for his or her description of the phenomena.

These concepts of space and time are so basic for our description of natural phenomena that their modification entailed a foundational alteration in the very framework that we use to describe nature, the most important consequence of this change being the realization that mass is nothing but a form of energy. Even an object at rest has energy stored in its mass, the relation between the two being given by the now famous equation $E = mc^2$ ("c" representing the speed of light).

The key to the answer of the wave–particle paradox came from quantum theory. It was Max Planck who discovered that the energy of heat radiation is not emitted continuously, but appears in the form of energy "packets." Einstein called these packets "quanta," and recognized them as a fundamental aspect of nature. He postulated that light appears not only as electromagnetic waves but also in the form of these quanta, which have since been accepted as true particles and are called "photons" (the photon remains an intriguing sort of particle, however, being massless and always traveling at the speed of light).

The puzzling wave–particle contradiction was solved in a very surprising and unexpected way, a way which called into question the very foundation of the mechanistic, Newtonian world-view—nothing less than the *reality of matter itself*. At the subatomic level: (a) matter does not exist with certainty at definite places, but rather shows "tendencies to exist," and (b) events do not occur with certainty at definite times, but rather show "tendencies to occur." In quantum theory, these tendencies are expressed as probabilities—mathematical quantities which take the form of waves. This is the way in which matter manifests itself as both particle and wave *at the same time*. These same tendencies are not actual three-dimensional waves (like sound or water), but are, rather, "probability waves"—abstract mathematical quantities (with all the characteristic properties of waves) which are related to the probabilities of finding the particles at particular points in space at particular times. All the laws of atomic physics are expressed in terms of these probabilities. One can never predict an atomic event with certainty; only how likely it is to occur.

This inability to predict precisely atomic events was addressed by the physicist–philosopher Werner Heisenberg. Heisenberg theorized and demonstrated that it is not possible, either in practice or *in principle*, to know enough about the present to make a complete and accurate prediction about the future. Even if one has the time, the determination, and the best possible measuring devices, *it is not possible.* The very nature of things is such that one must choose which aspect of the phenomenon one wishes to know best, for one can know only one aspect precisely. More specifically, in the subatomic realm, one cannot know both the position *and* the momentum of a particle with absolute precision. One can know both of them approximately, but the more that is known about one, the less one knows about the other. Either the position or momentum can be determined exactly; but, in that case, nothing can be determined about the other. This is Heisenberg's uncertainty principle.

The kind of universal reality revealed by these quantum-theory insights is nothing short of remarkable, awe-inspiring, almost incredible. Consider Capra's (1975) conclusion:

> Quantum theory has thus demolished the classical concepts of solid objects and of strictly deterministic laws of nature. At the subatomic level, the solid material objects of classical physics dissolve into wavelike patterns of probabilities, and these patterns, ultimately, do not represent probabilities of things, but rather probabilities of interconnections. A careful analysis of the process of observation in atomic physics has shown that the subatomic particles have *no meaning as isolated entities, but can be only understood as interconnections* between the preparation of an experiment and the subsequent measurement. Quantum theory thus reveals *a basic oneness of the universe.* It shows that we cannot decompose the world into independently existing smallest units. As we penetrate into matter, nature does not show us any isolated "basic building blocks," but rather appears as a complicated web of relations between the various parts of the whole. (pp. 56–57, italics added)

Capra is not alone. The physicist Henry Stapp (discussing the theory of relativity) apparently concurs, stating that the world appears

> not as a structure built out of independently existing, unanalyzable entities, but rather as a web of relationships between elements whose meanings arise entirely from their relationship to the whole. (Woodward & Lubenow, 1979, p. 85)

It seems that what we have come to know as objects and events are really *patterns* in a universal, cosmic process.

This train of thought has been carried further. Capra (1975) goes on to point out that these natural relationships

> always include the observer in an essential way. The human observer constitutes the final link in the chain of observational processes, and the properties of any atomic object can be understood only in terms of the object's interaction with the observer. This means that *the classical ideal of an objective description of nature is no longer valid.* The Cartesian partition between the I and the world, between the observer and the observed, cannot be made . . . we can never speak about nature without, at the same time, speaking about ourselves. (p. 57, italics added)

It is simply not possible to observe reality without, at the very same moment, changing it. Zukav (1979), in a similar vein, believes that the ancient philosophers of the East were right all along in their insistence that the observer and the observed are fundamentally one; that when we study nature there is no way to avoid the fact that nature is studying itself. Physicist Saul-Paul Sirag puts it this way: "If what we can know of the world is a function of the structure of the mind, then what we are elucidating in doing fundamental physics is the structure of the mind" (Woodward & Lubenow, 1979, pp. 85, 87). And, lastly, consider Sir Arthur Eddington (the renowned British astronomer), who once proclaimed that "the stuff of the world is mind-stuff."

From "waves," "particles," and "quanta" we have moved to "the observer," "the observed," and "the mind." Recalling that psychology ("psyche-ology") literally means "science of the mind," the natural flow at this point seems to be from physics to psychology. In fact, Zukav (1979) states quite matter-of-factly: "Physics has become a branch of psychology, or perhaps the other way round" (p. 56).

The Old and New Psychology

Let us now take a look at contemporary natural scientific psychology. Does the above discussion of the changing perspective (world-view) of physics have anything to offer the psychologist? The answer, as you may have guessed, is "Yes." If one places the approach of this natural scientific psychology in the context of the changing world-view of the physicist, an interesting pattern emerges.

Psychology, in an attempt to be rigorously "scientific" and objective, has made certain assumptions concerning what there is about the human individual that can be studied. These assumptions are essentially that any human phenomenon must be, in one way or another: (a) observable (i.e., one must be able to perceive the phenomenon with one or more of the senses), (b) measurable (i.e., one must be able to quantify the defined properties of the observed phenomenon), and (c) of a kind that it is possible for more than one observer to agree on its existence and characteristics. It is human *behavior* that fits these assumptions, and *behaviorism* that characterizes the work of contemporary psychology. Those of us engaged in psychological inquiry know very well the extensive range and all-pervading nature of this behavioristic approach. Even the new wave of cognitive psychologists with their entourage of internal mediating variables are eventually confronted with verbal behavior and the self-imposed necessity of remaining faithful to these three assumptions.

Examining psychology as behaviorism more closely, some further implications are revealed. It is often concluded that the object of the natural sciences is to investigate *spatio-temporal* entities and the interrelationships that exist among them (Colaizzi, 1973). Being behavioristic in its approach, does mainstream psychology also have spatio-temporal entities as its subject matter? Behavior, being both observable and measurable, is certainly spatial in nature (any individual, for example, occupies a given space). But in what sense is it temporal? One must examine the methodology of natural scientific psychology for a clue.

In the actual practice of behavioristic psychology, hypotheses are formed and then tested in a rigorous, experimental fashion. The formulation of hypotheses is the key. An hypothesis is, in general, a statement about the relationship between two entities or variables. In particular, it is a prediction about the *cause–effect* relationship between the first or independent variable (the proposed cause which the experimenter can manipulate) and the second or dependent variable (the proposed effect which is observed). Usually a proposed hypothesis will take this cause–effect form directly, as in this specific example: "Lack of sleep will lead to an increase in one's aggressive behavior"; that is, the cause (lack of sleep) will lead to an effect (an increase in aggressive behavior). A more general case would include two notions with which we are all too familiar: stimulus and response. The *stimulus* (that which impinges on the organism's senses) is usually thought to elicit (cause) the *response* (the motor, perceptual, or cognitive effect). In any case, the important point is that an unstated *linear temporality* is implied in any proposed attempt to determine a cause–effect (or stimulus–response) relationship. One predicts that the effect will follow directly in time the presence of the cause. Similarly, if the proposed cause is absent, the effect will not occur. Evidently, behavioristic psychology does in fact examine spatio-temporal relationships.

Some key terms should stand out for you, namely *space, time,* and *cause–effect*. Sound familiar? They should. They are the foundational concepts of the Newtonian physics reviewed above. In the same way, with the same conceptual foundation, psychology patterns itself after the "old physics," after that Newtonian world-view which the new physics has shown to be narrow and restrictive. Treating behavior as the only objective ("object-like") aspect of people has led psychologists to a profound reductionism. In the name of experiment, the search continues for the cause behind every effect, and the cause in one instance becomes the effect in the next. The dizzying process goes on until every postulated variable that can possibly be operationalized has been examined in great detail. This reduction is indeed quite a search! It is a search for the "basic building blocks" of human behavior. An intensive, microscopic, Newtonian search for the "atoms" that make us up, a search for those small, indestructible "truths" that will answer all the "whys" of what we do and how we act.

Further reflection and comparison reveals still more. The stimulus–response (S–R) model just discussed does indeed view the person as a passive entity just as Newton saw matter as passive. But S–R theory also sees the forces (stimuli) as separate from and independent of the person, as something (some *thing*) external which impinges. Even Newton himself believed force (the force of gravity) to be somehow intrinsic to the physical bodies involved, force as "rigidly connected with the bodies it acted upon." One must go back to Democritus to find discussion of "force'" as separate and independent. Behavioristic psychology is really patterned, therefore, not so much on pure Newtonian thought as on a pre-Newtonian Greek atomism. When one thinks of the change in the natural scientific world-view based on the insights of the new physics, it is staggering to see the modern self-proclaimed science of psychology floundering in the sea of Democritean atomism. Why this is so is beyond the scope of the present discussion, but the implications for change must be examined.

The new physicists have clearly pointed out that what may appear to be one thing may really be another—what seems to be a subatomic particle at one moment may be completely wave-like the next. The existential-phenomenologists remind us that people are not just objects in nature either. Rather, a total, indissoluble unity or interrelationship exists between the individual and his or her world. The existential man or woman is *more* than simply natural man or woman. In the truest sense, the person is viewed as having no existence apart from the world, and the world as having no existence apart from persons. Each individual and his or her world are said to *co-constitute* one another. In traditional psychology, people and their environment are seen, in effect, as two separate and distinct things or poles. This traditional conception is rejected by the existential-phenomenological psychologist, however, in favor of the above-mentioned unity. Capra's (1975) own conclusion appears to be consistent with this person–world view:

> The further we penetrate into the submicroscopic world, the more we shall realize how the modern physicist . . . has come to see the world as a system of inseparable, interacting, and ever-moving components, *with man as an integral part of this system.* (p. 11, italics added)

With these thoughts in mind, it is here suggested that a direct analogy can be made between the dual wave–particle nature of the above-mentioned phenomena in physics, and the nature of the human individual; that is, the nature of reality as perceived and understood on the *microscopic* level as examined by the particle physicist will have inescapable manifestations on the *macroscopic,* human level as well. Given the nature of interference patterns and the photoelectric effect, it is apparent that light will appear as a wave or as a particle *depending solely on the approach and subsequent method of the investigator*—the observer and the observed co-constituting the situation as it appears, neither one would be the same without the presence of the other. The same is true in psychology. Behavioristic psychology has chosen an objective, reductive approach with its attendent experimental method where the observer–experimenter is treated as a separate, neutral, and noninteractive agent in relation to the phenomenon (behavior) being observed. What this has revealed, powerfully and accurately, is the "object" side of human existence. The side of being human that can be, in fact, described objectively and investigated in a fashion consistent with the three assumptions discussed above. To borrow from the language of physics, the "particle" side of human nature has been and is now being revealed by these tactics. But is that all?

The answer is a resounding "No." That is not all. Just as mechanistic Newtonian atomism was found to be too narrow in scope to encompass the findings of the new physics (however efficiently and beautifully it handled many of the macroscopic phenomena of physical mechanics), so our objective behavioristic psychology, which is based on this Newtonian approach, appears as far too restrictive a model to deal successfully with any human phenomenon other than behavior. This seems especially true in light of the above-noted similarity between the existential-phenomenological insight that the individual and world co-constitute one another, and the conclusion reached by the new physicists that the observer and the observed are fundamentally one.

You may at this point say "Fine. The humanists, the phenomenologists, and the growth psychologists have all been saying this for years but without successfully providing an alternative. There is still no model for comparison." Not so. Such a model is there for the taking. That is, the conscious, thinking, behaving human being also has a "wave" side. If the approach one takes, if the place one "stands in," so to speak, is changed, then the "particle" side will dissolve, and the "wave-like" aspects will be revealed.

Our "wave" nature is revealed primarily in the apparent free choice we have in our decisions and in our actions (the adjective "apparent" is used only in present deference to the determinism which underlies the behavioristic school of thought). We have all experienced our sense of choice, our "free will," at one time or another. This sense is manifest in our cognizing, in our emotions, and through our intuitive faculties. Yet, however real it appears to be, it has proven to be inaccessible to the questioning and methods of our objective experimental psychology. The centuries-old "determinism versus free will" debate continues, therefore, with little sign of relief. This issue will be examined below at greater length.

It is here proposed that this "wave" side of ours can be best described as *volition*. Volition is chosen rather than free will for a number of reasons. The term "will" has a history of different uses with many different meanings. It has been used loosely and thrown about in a very sloppy, unrigorous fashion. In addition, the term brings to mind the notion of "will power," which implicitly implies only intensity. Volition, on the other hand, is being used here to describe a phenomenon which has not only intensity (or magnitude if you will), but also direction. In classical physics, the descriptive concept used to illustrate any entity that has both a magnitude and a direction is *vector* (a force vector is, for example, described as having a certain strength, given in measurable units, as well as an aim or direction). *Volition is vectorlike in nature*—one can decide not only how much one will attend to a given person or situation (that is, the magnitude or intensity of will) but also the degree of concentration one will evidence (that is, the focus or purity of direction). Just as in physics, where the wave equation is conceived to represent a vector on a matrix of particles, so the volitional aspects of a human being can be represented by a vector on the matrix of his or her behaviors.[2] That is, a vector describes what is necessary (in a mathematical sense) for the transformation from one state to another. Given this analogy, "state" may represent "particle" in the physical sense, or "operationalized behavior" in the psychological.

In this context, volition is also *intentional*. The existential-phenomenologist points out that we are never merely conscious but are always conscious *of*, that consciousness always has an object (whether that be a thing, another person, a dream, or an idea) (Valle & King, 1978b). Consciousness is said, therefore, to be intentional (it always has an intended object) or to be characterized by intentionality.[3] Given these insights, volition (as a vector) is not merely another "ghost in the machine," but, rather, can be thought of as *process*, as a "tending toward," as *engaged* consciousness, or engaged subjectivity—not simply as "will," but as a "will for." The possibility of achieving a transcendent state of *pure* consciousness, that is, consciousness without an object (Merrell-Wolff, 1973), is a valid and critically important issue to recognize, but one that is beyond the scope of the present discussion.

There is much evidence for these notions, both ancient and modern. Patanjali, in his *Yoga Sutras* (a classic text of yoga psychology written

[2]The author wishes to thank Karl Pribram for this particular insight.
[3]See Moss, Chapter 7, de Silva, Chapter 13, and R. von Eckartsberg and R. Valle, Chapter 14, for other discussions of *intentionality*.—Eds.

around 200 B.C.), discusses the continuous stream of thought-*waves*[4] which flow through the mind—what present-day psychologists refer to as the mind's stream of "associations." In this context, Arya (1978) described the Eastern philosophical notion of volition as "universal waves," waves of volition which are as inseparable a part of the universe as are matter and energy (as conceptualized by the special theory of relativity discussed above). Many schools of Eastern thought speak of the directional quality of volition (e.g., Swami Rama, 1976). They prescribe formal meditation (the continuing practice of clearing the mind of all thought and emotion) as a means of developing concentration, the goal being the ability to bring one's mind to "one-pointedness," or pure focus at will. In fact, Patanjali himself defines Yoga as "the control of the thought-waves in the mind" (Swami Ajaya, 1979, p. 13). One can practice directionality of will just as one might practice playing the piano. At any rate, it can now be asked, what are the implications of conceptualizing the "wave" side of human nature as a vectorlike volition?

Let us return to the controversial "determinism versus free will" debate and see how this knot may be unraveled, or at least revisioned, by the issues just discussed. Whether human behavior is completely predictable (based on our experimental skills in identifying all relevant variables and the cause–effect network they form), or is merely an aside to the free exercise of will is very much like the, at first, apparently unresolvable particle and wave nature of light. Just as the wave–particle issue was resolved by showing that both properties exist in the very nature of light—they co-constitute one another, they make each other up—so might the dichotomy between free will and determinism be seen more clearly in a different context.

Free will and determinism are commonly thought of as polar-opposite ends of a linear scale. Let us keep this semantic model for a moment. It is proposed that under two conditions the "totally determined" human being is, in fact, the reality that is evident. These conditions occur when volition is either (a) completely lacking in magnitude or intensity regarding the issue at hand (one might say that such an individual has no desire or motivation to act in or to think about the situation) or (b) completely lacking a focus or direction regarding the relevant issue (one could say that one's attention is gone or scattered, presenting a diffused, nondirectional volition regardless of its intensity). In either case, one's "wave" nature is somewhat irrelevant, and one is indeed merely "particle." As, however, the magnitude and direction of volition (one's "wave" nature) increases regarding the issue at hand, the purely objectified and predictable human subject (one's "particle" side) dis-

---

[4]See Swami Rama's, Chapter 15, descriptions of the "waves of consciousness."—Eds.

solves proportionately. Understandably, the person becomes less and less like a predictable, controllable "thing" and is seen to be more and more under his or her own control. This "wave–particle" nature of human existence cannot be stressed too strongly. In the very foundation of our nature these two aspects co-constitute one another in the strict existential-phenomenological sense. Neither side has meaning, neither side can exist as such without accounting for the other, just as "light" as a conceptual reflection of our experience would now be meaningless without mutual consideration of its wave and particle properties. As one who examines and questions, as one who asks and describes, as a scientific inquirer in the truest sense, you cannot separate these aspects in any way, shape, or form without ripping apart the very phenomenon you seek to understand—in this case, human being.

If these insights hold, then the reasons for the determinism–free will argument become clearer. More specifically, the strict determinists ignored the "wave" nature of human existence—their experimental method narrowing their view and allowing them to see only our "particle" side; and those clinging to strict free-will interpretations ignored the "particle" side of human existence—their introspectionistic methods allowing them to see only our "wave" side. One can venture even further and hypothesize that knowing more of our "particle" side in any given situation necessitates *in principle* knowing less about our "wave" side, and vice versa—investigating one's "wave-like" aspects at any given time demands the impossibility of accurately measuring the complementary "particle" factors. It seems that here, on the macroscopic, psychological level, we have a situation directly analogous to the one addressed by the Heisenberg uncertainty principle, verified repeatedly by experiment to hold true on the microscopic, subatomic level. The free will–determinism issue thus becomes just one more illusory dichotomy.

At this point, the new direction for psychology which was promised earlier can now be offered. The new physics mathematically describes matter as not existing with certainty at any definite place but rather showing a "tendency to exist," and atomic events as not occurring with certainty at definite times but revealing instead a "tendency to occur." These insights are directly tied in with the understanding of the wave–particle nature of material substance. So it will be with a new psychology that realizes the "wave–particle" nature of the human individual.[5] That is, human behavior and thought do not occur with certainty at definite times but show instead a "tendency to occur." This statement is based directly on the volitional, "wave" side of human nature just described. This probabilistic "tendency to act" is really based, however, on our "tendency to exercise directed volition" at any time. If one accepts that

[5]See Weber, Chapter 5, for reference to the "wave–particle" nature of consciousness.—Eds.

we, as human beings, demonstrate a "tendency to behave," rather than completely determined behavior, a startling conclusion is reached: *human behavior can never be predicted with certainty* because of its intrinsic "wave" nature. In fact, one can now see that the variance, the error that is evident in all experimental data, *is* the ignored volitional side of the human subject. Our "wave" side is the reason there is a "built-in" variability that can *never* be accounted for in the purely "particle" approach of an objective social science as psychology is presently conceived.

Earlier, Capra reminded us that the solid material objects of Newtonian physics dissolve into wave-like probabilities of "interconnections," and that nature does not show us any isolated "basic building blocks" but rather a complicated "web of relations" between the various parts of the whole. Capra (1975) expands on these points, describing a rather remarkable situation:

> Relativity theory has had a profound influence on our picture of matter by forcing us to modify our concept of a particle in an essential way. In classical physics, the mass of an object had always been associated with an indestructible material substance, with some "stuff" of which all things were thought to be made. Relativity theory showed that mass has nothing to do with any substance, but is a form of energy. Energy, however, is a dynamic quantity associated with activity, or with *processes*. The fact that the mass of a particle is equivalent to a certain amount of energy means that the particle can no longer be seen as a static object, but has to be conceived as a *dynamic pattern*, a process involving the energy which manifests itself as the particle's mass. (pp. 66–67, italics added)

It is proposed that the new psychology, obligated to account for the "wave" as well as the "particle" side of human nature, will see the human individual in purely *relational* terms.[6] Since we all are "wave-like" in nature and do indeed exist in a "social" situation (that is, as inescapably together on this planet), the account of one individual (his or her action, thought, and emotion) *must invariably include* those other persons with which this particular individual interacts. This condition of "interaction" is met whenever the individual being examined is directly engaged in intentional action directed at an other, is thinking in some way about an other, and/or has feelings and emotions which are clearly involved with an other's existence. To put it another way, the volition of one individual is directed toward another. Theoretical mathematics has successfully demonstrated that the wave aspect of any physical entity extends to *infinity*,[7] it goes on without end and only *seems to be* confined to the

---

[6]This is consistent with V. Valle and Kruger's, Chapter 19, insight that the "substance of reality" for feminine consciousness is our *relationship* with one another.—Eds.

[7]One argument for the "oneness" of all in the universe, for a universal interconnectedness of all that exists, is based on this mathematical demonstration that the wave components of all physical entities share a common meeting place in infinity, thereby comprising an inseparable Unity.

limited space in which its form is manifest. So it is with directed volition. The physical nearness of two "interacting" individuals becomes irrelevant. If the "wave" of volition is directed by one to another (we often say if one is *conscious* of the other) then they are said to be "interacting."

We find ourselves confronted with a cosmic social psychology of sorts, whose subject matter will necessarily include the dynamic patterns of human interaction and the processes involved in the formation of these patterns. This compares with traditional experimental social psychology which conceptualizes individuals as separate "subjects" who supposedly "interact" with methodologically predetermined or "allowable" paths of volition—an approach which is living out a self-fulfilling "particle" prophecy that will never reveal our "wave" nature as well. The new physicist describes the constantly occurring subatomic processes where matter and energy are clearly and completely interchangeable, where one particle (with a certain energy of motion and mass) can become any other particle or particles (with conserved but different motion and mass) when these particles collide—their true wave–particle nature being revealed in these collisions. When two individuals "collide," a similar outcome of this interaction also occurs with the very same revelation. Many psychologists, philosophers, and literary figures have, in fact, described how we seem to "die" and be "reborn" in every social encounter, the degree of "death" and "rebirth" being dependent on the intensity and importance of the interaction.

Descriptive analyses of human nature as a dynamic pattern of social interdependency have been undertaken in several different ways. The dialogal existentialists, a number of Jungian analysts, and the poet–writer Anaïs Nin have all, for example, described this aspect of human nature. One does not necessarily have to rely on description alone, however. As is true of all wave-like phenomena, volitional waves also create interference patterns when they cross. One can envision the new psychologist analyzing a complex pattern of "volitional interference" involving the directed volition of a number of human subjects via some psychological analogue to Fourier analysis, Fourier analysis being a sophisticated mathematical technique for extracting the "pure," individual wave-forms that comprise a complex interference pattern. A Fourier-type analysis of complex patterns of human interaction would be a giant step in our self-understanding.

The effects that the new physics can have on our psychological theorizing do not end here. For example, physicists are currently collecting compelling new evidence in support of Bell's Theorem, which assumes that separate parts of the universe may be connected at a fundamental level, and that things once connected remain attached over distance by some unknown force traveling *faster* than the speed of light.

Such findings have led the physicist Finkelstein to insist that: "We are about to undergo revisions of the concepts of space and time [even] *more drastic than those engendered by relativity and quantum physics*" (Woodward & Lubenow, 1979, p. 87, italics added). It should be most interesting to note the essentially unavoidable ramifications a theorem such as Bell's will eventually have on both physics and psychology.

There is, however, more than futuristic speculation involved here. Such fundamental theoretical change, with more obviously direct ties to psychology and philosophy, is already in the wind, as evidenced by the new holistic models of Karl Pribram and David Bohm. Pribram, noted neuropsychologist and brain researcher, has proposed that the human brain deals in wave-like neural interactions, interpreting the wave frequencies and storing the resulting image (much like a three-dimensional hologram), not in a localized fashion, but dispersed throughout the brain (Ferguson, 1978).[8] Bohm, a theoretical physicist, in describing an enfolding-unfolding holonomic universe, may be presenting not only a new model of consciousness but an entirely new cosmology based on an invisible flux of inseparable interconnectedness (Weber, 1978).[9] Bentov (1978) examines this state of infinite interconnectedness, relating it to Eastern concepts of reality and to the psychological process of individuation thereby demonstrating the relevance of the new holistic models to the understanding of human phenomena.

With this dual "wave–particle" approach to human nature in mind, all sorts of questions begin to form. Just as some examples, consider: "Is 'one-pointedness' of mind analogous to the speed of light constant 'c'?"; "Does successful psychotherapy invariably deal with a directing of volition?"; Will holistic approaches be the only ones that successfully account for our dual nature?"; and, recognizing that the breaking of particle bonds in an atom's nucleus releases tremendous amounts of energy, "Will breaking the 'bonds' of ego through meditative practices have an analogous and equally dramatic effect?"

When he introduced his section on "Modern Physics," Capra (1975) began:

> Two separate developments—that of relativity theory and of atomic physics—shattered all the principal concepts of the Newtonian world view: the notion of absolute space and time, the elementary solid particles, the strictly causal nature of physical phenomena, and the ideal of an objective description of nature. None of these concepts could be extended to the new domains into which physics was now penetrating. (p. 50)

In the presentation just completed above, there is an implicit, presumed belief that the accelerating conceptual change in physics will have an

[8]See Pribram, Chapter 6.—Eds.
[9]See Weber, Chapter 5.—Eds.

analogous and equally disruptive parallel in psychology. More specifically, psychologists will experience a dramatic change in their world-
view, including drastic alterations in concepts like the strictly causal
nature of behavioral (and experiential) phenomena, the notion of person
as "object" to be reduced in order to be understood, and the ideal of an
objective description of human nature. As the "New Age" progresses,
watching behavioral psychology slowly evolve into a relativistic quantum
psychology will be, as *Star Trek's* Mr. Spock so often said, "Fascinating!"

References

Arya, U. Personal communication, November, 1978.

Bentov, I. Comments on the holographic view of reality. *Re-Vision*, 1978, *1*(3 & 4), 96–97.

Capra, F. *The tao of physics.* New York: Bantam Books, 1975.

Colaizzi, P. F. *Reflection and research in psychology: A phenomenological study of learning.*
    Dubuque, Iowa: Kendall-Hunt, 1973.

Ferguson, M. Karl Pribram's changing reality. *Re-Vision*, 1978, *1*(3 & 4), 8–13.

Heisenberg, W. The representation of nature in contemporary physics. In R. May (Ed.),
    Symbolism in religion and literature. New York: Braziller, 1960.

LeShan, L. *The medium, the mystic, and the physicist.* New York: Ballantine Books, 1974.

Margenau, H. *The nature of physical reality.* Woodbridge, Conn.: Ox Bow Press, 1977.

Maslow, A. H. *Toward a psychology of being.* New York: Van Nostrand Reinhold, 1962.

Merrell-Wolff, F. *The philosophy of consciousness without an object.* New York: Julian Press,
    1973.

Needleman, J. *A sense of the cosmos.* New York: Dutton, 1965.

Postle, D. *Fabric of the universe.* New York: Crown, 1976.

Siu, R. G. *The tao of science.* Cambridge: The M.I.T. Press, 1957.

Swami Ajaya. Yoga psychology. *Himalayan News*, 1979, September, p. 13.

Swami Rama. A few glimpses of concentration. In Swami Rama, *Lectures on yoga.* Glenview,
    Ill.: Himalayan International Institute, 1976.

Tart, C. T. (Ed.), *Transpersonal psychologies.* New York: Harper & Row, 1975.

Thompson, W. I. Of physics and tantra yoga. In W. I. Thompson, *Passages about earth.* New
    York: Harper & Row, 1973.

Valle, R. S., & King, M. (Eds.), *Existential-phenomenological alternatives for psychology.* New
    York: Oxford University Press, 1978. (a)

Valle, R. S., & King, M. An introduction to existential-phenomenological thought in
    psychology. In R. S. Valle & M. King (Eds.), *Existential-phenomenological alternatives for
    psychology.* New York: Oxford University Press, 1978. (b)

Weber, R. Field consciousness and field ethics. *Re-Vision*, 1978, *1*(3 & 4), 19–23.

Woodward, K. L., & Lubenow, G. C. Physics and mysticism. *Newsweek*, 1979, July 23, 85–87.

Zukav, G. *The dancing Wu Li masters.* New York: Morrow, 1979.

22

Chemistry and Human Awareness
NATURAL SCIENTIFIC CONNECTIONS

Neil E. Schore

Chemistry? Chemistry and human awareness? A curious combination, especially in light of the oft-expressed public perception that science is somehow fundamentally unnatural or "anti-human." Certainly the application of scientific knowledge in hasty or ill-considered ways has fostered this attitude. Concerns over the use and misuse of scientific knowledge in the development of new technology have led to much discussion among scientists themselves. Such discussions will no doubt continue as the interrelationships between science, technology, and society in general are continually redefined in an attempt to derive the greatest mutual benefit from these relationships. Here, however, we look at the science itself: science as a field, as a human endeavor, as a mechanism by which one may investigate and interact with one's environment.

The primary activity in basic science is the pursuit of knowledge. Regardless of the individual field, of the specific information sought, or the methods employed, the same motivations operate. The scientist's quest is not unique to the scientist: it is a natural and fundamental human endeavor. Indeed, the desire to discover the true "nature of things" is so basic to the species that it can almost be considered an indispensable prerequisite of "humanness." It is not surprising, therefore, that philosophies of and methodologies for the elucidation of fundamental truths are to be found in virtually every culture, with innumerable influ-

Neil E. Schore • Department of Chemistry, University of California at Davis, Davis, California 95616.

ences of history and human condition combining to color what is meant by truth and what is accepted as "proper" methodology. Whether "truth" as defined by Culture "A" coincides with that as defined by Culture "B" is usually of little import unless the peoples involved happen to be neighbors and at least one is given to a high degree of aggressive behavior. On the other hand, similar truths, independently arrived at by disparate groups or individuals, may develop a sort of general acceptance by force of numbers. With the passage of time and the refinement of methodology, some of the original ideas may ultimately be recognized as part of a valid description of nature, and the insights thus developed may be used to expand further the body of knowledge in both its breadth and its depth. The joy of discovery and the exhilaration of "knowing," these peculiarly human feelings, have been shared by ancient scholars and prehistoric astronomers, by Eastern philosophers and Western physical scientists alike; and where these feelings kindled the desire to know more, significant advances in the state of knowledge became possible.

The Spectrum of Physical Sciences

When we speak of modern physical science, we refer to a large array of disciplines, each with its own history of insight and discovery, a history both of ideas that led to fruitful investigation and of ideas that proved to be dead ends. Physical science consists of much more than ideas, however; it requires the development of methodology to observe physical phenomena and to explain observations within a well-established framework. This framework is derived by combining new ideas with explanations of previously observed phenomena. When old explanations are supported by new experimentation, they are retained and amplified; otherwise, they are greatly modified or even discarded. Thus, sciences build upon themselves and each other.

We talk about individual disciplines, such as biology, physics, and chemistry, and, indeed, we introduce these to students in the typical educational curriculum as if they were independent entities. Of course, these labels do have a purpose: historically, development of these fields into mature sciences occurred more or less independently of one another, primarily over the course of the nineteenth century (Ravetz, 1974), and each name connotes in a general way an area of interest more or less distinct from the other two. In the last decades of the twentieth century, however, we recognize significant areas of practical overlap among these disciplines. Biochemistry, molecular biology, physical chemistry, and chemical physics all describe major fields on the "borderlines" of the traditional disciplines. Indeed, the very concept of "traditional disciplines" with "borderlines" is becoming obsolete. Rather than differing from one another in some fundamental, qualitative sense, these fields can be considered to be part of a physical-science continuum. The differences are, in reality, matters of degree: quantitative rather than qualitative in nature. Each discipline has specific objects of study, such as the cells of biology and the atoms of chemistry. The obvious qualitative differences between objects such as these cannot be minimized; nevertheless, as a practical matter, many of the most basic differences in methodology, instrumentation, and the general experimental approach are dictated by the quantitative differences: differences in size, in mass, in electric charge. The same can be said of other characteristic areas of investigation within these fields, such as the study of energy requirements for processes to take place and the rates of these processes. Using a somewhat crude one-dimensional diagram (Figure 1), let us locate some of these sciences, focusing on just those characteristics that illustrate the continuous nature of the scientific spectrum.

Horizontally, across the bottom of the chart, are listed a selection of fields representative of the range encompassed by physics, chemistry, and biology. The rest of the chart presents typical objects of investigation and some of their properties, corresponding to their position along the horizontal scale. Thus the most elementary objects physicists study are the pointlike leptons and quarks, currently favored as the elementary constituents of all physical matter. Understanding their interactions re-

QUANTUM EFFECTS

OBJECTS:	LEPTONS QUARKS	HADRONS (MESONS, BARYONS)	ATOMIC NUCLEI	ATOMS	SMALL MOLECULES	TYPICAL ORGANIC MOLECULES	MODERATE AND LARGE ORGANIC MOLECULES	ORGANIZED ENTITIES (E.G. VIRUSES ON UP)
SIZE:	VERY SMALL	10^{-13}cm	10^{-12}cm	10^{-8} cm		10^{-7} cm		$\geq 10^{-4}$cm
FORCES:	STRONG NUCLEAR ELECTROMAGNETIC WEAK NUCLEAR GRAVITATIONAL			ELECTROMAGNETIC WEAK NUCLEAR		ELECTROMAGNETIC		
RATES:	VERY FAST	$\leq 10^{23}$ sec^{-1}	$\leq 10^{21}$ sec^{-1}	$\leq 10^{15}$ sec^{-1}	$\leq 10^{12}$ sec^{-1}	$\leq 10^{9}$ sec^{-1}		
ENERGIES:	VERY LARGE	10^{10}eV	10^{6}eV	10eV		4eV		2eV
FIELD:	PARTICLE PHYSICS	NUCLEAR		CHEMICAL PHYSICS, PHYSICAL CHEMISTRY	CHEMISTRY (INORGANIC)	ORGANIC CHEMISTRY	BIOCHEMISTRY	MOLECULAR BIOLOGY, BIOLOGY

Figure 1. The scientific spectrum.

quires invoking the operation of the four known natural forces: the strong and weak nuclear, the electromagnetic, and the gravitational. All that we can say about the nature of the physical universe rests ultimately on the interactions brought about by these forces, for both in their origins and in their existence throughout time lies the basis for the properties of everything that any physical scientist studies.

Moving gradually to the right of our chart, we encounter the larger, composite objects of study. We associate each class of objects with the fastest rate at which one of their members is known to do something significant, as far as researchers in that particular area seem to be concerned. Thus the shortest-lived of the particles called hadrons may exist for only 10^{-23} sec (Schwitters, 1977) whereas the shortest-lived composite atomic nuclei persist for but 10^{-21} sec (Bromley, 1978). Measurements of time periods like this are not possible in a conventional sense. The inherent properties of matter at this level are of a nature totally foreign to our macroscopic and intuitive experience. Among the consequences of such a short lifetime is a measurable and predictable imprecision in the determination of energy content required by the Heisenberg uncertainty principle.[1] The shorter something lives, the less accurately may its energy be determined; thus lifetime limitations can be estimated on the basis of imprecisions in energy measurement that are shown not to be instrument-limited. The impressive energies involved (listed in Figure 1 in electron volts) refer to the approximate amount required to convert one hadron to another, and to induce the breakup of an atomic nucleus into smaller fragments.

We next leave the realm of subatomic particles and reach the level of the atom, entering the world of the chemist. The strong but short-ranged force that holds the tiny nucleus together is no longer a matter of concern; from this point, virtually all physical phenomena are under the control of the electromagnetic interactions, the attraction and repulsion of like- and unlike-charged particles respectively. Interactions of atoms with electromagnetic radiation can take place in as little as 10^{-15} sec, and involve energies of up to some 10 electron volts, an insignificant amount compared with the energies of physics, but still equivalent to quite high-energy ultraviolet light. Classical chemistry begins with the combination of atoms into molecules, linked by spring-like bonds composed of negative electrons mutually attracted to the positively charged nuclei, all vibrating up to 10^{12} times a second. We begin here to discern the bridging nature of chemistry, linking the puzzling and often bizarre world of physics, which is almost abstract and unreal compared with everyday

[1]See R. Valle, Chapter 21, for a discussion of Heisenberg's uncertainty principle and its implications for psychology and philosophy.—Eds.

experience, and the tangible, familiar, and very visible objects of biological study.

The chemistry of larger molecules, based on the linkage of multitudes of carbon atoms into the more and more sophisticated structures of life science, dominate the remainder of the chart. The areas of interest of the organic chemist begin with a relatively small number of basic combinations of atoms and lead up to the study of the complex biomolecules, the proteins, sugars, enzymes, and nucleic acid of the biochemist. The largest objects in our spectrum are the organized structures of the living entities themselves, the subject of biology. The chemical energy involved in the common processes linking respiration and food metabolism covers a mere 2-volt energy range, which stands in striking contrast to the massive hidden power holding the tiny fragments of the atoms together. How delicate a balance must exist in the distribution of these energies in a universe so constructed as to allow life processes to go on and thrive!

Finally, somewhat breathlessly, we have completed our traversal of an entire range of physical sciences in a more or less continuous and orderly fashion. Although some arbitrariness (as well as approximation) has gone into the numerical portions of Figure 1, certain generalities become clear. As we proceed from physics, through chemistry, to biology, we deal with larger and larger fundamental entities. Being more and more complex, they become more and more fragile, requiring less and less energy to engage in significant transformations. Their life-spans range from the inconceivably short existence of some of the most ephemeral particles of physics to the very respectable durations accorded to our own and numerous other species in nature.

Beginnings, In-betweens, and Endings

Well, now, where has all this gotten us? Before going any further, let us examine one more parallel to our chart of the sciences, one that is rooted in the very history of our physical universe itself. Modern theory describes the universe as we know it beginning some 15–20 billion years ago with the explosion, or "Big Bang," of an immense compressed mass containing all the matter now in existence. The enormous energy involved allowed the existence of only the most elementary fragments of matter. Now one might think that the results of such a catastrophic explosion would be to simply blow these elementary bits uniformly in all directions, leading to complete dissipation of its energy and matter. The universe would then cool over the eons, and its material would continue to fly apart in a sort of subatomic cloud, growing ever more tenuous, forever. In a partial sense this *does* describe the universe, its energy and mass as a whole constantly dissipating, but it is quite clearly grossly incorrect in detail. Under the influence of the fundamental forces that asserted themselves at different times after the Big Bang, particles coalesced forming atomic nuclei, atoms, and finally small molecules as temperatures dropped to levels compatible with their existence (Watson, 1977). Larger aggregates of matter formed as a result of turbulences and inhomogeneities, leading eventually to clouds contracted by gravitation which formed stars and galaxies. And, of course, planets, pumice, paramecia, pomegranates, and people followed. How did all this highly organized, highly sophisticated structure come about? It is almost as if Mother Nature started up with a career in particle physics just after the Big Bang, and has spent the ensuing 15 billion years or so patiently sampling each of the disciplines of our scientific spectrum in succession, winding up as the current reigning chief biologist. And, in doing so, she has presented us with a model for the continuum of physical science in the history of the universe itself.

As we will shortly see, there is a problem. At the beginning of all this, the basic nature of the laws, or rules, by which the universe was to be established was presumably determined. We know quite a lot about these rules, in particular the ones dealing with temperature, energy changes, and orderliness of a system. These topics are studied by scientists in the general area of physical chemistry and are encompassed under the general title of thermodynamics. By means of certain very specific laws, thermodynamics tells us that (1) hot things cool off and (2) organized things inevitably become disorganized, especially if they are left alone. Well, no one should be surprised that hot things cool off; thermodynamics is simply the rigorous mechanism by which we humans quantify such phenomena as the transfer of heat from a warmer system to a cooler one. Thermodynamics, however, participates in less obvious matters. An inherent tendency of all systems toward disorganization, toward randomness, is a cornerstone of thermodynamics. The inevitability of ever-increasing randomness, or *entropy*, to use the proper term, is so fundamental that entropy is often loosely referred to as "the arrow of time." This concept is an overriding one, pervasive in its influence in a surprising array of practical as well as theoretical matters.

Given these concepts, thermodynamics certainly predicts the *dissipation* of the universe after the Big Bang—the transition from a hot, compressed, distant past to a cold, dispersed, remote future. But does it predict the *structures* that have arisen along the way? If thermodynamics is right, if its laws are valid without exception, then it must allow for the creation of organized entities out of chaos: the appearance of "dissipative structures," in the terminology of Prigogine (Glansdorff & Prigogine, 1971). Can it do this?

Prigogine's own development of the thermodynamics involved in these phenomena has produced novel notions of the role of probability and uncertainty in all manner of systems that have conventionally been considered to be completely and precisely described by their initial conditions alone (Lepkowski, 1979). The extent to which probabilistic descriptions of nature are more valid than traditional deterministic ones is a matter of lively debate, and may rest partly on practical limitations in our ability to "know" completely the initial conditions themselves. Rather than pursue these questions, which exist on several levels, we are going to focus on one very specific phenomenon—a simple chemical model illustrating dissipative structure and demonstrating properties strikingly similar to much more complex natural systems.

Thermodynamics and Pretty Colors

DICK CAVETT: Let's talk about thermodynamics.
ALAN ARKIN: Thermodynamics is my field. Thermodynamics is *everybody's* field.

On second thought, let us digress. Throughout the history of science there stand examples of peculiar phenomena that failed to fit comfortably into the prevailing theories and concepts regarding nature. Often the study of such phenomena was considered to be, at the very least, unconventional. Acupuncture is an enlightening example. Rooted, as it is, in a tradition very different from that which gave rise to Western thinking, it is no surprise that Western thinkers had difficulty accepting the fact that it works. Of those few who accepted this fact, virtually none were comfortable with the traditional explanations of Chinese philosophy and medicine concerning *why* it works. To most Western ears, these reasons were simply too weird. Nevertheless, the past three years have seen a remarkable revolution in our understanding of pain in the Western physical science context. The chemistry of the brain and nervous system is one of the most exciting current areas of research in biological chemistry. The pain-killing mechanisms of the opiate drugs, of aspirin, and, yes, of acupuncture, are now being elucidated in terms of basic chemical concepts. In a sense, it is now "permissible" to believe that acupuncture works, now that its mode of action may be described by the chemistry of enkephalin, endorphin, and prostaglandin molecules instead of the traditional terminology involving "circulation of vital energy through meridians associated with each organ system" (Flanagan, 1979). We think we understand, so we decide it is O.K. to believe.

Early in this century, another phenomenon was discovered which, like acupuncture, was a phenomenon so bizarre, so implausible that it was immediately consigned to that curious periphery of science reserved for observations that are "inexplicable," "probably an artifact," or simply wrong. One J. S. Morgan (1916) published a study of the reaction of concentrated sulfuric acid (battery acid) with the common, natural organic molecule called formic acid. Like all chemical reactions, this one may be described by an equation in which each chemical substance is represented by a unique formula. The equation

$$\text{HCO}_2\text{H} \xrightarrow[\substack{\text{(sulfuric acid)} \\ 55°C}]{\text{H}_2\text{SO}_4} \text{H}_2\text{O} + \text{CO}$$
$$\text{(formic acid)} \qquad\qquad \text{(water)} \quad \text{(carbon monoxide)}$$

tells us that sulfuric acid is an agent acting to remove water from formic acid, leading to the production of the gas, carbon monoxide, which bubbles out of the liquid mixture. Superficially, this is a rather ordinary reaction: sulfuric acid is a well-known dehydrating agent for organic compounds. Morgan's report, however, is quite out of the ordinary. Upon mixing the reagents and stirring slowly, he reported observing a rapid initial evolution of carbon monoxide, slowing and nearly ceasing after a period of minutes, only to be followed by sudden, violent bursts of gas evolution taking place at fairly regular intervals, interspersed by relatively quiet periods displaying greatly reduced bubble formation. This periodic behavior continued over an extended period of time until all the formic acid was consumed.

Morgan's observations generated skeptical comments from several scientists, and, as late as 1976, lacked even a remotely accurate explanation. Vindication came with the work of R. M. Noyes (Showalter & Noyes, 1978), who presented powerful confirmation of Morgan's observations, and the first coherent explanation of the phenomenon within an elegant theoretical framework designed especially for processes of this kind. In addition, throughout the intervening decades a number of other periodic or oscillating chemical reactions were discovered, but the lack of a rigorous explanation kept these phenomena firmly in the dusty corner of scientific curiosity. As Noyes himself put it (Field & Noyes, 1977), "Although unambiguous examples of chemical oscillators were discovered over half a century ago, even a decade ago most chemists, *including ourselves*, were unaware that the phenomenon existed" (p. 220).

Now that a firm theoretical basis for chemical oscillation exists (one that we shall shortly look into in some detail), an ever-growing number of researchers are studying these processes, processes which are at times quite spectacular. In 1959, the Russian scientist B. P. Belousov reported periodic color changes in a reaction between citric acid and an oxidizing agent, potassium bromate, in the presence of sulfuric acid and a rare catalyst, ceric sulfate. Related systems were studied extensively over the next decade by his countryman A. M. Zhabotinsky (Zaikin & Zhabotinsky, 1970), and one of the variants of this "Belousov–Zhabotinsky" reaction is both the most well-known and the most visually striking example of the oscillation genre to the extent that it is a commonly used demonstration in classroom displays of "chemical magic." Let us examine this particular example in detail: its appearance, its theoretical basis, and its relationship to the principles of thermodynamics we have outlined above.

Chemical and Physical Oscillations: The Belousov–Zhabotinsky Reaction

If a solution of malonic acid in aqueous sulfuric acid is treated with sodium bromate and the iron-based catalyst, ferroin, it will initially take on the reddish-orange color of the iron compound. If it is left unstirred in a shallow dish, a rather peculiar event ensues. Seemingly without warning, spots of blue appear randomly against the otherwise uniform field of orange. The spots become circles and grow larger and larger, finally merging, whereupon the entire solution eventually becomes uniformly sky-blue in color (Figure 2). After a bit of time goes by, a spot or two of

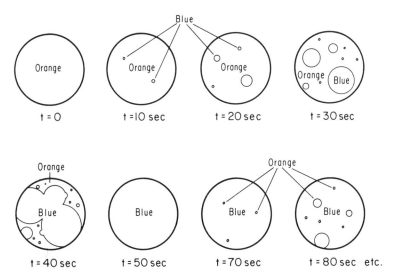

Figure 2. The Belousov-Zhabotinsky reaction depicted as it might be seen occurring in a shallow dish somewhat above room temperature. The upper left drawing represents the initial appearance, with the change occurring over a period of time as shown.

orange turns up in the blue solution, and these grow in circular patterns, merging eventually to reestablish the uniform orange color that was present initially. These changes occur in a cyclical fashion, and the oscillations from orange, to blue, and back again repeat themselves over and over in just the manner described, ceasing only when the limiting ingredients, bromate and malonic acid, are finally consumed, whereupon the solution settles back to the orange color it had at the start, just as if none of this bizarre sequence of transformations had ever taken place at all. Certainly, we must be dealing with a phenomenon that falls into the category of ". . . and now for something *completely* different." How does one begin to explain something like this? For starters, the colors need to be identified: as we said, the orange is due to the ferroin catalyst initially present. The blue color is that of the same catalyst, but in another form, called ferriin. Therefore, what we see in this process are many oscillations, over an extended period of time, between two distinct chemical forms, orange ferroin (technically called a "reduced" form) and blue ferriin ("oxidized"). The oscillations are not only temporal (in time), but spatial as well, as regions of one color are continually forming and expanding into regions of the other. While this is taking place, the malonic acid and sodium bromate are irreversibly being consumed, and when they are all gone, the pretty oscillations stop.

Perhaps a word first on the reasons that chemical reactions *should not* exhibit oscillations, before we try to find out why this one *does*. We

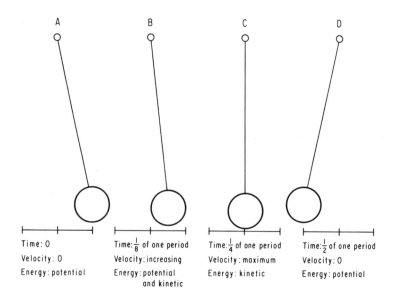

Figure 3. Motion of a pendulum.

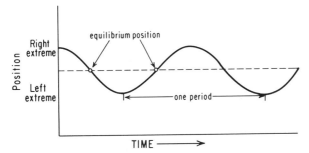

Figure 4. Motion of a pendulum graphically depicted. One period is represented by the distance between peaks or valleys.

are all familiar with mechanical oscillators, like the pendulum of a grandfather clock. Its motion may be divided up as shown in Figure 3. At the extreme of its pathway, it is suspended, motionless, with all of its energy locked in the potential energy of gravitation. As it falls from this point, it picks up speed, moving fastest when vertical where all its energy is kinetic, or energy of motion. Rising beyond vertical, this energy is reconverted to potential energy as the pendulum comes to a stop at the other extreme of its path. Its motion is oscillatory, with a period represented by the time required to swing back and forth once. Figures 4 and 5 show, graphically, the changes in the pendulum's position and energy over time. The point is that the ideal (frictionless) pendulum never loses any energy; it simply changes the energy from one form to another and therefore can maintain its oscillatory motion indefinitely. One further feature of significance is that, during each oscillation, the pendulum passes through the precise position that it would occupy if it had zero energy (neither kinetic nor potential), namely, hanging vertically. This position of minimum energy is labeled the equilibrium position, and it is in the nature of mechanical (and electrical) oscillators that they can pass through their equilibrium position and still maintain oscillatory behavior.

Chemical reactions are different. At the beginning of a chemical

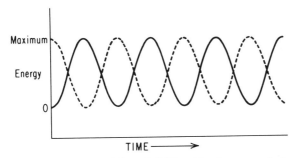

Figure 5. Energy changes for a pendulum. Solid line: kinetic energy; dashed line: potential energy.

reaction, the starting compounds possess potential energy of a chemical nature, to be sure, but, as they react, this energy is used to break bonds between atoms as old molecules are broken up so that new ones can form. Eventually energy may be lost as heat, manifesting itself as kinetic energy of the product and its surroundings. Unlike the pendulum, whose left and right extremes are essentially the same, the initial and final extremes of a typical chemical reaction are distinct, and there is no turning back. Energically, chemical reactions are dissipative in nature, turning some of the organized energy locked within molecular bonds into random heating of the surroundings. Figure 6 illustrates the progress of a typical chemical reaction where a hypothetical starting material "A" is smoothly and irreversibly converted to a product substance "B." The final outcome of the reaction, when all varying energetic parameters have been minimized, is called the equilibrium position, and the concentrations of all materials present then are called equilibrium concentrations. Any disturbance introduced into the chemical system to move it away from its equilibrium condition merely causes it to smoothly follow the path back to equilibrium. Once at equilibrium, all macroscopic observables cease to change: the reaction is done.

Although no two chemical processes will be identical in detail, this picture is qualitatively applicable in one form or another to virtually any reaction. The distinctions between reactions find expression in the detailed nature of each fundamental step involving the breaking or making of a chemical bond, and in the energetic (thermodynamic) considerations that apply to each step. The study of the minute details of chemical reactions is the study of reaction "mechanisms." The generality of Figure 6, on the face of it, made it very difficult for chemists to admit the existence of oscillating chemical reactions, let alone seriously attempt to understand them. How could chemicals interact so as to oscillate back and forth from one form to another, if it is a general feature of chemical reactions that they smoothly "wind down" to a final, stable equilibrium?

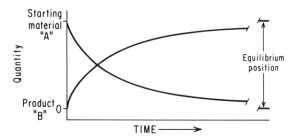

Figure 6. Progress of a typical chemical reaction.

Mechanisms of the Belousov–Zhabotinsky Reaction

Let us start, then, by stating that, in a gross sense, Figure 6 is perfectly adequate for describing the course of the Belousov–Zhabotinsky reaction! The reaction, overall, is dissipative: heat is given off, and the starting materials (malonic acid and bromate) are smoothly and irreversibly converted to products. No fundamental violation of thermodynamic principles is involved, and yet, over and over, the pretty colors came and went, seemingly mocking the first startled scientists who made these observations. One must turn to the detailed reaction mechanism for an answer, and it is in this regard that Noyes and his co-workers have done so much to enlighten us and reveal some of the complex possibilities inherent in our already existing notions of the course of chemical reactions.

Even the most simple of reaction processes may proceed via complex, multistep mechanistic pathways. The pathway chosen by nature is the most favorable one from an energic standpoint, and the evaluation of the variables involved is a qualitatively well-understood area of chemistry. The mechanism of the Belousov–Zhabotinsky reaction involves no less than *five* steps. Moreover, the five-step mechanism is a general one and may be applied to a number of other oscillating processes (chemical or otherwise). Pared down to its essentials, this is how it goes:

Group A
$$
\begin{cases}
\text{1. Reactant}^2 + Y \rightarrow X \\
\text{2.} \quad\quad X \quad + Y \rightarrow \text{product}
\end{cases}
\left.\begin{array}{l}
\text{Color: orange (ferroin present)} \\
\text{Concentration of Y: large} \\
\text{Concentration of X: small}
\end{array}\right.
$$

Group B
$$
\begin{cases}
\text{3. Reactant} + X + \text{ferroin} \\
\quad\quad \rightarrow\;\; 2X \;\;+ \text{ferriin} \\
\text{4.} \quad\quad X \quad + X \rightarrow \text{product}
\end{cases}
\left.\begin{array}{l}
\text{Color: blue (ferriin produced)} \\
\text{Concentration of Y: small} \\
\text{Concentration of X: large}
\end{array}\right.
$$

$$
\text{5. Reactant + ferriin} \longrightarrow \text{product} + Y + \text{ferroin}
$$

In these five equations, X and Y are chemical intermediates different from the initial reactants and final products, but intimately involved in the overall conversion of reactants to products. The equations are best grouped as shown, 1 and 2 together (Group A), 3 and 4 together (Group B), and 5 by itself. Notice that, in all three groups, reactants are converted to products. Thus, overall, the quantity of reactant present continuously decreases whereas the quantity of product present always increases. The reaction outline of Figure 6 is followed. The *intermediates* X and Y are the

---

^{2}Reactant refers, in general, to any of the chemical species initially present that are eventually converted to products during the course of the overall chemical process.—Eds.

species whose quantities oscillate. We see here one key feature in this phenomenon: the oscillations are restricted to transient intermediate substances and are never observed in the reactants or products themselves.

In the setup of this reaction, we begin with reactants in the presence of enough critical intermediate Y, so that equation 1 can proceed. Intermediate X is produced by equation 1, but its concentration does not build up because it reacts with Y, yielding products (equation 2). As the reactions in equations 1 and 2 (Group A) proceed, therefore, reactant is converted to product, intermediate X comes and goes, and intermediate Y is consumed.

When the amount of Y drops below the amount required to take away X according to equation 2, the residual X, having nothing better to do, begins to react according to equation 3. Equation 3 is unusual and important in one key respect: *it produces (from reactant molecules) more X than it consumes.* Such a process is called *autocatalytic,* and the result is a tremendous burst in the quantity of X present. Almost incidentally, this equation 3 contains the conversion of orange ferroin to blue ferriin as a part of its process. Any residual Y is now rapidly consumed by reaction with the large quantity of X now present (equation 2), and, eventually, molecules of X react with each other, yielding products (equation 4). The system has suddenly, and literally, switched from a condition where much Y is present and only a little X (Group A reactions predominating) to a condition where the concentration of X is high and the Y is practically all gone (Group B reactions taking over). In the former case, the mixture is orange, and in the latter, it is blue.

What, then, takes place? After a delay period, the large quantity of blue ferriin produced in equation 3 finally begins to react according to equation 5, regenerating a tremendous quantity of intermediate Y, and, in the process, is itself converted to orange ferroin. So the system changes back to its original orange color, and, due to the renewed quantity of Y present, is switched back into the regime of the Group A equations, allowing the cycle to begin again. The repetitions of this complex cycle of processes are the underlying basis for the visible color oscillations. Specific relationships between the rates of the individual steps contribute to the persistence of the oscillatory behavior, and well-defined mathematical bounds have been derived as prerequisites for oscillations (Pacault, Hanusse, DeKepper, Vidal, & Beissonade, 1976). As this mechanism demonstrates, these oscillations occur in a parallel sense to the inexorable conversion of reactants to products, and, upon completion of the latter process (i.e., the attainment of final chemical equilibrium), they must cease. In this regard, it should be noted that, contrary to the mechanical oscillator which passes through its equilibrium position periodically, the chemical oscillation ceases upon attainment of equilibrium: as long as active, ongoing chemical oscillation is taking place, the equilibrium position must *not* be encountered.

As involved as this chemical oscillation appears, it is infinitely simpler than the biochemical processes that maintain all the periodically repeating phenomena of a living system. The chemical system has the value of being a powerful model for any essentially dissipative phenomenon in which organized structures (e.g., bursts of gas, colorful oscillations, the birth of a star or galaxy, the beat of a living heart) are observed to arise. The chemical system shows a great deal in terms of the requirements for such phenomena. Most critically, they can only occur far from equilibrium. Although, superficially, they seem to occur in spite of the ultimate dissipative tendencies dictated by thermodynamics, they are in reality governed by those same thermodynamic principles. All five steps in the Noyes mechanism are conventional chemical reactions of no great note individually. Each one proceeds in a perfectly well-behaved manner according to the normal concepts of energy change and molecular rearrangement that apply to all chemical reactions. The superposition of oscillations on the overall chemical process is due to an unusual but by no means unique combination of energetic, kinetic, and concentration factors that place the entire system within well-defined mathematical bounds for periodic behavior. It works!

Order Out of Chaos

And, obviously, so will any system with intermediate components whose interactions fall within similar mathematical boundaries and which is, as a whole, far enough from equilibrium. This, then, is the focus of the work of Prigogine over the last decade: the range of phenomena which display dissipative structure, order arising out of chaos. We have given several examples of such phenomena taken from the spectrum of physical science, and numerous others can be cited. The question that arises concerns the applicability of this sort of concept, presumably codified within a well-defined mathematical framework, to other areas of human experience and study.

Lots of examples of order in the presence of chaos can be plucked out of the context of our everyday lives. From the point of view of the average shopper, sale day at Bloomingdale's is indeed chaotic, as well as truly dissipative with regard to the status of one's wallet. Perhaps the line to the cash register would serve as a sort of order in the midst of so much tumult. Here, however, we have an example of order imposed from without on a chaotic situation, and not arising as a natural result of the chaos itself. Nevertheless, much effort has gone into, of all things, mathematical modeling of cash register lines and the like under the broad heading of queue theory (Takacs, 1962).

The relationship between such analyses of everyday events of a societal nature and the principles of nonequilibrium thermodynamics that govern the behavior of the bulk of the physical universe are just beginning to emerge from the work of a number of investigators (Lepkowski, 1979). It is, as yet, by no means clear whether a comfortable synthesis of these concepts will be the ultimate result. We may find great difficulty in applying physical laws to forces that govern societies in general. Perhaps only selected microcosms will accept the descriptions those laws present, and not without much kicking and screaming.

We mentioned previously that Prigogine has devoted a good deal of study to the development of parallels between the probabilistic aspects of the physical and the social sciences. In postulating the likelihood of multiple trajectories in time for a physical system given a specific set of initial conditions, he anticipates comparison with the typical social situation whose outcome is naturally and intuitively considered to be uncertain to some degree. At the various levels, the uncertainites may have very different origins. In the subatomic regime, uncertainty is an inherent consequence of the quantum nature of matter. In larger aggregates, quantum effects are gradually suppressed as materials take on, to a greater and greater extent, the characteristic of bulk materials with which we are more intuitively familiar (Figure 1). Here we treat collections of individual units according to well-established statistical models: after all, entropy, one of the cornerstones of thermodynamics, is essentially statistical in nature.

A number of examples may be used to illustrate the very important role of statistics in these matters. Given a bulk radioactive material, we are able to say *precisely* how long it will take for half of the atoms to undergo radioactive decay, even though we *cannot* predict with any certainty the time that one particular atom will decay. In a macroscopic, chemically reactive system, the course of events may be predicted very accurately using thermodynamic considerations as a basis. Still, at the level of the individual molecule, the likelihood of reaction at a given time is uncertain and may only be assigned a certain level of probability. Likewise, predictions relating to the likely actions to be taken by groups of people can be made with much more confidence than can similar predictions relating to a single individual. In each example, a reasonable degree of well-behaved order associated with the system as a whole is, in fact, shown to be the result of the statistical summation of rather chaotic activity at the individual level. The analysis of the behavior of aggregates based on our knowledge of the properties of the individual entities is a very general link between physical and social science. There are, however, much more specific analogies which show, even more strikingly, how powerful a model the chemical example of dissipative structure really is.

Triggers, Thresholds, Autocatalysis, and . . .

We have described in detail the mechanism of the Belousov–Zhabotinsky reaction, an archetypal chemical oscillator, and a molecular model of the natural generation of organized structure while the dissipative process runs its course. We did not tell the whole story, however. In particular, there are several key features of this system that are absolute necessities for the occurrence of any phenomena of this type.

1. Referring to the sequence of five reactions that describes the mechanism of this process, we stated that the oscillation actually involves fluctuations in the quantities of the intermediates X and Y present at any given time in the system. A basic property of such systems is their sensitivity toward perturbation. If we refer back to step 3 of the mechanism, we recall that it is an example of an autocatalytic process: more X is created than is consumed. Therefore, if we were to add some X to this reaction mixture, our addition would essentially be greatly magnified by the presence of this step, and the overall effect on the system as a whole would be the promotion and enhancement of oscillatory behavior far out of proportion to the magnitude of the original perturbation. One should recognize that this result is highly unusual and very much in contrast to our intuitive ideas about the effects brought about by small disturbances. For example, if we disturb the average rock by picking it up off the ground, its typical response when we let it go is to fall straight down again. If said rock were to respond to the perturbation of being picked up in a manner similar to the response of our oscillating reaction to perturbation, it might fly off into the sky as soon as we let it go. This autocatalytic feature which works to magnify the response of the system to perturbation is one key feature that characterizes these processes.

2. The time scale of oscillation is very short relative to the duration of the reaction as a whole. Transitions from one reaction regime to another (i.e., blue to orange, or back again) are relatively sudden events: the system switches from one predominant mode to another. No intermediate states are observed—the transitions are not gradual but discontinuous. Once a threshold is reached, such as a critical concentration of one of the key intermediates, the shift from one regime to another is autocatalytically driven and very rapid.

3. Transitions of this sort may be spontaneous, or, alternatively, may be triggered by outside influences. Color changes in the Belousov–

Zhabotinsky reaction may be induced by heating, by physical disturbance of the solution, or by electrical stimulation, any of which is capable of inducing local or general perturbation of the system.

Where else do we find systems possessing a high degree of naturally generated organization that are highly sensitive to perturbation, switch rapidly from one state to another, and operate both spontaneously as well as upon external triggering? Whether physical, biological, or social, what are the implications of these systems, and what are their unique properties with respect to the universe and our perception of it?

In the biological/biochemical domain, the answer is in a sense obvious. Indeed, the archetypal examples of systems displaying these properties are the various interacting subunits that make up living organisms. Although their detailed mechanisms are not all equally well understood, the many biochemical "cycles" involved in the actual carrying out of biological functions all seem to have highly interconnected individual steps operating under various kinds of self-generated control mechanisms. For example, the autocatalysis we've already talked about with regard to our simple model chemical oscillator is one particular form of feedback system, a commonly encountered biochemical device whereby the products of a biochemical process exert, directly or indirectly, a positive or negative influence on their own further generation.

As one might expect, biological units also display oscillatory behavior as an ultimate consequence of these basic mechanistic properties. We can cite both long- and short-term cycles in both plants and animals, cycles that undergo both internal (e.g., hormonal) and external (environmental) triggering. From the level of individual biochemical systems, through cells, to individual organ systems and entire organisms, the presence of regular rhythms is a dominant feature, an ever-present quality of the organized living structure. We readily recognize the physical rhythms of heartbeat and breathing. The more subtle oscillations in the ever-active processes of the central nervous system provide physical evidence for the rhythms that interconnect chemical, electrical, and ultimately integrated neural controls in the living organism as a whole. The human brain provides the most sophisticated physical bridge, the ultimate link between self-organized systems of all sizes, on all scales.

From a totally objective, physical point of view, the brain is an intricate electrochemical unit, ostensibly receiving input and transmitting signals over its auxiliary nervous system network. Yet even on the most superficial level this description is hopelessly inadequate, leading one to characterize the brain simply as a glorified computer mechanism. Consider the fact that we view ourselves as aware, conscious beings. Is it possible for the human brain to be capable of generating this quality of consciousness or awareness, and still, essentially, be considered a glorified computer? Or does it differ in some fundamental, qualitative way from the Univacs and IBMs, HPs and TIs that seem to run so much of the daily show?

Recent evidence (e.g., Pribram's holographic neurology—see Ferguson, 1978; Pribram, 1978)[3] indicates that there is much more to the brain than just number crunching. And no wonder: just consider the striking parallels between the physical systems that comprise the brain, and the familiar characteristics of those properties of consciousness and awareness that we all experience. The brain is chemical and electrical; it is organized along the same physical lines that describe both our model chemical oscillator and other biochemical systems. Thus, in a microscopic sense it can be shown to display trigger phenomena, sensitivity to critical or threshold levels of numerous substances, and feedback effects of various types. Remarkably, these same characteristics are manifest in the workings of the mind itself. Consider a very simple example. How do we become "aware" of something? In the case of a very low level sound, for instance, it is perfectly possible for our hearing mechanism to respond, and to transmit neural impulses to the brain, without our being consciously aware of the sound at all. All the physiological responses for hearing have taken place, *but we do not hear.* Only upon reaching a certain threshold level (which will vary according to a number of factors) will the impulses entering the brain emerge into our "awareness." Thus, our conscious response to sensory input is, first, distinctly nonlinear, especially at the extremes of intensity, and, second and more specifically, displays a threshold-type response whose threshold level is critically dependent on both external factors, such as intensity and quality of other sensory input, and internal factors like mood or attentiveness. Quite a contrast with typical calculating devices!

Threshold response implies discontinuity: a shift is taking place from a condition in which the individual is not consciously aware of a sensory input to a condition in which he is. In a sense, a focus of attention is suddenly switched on. As we have said, this "switch" from an unresponsive state to one of full awareness may occur upon either an increase in intensity of the stimulus, a lowering of the sensory threshold level, or a combination of the two. The sudden movement of an object catching our attention in an otherwise motionless visual field is a simple example of both effects working in tandem. This sudden shifting or switching nature of our sensory responses is strikingly similar to the responses of the organized chemical system when the threshold quantity of a key intermediate is reached.

The input need not be externally generated in the conventional sense

[3]See Pribram, Chapter 6.—Eds.

for a threshold to be reached and our awareness to be "switched on." In the course of any intellectual exercise, a certain amount of progress toward solving a problem will result from careful, step-by-step evaluation of the problem, consideration of alternative methods of approach, and a final, rational working out of the solution—number crunching. And then, there's insight—the sudden intuitive flash that can and so often does shortcut the conventional process leading to the answer. Where could this be coming from? Is it truly internally generated from a subconsciously ordered body of facts, or is there indeed something external involved, something subtle, allowing "the idea" to surmount the threshold of awareness?

As a next step, consider the more fundamental transitions between generalized states of consciousness: sleeping and waking, hypnotic states, and other levels of awareness, either self-induced (e.g., states of consciousness brought about as a result of sophisticated meditational techniques) or triggered externally (as a result of chemical hallucinogens). Each has its own characteristic rhythm, for example, a brain wave frequency associated with a certain level and quality of brain activity. Likewise, the shifts between these states have been repeatedly described as sudden, rapid, or even instantaneous rather than gentle or gradual. Suddenly we recognize something as "nonphysical" as consciousness, in all its forms, displaying either spontaneous or triggered organization into various states, each with its characteristic oscillation frequency, linked by discontinuous, almost wrenchingly sudden transitional mechanisms. Anyone for changing grape soda into orange? There is something very natural, perhaps all-encompassing, about these particular properties. They show up throughout the physical realm: from our simple chemical model through the heightened structure of living systems. But can they be applied to consciousness itself? What a strange link: the physical and tangible with the mechanisms of our perception of the physical and tangible. But if they are all of the same stuff, all similar types of manifestations (of what?), then it is natural and sensible for a physical brain, creating perception of a physical universe, to utilize methods which are *perceived* to possess the same sorts of physical characteristics.

The "of what?" above, is a good question. Suppose we assign similar properties to the physical or "tangible" and to the stuff of the mind or the "intangible," and then extend the argument to the various kinds of "stuff" the mind puts out, so to speak—the various states of awareness and consciousness. Where, then, do we draw the lines as to validity? Or is there a line to be drawn at all? Take the logical extreme: it is either all equally real—the rock, the tree, the sound, the image, the dream—or perhaps it's all equally unreal, just being some construct, some manifestation of the "real" that, as Bohm (see Weber, 1978) would say, is not spoken of or written about because the act of focusing upon it is incompatible with our "being there".[4]

Lastly, keeping in mind the above statement made in reference to processes like the Belousov–Zhabotinsky reaction that "there is something very natural, perhaps all-encompassing, about these particular properties," let us consider an analogous process from the "psychological" realm which bears a remarkable resemblance to these dissipative structure phenomena of chemistry. More specifically, many philosophers and sages (particularly those of the East) make constant reference to the uniquely human *process* of self-realization, that life-long endeavor of attempting to dissolve one's identification with the ego or self by breaking its desires for and attachments to both material things and emotional states—the goal being to attain that highest state of pure, selfless awareness variously called *nirvana, samadhi,* or *Self.*[5] This process of increasing self-awareness, what the Chinese called recognition of the "Tao" or "path,"[6] traditionally involves a meditational practice to quiet the random "noise" of the mind, and a conscious effort to apply the insights one gains in meditation to the task of learning from our everyday experiences. That is, one comes to respond to these experiences, whether they be joyful, neutral, or pain-producing, so as to remain in the Tao or rightful "flow of things," thereby easing one's task of rising above the *self*ish attachments and becoming free of what Paramahansa Yogananda (1969) outrightly calls the "ego-prison."

Another important aspect of this "prison" is evident in the following description offered by Gurudev Chitrabhanu (1978), Jain teacher and spiritual leader:

> The ego is a very subtle form of intoxication. It is very difficult to cross and go beyond. It is a thin veil whose nature is opaque; sometimes we may see through it to the other side and we know we are being held back by it, but still we cannot go beyond it.
>
> The deeper meaning of meditation is to overcome the ego which holds us back and makes us miserable. (p. 26)

Evident here is the insight that the ego does not simply yield to our attempts to rise above it and be free of its influence; it is "difficult to cross," something which we at times "cannot go beyond"—being an entity whose roots lie deep in our very nature, it does not easily relinquish its hold.

[4]The following five paragraphs of this chapter were written by Ronald S. Valle, and are included with the author's permission and approval.—Eds.

[5]Keep in mind that there are many real and subtle differences both between and among these differently named states of awareness.—Eds.

[6]See R. von Eckartsberg and R. Valle, Chapter 14, for a discussion of "path" in Heideggerian and other terms.—Eds.

One should now realize that the process of self-realization, one's "path," is not a simply linear process, but rather a complex, oscillatory phenomenon where the ego structure, whose roots have been slowly pried loose in meditation, begins to react in a more flexible, freer manner to those positive and negative life experiences we all face each and every day. Reacting in this less restrictive way, the ego begins to periodically "collapse" as one meets his or her life situations. This "collapse" is not, however, a permanent one. The ego, with its entourage of defenses, desires, and attachments, restructures itself and rises once again to "run the show." As meditation continues, however, the ego becomes more prone to change and will indeed undergo this process of restructuration again and again, each time its new structure being a bit looser and less clinging than the last. In addition, as this cycle of birth, death, and rebirth continues, one begins to notice a parallel occurrence of increasing calmness—an understandable decrease in anxiety as the entity which responds to things in an anxious, concerned way (i.e., the ego) slowly dissolves. Along with this steadily increasing calmness comes a new sensitivity. While engaged in one's own seemingly chaotic, anxiety-filled, day-to-day existence, one slowly becomes aware of an emerging pattern—the regular, periodic, and oscillatory pattern of ego dissolution and rejuvenation. Sound at all familiar? It should. We appear to have a nonphysical, yet rather direct parallel to the dissipative structure phenomena of chemistry.

Look once again at the five equations describing the Belousov–Zhabotinsky reaction presented above. If we substitute "ego" for "reactant," "life experiences" for the intermediates "X" and "Y," and "centeredness" or increasing "awareness of Self" for "product," the analogy seems complete. In fact, one can even treat intermediate "X" as "positive" life experiences, and intermediate "Y" as "negative" life experiences—it seems no accident that two intermediates are needed to describe this apparently universal process in the metaphorical language of chemistry. We now have a continuing process where, as the amount of reactant (ego) slowly decreases, the amount of product (self-realization) slowly increases, with the negatively correlated intermediates X and Y (positive and negative experiences) oscillating back and forth between a maximum and a minimum. Who has not noticed the pattern in life of how things seem to go so well for a time only to be followed inexorably by bad times where nothing seems to work out well, the intermediate spaces being times of balance between the favorable (intermediate X) and unfavorable (intermediate Y)?

There are other common features as well. Both processes, for example, begin far from "equilibrium," the chemical process ending when all of the initial reactant has undergone the appropriate change and become product, the awareness process ending when the self, undergoing its metamorphosis, becomes Self.[7] In addition, both processes are irreversible; that is, once they have run their course, they reach a final resting state of sorts. The conclusion reached above concerning the chemical process can just as easily describe the self-realization process: "Once at equilibrium, all macroscopic observables cease to change: the reaction is done." Once one becomes aware of the ego-self's true nature, never again will it create "reality." Once realized, its power is gone. In any case, dissipative structure is extremely useful in helping one understand how the order and calmness of "one-pointedness of mind" can arise out of the seemingly chaotic and random strivings of the selfish (self-ish) ego.

So, in the end, where have we come to? Maybe nowhere—after all, the reason for speculation is ignorance in the first place. But, then again, maybe there *is* something to analyzing things the way we've tried to do here. We have taken properties of the physical world and found them strangely to mirror properties of the intangible mind. The next logical step has been simply to reverse the process: borrow from the most recent ideas concerning the nature of the ego, the mind, and consciousness itself, and declare them to be applicable to what we call the tangible universe. What does this imply concerning the universal theories of Bohm[8] and others? To say that it requires them to be correct in detail is much too extreme, at least given the body of evidence we have presented. Nonetheless, the parallel natures of such disparate manifestations do point toward some sort of unifying concept between the physical and the psychological realms. Although the details of this unification may not be either completely or even very accurately defined at present, it is satisfying to recognize evidence that it does in fact exist.

References

Bromley, D. Nuclear molecules. *Scientific American*, 1978, 239(6), 58–69.

Ferguson, M. Karl Pribram's changing reality. *Re-Vision*, 1978, 1(3 & 4), 8–13.

Field, R., & Noyes, R. M. Mechanisms of chemical oscillators: Conceptual bases. *Accounts of Chemical Research*, 1977, 10, 214–221.

Flanagan, D. (Ed.). The chemistry of acupuncture. *Scientific American*, 1979, 241(1), 79A–80.

Glansdorff, P., & Prigogine, I. *Thermodynamic theory of structure, stability, and fluctuations*. New York: Wiley, 1971.

Gurudev Chitrabhanu. *Realize what you are: The dynamics of Jain meditation*. New York: Dodd, Mead, 1978.

Lepkowski, W. The social thermodynamics of Ilya Prigogine. *Chemical and Engineering News*, 1979, 57(16), 30–33.

[7]See Marlan's, Chapter 11, discussion of ego (self) transcendence.—Eds.

[8]See Weber, Chapter 5, for a presentation of David Bohm's theories.—Eds.

Morgan, J. S. The periodic evolution of carbon monoxide. *Journal of the Chemical Society*, 1916, *109*, 274–283.

Pacault, A., Hanusse, P., DeKepper, P., Vidal, C., & Beissonade, J. Phenomena in homogeneous chemical systems far from equilibrium. *Accounts of Chemical Research*, 1976, *9*, 438–445.

Paramahansa Yogananda. *Autobiography of a yogi*. Los Angeles: Self-Realization Fellowship, 1969.

Pribram, K. H. What the fuss is all about. *Re-Vision*, 1978, *1*(3 & 4), 14–18.

Ravetz, J. History of science. In *Encyclopedia Brittanica (15th ed.)*, *Macropaedia, Vol. 16*. Chicago: William Benton, 1974.

Schwitters, R. Fundamental particles with charm. *Scientific American*, 1977, *237*(4), 56–70.

Showalter, K., & Noyes, R. M. Oscillations in chemical systems. 24. Oscillatory decompositions of formic acid in sulfuric acid. *Journal of the American Chemical Society*, 1978, *100*, 1042–1049.

Takacs, L. *Introduction to the theory of queues*. New York: Oxford University Press, 1962.

Watson, W. Interstellar chemistry. *Accounts of Chemical Research*, 1977, *10*, 221–226.

Weber, R. The enfolding-unfolding universe: A conversation with David Bohm. *Re-Vision*, 1978, *1*(3 & 4), 24–51.

Zaikin, A., & Zhabotinsky, A. Concentration wave propagation in two-dimensional liquid-phase self-oscillating systems. *Nature*, 1970, *225*, 535–537.

23

On the Shifting Structure of Mathematical Paradigms

John M. Carpenter

Mathematics. The word brings many images to mind: strange symbols, difficult problems, absent-minded professors. For the average man, however, the word first implies some type of computation problem. It may be finding areas or percentages or simply adding and subtracting, but the main impression is of some type of practical arithmetic problem. This viewpoint has a lot of historical legitimacy. The earliest written mathematical records that we have date from more than 5,000 years ago. For the overwhelmingly greater part of this time, the importance of mathematics (and indeed its very truth) was perceived as stemming from the fact that mathematics was one way of describing the nature of the real world. In other words, mathematical statements are true because they describe or agree with or predict our perceptions of the real world, and mathematics is important because it lets us make statements and predictions about the real world more easily than we might otherwise be able to do.

The majority of professional mathematicians no longer completely accept this view as the sole nature of mathematics. Some of the changes are quite recent (within the last fifty years), although their beginnings can be traced back a long time. The changes in the mathematicians' view of the nature of mathematics imply changes in our view of the nature of the world and of mathematics' relationship to the world.

John M. Carpenter • 1017 Milton Avenue, Pittsburgh, Pennsylvania 15218.

The story begins in Greece about 2,500 years ago.[1] The major contribution of Greek mathematics in antiquity was the systematic introduction of deductive reasoning as a means of establishing the truth of mathematical statements. The method involved starting with some statements (called postulates) that were accepted as being clearly true. Then, by using forms of argument developed by the Greeks in their philosophical studies, other statements could be deduced. The truth of these statements followed inexorably from the truth of the postulates and the correctness of the reasoning methods. For example, if we postulate that the diagonals of a rectangle are the same length and show that a square is a special kind of rectangle, then we know that the diagonals of a square are also the same length. Further, we know this without ever having examined the diagonals of any square.

This last statement is important for two reasons. First, it implies that the world is not made up of a jumble of separate unconnected facts. Rather, many of these facts are connected in such a way that, given the right starting place, the entire structure is implicit in that starting place. Second, the Greeks realized that their geometry was dealing with an abstraction of the real world. For example, no matter how fine the point on your drawing implement or how finely divided your protractor, it is not possible to draw an angle measuring exactly 90°. There is always some error. It is therefore impossible to show that the diagonals of a square are the same length by looking at a particular square, since it is not possible to draw a perfect square.

Another tool in this method was a form of reasoning that we know as *reductio ad absurdum,* or proof by contradiction. In effect, the idea is to show that a particular statement, possibly in conjunction with other true statements, leads deductively to some statement that contradicts a known truth. The conclusion is that the original statement must then be false. For example, suppose that there is a freshly painted wall in a room that contains only one entrance. I watch two people enter the room and one of them comes back out. When I enter the room, I see a handprint on the freshly painted wall. I assume that it was put there by the person remaining in the room. This assumption, together with the other facts, allows me to deduce that the person remaining in the room has paint on his hand. I check and find no paint. This contradiction leads me to conclude that my assumption was false; this person did not put the handprint on the wall. Implicit in this method of reasoning is the assumption that contradictions do not exist in the real world. A statement is either true or not true; it can't be both at the same time.

The Greeks made enormous advances with their new methodology.

[1]The historical treatment of mathematics which comprises the first section of this chapter relies on the scholarly reviews of both Eves (1969) and Newman (1956).

Archimedes established, among other things, the correct formulas for the area of a circle, the volume and surface area of a sphere, the volume and surface area of a cylinder, and the volume of a cone. Archimedes also anticipated by 1,900 years some of the key ideas in Isaac Newton's calculus. Euclid's *Elements* was considered such an outstanding example of clear, concise, and correct reasoning that until about 50 years ago virtually every geometry text was either a translation or a close adaptation of parts of this work. It has appeared in more than 1,000 editions since its first printing in 1482.

A key part of this method of deductive reasoning is the fact that the postulates are statements whose truth must be assumed or verified by some other method. The postulates themselves are not established by deductive reasoning. The Greeks felt that it was important to have as few postulates as possible. This made the theory more aesthetic and, more significantly, it also reduced the chance of error. The truth of all the statements established deductively rests on the truth of the postulates. Therefore, the fewer postulates you have, the smaller the possibility that you made a mistake.

Almost immediately after *Elements* was written, mathematicians began leveling criticisms at Euclid's fifth postulate:

> If a straight line intersects two straight lines so as to make the interior angles on one side of it together less than two right angles, these straight lines will intersect, if indefinitely produced, on the side on which are the angles which are together less than two right angles.

Nobody charged that this statement was false. The question was whether it should be a postulate or a theorem (a statement proved deductively from the postulates). The statement is considerably longer than the first four postulates. In complexity it is much more similar to Euclid's theorems than to his other postulates. In fact, Euclid did prove the converse of this statement (the statement obtained by interchanging the hypothesis and the conclusion) using only the first four postulates. Euclid himself seems to have had some reservations about this postulate since he avoided using it in proofs until more than halfway through the first of *Elements'* thirteen books.

Thus began a more-than-two-millenia attempt to prove this fifth postulate from the other four. Many a mathematician thought he had found a proof, but each of these proofs was shown to contain one or another implicit assumption that was logically equivalent to the fifth postulate. It began to be apparent that at least one of Euclid's achievements was his awareness that this postulate was a necessary one.

In 1733, an Italian priest named Girolamo Saccheri took a slightly different tack. Instead of trying to prove Euclid's fifth postulate directly, Saccheri used the first four postulates to prove a statement about rectangles. This statement allowed for three possibilities, one of which implied Euclid's fifth postulate. Saccheri attempted to show that each of the remaining two possibilities led to contradictions and was therefore false. He succeeded with one of the possibilities by implicitly assuming that a straight line is infinitely long. (Euclid's second postulate assumes only that a line is unbounded, that is, that it can be extended as far as you like in the same direction. A circle is an example showing that these two ideas are distinct. The circle is clearly finite, but it is unbounded. You can continue on it as far as you like without ever coming to an end.) Saccheri was unable to show that the second possibility led to a contradiction. He was, however, either unwilling or unable to admit this, and he hedged about his results.

The question was approached again 100 years later by three mathematicians: Carl Friedrich Gauss, Janos Bolyai, and Nicolai Lobachevsky. Working independently, each of the three used a method of attack similar to that used by Saccheri. Each of the three men came to the conclusion that from one of the alternatives to Euclid's fifth postulate, no contradictions were possible. In other words, there were two different geometries. They shared some theorems, those proved using only the first four postulates. However, some theorems from one geometry (those whose proof depended upon the fifth postulate) differed from the corresponding theorems in the other geometry. For example, in one geometry the sum of the angles in any triangle is 180°, whereas in the other geometry the sum of the angles in any triangle is always less than 180°.

Gauss is universally regarded as the greatest mathematician who ever lived. Interestingly, Bolyai and Lobachevsky published these results as relatively young men. Gauss was an elderly man at the time and did not publish, although he had discovered the same results many years earlier. He knew the implications of the results and stated in a letter that he wanted to avoid the controversy that would certainly ensue.

What were these controversial implications? For more than 2,000 years, Euclid's geometry had been accepted as the description of physical space, the real world. Here now was a competitor that contradicted many aspects of it, and there appeared to be no purely mathematical reason for preferring one over the other. Serious questions were being raised about the nature of mathematical truth and its relationship with the real world.

Any last diehard hopes for the absolute truth of Euclidean geometry were dashed a few years later when several mathematicians published proofs that if there were contradictions derivable in non-Euclidean geometry, then there were also contradictions derivable in Euclid's geometry. The method for this proof involved giving a different interpretation to the elementary terms "point," "line," "plane," "distance," and so forth. Under the new interpretations of these terms, statements in non-Euclidean geometry turned into true statements about a part of Euclidean space.

This proof method laid some questions to rest while simultaneously raising others. The mathematicians were able to salvage geometry's role as a description of the real world, but only at the cost of denying both a single universal interpretation for the elementary terms and the absolute truth of the postulates. In other words, if we assign certain meanings to the terms and accept certain postulates, then we get a true description of some part of the real world. If we assign other meanings to the terms and accept other postulates, then we get a true description of some other part of the real world.

In the mid-1800s, therefore, there began to arise the awareness and conviction that our assignment of meaning to a particular term and our choice of postulates is, to a large degree, arbitrary. Once we choose our postulates, we then investigate what statements can be deduced from them. If we can find a real-world assignment of meanings for our terms which makes the postulates true, then our theorems also become true statements about the world. The collection of postulates and theorems has, however, an existence and a truth independent of any real-world application. By the early part of the twentieth century, extreme versions of this viewpoint were widely enough accepted that many mathematicians were willing to actually equate mathematics with these completely abstract deductive systems. Any type of practical application was deemed not to be "pure mathematics."

We are, however, getting a little ahead of our story. By 1854 Georg Bernhard Riemann had published a second non-Euclidean geometry. It was not very long until there was a whole host of non-Euclidean geometries, each of them different, and each of them shown to be contradiction-free so long as Euclidean geometry was contradiction-free. Of course everyone was sure that Euclidean geometry was contradiction-free because it described the real world. Although the real world might contain apparent contradictions, if you looked closely enough there were no contradictions there. The proliferation of non-Euclidean geometries (all resting on Euclid) did finally, however, cause the consistency of Euclidean geometry to be called into question. By elaborating on René Descartes's analytic geometry, it was shown that the existence of contradictions in Euclidean geometry would imply the existence of contradictions in arithmetic. Now, the human race has probably been doing at least simple arithmetic for a longer period of time than it has been writing. Relying on a probable minimum of 10,000 years of experience, most people would be pretty ready to say that there are no contradictions in arithmetic. But the question was raised.

Mathematicians had long been rather carelessly brushing questions about infinite quantities under the rug. In the last half of the nineteenth century, Georg Cantor produced a highly original and beautiful theory of infinite quantities that squarely faced the difficulties and resolved them. The basis of his treatment was his equally revolutionary theory of sets (yes, the same sets and unions and intersections that you or your children may have had trouble with in grade-school arithmetic). Now, it is difficult to conceive of a more simple idea than that of a group of things. Indeed, most mathematicians today would describe the idea of a set as being the most fundamental concept in mathematics. Gottlob Frege, in an extremely lengthy book, succeeded in deriving arithmetic from Cantor's theory of sets. In other words, any contradiction in arithmetic meant that there had to be a contradiction in set theory. Frege claimed at the end of his book to have set the foundations of all mathematics on firm, unshakable, and trustworthy ground. Just a few days after his book went to press, Frege received a letter from Bertrand Russell that burst the whole gigantic bubble. Russell had discovered a paradox in set theory.

A paradox is a special type of contradiction. One form of Russell's paradox deals with sets that have other sets as members. For example, the collection of all sets of silverware is a set each of whose members is also a set. Now we can consider the question of whether or not one of these sets is the original set itself, that is, whether or not the set is a member of itself. For example, consider the set of all sets that have exactly three elements. Clearly there are many sets with exactly three elements; in particular, there are more than three such sets. So the set of all sets containing exactly three elements itself contains more than three elements. This set is not a member of itself. On the other hand, consider the set of all sets that have more than three elements. We can write many different sets that contain more than three elements; in particular, there are more than three such sets. Therefore, the set of all sets containing more than three elements itself contains more than three elements. This means that the set is a member of itself.

Now every set is either a member of itself or is not a member of itself. So consider finally the set of all those sets that are *not* members of themselves. We will call this Russell's set. The critical question is whether or not Russell's set is a member of itself. If it is a member of itself, then by its defining property it is not a member of itself (Russell's set contains only those sets that are *not* members of themselves.) On the other hand, if Russell's set is not a member of itself, then it must be a member of itself (Russell's set contains all sets that are not members of themselves.)

Mathematicians thus found themselves faced with two statements in set theory. Each of the statements led to a contradiction, and yet one of the statements was necessarily true. As we mentioned above, the concept of mathematics as an abstract deductive system had been growing in importance for perhaps seventy years. Its truth did not depend on any particular assignment of meanings to the terms (nor therefore on any necessary relationships to the real or concrete world). Its truth derived solely from the deductive structure and the assumed truth of the postulates. The absence of contradictions in deductive mathematics depended on the absence of contradictions in set theory, and now a gaping settlement crack had been discovered in this foundation of mathematics. It threatened the integrity of the entire structure.

There ensued a number of different attempts to patch the crack, with varying degrees of limited success. Alfred North Whitehead and Bertrand Russell made an attempt in their *Principia Mathematica* (1925–1927) with a concept even more basic than that of set. Based on the work of several men over a period of more than two hundred years, deductive logic had been reformulated as a collection of operations on abstract symbols. Whitehead and Russell, drawing heavily on their philosophical background, tried carefully to construct a contradiction-free set theory solely out of this symbolic logic. They succeeded in disposing of Russell's paradox, but only at the cost of introducing what seemed to many mathematicians to be a highly artificial and limiting restriction. They made a distinction between hierarchies of sets that effectively prohibited the discussion of such concepts as the set of all sets.

Other mathematicians (notably Ernst Zermelo) felt that insufficient care had been given to the choice of postulates and the interpretation of the term "set" in Cantor's theory. Cantor's set theory is now often called naive set theory to distinguish it from its more rigorous successors. In order to establish certain results necessary for the development of calculus, Zermelo was forced to introduce a postulate called the axiom of choice. This postulate sanctioned a particular method of constructing infinite sets and immediately drew a great furor of criticism.

A school of mathematics called intuitionism, more or less founded by the Dutch mathematician L. E. Brouwer, objected strenuously. Basically, the intuitionists refuse to accept any method of proof that is not concretely verifiable in a finite amount of time. They will not, therefore, accept any process that would require an infinite number of steps. They also refuse to accept proof by contradiction. While these restrictions eliminate Russell's paradox, they also unfortunately eliminate huge areas of very useful mathematics. Consequently, the intuitionist school, while still surviving today, is presently an extremely small minority of mathematics.

Still another approach was tried by a group called the formalists, led by David Hilbert. Hilbert's group maintained that mathematics in its entirety was nothing more than a collection of abstract symbols and operations on these symbols. Insofar as there was any attempt to attach any meaning whatever to the symbols, you were not doing mathematics. The formalists did achieve some successes. They were able to prove conclusively that certain very simple mathematical systems (most notably a small part of symbolic logic known as statement calculus) were consistent and complete. Consistency means that no contradictions are derivable from the postulates. Completeness means that any true statement expressible in the system is provable from the postulates. Hilbert's success with the statement calculus led to high hopes in the late 1920s that the consistency and completeness of all mathematics would soon be demonstrated, that is, that all of mathematics would be derivable from one set of a few postulates.

Those hopes were exploded forever by an Austrian mathematician named Kurt Gödel. The symbolic logic used in most of Whitehead and Russell's *Principia Mathematica* (1925–1927) is called first-order predicate calculus. In an epoch-making paper, Gödel (1931) proved that any deductive system at least as complex as first-order predicate calculus is *inherently either inconsistent or incomplete, and, further that we can never know which.*[2] For a detailed explanation of this proof, the interested reader is referred to Nagel and Newman (1958) and Hofstadter (1979). A more general discussion follows.

Let us take a slightly closer look at this—Gödel's incompleteness theorem. Gödel's theorem does not apply to very simple postulational systems, such as the statement calculus. It only discusses systems that have passed a certain threshold level of complexity, that is, systems like the logic in *Principia Mathematica* that are sufficiently complex to support arithmetic and, by extension, the rest of mathematics. Gödel showed that if such deductive systems were free of contradiction, then they had to contain true statements that were not provable from the posulates. He further showed that there was no way to prove that such systems were contradiction-free by working solely within the system itself. In short, one cannot prove that these systems are consistent (contradiction-free); but if they are consistent, then they are also incomplete (contain true statements that are not provable.)

A particular analogy may be helpful to the lay mathematician. Hofstadter (1979) sees Gödel's discovery, in its barest form, as a translation of an ancient philosophical paradox—the Epimenides or liar paradox—into mathematical terms. This now famous statement attributed to Epimenides is: "This statement is false." Hofstadter clearly describes this statement's paradoxical nature:

[2]Stated in this way, Gödel's imcompleteness theorem bears a striking resemblance to the Heisenberg uncertainty principle in physics. See R. Valle, Chapter 21, for a discussion of this analogous principle and its implications for psychology and philosophy.—Eds.

> It is a statement which rudely violates the usually assumed dichotomy of statements into true and false, because if you tentatively think it is true, then it immediately backfires on you and makes you think it is false. But once you've decided it is false, a similar backfiring returns you to the idea that it must be true. (p. 17)

What, you may ask, does this have to do with mathematics? Read on, as this is what, in fact, Gödel discovered.[3] Resting on Hilbert's idea of metamathematics, Gödel used mathematical reasoning to investigate mathematical reasoning itself. It was this notion, that is, making mathematics "introspective," that led to the incompleteness theorem described above. It seems that the proof of the theorem depends upon the necessary appearance of a self-referential mathematical statement, similar in kind to Epimenides' paradox which is a self-referential statement of language. Needless to say, it is not easy to understand how a statement about numbers can talk about itself, but this was Gödel's genius—to connect the idea of self-referential statements with number theory.

Gödel's reasoning continued with his realization that a statement of number theory could be *about* a statement of number theory (even itself), if only numbers could somehow be used to stand for or represent statements. In short, this was accomplished by using a clever coding system called "Gödel-numbering," where numbers are used in place of symbols and sequences of symbols. In this way, each statement of number theory, being a sequence of specialized symbols, acquires its own Gödel number. What this coding allowed was that statements of number theory could be understood not only *as* statements of number theory, but also as *statements about statements* of number theory—meta-statements! Gödel could then translate Epimenides' paradox into mathematical formalism as: "This statement of number theory does not have any proof." Keeping in mind that "proofs" are demonstrations within fixed systems of propositions, and that, in Gödel's work, the fixed system of number-theoretical reasoning referred to is that of Whitehead and Russell's *Principia Mathematica,* Gödel's transposition of the liar paradox can be more properly written as: "This statement of number theory does not have any proof in the system of *Principia Mathematica.*" What, then, is the final conclusion? Namely, "That the system of *Principia Mathematica* is incomplete—there are true statements of number theory which its methods of proof are too weak to demonstrate" (Hofstadter, 1979, p. 18).

What are the implications of all this for mathematics? Almost all present-day mathematicians save the handful of remaining intuitionists, choose to believe that mathematics is consistent and therefore incom-

---

[3]The presentation and explanation of Gödel's theorem which follow rely on Hofstadter's (1979) clear exposition of these ideas.

plete. There is a very good pragmatic reason for this choice. If a contradiction is derivable from a set of postulates, then a very simple rule of deductive logic states that any statement at all in the system can be proved true. This would be a very disturbing state of affairs if mathematics is to have any meaning at all. For example, if mathematics is not consistent, then it is possible to prove that a whole number can be both even and odd at the same time. From the assumption that mathematics is consistent but incomplete, it follows that it will never be possible to express all of mathematics in one unified deductive system. As Hofstadter (1979) says, "Gödel showed that provability is a weaker notion than truth, no matter what axiomatic system is involved." In other words, the method of deductive proof has some very sharp limits. No matter what postulates you start from, there will be true statements not provable from those postulates (provided you accept the assumption that the postulates are consistent).

We are, therefore, forced to another revision of what it means to say that a mathematical statement is true. We started with the criterion that a mathematical statement was true because it described the real world. With the introduction of the deductive method, we extended that criterion to confer truth on statements that were correctly deduced from other true statements. We then moved to a recognition that our choice of starting places or postulates was to some degree arbitrary. Mathematical statements had an existence and a truth or falsehood of their own, independent of the "real" world. The sole determinant of that truth or falsehood was whether or not a deductive proof of that statement was constructible starting from the postulates. When you assigned definitions to the terms in such a way that the postulates became meaningful statements about the "real" world, the provable statements also became true statements about the "real" world. We have now come to the idea that for mathematical statements, anyway, provability is no longer a necessary criterion of truth (although it is highly doubtful that any mathematician would accept any specific statement as true without seeing a proof of it). In part, this fact seems to necessitate a greater reliance on the correspondence between mathematical statements and the "real" world. And yet, Gödel and the majority of mathematicians believe that the human mind, or the rational mind if you will, is more powerful than deductive logic. They do not rule out the possibility of the discovery of methods of proof more powerful than deductive logic.

It is necessary to be very careful in discussing the meanings of Gödel's results. Many people have used the theorem to justify many different metaphysical arguments. For example, it has been alleged that the theorem shows that there are limits to the rational mind. The theorem, however, does not discuss the rational mind; it only discusses the axiomatic method. Referring again to Hofstadter (1979):

> If one uses Gödel's Theorem as a *metaphor*, as a source of inspiration, rather than trying to translate it literally into the language of psychology or of any other discipline, then perhaps it can suggest new truths in psychology or other areas. But it is quite unjustifiable to translate it directly into a statement of another discipline and take that as equally valid. It would be a large mistake to think that what has been worked out with the utmost delicacy in mathematical logic should hold without modification in a completely different area. (p. 696, italics added)

Even with this note of caution, Hofstadter does go on to offer speculations in several different areas. He is a computer scientist, though, and is very careful to maintain a clear distinction between implications of Gödel's results in a mathematical context and metaphorical discussions.

Do recall, however, that Gödel's theorem applies only to deductive systems that have reached a certain threshold level of complexity; and recall also that in Russell's paradox, the difficulties began to arise when we talked about sets that were members of themselves. Hofstadter speculates that the critical level of complexity appears to occur when the system becomes capable of making statements concerning itself, or, in other words, capable of *self-reference* (self-reference being the same issue presented earlier with regard to the generation of meta-statements).[4]

Self-reference speaks directly to the issue of human consciousness. When human beings explore the external world, the world of objects, events, and their interrelationships, the system of logic and scientific reasoning being used is not self-referent and, therefore, Gödel's theorem is irrelevant. However, whenever we have attempted to explore the nature of our own thought processes and consciousness (that is, the nature of ourselves), we act in a self-referent manner. At this point, Gödel's theorem takes on *metaphorical* relevance. It suggests that when the human individual attempts to understand him- or herself, truth must have a definition apart from logical provability.

Where does this awareness of the nature of self-reference lead us? It is here suggested that it leads us to a classic borderline—the borderline between the rational, thinking, conceptual mind, the realm of the Jungian masculine, the phenomenal divider, the subject–object dichotomizer, and the intuitive, feeling, wisdom-seeking higher faculty, the realm of the Jungian feminine, the noumenal congealer, the dissolver of all apparent difference.[5] This is the same distinction that exists in each of us, a

---

[4]The remainder of this chapter was written by Ronald S. Valle, and is included with the author's permission and approval.—Eds.

[5]See V. Valle and Kruger, Chapter 19, for a dicsussion of the Jungian masculine and feminine.—Eds.

distinction which the ancient Hindu philosophers called *manas* (the lower mind) and *buddhi* (the higher wisdom). If deductive mathematical reasoning is in fact an emergent phenomenon of manas, then provability (a product of our rational faculties) is indeed a weaker notion than truth (our descriptive conceptualization of the foundational characteristic of buddhi). In words which seem to mirror both the Platonic doctrine of disembodied, eternal Forms and the Jungian notion of archetypes, Gödel (1944) himself once said:

> Classes and concepts may . . . be conceived as real objects [Forms, archetypes] . . . existing independently of our definitions and constructions. It seems to me that the assumption of such objects is quite legitimate . . . and there is much reason to believe in their existence. (p. 137)

When one examines the nature of "truth" as Gödel apparently has, one is left with more questions than answers. Given Gödel's insights, consider: "What is the nature of probability, particularly as used by the new physicists to explain subatomic phenomena?",[6] "What are the limits of man-made computers and of the attempts to create a true artificial human intelligence?",[7] and "Does this lend credibility to the many psychological and other theories which describe transpersonal faculties of higher consciousness?"

References

Eves, H. *An introduction to the history of mathematics.* New York: Holt, Rinehart, & Winston, 1969.

Gödel, K. Uber Formal Unentscheidbare Sätze der *Principia Mathematica* und Verwandter Systeme, I. *Monatshefte für Mathematik und Physik,* 1931, *38,* 173–198.

Gödel, K. Russell's mathematical logic. In P. A. Schilpp (Ed.), *The philsophy of Bertrand Russell.* La Salle, Ill.: Open Court, 1944.

Hofstadter, D. *Gödel, Escher, Bach: An eternal golden braid.* New York: Basic Books, 1979.

Nagel, E., & Newman, J. *Gödel's proof.* New York: New York University Press, 1958.

Newman, J. *The world of mathematics.* New York: Simon & Schuster, 1956.

Whitehead, A. N., & Russell, B. *Principia mathematica.* Cambridge: Cambridge University Press, 1925–1927.

[6]See R. Valle, Chapter 21.—Eds.
[7]See Bair, Chapter 24.—Eds.

24

Computer Metaphors for Consciousness

Puran Khan Bair

Introduction

The Landmark Events of Our Times

This age represents a new stage in the awakening of humanity, and its effects are being seen in every aspect of life. In particular, there have been several landmark events that are both a product of the consciousness of our age, and also so monumental in their implications that they have a transforming effect upon our consciousness.

One of these events is our landing on the moon. Through the eyes of the cameras, we had a shared experience of standing on the moon, looking at planet earth. We will never think of ourselves in the old way again—our vision has a new sense of the unity of earth's passengers, their fragility and interdependence, and the detachment of the cosmic perspective.

The development of nuclear weaponry, giving us the ability to virtually eradicate human life on this planet, is a second landmark event. It has been deeply impressed on us, although for most it has become unconscious, that our individual will must be limited; that the question of the continuance of the grand human experiment is not predetermined by some external deity, but is our responsibility.

The development of the computer is a third event of this universal

Puran Khan Bair • Serapis Corporation, 84 State Street, Boston, Massachusetts 02109.

scope, because it is a new level of machine, unlike anything that mankind has ever created before. Of course, the computer was essential to the accomplishment of the events above, but its very profound implications for humanity go far beyond its use as a tool.

The Impact of the Computer

The impact of computers is felt in various ways:

1. The computer represents such a serious challenge to our identity as "beings that think," that it pushes us to discover our true identity in the consciousness beyond our thinking process.

2. By studying computers, we can learn a tremendous amount about the function, operation, organization, and physical construction of our human brain and nervous system. In fact, the knowledge about the working of the mind that was taught by a great mystic of our time corresponds exactly to the way that computers have been constructed.

3. Computer organization models human sociology; the advantages and disadvantages of different systems of social organization and types of human relationships can be clearly observed, quantified, and analyzed in systems of multiple computers.

4. There is a definite path of evolutionary growth of computers that may give us some hint of our own evolutionary path.

Implications for Human Evolution

The Path of the Evolution of Technology

Peeking ahead into the future, let us look at the conclusion before the analysis. In the background material that will be presented in later sections will be found some evidence of a clear path of evolution which computers have followed and continue to follow. It seems reasonable to believe that all technology follows this same path, but that the limitations inherent in the physical machines (noncomputer machines) are so great that we had only observed a very small part of the technological evolutionary chain before the computer. In the 30-year life of the computer so far, there have been radical changes that show us, in a short time, a very long section of the evolutionary chain of technology by comparison with what we saw before.

Translated into Human Terms

What follows is not an extrapolation of that line of evolution; it is only a translation of the evolution of technology into human terms. If we assume that human evolution will proceed in the same direction as technology has, then we can expect the following for humanity in the future:

1. The body will be continually refined, eventually incorporating light into and with its material substance.

2. This refinement in the body will support a much faster and more expansive mental process, giving the ability to think with greater speed and precision.

3. Much of the body's substance will be dedicated to memory. This, together with more efficient means of storing information, will result in a much expanded memory.

4. We will have the ability to access at will the information stored in the different levels of our memory: the unconscious storage, and the memory of the muscles, nerves, skin, and other tissues.[1]

5. Emotions will be used consciously for a kind of holographic,[2] coded, condensed storage of a large amount of thought.

6. Discrimination will become very fine, owing to the very fast processing of comparisons. This will give a fine sense of judgment and a much greater ability to predict the consequences of actions.

7. The experience and memory of others will be instantly available to us through direct communication without the need for expression.

8. Once memory-sharing becomes efficient, we will begin to depend on it, deliberately forgetting whole areas of expertise in order to concentrate all available personal memory on our own work. This would amount to a decision to store the "forgotten" material in the memory of another, which could then be retrieved by a mental connection with that person.

9. Information will be stored increasingly in people's minds rather than in books. To retrieve a piece of information, one will contact a particular person rather than using the senses to input the information (seeing and listening).

10. The senses will become much more sensitive owing to the mind's ability to consciously suppress their signals when the input is not desired. The senses always develop to the extent of the mind's ability to deal with the volume of input.

11. The senses will be used primarily to communicate emotion, the melting pot in which thoughts can be mixed to create a new order of thinking that does not come logically from the ingredient thoughts.

12. The single-purpose organs of the body will be replaced by general-purpose tissue (perhaps glands) that can perform many different functions under conscious control.

13. Physical life will be much longer because of the high degree of

---

[1]See Moss and Keen, Chapter 4, for a discussion of *embodied* consciousness.—Eds.
[2]See Pribram, Chapter 6, for a discussion of the holographic nature of memory.—Eds.

redundancy in a body that is composed of general-purpose tissue and the ability to direct it consciously.

The Challenge of the Computer

The Created Manifests the Creator

> Man—*the created creator and the creating creature.*
>
> —AL HALLAJ

All of our creations are receptacles and vehicles for our own qualities as we are vehicles for the Qualities of the Creator. Our art and science express that beauty, grace, wisdom, power, love, etc. which is manifested in us. When we create, we act on behalf of creation.

In the computer, we have the best vehicle that we have created so far for carrying that intelligence that we hold. It manifests intelligence just as a canvas painting manifests beauty and an atomic bomb manifests power. In each case, the created object is able to pass on its quality in some way: the beautiful painting makes the observer feel beautiful, the bomb creates chain reactions of powerful explosions in other objects, the computer can solve problems that the human mind cannot solve.

As a contrast, many of our creations have a kind of "life" to them, but we have not yet succeeded in creating something that "lives." That is, the quality of life is not one of our qualitites that we have learned how to pass on as yet. Someday we will do it—we will create something that lives. But already we have created something that "thinks."

The Accomplishments of the Computer

In the first 30 years of its existence, the computer has been instructed to compete at chess at a master level, discover new proofs of theorems of geometry and symbolic logic, play the pattern-discovery game much better than chimpanzees, demonstrate a good understanding of the meaning in English-language sentences within certain contexts, and decipher the human voice, given a large sample of the same voice within a limited vocabulary.

The Limitations of the Computer (So Far)

So far, a computer has not been able to make an acceptable translation of one natural language to another, decipher the voice of a stranger, retrieve information on an association-basis as fast as the human mind with the same capacity, and make an acceptable attempt at the Turing test.

Turing proposed in 1950 that we substitute, for the loaded question of whether or not a computer can think, an observable criterion—namely, whether an interrogator can determine which of two rooms contains a man and which contains a computer when the interrogator is only permitted to interact with the rooms through a teletypewriter. If the interrogator cannot tell, then let us say that the computer thinks like a human being, even though the actual process that it goes through may be different. So we cannot yet say, by this criterion, that computers think like humans. But the general question is still open.

Can Computers Think?[3]

"Some say animals have no mind. But that is a wrong conception. Wherever there is a body there is mind; even the tree has a mind" (Hazrat Inayat Khan, 1961, p. 134).[4]

Some people deny that a computer can think; some say that animals cannot think. We are challenged here to understand what "thinking" is, and what our unique capability is as humans. In our need for a unique position in creation, we have clung to the title of "the one who thinks, reasons, plans, and makes judgments." But it is a futile attempt to defend a province that does not belong to us alone. We stubbornly try to define "thinking" as that which humans do. The truth is that computers can do many things that, had they been done by humans, would be called intelligent, rational, even creative thinking.

Again, considering the inevitability of the moment when we create life in a test tube, will we deny that it is living because it doesn't enjoy going out to a movie? No, because biologists have defined a few very specific criteria that define "living": the organism must take in food, grow, reproduce, etc. But we are not threatened by something that lives, even if we create it, because we do not identify ourselves with that which lives—we identify with that which thinks.

When a specific set of criteria for thinking is defined, a computer can be made to pass it, because as soon as we understand precisely something of what thinking is, we understand enough to be able to program a computer to do it. This has happened repeatedly, and each time, of course, we then stand on such an understanding and reach for a still higher criterion of thinking. At the same time, we repudiate our earlier

---

[3]See Leavitt, Chapter 20, for a review and discussion of the science-fiction literature which has addressed itself to the idea of *sentient* computers.—Eds.

[4]Pir-o-Murshid Hazrat Inayat Khan founded the Sufi Order in the West in 1910.

approximations as trivial. We shall never be satisfied with a model of thinking that we can think up.

The View of the Mind from Above

This is where our higher consciousness can come to the rescue. In our anxious flailings about within the mind, trying to push its functional description beyond the point of competition, we fail to see that the mind is not the center of identity. Indeed, we continue to exist even though we go through very great mind changes.

Meditation can open the experience of existence beyond life: as it was and will be when the mind is not supported by a brain.[5] Furthermore, meditation can provide the experience of nonlocal and nontemporal existence, that is, "seeing without the lens,"[6] or being conscious of the whole without being centered at a point in space–time. The experience is the same as that described by people who have gone through a clinical death and then been revived, and it is further substantiated by verifying the reality of one's intuitions and visions.

The meditation called *Satipathana*, for example, which is part of the teaching of the Buddha, describes the technique for looking upon one's mind as also peripheral.

When one watches the mind from the consciousness of an eternal, essential identity, it appears very clearly as a mechanical, though very clever, computerlike device. It functions at a level determined by the consciousness, follows a direction set by the emotions, and works under the direction of the interest.

"Plainly, it may be said that the mind is the instrument of the soul and the body is the instrument of the mind" (Hazrat Inayat Khan).

Rising to the Challenge

Instead of trying to define "thinking" as "that which human beings do," we could surrender the thinking identity and push the standard of "human" much higher. When we are threatened by computers, we cannot learn from them, and that is a pity because they have so much to show us about how we work. It is not insulting to think of the mind as a computer and to study computers to get insights into ourselves any more

[5]Compare this with the "mind-contained" hypothesis described by Lilly, Chapter 8. Once again we are faced with the distinction between intentional mind (see R. von Eckartsberg and R. Valle, Chapter 14) and pure consciousness (see Swami Rama, Chapter 15).—Eds.

[6]See Weber, Chapter 5, for a discussion of "lenseless vision."—Eds.

than it is insulting to study the bodies of monkeys and dogs to gain knowledge about our body. But we must center our identity beyond our mind and know that essence of ourselves which is not physical or mental in order to look objectively upon the mind. When we do that, we will find that this creation of ours, the computer, is a remarkably clear mirror of the way that intelligence functions within us.

Analogies Between the Computer and the Mind

Hardware and Software

"Hardware" in a computer is the physical machinery. "Software" is the programming that directs the computer to do a function. The software resides in the memory of the computer either having been placed there at the time of manufacture by impressing a certain pattern on the memory which is then not erasable or having been loaded into memory temporarily from some storage device.

The hardware, or physical component, of the mind is the brain and nervous system. The software is that which distinguishes two minds, even though the brains may look physically similar. Furthermore, any mind's change in point of view in a relatively short period of time is the result of new software, not new hardware. The human software exists in the form of conditionings, opinions, experiences, understandings, etc. —that which makes one think as one does.

Gates Are Cells

The hardware of the computer is composed of basic elements called "gates," just as the hardware of the mind, the body, is composed of cells. A gate is a device that allows a small force to start or stop the flow of a large force, as a light turn on the handle of a faucet can control a very forceful stream of water. As the intelligence residing in human beings is supported by structures of cells in the brain, so the intelligence residing in a computer is supported by structures of gates.

The Refinement of the Cells

As computers have evolved, the construction of gates has gone through a very rapid refinement. In fact, the computer has gone through what are called "generations," which are defined by the construction of the basic gates in the machine:

Generation 0: electromagnetic relays
Generation 1: vacuum tubes
Generation 2: transistors
Generation 3: integrated circuits on silicone

The function of the gate has not changed, but the weight, size, power consumption, and speed of the gate has changed by at least a factor of 10 at every generation.

Here is the most rapid evolution of any machine ever created. Notice how the body of the computer has changed from a series of metal switches that are physically moved by electromagnets, to the flow of electrons that are boiled off of a metal at high temperature to travel through a vacuum space, to the flow of electrons within a crystal. At each step, the mass of the moving material is decreased, its travel distance is decreased, and the speed is increased.

Active and Passive Thinking

Gates are used to create all the circuits of the computer. There are two principal kinds of circuits—processor and memory. The processor circuits combine two numbers, expressed as electrical signals, to create a new number. The memory retains numbers. The software, the computer's list of instructions, is stored in memory.

Computer memory is made of pairs of interconnecting gates, such that the controlled force in one is the controlling force in the other, and vice versa. Processor circuits are made of pairs of connected gates such that the controlling forces are combined or the controlled forces are combined. Furthermore, a memory circuit can be made from several processing circuits, and a processing circuit can be made from several memory circuits.

This demonstrates the relationship between active and passive modes of thinking. Our productive thinking may be seen as simply memory recall, that is, our "creative" process is actually a listening process. And our memory operations may be seen as the result of active processes that *create* the images that we "remember," that is, our memory is "living."

> One characteristic of the mind is that it is like a gramophone-record: whatever is impressed upon it, it is able to reproduce; and another characteristic of the mind is that it does not only reproduce something, but it creates what is impressed upon it. (Hazrat Inayat Khan, 1961, p. 155)

The Generalization of the Hardware

The hardware of the computer is actually exceedingly simple, and the trend is toward an even greater simplification. Software is being introduced at an even more basic level than before, such that the elemental computer operation that used to rest on a hardware structure is now actually a software operation of an even more elemental hardware. That is, a certain number of gates are needed to perform any simple computer operation, like "add." The number of gates required for the whole computer can be greatly reduced by using the same gates in other processing circuits as well.

The gates are programmed to act one way for "add" and a different way for other operations, and this "microprogram" is held in a computer memory. Now the gates must open and close much faster because a series of operations of the general-purpose gates is required instead of the single operation of fixed-purpose, dedicated gates. The general-purpose gates actually form a computer within the computer.

As the hardware becomes faster, it can be used in a more general way, and *less of it is needed*. A computer-processing operation in hardware can be reduced to a software program of a more elemental hardware. We do not know what the limit is to this principle.

In the human body, we see the same DNA in all cells, which is sometimes programmed to act one way and sometimes another, producing cells of different types and functions. The conscious control of the DNA would allow us to regenerate one type of cell from another.

The Five Functions of Mind

One of the clearest parallels between the computer and the mind can be seen through the teachings of Hazrat Inayat Khan, a great mystic who lived in the West for 17 years before his death in 1927, almost 20 years before the computer era. His descriptions of the action of the mind, taken from his extensive teachings on the mind, describe exactly the construction and operation of the computer. This teaching is quoted here so that we can use it as a framework in examining further the analogies between the mind and the computer.

> There are five different actions of the mind which can be distinguished: the creating of thought; the sense of discrimination; memory; the factor of feeling; and the principal faculty, the feeling of "I-ness" or ego. (Hazrat Inayat Khan, 1961, p. 135)

The Creating of Thought. This element in the computer is called the Processor Unit, and it is the one that performs all the arithmetic and logical computations, like the sum, difference, or combination of two numbers. It does not create a wholly new result, it only operates on one or more "old thoughts" to produce a logical combination or manipulation like the converse of an argument or the association of two ideas. Larger mental operations are built up by repetitions of the basic operations that the Processor performs. The Processor does not seem to add any information, since all of the information contained in the result is already present in the input.

"Every thought that the mind creates has some connection with some idea already recorded, not exactly similar but akin to it" (Hazrat Inayat Khan).

However, it does add information by ordering and organizing the input. Consider two lists of the names and telephone numbers of the residents of Boston: one is in no particular order, and one is in order by name. The ordered list is useable and valuable. It contains more "information" than the unordered list.

Sorting is one of the most fundamental operations of the computer. People do sorting, a basic thought process, by selectively forgetting, by going over and over the same information, and by labeling, to give a few examples. Labeling is the process of creating names for classes of things and then placing objects into those classes by some judgment based on the object and the definition of the class. Computers use models of these and other methods to accomplish sorting.

Sorting is an example of a process that takes energy and creates order. Order stores energy in the sense that it takes less energy to do something in the future, like looking up a telephone number.

The Sense of Discrimination. We discriminate by making decisions which lead us from one thought to the next of several. According to Webster, "to discriminate" means "to detect as different, to distinguish, to select." Discrimination is "a difference in treatment between things."

The mechanism of selection and decision in a computer is called the Control Unit. It determines which instruction to take next based on comparisons or judgments that have been made by the Processor. The ability to take one of two possible alternatives lies here.

Memory. The two major divisions of computer memory are called the "Random-Access Memory" (RAM), and the "Storage." This corresponds exactly to the divisions described by Hazrat Inayat Khan:

> Memory can also be divided into two parts. There are certain things we need not look for, but which are always clear in our memory. We can recall them at any moment we wish; they are always living in our memory. But then there is the second part of memory which is sometimes called the subconscious mind, though in reality it is the bottom of the memory. In this part of the memory a photograph is made of everything we have seen or heard, even once just like a flash, and it remains there. There we can find it at some time or other, either with difficulty or easily, as the case may be. (1961, p. 137)

The computer's Random-Access Memory is so called because all of its contents are available immediately and can be transferred to the

Processor Unit without holding up the processing. All of its contents are equally accessible—there are not some parts of it that are slower to access than others.

The computer Storage, on the other hand, requires some time for access, the delay depending on what it is that is being retrieved and how closely it is related to what was retrieved last. The capacity of this Storage is much larger than the RAM, at least a million times larger. And it contains, generally, all the data that the computer has ever used or generated. The computer operator may elect to erase some data in order to reuse that storage media for other data, but the ability is there to preserve all the data indefinitely.

The Factor of Feeling. The next element of a computer is the Input/Output Unit. It is the interface between the other parts of the computer (described above) and the computer's "peripherals"—the input and output devices like keyboards, printers, video displays, and other sensors and controllers. These devices are the "senses" of the computer, and they are all attached to the Input/Output Unit.

> Beneath the five senses there is one principal sense that works through the others. It is through this sense that one feels deeply and distinguishes between the impressions which come from outside. (Hazrat Inayat Khan)

The one principal sense is the Input/Output Unit. Hazrat Inayat Khan makes it clear that the factor of feeling comes through the principal sense. This corresponds to the teaching of the Buddha that the senses trigger the emotions.[7]

The Ego. The Ego of a computer is so clear that it is not ever mentioned. Ego is a sense of separateness. The separateness of one computer from another is much more obvious than the separateness of one human being from another.

Computer Models of Human Sociology

Not only do we learn about ourselves by studying computers, but we learn about computers by studying ourselves. We can build better computers by basing our designs on natural and, particularly, human behavior. In constructing computers and computer systems, we have a great deal of latitude to do it however we wish—we can model as high a conception as we can understand. The problems with computers today come from our not implementing very much of what we know.

[7]See Levin, Chapter 12, and de Silva, Chapter 13, for discussions of Buddhist teachings.— Eds.

For example, consider the problem of interconnecting computers in order to form a much greater system capacity. The machines can work on independent parts of one problem, signaling each other for coordination and information.

The Master–Slave Relationship

The first multicomputer installations were based on a model of master and slave. One computer was always in control of the others. Usually the master computers were built differently from the slave computers, so that it was not possible to switch functions. Not surprisingly, computer systems of this type have all the inefficiencies that master–slave relationships have among people. The roles are so structured that one cannot help the other do its job.

The Leaderless Group

Another model used for computer interconnection is the democratic, leaderless-group model popular in some communes. There is strong autonomy of the individuals who organize themselves in a group for efficiency. The computers all keep in a common memory the equivalent of the "list-on-the-refrigerator-door" of jobs-to-be-done. Whoever has spare time goes to that list and removes one item.

The Army

Another model used is the army, which is an improvement over the master–slave model in that slaves can become masters, and there are many levels of masters (or slaves).

Whether these models are applied to groups of computers or human societies, they show the same shortcomings. But none of these models represents the best of what we know about how groups operate. As we more fully understand better sociological models, they can be implemented and tested among computers. Not only will the computer systems work more efficiently and reliably with greater throughput,[8] but we will learn a tremendous amount about the model by specifying it in precise detail and by tuning that specification to improve the computer's performance.

---

[8]"Throughput" is a term used to refer to the information currently being processed *within* the computer (compared to "input" and "output").—Eds.

Higher Level Examples

Some examples of better models for interconnected intelligence are the way the brain cooperates with the rest of the nervous system, particularly the spine, to distribute the control and memory functions, and the kind of hierarchical structure that exists among the masters, saints, and prophets who form the spiritual government of the universe.

Conclusion

The alchemists of the Middle Ages were forced to conduct their research into human consciousness through a coded language that allowed communication about the mystical experience, but hid the real nature of their work. The language uses the names of material objects to represent different aspects of the human essence or stages of human consciousness. For instance, salt represents the body, mercury the mind, and sulphur the spirit.

There must have been a very dynamic flow of ideas in both directions, as they discovered the fundamentals of chemistry through working with these material analogues of consciousness, and as they had new realizations into the process of transformation through their physical experiments.

The metaphor of alchemy works in the light of the realization that there is one basic method of transformation; that all matter goes through the same process to change states: dissolution and then coagulation, or disintegration followed by rebirth.[9]

The computer gives us another vocabulary with which to discuss our essence, plus a working mechanism that embodies and demonstrates the concepts. In our case, the science that is being discovered is the science of thinking, which we now call Computer Science. As the alchemists discovered transformation, we are discovering evolution—conscious evolution—or the development of latent potentials by making conscious that which is unconscious.

Reference

Hazrat Inayat Khan. *The Sufi Message* (Vol. 4). London: Barrie & Jenkins, 1961.

[9]This process bears a remarkable semblance to the Belousov–Zhabotinsky reaction (dissipative structure phenomena) described by Schore, Chapter 22.—Eds.

25

Thymós as Biopsychological Metaphor
THE VITAL ROOT OF CONSCIOUSNESS

Paul A. Lee

When I started to take an interest in botany and the plant kingdom, a friend introduced me to the botanical writings of Goethe, after Alan Chadwick had made me aware of the Vitalist tradition in horticulture, in particular the biodynamic system developed by Rudolf Steiner. My friend gave me a copy of Agnes Arber's edition of Goethe's *Metamorphosis of Plants*, which was to open the theme of metamorphoses, of changes, as though the main text for botany were the *I Ching*.

I read Goethe's essay and did not understand it. I read Rudolf Steiner on Goethe (he was the editor of Goethe's scientific writings at the Weimar Archive) and did not understand him. But I plugged along.

As the pieces began to fall into place, where fragments never became more than fragments, even though they suggested some larger design, the larger design continued to shift and I never knew exactly how to put it until I found the key: Physicalism versus Vitalism.[1]

I was aware of the implications of this larger design for the philosophy of science and the theme of the structure of scientific revolutions. Although Thomas Kuhn (1962) the proponent of the theme, could assume the structure of Physicalism as *the* structure of scientific revolutions and write a purely formalistic account of the revolution, as though the Physicalist camp were all there was, I had picked up the Vitalist

---

[1]The best introduction to this conflict is E. Cassirer's (1950) *The Problem of Knowledge*, J. Merz's (1978) *A History of European Scientific Thought in the Nineteenth Century*, and T. Kuhn's (1962) *The Structure of Scientific Revolutions*.

Paul A. Lee • The Platonic Academy, Box 409, Santa Cruz, California 95061.

thread, the defeated point of view, the refutation of which defined Physicalism. It was a negative definition: you are defined by what you reject. The rejection of Vitalism by Physicalism thus became, for me, a key to our culture.

While I was studying philosophy and theology at Harvard, Paul Tillich introduced me to a theology of culture and prepared the way for my intellectual path. He gave me the definition of industrial society as "a world above the given world of nature," where I came to see how the "above" was brought about through "artificial synthesis," as in the isolation of active ingredients and their synthetic counterparts. The role of synthetics in industrial society was comparable to the role of plastics and the emphasis on simulation. All this took on an ersatz odor for me, thanks to the teaching of my German-born theologian.

In the tradition of Friedrich Wilhelm von Schelling, Tillich (1975) was looking for the means to do philosophy of nature again. He tried, in his *Systematic Theology*, to work out a philosophy of life (following Nietzsche), but the transmission from Schelling never seemed to find expression. Tillich's most important paper on Schelling still remains untranslated, although his two early works, expounding Schelling's theory of guilt and of religious symbolism in antiquity, are now in English.

I began to think of Schelling (one of the most neglected of all the major Western philosophers) as the key to the last century and a half, so much so, that I toyed with the notion of being in some strange relation with him. I thought that to me had fallen the opportunity to discuss the theory of vital roots and their replanting as a new hope for the philosophy of nature especially in this late stage of the self-destructive tendency of our industrial society.

Neo-Vitalism is not a term I should like to live with, but it expresses the resurgence of movements and forces (since 1970 and the Earth Day Celebration) which were thought to be dead and buried after 1828 and the artificial synthesis of urea by Friedrich Wöhler, one of the fathers of organic chemistry.

The Physicalist–Vitalist conflict is the deepest conflict in our culture. It is now possible to delineate it because we are now able to grasp its history, thanks to the resurgence of the Vitalist point of view in the form of the environmental and ecology movements. I cling to the notion that the clarity with which we can grasp this past struggle indicates our distance from it, even though we continue to read its truth every day in countless guises.

The theatre of ideas I have called into play is determined by two masks—the Vitalist Smile and the Physicalist Frown: it is the comic and tragic together. Why they are split apart in science, as in drama, I do not know; all I know is the expression on the masks.

These expressions are paradigm features—they define the point of view. From these central masks, countless other masks may be assumed. Actors can even change places, representing now one, now the other point of view. But the fixity and precision of the initial determination remain. The Physicalist and Vitalist shall come to center stage and state their views. In our effort to develop a leading metaphor for consciousness, we shall see that the Vitalist Smile takes us back to "vital roots."

The Kantian Recoil from Vital Roots

Issac Newton and Goethe are the supreme embodiment of the Physicalist and the Vitalist, even though Newton kept cabbalistic esoterica locked in a trunk (as though his Vitalist side could not come out of the closet) and Goethe carried on his exacting experiments in the development of his theory of color for the express purpose of refuting Newton's Optics. Everything follows from these two in terms of characterizing the victory of one trend over another. In order to add to the symmetry, we will give Kant to Newton and Schelling to Goethe.

Kant knew what was coming. Perhaps it was Kant whom Goethe had in mind as the figure for Faust. Then the pact with the Devil becomes the sin against the Holy Spirit, otherwise known as the vital root of existence. The quandary over whether existence is a predicate, a technical problem in philosophy which Kant decided in the negative, comes in here. It is the background for the plight of existence in industrial society and the origins of existentialism as the protest against industrial society.

Kant decided against existence as a predicate, and, if we are to follow Heidegger on Kant, this was because of the Kantian recoil from the unknown root of existence. Kant betrayed the existential root. It was the price he had to pay for his "Copernican Revolution" and accommodation of philosophy to the protocols of a physicalistically oriented natural science. From Kant onward, German philosophers tried to find the root again, and failed. The leading theme of German philosophy became the "prison of finitude" as an expression of life in industrial society.

Martin Heidegger inherited this Kantian recoil from "vital roots," a recoil necessary for the development of industrial society as a world "above" nature and therefore devoid of vital roots. This recoil is the Copernican Revolution in philosophy. Kuhn's book on the structure of scientific revolution is an effort to make us feel comfortable about the "recoil." The recoil is the revulsion of the mind over its own unknown root. As Heidegger (1962a) puts it—it is more familiar to us than we are to ourselves:

> This fundamental constitution of the essence of man, "rooted" in the transcendental imagination, is the "unknown" of which Kant must have had an intimation when he spoke of "the root unknown to us"; for the unknown is not that of which we know absolutely nothing but that of which the knowledge makes us uneasy. However, Kant did not carry out the primordial interpretation of the transcendental imagination; indeed, he did not even make the attempt, despite the clear indications he gave us concerning such an analytic . . . . Kant recoiled from this unknown root. (Heidegger, 1962a, pp. 166, 167)

It is the flight from our own ground!

Heidegger retired to the Black Forest, in a forester's hut, with his water spout of pure mountain water dripping into its trough, walking the path back to the vital root. From Goethe's journey to Italy to Heidegger in his woods, from the journey to the Ur-plant to the path to the vital root, we have the hidden movement of Vitalism in a world determined by the Physicalist victory.

This impulse—to find the root again—was shared by Alan Chadwick and myself, when we started the Student Garden Project at the University of California in Santa Cruz. In order to find it, we had to "double dig."

The Renewal of the Philosophy of Nature

Double digging is a horticultural technique practiced by Chadwick. It is clearly set forth in John Jeavon's *How to Grow More Vegetables than You Ever Thought Possible on Less Land than You Can Imagine*, and Tom Cuthbertson's *Alan Chadwick's Enchanted Garden*.

We would also like to use "double digging" metaphorically. The upper crust is not all there is; like Ahab, we have to go to a little lower layer. This opening of the subsoil, for roots, is the basis for a renewed philosophy of nature. The linkage, for me, has been something like this: Schelling represents the breaking point in the defense against the rise of industrial society. Countless critics and witnesses inveigh against it. One of the most powerful, Simone Weil, who was drawn to work in a Renault factory as a missionary to some heathen tribe, wrote the central meditation on this revolt: *The Need for Roots* (Weil, 1979).

Schelling is the breaking point because of his turn from *Natürphilosophie*, and his alliance with Hegel, to existentialism (in his Berlin Lectures of 1841–1842), where the audience seemed to sense that a historic move was being made, initiating a philosophical position for the coming century and a half—so much excitement was there in the packed class-room, with Kierkegaard taking notes.[2]

This breaking point was to continue until the rejected forces could resummon themselves in trying to put things right, when the "unfore-seen" consequences of industrial society would provoke the environmen-tal movement. For historical dating purposes, existentialism plays the role of chief mourner for defeated Vitalism (and *Natürphilosophie*) until the Earth Day Celebration in April of 1970. This past decade has seen the groundwork for a renewed philosophy of nature, now that science has actually succeeded in unveiling nature's mysteries in the DNA code of the double helix and in the structure of the atom. Nature's mysteries were turned into scientific problems to be solved. The mystery became a secret. Those who penetrate to the secret receive Nobel prizes (the story is begun by Watson, 1968, and told in full by Judson, 1979).

The breaking point, represented in the turn of Schelling, is only shared by those who, so far, assume a minority view in their reaction against the pursuit of science under Physicalist protocols defined by the rejection and elimination of Vitalism.

The environmental and ecology movements are contemporaneous with the penetration to the secret of life. Think of the moment when Francis Crick, in a loud voice in a pub near Cambridge University, announced that he had solved the secret of life. Given the forces that are ranged against them, the ecology and environmental movements have achieved only partial toeholds. Look at the Environmental Studies Pro-gram at your local university—they are beleaguered enclaves in the midst of a hostile, science-determined organization of knowledge whose pur-pose is to train servants of industrial society.

However, all the signs are clear about our being in an advanced stage of the self-destruction of industrial society, as we know it. The economy of the United States is a symptom of this self-destruction. The organized system of industrial society is best expressed on the faces of unemployed blacks in the inner city in Milwaukee, Wisconsin. Once having driven through these areas, replicated in every major industrial city in the United States, one never forgets it. It is like escaping from an armed camp.

For this reason, we have tried to elucidate the metaphor—vital roots—as a leading metaphor of consciousness, and we have moved from applying the metaphor in a critique of industrial society to an uncovering of the metaphor in the origins of our culture in ancient Greece.

It should be obvious that this metaphor was discovered in the actual

[2]Kierkegaard's notes are contained in his *Papers and Diaries* (an unpublished manuscript amounting to some 75 pages in Danish). For other references to his attendance at Schel-ling's lectures, see the last volume of his papers, translated by Howard and Edna Hong. Paul Tillich calls these notes the "Ur-text of Existentialism."

development of a university garden project where countless students rediscovered their roots. In this sense, horticulture and agriculture, seen in the light of the ecology movement, are prerequisites for the development of any culture worthy of the name. Industrial society alienates us from this ground and provokes in us the longing for roots. Only in a discussion of the metaphors of consciousness do such considerations take on the meaning they deserve.

The Metaphors: "Vital Roots" and "Thymós"

According to Freud, the metaphor for consciousness is the neurone, an electrical charge along a nerve pathway. In order to distinguish the neurones appropriate to consciousness, Freud tried to postulate a qualitative charge in the neurone, but it did not work, and he sent his famous "Project for A Scientific Psychology" off to his cohort—Wilhelm Fliess—and never asked for it back. It was found among Fliess's papers, and came to light only a few decades ago in the publication of the Freud–Fliess correspondence as the *Origins of Psychoanalysis* (Freud, 1954).

Freud would have done better with a metaphor like "vital root" rather than "neurone," but his Physicalist training under Ernst Brücke prevented him from using a vitalist metaphor. Why? Because Physicalism in alliance with positivism eschewed terms with a metaphysical ring. Neurone is a nice empirical word; "vital root" is a metaphysical metaphor.

I have been working with the metaphor, as a metaphor for consciousness, ever since teaming up with a man who assumed responsibility for replanting it—Alan Chadwick, sometimes referred to as the world's greatest living gardener. When we started the Student Garden Project at the University of California at Santa Cruz in 1967, I witnessed Alan Chadwick's singular devotion to creating a garden, working fifteen to eighteen hours a day, seven days a week, without a break. I had to think of some way of putting it. The formulation appropriate to the phenomenon was to say that Alan Chadwick had been uniquely appointed to replant the vital root of existence. The supposition was that if it could happen somewhere, and it had to happen somewhere in order to prove that it was possible in a world where vital roots were endangered and in jeopardy, then it could happen elsewhere, as has been the case, given the thousands of students who have been trained in the methods and systems devoted to the replanting of the vital root, practiced by Chadwick, the French Intensive and Biodynamic. I came to appreciate that these were more than names for styles of hand-intensive systems of horticulture and agriculture, they were forms for the replanting of what industrial society had uprooted.

In fact, they were new forms for the *supplanting* of industrial society! We had joined a revolutionary movement which erupted nationally in 1970, on a given weekend, when countless Americans celebrated Earth Day I—April 22, 1970. We were ready for it in our garden in Santa Cruz.

After 1970, prompted by the inspiration of Earth Day, I started to think through what historical forces we were opposing in order to get a clear view of what we were up against. It became a marvelous detective story as I began to unravel the clues. Now that I have it mostly figured out, I can see that it has given me the central metaphor for consciousness in the notion of the "vital roots" of consciousness.

Here is how it goes: the ancient Greek term for the "vital root" is *thymós*, a Homeric word meaning vitality, courage, or spirit. There is now a fairly extensive philological and philosophical literature on *thymós*, but no one has fully elucidated its philosophical significance, although there have been a number of good attempts, beginning with Tillich (1952), Ricoeur (1965), and Strasser (1977). A new contribution was added by Julian Jaynes (1977) in his book, *The Origin of Consciousness in the Breakdown of the Bicameral Mind*. He utilized what was well known to anyone interested in classical philology, namely, the work of Bruno Snell and the linguistic approach to Homeric anthropology through the analysis of the metaphors for consciousness in the *Iliad* and *Odyssey*. Snell found that all the words for consciousness were words that referred to organs or quasi-organs—they had a material ring to them that had to be appreciated in order not to read back into them the subsequent linguistic elaborations of the terminology for consciousness. When Homer said *"psyche"* he meant the breath, consciousness was "breathing" in the sense of "one gasped one's last," the literal meaning of consciousness or *"psyche."* Consciousness (*"psyche"*) is only mentioned in reference to death; there is no *"psyche"* but this "last gasp." By the time we get to Plato, *"psyche"* is the name for a structured consciousness with three parts—the rational, the vital, and the appetitive. Plato's words are *nous*, *thymós*, and *epithymia*.

So from Homer to Plato we can catch the growing density in the linguistic evolution of rational self-consciousness—from "vital breath" (in the moment of death, as in, "he blew his life away"), to a structured self-consciousness ruled by reason. The carriers of this development are the pre-Socratic philosophers, about twenty of them, who prepared the way to Socrates as if he was what they meant. I like this existential reference. It has been immortalized in the syllogism:

> All men are mortal.
> Socrates is a man.
> Therefore, Socrates is mortal.

The second line in the syllogism is called an enthymeme, when it is understood, in which case the syllogism would read:

All men are mortal.

....

Therefore, Socrates is mortal.

An enthymeme, derived from *thymós*, is in the middle. In principle, we take it for granted. I have come to develop a whole philosophy out of it. I have moved from thinking of *thymós* as in the middle to thinking of *thymós* as "vital root." I had my metaphor for consciousness.

In order to develop a metaphor for consciousness, it is good practice to go back to Homer, where all the terms are metaphors, because Homeric culture is an oral culture, preliterate, and preconceptual. The Homeric metaphors for consciousness are *phrenes, thymós, psyche,* and *nous,* etc. They can be considered protoconcepts, or the metaphorical roots of concepts, in the sense that these metaphors for consciousness, based on organs in the body, become the concepts of Plato with no bodily references.

The key metaphor in Homer is *thymós,* the most widely used term in the *Iliad.* Imagine my delight when I began to excavate this central term, rather like Schliemann digging up Troy. Forgotten and buried under the successive layers of language, representing the linguistic evolution of rational self-consciousness, *thymós* was waiting to be found. I was able to dig down to the vital root of consciousness.

When I saw the book by Jaynes (1977), one day as I walked through a local bookstore, I thought—"oh–oh"—somebody got there before me. I saw from the index a number of entries on *thymós.* I held my breath. When I got to his definition of *thymós,* I exhaled. He had missed it by a step. He calls *thymós* the adrenalin-based reaction to an emergency situation, which is not bad for defining vitality, but more appropriate to *epithymia,* or the "lesser *thymós,*" the region of longing—drives, desires, and appetites, below the region of "spirit."

What step had Jaynes missed? No one in the area of classics had made the obvious connection between the word and the bodily organ, even though Snell had specified the relation between *psyche* and breath, *phrenes* and liver, etc. Even Snell had missed the obvious. *Thymós* is the thymus gland. I had found the vital root of consciousness in the thymus gland.

The thymus, therefore, is what Homer referred to when he used the word *thymós.* This is the hypothesis for unravelling the mystery of the vital root. Although the gland was formally named by Rufus of Ephesus (c. 100 A.D.), the correlation, in Homeric terms, between *thymós* and thymus carries through the principle of organs, or quasi-organs, as the basis for words for consciousness.

My speculative faculty was set into play when I went on to make the connection with the herb thyme, also derived from *thymós.* Now I really had a connection with vital roots, although the thymus, as the center of the immune system, was vital root enough.

The herb grows wild all over Greece, and its highly volatile essential oil makes it one of the great germicidal and antiseptic herbs. Therefore, its vital function. Like the thymus, it is a guardian of vitality in the defense against disease and illness. In this role, thyme has always been associated with courage.

The more this configuration of ideas came into focus, the more I was convinced that I had lucked into a key to the riddle of "vital roots" as the leading metaphor for consciousness where *thymós* was the root. I knew I had to extend the work of Tillich, Ricoeur, Strasser, and Jaynes into further areas of exploration in order to develop a Thymós Doctrine, drawing, as well, from the work of classical philologists—Snell, Onions, Havelock, Dodds, and Adkins.

Origin of the Word Thymós

Thymós is a Greek word meaning the raising of the soul, passion, courage, spirit. Its origin should be found in the Indo-European root *dheu*—to rise in a cloud, as dust, vapor or smoke (relation with breath). In Sanskrit, *dhumah* (dhumo-) means smoke or vapor, giving in Latin "fumus," in English "fume," "fumigate," "perfume." There is also the idea of undulation, waving, and ebullition. In Irish, *dumhach* means foggy. In Sanskrit, *dhulih* (dhuli) means dust or dusty soil or pollen. In middle Irish, *duil* means desire, movement of the soul. The root *dheu* (dheua) has the connotation of "being animated by swift movements," to swirl or whirl. In Sanskrit, *dhutah* means shaken. In Greek, *thuella* means storm, whirlwind; *thuein:* to sacrifice; *thuos:* incense for sacrifice; *thumos:* soul, courage, anger. Some authors think that *dheues* (dhes) belongs to the same root; it became in Greek, *theos:* God, and *theion:* smoke or sulfur. *Thuo* originally denotes a violent movement of air, water, the ground, animals, or men. From the sense of "to well up," "to boil up," it went to "to smoke" then "to cause to go up in smoke," "to sacrifice." *Thumos* is "that which is moved and which moves," "vital force"! The meaning of *thumos* is quite extensive: desire, impulse, inclination, consideration. Later on, *thumos* took the meaning of "wrath," particularly in the New Testament.

The Continuing Struggle between Physicalism and Vitalism

The vital root of consciousness is more than the elucidation of a word, although even that is a prodigious task and beyond any single effort. Tillich's *Courage to Be* begins the work in his masterful elucidation of the meaning of *thymós* in Plato, the Stoics, Spinoza, Nietzsche, etc. It is as though Tillich was able to carry through Kant's failed attempt at developing the transcendental imagination. As we mentioned, according to Heidegger, something happened to Kant to make him recoil from carrying through his interest in the vital root of consciousness in the constitution of the transcendental imagination.

If the problem is the vital root, then we can understand why metaphysics was abandoned and even rejected by the Physicalist trend in the system of the sciences, as if the best way to deal with a problem one has renounced the language for formulating is to bracket it and hope it goes away, as in the Positivist and Linguistic revision of language for the purpose of excluding such issues as "pseudoproblems." If Kant intuited this and recoiled from it, if Kant saw what was coming—industrial society—and that philosophy would have to accommodate itself to it, then Kant is part of the problem.

When I found the passage in Heidegger, I thought it was too good to be true. Here was Heidegger (1962a), as though complaining about himself and his inability to carry through the project of *Being and Time* (Heidegger, 1962b), isolating the moment in Kant where the recoil from the unknown root occurred—a recoil he was to inherit. It is a commentary, buried in philosophy, of the uprooting of our modern period as a result of the rise and triumph of industrial society. It is the story of how our "courage to be" was undermined and eroded as a result of losing touch with "vital roots."

So our metaphor for consciousness is indicative of the deepest perplexity in the depths of our culture. We are all worried to death about the outcome of this revived debate, thought settled in 1828 when Physicalism defeated Vitalism (a view repeated throughout the literature, as though a war had been fought to decide the issue). This assumption reigned supreme for a century and a half. Should you look up any references to Vitalism in the literature, including references to philosophy of life (Nietzsche) and philosophy of nature (Schelling), they will uniformly refer to names of defeated points of view—with existentialism inheriting the defeat and presiding over the last rites.

No one could have predicted the reemergence, historically, of defeated Vitalism in the celebration of Earth Day. It is the historical end of existentialism as chief mourner for defeated Vitalism. Even though the nails may not have given way, the coffin came unglued, and we witnessed the return of a point of view thought dead and buried.

This neo-Vitalist resurgence in the environmental and ecology movements reenjoined the debate. It has lead to the realization of the necessity for dismantling industrial society in order to minimize the damage due to its self-destruction.

What we need now is the amplification of this renewal in a new view of consciousness. For our own point of view, by renewal we mean discovering your thymus gland as the biological basis of your spirit, and we mean discovering the medicinal properties of herbs, as in the herb thyme. These two roots, glandular and herbal, will put you in touch with *thymós*, the vital root of consciousness.

I can sum it up in a parable:

> Once upon a time, a famous poet and man of letters, who was also an accomplished scientist, particularly in botany, dropped out of German society to take a long walk as though he went in search of something as profound as the vital root of existence, although he was not able to put his longing into words. He went south, to Italy, as though in search of cultural roots, mindful of the danger they were in which he foresaw. Based on his botanical studies, he was actually in search of his own version of the vital root—what he called the *Ur*-plant. He had formulated a theory of plant metamorphosis based on the relation of leaf to stem. He had envisaged a primal plant exemplifying his theory, a plant that would be the morphological prototype of all possible plant development. He wanted to find one.
>
> When he entered the oldest botanical garden in the Western world, in Padua, founded in 1545, he sensed that his quest was realized.
>
> When he gazed upon the palm growing in the middle of the garden— *Chaemerops humilis*—he designated it the *Ur*-plant.
>
> To commemorate the finding of the *Ur*-plant in their garden, the Paduans built a glass case to cover it. They called it "Goethe's Palm."
>
> The vital root of existence in the form of the *Ur*-plant was squirreled away under glass in the oldest botanical garden in the Western world to wait out the triumphant rise and self-destructive demise of industrial society as a world above the given world of nature and therefore devoid of vital roots.
>
> The vital root is alive and well in Padua.

The Physicalist–Vitalist Conflict in Psychology[3]

The physicalist–vitalist conflict also pervades the discipline of psychology. On the one hand, we find the "hardheaded" and natural science-inspired approaches in psychology (e.g., physiological psychology, behaviorism, and cognitive psychology), which follow the strictly experimental approach of rigorous scientific causal analysis. This approach seeks to uncover the roots of behavior in the prepersonal terms of physiological and psychological functions, without appeal to the experi-

[3]The remainder of this chapter was written by Rolf von Eckartsberg, and is included with the author's permission and approval.—Eds.

enced reality of consciousness and personal self-agency. In this view, behavior is a consequence of antecedent reinforcement and situational manipulation circumventing the awareness and choice of the participants; action is the result of the operation of certain information-processing loops steered by feedback. The physicalistic-positivistic approach is the serious attempt to simulate man as an assembly of variables and response tendencies with a general information-processing capability of an "artificial" intelligence with emergent properties. The ideal of the Physicalist view is the complete simulation of man, the creation of the android under scientific management and control.

On the other side of the psychological spectrum, there are the "soft" humanistic and existential approaches which insist on the reality of selfhood, self-realization, and self-agency, and which emphasize the importance of personal consciousness, of meaning and values. The activities of each human individual require an "intentional analysis" and interpretational reading, a "hermeneutics of existence," rather than a causal analysis. Human reality is preinterpreted reality; people act on the meanings they perceive the situation to have. Action implies choices between alternatives, choices of direction leading into the future and ultimately to the creation of a way of life. The Vitalist emphasis in psychology stresses the reality of *embodiment,* meaningfulness and intensity of experience. It is thus sympathetic with both the human-potential movement in humanistic psychology and its emphasis on the experience of the body, and transpersonal psychology, which retains an appreciation for man's vital connectedness with the realities of the spirit, of values, and ultimately with the realm of the Divine. The existential emphasis on authenticity, on the right relationship of the person to others and to his/her world, also represents the Vitalist position of insistence on quality, on will, and on commitment, on the courage to be, the courage to incarnate values.

Methodologically the humanistic and existential approaches emphasize case studies, descriptions of experiences, and personal stories, working directly on one's involvement and experiences in the sense of a spiritual and psychological praxis. The expression of experience becomes important; the use of personal testimony, of symbols and metaphors, is seen as helping the interpretation and serving as guiding images and is favored over conceptual classification, measurement, and the expression of knowledge as cognitive objects. Although the natural scientific approach moves in a denotative way, using specified operational definitions, the humanistic-existential approach favors connotative ways, which are suggestive, which invite participation, and which emphasize the plurality of meanings that symbols can carry.

Although the physicalist-positivist psychologies aim for mastery and control by a professional scientific elite (e.g., computer diagnostics), the vitalist psychologies seem to favor and further emancipation, self-development, and taking matters in one's own hands. The search for the appropriate metaphor and symbol to live by and the task to embody spiritual insight, wisdom, and knowledge in a viable and responsible assembly of activities and in collaboration with a social ensemble, defines the vitalist task in psychology: to create an optimal way of life together, on Earth, from within the conditions in which we find ourselves. In this day and age, the issues are defined by the limits to technological carrying capacity in a limited earth-resource environment, a historical development that has brought our very rootedness in the land, in our body, and in our spirit (as the source of illumination as to the right way on earth) into question and existential jeopardy.

The journey and account of one person through this complex interdisciplinary terrain of issues and ruling metaphors, and his discovery of a root of renewed existence in "double digging" (the biodynamic French-intensive mode of horticulture), in the ecology movement, in the Greek word *thymós*, in the herb thyme, and in the human thymus gland, offers a Vitalist testimonial and a summons to everyone to become involved with roots again. The story of the journey evokes our personal and collective existence in its unfolding. *Thymós* is a vital reality and a biopsychological metaphor that may keep us on the right track by calling us to our roots and to the sources of our vitality, to the ground of our life-making.

References

Cassirer, E. *The problem of knowledge.* New Haven: Yale University Press, 1950.

Cuthbertson, T. *Alan Chadwick's enchanted garden.* New York: Dutton, 1978.

Freud, S. Letters to Wilhelm Fliess. In M. Bonaparte, A. Freud, & E. Kris (Eds.), *Origins of Psychoanalysis.* New York: Basic Books, 1954.

Heidegger, M. *Kant and the problem of metaphysics.* Bloomington: Indiana University Press, 1962. (a)

Heidegger, M. *Being and time.* New York: Harper & Row, 1962. (b)

Jaynes, J. *The origin of consciousness in the breakdown of the bicameral mind.* Boston: Houghton-Mifflin, 1977.

Jeavon, J. *How to grow more vegetables than you ever thought possible on less land than you can imagine.* Berkeley, Calif.: Ten Speed Press, 1979.

Judson, H. *The eighth day of creation: The makers of revolution in biology.* New York: Simon & Schuster, 1979.

Kuhn, T. H. *The structure of scientific revolutions.* Chicago: University of Chicago Press, 1962.

Merz, J. *History of European thought in the nineteenth century.* Darby, Penna.: Arden Library, 1978.

Ricoeur, P. *Fallible man.* Chicago: Henry Regnery, 1965.

Strasser, S. *Phenomenology of feeling*. Atlantic Highlands, N. J.: Duquesne University Press, 1977.
Tillich, P. *The courage to be*. New Haven: Yale University Press, 1952.
Tillich, P. *Systematic theology*. Chicago: University of Chicago Press, 1975.
Watson, J. D. *The double helix*. New York: New American Library, 1968.
Weil, S. *The need for roots*. New York: Harper & Row, 1979.

Additional Reference

For the best introduction to the botanical origins of modern science, see:

Armytage, W. H. *The rise of the technocrats, a social history*. Toronto: University of Toronto Press, 1965.

Author Index

Subject Index